Contemporary Ethnic Families in the United States

Characteristics, Variations, and Dynamics

Nijole V. Benokraitis
University of Baltimore

Prentice
Hall

Upper Saddle River, New Jersey 07458

Library of Congress Cataloging-in-Publication Data

Contemporary ethnic families in the United States : characteristics, variations, and
dynamics / [edited] by Nijole V. Benokraitis.
  p. cm.
  ISBN 0-13-089326-9
  1. Minorities—United States—Social conditions.   2. Minorities—United States—Family
relationships.   3. Family—United States.   4. Ethnology—United States.   5. United
States—Social conditions—1980– .   6. United States—Ethnic relations.   7. Ethnic families
I. Benokraitis, Nijole V. (Nijole Vaicaitis)   II. Title.

E184.A1 C597 2001
305.8′00973—dc21

                                                    00-052847

VP, Editorial Director: *Laura Pearson*

AVP, Publisher: *Nancy Roberts*

Editorial Assistant: *Lee Peterson*

Project Manager: *Merrill Peterson*

Cover Director: *Jayne Conte*

Cover Photo: Margaret Cusack/Stock Illustration
  Source, Inc.

Manager of Line Art: *Guy Ruggiero*

Interior Image Specialist: *Beth Boyd*

Manager, Rights and Permissions: *Kay Dellosa*

Director, Image Resource Center: *Melinda Reo*

Marketing Manager: *Chris Barker*

Prepress and Manufacturing Buyer: *Mary Ann Gloriande*

This Book Is Dedicated to My Husband, Vitalius

This book was set in 10/12 Times by NK Graphics,
and was printed and bound by RR Donnelley & Sons Company.
The cover was printed by Phoenix Color Corp.

© 2002 by Pearson Education, Inc.
Upper Saddle River, New Jersey 07458

ISBN   0-13-089326-9

PRENTICE-HALL INTERNATIONAL (UK) LIMITED, *London*

PRENTICE-HALL OF AUSTRALIA PTY. LIMITED, *Sydney*

PRENTICE-HALL CANADA INC., *Toronto*

PRENTICE-HALL HISPANOAMERICANA, S.A., *Mexico*

PRENTICE-HALL OF INDIA PRIVATE LIMITED, *New Delhi*

PRENTICE-HALL OF JAPAN, INC., *Tokyo*

PEARSON EDUCATION ASIA PTE. LTD., *Singapore*

EDITORA PRENTICE-HALL DO BRASIL, LTDA., *Rio de Janeiro*

Contents

Preface   vii

Contributors   xii

About the Editor   xv

1. The Changing Ethnic Profile of U.S.
   Families in the Twenty-First Century
   Nijole V. Benokraitis   1

CHAPTER 1
Socialization and Family Values   15

2. Socialization Concerns in African
   American, American Indian, Asian
   American, and Latino Families
   Ross D. Parke and Raymond Buriel   18

3. African American Family Values
   Ramona W. Denby   29

4. Filipino American Culture and Family
   Values
   Pauline Agbayani-Siewart   36

5. Taiwanese American Family Values
   and Socialization
   Franklin Ng   43

6. Grandmother to Granddaughter: Learning
   to Be a Dakota Woman
   Angela Cavender Wilson   49

CHAPTER 2
Gender Roles   55

7. Behind, beside, in front of Him? Black
   Women Talk about Their Men
   Earl Ofari Hutchinson   58

8. Grappling with Changing Gender Roles
   in Dominican American Families
   Patricia R. Pessar   66

9. Appropriate Gender Roles in Vietnamese
   American Families
   Min Zhou and Carl L. Bankston III   71

10. Coping with Gender Role Strains
    in Korean American Families
    Moon H. Jo   78

11. To Be an Asian Indian Woman in America
    Monisha Das Gupta   83

CHAPTER 3
Cohabitation, Marriage, and Intermarriage   93

12. Black Couples and the "Big C": The Ring,
    the Ceremony, Forever
    Denene Millner and Nick Chiles   96

13. Asian Indian Marriages—Arranged,
    Semi-Arranged, or Based on Love?
    Johanna Lessinger   101

14. Changes in Marital Satisfaction
    in Three Generations
    of Mexican Americans
    Kyriakos S. Markides,
    Jan Roberts-Jolly,
    Laura A. Ray, Sue K. Hoppe, and
    Laura Rudkin 105

15. Intermarriage and Ethnic Identity
    among Second-Generation Chinese
    and Korean Americans
    Nazli Kibria 110

16. Turkish American Intermarriage
    Barbara Bilgé 120

CHAPTER 4
Parenting 127

17. Fathers' Child-Rearing
    Involvement in African American,
    Latino, and White Families
    John F. Toth Jr. and Xiaohe Xu 130

18. Parenting in Middle-Class
    Black Families
    Susan D. Toliver 141

19. *Las Comadres* as a Parenting Support
    System
    Rebecca A. López 149

20. Perspectives of Asian American Parents
    with Gay and Lesbian Children
    Alice Y. Hom 156

21. Parenting and the Stress
    of Immigration
    among Jordanian Mothers
    Marianne Hattar-Pollara
    and Afaf I. Meleis 162

CHAPTER 5
Work Experiences, Discrimination,
and Family Life 171

22. Some Benefits and Costs of Black
    Dual-Career Commuter Marriages
    Anita P. Jackson, Ronald P. Brown,
    and Karen E. Patterson-Stewart 174

23. Chicanas in White-Collar Jobs: "You Have
    to Prove Yourself More"
    Denise A. Segura 189

24. Struggling to Succeed: Haitians in South
    Florida
    Alex Stepick 199

25. Central American Workers: New Roles
    in a New Landscape
    Terry A. Repak 205

26. Family and Traditional Values: The
    Bedrock of Chinese American Business
    Bernard Wong 212

CHAPTER 6
The Impact of Social Class 217

27. Are Ethnic and White Middle Classes
    Booming?
    Alison Stein Wellner 220

28. Explaining Cuban Americans' Success
    Roberto Suro 226

29. Puerto Rican Migrants: Juggling Family
    and Work Roles
    Maura I. Toro-Morn 232

30. Living Poor: Family Life among Single
    Parent African American Women
    Robin L. Jarrett 240

31. Social Class, Interaction, and Perceptions about Other Ethnic Groups: The Case of Korean Americans
Kyeyoung Park 251

CHAPTER 7
Violence and Other Family Crises 259

32. Risk-Taking Behavior among American Indian, Black, and White Adolescents
Enid Gruber, Ralph J. DiClemente, and Martin M. Anderson 263

33. Intergenerational Conflict, Acculturation, and Drug Use among Asian Indian Adolescents
Gauri Bhattacharya 269

34. Eating Problems among African American, Latina, and White Women
Becky W. Thompson 279

35. Domestic Violence in African American, Asian American, and Latino Communities
Doris Williams Campbell, Beckie Masaki, and Sara Torres 289

36. Mistreatment of Vietnamese Elderly by Their Families in the United States
Quyen Kim Le 299

CHAPTER 8
Marital Conflict, Divorce, and Remarriage 307

37. Divorce and Iranian Immigrants' Attitudes about Gender Roles and Marriage
Mohammadreza Hojat, Reza Shapurian, Danesh Foroughi, Habib Nayerahmadi, Mitra Farzaneh, Mahmood Shafieyan, and Mohin Parsi 310

38. Separation and Divorce in Brazilian Immigrant Families
Maxine L. Margolis 318

39. Black Men and the Divorce Experience
Erma Jean Lawson and Aaron Thompson 322

40. Divorce Mediation among Asian Americans
Roger R. Wong 331

41. Latino Fathers and the Child Support Enforcement Experience
Kimberly A. Folse 341

CHAPTER 9
Grandparenting, Aging, and Family Caregiving 351

42. Sixty-Five Plus in the United States
Robert Bernstein 354

43. Intergenerational Assistance within the Mexican American Family
Tracy L. Dietz 360

44. Elder Care in Pueblo Indian Families
Catherine Hagan Hennessy and Robert John 368

45. Black Grandmothers Raising Their Grandchildren
Antoinette Y. Rodgers-Farmer and Rosa L. Jones 378

46. Variations in Asian Grandparenting
Yoshinori Kamo 385

Internet Resources 395

Photo Credits 400

Preface

The proportion of ethnic minority families in the United States is growing at a breathtaking pace. By 2025, according to Census Bureau projections, 62 percent of the U.S. population will be white, down from 76 percent in 1990 and 86 percent in 1950 (see Reading 1). The increasing cultural, racial, and ethnic diversity of U.S. families is generating much interest among scholars, journalists, politicians, and students. During the mid-1980s, "Racial and Ethnic Relations" courses often were canceled because of low enrollments, but a decade later, classes were overflowing. During end-of-semester course evaluations, moreover, a number of students offered (unsolicited) comments like "I never realized I stereotyped until I took this course" or "This course should be required for *all* University of Baltimore students because we don't know very much about our classmates and coworkers."

Such remarks were gratifying, of course, but despite many students' enthusiastic reactions, I felt frustrated when choosing textbooks—for several reasons. First, although there are several excellent race and ethnic textbooks on the market, they typically offer scope rather than depth because it's nearly impossible to provide both.

Second, when I searched for edited volumes that would provide the depth I wanted, I discovered several shortcomings. The books typically devoted much space to European American families, but I wanted more coverage of ethnic minority families. The books tended to focus on low-socioeconomic households—especially those in black and Latino communities—but I was interested in increasing students' awareness of healthful family processes across and within ethnic households, whether poor, middle-class, or affluent. And all of the anthologies failed to recognize what I call the "heterogeneity of diversity" of U.S. families. For example, in 1990 Chinese, Filipinos, and Japanese ranked as the largest Asian American groups, but Southeast Asians, Indians, Koreans, and Pakistanis have been registering much faster growth. Mexicans, Puerto Ricans, and Cubans have been the dominant groups among Latinos, but their growth rate, too, is being outpaced by immigration from Central and South American countries such as El Salvador, Guatemala, and Brazil. Similarly, we rarely read or hear about the influx of Middle Eastern or Caribbean families. Ignoring many of the relatively small ethnic groups gives a skewed picture of diversity and increases the invisibility of significant numbers of U.S. households.

Third, many of the edited volumes focus on demographic characteristics, migration patterns, and the history of the immigrants' country of origin. I wanted students to learn more about *families* and *family processes*—how ethnic families interact on a daily basis, cope with difficulties, and adjust to a new environment. Selections that emphasize historical backgrounds do not capture recent intergenerational changes.

Fourth, I found that many of the anthologies contained articles based on 1970s and 1980s data. Although there is nothing wrong with using older selections when necessary, ethnic families changed considerably—demographically and culturally—during the 1990s.

Purpose of the Book

Contemporary Ethnic Families in the United States will broaden students' awareness of the increasing heterogeneity of diversity in U.S. society. This anthology provides representative articles about African Americans; families with Latino roots (including Mexican Americans, Central Americans, and Latin Americans); Caribbean families; families from East Asia, South Asia, and Southeast Asia; and families from the Mideast. I would have liked to include selections about many of the subgroups within each major ethnic group (such as Laotian Americans for Southeast Asian families) and for each of the topics I cover. But substantive articles are not available for all of the subgroups, and there are length limits for every textbook. Despite those constraints, the selections here are more representative of the diversity of ethnic families in the United States than the selections that any other reader offers. In addition, the chapter introductions present material on smaller ethnic groups that are not covered in the articles.

Criteria for Selecting the Readings

My selection criteria included the following: (1) readability, or articles written in a clear and nontechnical manner; (2) a balance of selections that examine both large and small immigrant populations; (3) a mixture of national-level surveys as well as in-depth analyses based on small, exploratory studies; (4) a variety of research approaches to show students the many ways in which social scientists collect data; (5) selections that use the most recent data; and (6) articles that describe how ethnic families change over time as they interact with the dominant culture. These criteria reflect reviewers' suggestions to choose articles that compare ethnic families but also to include non-Latin white families. As one reviewer noted, "Students look for themselves in texts like these and enjoy recognizing their own families."

Some publishers now offer series of volumes that highlight specific ethnic families, such as Filipino Americans, Cuban Americans, and Taiwanese Americans. In addition, periodicals on ethnic groups have recently mushroomed—for example, *Amerasia Journal, American Indian Quarterly, Journal of Comparative Family Studies, Journal of Black Studies, Hispanic Journal of Behavior Sciences,* and *Ethnic and Racial Studies.* In some cases, though they were relatively rare, there were several equally enticing candidates for inclusion here. In these situations, I picked a selection in which the author discussed the research in a way that I felt would offer students the greatest insights in understanding what ethnic families experience on a daily basis.

I do not assume that students are familiar with sophisticated statistical techniques. I made a concerted attempt, therefore, to avoid using articles that are highly quantitative and "number crunching." My goal is to provide scholarly and thought-provoking materials that are interesting, conceptually accessible, and free of unnecessary jargon.

Topics and Organization

Contemporary Ethnic Families in the United States focuses on nine important topics: (1) socialization and family values; (2) gender roles; (3) cohabitation, marriage, and intermarriage; (4) parenting; (5) work experiences, discrimination, and family life; (6) the impact of social class; (7) violence and other family crises; (8) marital conflict, divorce, and remarriage; and (9) grandparenting, aging, and family caregiving. These topics are among the most important issues that many marriage and family courses cover. Whenever possible, I chose selections that examine the intersection of social class, age, gender roles, and intragroup variations within ethnic families.

Usually, each chapter begins with a general or comparative article that discusses two or more ethnic families. In Chapter 1 on socialization and family values, for example, the first reading describes socialization practices and concerns in black, American Indian, Asian American, and Latino families. This selection is followed by an examination of black family values (Reading 3), Filipino American culture and socialization (Reading 4), Taiwanese American family values (Reading 5), and American Indian grandmothers' transmission of cultural beliefs and practices to their daughters and granddaughters (Reading 6).

In some chapters, the articles are organized around the life course. Chapter 3, for instance, begins with a discussion of the merits and disadvantages of cohabitation versus marriage from the perspective of a black married couple. "She" thinks black men fear marriage; "he" argues that many black men avoid commitment ("the big C") because they think Ms. Right might be just around the corner (Reading 12). We then look at marriage—arranged, semi-arranged, and based on love—among Asian Indian partners (Reading 13), examine changes in marital satisfaction in three generations of Mexican Americans (Reading 14), and consider two articles on the benefits and difficulties of intermarriage in Chinese American, Korean American, and Turkish American marriages (Readings 15 and 16). The life cycle perspective is also used in analyzing marital conflict, divorce, and remarriage (Chapter 8) and grandparenting, aging, and family caregiving (Chapter 9).

A third organizing principle considers some of the problems that immigrant families face, how they deal with everyday stresses and cope with ethnic identity issues in a new environment. In Chapter 7 on violence and other family crises, for example, the selections compare the risk-taking behavior of American Indian, black, and white adolescents (Reading 32) and explain why Asian Indian adolescents sometimes turn to drugs in an effort to cope with identity problems and intergenerational conflict (Reading 33). The authors of Reading 34 argue that black women, Latinas, and white girls, as well as young women, may develop self-destructive eating problems to survive in a society fraught with sexism and racism. Family problems aren't limited to adolescence, however. Domestic violence is widespread in black, Asian American, and Latino communities (Reading 35). The violence manifests itself, moreover, in the mistreatment of some elderly, such as Vietnamese Americans (Reading 36).

Teaching and Learning Features

Contemporary Ethnic Families in the United States offers four tools to facilitate both teaching and learning. First, chapter introductions suggest some of the similarities, differences, and overlap (when it occurs) across the various ethnic families. They also include supporting or supplementary information that (1) updates data cited in some of the readings, (2) integrates recent empirical findings, and (3) incorporates relevant or well-known studies that enhance students' understanding of the selections.

Second, brief headnotes highlight the key issues that students should keep in mind while reading a selection or a set of selections. In many instances, the introductions "bridge" or contrast the experiences of ethnic families. These bridges encourage students to think about all the readings in a chapter rather than seeing each reading as describing an isolated occurrence in a particular ethnic family.

Third, three "Think about It" questions follow each reading. Some of these questions simply "test" students' understanding of the material. Most, however, invite students to compare and contrast the experiences of ethnic families, to organize their reading, and to consider the issues thoughtfully. The questions should stimulate critical thinking and provide catalysts for class discussion.

Fourth, the "Internet Resources" section identifies Web sites that students can use for their research, class discussions, course projects, or intellectual enhancement. Because URLs come and go, I recommend only the sites that I think will continue into the future. They represent well-established organizations or devoted homepage "owners," were constructed four or five years ago, are frequently updated, and probably won't disappear in the cyberspace cemetery after this book is published.

Because *Contemporary Ethnic Families in the United States* is a one-of-a-kind anthology, I expect that it will be useful for a variety of courses to supplement textbooks in "Sociology of the Family," "Marriage and Family," race/ethnic courses, women's studies, social work, and American studies programs. As I noted earlier, this reader will add depth to survey courses and enhance students' understanding of a variety of ethnic families. Faculty who are using a textbook (including my *Marriages and Families: Changes, Choices, and Constraints*) might also consider using this anthology to supplement students' readings.

A Note about Language

Both faculty and students might sometimes be put off by the contributors' language—such as using *Hispanic* rather than *Latino, Indo-Asian* rather than *Asian Indian* or vice versa, *Pilipino* rather than *Filipino,* or *Oriental* rather than *Asian.* Because this book is an edited volume and the articles come from numerous sources, readers might also notice differences in spelling and writing styles. Articles and books published in Canada or Great Britain, for example, often use different spellings of a word (such as "labour" instead of "labor"). Some contemporary writers still use "his," "him," or "he" instead of less exclusionary pronouns that include women. I decided not to edit such language usage because, after all, how we write is data. Finally, some social scientists feel that using *they* and *one* instead of *we* and *our* objectifies immigrants, excludes racial and ethnic groups from "mainstream" (whatever that means) analyses, and treats people as outsiders. I don't feel comfortable, however, in using *we* and *our* because I think it's presumptuous to speak for any group or to assume that I can identify with the experiences of specific communities.

Acknowledgments

I am indebted to a number of people who helped shape and produce this book. At Prentice Hall, Nancy Roberts, publisher for sociology and anthropology, guided and supported this project from beginning to end. Lee Peterson, Nancy's administrative assistant, solicited reviewer comments and responded, always quickly, to my requests for information. Merrill Peterson, production editor, orchestrated the myriad tasks involved in turning out a textbook. I am also grateful to Pat Herbst, copyeditor, for providing many valuable suggestions.

At the University of Baltimore, Brandi Hammond, my graduate assistant, provided valuable research assistance. Linda Fair, our departmental guru, was always good-natured and responsive in solving everyday office-related glitches and facilitating correspondence. At Langsdale Library, Mary Atwater, Tammy Taylor, and Brian Chetelet kept track of hundreds of books borrowed from other libraries as the materials crossed the circulation desk into my shopping bags. I am especially grateful to our excellent reference librarians— Stephen LaBash, Mary Schwartz, Randy Smith, and Lucy Holman. They continue, year after year, to be an invaluable resource for locating information, solving online problems, and tracking down articles and books. Carol Vaeth, our interlibrary loan specialist, deserves special thanks. As always, Carol managed to find articles when I had only a partial citation, persevered in obtaining books that many out-of-state libraries didn't want to lend, and was responsive to my weekly deluge of requests.

I am especially grateful to the following reviewers for their thoughtful comments and suggestions on the initial proposal for this book: Walter F. Carroll, Bridgewater State College; Jan DeAmicis, Utica College; Jennifer E. Glick, Arizona State University and Anne Rankin Mahoney, University of Denver. Their reactions and excellent recommendations helped me considerably in preparing *Contemporary Ethnic Families in the United States*.

I look forward to, and will respond to, comments on this book. I can be contacted at

University of Baltimore
1420 N. Charles Street
Baltimore, MD 21201
Voice mail: 410-837-5294
Fax: (410) 837-5061
E-mail: nbenokraitis@ubmail.ubalt.edu

Contributors

Pauline Agbayani-Siewart is Assistant Professor, School of Social Welfare, University of Washington, Seattle.

Martin M. Anderson is Associate Professor, Adolescent Medicine Program, Division of General Pediatrics, University of California at Los Angeles.

Carl L. Bankston III is Assistant Professor of Sociology at the University of Southwestern Louisiana.

Robert Bernstein is a Public Affairs Specialist in the Public Information Office, U.S. Bureau of the Census, Washington, DC.

Gauri Bhattacharya is Principal Investigator, National Development and Research Institutes, Inc., New York, New York.

Barbara Bilgé is a Lecturer of Anthropology at Eastern Michigan University.

Ronald P. Brown is President and CEO of JOPARO Company, a consulting group that specializes in cultural diversity training, motivational speaking, and applied strategic planning.

Raymond Buriel is Professor of Psychology and Chicano Studies at Pomona College, Claremont, California.

Doris Williams Campbell is Director of Diversity Initiatives for the University of South Florida Health Sciences Center, Tampa, Florida, and Professor in the Colleges of Nursing and Public Health.

Nick Chiles is a reporter for the *Star Ledger* of Newark, New Jersey.

Monisha Das Gupta is Assistant Professor in the Department of Sociology at Syracuse University.

Ramona W. Denby is Assistant Professor in the School of Social Work at the University of Nevada, Las Vegas.

Ralph J. DiClemente is Professor and Chair, Rollins School of Public Health, Emory University.

Tracy L. Dietz is Assistant Professor in the Department of Sociology and Anthropology at the University of Central Florida.

Mitra Farzaneh is a Senior Psychologist at the New Lisbon Development Center, New Jersey.

Kimberly A. Folse is Assistant Professor in the Department of Sociology at Southwest Texas State University.

Danesh Foroughi is a family therapist in private practice and works at the Department of Children and Family Services in Los Angeles.

Enid Gruber teaches in the Department of Psychiatry at the University of California at Los Angeles.

Marianne Hattar-Pollara is Assistant Chair/Lecturer, Statewide Nursing Program, California State University, Dominguez Hills.

Catherine Hagan Hennessy is a researcher at the Aging Studies Branch, Centers for Disease Control and Prevention.

Mohammadreza Hojat is Professor in the Department of Psychiatry and Human Behavior at Jefferson Medical College, Philadelphia.

Alice Y. Hom is an author and a doctoral candidate in History/American Studies at Claremont Graduate University, Los Angeles.

Sue K. Hoppe is Professor and Chief of the Division of Sociology in the Department of Psychiatry at the University of Texas Health Service Center in San Antonio.

Earl Ofari Hutchinson is an author and lecturer.

Anita P. Jackson is Associate Professor, Counseling and Human Development Services, Kent State University.

Robin L. Jarrett is Associate Professor of Family Studies in the Department of Human and Community Development at the University of Illinois, Champaign-Urbana.

Moon H. Jo is a retired Professor of Sociology at Lycoming College in Williamsport, Pennsylvania.

Robert John is Chair in Gerontology at the University of Louisiana at Monroe.

Rosa L. Jones is Vice Provost and Dean of Undergraduate Studies and Associate Professor in the School of Social Work at Florida International University, Miami.

Yoshinori Kamo is Associate Professor of Sociology at Louisiana State University.

Nazli Kibria is Assistant Professor of Sociology at Boston University.

Erma Jean Lawson is Assistant Professor of Sociology at the University of North Texas.

Quyen Kim Le is affiliated with the John XXIII Multi-Service Center in San Jose, California.

Johanna Lessinger is a Research Associate in the Anthropology Department at Columbia University.

Rebecca A. López is Assistant Professor in the Department of Social Work, California State University, Long Beach.

Maxine L. Margolis is Professor of Anthropology at the University of Florida.

Kyriakos S. Markides is Professor and Director of the Division of Sociomedical Sciences in the Department of Preventive Medicine and Community Health at the University of Texas Medical Branch at Galveston.

Beckie Masaki is Co-Founder and Executive Director of the Asian Women's Shelter in San Francisco.

Afaf I. Meleis is Professor in the Department of Mental Health, Community, and Administrative Nursing, University of California at San Francisco.

Denene Millner is a reporter for the *New York Daily News*.

Habib Nayerahmadi is Senior Psychologist at the New Lisbon Developmental Center, New Jersey.

Franklin Ng is Professor of Anthropology at California State University, Fresno.

Kyeyoung Park is Assistant Professor of Anthropology and Asian American Studies at the University of California at Los Angeles.

Ross D. Parke is Professor of Psychology at the University of California at Riverside.

Mohin Parsi is a doctoral candidate in the Department of Psychology at the School of Professional Psychology, Los Angeles.

Karen E. Patterson-Stewart teaches in the interdisciplinary Leadership Studies Doctoral Program at Bowling Green State University.

Patricia R. Pessar is Associate Professor in American Studies and Anthropology at Yale University.

Laura A. Ray is Project Director of the Hispanic Established Population of Epidemiologic Studies of the Elderly study.

Terry A. Repak is a freelance writer.

Jan Roberts-Jolly is Executive Director of the Southwest Alabama Area Health Education Center in McIntosh, Alabama.

Antoinette Y. Rodgers-Farmer is Assistant Professor in the School of Social Work at Rutgers University.

Laura Rudkin is Assistant Professor in the Department of Preventive Medicine and Community Health at the University of Texas Medical Branch at Galveston.

Denise A. Segura is Associate Professor of Sociology at the University of California at Santa Barbara.

Mahmood Shafieyan is Senior Psychologist at the Trenton Psychiatric Hospital, New Jersey.

Reza Shapurian is Emeritus Professor of Psychology at the University of Shiraz; he now lives in Boston.

Alex Stepick is Director of the Immigration and Ethnicity Institute and Professor of Anthropology and Sociology at Florida International University in Miami.

Roberto Suro is a journalist and reporter at the *Washington Post*.

Aaron Thompson is Associate Professor of Sociology and Coordinator for Academic Success at Eastern Kentucky University.

Becky W. Thompson is Visiting Assistant Professor of African American Studies and American Studies at Wesleyan University.

Susan D. Toliver is Associate Professor of Sociology and Director of Women's Studies at Iona College in New Rochelle, New York.

Maura I. Toro-Morn is Associate Professor in the Department of Sociology and Anthropology at Illinois State University.

Sara Torres is Associate Professor and Chair of the Department of Psychiatric, Community Health, and Adult Primary Care at the School of Nursing, University of Maryland at Baltimore.

John F. Toth Jr. is Assistant Professor of Sociology at West Virginia Wesleyan College.

Alison Stein Wellner is an author and regular contributor to *American Demographics* who specializes in consumer trends.

Angela Cavender Wilson, Tawapaha Tanka Win (Her Big Hat Woman), is Assistant Professor in American Indian History at Arizona State University.

Bernard Wong is Professor of Anthropology at San Francisco State University.

Roger R. Wong is an attorney practicing law in Guam.

Xiaohe Xu is Associate Professor of Sociology at Mississippi State University.

Min Zhou is Associate Professor of Sociology and Asian American Studies at the University of California at Los Angeles.

About the Editor

Nijole V. Benokraitis received her Ph.D. in sociology from the University of Texas, Austin. She is currently Professor of Sociology at the University of Baltimore. Dr. Benokraitis has authored, coauthored, edited, or coedited *Feuds about Families: Conservative, Centrist, Liberal, and Feminist Perspectives; Subtle Sexism: Current Practices and Prospects for Change; Marriages and Families: Changes, Choices and Constraints* (3d ed.); *Modern Sexism: Blatant, Subtle, and Covert Discrimination* (2d ed.); *Seeing Ourselves: Classic, Contemporary and Cross-Cultural Readings in Sociology* (5th ed.); and *Affirmative Action and Equal Opportunity: Action, Inaction, and Reaction.* She is a member of the editorial board of *Women and Criminal Justice,* reviews manuscripts for several periodicals, and has published numerous journal articles in the areas of institutional racism, discrimination in government and higher education, and social policy. She has for some time served as a consultant in the areas of sex and race discrimination to women's commissions, business groups, colleges and universities, and state and federal government programs.

1

The Changing Ethnic Profile of U.S. Families in the Twenty-First Century

Nijole V. Benokraitis

The rapid shift in the racial and ethnic composition of the U.S. population is transforming families. As the number and variety of immigrants increase, the way we relate to each other may become both more interesting and more complex. As the selections in this book show, ethnic families from a certain region (such as Southeast Asia, the Mideast, or Central America) may share similar histories, traditions, immigration experiences, and religious or cultural values that shape family life. There is also a rich diversity *within* ethnic groups. As I note in the preface to this collection, it is important to recognize the "heterogeneity of diversity" of U.S. families. Ignoring many of the smaller ethnic groups or assuming, for example, that Asian American families are "the same" gives a skewed picture of diversity and decreases the visibility of a significant number of U.S. households. Later selections provide an up close and personal introduction to the increasingly heterogeneous diversity of contemporary ethnic families. Here, in contrast, I present a broad overview of the range of ethnic family characteristics—the size and growth of minority groups, countries of origin, and the effect of immigration laws, place and length of residence, family structure and living arrangements, and socioeconomic status. I conclude with a brief discussion of whether the

United States is becoming a melting pot or, rather, a tossed salad.

Before we begin, several caveats are in order. First, the U.S. Census Bureau has used different categories of race and ethnicity over the years. The 1970 census, for example, was the first to collect data on Hispanic origin. In the 1980 and 1990 censuses, information was collected on whites and four racial and ethnic minorities—African Americans, Hispanics, Asians and Pacific Islanders, and American Indians (including Alaska Natives). The 2000 census ushered in more changes: respondents could identify themselves as members of more than one race, as either Hispanic or non-Hispanic, and as members of a specific ethnic group. Until the 2000 census data are available, however, we must rely on the Census Bureau's standard categories for classifying ethnic and racial groups.

A second limitation is that Census Bureau categories such as "Hispanic" and "Asian and Pacific Islander" typically encompass very heterogeneous groups. Hispanic Americans, for example, include persons of Mexican, Puerto Rican, Cuban, and Salvadoran descent—people who have different cultural backgrounds, migration patterns, and reasons for immigrating to the United States or elsewhere.[1] Hispanics, according to U.S. government guidelines, are an ethnic group, not a racial group. Most classify themselves as white, a minority classify themselves as black, and an increasing number identify their race as "other," which "underscores the ambiguity of race and ethnic-group definitions in the United States."[2] Asian Americans also include people from locations as disparate as India, Manchuria, and Samoa. They follow different religions, speak different languages, and even use different alphabets.[3]

Many of the Census Bureau's demographic and socioeconomic measures aren't broken down by subgroups within an ethnic group because the populations are very small and comparisons may be unreliable. Whenever possible and appropriate, however, I provide information about some of the subgroups (for the sake of brevity, I use *white* instead of *non-Hispanic white,* and I use *Hispanic* and *Latino* interchangeably.)[4]

SIZE AND GROWTH OF ETHNIC GROUPS

Over the last several decades, the number of culturally diverse groups in the U.S. population has changed significantly. Nearly 70,000 foreign-born[5] people arrive in the United States every day. More than 60,000 are tourists, businesspeople, students, or foreign workers; about 2,200 are immigrants or refugees who will probably become permanent residents of the United States; and an estimated 5,000 make unauthorized entries every day. About 4,000 in the last group are apprehended after crossing the U.S. border. Of the nearly 1,000 who elude detection, many remain while others return to their home countries.[6] Whether they are U.S. citizens or not, many of the current residents are foreign-born. In 1997, for example, 6 in 10 Asians and Pacific Islanders in the United States were foreign-born.[7]

Racial and ethnic minorities now account for approximately 28 percent of the U.S. population, or 73.1 million people. In 2000, 72 percent of the population was white, 12 percent black, 11 per-

cent Latino, 4 percent Asian, and 1 percent American Indian (see Figure 1). Nearly two-thirds of all Latinos were of Mexican origin (65 percent). People of Puerto Rican origin accounted for almost 10 percent of the total Hispanic population; people of Cuban origin, Central and South American origin, and other Latinos each accounted for 4 percent, 14 percent, and 7 percent, respectively.[8] Asians and Pacific Islanders are the most diverse U.S. minority group. The 1990 census included population characteristics for thirteen Asian ethnic groups and six Pacific Islander groups. In 1997, six groups numbered 900,000 or more: Chinese, Filipino, Vietnamese, Asian Indian, Korean, and Japanese. These six groups made up 84 percent of Asians and Pacific Islanders. Hawaiians and other Pacific Islanders accounted for only 5 percent of the Asian and Pacific Islander population.[9] In the same year, the Philippines, China, and Vietnam were among the ten leading countries of birth of the foreign-born population.[10] The Census Bureau estimates that there were 2.4 million American Indians and Alaska Natives in 1998, including 347,000 Hispanic Indians. There are more than 500 recognized American Indian tribes, but one-half of all American Indians identify with one of the eight largest tribes.[11] About 160 distinct languages are still spoken in the United States and Canada.[12]

The U.S. population is expected to grow to 394 million by 2050—a 58 percent increase from its 1990 size of 249 million. By 2050, only slightly more than half of the population will be white. The proportions of other racial and ethnic groups will increase: 15 percent black, almost 25 percent Latino, almost 9 percent Asian and Pacific Islander, and slightly over 1 percent American Indian, Eskimo, and Aleut (see Figure 1). According to Census Bureau projections, the black population will nearly double its present size to 61 million in 2050. The Asian population is expected to be the fastest-growing group. By 2050, it will be 34 million, three and a half times its 1995 level of 9.3 million. Although Asians are the fastest-growing group, Latinos will show the largest nu-

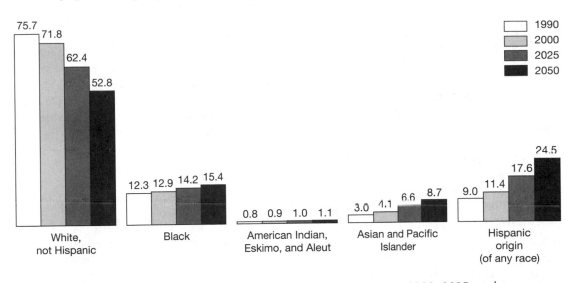

FIGURE 1 Percent of the Population, by Race and Hispanic Origin: 1990, 2000, 2025, and 2050 (Middle-series projections)

Source: U.S. Census Bureau, Current Population Reports, Series P23-194, *Population Profile of the United States: 1997* (Washington, DC: Government Printing Office, 1998), 9.

meric increases of any group—that is, by 2050, Latinos will increase to 97 million, three and a half times their 1995 population.[13] Besides high immigration rates, the acceleration of minority growth also reflects higher birthrates compared with rates in the native-born population. Although fertility rates vary across Hispanic groups, the large number of foreign-born Latinos, who tend to be younger than whites and in their reproductive years, is expected to keep birthrates high.

COUNTRY OF BIRTH

American Indians were the original inhabitants of North America, to which English settlers and subsequent groups migrated. African Americans, of course, were involuntary immigrants to the United States. About 4 million enslaved African Americans swelled population rates between the 1600s and 1800s. Most people who have entered the United States, however, have done so for a

combination of push-and-pull reasons: they seek economic opportunities, hope to reunite with family members who immigrated earlier, or are refugees from brutal political regimes and oppressive religious bigotry.

U.S. immigrants have come from every country in the world. The largest ethnic groups include families with Latino roots (often mixed with African and American Indian stock) in North America (primarily Mexico), Central America (Guatemala, Honduras, El Salvador, Nicaragua, Costa Rica, Panama, and Colombia), Latin America (Brazil, Argentina, Peru, and Ecuador), and the Caribbean (Cuba, Haiti, Puerto Rico, Jamaica, and the Dominican Republic). The largest numbers of families with Asian roots have come from East Asia (China, Japan, and Korea), South Asia (India, Pakistan, Sri Lanka, and Bangladesh), and Southeast Asia (Cambodia, Laos, Vietnam, Thailand, and the Philippines). The largest numbers of families with Middle Eastern roots have come from Syria, Lebanon, Palestine, Iran, Iraq, Jordan, and Turkey. Native Hawaiians and Samoans make up the largest population of Pacific Islanders in the United States. And, especially since 1981, the largest numbers of immigrants from African countries have come from Egypt, Ethiopia, Ghana, and Nigeria.[14]

At each census from 1850 through 1960, the ten leading countries of birth of the foreign-born population were predominantly European countries and Canada. The only exceptions were Mexico (1850–1860, 1920–1960) and China (1860–1880). Europe was the major source of immigration in the United States until 1970. In contrast to the nineteenth century and the latter part of the twentieth century, since 1980 many of the foreign-born who plan to establish permanent U.S. residency are from Asia and Latin America (see Figure 2).

In 1997, people from Mexico, Central America, and South America (combined under "Latin America" in Figure 2) accounted for 51 percent of the foreign-born population.[15] People born in Mexico accounted for 28 percent of the foreign-born population in 1997 and were about 6 times more numerous than immigrants from the Philippines, the next highest ranked country (see Figure 3). While the foreign-born population of Germany and Canada decreased between 1990 and 1997, there were increases of half a million or more from several other countries: China, Cuba, Vietnam, India, the Soviet Union, the Dominican Republic, and El Salvador.[16] Thus, the countries of birth reflect a great diversity of cultural backgrounds, languages, and religions.

SOME EFFECTS OF IMMIGRATION LAWS

The United States is a nation of immigrants, as reflected in its motto *e pluribus unum*—"from many, one." In 1886 President Grover Cleveland dedicated the Statue of Liberty in New York Harbor. On its pedestal are inscribed Emma Lazarus's famous welcoming words: "Give me your tired, your poor, your huddled masses yearning to breathe

free. . . ." Older arrivals, however, have not always welcomed newcomers. Although it is beyond the scope of this essay to summarize U.S. immigration laws, it can be said that since the 1800s a number of immigration and naturalization policies have either restricted or encouraged entrants from other countries when doing so seemed economically and politically desirable.[17] For example,

- In 1882, Congress enacted the Chinese Exclusion Act that outlawed Chinese immigration for ten years and denied citizenship to those Chinese already in the United States.
- In 1913, the California Alien Land Act barred aliens, mostly Japanese farmers, from owning land. Further restrictions were added in 1921 and 1923; the act was repealed in 1948.
- The Immigration Act of 1921 introduced a quota system based on the 1910 census. Each nation was allowed an annual quota of 3 percent of that nationality's U.S. population in 1910. In effect, this law kept the majority the majority. Beginning in 1921, a series of measures created a national origins system that remained the basis of immigration until 1965. This system used the country of birth to determine whether an individual could enter as a legal alien, and the number of previous immigrants and their descendants was used to set the quota of how many people from a country could enter annually.
- The Immigration Act of 1924, also called the National Origins Act, amended the Immigration Act of 1921 by lowering the annual quota to 2 percent. It also barred entry to any "alien ineligible to citizenship." Since Asian immigrants weren't eligible for citizenship, this law effectively ended Asian immigration until after World War II. In effect, the National Origins Act of 1924 and similar legislation boosted immigration from Great Britain, Ireland, and Germany and restricted immigration from southern and eastern Europe and many other parts of the world. The national origins system was abandoned with the passage of the 1965 Immigration and Naturalization Act (see below).
- In 1934, the Tydings-McDuffie Act closed the door to Filipino immigration by reclassifying all Philippine-born Filipinos as aliens and limiting their immigration to 50 people per year.

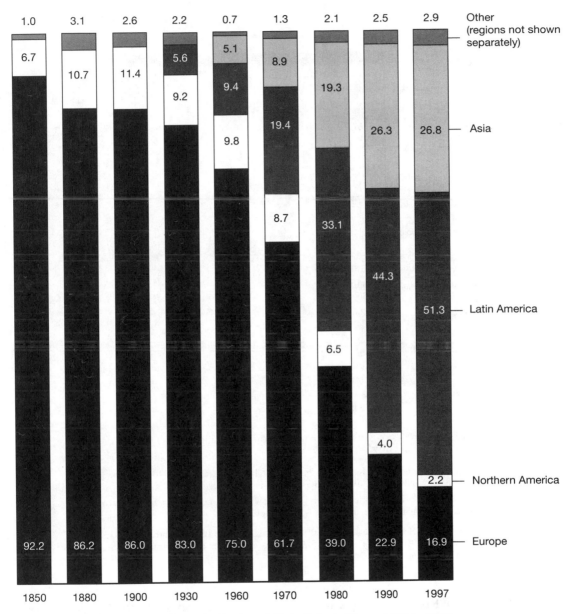

FIGURE 2 Foreign-Born Population by Region of Birth: Selected Years, 1850 to 1997

Source: Dianne A. Schmidley and Campbell Gibson, U.S. Census Bureau, Current Population Reports, Series P23-195, *Profile of the Foreign-Born Population in the United States: 1997* (Washington, DC: Government Printing Office, 1999), 11.

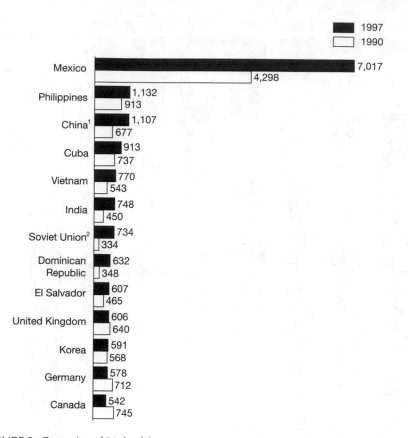

FIGURE 3 Countries of Birth of the Foreign-Born Population, with 500,000 or More in 1997: 1990 and 1997

[1]Including Hong Kong and excluding Taiwan. Data for Taiwan corresponding to the format in Figure 3 are (in thousands) 244 for 1990 and 360 (260–461) for 1997.

[2]The Soviet Union as defined prior to January 1, 1992, when the United States formally recognized 12 independent republics within the former Soviet Union.

Source: Dianne A. Schmidley and Campbell Gibson, U.S. Census Bureau, Current Population Reports, Series P23-195, *Profile of the Foreign-Born Population in the United States: 1997* (Washington, DC: Government Printing Office, 1999), 12.

- The Luce-Celler Bill of 1946, also called the Filipino Naturalization Act, allowed people to immigrate from the Philippines and India. It also allowed Filipinos and Indians to become naturalized citizens. Quotas were set at 100 people per country per year.
- The 1965 Immigration and Naturalization Act eliminated national origins quotas and instituted a series of preferences based largely on two goals: relieving occupational shortages and achieving family reunification. The 1965 law capped annual immigration from the Eastern Hemisphere at 170,000 per year and imposed a 20,000-per-country maximum. It set an annual limit of 120,000 persons from the Western Hemisphere.
- The Immigration Reform and Control Act of 1986 legalized undocumented immigrants who had resided in the United States continuously since 1982. It also authorized special programs to bring in agricultural laborers, enhanced Border

Patrol activities between the United States and Mexico, and implemented stronger sanctions against employers who hired illegal immigrants.

- The Civil Liberties Act of 1988 apologized to the thousands of Japanese Americans who had been detained in internment camps during World War II.
- The Immigration Act of 1990 capped total annual immigration at 700,000 (this number was lowered to 675,000 in 1995). The act established several visa categories, the largest of which is reserved for family members of legal U.S. residents to facilitate family reunification. Another 140,000 employment-based visas are reserved mostly for highly skilled workers.

WHERE ETHNIC GROUPS LIVE

The regional location of different ethnic groups is linked to economic opportunities, historical circumstances, and migration streams (see also Readings 24 and 29). At the beginning of the twentieth century, approximately 90 percent of blacks lived in the South. Blacks started to move to the industrial cities of the North when the cheap labor supplied by European immigrants was reduced during World War I. In addition, difficult economic times in the South led to a migration of blacks to the Northeast and Midwest in the 1930s and 1940s. From 1970 into the late 1990s this trend reversed itself, and African Americans moved back to the South. Now, approximately 53 percent of blacks live in the South, about 10 percent are in the West, and the remaining 37 percent are evenly split between the Midwest and Northeast.[18]

In 1900 and 1930, over 80 percent of the foreign-born population of the United States lived in the Northeast and Midwest. In 1930, 51 percent lived in the Northeast alone. By 1997, the proportion of foreign-born exceeded the national average of 10 percent in nine states: California (25 percent), Hawaii (18 percent), New York (20 percent), Florida (16 percent), New Jersey (15 percent), Arizona (14 percent), Texas (11 percent), and Nevada and Rhode Island (11 percent in each).[19] Thus, by the end of the twentieth century, much of the foreign-born residence had shifted from the Northeast and Midwest to the South, West, and Southwest.

For the most part, historical origins and point of entry into the United States have determined the geographical distribution of the various Latino groups. About 85 percent of all Latinos are concentrated in nine states: California, Texas, New York, Florida, Illinois, New Jersey, Arizona, New Mexico, and Colorado. More than one-half of the Latino population resides in California and Texas. Many southwestern Latinos are recent immigrants, but others identify themselves as *Hispanos*—descendants of Mexican and Spanish settlers who lived in the territory before it was taken by the United States.[20]

Mexicans and Central Americans are drawn to the Southwest because of its proximity to their home countries, job opportunities, and established Latino communities that can help newcomers find jobs. Recent Latino migration waves, however, have enlarged some metropolitan areas. In 2000, for example, nearly 60 percent of Latino immigrants in the Washington, D.C., area identified themselves as Central Americans, and about 31 percent described themselves as Salvadorans[21] (see also Reading 25).

Puerto Ricans, the second largest Latino group, are concentrated primarily in the Northeast, particularly in the New York metropolitan area. Central and South Americans, though entering the United States typically through California, live in the Northeast, while two-thirds of Cubans live in southern Florida. New job opportunities in industries such as meat processing have brought Hispanic immigrants to small towns and rural areas in Georgia, Illinois, Iowa, Michigan, New York, Tennessee, Wisconsin, and Washington.[22]

Historically and at the present time, Asians and Pacific Islanders are also concentrated in the western region of the United States. A majority (57 percent) live in just three states: California, New York, and Hawaii. Most (94 percent) live in metropolitan areas. Of these, one-half lives in the suburbs of metropolitan areas.[23] Some Asian Americans are descendants of Chinese workers brought to the western states beginning in the mid-1800s to work as laborers on the railroads. Others are descendants of Japanese who came in various immigration waves in the late nineteenth and early twentieth centuries. Most Asians, however, as described earlier, immigrated to the United States after passage of the 1965 Immigration and Naturalization Act. In 1998, approximately 39 percent of all Asians and Pacific Islanders lived in California, 10 percent lived in New York, and 7 percent lived in Hawaii.[24]

Over 60 percent of Chinese Americans live in California or New York; about two-thirds of Filipinos and Japanese live in California or Hawaii. Asian Indian and Korean populations are somewhat less concentrated geographically, although large communities live in a handful of states including Illinois, New Jersey, Texas, California, and New York. Southeast Asians have a different settlement pattern because federal resettlement practices created pockets of Southeast Asian refugees in a few states. In 1990, for example, nearly 40 percent of the U.S. Hmong population lived in Minnesota and Wisconsin. One-tenth of American Vietnamese lived in Texas—the largest concentration of Vietnamese outside of California (see also Reading 9).[25]

About 48 percent of American Indians, Eskimos, and Aleuts are concentrated in the West. The geographic concentration of American Indian populations reflects government policies and private practices that reduced the American Indian population in the eastern part of the United States during the 1880s. Many Indians were killed, and others were forced to move to reservations in the West. The Navajo Reservation and Trust Lands, which extend from Arizona to New Mexico and Utah, contain the largest Indian enclave in the country.

In 1930, just 10 percent of American Indians lived in urban areas, compared with 56 percent of all Americans. World War II and federal urban relocation policies from the 1950s through the 1970s brought large numbers of Indians to cities. More than 25,000 American Indians served in the armed forces during World War II and another 50,000 left reservations to work in war-related industries.

Many remained in urban areas after the war. Some took advantage of job opportunities or education benefits through the GI Bill. By the 1990s, about one-half of American Indians lived in urban areas, compared with three-fourths of all Americans.[26] In 1995, more of the nation's American Indians, Eskimos, and Aleuts lived in Oklahoma than in any other state (257,000 or 13 percent). Arizona, California, New Mexico, and Alaska were the next most popular states of residence.[27]

FAMILIES AND HOUSEHOLD STRUCTURES

The Census Bureau divides households into two major categories: family and nonfamily. A *family household* consists of two or more persons living together who are related through marriage, birth, or adoption. It may or may not include dependent children. *Nonfamily households* consist of two or more unrelated people who share living quarters. The count of unmarried-couple households is intended mainly to estimate the number of cohabiting couples, but it also includes the small number of households with a roommate, boarder, or paid employee of the opposite sex.

Household structures and living arrangements vary among and across ethnic groups. Primarily because minorities are younger and have higher birthrates than the white population, they are more likely to live in family households and to have dependent children (see Table 1). In 1998, differences in living arrangements among ethnic families often were as large as the difference between minority and white families. For example, nearly 30 percent of both white and black households consisted of a single person in 1998, compared with just 14 percent of Hispanic and 18 percent of Asian households. Elderly people, particularly widows, often live alone. This might partially explain the lower incidence of single-person households among the relatively young Hispanic and Asian populations. The 23 percent of single-person households among American Indians might be

TABLE 1　Household and Family Structure by Race and Ethnicity, 1998

Race/Ethnicity	Non-Hispanic				Hispanic
	White	African American	Asian	American Indian	
Number of households (millions)	77.9	12.2	3.1	0.7	8.6
Family households (%)	68	67	77	70	81
Nonfamily households (%)	32	33	23	30	19
Single-person households (%)	27	29	18	23	14
	Percent Distribution of Family Households				
With own children, total	46	57	53	52	64
Married couple	36	24	47	33	45
Male head (no wife)	2	3	1	6	3
Female head (no husband)	7	30	5	13	16
Without own children (total)	54	43	47	48	36
Married couple	48	22	35	34	24
Male head (no wife)	3	4	5	3	4
Female head (no husband)	6	16	6	11	7

Note: Subtotals may not add to totals because of rounding. Hispanics may be of any race. Asian includes Pacific Islanders. American Indian includes Eskimos and Aleuts.

Source: Kelvin M. Pollard and William P. O'Hare, "America's Racial and Ethnic Minorities," *Population Bulletin* 54 (September 1999), www.prb.org/pubs/bulletin/bu54-3/part4.htm (accessed June 22, 2000). Reprinted by permission of the Population Reference Bureau.

due to younger members' leaving reservations to search for jobs in the city while an elderly parent, usually a mother, lives alone on the reservation.

On average, foreign-born households are larger than native-born households. In 1997, the average size of foreign-born households (3.32) was considerably larger than the size of native households (2.56). Among households with a foreign-born householder, average household size was smallest where length of residence in the United States was twenty years and over. Household size also varies by country of origin. In 1997, the average household size among families from Mexico was 4.38, compared with 3.32 for all foreign-born households, 3.26 for Asian families, and 2.41 for households from Europe.[28] The higher figure for Mexican American households reflects, in part, higher birthrates among women and the lower proportion of people 65 years and over living in the home. The higher figure for

Asian families, especially recent immigrants, may reflect extended-family members who live under the same roof.

In 1999, nearly 32 percent of Latino families and 53 percent of black families were composed of a single parent with dependent children. Such families composed only 6 percent of Asian families and 9 percent of white families. Except for Asian Americans, minority families were more likely than white families to be headed by a single parent, usually a woman, living with dependent children. Female-headed households with children were the most common family arrangement for African Americans. They accounted for 45 percent of black family households in 1999, compared with 35 percent of American Indian families, 24 percent of Latino families, 13 percent of white families, and 13 percent of Asian American families.[29]

White women (especially cohabitants) are highly likely to marry before the birth of a child, which decreases the number of single-mother families. Black women are much less likely than white women to be cohabiting or to marry when they become mothers, which increases the number of single-mother families.[30] Cohabitation and out-of-wedlock birth are more complex among Latinas. In 1998, almost 38 percent of Puerto Rican families were headed by single mothers, compared with 15 percent of Cuban families, 20 percent of Mexican American families, and 23 percent of Central and South American families.[31] This difference may be partially explained by Puerto Rican Americans' being more accepting of cohabitation, which leads to nonmarital childbearing, while Mexican Americans expect cohabitation and nonmarital childbearing to be a precursor to marriage.[32]

SOCIOECONOMIC CHARACTERISTICS

Most social scientists use income, education, and occupation to measure socioeconomic status (SES). The U.S. median household income in 1998 was $38,885. Asians and Pacific Islanders have the highest median household income among all racial groups (see Figure 4). Household income reflects the number of earners in a household, as well as the income of each earner. In 1997, for example, 58 percent of white families had two or more household members working, compared with 45 percent of black households and 49 percent of Latino households. But 18 percent of Asian families had three or more earners, compared with 13 percent of white families.[33] Median incomes also reflect nativity—that is, in 1998 the median income of households maintained by a native-born person was $39,677, compared with $28,278 for households maintained by a person foreign-born and not a citizen of the United States.[34] This difference in income can be partially explained by the recency of immigration as well as by educational and occupational variations across and within ethnic groups.

In educational attainment, there's considerable variation. In 1999, 42 percent of Asians ages 25

and over had a bachelor's degree or higher, compared with 28 percent of whites, 16 percent of blacks, 11 percent of American Indians, and 12 percent of Latinos.[35] Variation also is evident within groups. Across Latino subgroups, for example, almost 25 percent of Cubans ages 25 and over had a bachelor's degree, compared with 18 percent for Central and South Americans, 11 percent for Puerto Ricans, and 7 percent for Mexicans.[36] Although figures are not available for specific Asian groups, those who have been in the United States for several generations, such as the Chinese and Japanese, have higher educational attainment rates than others—such as the Hmong, Vietnamese, Laotians, and Cambodians—who immigrated to the United States comparatively recently.[37] Similarly, many Asian Indians who arrived soon after 1965 were well-educated professionals, and more recent entrants have tended to be blue-collar workers and economically more diverse[38] (see also Reading 33).

Education provides access to income and economic opportunities. Although the occupational status of ethnic groups has improved slowly over the past decade, Latinos, blacks, and American Indians are more likely than whites or Asians to work in low-paying, semiskilled jobs or as service workers (see Table 2). Minorities who hold white-collar jobs are more likely than whites or Asians to work in clerical positions or in sales rather than as higher-earning managers or professionals. And although the number of U.S. workers in farming, fishing, or forestry is very small, it is greatest among Latinos, reflecting the large number of Hispanics who work in agriculture or have rural backgrounds.

These data mask striking differences within ethnic subgroups, however. Although many Asian Americans have prospered, Laotians, Cambodians, and Vietnamese remain at the low end of the SES scale. Asian Indians, Japanese, and Chinese Americans have a high rate of managerial and professional positions (44, 37, and 36 percent, respectively) while more than 20 percent of Vietnamese and 37 percent of Southeast Asian Amer-

Income in thousands of 1998 dollars

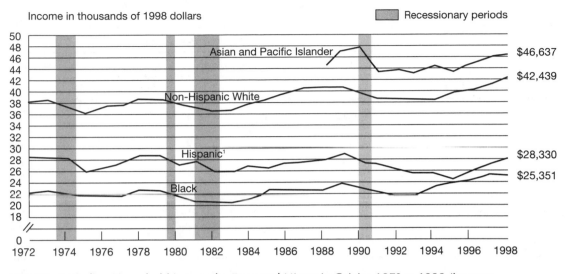

FIGURE 4 Median Household Income by Race and Hispanic Origin: 1972 to 1998 (Income in thousands of 1998 dollars)

Note: The Population Reference Bureau cites $29,000 as the median household income for American Indians, Eskimos, and Aleuts for 1997; www.prb.org/pubs/bulletin/bu54-3/part6.htm (accessed June 18, 2000).

[1]Hispanics may be of any race.

Source: U.S. Census Bureau, Current Population Reports, Series P60-206, *Money Income in the United States: 1998* (Washington, DC: Government Printing Office, 1999), ix.

icans work in low-skilled or unskilled jobs. In addition, recent immigrants from China, Laos, Thailand, and Cambodia tend to earn lower incomes than native-born Asian Americans.[39]

There are occupational differences within Latino subgroups as well. For example, Cubans and native-born Latinos are much more likely than other Hispanics to work in managerial, professional, technical, and administrative positions.[40] While many Cuban Americans are doing well economically, 11 percent of Cuban American families live below the poverty level. This poverty rate is about twice as high as that of white families (6 percent) but lower than that of many other Latino families (e.g., 24 percent for Mexican American families, 27 percent for Puerto Rican families, and almost 19 percent for families from Central and South America).[41] Although many ethnic groups have made great strides in business, academia, and other sectors, they continue to face

discrimination across all socioeconomic levels (see Chapters 5 and 6).

A MELTING POT OR A TOSSED SALAD?

During much of the twentieth century, social scientists and popular writers embraced the notion of a "melting pot" in which immigrants would assimilate by conforming to the dominant Euro-American (or British American) cultural values, language, and customs.[42] By the 1980s more of my colleagues and students were describing U.S. society as a "smorgasbord," a "potpourri," and a "tossed salad" where different vegetables were mixed together but maintained their own color, flavor, shape, and texture. In a similar vein, one researcher observed that "If the United States is a 'melting pot,' it could be getting harder to stir."[43] The end of the twentieth century witnessed

TABLE 2   Occupational Distribution by Race and Ethnicity, 1998

| | *Percent of Employed Persons, Ages 16+* | | | | |
| | Non-Hispanic | | | | Hispanic |
Occupation	White	African American	Asian	American Indian	
Total (thousands)	97,162	14,028	4,942	892	12,983
White collar					
Managerial and professional[1]	33	20	34	20	15
Technical and administrators[2]	30	30	31	31	23
Blue collar					
Skilled labor[3]	11	8	8	12	13
Semi-skilled and unskilled labor[4]	12	20	11	17	22
Services[5]	12	21	15	17	21
Farming, fishing, and forestry	2	1	1	2	5

Note: Hispanics may be of any race. Asian includes Pacific Islanders. American Indian includes Eskimos and Aleuts. Percentages may not add to 100 because of rounding.

[1]Includes managers, administrators, professionals, and teachers.

[2]Includes technicians and related support staff, administrative and clerical support, and sales.

[3]Includes precision production, craft, and repair workers.

[4]Includes machine operators, assemblers, inspectors, transportation workers, handlers, equipment cleaners, helpers, and laborers.

[5]Includes private household workers, protective services, and other service workers.

Source: Kelvin M. Pollard and William P. O'Hare, "America's Racial and Ethnic Minorities," *Population Bulletin* 54 (September 1999), www.prb.org/pubs/bulletin/bu54-3/part6.htm (accessed June 22, 2000). Reprinted by permission of the Population Reference Bureau.

increased interest in supporting "diversity" and "multiculturalism," respecting the differences between racial and ethnic groups, and recognizing the many contributions that non-European immigrants have made and continue to make to U.S. society.

This cultural pluralism perspective is probably due to many factors: the rise in immigration rates when restrictive immigration quotas for non-Western groups were relaxed; the growth of racial and ethnic protest movements by African Americans, Mexican Americans, and American Indians during the 1960s and 1970s; the general population's concern about an increase in hate crimes and racial violence that have created divisiveness and strife; a push on college faculties by many scholars and educators (with roots in African, Asian, and Latin American countries) who have

endorsed multicultural studies and programs; the dominant culture's respect (albeit stereotypical, as you will see in several readings) for Asians as the "model minority"; and the high visibility of well-educated, highly skilled, and successful Internet entrepreneurs (many of Asian heritage) who played an important role in propelling U.S. society into the high-tech era during the late 1990s. As a result, and although the efforts are modest, many corporations, schools, and other institutions have implemented programs to teach tolerance and greater appreciation of cultural differences.

Not everyone is enthusiastic about the recognition of U.S. cultural diversity, of course. Historian Arthur Schlesinger Jr., for example, denounced multiculturalism perspectives because they repudiate the idea of a melting pot: "The contemporary ideal is not assimilation but ethnicity. We used to say *e pluribus unum.* Now we glorify *pluribus* and belittle *unum.* The melting pot yields to the Tower of Babel."[44] Others feel (or hope) that diversity is a passing fad.

While preparing this anthology, I saw much evidence that some ethnic and racial group *individuals* have been upwardly mobile economically (see Table 2 and Readings 26 through 28) or have penetrated some political offices, especially at local levels. But many ethnic and racial families still face enormous prejudice and discrimination across most U.S. institutions. Also, it's not clear that cultural assimilation is desirable. As many of the selections in Chapter 7 show, assimilative efforts often produce unavoidable intergenerational conflict and unhealthy risk-taking behavior among many adolescents. Nevertheless, I haven't seen much data to support the notion that diversity is a passing fad. Quite to the contrary, there is more heterogeneity across and within diverse ethnic and racial families than many of us realize. And, as the authors of many of the readings show, heterogeneity enriches and strengthens U.S. society.

Despite immigrants' many contributions, ethnic families should not be romanticized (see Reading 43). As scholars and members of ethnic groups speak for themselves in this book, they describe a clash of cultural values, gender role strains, parenting stress, and family crises. Despite such difficulties, however, many of the selections also document enormous resiliency, determination to succeed, and strong family ties that help individuals overcome considerable adversity.

NOTES

1. "*Hispanic* is an English-language word derived from *Hispania,* the Roman name for Spain. . . . *Latino,* an alternative collective designation which recognizes the Latin American origins of many groups, is a Spanish-language word and therefore more acceptable to many Spanish-speaking Americans"; Joe R. Feagin and Clairece Booher Feagin, *Racial and Ethnic Relations,* 6th ed. (Upper Saddle River, NJ: Prentice Hall, 1999), 291.

2. Jorge del Pinal and Audrey Singer, "Generations of Diversity: Latinos in the United States," *Population Bulletin* 52

(October 1997): 1–2, www.prb.org/pubs/bulletin/bu52-3.htm (accessed June 21, 2000).

3. Kelvin M. Pollard and William P. O'Hare, "America's Racial and Ethnic Minorities," *Population Bulletin* 54 (September 1999), www.prb.org/pubs/bulletin/bu54-3.htm (accessed June 22, 2000).

4. Beginning on January 1, 2003, the Census Bureau will use a new terminology that includes the terms *Hispanic* and *Latino.*

5. The Census Bureau defines the *native population* as residents who were born in the United States or in an outlying area of the United States and U.S. residents who were born in a foreign country but had at least one parent who was a U.S. citizen. All other residents of the United States are classified as foreign-born. The *foreign-born population* includes immigrants (defined by the Immigration and Naturalization Service as aliens admitted to the United States for lawful permanent residence), legal nonimmigrants (e.g., refugees and persons on student or work visas), and persons residing in the United States illegally (undocumented aliens); Dianne A. Schmidley and Campbell Gibson, U.S. Census Bureau, Current Population Reports, Series P23-195, *Profile of the Foreign-Born Population in the United States: 1997* (Washington, DC: Government Printing Office, 1999), 2, 8.

6. Philip Martin and Elizabeth Midgley, "Immigration to the United States," *Population Bulletin* 54 (June 1999): 1–4, www.prb.org/pubs/bulletin/bu54-2.htm (accessed June 23, 2000).

7. U.S. Department of Commerce News Release, "Region of Birth a Key Indicator of Well-Being for America's Foreign-Born Population, Census Bureau Reports," www.census.gov/Press-Release/www/1999/cb99-195.html (accessed June 23, 2000).

8. Roberto R. Ramirez, "The Hispanic Population in the United States: March 1999," U.S. Census Bureau, www.census.gov/prod/2000pubs/p20.527pdf (accessed June 29, 2000).

9. Pollard and O'Hare.

10. U.S. Census Bureau, "Census Bureau Facts for Features," www.census.gov/Press-Release/www/2000/cb00ff05.html (accessed July 2, 2000).

11. The largest tribes are the Cherokee (308,000), Navajo (219,000), Chippewa (104,000), Sioux (103,000), Choctaw (82,000), Pueblo (53,000), Apache (50,000), and Iroquois (49,000). U.S. Census Bureau, press releases CB91-215 (June 12, 1991) and CB92-244 (November 14, 1992).

12. J. A. Price, "North American Indian Families," in *Ethnic Families in America: Patterns and Variations,* ed. C. H. Mindel and R. W. Habenstein (New York: Elsevier, 1981), 245–68.

13. Gregory Spencer and Frederick W. Hollmann, "National Population Projections," U.S. Census Bureau, Current Population Reports, Series P23-194, *Population Profile of the United States: 1997* (Washington, DC: Government Printing Office, 1998), 8–9.

14. U.S. Census Bureau, *Statistical Abstract of the United States: 1999* (Washington, DC: Government Printing Office,

1999), 11–12. For good overviews of the immigration waves, values, religious beliefs, family roles, and language of some of these groups see Eleanor W. Lynch and Marci J. Hanson, eds., *Developing Cross-Cultural Competence: A Guide for Working with Children and Their Families,* 2d ed. (Baltimore: Paul H. Brookes Publishing Co., 1998), and Monica McGoldrick, Joe Giordano, and John K. Pearce, eds., *Ethnicity and Family Therapy* (New York: Guilford Press, 1996).

15. The Census Bureau data in Figure 2 use the six regions of the world as defined by the United Nations. These regions are Europe, Asia, Africa, Oceania, Latin America, and Northern [sic] America.

16. Schmidley and Gibson, 12–13.

17. Hundreds of books examine immigration and migration history, immigration laws, and settlement patterns. Volumes that address immigration, assimilation, and ethnic identity include the following: Robert M. Jiobu, *Ethnicity and Assimilation* (Albany: State University of New York Press, 1988); Ernest McCarus, ed., *The Development of Arab-American Identity* (Ann Arbor: University of Michigan Press, 1994); Alejandro Portes, ed., *The New Second Generation* (New York: Russell Sage Foundation, 1996); Jean Bacon, *Life Lines: Community, Family, and Assimilation among Asian Indian Immigrants* (New York: Oxford University Press, 1996); Juanita Tamayo Lott, *Asian Americans: From Racial Category to Multiple Identities* (Walnut Creek, CA: AltaMira Press, 1998); Frank D. Bean and Stephanie Bell-Rose, eds., *Immigration and Opportunity: Race, Ethnicity, and Employment in the United States* (New York: Russell Sage Foundation, 1999); Vijay Prashad, *The Karma of Brown Folk* (Minneapolis: University of Minnesota Press, 2000); and Meri Nana-Ama Danquah, ed., *Becoming American: Personal Essays by First Generation Immigrant Women* (New York: Hyperion, 2000).

18. U.S. Census Bureau, www.census.gov/Press-Release/www/2000/cb00-27.html (accessed June 29, 2000).

19. Schmidley and Gibson, 14–15.

20. Pollard and O'Hare.

21. Rose Ann M. Rentería, "A Vibrant Latino Presence in Washington, DC," *Footnotes* 28 (May/June 2000): 1, 41.

22. Ibid.

23. Claudette E. Bennett and Kymberly A. Debarros, "The Asian and Pacific Islander Population," U.S. Census Bureau, Current Population Reports, Series P23-194, *Population Profile of the United States: 1997* (Washington, DC: Government Printing Office, 1998), 46–47.

24. Based on U.S. Census Bureau data presented in www.census.gov/population/estimates/state/rank/strnktb4.txt (accessed June 29, 2000).

25. Pollard and O'Hare.

26. Ibid.

27. U.S. Census Bureau, www.census.gov/Press-Release/cb96-36.html (accessed June 29, 2000).

28. Schmidley and Gibson, 28–29.

29. Ramirez;   www.census.gov/population/socdemo/race/api99/table03.txt; U.S. Department of Commerce News, www.census.gov/Press-Release/www/2000/cb00-27.html (accessed June 29, 2000).

30. W. D. Manning and N. S. Landale, "Racial and Ethnic Differences in the Role of Cohabitation in Premarital Childbearing," *Journal of Marriage and the Family* 58 (February 1996): 63–77.

31. U.S. Census Bureau, *Statistical Abstract of the United States: 1999* (Washington, DC: Government Printing Office, 1999), Table 55.

32. R. S. Oropesa, "Normative Beliefs about Marriage and Cohabitation: A Comparison of Non-Latino Whites, Mexican Americans, and Puerto Ricans," *Journal of Marriage and the Family* 56 (February 1996): 49–62.

33. Census data cited in Pollard and O'Hare.

34. U.S. Census Bureau, Current Population Reports, Series P60-206, *Money Income in the United States: 1998* (Washington, DC: Government Printing Office, 1999).

35. Ramirez;   www.census.gov/population/socdemo/race/api99/table03.txt; U.S. Department of Commerce News, www.census.gov/Press-Release/www/2000/cb00-27.html (accessed June 29, 2000). The figure for American Indians is based on ages 25 to 44 and is for 1998; Pollard and O'Hare.

36. Ramirez.

37. U.S. Department of Commerce News, "2 in 5 of Asians and Pacific Islanders Have Bachelor Degrees or Higher, Census Bureau Reports," www.census.gov/Press-Release/www/2000/cb00-76.html (accessed June 23, 2000).

38. See, for example, Gregory L. Pettys and Pallassana R. Balgopal, "Multigenerational Conflicts and New Immigrants: An Indo-American Experience," *Families in Society* 79 (July–August 1998): 410–22.

39. Sharon M. Lee, "Asian Americans: Diverse and Growing," *Population Bulletin* 53 (June 1998): 1–40.

40. Jorge del Pinal and Audrey Singer, "Generations of Diversity: Latinos in the United States," *Population Bulletin* 52 (1997): 1–48.

41. Ramirez.

42. See, for example, Israel Zangwill, *The Melting Pot* (New York: Macmillan, 1925); Milton M. Gordon, *Assimilation in American Life: The Role of Race, Religion, and National Origins* (New York: Oxford University Press, 1964); and Nathan Glazer and Daniel Patrick Moynihan, *Beyond the Melting Pot: The Negroes, Puerto Ricans, Jews, Italians, and Irish of New York City* (Cambridge: MIT Press, 1963).

43. Kelvin Pollard, "U.S. Diversity Is More Than Black and White," Population Reference Bureau, www.prb.org/pubs/usds99.htm (accessed June 26, 2000).

44. Quoted in Feagin and Feagin, 464.

CHAPTER 1

Socialization and Family Values

This chapter is about children's ethnic socialization, or the ways in which ethnic group membership and values affect children's development. The peer group plays an important role in the socialization process as the child matures:

> An Asian girl whose family recently has arrived from Vietnam attends a primarily White school. She studies hard and takes special English classes. Soon she is speaking English well, getting good grades in school, and translating for her parents. From her White friends she learns the latest fads in clothing and popular music. She begins to spend more time with her friends and studies less. Her parents worry that she is losing her culture.[1]

The mass media, especially television, also provide children with "an unending array of values and ideas about the world, people like themselves, and those who are different from them."[2] But, although peers, television, the school, and religious organizations are important socialization agents, parents and the family remain the major transmitters of values within the socialization process.

As the five readings in Chapter 1 show, children acquire the behaviors, perceptions, attitudes, and values of an ethnic group, and come to see themselves and others as members of such groups, primarily through their parents. In an overview of ethnic families, Ross D. Parke and Raymond Buriel show that the socialization concerns of black, American Indian, Asian American, and Latino families are similar in many ways (Reading 2). Most native-born and immigrant parents try to instill similar values in their children: racial pride and a strong ethnic identity, self-discipline, cooperation within the family unit, respect for extended-family members, and the achievement of success in the dominant society despite widespread prejudice and discrimination.[3]

Readings 3 through 6 take a closer look at parental socialization within ethnic families. Since the mid-1960s, some social scientists have described the rise of mother-headed black families in the United States as "pathological" and resulting in negative effects for children.[4] More recently, many researchers and theorists have argued that poverty and economic discrimination, rather than family structure, have a negative effect on the outcomes of many black children (see Chapters 5 and 6).[5] Ramona W. Denby argues that, regardless of family structure, most black parents embrace child-rearing strategies that emphasize adapting to the majority culture's views on being successful without sacrificing their children's racial identity (Reading 3). Denby attributes many black parents' successful socialization processes to a "core set of values" that include intergenerational shared parenting, emphasis on parenthood, community support structures, and a close relationship with black churches that promote and intensify family solidarity.

Unlike black families, many immigrant Asian American parents are raising their children in a "foreign" culture. In the case of Filipino immigrants, for example, parents may experience socialization conflicts "when the differing values of Filipino parents and their American-reared children collide."[6] In Reading 4, Pauline Agbayani-Siewart examines some of the collisions between traditional Filipino family cultural practices and many children's Americanized behavior. Like Denby in Reading 3 on black parents, Agbayani-Siewart argues that *fictive kin* (nonrelatives who are accepted as part of the family) play a critical role in dealing with acculturative stress while providing important resources for the immigrant family.

Many Filipinos could enter the United States without restriction after 1934 because the U.S. government seized the Philippines between 1901 and 1913. Unlike Filipinos, however, other Asian groups—such as the Taiwanese—immigrated to the United States only after 1965, when President Lyndon B. Johnson signed the Immigration and Nationality Act of 1965 (see Reading 1). This act allowed family reunification, tried to reduce the backlog of individuals who were waiting for admission, and corrected a previous legacy of anti-Asian bias in the nation's immigration laws.[7] Have recent immigration waves influenced socialization patterns? Franklin Ng shows that Confucian values still shape the important ties that maintain a family (Reading 5). Because of the need to adapt to a new environment and the small number of extended families in the United States, however, some Taiwanese families are less traditional in their approach to family roles and the father's unquestioned authority in the family.[8]

Many (though not all) ethnic families initially reside in "ethnic enclaves" that provide jobs (see Reading 1 and Chapters 5 and 6). About one-third of American Indians live on reservations. The majority, however, have migrated to cities to find employment or educational training and have married outside of their ethnic group. A few have established lucrative gambling establishments that create jobs, health clinics, new schools, sanitation systems, and services for the elderly.[9] Despite the geographic dispersion of many American Indians, Angela Cavender Wilson maintains that much of the survival of American Indian culture is a result of indirect rather than direct socialization (Reading 6). She argues that indirect socialization, especially in stories transmitted from grandmothers to granddaughters, enhances an American Indian's sense of heritage, roots, and an enduring sense of responsibility to ensure cultural survival.

As you read Chapter 2, it's important to note that many ethnic families emphasize common themes, such as cooperation in extended families, reliance on spiritual values that reinforce family relationships, and a focus on discipline to ensure success in the United States in accordance with the majority culture's values. In addition, many ethnic parents must teach their children about ethnic prejudice, discrimination, or biracial identity.[10] You'll see also that across ethnic families ethnic socialization may vary quite a bit in attitudes about discipline and gender roles.[11]

NOTES

1. Mary Jane Rotheram and Jean S. Phinney, "Introduction: Definitions and Perspectives in the Study of Children's Ethnic Socialization," in *Children's Ethnic Socialization: Pluralism and Development,* ed. Jean S. Phinney and Mary Jane Rotheram (Newbury Park, CA: Sage 1987), 10.
2. Gordon L. Berry, "Black Family Life on Television and the Socialization of the African American Child: Images of Marginality," *Journal of Comparative Family Studies* 29 (Summer 1998): 234.
3. Socialization values may differ within ethnic subgroups, depending on the parent's social class. See, for example, Robin L. Harwood, Axel Schoelmerich, Elizabeth Ventura-Cook, Pamela A. Schulze, and Stephanie P. Wilson, "Culture and Class Influences on Anglo and Puerto Rican Mothers' Beliefs Regarding Long-Term Socialization Goals and Child Behavior," *Child Development* 67 (1996): 2446–61. Socioeconomic differences in parenting styles are discussed in Chapter IV.
4. Daniel P. Moynihan, *The Negro Family: The Case for National Action* (Washington, DC: Government Printing Office, 1965).
5. For a summary of ideological and political perspectives on the "deterioration" of the black family, see Nijole V. Benokraitis, ed., *Feuds about Families: Conservative, Centrist, Liberal, and Feminist Perspectives* (Upper Saddle River, NJ: Prentice Hall, 2000).
6. Barbara M. Posadas, *The Filipino Americans* (Westport, CT: Greenwood Press, 1999), 48.
7. See Hsiang-shui Chen, *Chinatown No More: Taiwan Immigrants in Contemporary New York* (Ithaca, NY: Cornell University Press, 1992).
8. Other researchers have noted that although Filipinas observe male dominance/female submissiveness in public behavior, there is often a more egalitarian approach to family life in the home. See Rocco A. Cimmarusti, "Exploring Aspects of Filipino-American Families," *Journal of Marital and Family Therapy* 22 (April 1996): 205–17.
9. See, for example, D. Holmstrom, "Gambling Ventures Reverse Poverty for Only Some Indians," *Christian Science Monitor* (July 8, 1994): 3.
10. See Jean S. Phinney and Victor Chavira, "Parental Ethnic Socialization and Adolescent Coping with Problems Related to Ethnicity," *Journal of Research on Adolescence* 5 (1995): 31–53; Stephen M. Quintana and Elizabeth M. Vera, "Mexican American Children's Ethnic Identity, Understanding Ethnic Prejudice, and Parental Ethnic Socialization," *Hispanic Journal of Behavioral Sciences* 21 (November 1999): 387–404; Teresa Kay

Williams and Michael C. Thornton, "Social Construction of Ethnicity versus Personal Experience: The Case of Afro-Amerasians," *Journal of Comparative Family Studies* 29 (Summer 1998): 225–67. Racial socialization may vary, however, by socioeconomic status. For example, Anita Jones Thomas and Suzette L. Speight, "Racial Identities and Racial Socialization Attitudes of African American Parents," *Journal of Black Psychology* 25 (May 1999): 152–70, found that middle-class black parents are more likely to racially socialize their children than are parents from lower socioeconomic levels.

11. A number of recently published monographs explore socialization and family values in specific ethnic groups. The "New American" series published by Greenwood Press, for example, includes the following titles: Hien Duc Do, *The Vietnamese Americans* (1999); Won Moo Hurh, *The Korean Americans* (1998); Karen Isaksen Leonard, *The South Asian Americans* (1997); and Silvio Torres-Saillant and Ramona Hernández, *The Dominican Americans* (1998).

2 | Socialization Concerns in African American, American Indian, Asian American, and Latino Families

Ross D. Parke and Raymond Buriel

Socialization is a process through which a child acquires the beliefs, attitudes, behavior, and values of a culture and learns the social and interpersonal skills needed to function effectively in society. Ross D. Parke and Raymond Buriel show that ethnic families, like all families, have an early, pervasive, and highly influential effect on their children and on other family members.

AFRICAN AMERICAN FAMILIES

... Nobles, Goddard, Cavil, and George (1987) have defined the African American family as follows: "The African American family is a term used to characterize a group of people who are biologically and spiritually bonded or connected and whose members' relations to each other and the outside world are governed by a particular set of cultural beliefs, historical experiences and behavioral practices" (p. 22). Sudarkasa (1993) notes that

Source: From Ross D. Parke and Raymond Buriel, "Socialization in the Family: Ethnic and Ecological Perspectives," in *Handbook of Child Psychology,* 5th ed., ed. William Damon (New York: Wiley, 1998), 502–09. Copyright © 1998 John Wiley & Sons, Inc. Adapted by permission of John Wiley and Sons, Inc.

to understand families, households, and socialization of children among African Americans, it is important to understand that these groupings evolved from African family structure in which coresidential families were the norm. Sudarkasa suggests that the type and quality of adaptations to slavery and life in America were perhaps facilitated by the West African heritage of African Americans. From her studies of West African culture, she contends that African extended-family traditions may have proved useful in preserving family ties and for the socialization of children in the face of the disruptive aspects of slavery and its aftermath. Greenfield and Cocking (1994) have also argued that more attention needs to be paid to the positive heritage that ethnic minority socialization practices owe to their culture of origin. Characteristics of African American extended-kin systems noted most frequently in the literature include: (a) a high degree of geographical propinquity; (b) a strong sense of family and familial obligation; (c) fluidity of household boundaries, with great willingness to absorb relatives, both real and fictive; (d) frequent interaction with relatives; (e) frequent extended-family get-togethers for special occasions and holidays; and (f) a system of mutual aid (Harrison et al., 1990; Hatchett & Jackson, 1993). Some might surmise that extended-kin behavior among African Americans is a response to poverty rather than an authentic cultural characteristic of the group. However, there is evidence (H. McAdoo, 1978) that higher-SES African Americans have greater activity within kin networks than their lower-SES counterparts. This suggests that higher-SES African Americans continue to derive physical and psychological benefits from these behaviors. Boykin (1983; Boykin & Toms, 1985) has also noted similarities between the West African traditions of spirituality, harmony, affect, and communalism and African American culture.

The influence of the extended family among African Americans is important because of the large number of female-headed households that require child-rearing assistance and economic support (M. Wilson, 1992). The proportion of African American households with elderly heads that have young family members is also high, about one in three families (Pearson, Hunter, Ensminger, & Kellam, 1990) When coupled with the fact that many African American grandparents live in close proximity to their married children and families, it is obvious that African American grandparents have many opportunities to influence the development of their grandchildren. Pearson et al. (1990) found that in multigenerational households, mothers were the primary caregivers, followed by grandmothers and then fathers. Grandmothers also showed more supportive behaviors in mother/grandmother families than in mother/father/grandmother families. In

mother-absent families, grandmothers were more involved in control and punishment of children. Tolson and Wilson (1990) found that the presence of grandmothers in African American families increases the moral–religious emphasis in the household. Nobles et al. (1987) note that such religious emphasis helps to sustain the African American family and reinforce the sense of family and family solidarity. While some research suggests that children are better adjusted in grandmother households (Staples & Johnson, 1993), other research suggests that intergenerational conflict may offset the positive effects of grandmother presence.

Male-present households were the norm in poor African American communities in the period between 1880 and 1925 (Staples & Johnson, 1993). Until the 1980s, most African American families included two parents; today, approximately 42% of all African American children live in two-parent families (U.S. Census Bureau, 1994). Despite the statistical norm of two-parent families until recently, much of the research on African American fathers focused either on fathers' absence or their maladaptive responses to familial roles (Bowman, 1993). Now, a small but growing body of research is beginning to focus on African American husband-fathers who remain with their families. Bowman (1993) notes that researchers are beginning to document the high level of involvement among African American husband-fathers in child rearing, family decision making, and the economic provider role. J. McAdoo (1993) notes that across several studies, African American spouses share equally in the major decisions in the family. From an exchange theory perspective, cooperation in decision making has been essential because in most families both spouses have had to work to overcome the lower wages earned by the husband (J. McAdoo, 1993).

Previous research suggests that persistent economic marginality among African American fathers may lessen their perceptions of the quality of family life and contribute to their separation from their families (Farley & Allen, 1987; W. Wilson, 1987). Bowman (1993) has adopted a role strain model to investigate how African American males perceive economic marginality and how cultural resources facilitate adaptive modes of coping. He has shown that subjective cultural strengths, which are transmitted across generations, appear to reduce harmful effects of provider role barriers among husband-fathers and to facilitate adaptive coping. In particular, religious beliefs appear to be strongly associated with effective coping. Bowman also found that in his national sample, African American husband-fathers were much more likely to have jobs (75%) than unmarried fathers (58%). Among African American fathers, joblessness appears to be a major factor distinguishing the growing numbers of unmarried fathers from traditional husband-fathers.

When African American fathers from working-class backgrounds discipline children, the discipline is more often physical than verbal and delivered in accordance to the transgression's consequences rather than the child's intent (Staples & Johnson, 1993). Although these parents may use physical discipline, they rarely couple this with withdrawal of love from children, which may eliminate some of the anxiety and resentment associated with this disciplinary method. Because African American socialization stresses obedience to adults and may involve physical discipline, parents have often been described as harsh, rigid, and strict (P. Portes, Dunham, & Williams, 1986). The disciplinary style of African American parents is sometimes referred to as being parent-centered rather than child-centered because it does not primarily take into account the desires of the child (Kelley, Power, & Wimbush, 1992). These descriptions of African American parents and their disciplinary style fail to take into account the settings in which parents must raise children and the adaptive value connected to their parent-centered approach to child rearing. Growing up in dangerous neighborhoods brings with it greater risks for involvement in antisocial behavior, which can have serious personal consequences, whether one is a victim or a perpetrator. Under these circumstances, strict obedience to parental authority is an adaptive strategy that parents may

endeavor to maintain through physical discipline (Kelley et al., 1992).This disciplinary method may also serve to impress upon children the importance of following rules in society and the consequences incurred from breaking those rules when one is a member of an ethnic or racial group that is unfairly stereotyped as violent (Willis, 1992). Kelley and her colleagues (Kelley et al., 1992; Kelley, Sanchez-Hucies, & Walker, 1993) note, however, that there is considerable diversity in the disciplinary methods used by African American parents. Younger mothers and mothers raising their children alone use more physical discipline. Mothers with less education use more restrictive disciplinary practices that include insensitivity, inflexibility, and inconsistent parent behavior. Mothers who are more involved in organized religion also express more child-oriented disciplinary attitudes (Kelley et al., 1992; Kelley et al., 1993).

An important socialization goal of many ethnic minority parents is fostering a sense of ethnic pride in children (Harrison et al., 1990). Some parents believe that in order for their children to successfully confront the hostile social environment they will encounter as African Americans, it is necessary to teach them to be comfortable with their Blackness (Harrison, 1985; Peters, 1985). Bowman and Howard's (1985) study of a national sample of African American three-generational families indicated that the manner in which parents oriented their children toward racial barriers was a significant element in children's motivation, achievement, and prospects for upward mobility. Parents of successful children emphasized ethnic pride, self-development, awareness of racial barriers, and egalitarianism in their socialization practices. Using a national sample, Thornton, Chatters, Taylor, and Allen (1990) also report that two out of three African American parents indicate that they either spoke or acted in a manner intended to racially socialize children. African American parents envisioned racial socialization as involving messages regarding their experiences as minority group members, themes emphasizing individual character and goals, and information related to African American cultural heritage. In addition, Thorton et al. found that (a) older parents were more likely than younger parents to view racial socialization information as a necessary element of the socialization process; (b) that mothers were more likely than fathers to educate children about race; (c) that never-married parents, both women and men, were less likely than their married counterparts to racially socialize their children; (d) that fathers residing in the Northeast were more likely than those living in the South to racially socialize children; and (e) that mothers living in racially integrated neighborhoods were more likely to socialize their children to racial matters than were mothers living in all–African American communities.

AMERICAN INDIAN FAMILIES

At one time in the recent past American Indians were known as the "Vanishing Americans." Since 1940, however, the American Indian population has increased at every census count. The Indian population was 345,000 in 1940, but in 1990 numbered nearly 2,000,000 American Indians and Alaska Natives. American Indians are a socioculturally diverse group consisting of over 450 distinct tribal units who speak over 100 different languages (Trimble & Medicine, 1993). Typically, American Indians prefer their tribal designation over the term American Indian (Burgess, 1980).The Navajo of New Mexico and Arizona is the largest tribe, with more than 170,000 members. Other large tribes include the Cherokee, Sioux, and Chippewa, as well as the Aleuts and Eskimos.

Today, approximately 70% of American Indians live off reservations (Banks, 1991), mostly in urban areas. For example, Los Angeles, California, has the largest concentration of American Indians in the United States. Despite this, most research on American Indians focuses on those living on reservations. Due to cultural differences and discrimination, many Indians have a difficult time adjusting to life in urban areas. For this rea-

son, many reservation Indians who migrate to urban areas tend to settle in cities and towns near reservations and to maintain contact with family on the reservation (Banks, 1991). Such living arrangements close to the reservation are more conducive to the development of biculturalism than when Indians live in large urban areas further removed from reservations. Contact with Euro-Americans and other cultural groups such as Latinos have introduced changes in traditional Indian values and behaviors. . . .

American Indian families may be characterized as a collective cooperative social network that extends from the mother and father union to the extended family and ultimately the community and tribe (Burgess, 1980). American Indian tribes are resilient in that they have withstood attempts at extermination, removal from their traditional lands, extreme poverty, removal of their children to boarding schools, loss of self governance, and assimilationist policies aimed at destroying Indian languages, traditions, dress, religions, and occupations (Harjo, 1993). A strong extended-family system and tribal identity characterizes many urban and rural American Indian families (Harrison et al., 1990). Extended-family systems have helped American Indians cope with adversity both on and off the reservation. American Indian patterns of extended family include several households representing significant relatives that give rise to village-like characteristics even in urban areas. In such families, grandparents retain an official and symbolic leadership role. Children seek daily contact with grandparents and grandparents monitor children's behavior and have a voice in child rearing (Lum, 1986). Despite the many social problems faced by American Indian families, such as poverty, alcoholism, accidents, and adolescent suicide, the majority are two-parent families. In 1980, 7 out of 10 American Indian families included married couples living together (Banks, 1991).

Although there are variations among tribes in their value orientations, there are nevertheless some common themes across many groups that can be characterized as traditional American Indian values. These include (a) present-time orienta-tion—a primary concern for the present and ac-ceptance of time as fluid and not segmented; (b) respect for elders—with age comes experience that is transmitted as knowledge that is essential for group survival and harmony in life; (c) iden-tity with the group—self-awareness has meaning only within the context of the family and tribe so that the interests of the family and tribe are the same as one's own self-interest; (d) cooperation and partnership—among the Pueblo Indians a common saying is "Help each other so the burden won't be so heavy" (Suina & Smolkin, 1994, p. 121); the concept of partnership and sharing is stressed as the desirable way of conducting most activities; and (e) living in harmony with nature—nature, like time, is indivisible, and the person is an integral part of the flow of nature and time. . . .

Within traditional-oriented Indian culture, the uses of knowledge and learning are prescribed to help individuals live fulfilling lives as fully inte-grated members of the family and tribe. For exam-ple, among the Navajo, knowledge is organized around three life goals. First there is knowledge that lasts throughout one's lifetime and has to do with language, kinship, religion, customs, values, beliefs, and the purpose of life (Joe, 1994). This kind of knowledge is usually taught informally and using a variety of sources. Among the Pueblo Indians, teaching and learning at this stage is thought to be the responsibility of all Pueblo members (Suina & Smolkin, 1994). The second area of knowledge involves learning an occupa-tion or the means to making a living. This learning often requires an apprenticeship and involves a narrower range of teaching experts such as herders, weavers, and hunters. Learning is through listen-ing, watching, and doing, with a strong emphasis placed on modeling and private practicing of the emerging skill (Suina & Smolkin, 1994). At this stage, children also learn the appropriate context for the use of their knowledge. The person learns how one's knowledge is enmeshed with the his-tory, culture, and survival goals of the tribe. The third category of knowledge is the most restrictive because it is reserved for those interested in be-coming healers and religious leaders (Joe, 1994). These are lifetime commitments involving spe-cialized instruction that is usually in addition to learning other means of livelihood.

The influence of traditional-oriented Indian culture on child rearing varies from tribe to tribe and from family to family depending on their con-tact with Euro-American society. The establish-ment of boarding schools for American Indian children, far removed from the reservation, was a deliberate attempt to destroy traditional child-rearing practices. Between 1890 and 1920, chil-dren were forcibly removed from their families for up to 12 years, and parents and relatives were not allowed to visit children during the school year. From 1920 to the 1970s, boarding schools were still a usual part of the childhood and ado-lescent experience of most Indian children. Among the many deleterious effects of boarding schools were the deprivation of children from adult parenting models and an undermining of parental authority. Today most Indian grandpar-ents and parents are products of government boarding schools, which impacts on the quality of their parenting. Child abuse, particularly in the form of neglect, is cited as a major reason for the removal of Indian children from their families and tribes. As recently as 1980, Indian children were placed out of homes at a rate five times higher than other children (Harjo, 1993).

According to Berlin (1987), a major concern of some tribes is the infant- and child-rearing abili-ties of adolescents, which are critical for the tribes' survival. Greater tribal self-determination in the areas of education (the Indian Self-Determination and Education Assistance Act of 1975), family life (the Indian Child Welfare Act of 1978), and culture (the American Indian Religious Freedom Act of 1978) have made it possible for some In-dian tribes and families to recover traditional child-rearing practices. The socialization goal is to prepare children to be proud and competent members of an integrated family and tribal sys-tem, and to selectively adopt those aspects of Euro-American culture that can contribute to the well-being of the group (Berlin, 1987).

ASIAN AMERICAN FAMILIES

The Asian American population includes people from 28 Asian countries or ethnic groups (Takanishi, 1994). It is a very diverse group in terms of languages, cultures, generations in the United States, and reasons for immigrating to the United States. . . .

Historically, Japanese, Chinese, and Filipino immigrants came to the United States primarily to improve their economic status. However, Indo-Chinese have arrived primarily as political immigrants or refugees. At the end of the Vietnam War in 1975, 130,000 refugees found asylum in the United States. Beginning in 1978, a massive flow of Indo-Chinese refugees (boat people or second wave) occurred, abruptly ending in 1992 (Rumbaut, 1995). Unlike economic immigrants, political immigrants leave their homelands involuntarily. Usually refugees suffer more psychological problems and have a more difficult time adjusting to life in the United States than economic immigrants. In addition, they tend to experience more undesirable change in the process of acculturation, a greater threat of danger, and a decreasing sense of control over their lives (Rumbaut, 1991).

Little empirical research exists on the structure and process of Asian American families. Among the studies in this area, most have sampled from Chinese and Japanese American populations. Often, examination of Asian American families is for the purpose of identifying the family characteristics that contribute to children's academic performance. Consequently, there is very little research on the adaptive strategies and socialization goals of Asian American parents that bears on the socioemotional development of children. Discussions of Asian American families usually invoke Confucian principles to explain family structure and roles. Confucius developed a hierarchy defining one's role, duties, and moral obligations within the state. This hierarchical structure is also applied to the family and each member's role is dictated by age and gender. Typically Asian American families are seen as patriarchal, with the father maintaining authority and emotional

distance from other members (Ho, 1986; Wong, 1988, 1995). Wives are subordinate to their husbands, but in their role as mothers they have considerable authority and autonomy in child rearing. Traditionally, the family exerts control over family members, who are taught to place family needs before individual needs. Children show obedience and loyalty to their parents and, especially in the case of male children, are expected to take care of elderly parents (filial piety). Confucian influences on family life are stronger in some Asian American populations (e.g., Chinese and Vietnamese) than others (e.g., Japanese) due to differences in immigration patterns and degree of Westernization of the country of origin. Length of U.S. residence and acculturation also contribute to extensive within-group differences in family structure and roles. Kibria (1993) found that large Vietnamese families varying in age and gender fared better economically than smaller nuclear families. The larger extended family enabled households to connect to a variety of social and economic resources. In Vietnamese families, the kin group is seen as more important than the individual. This perspective has its source in Confucian principles, especially ancestor worship (Kibria, 1993). Ancestor worship for Vietnamese Americans consists of devotion in caring for an altar containing pictures of deceased family members and praying at ritually prescribed times (C. Chao, 1992). This act affirms the sacredness, unity, and timelessness of the kin group. It is this belief that one's kin group is an economic safety net that creates extended families and multiple-family households.

Aspects of traditional Asian child-rearing practices appear to be continued by Asian American families (Uba, 1994). Studies tend to be focused primarily upon characteristics of parental control. Chiu (1987) compared the child-rearing attitudes of Chinese, Chinese American, and Euro-American mothers. Chinese mothers endorsed restrictive and controlling behavior more than Chinese American and Euro-American mothers, and Chinese American mothers were more restrictive and controlling in their child-rearing attitudes than Euro-American mothers. The intermediate position of Chinese American mothers suggests that their child-rearing attitudes are shifting toward Euro-American norms due to acculturation.

R. Chao (1994) has argued that the traditional view of Chinese parents as authoritarian, restrictive, and controlling is misleading because these parenting behaviors do not have cross-cultural equivalence for Euro-Americans and Chinese: these child-rearing concepts are rooted in Euro-American culture and are not relevant for describing the socialization styles and goals of Chinese parents. According to R. Chao (1994), "The 'authoritarian' concept has evolved from American cultures and psychology that is rooted in both evangelical and Puritan religious influences" (p. 1116). Instead, Chinese parenting should be viewed from the concepts of *chiao shun* and *guan*. *Chiao shun* means "training" or "teaching in appropriate behaviors." Parents and teachers are responsible for training children by exposing them to examples of proper behavior and limiting their view of undesirable behaviors. However, training in the Euro-American sense is conceptualized in terms of strict discipline. This is not the case for Chinese, for whom training is accomplished in the context of a supportive and concerned parent or teacher. The word *guan* means "to govern," "to care for or to love," and parental care and involvement is seen as an aspect of *guan*. Thus, control and governance have positive connotations for the Chinese. Using a middle-class sample, R. Chao (1994) compared Euro-American and immigrant Chinese American mothers on standard measures of control and authoritarian parenting, as well as measures of *chiao shun* and *guan*. R. Chao found that Chinese American mothers scored higher on standard measures of parental control and authoritarian parenting. However, they also scored higher on measures reflecting the concepts of *chiao shun* and *guan*. Thus, although Chinese American mothers scored high on the Euro-American concepts of parental control and authoritarian parenting, their parenting style could not be described using Euro-American concepts. Instead, the style of parenting used by the Chinese American moth-

ers is conceptualized as a type of training performed by parents who are deeply concerned and involved in the lives of their children.

The value of this approach is that it helps resolve paradoxes in the current literature. In a series of studies of ethnicity and achievement, Steinberg, Dornbusch, and Brown (1992) have found that Asian American students rated their parents as higher on authoritarian parenting than Euro-American or Hispanic groups. Although their parents scored lower on the optimal parental style of authoritativeness, Asian students had the highest achievement scores (Steinberg et al., 1992). The R. Chao (1994) study suggests that confusion between authoritarian and training child-rearing concepts among Chinese respondents may account for the paradox. In short, Chinese simply have a different set of child-rearing values and styles that are distinct from the traditional U.S. child-rearing schemes. . . .

LATINO FAMILIES

The term *Latino* is used here to describe those persons often referred to as Hispanics. *Hispanic* is a word coined by the Department of Commerce to enumerate persons in the United States whose ancestry derives from the Spanish-speaking countries and peoples of the Americas. Many people in this group prefer Latino over Hispanic because Latino is the Spanish word for describing this group, whereas Hispanic is an English word imposed on the group. The Latino population consists primarily of Mestizo peoples born of the Spanish conquest of the Americas who intermixed with populations indigenous to the geographic areas. Although the language of Mestizos is Spanish, much of their culture is a hybrid of Spanish and Native American influences. Child rearing, in particular, is heavily influenced by Native American cultures because it was the Native American women who bore the children of the Spanish conquistadores and raised them in their extended families. As these children grew, they formed unions with other Mestizos and Native Americans and extended the predominately Native American child-rearing practices across generations through their children. . . .

Ramirez and Castaneda (1974) have described the cultural values of Latinos in terms of four conceptual categories: (a) identification with family, community, and ethnic group; (b) personalization of interpersonal relationships; (c) status and roles based on age and gender; and (d) Latino Catholic ideology. The following discussion of these values is with the understanding that there are important subgroup (Cuban American, Mexican American, Puerto Rican, Central and South American) variations as well as variations due to acculturation, generation, and social class.

Identification with Family, Community, and Ethnic Group

Latino child-rearing practices encourage the development of a self-identity embedded firmly within the context of the *familia* (family). One's individual identity is therefore part of a larger identity with the familia.

The desire to be close to the familia often results in many members of the same familia living in the same community. The familia network extends further into the community through kinships formed by intermarriage among familias and *el compadrazco,* which is the cultural practice of having special friends become godparents of children in baptisms. Adults united through el compadrazco, called *compadres* and *comadres,* have mutual obligations to each other similar to those of brothers and sisters. Vidal (1988) found that Puerto Rican godparents served as role models and social supports for their godchildren, and regarded themselves as potential surrogate parents in the event of the parents' death. Extended familia ties in the community give rise to a sense of identity with one's community.

The worldview of many Latinos includes a sense of identity with *La Raza* (the Race), which is a sense of peoplehood shared by persons of the Americas who are of Mestizo ancestry.

Personalization of Interpersonal Relationships

Latino culture places a heavy emphasis on sensitivity to the social domain of the human experience. Individuals are socialized to be sensitive to the feelings and needs of others and to personalize interpersonal relationships (*personalismo*). This socialization goal encourages the development of cooperative social motives while discouraging individual competitive behaviors that set apart the individual from the group (Kagan, 1984). In a collectivist culture where working as a group is important, knowing how to cooperate is a valuable social skill.

The paramount importance of the social domain for Latinos is reflected in the term *bien educado,* which literally translated means "well-educated." In Latino culture, however, the term is used to refer not only to someone with a good formal education but also to a person who can function successfully in any interpersonal situation without being disrespectful or rude. Okagaki and Sternberg (1993) found that Mexican immigrant parents emphasized social skills as equal to or more important than cognitive skills in defining an "intelligent" child. Children in particular are expected to be bien educados in their relations with adults. Addressing adults in Spanish with the formal "you" (*usted*) rather than the informal "you" (*tu*) is an example of being bien educado. Thus, if children lose Spanish and cannot communicate with Spanish monolingual adults, they may be unable to achieve the status of being bien educado in their community.

Status and Roles Based on Age and Gender

Latino culture has clearly defined norms of behavior governing an individual's actions within the familia and the community. Age and gender are important determinants of status and respect. Children are expected to be obedient and respectful toward their parents, even after they are grown and have children of their own. An authoritarian parenting style has been reported among Latinos (Dornbusch, Ritter, Leiderman, Roberts, & Fraleigh, 1987; Schumm et al., 1988). Yet, as R. Chao (1994) has shown, in the context of non-Western cultures, this parenting style may be experienced as parental support and concern. Grandparents, and older persons in general, receive much respect and have considerable status owing to their knowledge of life. Consequently, children are taught to "model" themselves after adults, and as a result modeling becomes a preferred teaching style (Laosa, 1980).

Gender also influences a person's role in the familia and community. Males are expected to have more knowledge about politics and business, while females are expected to know more about child rearing, health care, and education. Because politics and business expose males more to the outside world, they are often perceived as the dominant figures in the familia. However, decision-making studies in the United States reveal that Latino husbands and wives most often share responsibility for major family decisions (R. Cooney, Rogler, Hurrell, & Ortiz, 1982; Ybarra, 1982; Zavella, 1987). These findings challenge the stereotype of the macho Latino male. Another stereotype is that Latino gender roles prevent women from working outside the home. However, U.S. Department of Commerce (1988) statistics show 51% of Latinas in the labor force compared to 56% for non-Latinas. Among young women, the percentage of working Latinas actually exceeds that of non-Latinas.

Latino Catholic Ideology

Religion strongly influences the lives of Latinos inasmuch as Latino Catholicism reinforces and supports cultural values. Latino Catholicism is a synthesis of Spanish European Catholicism and indigenous religious beliefs and practices. Identity with family and community is facilitated through such religious practices as weddings and el compadrazco, which help extend family networks. Identity with the ethnic group is reinforced by the common Catholic religion shared by more than 80% of La Raza. Religious symbols are often used as markers of ethnic identity. For example, the image of the Virgen of Guadalupe, the Mestizo equivalent of the Virgin Mary, is both a religious symbol and a symbol for La Raza. The cultural emphasis on respect, group harmony, and cooperation in interpersonal relations is in line with the religious themes of peace, community, and self-denial.

REFERENCES

Banks, J. A. (1991). *Teaching strategies for ethnic studies* (5th ed.). Boston: Allyn & Bacon.

Berlin, I. N. (1987). Effects of changing Native American cultures on child development. *Journal of Community Psychology, 15,* 299–306.

Bowman, P. J. (1993). The impact of economic marginality among African American husbands and fathers. In H. P. McAdoo (Ed.), *Family ethnicity* (pp. 120–137). Newbury Park, CA: Sage.

Bowman, P. J., & Howard, C. S. (1985). Race-related socialization, motivation and academic achievement: A study of Black youth in three-generation families. *Journal of the American Academy of Child Psychiatry, 24,* 134–141.

Boykin, A. W. (1983). The academic performance of Afro-American children. In J. Spence (Ed.), *Achievement and achievement motives* (pp. 321–371). San Francisco: Freeman.

Boykin, A. W., & Toms, F. D. (1985). Black child socialization: A conceptual framework. In H. P. McAdoo & J. L. McAdoo (Eds.), *Black children: Social, educational, and parental environments* (pp. 33–51). Newbury Park, CA: Sage.

Burgess, B. J. (1980). Parenting in the Native American community. In M. D. Fantini & R. Cardenas (Eds.), *Parenting in a multicultural society* (pp. 63–73). New York: Longman.

Chao, C. M. (1992). The inner heart: Therapy with Southeast Asian families. In L. A. Vargas & J. D.

Koss-Chioino (Eds.), *Working with culture: Psychotherapeutic intervention with ethnic minority children and adolescents* (pp. 157–181). San Francisco: Jossey-Bass.

Chao, R. K. (1994). Beyond parental control and authoritarian parenting style: Understanding Chinese parenting through the cultural notion of training. *Child Development, 65,* 1111–1119.

Chiu, L. H. (1987). Child-rearing attitudes of Chinese, Chinese-American, and Anglo-American mothers. *International Journal of Psychology, 22,* 409–419.

Cooney, R. S., Rogler, L. H., Hurrell, R., & Ortiz, V. (1982). Decision making in intergenerational Puerto Rican families. *Journal of Marriage and the Family, 44,* 621–631.

Dornbusch, S. M., Ritter, P. L., Leiderman, P. H., Roberts, D. F., & Fraleigh, M. J. (1987). The relation of parenting style to adolescent school performance. *Child Development, 58,* 1244–1257.

Farley, R., & Allen, W. R. (1987). *The color line and the quality of American life.* New York: Russell Sage Foundation.

Greenfield, P.M., & Cocking, R. R. (1994). *Cross-cultural roots of minority child development.* Hillsdale, NJ: Erlbaum.

Harjo, S. S. (1993). The American Indian experience. In H. P. McAdoo (Ed.), *Family ethnicity* (pp. 199–207). Newbury Park, CA: Sage.

Harrison, A. O. (1985). The black family's socializing environment. In H. McAdoo & J. McAdoo (Eds.), *Black children* (pp. 174–193). Beverly Hills, CA: Sage.

Harrison, A. O., Wilson, M. N., Pine, C. J., Chan, S. Q., & Buriel, R. (1990). Family ecologies of ethnic minority children. *Child Development, 61,* 347–362.

Hatchett, S. J., & Jackson, J. S. (1993). African American extended kin systems: An assessment. In H. P. McAdoo (Ed.), *Family ethnicity.* Newbury Park, CA: Sage.

Ho, D. Y. F. (1986). Chinese patterns of socialization: A critical review. In M. H. Bond (Ed.), *The psychology of the Chinese people* (pp. 1–37). Hong Kong: Oxford University Press.

Joe, J. R. (1994). Revaluing Native-American concepts of development and education. In P. M. Greenfield & R. R. Cocking (Eds.), *Cross-cultural roots of minority child development* (pp. 107–113). Hillsdale, NJ: Erlbaum.

Kagan, S. (1984). Interpreting Chicano cooperativeness: Methodological and theoretical considerations. In J. L. Martinez, Sr. & R. H. Mendoza (Eds.) *Chicano psychology* (2nd ed., pp. 289–333). New York: Academic Press.

Kelley, M. L., Power, T. G., & Wimbush, D. D. (1992). Determinants of disciplinary practices in low-income Black mothers. *Child Development, 63,* 573–582.

Kelley, M. L., Sanchez-Hucies, J., & Walker, R. (1993). Correlates of disciplinary practices in working- to middle-class African-American mothers. *Merrill-Palmer Quarterly, 39,* 252–264.

Kibria, N. (1993). *Family tightrope: The changing lives of Vietnamese Americans.* Princeton, NJ: Princeton University Press.

Laosa, L. M. (1980). Maternal teaching strategies in Chicano and Anglo-American families: The influence of culture and education on maternal behaviors. *Child Development, 51,* 759–765.

Lum, D. (1986). *Social work practice and people of color: A process-stage approach.* Monterey, CA: Brooks/Cole.

McAdoo, H. P. (1978). Factors related to stability in upwardly mobile black families. *Journal of Marriage and the Family, 40,* 761–776.

McAdoo, J. L. (1993). The roles of African-American fathers: An ecological perspective. *Families in Society: The Journal of Contemporary Human Services, 74,* 28–34.

Nobles, W. W., Goddard, L. L., Cavil, W. E., & George, P. Y. (1987). *African-American families: Issues, insight, and directions.* Oakland, CA: Black Family Institute.

Okagaki, L., & Sternberg, R. J. (1993). Parental beliefs and children's school performance. *Child Development, 64,* 36–56.

Pearson, J. L., Hunter, A. G., Ensminger, M. E., & Kellam, S. G. (1990). Black grandmothers in multigenerational households: Diversity in family structure and parenting involvement in the Woodlawn community. *Child Development, 61,* 434–442.

Peters, M. (1985). Racial socialization of young black children. In H. McAdoo & J. McAdoo (Eds.), *Black children* (pp. 159–173). Beverly Hills, CA: Sage.

Portes, P. R., Dunham, R. M., & Williams, S. (1986). Assessing childrearing style in ecological settings: Its relation to culture, social class, early age intervention, and scholastic achievement. *Adolescence, 21,* 723–735.

Ramirez, M., III, & Castaneda, A. (1974). *Cultural democracy, bicognitive development and education.* New York: Academic Press.

Rumbaut, R. G. (1991). The agony of exile: A study of the migration and adaptation of Southeast Asian refugee adults and children. In F. L. Ahearn Jr. & J. A. Garrison (Eds.), *Refugee children: Theory, research, and practice* (pp. 53–91). Baltimore: Johns Hopkins University Press.

Rumbaut, R. G. (1995). Vietnamese, Laotian, and Cambodian Americans. In P. G. Min (Ed.), *Asian Americans: Contemporary trends and issues* (pp. 232–270). Thousand Oaks, CA: Sage.

Schumm, W. R., McCollum, E. E., Bughaighis, M. A., Jurich, A. P., Bollman, S. R., & Reitz, J. (1988). Differences between Anglo and Mexican American family members on satisfaction with family life. *Hispanic Journal of Behavioral Sciences, 10,* 39–53.

Staples, R., & Johnson, L. B. (1993). *Black families at the crossroads.* San Francisco: Jossey-Bass.

Steinberg, L., Dornbusch, S., & Brown, B. (1992). Ethnic differences in adolescent achievement: An ecological perspective. *American Psychologist, 47,* 723–729.

Sudarkasa, N. (1993). Female-headed African American households: Some neglected dimensions. In H. P. McAdoo (Ed.), *Family ethnicity* (pp. 81–89). Newbury Park, CA: Sage.

Suina, J. H., & Smolkin, L. B. (1994). From natural culture to school culture to dominant society culture: Supporting transitions for Pueblo Indian students. In P. M. Greenfield & R. R. Cocking (Eds.), *Cross-cultural roots of minority child development* (pp. 115–130). Hillsdale, NJ: Erlbaum.

Takanishi, R. (1994). Continuities and discontinuities in the cognitive socialization of Asian-originated children: The case of Japanese Americans. In P. M. Greenfield & R. R. Cocking (Eds.), *Cross-cultural roots of minority child development* (pp. 351–362). Hillsdale, NJ: Erlbaum.

Thornton, M. C., Chatters, L. M., Taylor, R. J., & Allen, W. R. (1990). Sociodemographic and environmental correlates of racial socialization by Black parents. *Child Development, 61,* 401–409.

Tolson, T. F. J., & Wilson, M. N. (1990). The impact of two and three generational Black family structure on perceived family climate. *Child Development, 61,* 416–428.

Trimble, J. E., & Medicine, B. (1993). Diversification of American Indians: Forming an indigenous perspective. In U. Kim & J. W. Berry (Eds.), *Indigenous psychologies* (pp. 133–151). Newbury Park, CA: Sage.

Uba, L. (1994). *Asian Americans: Personality patterns, identity and mental health.* New York: Guilford Press.

U.S. Census Bureau. (1994). *The diverse living arrangements of children: Summer 1991.* Washington, DC: U.S. Government Printing Office.

U.S. Department of Commerce. (1988). *The Hispanic population in the United States: March 1988* (Current Population Reports, Series P-20, No. 431). Washington, DC: U.S. Government Printing Office.

Vidal, C. (1988). Godparenting among Hispanic Americans. *Child Welfare, 67,* 453–459.

Willis, W. (1992). Families with African American roots. In E. W. Lynch & M. J. Hanson (Eds.), *Developing cross-cultural competence: A guide for working with young children and their families* (pp. 121–150). Baltimore: Brookes.

Wilson, M. N. (1992). Perceived parental activity of mothers, fathers, and grandmothers in three generational Black families. In A. K. Hoard Burlew, W. C. Banks, H. P. McAdoo, & D. A. Azibo (Eds.), *African American psychology* (pp. 87–104). Newbury Park, CA: Sage.

Wilson, W. J. (1987). *The truly disadvantaged: The inner city, the underclass, and public policy.* Chicago: University of Chicago Press.

Wong, M. G. (1988). The Chinese American family. In C. H. Mindel, R. W. Habenstein, & R. Wright, Jr. (Eds.), *Ethnic families in America: Patterns and variations* (3rd ed., pp. 230–257). New York: Elsevier.

Wong, M. G. (1995). Chinese Americans. In P. G. Min (Ed.), *Asian Americans: Contemporary trends and issues* (pp. 58–94). Thousand Oaks, CA: Sage.

Ybarra, L. (1982). When wives work: The impact on the Chicano family. *Journal of Marriage and the Family, 44,* 169–177.

Zavella, P. (1987). *Women's work and Chicano families: Cannery workers of the Santa Clara Valley.* Ithaca, NY: Cornell University Press.

? *Think about It*

1. How are black, American Indian, Asian American and Latino families similar in their socialization goals? How do they differ because of historical influences, religious beliefs, or immigration experiences?

2. Explain why the influence of the extended and multigenerational family is important for many ethnic families.

3. Why do Parke and Buriel feel that Euro-American norms of disciplining children often stereotype the child-rearing practices of ethnic families?

3 *African American Family Values*

Ramona W. Denby

In Reading 2, Parke and Buriel note the importance of extended family members in socializing African American children. Here Ramona W. Denby describes a "core set of values" that characterize black family life. These values include intergenerational support in child rearing, an emphasis on parenting, instilling racial pride, communalism, and the importance of spirituality in strengthening the family unit.

It is sometimes forgotten that most African American families live and prosper as intact units. "On any given day, fully 75 percent of African-American people will be found living in families of one kind or another" (Billingsley, 1990, pp. 90–91). What can be learned from these families? How can family preservation programs devise a value base that is more applicable to African Americans? This section highlights key characteristics, values, and strategies already employed by African American families that help to strengthen and preserve the family unit. The values presented are the culmination of an extensive review of current knowledge about African American families. Table 1 displays a collection of African American values and characteristics as cited by numerous scholars

Source: From Ramona W. Denby, "Resiliency and the African American Family: A Model of Family Preservation," in *The Black Family: Strengths, Self-Help, and Positive Change,* ed. Sadye L. Logan (Boulder, CO: Westview Press, 1996), 144–63. Reprinted by permission of Westview Press, a member of Perseus Books, L.L.C.

in the literature. The five areas discussed have been taken from Table 1 and chosen for their specific relevance to family preservation programs.

CHILDREARING

Among the many strategies that African Americans have successfully employed to strengthen the family unit is their approach to childrearing. Three aspects of African American childrearing are offered as examples of successful strategies to preserve the family unit: (1) shared parenting, (2) pride in children, and (3) "nurturing firmness" in discipline.

An African cultural residual employed by African American families is the use of "collective" or "shared" parenting (Carson, 1981; Hall & King, 1982; Hays & Mindel, 1973; Hill, 1977; Martin & Martin, 1978; Stack, 1974; Sudarkasa, 1988). This occurrence is exemplified in the extensive use of

TABLE 1   Values, Characteristics, and Belief Systems That Have Sustained African American Families

Billingsley, 1968, 1992	Boykin, 1983	Christopherson, 1979	Gary et al., 1983	Hill, 1971	Martin & Martin, 1985	McAdoo, 1988	Nobles, 1976, 1979, 1988	Scanzoni, 1971 Staples, 1994	Stack, 1974 Aschenbrenner, 1973

• Value of learning, knowledge, education, and skill development
• Deep spiritual values
• Quest for self-governance
• Service to others
• Cooperative economics, politics, and social goals
• Race pride
• Strong Black-owned, private enterprises
• Family ties
	• Spirituality
	• Harmony
	• Movement
	• Verve
	• Affect
	• Communalism
	• Expressive individualism
	• Orality
	• Social time perspective
		• Love of children
		• Acceptance of children born out of wedlock
		• Strong resilience
		• Adaptability of family coping skills
			• Strong kinship bonds
			• Strong achievement orientation
			• Parenting skills
			• Strong religious–philosophical orientation
			• Intellectual–cultural orientation
			• Ability to deal with crises
			• Strong work orientation
			• Independence
			• Organization
			• Active recreation orientation
			• Appreciation for each other
			• Adaptability of family roles
			• Self-expression
			• Love, kindness, and compassion
			• Supportiveness and caring
				• Strong kinship bonds
				• Strong work orientation
				• Adaptability of family roles
				• Strong achievement orientation
				• Strong religious orientation
					• Elements of extended family
					  1. Mutual aid
					  2. Social class cooperation
					  3. Male–female cooperation
					  4. Pro-socialization of children
					• Extension of extended family elements
					  1. Fictive kinship
					  2. Racial consciousness
					  3. Religious consciousness
					• Institutions of Black helping tradition
					  1. Black churches
					  2. Mutual aid societies
					  3. Fraternal orders
					  4. Women's clubs
					  5. Unions
					  6. Orphanages, senior homes, and hospitals
					  7. Schools
					  8. Protest movements
					  9. Race-consciousness organizations
						• Kinship and mutual assistance are more than provision of basic needs	• Strong family ties
							• Unconditional love of children
							• Respect for self and others
							• Assumed natural goodness of children
							• Legitimation of beingness
							• Provision of a family code
							• Elasticity of boundaries
							• Provision of information and knowledge
							• Mediation of concrete conditions
								• Strong mother–child bonds
								• Heavy emotional nurturance
									• Relationship and kinship ties
									• Reciprocity
									• Fidelity to family obligations
									• Strong commitment to children

the entire family in childrearing, the use of older siblings in caregiving, and intergenerational support-giving (usually grandmother or aunt to a younger mother). Researchers have noted that such a practice is a direct carryover from African tribal life, whereby the general orientation was that of "we" as opposed to "I" (Franklin & Boyd-Franklin, 1985; Mbiti, 1970; Nobles, 1980). In addition, the notion of shared parenting permeates the biological family to include the practice of "nonblood" relatives caring for, providing for, and rearing children (Boyd, 1982; Hines & Boyd-Franklin, 1982).

A second component of the African American approach to childrearing that has maintained the family unit and is worthy of emulation is the high value placed on children. A family's esteem and worth are often related to the presence of children. Many African American parents consider their children to be their contribution to society. This elevation is necessary because society has devalued, depreciated, and marginalized African American people. As a result, African American families tend to exercise unconditional, positive regard for their children. The existence of children in a family allows African Americans to leave their legacy by transferring "traditions, beliefs, symbols, language, ways of thinking, rules for interacting within Black cultures, and providing a foundation for what it means to be Black" (Dilworth-Anderson, 1992, p. 29). The significance African Americans place on children, family, and family bonds has been noted by several researchers (Bell, 1971; Gary et al., 1983; Nolle, 1972; Scanzoni, 1971; Staples, 1994). Their writings corroborate the sanctity and inherent worth of children in the African American community.

The third aspect of African American childrearing that sustains the family unit is the discipline style nurturing firmness. "Discipline styles among African-American parents are closely scrutinized; yet, they may be among the most positive aspects of African-American childrearing" (Denby & Alford, 1996, p. 1). African American discipline is characterized as firm, caring, and uncompromising. Staples (1994) observed that African American mothers of lower socioeconomic standing

combine physical measures with "very high doses of emotional nurturance" (p. 12). Although this combination may prove more effective than a withdrawal of love (often employed by middle-class parents), it is not given merit.

Child discipline in African American families goes beyond the purpose of correcting undesirable behavior. Discipline is largely considered to be a means of socializing children about issues related to race differentials. Staples (1994) noted in his observations of childrearing and parental roles in African American families that parents must socialize their children to adapt successfully to the majority culture's values while simultaneously readying them to know their own ethnicity. Many researchers have observed the strength, creativity, and brilliance employed by African Americans in providing their children with a dual socialization (Brown, 1988; Denby & Alford, 1996; Devore, 1983).

EMPHASIS ON PARENTHOOD (MOTHERHOOD)

In addition to childrearing patterns, a theoretical model for preserving African American families would concentrate on the culture's emphasis on motherhood. Like the value given to children, much significance and honor are given to mothers. Discussion of motherhood as an underpinning in African American family life focuses on two main points: (1) centrality of African American motherhood and (2) centrality of grandmothers.

In exploring the meaning of motherhood in the African American culture, Collins (1994) discusses four common themes: women-centered networks, providing as part of mothering, community "other mothers" and social activism, and motherhood as a symbol of power. Women-centered networks—inclusive of mothers, sisters, aunts, godmothers, and grandmothers—have been a force, as well as an unchanging presence, in African American family life. Such networks fulfill varied roles: nurturer, financial provider, teacher, caregiver, and community and family stabilizer. These roles are indicative of the self-reliance, resourcefulness, and strength that are inherent in Black motherhood.

Second, the centrality of grandmothers is critical in bolstering African American family functioning. Flaherty, Facteau, and Garner (1994) found seven key functions of grandmothers in their study of multigenerational African American families: managing, caretaking, coaching, assessing, nurturing, assigning, and patrolling. Grandmothers are often the glue that holds generations of family members together. They are referred to for guidance in both major and minor family matters. Such eminence is not granted to the grandmother simply because of African Americans' regard and respect for elders but also because she epitomizes endurance, wisdom, and spirituality.

EMPHASIS ON PARENTHOOD (FATHERHOOD)

Juxtaposed with the role of motherhood, the parameters of fatherhood are broad in the African American community. Uncles, ministers, deacons, elders of the church, and male teachers can all be viewed as father figures. These men play a significant part in solidifying the foundation of African American communities.

Contrary to popular belief, many biological fathers embrace their fatherly duties with sincerity and thoroughness. In his discussion of father–child interaction in the African American family, J. McAdoo (1988) noted that given economic and social supports, African American fathers welcome the responsibilities of childrearing: "Black fathers, like fathers of all ethnic groups, take an equal part in the childrearing decisions in the family. Their expectations for their child's behavior in the home also appear to be similar given socioeconomic status patterns. . . . [The father's] predominant relationship and interaction pattern appears to be nurturant, warm, and loving toward his children" (p. 266).

In the case of the dubious father who may require extra incentive to fulfill his rightful responsibilities, elders or male fictive kin fill in the gaps by encouraging and redirecting him toward familial matters of importance. They also serve as role models, caretakers, tutors, and informal counselors for the youth of the community. Unselfish efforts such as these are performed to facilitate interest and shore up successful possibilities for young people who are victims of social, economic, and educational disenfranchisement. Several African American men's groups have initiated service projects to help improve the economic and social plights of deprived children and families. The Black Masons, for instance, have a long-standing reputation for their charitable activities (Martin & Martin, 1985). Other groups of similar distinction include 100 Committed Black Men, the Elks, Male Africentric Rites of Passage Programs, and African-American Church Groups. In addition, African American fraternities (Alpha Phi Alpha, Omega Psi Phi, Kappa Alpha Psi, and Phi Beta Sigma) extend their purview in the form of graduate chapters so members can continue their service to humankind beyond undergraduate studies through altruistic deeds and scholarship enhancement. Big-brother mentoring and man-to-man "rap sessions" offered by these fraternal organizations provide opportunities for cathartic release and curative redirection.

RACIAL PRIDE AND STRONG ETHNIC IDENTITY

Building racial pride, self-respect, and a strong sense of racial identity are key components in cultivating the family unit. In a study of young African American children and parents, Peters (1985) noted that "racial identity undergirds every parent's child-rearing philosophy" (p. 165). Harrison (1985) noted that a major task for African Americans in the family environment is to socialize children to acquire a positive attitude toward their ethnicity. African American families realize that cultural preservation begins with family preservation. Research has noted the positive results of instilling African American consciousness and self-pride within the African American community (Fox & Barnes, 1971; Hraba & Grant, 1970; Lipscomb, 1975; McAdoo, 1970; Ward & Braun, 1972). Similarly, McAdoo (1985) countered claims that African American children do not value themselves because of negative environmental messages and found, to the contrary, that children felt competent and valued and believed they were perceived positively by their mothers. By instilling a strong sense of ethnic pride, Black families communicate to their children that they matter and that they are important to their communities and families.

COMMUNALISM

A discussion of African American family characteristics that help to enhance the family system is incomplete without mention of the strong sense of communalism that is prevalent in most African American families. Much has been written about the nature of communalism in the African American family (Billingsley, 1968; Gutman, 1976; Hill, 1972; Ladner, 1971, 1973; Martin & Martin, 1978, 1985; McAdoo, 1981; Nobles, 1986; Staples, 1971). This discussion of communalism focuses on two points: (1) family support structures and (2) community support structures.

Two key elements in family support structures that enrich African American families are kinship networks and egalitarian family units. African American families tend to rely on kinship ties in maintaining the family unit. Many researchers have discovered the importance of kin networks in the African American family (Allen, 1979; Angel & Tienda, 1982; Hays & Mindel, 1973; Hofferth, 1984; McAdoo, 1980; Stack, 1974). Strong kinship networks provide not only such concrete necessities as child care, finances, and transportation but also provide emotional support that acts as a buffer to outside stressors and eventually helps to preserve the family unit. The flagrant use of kin in the African American family has also been described as use of a "mutual aid system." It has been noted that the contemporary mutual aid system in African American families "continues

to absorb needy and dependent members, using few, if any, formal services to support the family" (Dilworth-Anderson, 1992, p. 30). The use of kin networks not only preserves and supports the family but is also a prevention mechanism employed in the African American culture to avoid intervention by official agencies into families.

Although shared roles between husbands and wives may be a relatively new phenomenon within the dominant, middle-class culture, this egalitarian practice has been an enduring tradition in African American families (Hill, 1973; Scanzoni, 1971; Willie, 1976). The sharing of roles lessens the pressures associated with raising a family and ultimately promotes family cohesion and strength.

The second point related to the use of communalism involves community support structures within the African American culture. Indigenous community support structures have assisted African American families in ensuring that the family remains intact. These resources, also referred to as mediating structures, help families withstand the impact of stresses brought on by the larger community (Leigh & Green, 1982). Although some question the viability of contemporary African American community support structures, evidence suggests the existence of a strong, capable, and nurturing community. Billingsley (1992) postulates that African Americans constitute a community in four ways: (1) Geographically, most Blacks live in neighborhoods in which most of their neighbors are Black; (2) there is a shared set of values; (3) most Black people strongly identify with their heritage; and (4) there is a set of institutions and organizations that grew out of the African American heritage, that identify with that heritage, and that serve primarily African American people and families (pp. 71–73).

RESILIENCY THROUGH SPIRITUALITY

One final value found within the African American culture that has a lasting legacy in strengthening the family unit is spirituality. Spirituality can assume multiple meanings; for example, spirituality can be manifested in a belief structure of perpetual optimism and the ability to recover from adversity. African Americans' undaunted belief in "a better day" is said to be based on a strong religious orientation. Such a belief system sustains the family unit, because this belief is transferred and transposed onto children. Likewise, spirituality leads to parental hopefulness, which is undergirded by love, support, and commitment to children.

A more concrete example of spirituality is that of the African American church. This institution is viewed as a major ingredient in preserving the family. The church often serves as a vehicle of renewal and solace. In addition to providing spiritual guidance, church activities (e.g., church "welfare" programs, libraries, nurseries, preschools, Saturday and Sunday schools) intensify the bonding and solidarity of African American families (Scott & Black, 1994).

REFERENCES

Allen, W. R. (1979). Class, culture and family organization: The effects of class and race on family structure in urban America. *Journal of Comparative Family Studies, 10,* 301–313.

Angel, R. J., & M. Tienda (1982). Determinants of extended household structure: Cultural pattern of economic need? *American Journal of Sociology, 87,* 1360–1383.

Aschenbrenner, J. (1973). Extended families among Black Americans. *Journal of Comparative Family Studies, 4,* 257–268.

Bell, R. (1971). The related importance of mother and wife roles among Black lower class women. In R. Staples (Ed.), *The Black family: Essays and studies* (2d ed.) (pp. 248–255). Belmont, CA: Wadsworth.

Billingsley, A. (1968). *Black families in white America.* Englewood Cliffs, NJ: Prentice-Hall.

Billingsley, A. (1990). Understanding African-American family diversity. In J. Deward (Ed.), *The state of Black America* (pp. 85–108). New York: National Urban League.

Billingsley, A. (1992). *Climbing Jacob's ladder: The enduring legacy of African-American families.* New York: Simon and Schuster.

Boyd, N. (1982). Family therapy with Black families.

In E. Jones and S. Korchin (Eds.), *Minority mental health* (pp. 227–249). New York: Praeger.

Boykin. A. W. (1983). The academic performance of Afro-American children. In J. Spence (Ed.), *Achievement and achievement motives* (pp. 321–371). San Francisco: Freeman.

Brown, A. (Spring 1988). Duality: The need to consider this characteristic when treating Black families. *The Family, 8,* 88.

Carson, N.H.D. (1981). *Informal adoption among Black families in the rural south.* Unpublished Ph.D. dissertation, Northwestern University, Chicago.

Christopherson, V. (1979). Implications for strengthening family life: Rural Black families. In N. Stinnett, B. Chesser, & J. Defrain (Eds.), *Building family strengths: Blueprints for action* (pp. 63–73). Lincoln, Neb.: Lincoln University Press.

Collins, P. H. (1994). The meaning of motherhood in Black culture. In R. Staples (Ed.), *The Black family: Essays and studies* (5th ed.) (pp. 165–173). Belmont, CA: Wadsworth.

Denby R., & K. Alford (1996). Understanding African-American discipline styles: Suggestions for effective social work intervention. *Journal of Multicultural Social Work, 4*(3).

Devore, W. (1983). Ethnic reality: The Life Model and work with Black families. *Social Casework: The Journal of Contemporary Social Work, 64,* 525–531.

Dilworth-Anderson, P. (Summer 1992). Extended kin networks in Black families, *Generations, 16,* 29–32.

Flaherty, M. J., L. Facteau, & P. Garner, (1994). Grandmother functions in multigenerational families: An exploratory study of Black adolescent mothers and their infants. In R. Staples (Ed.), *The Black family: Essays and studies* (5th ed.) (pp. 195–203). Belmont, CA: Wadsworth.

Fox, D., & U. Barnes (April 1971). Racial preference and identification of Blacks, Chinese, and white children. Paper presented at the American Educational Research Association Meeting, New York, New York.

Franklin, A. J., & N. Boyd-Franklin (1985). A psychoeducational perspective on Black parenting. In H. P. McAdoo and J. L. McAdoo (Eds.), *Black children* (pp. 194–210). Newbury Park, CA: Sage Publications.

Gary L., L. Beatty, G. Berry, & M. Price (1983). *Stable Black families: Final Report, Institute for Urban Affairs and Research.* Washington, DC.: Howard University.

Gutman, H. (1976). *The Black family in slavery and freedom, 1750–1925.* New York: Pantheon.

Hall, E., & G. King (1982). Working with the strengths of Black families. *Child Welfare, 61,* 536–544.

Harrison, A. O. (1985). The Black family's socializing environment. In H. P. McAdoo and J. L. McAdoo (Eds.), *Black children* (pp. 174–193). Newbury Park, CA: Sage Publications.

Hays, W. C., & C. H. Mindel (1973). Extended kinship relations in Black and white families. *Journal of Marriage and the Family, 35,* 51–57.

Hill, R. B. (1971). *The strengths of Black families.* New York: Emerson Hall.

Hill, R. B. (1972). *The strengths of Black families.* New York: Emerson Hall.

Hill, R. B. (1973). *Strengths of Black families.* New York: National Urban League.

Hill, R. B. (1977). *Informal adoption among Black families.* Washington, DC: National Urban League.

Hines, P., & N. Boyd-Franklin (1982). Black families. In M. McGoldrick, J. K. Pearce, & J. Giordano (Eds.), *Ethnicity and family therapy.* New York: Guilford.

Hofferth, S. L. (1984). Kin networks, race, and family structure. *Journal of Marriage and the Family, 46,* 791–806.

Hraba, J., & G. Grant (1970). Black is beautiful: A re-examination of racial preference and identification. *Journal of Personality and Social Psychology, 16,* 398–402.

Ladner, J. (1971). *Tomorrow's tomorrow.* New York: Anchor Press.

Ladner, J. (1973). *The death of white sociology.* New York: Vintage Books.

Leigh, J. W., & J. W. Green (1982). The structure of the Black community: The knowledge base for social services. In J. W. Green (Ed.), *Cultural awareness in the human services* (pp. 24–37). Englewood Cliffs, NJ: Prentice–Hall.

Lipscomb, I. (May 1975). Parental influences in the development of Black children's racial self-esteem. Paper presented at the meeting of the American Sociological Association, San Francisco, California.

Martin, J. M., & E. P. Martin (1978). *The Black extended family.* Chicago: University of Chicago Press.

Martin, J. M., & E. P. Martin (1985). *The helping tradition in the Black family community.* Silver Spring, MD: National Association of Social Workers.

Mbiti, J. S. (1970). *African religions and philosophies.* Garden City, NY: Anchor.

McAdoo, H. P. (1980). Black mothers and the extended family support network. In L. Rodgers-Rose (Ed.), *The Black woman* (pp. 125–144). Beverly Hills, CA: Sage Publications.

McAdoo, H. P. (Ed.) (1981). *Black families.* Beverly Hills, CA: Sage Publications

McAdoo, H. P. (1985). Racial attitude and self-concept of young Black children over time. In H. P. McAdoo and J. L. McAdoo (Eds.), *Black children* (pp. 213–242). Newbury Park, CA: Sage Publications.

McAdoo, H. P. (1988). Transgenerational patterns of upward mobility in African-American families. In H. P. McAdoo (Ed.), *Black families* (2d ed.) (pp. 148–168). Newbury Park, CA: Sage Publications.

McAdoo, J. L. (1970). *An exploratory study of racial attitude change in Black preschool children, using differential treatment.* Ph.D. dissertation, University of Michigan, Ann Arbor (University Microfilms 71-468).

McAdoo, J. L. (1988). The roles of Black fathers in the socialization of Black children. In H. P. McAdoo (Ed.), *Black families* (2d ed.) (pp. 257–269). Newbury Park, CA: Sage Publications.

Nobles, W. W. (1976). *A formulative and empirical study of Black families.* Washington, DC: U.S. Department of Health, Education, and Welfare.

Nobles, W. W. (1979). *Mental health support systems in Black families.* Washington, D.C.: U.S. Department of Health, Education, and Welfare.

Nobles, W. W. (1980). African philosophy: Foundations for Black psychology. In R. Jones (Ed.), *Black psychology* (pp. 23–36). New York: Harper and Row.

Nobles, W. W. (1986). *African psychology: Toward its reclamation, reascension and revitalization.* Oakland, CA: Black Family Institute.

Nobles, W. W. (1988). African-American family life: An instrument of culture. In H. P. McAdoo (Ed.), *Black families* (2d ed.) (pp. 44–53). Newbury Park, CA: Sage Publications.

Nolle, D. (1972). Changes in Black sons and daughters: A panel analysis of Black adolescents' orientation toward their parents. *Journal of Marriage and the Family, 34,* 443–447.

Peters, M. F. (1985). Racial socialization of young Black children. In H. P. McAdoo and J. L. McAdoo (Eds.), *Black children* (pp. 159–173). Newbury Park, CA: Sage Publications.

Scanzoni, J. (1971). *The Black family in modern society.* Boston: Allyn and Bacon.

Scott, J. W. & A. Black (1994). Deep structures of African American family life: Female and male kin networks. In R. Staples (Ed.), *The Black family:*

Essays and studies. (pp. 204–213). Belmont, CA: Wadsworth.

Stack, C. (1974). *All our kin: Strategies for survival in a Black community.* New York: Harper and Row.

Staples, R. (1971). Toward a sociology of the Black family: A theoretical and methodological assessment. *Journal of Marriage and the Family, 33,* 119–138.

Staples, R. (1994). Changes in Black family structure: The conflict between family ideology and structural conditions. In R. Staples (Ed.), *The Black family: Essays and studies* (5th ed.) (pp. 11–19). Belmont, CA: Wadsworth.

Sudarkasa, N. (Summer 1988). Reassessing the Black family: Dispelling the myths, reaffirming the values. *Sisters 1,* 1, 22–23, 38–39.

Ward, S. H., & J. Braun (1972). Self-esteem and racial preference in Black children. *American Journal of Orthopsychiatry, 42,* 644–647.

Willie, C. (Ed.) (1976). *The family life of Black people.* Columbus, OH: C. E. Merrill.

? Think about It

1. Denby describes three aspects of black child-rearing strategies. Are these strategies similar to or different from those used in your own family?
2. How do "fictive kin" and communalism support and sustain the family?
3. Why, according to Denby, is spirituality an important core value in many black families?

4 Filipino American Culture and Family Values

Pauline Agbayani-Siewart

Filipinos make up one of the largest Asian American subgroups in the United States today (see Reading 1), but they are one of the least understood and least researched groups. In this description of Filipino American values, marital relations, and children's socialization, Pauline Agbayani-Siewart provides a framework for understanding how acculturation may be changing traditional family beliefs and behavior.

FILIPINO FAMILY AND CULTURAL VALUES

In Filipino American families, members depend on one another for emotional, psychological, and financial support (Affonso, 1978; Almirol, 1982; Bulatao, 1981; Duff & Arthur, 1973; Guthrie, 1968; Guthrie & Jacobs, 1966; Hollnsteiner,

Source: From Pauline Agbayani-Siewart, "Filipino American Culture and Family: Guidelines for Practitioners," *Families in Society: The Journal of Contemporary Human Services* 75.5 (September 1994): 429–38. Copyright © 1994. Reprinted by permission of Families in Society: The Journal of Contemporary Services.

1981; Lynch, 1981; Peterson, 1978; Santiago, 1953; Yu & Liu, 1980). Filipino family structure is built on cultural values that reflect a system of co-operation and mutual support that members depend on for a sense of belonging. Kinship relations are highly valued and are regarded as familial whether defined by blood, marriage, or fictive kinship (Almirol, 1982; Bulatao, 1981: Duff & Arthur, 1973; Guthrie, 1968; Hollnsteiner, 1981; Lynch, 1981; Peterson, 1978; Takagi & Ishisaka, 1982). Filipino families place a high priority on dependence on, loyalty to, and solidarity with the family and kin group. The interests or desires of the individual are sacrificed for the good of the family, and cooperation among family members is stressed over individualism. Underlying this strong sense of family is the dominant cultural value of smooth interpersonal relationships, which permeates and guides the everyday lives and behaviors of Filipinos. Lynch (1981) describes smooth interpersonal relationships as the ability to get along with others without creating open conflict. Open displays of anger or aggression are discouraged, and passive and cooperative behaviors are encouraged (Varies, 1963). Smooth interpersonal relationships serve to bind the family and create a system of support and cooperation. Such relationships are maintained primarily through four means: *utang ng loob* (reciprocal obligation), *hiya* (shame), *amor proprio* (self-esteem), and *pakikisama* (getting along with).

Binding relationships are created through reciprocal obligations (*utang ng loob*), whereby moral principle dictates that when an individual recognizes a favor or service, he or she must reciprocate (Almirol, 1982). *Utang ng loob* works most strongly within the family unit. Because reciprocal obligations are based on services rather than goods, it is difficult to know whether a debt has been paid. Failure to meet reciprocal obligations engenders feelings of guilt (Duff & Arthur, 1973). Children are eternally indebted to parents for having given birth to them, and life is considered an unsolicited gift that can never be repaid. *Utang ng loob* is a form of social control that offers individuals help and protection under the auspices of the family group. However, if the individual expects to receive support from others, he or she must be prepared to return such support or suffer *hiya*.

Loosely translated, *hiya* means shame. *Hiya* occurs when the individual fails to meet an expected goal or performs in ways that result in disapproval from the family or others (Almirol, 1982). *Hiya* is tied to conformity (Hollnsteiner, 1963) and serves to maintain the importance of the group over the individual.

Amor proprio, which is related to *hiya,* refers to one's self-esteem (Lynch, 1981). Filipinos are highly sensitive to criticism and are easily humiliated. Criticism may be taken as a personal insult. Affronts to one's *amor proprio* may require the individual to take aggressive action to protect the self. However, *hiya* serves to repress aggressive behavior and to protect against shaming of others. Filipinos are careful not to criticize, complain about, or question others.

Pakikisama means going along with others even if doing so contradicts one's own desires. One who possesses *pakikisama* also possesses *pakiradam*—the ability to sense things, especially other people's wants and needs (Hippler, 1985). Anticipation of other peoples' desires is often accomplished by understanding subtle subverbal and nonverbal cues such as body language and tone of voice. *Pakikisama* assures that good feelings and cooperation are maintained. The individual's interests, desires, and relationships outside the family unit must be sacrificed for the needs of the family unit (Hollnsteiner, 1963).

Within the family hierarchy, age is important but does not necessarily connote authority. Grandparents are respected and indulged but do not maintain authority over family members as occurs in most Asian groups. The advice of grandparents is considered valuable, and they are frequently consulted on important family matters. They assist in household chores and in caring for the children. If it is possible for them to do so, the elderly will contribute to the educational expenses of grandchildren. In turn, most children feel responsible for taking care of their elderly parents (Peterson, 1978).

The U.S. Bureau of the Census (1980) indicates that compared with whites and other Asian groups, immigrant Filipino families have more ($N = 1.5$) extended family members residing with them. The average family size is 4.04 persons. Through bilateral descent and the compadre system (see the following paragraph for a definition), an individual may have more than 100 identified relations (Guthrie, 1968). The *bilateral extended family* provides mutual support, protection, and interdependence to all its members, and the kin group takes precedence over unrelated persons, the community, and the law. When a member is threatened, the family will rally around the individual to provide protection and support. Through the concept of reciprocal obligation, the extended family will provide financial aid and career favors.

Fictive relatives are brought into the family through the *compadre* (co-parent) system. They are incorporated into the kinship network through Catholic religious rites of passage: baptism, confirmation, and marriage (Affonso, 1978). These religious practices are highly congruent with Filipino family culture and values. The system is characterized by reciprocal obligations that increase the number of people in the individual's support network. Godparents are expected to contribute to the child's education, provide financial assistance, and to be attentive. The compadre system extends and binds familial ties, loyalties, and interdependence in the community (Anderson, 1984). Early Filipino immigrants to the United States (between 1920 and 1950) made functional use of the compadre system (Sharma, 1980). Greater than 90% of the early Filipino immigrants were men. The absence of Filipino women and the racist attitudes and behaviors (e.g., antimiscegenation laws) in the United States resulted in few marriages. Coming from a society that placed a high value on familial relationships, the compadre system allowed many single men to be incorporated into a family system. . . .

MARITAL RELATIONSHIPS

The acculturation process can create family and marital conflict (Tyron & Briones, 1985; Agbayani-Siewert, 1991). Traditional Filipino values and adherence to cultural norms of smooth interpersonal relationships and clear, well-defined family roles help minimize potential conflicts between spouses (Tyron & Briones, 1985). Agbayani-Siewert (1991) studied immigrant Filipino American married couples and found that the majority

of couples reported role strain as a result of non-reciprocity in their relationship. Nonreciprocal situations included a spouse who insisted on having his or her way, a spouse who expected more than he or she was willing to give back, always giving in to one's spouse, and having a spouse who acted as if he or she were the only important person in the family. Both males and females reported nonreciprocity as a primary source of marital strain. These findings suggest a breakdown in the cooperative structure of immigrant Filipino American families. The study also reported that Filipino couples were willing to negotiate on difficulties related to nonreciprocity.

Pierse (1976) described Filipino couples as being noncommunicative. The pressure of being a new immigrant may place new demands and stresses on traditional styles of communication, and the acculturation process may introduce new values and roles that conflict with traditional ones and thus strain the marital relationship. In a study of married Filipino couples, Card (1978) reported that verbal communication between spouses occurred infrequently. Moreover, spouses are hesitant to confront each other with their own individual problems. They will, however, discuss personal problems that involve their children. Lack of verbal communication may become dysfunctional in new situations that require more direct and confrontational negotiations, new understandings and clarification.

Filipino American couples tend to keep marital difficulties private. They use the term *tayo-tayo* (just among us) to express the sentiment that disagreements should not be made public (Guthrie, 1968). Most couples do not seek advice as a way of coping with marital strains. Professional or religious counseling is rarely sought (Agbayani-Siewert, 1991), although reading materials may be used. In a survey of social service agencies serving Asian Americans in Los Angeles County, changes in child-rearing practices and spousal sex-role expectations were a major source of marital role strain and domestic violence directed toward Filipino women (Agbayani-Siewert, 1988).

Filipino women are responsible for nurturing and caring for children. Most married Filipino American women with children work to survive economically (Gardner et al., 1985). Couples may feel overburdened if they lack support from other family members, which in turn creates conflict within the family and the marital relationship. In the Philippines, the large extended-family network serves as a buffer from daily life strains. Relatives often assist in child care and sometimes serve as mediators to facilitate communication among family members. The immigrant family, however, may not have an established support network. The loss of a strong, supportive family network combined with the lack of verbal communication may exacerbate the acculturative stress experienced by Filipino couples.

Filipinos differ from other Asian groups in two important ways. Unlike other Asian groups, Filipino families are founded on egalitarian rather than patrilineal principles (Andres & Illada-Andres, 1987; Pido, 1986; Yap, 1986); ancestry is traced bilaterally. Filipino Americans also differ from other Asian Americans in their religious background. The majority of Filipinos are Catholic. In a manner similar to that of egalitarian societies such as the United States, Filipino families have liberalized traditional Catholic beliefs with regard to male and female roles (Yap, 1986). Filipinos have been described as having "Filipinized" Western culture and institutions to fit Filipino structures, values, and norms (Pido, 1986). Reportedly, the egalitarian structure between the sexes predated Western influences (Pido, 1986; Yap, 1983, 1986). Moreover, some Filipino historians argue that Filipinos were a matriarchal society prior to the arrival of the Spanish (Pido, 1986). Filipino legend describes both man and woman emerging simultaneously from a bamboo stalk (Andres & Illada-Andres, 1987). Women share equally in power, decision making, and finances (Nydegger & Nydegger, 1966; Pido, 1986). Regardless of sex, Filipino families will give recognition, opportunities, and deference to any family member who shows the potential to increase the

family's resources or standing in the community (Pido, 1986). Thus, females as well as males are expected to contribute toward increasing the family's resources. This expectation reflects the values of cooperation with and obligation to the family and interdependency among its members.

Although the family is structured along egalitarian principles, male and female sex-role behavior has also been influenced by Spanish cultural values. Women are the primary nurturers and caretakers of children. They also form stronger emotional attachments with children than do males. Males are also socialized to be more aggressive than females (Guthrie & Jacobs, 1966). The Spanish influence also dictates that males should exhibit "machismo" mannerisms and behaviors. The seemingly incongruent orientations of egalitarian and "machismo" principles have been described as paradoxical and inconsistent (Yap, 1986). Filipino social workers contend that machismo is surface behavior used mainly for public display (V. Claravall & I. Irigon, personal communication, May 1993). Moreover, it has been argued that Filipino women take an active role in directing this display of public behavior by acting submissive and passive (Andres & Illada-Andres, 1987).

This seemingly inconsistent behavior of Filipino couples is understandable when one realizes that beneath the cultural values and behaviors imposed by the Spanish influence lies an indigenous cultural ethos. Public displays of machismo may have developed as an adaptive response to Spanish colonial rule but never fully integrated into traditional Filipino family structure. For example, the Filipino family structure does not allow male domination of the family, and the principles of egalitarianism are reflected in Filipino law. The Philippine Constitution provides equal opportunities in employment, regardless of sex. Under family law, the rights of women to assume management of domestic affairs are assured. Family-leave law also allows both maternity and paternity leave. Neither member of a married couple can dispose of property without the consent of the spouse. Andres and Illada-

Andres (1987) state, "Equality with men is a birthright of the Filipino woman" (p. 61). . . .

FILIPINO CHILDREN

Children are highly valued and referred to as "precious gifts from God." In a study conducted in the Philippines, Arnold et al. (1975) found that the most frequently mentioned reasons for having children were family happiness, companionship, love, and comfort in old age. This finding was consistent across all socioeconomic groups.

Children are expected to be obedient to parents, older relatives, and older siblings and to be dependent on the family (Guthrie, 1966; Guthrie & Jacobs, 1966; Javier, 1969). Andres and Illada-Andres (1987) contend that Filipino children enjoy a "pampered" and prolonged childhood in which they are absolved from adult responsibilities. Such socialization fosters dependency upon the group (Guthrie & Jacobs, 1966). In a comparative study, Kieth and Barrando (1969) reported that Filipinos are less autonomous and more dependent on the primary family group than are Americans and that Filipino adolescents have later-age norms for independent behavior than do Americans. Filipino adolescents tend to date, go steady, become engaged, and marry between three to seven years later than do American youth. In another comparative study of white and Filipino childbearing practices, Guthrie (1966) found that Filipino parents devoted more time to establishing control over their children, whereas white parents were more concerned about establishing independent behavior.

The acculturative process introduces conflict between Filipino parents' traditional values and the new values and behaviors adopted by their children (Kieth & Barrando, 1969). Children often acculturate at a faster rate than do their parents (Forman, 1990; Tamayo-Lott, 1980).

American middle-class values of individualism, independence, and assertiveness are in direct opposition to traditional Filipino values of smooth interpersonal relationships, familial cooperation,

and interdependence (Forman, 1990). As with most children, Filipino American youth want to be accepted, which requires that they adopt behaviors and values similar to the larger group. American adolescent behaviors and norms such as all-night prom parties and "hanging out" with peers rather than with family members are not readily accepted or understood by most traditional Filipino parents, who value behaviors that reflect family cooperation and interdependency. A young adult's request to establish a residence of his or her own may be met with strong resistance from his or her parents. Parents may perceive such behaviors as stemming from a lack of obedience and dependence, which in turn challenges their parental role (Forman, 1990). Santos (1983) states that parents may intensify their traditional hierarchical stance, which may lead to a breakdown in family communication. In response to their feeling parental role strain caused by children's nonconformity to their values, parents may seek advice through literature, followed by seeking advice from relatives, friends, and neighbors (Agbayani-Siewert, 1991).

Economic issues have also created problems for Filipino American families. In Filipino American households with children, both parents are likely to be employed full time. Most Asian immigrants' adjustment to economic life in the United States is accomplished in part by strong family support, whereby the majority of adult members are employed and contribute to the family income (Gardner et al., 1985). Filipino community leaders and social service workers in Los Angeles and Seattle have reported increasing adolescent gang problems and the increasing practice of sending problematic children to the Philippines to live with extended-family members. Card (1978) states that the primary reasons given by immigrant Filipino American couples as to why they have fewer children than people do in the Philippines was the lack of available child care by family members and others. Working parents spend relatively little time with their children. The lack of parental supervision and support from extended family in the United States, economic issues, and the stress stemming from the acculturation process compel some parents to seek the help of extended family members in the Philippines. . . .

CONCLUSION

An increasing need exists for up-to-date research on Filipino American families. Although empirical data about the Filipino family and cultural values are available in the Philippines, little information is available on Filipino American families. More than half of the studies chosen for inclusion in this article were conducted in the Philippines; although the majority of these studies appeared to be empirically valid, their applicability to Filipino Americans is questionable in that they do not concern themselves with problems that the immigrant Filipino American may encounter with family, work, social service needs, and life in general in the United States.

It is difficult to offer generalizations that apply to the Filipino community as a whole. Filipino Americans are a diverse population comprising four main groups: (1) Filipinos who immigrated during the 1920s and who are mainly farm laborers with little or no education, (2) American-born children and grandchildren of the first group of immigrants, (3) early post–World-War-II immigrants who served in the United States Navy, generally as stewards, and (4) educated professionals who emigrated after 1965 (Cordova, 1973; Kitano, 1980). These groups are differentiated by socioeconomic background, education level, language, and factors surrounding immigration. Minimal interaction takes place among the groups, whose only perception of commonality is based on ethnic origin (Kitano, 1980). Moreover, within each group, Filipinos differ in dialect, geographical origin, and social class, and levels of acculturation may vary depending on age, education, and socioeconomic level. Little research is available on these immigrant groups, with the exception of the first group. . . .

REFERENCES

Affonso, D. (1978). The Filipino American. In A. L. Clark (Ed.), *Culture in childrearing health professionals* (pp. 128–153). Philadelphia: F. A. Davis.

Agbayani-Siewert, P. (1988). *Social service utilization of Filipino Americans in Los Angeles.* Unpublished manuscript, School of Social Welfare, University of California, Los Angeles.

Agbayani-Siewert, P. (1991). *Filipino American role strain, self-esteem, locus of control, social networks, coping, stress, and mental health outcome.* Unpublished doctoral diss., School of Social Welfare, University of California, Los Angeles.

Almirol, E. (1982). Rights and obligation in Filipino American families. *Journal of Comparative Family Studies, 13,* 291–306.

Anderson, R. (1984). *Filipinos in rural Hawaii* (pp. 79–85). Honolulu: University of Hawaii Press.

Andres, T., & Illada-Andres, P. (1987). *Understanding the Filipino.* Quezon City, Philippines: New Day Publishers.

Arnold, F., Bulatao, R., Burpakdi, C., Chung, B., Fawcett, J., Iritani, T., Lee, S., & Wu, T-S. (1975). *The value of children: A cross national study* (Vol. 1). Honolulu: East–West Population Institute.

Bulatao, J. (1981). The Manilino mainsprings. In F. Lynch & A. de Guzman, II (Eds.), *Four readings on Filipino values* (4th ed., pp. 70–118). Quezon City, Philippines: Ateneo de Manila University.

Card, J. (1978). Correspondence of data gathered from husband and wife: Implications for family planning studies. *Social Biology, 25,* 196–204.

Cordova, F. (1973). The Filipino identity: There's always an identity crisis. In S. Sue & N. Wagner (Eds.), *Asian American psychological perspectives.* Palo Alto, CA: Science and Behavior Books.

Duff, D., & Arthur, R. J. (1973). Between two worlds: Filipinos in the U.S. Navy. In S. Sue & N. Wagner (Eds.), *Asian American psychological perspectives* (pp. 202–211). Palo Alto, CA: Science and Behavior Books.

Forman, S. (1990). Hawaii's immigrants from the Philippines. In J. McDermott, T. Tseng, & T. Maretzki (Eds.), *People and culture of Hawaii* (pp. 155–183). Honolulu: University of Hawaii Press.

Gardner, R., Robey, W., & Smith, C. (1985). Asian Americans: Growth, change, and diversity. *Population Bulletin, 40*(4), 1–43.

Guthrie, G. (1966). Structure of maternal attitudes in two cultures. *Journal of Psychology, 62,* 155–165.

Guthrie, G. (1968). *The Philippine temperament: Six perspectives on the Philippines.* Manila, Philippines: Bookmark Publishers.

Guthrie, G., & Jacobs, P. (1966). *Child-rearing and personality in the Philippines.* University Park, PA: Pennsylvania State University.

Hippler, A. (1985). Culture and personality studies of the Pilipinos of northern Luzon: A case of pragmatic erosion. *Journal of Psychoanalytic Anthropology, 8,* 115–155.

Hollnsteiner, M. (1963). Social control and Filipino personality. *Philippine Sociological Review, 11*(3–4), 184–188.

Hollnsteiner, M. (1981). Reciprocity in the lowland Philippines. In F. Lynch & A. de Guzman, II (Eds.), *Four readings on Philippine values* (4th ed., pp. 69–92). Quezon City, Philippines: Institute of Philippine Culture, Ateneo de Manila University.

Javier, A. (1969). Personality development of a Filipino adult. *Pennsylvania Psychiatric Quarterly, 9*(2), 41–47.

Kieth R., & Barrando, E. (1969). Age independence norms in American and Filipino adolescents. *Journal of Social Psychology, 78,* 285–286.

Kitano, H. (1980). *Race relations* (2nd ed.). Englewood Cliffs, NJ: Prentice-Hall.

Lynch, F. (1981). Social acceptance reconsidered. In F. Lynch & A. de Guzman, II (Eds.), *Four readings on Philippine values* (4th ed., pp. 1–68). Quezon City, Philippines: Institute of Philippine Culture, Ateneo de Manila University.

Nydegger, W., & Nydegger, C. (1966). *Tarong: An Illocos barrio in the Philippines.* New York: John Wiley.

Peterson, R. (1978). *The elder Filipino.* San Diego, CA: Companile.

Pido, A. (1986). *The Pilipinos in America: Macro/micro dimensions of immigration and integration.* New York: Center for Migration Studies

Pierse, G. (1976). Philippine culture patterns and psychopathology. *Philippine Journal of Mental Health, 7*(1), 44–46.

Santiago, C. (1953). Welfare functions of the Filipino family. *Philippine Sociological Review, 1*(1), 12–15.

Santos, R. (1983). The social and emotional development of Filipino American children. In G. Powell (Ed.), *The psychological development of minority group children* (pp. 131–146). New York: Brunner/Mazel.

Sharma, M. (1980). Pinoy in paradise: Environment and adaptation of Philipinos in Hawaii, 1906–1946. *Amerasia, 7,* 91–117.

Takagi, C., & Ishisaka, H. (1982). Social work with Asian- and Pacific-Americans. In J. Green (Ed.), *Cultural awareness in the human services* (pp. 138–144). Englewood Cliffs, NJ: Prentice-Hall.

Tamayo-Lott, J. (1980). Migration of a mentality: The Pilipino community. In R. Endo, S. Sue, & N. Wagner (Eds.), *Asian Americans: Social and psychological perspectives* (vol. 2, pp. 132–140). Palo Alto, CA: Science and Behavior Books.

Tyron, W., & Briones, R. (1985). Higher order semantic counter conditioning of Filipino women's evaluation of heterosexual behavior. *Psychology, 16*(12), 125–131.

U.S. Bureau of the Census. (1980). *Detailed population characteristics, 10.* Washington, DC: U.S. Government Printing Office.

Varies, R. (1963). Psychiatry and the Filipino personality. *Philippine Sociological Review, 11*(3–4), 179–184.

Yap, J. (1983, May). Sex and the Filipino psyche. *Asian-American News, 8*(8), 1–15.

Yap, J. (1986). Philippine ethnoculture and human sexuality. *Journal of Social Work and Human Sexuality, 4*(3), 121–134.

Yu, E., & Liu, W. J. (1980). *Fertility and kinship in the Philippines.* Notre Dame, IN: University of Notre Dame Press.

? Think about It

1 How do Filipino American cultural values about cooperation and mutual support strengthen the ties between wives and husbands as well as between children and parents? How do they exclude outsiders?

2. Compare the fictive relatives of Filipino American families with those of black families described in Reading 3.

3. What kinds of conflicts and stress do traditional Filipino American parents and their children experience as they become Americanized?

5 Taiwanese American Family Values and Socialization

Franklin Ng

The family is an important unit in Taiwanese American families. As Franklin Ng shows, Chinese values define familial relationships and responsibilities. They also emphasize the significance of filial piety, family harmony, respect for elders, and achieving success in education and employment.

The family was the building block of traditional Chinese society. Much of this was due to Confucian values, which tended to place a premium on the importance of family. As a result, in traditional China, clans and lineages were significant factors in local politics. They could mobilize resources, financial or human labor as the situation demanded. They could provide tutors or an education for the gifted children of the clan. On the whole, those clans and lineages in Southern China were more extensive and complete than those in the north.

Confucian values are associated with the five relationships that specify the important ties that maintain a family and society. The first is of subject and ruler: the subject is to obey the ruler. The second is of the father to the son: the son is to obey the father. The third is of the wife to the husband: the wife is to be obedient to her husband. The fourth is of the younger brother to the older brother: the younger brother should obey the older brother. Finally, in the fifth, a friend should respect a friend.

According to some interpreters of Confucian values, of the five relationships, three pertain to the family. Moreover, it has been noticed that of the five bonds, four are from the top down. That is,

one of the two in each dyad is subordinate, while the other is dominant. Some scholars explain, however, that the five bonds are not to subjugate. Rather they claim that there must be reciprocal responsibility. A ruler to merit being called a ruler must take care of his subjects. To win respect from his son a father must deport himself as a father. To keep his wife a husband must be solicitous of her needs. A younger brother is expected to defer or learn from the experience of his older brother, but the older brother must be aware of what he is doing wrong. Finally, a friend must reciprocate acts by his friend to maintain the tie.

THE STATUS OF FAMILY MEMBERS

Traditional family values placed an emphasis on the continuity of the family name. The family was patrilineal in the sense that the male line continued through the sons. For this reason, having sons was stressed: they could ensure the duration of the family line. Sons could carry on the rites to respect the ancestors. In fact, in the rites to commemorate ancestors, only males could conduct the ceremonies.

Also, in an agricultural society, having many sons meant that there would be a larger reservoir of labor to help in the fields. In other endeavors, it meant that there might be more to help in the family business. Finally, sons could be deployed to

Source: From Franklin Ng, *The Taiwanese Americans* (Westport, CT: Greenwood, 1998), 24–32. Copyright © 1998 by Greenwood Publishing Group, Inc. Reproduced with permission of Greenwood Publishing Group, Inc., Westport, CT.

diversify the family's resources and to enhance the family's economic and social status. A very talented son, for example, might be schooled to master the classics for the imperial examinations. Success in the examinations might lead to appointment to a post in the imperial bureaucracy, thereby conferring prestige and power to the family.

The family was hierarchical and respected seniority. A generation should respect the generations above it. Thus, a father should respect his own father; a grandson, his grandfather. A younger brother should respect the older brother; a younger sister, the older one. Those who were older had the benefit of greater experience and wisdom and should therefore be heeded.

Women who married were seen as marrying out of the family. They were marrying into another family and were to bear children for that family. In her new home, the new wife was expected to help out with the chores and to assist the mother of her husband. When she bore a son, her status in the family was elevated, for she had borne another male who could carry on the name of her husband's family.

Chinese society was considered patriarchal as men held the formal authority in the family. The position of women was noted in the "three obediences." According to this perspective, when a woman was young, she obeyed her father. When she was married, she obeyed her husband. And, when she was a widow, she obeyed her son. This is not to say, however, that women did not have informal power.

Children were seen as the raison d'etre for the family. In traditional China, an abundance of children was seen as a blessing. It suggested a prosperous and lucky household, with many members to assure the biological continuity and the economic success of the family. Of course, having many children was only desirable if the family had the means to support them. Otherwise, there would be problems in feeding so many mouths. Children were also a form of insurance to support parents in their old age in a society where there was no assurance of financial security or assistance upon retirement from work. . . .

CHANGES IN . . . THE UNITED STATES

. . . In the United States, family is also an important theme for the Taiwanese. The ideal family was traditionally envisioned to be an extended family. This might be a family with three generations under one roof—grandparents, their children and their wives, and their grandchildren. Or, it might be a joint family, including two brothers, their wives, and their children. Particularly in a traditional society that emphasized agriculture, a large family in one household was considered a benefit.

In the United States, the extended family may be found, but it often is the nuclear family. In Taiwan, important economic changes have deemphasized the need for large families as was required in agriculture. With movement from rural to urban areas, many are now employed in sectors other than farming. Changes bringing prosperity to Taiwan society also mitigate the need for many sons to take care of the security of parents after their retirement.

In the United States, there are even fewer extended families. Couples migrating to America often have left their parents and siblings behind in Taiwan. As a result, they live by themselves even as their parents continue to reside in Taiwan. But they try to maintain relations with their parents by constantly phoning back home to Taiwan. Moreover, if the circumstances permit, there may be occasional trips to visit parents and relatives. As a result, even though there may be physical separation, an emotional intimacy bridges the gulf in distance.

In some households, other relatives may live with the nuclear family comprised of the parents and their children. For example, a sister's family may be residing in the Midwest of the United States. But the other sister lives on the West Coast in California. The nephew from the Midwest may live with the aunt and uncle on the West Coast as he attends a university in the neighborhood in which they live. This is a way of conserving financial resources and also insuring that the nephew even at college will be under the careful guidance of family members. It is also a way of rekindling familial relationships.

Within a household of a first-generation family from Taiwan, Chinese kinship terminology is likely to be used. This type of family terminology is much more specific and precise than that of the general American society. Thus, the words for grandparents will denote whether they are the relations of the father or the mother. *Zufumu* is the term for parents of one's father, while *waizufumu* is the term for parents of one's mother. Or, the words for brother and sister will denote their rank and seniority, whether they are younger or older than the speaker. *Gege* is the term for an older brother, while *didi* is the term for a younger brother. *Jiejie* is the term for an older sister; *meimei,* for a younger sister.

In the case of terms for uncles and aunts, there will be embedded in the words the indication of whether they are from the father or mother's side, and their rank or seniority as the oldest uncle or youngest aunt as well. *Bofu* is the older brother of one's father, while *shufu* is the father's younger brother. *Jiufu* is the brother of one's mother. *Bofu, zufu,* and *jiufu* in the United States are simply referred to as "uncles." *Gumu* is the sister of one's father; *yimu,* the sister of one's mother. In the United States, both *gumu* and *yimu* are simply referred to as "aunts." In the case of cousins, the terms used will signify whether they are older or younger and whether they come from the father or mother's family.

Often a family in which there is a second generation will not be as precise in their use of the kinship terminology. Not as familiar with the Chinese or Taiwanese language, they may have trouble keeping track of the precise usage of the terms for relatives. The more acculturated they are, the more likely they are to adopt the more generalized American kinship terminology of just saying "aunt" or "uncle," which do not recognize their link to the father or mother's side of the relatives or their rank in terms of age or seniority.

In the United States, family relations are modified compared to the situation in Taiwan. In the United States, the situation may vary according to the economic situation of the families. Broadly speaking, it may be said that there are two kinds of families. One would be the Chinatown family of those who are employed by others, often in a Chinatown or urban area. The members of such a family would often be working class, laboring in a garment factory, restaurant, or tourist shop, in manufacturing, service, or some other small business.

For those in this scenario, the hours may be long and the wages not that high. In a garment factory, the women sit poised before their machines, sewing or assembling the clothing that must be conveyed from the subcontractors to the larger outlets or department stores. In a restaurant, the waiters, cooks, and busboys must contend with long hours and a wide variety of chores. Competition is fierce, and the flow of customers when it comes is fast and frenetic. In the tourist and curio shops, success is dependent on the economy and the tourist traffic. High rents dictate that there must be a sizable volume of window-shoppers and tourists, or else the businesses will not be able to recoup their costs of operation.

Typically there are two wage earners as their income is not in a high range. For this reason, the male and female may be coequal breadwinners as they both have an important role to play in securing income for the family. In such a situation, the husband and wife may not see each other frequently. Children may be left to fend for themselves, with perhaps the oldest ones entrusted to take care of the younger siblings. If it is an extended family, the grandparents may help in the care of the younger children.

In such a family, the roles may be much more traditional. The father may have a stronger, more dominant status. His opinions are more likely to carry weight, and the mother may echo his views. Because of their heavy involvement with work, they may not have much time with their children. As a result, there may be misunderstanding, a lack of communication, and even a widened generation gap between the parents and their children who are much more acculturated.

Another type of family is the professional family. In this type of family, the couple are usually of the middle class and engaged in white-collar employment. They have a college level education and perhaps postgraduate as well from Taiwan or the United States. They might be accountants, engineers, computer scientists, insurance agents, or financial managers. With this type of employment, the family enjoys a high level of income and a respectable social status. Their homes may be in suburban areas or in urban neighborhoods away from Chinatowns.

For the professional family, the relations between the husband and wife are more egalitarian. They are more acquainted with middle-class mores and are more acculturated than their Chinatown or working-class counterparts. Their lifestyle affords them more leisure and time for recreation. It also means that they may spend more time with their children, participating in their school and extracurricular activities. They are more able to participate in community activities and to network with others in the Chinese or non-Chinese community.

VALUES AND CUSTOMS

The families of immigrants from Taiwan, regardless of whether they are of the working or professional class, are likely to emphasize traditional Chinese values to their children. Although there may be a diversity in the degree of practice, the ideals are nonetheless common to many of these families. The ideals are likely to focus on the significance of family, filial piety, and respect for elders.

Children are told from an early age that the family is important. In Taiwanese society, an individual is nothing unless he or she is affiliated with a group. Of these groups, the family assumes paramount significance. But the family is not merely the nuclear family. It also extends to relatives beyond the nuclear family to those on the father's and mother's side. Kinship ties form a vast network that can help in many situations, so children are urged to always value relatives. . . .

One of the values that the parents are likely to pass on to their children is the importance of filial piety. Parents are the ones who are endowed with more experience and wisdom. They bring food to the table, shelter the children, and have made the sacrifice of coming to the United States so that the family could have a better life. Above all, they have brought the children into this world and have nurtured them.

For this reason, the children are obligated to obey their parents. The obligation of children to parents is one that can never be repaid. Their duties and responsibilities are to try to satisfy their parents by doing well in school, and to excel in their endeavors so as to bring honor to the family name. Older siblings should try to watch and help their younger brothers and sisters, and finally, they should try to avoid conflict with one another. As a family, they should try to be a cohesive and harmonious unit.

Children are taught how to deport themselves. That means that in the presence of family members, adults, and those in authority, children should observe proper etiquette and demonstrate correct manners. Children are warned that people can easily distinguish between those who have good breeding and teaching and those who do not. When in the public gaze, when at the meal table, or whatever setting it might be, children should always conduct themselves properly with appropriate propriety and decorum.

Another important value for the children that parents emphasize is the importance of education. This theme is consistent with Confucian values, and the parents have no problem in conveying it. They may mention how Taiwan used to be a developing country. They may emphasize that education helped in the transformation of Taiwan. They may also talk about how difficult it is to secure entry into one of Taiwan's prestigious universities. In the United States, the competition is much less fierce, but the children should still try their best to get into a prestigious college or university. One important change is that whereas in the past a high level of education was not seen as necessary or even desirable for a woman, that is no longer the case.

A great deal of emphasis is placed on success in achievement or accomplishment. Children are enjoined to strive to do well in whatever field of endeavor they enter. Whether it be a public or private career, whether it be education or extracurricular activities, they should try to do their best. The obverse side of this is that individuals should not bring shame or dishonor to the family. One should be aware that whatever is done will reflect upon the parents and others who are associated with that person. When there is success, it bestows prestige on the family. But when something brings shame or the loss of face, it hurts the family and those linked to that individual.

A person or a family encounters different stages through life. Marriage can be an important phase in one's life course. In traditional China, marriages were arranged by the parents of the two families. It was viewed as an alliance involving the joining of resources, so it was too important to be left to individuals. The young couple had little say in the arranged marriage, and romantic love was not a major concern. If the couple was lucky, love and affection would develop over the course of the marriage. In any event, it was important to bear heirs to the family name and to insure the continuity of the family.

But in the twentieth century, the place of love and romance in marriage has assumed a central position. In this sense, the desires and interests of the couple are now seen as the major determinant of a marriage. A couple may meet in the course of their education or in a place of employment, or through an introduction by others. As a result, in Taiwan and in the United States, marriages are now conducted in a manner familiar to other Americans.

While many Taiwanese marry other Taiwanese, intermarriages are on the rise. In the United States, there are many instances of marriage of those from Taiwan marrying other Chinese. Thus, for example, many Taiwanese have married Cantonese. There are also marriages with Chinese from Hong Kong, Singapore, Southeast Asia, and other areas. In addition, in the United States, many Asian Americans are marrying other Asian Americans who are outside their specific ethnic group. An example might be a Taiwanese American marrying a Japanese American, or a Vietnamese American marrying a Filipino American.

On the other hand, there are also rising numbers of marriage with those who are not Chinese or Asians. Familiarity with others through schools, work, and other encounters provides opportunities for a wider choice in marriage. As a result, in almost every community, there are mixed marriages of those from Taiwan with non-Chinese. In this sense, the Taiwan Chinese mirror the intermarriage that has been occurring with other Chinese Americans and Asian Americans.

With such a development, there are increasing numbers of mixed-race children. In a pluralistic society such as the United States, this is hardly a surprising situation. Many third- or fourth-generation descendants of immigrants are a rich mix of different heritages or ethnicities. This trend means that the parents must negotiate how they will raise the children and the type of religious orientation that the children may assume. It also has led to suggestions that the U.S. Census should henceforth adopt a category for those of mixed parentage. At the present time, one can only check off a single category such as "Asian American," "Hispanic," "American Indian," "African American," and so on. A mixed parentage category would permit people to check off their identity as being exactly that instead of being a single ethnic category. Or, they could check off several categories as a way of indicating their multiple identities. They would then not have to deny any facet of their interracial ancestry.

Within the family, a number of customs are observed with the corresponding rite of passage. That is to say, certain customs may be followed with the different stages in the life of a family. These rites of passage pertain to marriage, birth of a child, the celebration of a birthday, and funerals. Depending upon the family, there may be variations in the observance of these family customs.

The marriage is a good example of the influence of family customs. Marriage is the union of two individuals and two households. When a couple marries, their families are also joined as relatives. For many families, the hope for an auspicious marriage will lead them to check an almanac. Their parents especially, whether in Taiwan or the United States, are likely to consult it and offer advice to the prospective couple. The almanac will describe whether they are a lucky match according to the years of their birth. It functions thus as a horoscope.

For example, the Chinese calendar is based on the lunar year. It has a zodiac of a twelve-year cycle in which there are twelve different animals for each year. These animals are the rat, ox, tiger, rabbit, dragon, snake, horse, sheep, monkey, chicken, dog, and pig. Each animal is then paired with five elements, which are metal, wood, earth, water, and fire. It takes sixty years to complete a full cosmic cycle, which then repeats itself. The Chinese almanac helps to interpret what will be an appropriate day for an event and also offers a suggestion as to whether a marriage will be a lucky one. Individuals born in a year associated with a particular animal will have certain traits that may or may not match with others. Those persons born in the Year of the Rat should marry those born in the Year of the Dragon, Monkey, or the Ox. They should not marry those born in the Year of the Horse. But if a couple really wants to wed, such traditional practices are not likely to deter them.

A wedding is a joyous affair to be celebrated. It signals the start of a family, an important rite of passage in Chinese society. A church wedding or a civil wedding at city hall is followed with a banquet. The guests parade into the restaurant to offer their greetings and wishes for a happy marriage. They may bestow envelopes of money or gifts to the new couple. In the United States, the new couple may have opened a bridal registry with a department store so that they can receive chinaware, linen, appliances, and other needed items without duplication. In the course of the wedding banquet,

there may be games and teasing by well-wishers who try to add levity to the event.

In a few cases, if the finances permit and the parents desire it, there may be two wedding banquets—one in the United States and one in Taiwan. This may occur if one or two sets of parents are in Taiwan. One banquet is held for their benefit, while the other is held in the United States for the friends of the couple. During the 1980s, for a while, it was the practice to send the bride off to Taiwan to a cooking class so that she could learn how to prepare traditional Chinese dishes for her new family.

The birth of children is a happy occurrence. Before the birth, the mother is provided with foods that will strengthen her body. There are also food taboos of items that should not be consumed during this time, such as the consumption of lamb. After the birth, foods to restore her strength will be prepared. In this way, the health of mother and child are ensured. The birth of a baby is sure to touch off great excitement, and when the baby is one month old many families celebrate with a first-month party.

? Think about It

1. How do Confucian values emphasize the important ties that maintain a family? What does Ng mean when he describes some of these values as coming "from the top down"?
2. Why has immigration changed the structure of the Taiwanese family in the United States? Describe how acculturation is transforming kinship terminology, family roles, and the father's patriarchal authority in the Taiwanese American family.
3. Which traditional Chinese values do many Taiwanese American parents still teach their children?

6 Grandmother to Granddaughter: Learning to Be a Dakota Woman

Angela Cavender Wilson

As Readings 3, 4, and 5 suggest, much of our socialization is unconscious. We internalize values based on observation, religious beliefs, rewards and punishments, or the expectations of family members and other significant people in our lives. Socialization can also be conscious and deliberate. Angela Cavender Wilson shows, for example, that oral histories handed down from generation to generation teach valuable lessons about kinship responsibility and ethnic pride and provide an understanding of where we come from, who we are, and what is expected of us.

The intimate hours I spent with my grandmother listening to her stories are reflections of more than a simple educational process. The stories handed down from grandmother to granddaughter are rooted in a deep sense of kinship responsibility, a responsibility that relays a culture, an identity, and a sense of belonging essential to my life. It is through the stories of my grandmother, my grandmother's grandmother, and my grandmother's grandmother's grandmother and their lives that I learned what it means to be a Dakota woman, and the responsibility, pain, and pride associated with such a role. These stories in our oral tradition, then, must be appreciated by historians not simply for the illumination they bring to the broader historical picture but also as an essential component in the survival of culture.

Maza Okiye Win (Woman Who Talks To Iron) was ten years old at the time of the Unites States–Dakota Conflict of 1862. She saw her father, Chief Mazomani (Walking Iron), die from wounds suffered in the Battle of Wood Lake. White soldiers wounded him while he was carrying a white

Source: From Angela Cavender Wilson, "Grandmother to Granddaughter: Generations of Oral History in a Dakota Family," *American Indian Quarterly* 20 (Winter 1996): 7–13. Reprinted by permission of the University of Nebraska Press. Copyright © 1996 by the University of Nebraska Press.

flag of truce. She also witnessed the fatal stabbing of her grandmother by a soldier during the forced march to Fort Snelling in the first phase of the Dakota removal to Crow Creek, South Dakota. For three years Maza Okiye Win stayed in Crow Creek before she moved to Sisseton, South Dakota. Finally, after more than twenty-five years of banishment from Minnesota, she returned with her second husband, Inyangmani Hoksida (Running Walker Boy) to the ancient Dakota homeland of Mni-Sota Makoce, or Land Where the Waters Reflect the Heavens.[1] By this time both she and her husband had become Christians, and were known in English as John and Isabel Roberts. There they raised their children and three of their grandchildren.

Elsie Two Bear Cavender was born in Pezihuta zizi village in 1906 to Anna Roberts and Joseph Two Bear. She was raised by her grandparents, John and Isabel Roberts. Her Dakota name was Wiko (Beautiful), given to her by one of her great aunts when she was just a girl. Grandma always seemed embarrassed by that name—as though she didn't believe she was beautiful enough to possess it and certainly too modest to introduce herself that way. But now that she is gone, I can use what I perceive to be a fitting name without embarrassing her. To me, she was always *Kunsi,* or Grandma. She had eight children, four of whom she buried in her lifetime. She was well-known for her generosity, her wonderful pies and rolls, and her stories.

Grandma grew up in a rich oral tradition. Not only was she well-acquainted with many of the myths and legends of our people, she also possessed an amazing comprehension of our history, and many of her stories revolved around the events of the United States–Dakota Conflict of 1862. Her grandmother, in particular, had carried vivid, painful memories of those traumatic times. Over time, those painful memories of my great-great-grandmother became the memories of my grandmother and, then, they became my memories.

Early on, when I first began thinking about these stories in an academic context, I realized my understandings of oral tradition and oral history were incomparable with those I was finding in other texts. This incompatibility was largely because of terminology. David Henige, in his book *Oral Historiography,* differentiates between oral history and oral tradition, conveying an understanding that seems to be representative of most scholars in the field, when he says, "As normally used nowadays, 'oral history' refers to the study of the recent past by means of life histories or personal recollections, where informants speak about their own experiences . . . oral tradition should be widely practiced or understood in a society and it must be handed down for at least a few generations."[2] These definitions are applicable to Native American oral history and oral tradition only in a very limited way. Native peoples' life histories, for example, often incorporate the experiences of both human and non-human beings. In addition, this definition would not allow for the incorporation of new materials because it would then be outside the "tradition."

From a Native perspective, I would suggest instead that oral history is contained within oral tradition. For the Dakota, "oral tradition" refers to the way in which information is passed on rather than the length of time something has been told. Personal experiences, pieces of information, events, incidents, etc., can become a part of the oral tradition at the moment it happens or the moment it is told, as long as the person adopting the memory is part of an oral tradition.

Who belongs to an oral tradition? Charles Eastman, a Wahpetonwan Dakota, reveals in his autobiography *Indian Boyhood* the distinct way in which the oral tradition was developed:

> Very early, the Indian boy assumed the task of preserving and transmitting the legends of his ancestors and his race. Almost every evening a myth, or a true story of some deed done in the past, was narrated by one of the parents or grandparents, while the boy listened with parted lips and glistening eyes. On the following evening, he was usually required to repeat it. If he was not an apt scholar, he struggled long with his task; but as a rule, the Indian boy is a good listener and has a good memory, so that his stories are tolerably well mastered. The household became his audience, by which he was alternately criticized and applauded.[3]

This excerpt highlights the rigorous and extensive training required of young Dakota people. The Dakota oral tradition is based on the assumption that the ability to remember is an acquired skill—one that may be acutely developed or neglected. Eastman also describes the differentiation between myths and true stories, necessitating an understanding of history as being encompassed in oral tradition. However, few scholars working in oral history make any distinction between oral information collected from those belonging to a written culture and those belonging to an oral tradition. This is an area that is yet to be explored.

My grandmother, Elsie Cavender, received this type of training. She had much to tell about some of our more popular characters, stories starring our mythical trickster figure, Unktomi, as well as stories about Dakota men and women—mostly belonging to my lineage—who lived and died long before I was born.

In my own family, the importance of specific stories as interpreted by my grandmother was expressed by the frequency with which those were told. As a girl I was acquainted with an assortment of stories from these categories, and I remember having to request specifically those which were not in the historical realm. But I didn't have to request the stories we classify as "history." Those she offered freely and frequently. Especially in the last years of her life, on every visit she would tell stories about the Conflict of 1862, as if to reassure herself that she had fulfilled her obligations and that these stories would not be forgotten.

One of these stories has become particularly important to me since my grandmother's death because it deals with grandmothers and granddaughters, of which I am the seventh generation. Aspects of this story have helped shape my perception of what my responsibility is, as a mother and eventual grandmother, and as a Dakota. This particular story is an excerpt taken from an oral history project I began with my grandmother in 1990. This is an edited version with much of the repetition cut for the sake of clarity and conciseness in this presentation. However, under usual storytelling circumstances, the repetition is part of the storytelling procedure, often added for emphasis. Grandmother titled this portion of the United States–Dakota Conflict "Death March," consciously drawing on the similarities between the removal of Dakota from the Lower Sioux Agency, first to Fort Snelling and then on to Crow Creek, South Dakota, with the Bataan Death March in World War II. After one of our Dakota relatives who had participated in that march related to her his experiences she saw many parallels with 1862 and thought "Death March" a fitting title. This passage is in my grandmother's voice:

Right after the 1862 Conflict, most of the Sioux people were driven out of Minnesota. A lot of our people left to other states. This must have been heartbreaking for them, as this valley had always been their home.

My grandmother, Isabel Roberts (Maza-Okiye-Win is her Indian name) and her family were taken as captives down to Fort Snelling. On the way most of them [the people] walked, but some of the older ones and the children rode on a cart. In Indian the cart was called *canpahmihma-kawitkotkoka*. That means crazy cart in Indian. The reason they called the cart that is because it had one big wheel that didn't have any spokes. It was just one big round board. When they went they didn't grease it just right so it squeaked. You could just hear that noise about a mile away. The poor men, women, old people, and children who had to listen to it got sick from it. They would get headaches real bad. It carried the old people and the children so they wouldn't have to walk.

They passed through a lot of towns and they went through some where the people were real hostile to them. They would throw rocks, cans, sticks, and everything they could think of: potatoes, even rotten tomatoes and eggs. New Ulm was one of the worst towns they had to go through.

When they came through there they threw cans, potatoes, and sticks. They went on through the town anyway. The old people were in the cart. They were coming to the end of the town and they thought they were out of trouble. Then there was a big building at the end of the street. The windows were open. Someone threw hot, scalding water on them. The children were all burned and the old people too. As soon as they started to rub their arms the skin just peeled off. Their faces were like that, too. The children were all crying, even the old ladies started to cry, too. It was so hard it really hurt them but they went on.

They would camp someplace at night. They would feed them, giving them meat, potatoes, or bread. But they brought the bread in on big lumber wagons with no wrapping on them. They had to eat food like that. So, they would just brush off the dust and eat it that way. The meat was the same way. They had to wash it and eat it. A lot of them got sick. They would get dysentery and diarrhea and some had cases of whooping cough and small pox. This went on for several days. A lot of them were complaining that they drank the water and got sick. It was just like a nightmare going on this trip.

It was on this trip that my maternal grandmother's grandmother was killed by white soldiers. My grandmother, Maza Okiye Win, was ten years old at the time and she remembers everything that happened on this journey. The killing took place when they came to a bridge that had no guard rails. The horses or stock were getting restless and were very thirsty. So, when they saw water they wanted to get down to the water right away, and they couldn't hold them still. So, the women and children all got out, including my grandmother, her mother, and her grandmother.

When all this commotion started the soldiers came running to the scene and demanded to know what was wrong. But most of them [the Dakota] couldn't speak English and so couldn't talk. This irritated them and right away they wanted to get rough and tried to push my grandmother's mother and her grandmother off the bridge, but they only succeeded in pushing the older one off and she fell in the water. Her daughter ran down and got her out and she was all wet, so she took her shawl off and put it around her. After this they both got back up on the bridge with the help of the others who were waiting there, including the small daughter, Maza Okiye Win.

She was going to put her mother in the wagon, but it was gone. They stood there not knowing what to do. She wanted to put her mother someplace where she could be warm, but before they could get away, the soldier came again and stabbed her mother with a saber. She screamed and hollered in pain, so she [her daughter] stooped down to help her. But, her mother said, "Please daughter, go. Don't mind me. Take your daughter and go before they do the same thing to you. I'm done for anyway. If they kill you the children will have no one." Though she was in pain and dying she was still concerned about her daughter and little granddaughter who was standing there and witnessed all this. The daughter left her mother there at the mercy of the soldiers, as she knew she had a responsibility as a mother to take care of her small daughter.

"Up to today we don't even know where my grandmother's body is. If only they had given the body back to us we could have given her a decent funeral," Grandma said. They didn't though. So, at night, Grandma's mother had gone back to the bridge where her mother had fallen. She went there but there was no body. There was blood all over the bridge but the body was gone. She went down to the bank. She walked up and down the bank. She even waded across to see if she could see anything on the other side, but no body, nothing. So she came back up. She went on from there not knowing what hap-

pened to her or what they did with the body. So she really felt bad about it. When we were small Grandma used to talk about it. She used to cry. We used to cry with her.

Things happened like this but they always say the Indians are ruthless killers and that they massacred white people. The white people are just as bad, even worse. You never hear about the things that happened to our people because it was never written in the history books. They say it is always the Indians who are at fault.[4]

An excerpt such as this challenges the emphasis of the *status quo*. This account does not contradict the many written texts on the subject, but contributes details not seen elsewhere, details that shift the focus from the "Indian atrocities," which are provided in rich detail in histories written by non-Indians, to "white atrocities" and Indian courage. It exemplifies the nature of the oral tradition in Dakota culture, as it is the story of one family, one lineage, reflecting the ancient village structure and the community that united those with a collective identity and memory. This account by itself will not change the course of American history, or create a theory for or framework from which the rest of the Plains wars may be interpreted. It is not even representative of the "Dakota perspective." Instead, it is one family's perspective that in combination with other families' stories might help to create an understanding of Dakota views on this event and time period. Certainly these stories shed light on the behavior and actions of members of my family that have led up to the present moment.

As I listened to my grandmother telling the last words spoken by her great-great-grandmother, and my grandmother's interpretation, "Though she was in pain and dying, she was still concerned about her daughter and little granddaughter who was standing there and witnessed all this," I understood that our most important role as women is making sure our young ones are taken care of so that our future as Dakota people is assured. I learned that sometimes that means self-sacrifice and putting the interests of others above your own. It was also clear through this story and others that although these were and continue to be hard memories to deal with, always there is pride and dignity in the actions of our women.

In addition, my connection to land and place is solidified with each telling of the story. As a Dakota I understand that not only is Mni-sota a homeland worth defending, but through the stories I learn where the blood of my ancestors was spilt for the sake of the future generations, for me, my children, and grandchildren.

Because these stories are typically not told in the history texts, we also must recognize we are responsible for their repetition. The written archival records will not produce this information. These stories are not told by people who have been "conquered," but by people who have a great desire to survive as a nation, as Dakota people. Consequently, these are not merely interesting stories or even the simple dissemination of historical facts. They are, more importantly, transmissions of culture upon which our survival as a people depends. When our stories die, so will we.

In my last real visit with my grandmother, several months before she was hospitalized in her final days, she recited this story again. I was moving to New York to begin my graduate education, and it was as if she were reminding me where I come from. In the same way, these stories served to validate my identity in a positive way when, as a girl, I was confronted with contrasting negative images of the "Sioux" in school texts. These stories have stabilized me through graduate school and reminded me why I am involved in this sometimes painful process. One of the last video clips we have of my grandmother is of her telling one of our Unktomi stories to my daughter in Dakota. When I watch that scene it becomes apparent to me that the learning of these stories is a lifelong process and, likewise, the rewards of that process last a lifetime.

The contributions of stories such as this should be recognized as celebrations of culture, as declarations of the amazing resiliency and tenacity of a people who have survived horrible circumstances and destructive forces. Some of the greatest stories are those told by Native people and serve as challenges to the rest of the world to be so strong. Native people have an unbreakable belief in the beauty and the significance of our cultures, and this is reflected in our stories. They are testimony to the richness, variety, detail, and complexity of the interpretations of history. Our role as historians should be to examine as many perspectives of the past as possible—not to become the validators or verifiers of stories, but instead to put forth as many perspectives as possible. But, the greatest lessons of these stories are to the young people, the children, and grandchildren of the elders and storytellers, who will gain an understanding of where they came from, who they are, and what is expected of them as a Dine, as an Apache, as a Laguna, as a Choctaw, and as a Dakota.

NOTES

1. Chris C. Cavender, "The Dakota People of Minnesota," in *Hennepin County History* (Summer 1988, Volume 47, Number 3), p. 11.
2. David Henige, *Oral Historiography* (London: Longman, Inc., 1982), p. 2.
3. Charles Eastman, *Indian Boyhood* (New York: Dover Publications, Inc., 1971, originally published by McClure, Phillips & Company, 1902), p. 43.
4. Elsie Cavender, Oral History Project with Angela Cavender Wilson, Fall, 1990.

[?] *Think about It*

1. Why does Wilson describe oral history as "an essential component" in the survival of a culture? Is this characterization more applicable to American Indian families than to other ethnic families in the United States?
2. According to Wilson, what are the purposes of oral history—especially for American Indians?
3. What, specifically, did the grandmother-to-granddaughter stories teach Wilson about being a Dakota woman and mother?

CHAPTER 2

Gender Roles

As you saw in Chapter 1, one function of the family is to teach family members appropriate social roles. Among the most important of these are *gender roles*—characteristics, attitudes, feelings, and behaviors that society expects of females and males. We learn to become male or female through interaction with family members and the larger society. In this sense, gender roles are socially constructed rather than reflecting innate or inherent traits. Gender roles vary across cultures as well as within a culture. The purpose of the five selections in Chapter 2 is to examine some of the ways in which gender experiences and expectations vary across different racial and ethnic families in the United States.

In recent years, gender roles and identities in black families have received a great deal of scholarly and mass media attention. Black males are stereotypically perceived as financially irresponsible, uninvolved in their children's lives, unwilling to marry their children's mothers, or inclined to ignore their spousal obligations.[1] Such depictions ignore the broad diversity of family, spousal, and parental roles that black men perform. Many black men report being very satisfied with their family lives, for example, and are more likely than their white counterparts to share in household chores and child care.[2]

This is not to say that gender roles in the black family are problem free. As Earl Ofari Hutchinson (Reading 7) points out, much of American society is hostile to black men. Many black men must contend with racism, educational failure, and high unemployment rates. High-paying manufacturing jobs have dwindled because of computerization and many U.S. corporations have been exporting white-collar and blue-collar jobs overseas or to third world countries. In addition, the shortage of eligible men is especially acute among blacks because of AIDS, crime, and incarceration. As a result, many black women doubt whether black men are truly living up to their abilities. Many black men, on the other hand, question whether black women will support them when they try to achieve.[3]

Latino men often bear the stereotype of *machismo,* a concept of masculinity that emphasizes characteristics such as dominance, aggression, and womanizing. Positive elements of machismo—such as courage, honor, respect for others, and protection of one's family and nurturing of children—are often ignored by the literature and the popular press.[4] In Reading 8, for example, Patricia R. Pessar's study of Dominicans shows that these immigrant families differ from those back home in gender relations. Although there is no evidence that gender egalitarianism prevails in Latino families, Pessar's research of the daily practices of Dominicans contradicts the stereotypical image of *machismo* in Latino families. While some aspects of gender roles are still patriarchal, women's entry into the labor force is redefining traditional expectations about household authority, budgetary control, and the allocation of housework tasks. During and after the migration process, Latino women often gain power and autonomy while men may lose much of their traditional authority and privilege in the family.[5]

Many Asian immigrants, similarly, are grappling with changes in gender roles due to necessity and opportunity. In their study of a low-income urban community in New Orleans (the second largest Vietnamese settlement outside of California), Min Zhou and Carl L. Bankston III (Reading 9) found that "old" and "new" gender roles are often combined.[6] Because parents see educational success as a major avenue for upward mobility, they encourage both their daughters and their sons to pursue academic excellence. At the same time, however, parents accept a sexual double standard and expect greater obedience and domestic responsibilities from daughters than from sons. Zhou and Bankston suggest that pushing daughters toward academic achievement may result in girls' challenging their parents' controlling behavior and setting higher moral and behavioral standards for daughters than for sons (see also Reading 11).

Moon H. Jo's in-depth interviews with Korean immigrants also show a complex system of gender role relations and adjustment to a more egalitarian family system in the United States (Reading 10). Like Zhou and Bankston, Jo found that traditional gender roles sometimes conflict with the need for two incomes. Sources of strain in the Korean immigrant family include wives gaining economic power and independence. Such strains are worsened because many husbands experience downward social mobility. After migration, many Korean men encounter difficulties due to language problems, underemployment of immigrant professionals, barriers in borrowing money to start businesses, and stiff competition from other local storeowners. Reporters and the mass media praise Korean immigrants for their hard work and strong family values, but Jo shows that many Korean families experience conflict and tension in gender role relationships.[7]

In Reading 11, Monisha Das Gupta raises some interesting issues about Asian Indian gender roles that are probably applicable to other immigrant families as well. As you saw in Reading 1, immigrant experiences vary quite a bit, depending on factors such as language skills, socioeconomic status, migration period, historical immigration policies, and length of residence in the United States. Das Gupta shows that gender is another important variable in shaping one's ethnic identity and immigrant experiences. She notes, for example, that Asian Indian families or individuals who migrated before 1965 were often socially isolated from the larger society as well as from their own ethnic group in U.S. communities and in India. Such isolation often encouraged parents to "invent" and maintain traditional gender role expectations to protect their daughters from many of the negative American influences that would jeopardize women's values and prospective marriageability to suitable Indian or Asian Indian men. Conflict arises in families, Das Gupta maintains, when the second generation of women redefines their cultural identity and challenges their parents' expectations of what is Indian.

NOTES

1. See, for example, David Blankenhorn, *Fatherless America: Confronting Our Most Urgent Social Problem* (New York: HarperCollins, 1995), and David Popenoe, *Life without Father: Compelling New Evidence That Fatherhood and Marriage Are Indispensable for the Good of Children and Society* (New York: Free Press, 1996).
2. See V. Phena-Lopes, "'Make Room for Daddy': Patterns of Family Involvement among Contemporary African American Men," in *American Families: Issues in Race and Ethnicity,* ed. C. K. Jacobson (New York: Garland Publishing, 1993), 179–99, and Robert Joseph Taylor and Waldo E. Johnson Jr., "Family Roles and Family Satisfaction among Black Men," in *Family Life in Black America,* ed. Robert Joseph Taylor, James S. Jackson, and Linda M. Chatters (Thousand Oaks, CA: Sage, 1997), 248–61.
3. For a discussion of black male sexism, see *Black Families at the Crossroads: Challenges and Prospects,* ed. Robert Staples and Leanor Boulin Johnson (San Francisco: Jossey-Bass, 1993), 121–38.
4. Yolanda Mayo, "Machismo, Fatherhood and the Latino Family: Understanding the Concept," *Journal of Multicultural Social Work* 5 (1997): 49–61.
5. See, for example, Pierrette Hondagneu-Sotelo, "Overcoming Patriarchal Constraints: The Reconstruction of Gender Relations among Mexican Immigrant Women and Men," *Gender and Society* 6 (September 1992): 393–415.
6. Some researchers note that many recent Asian immigrants were sharing household responsibilities before migrating to the United States. See Phyllis J. Johnson, "Performance of Household Tasks by Vietnamese and Laotian Refugees," *Journal of Family Issues* 19 (May 1998): 245–73.
7. For other analyses of gender role conflict in Asian American families, see Allan L. Bergano and Barbara L. Bergano-Kinney, "Images, Roles, and Expectations of Filipino Americans by Filipino Americans," in *Filipino Americans: Transformation and Identity,* ed. Maria P. P. Root (Thousand Oaks, CA: Sage, 1997), 198–207; Sucheng Chan, ed., *Hmong Means Free: Life in Laos and America* (Philadelphia: Temple University Press, 1994); Anthony S. Chen, "Lives at the Center of the Periphery, Lives at the Periphery of the Center: Chinese American Masculinities and Bargaining with Hegemony," *Gender and Society* 13 (October 1999): 584–607; and Eunjung Kim, "Sexual Division of Labor in the Korean American Family" (paper presented at the annual meeting of the National Council on Family Relations, Washington, DC, November, 1999).

Behind, beside, in front of Him? Black Women Talk about Their Men

Earl Ofari Hutchinson

Earl Ofari Hutchinson considers why relationships between many black women and black men often are fragile. Are black men still recovering from hundreds of years of slavery and emasculation? Do black women expect too much from black men? Hutchinson describes the five black women he interviewed as "sometimes tender, sometimes harsh" but as wanting "to preserve what is best in African-American males."

It was a raucous scene in the college auditorium. A young woman rose and asked then Black Panther Party leader, Eldridge Cleaver, what the role of women should be in the Black Power movement. Cleaver did not miss a beat, he answered "prone." He was met with a torrent of hisses and shouts from the women in the audience. Others promptly headed for the exits.

Whether Cleaver expressed his own personal view or was speaking for his Party, was not clear. He did, however, reflect the thinking of many black men during the 1960s. That was a time when men routinely believed that the place of the woman was always "two steps behind her man."

When black women protested and accused men of being male chauvinist or sexist, some men retorted that it's part of "African history and tradition." The way these men read that history, men made all the decisions in society and women served dutifully.

In black organizations, men commonly would argue philosophy, set policy and plan strategy. Women would take notes, file papers and answer the telephones. The message was clear. Black women not only were second class citizens in America, they were second class citizens in the movement, too.

Source: From Earl Ofari Hutchinson, *Black Fatherhood II: Black Women Talk about Their Men* (Los Angeles: Middle Passage Press, 1994), 53–75. Reprinted by permission of Middle Passage Press, Inc.

ROSETTA: *The man should be king of his castle. When a major decision has to be made, I would want him to discuss it with me, but if his beliefs are stronger than mine, I would defer to him.*

BEHIND HIM?

During the 1960s, many women weren't buying that history. They knew that even in those patrilineal African societies, women held an honored place. Taking care of the children, food production and household management required great skill and organization. It was not considered by men as incidental or frivolous. Women were central to the maintenance of a smooth and orderly society.

Moreover, women understood American history. They knew that society had used every device to deny black men their manhood. Now times had changed. Black men saw opportunities to be their own men, to make their own decisions, and stamp their seal on history. Many black women were sympathetic and believed that black men should have their opportunity to lead. All they wanted was some assurance that it wouldn't come at their expense. Black men should be leaders but they must understand that black women were not the enemy. It was a tenuous balance that many women tried to walk.

CARLA: *I let my first husband make all the major decisions. He chose the school our daughter went to, how much rent we paid, how much money we spent, the kind of car we bought and even the kind of clothes that he wanted me to wear. I didn't object to it then. I trusted his judgment and was confident that he would make the right choices.*

There is a scene in Lorraine Hansberry's powerful play, *Raisin in the Sun,* about a working class black family's struggle for survival that sticks in my mind. Walter, who drives a cab for a living, and his wife Ruth are sitting at the breakfast table. Walter tries to convince his wife that his scheme to buy a liquor store with the insurance money his mother was due to receive will make them all rich.

When Ruth interrupts him in mid-sentence and tells him to eat his eggs, Walter explodes. He shouts at her that that's what's wrong with black women, they don't ever do anything to "build up their men." Ruth fires back that black women do support their men when they accomplish things. Walter, out of frustration, mumbles loudly that black men are "tied to a race of women with small minds."

Maybe that's one of the problems. Many black women question whether their Walters are truly achieving to their abilities. While many black men question whether their Ruths will support them when they try or do achieve.

ANDREA: *I try to support my man by being involved with his activities. He belongs to a club and I go to most of the events it has. Sometimes I would rather stay home or do something else, but I know it's important to him that I be with him. If that's what he needs to make him a more complete person, I'm for it.*

Sid was a good candidate for the "headstrong" award of the year. He prided himself on being able to make firm and decisive decisions. At the office, his coworkers admired him for his leadership qualities. When disputes arose, Sid stepped in immediately and settled matters quickly and resolutely. When he made a decision, rarely was it questioned or challenged. Sid always had the final word.

Sid's wife was just the opposite. She was soft-spoken and always listened carefully to what others had to say about their problems. She always approached things with diplomacy and tact. She was a good complement to Sid. She understood his personality. She knew that he had a need to be firmly in control. But she also knew that Sid always had their best interests in mind. So when there was a problem or dispute, and she felt strongly that she was right, she was at her best.

She knew exactly how to handle the situation and him. She let him do most of the talking as she knew he would. She was careful not to interrupt or challenge him. This would only result in an argument. When he finished, she quietly stated her points. Usually, they were on the mark and Sid knew it. She knew that he might protest or stomp around a little, but she was prepared to wait him out. She knew that he would see the logic in her argument. When Sid "made" the final decision, it was surprisingly close to what she wanted or had suggested they do.

CARLA: *There are ways to make a man feel like he's "a real man" and still get your way. My daughter was an example. When it came to discipline, my husband was more of a hands on person than me. I thought he was a little too aggressive. Rather than confront him directly and end up in an argument, I would leave little clippings from newspapers and magazines on child discipline around the house that agreed with my views.*

I would talk to mutual friends who agreed with me and when they came over, I would maneuver the discussion around to the subject, so that they could have their say when he was in the room. I never said a word. After a while I noticed that he was talking to our daughter rather than punishing her every time she misbehaved.

Most black women agree that black men have had a terrible way to go. Millions were lost during

African captivity and the passage to America. On the plantation, the slave master's word was the law not only in the field, but also in the family. He put the food and clothes on the table for black women and children, not the black man. He said when the black woman could rest, sing, and dance, not the black man. He said when the black woman could marry, not the black man. He said when the black woman could rest or pray, not the black man.

He could sell, beat and even kill the black woman, while the black man was helpless to act. He had to watch while the slave master stole into his cabin or took his woman up to the big house and raped or physically assaulted her.

The black man had to be taught obedience or broken into submission. The master had to break not only his spirit, but also his manhood. There was never room on the plantation for two masters.

ROSETTA: *If I had my wish, I would love to stay home and take care of the house and kids. I don't need to be a modern woman. If he's watching the game, I won't bother him. Even though I used to hate cooking and dishwashing because of the stigma of women in the kitchen, if that's what he wants, I'll do it.*

The list of those black men who did rebel and refused to submit would fill many pages. Black abolitionist leader Frederick Douglass tells of his day-long epic personal struggle with Covey, "the Negro breaker." The custom was when a black man was especially stubborn or rebellious, a master would send him out to a slave breaker to be "broken." Douglass was sent to Covey. After a series of beatings, Douglass challenged Covey. They fought for several hours. It was a battle of wills and the prize was Douglass' manhood, "I was a changed being after that fight. I was nothing before—I was a man now."

ROSETTA: *If I have a good relationship with a man, I don't regard doing things to please him as "selling-out" or being dominated by him. I made*

the decision to devote myself to the house, kids and him because I want to do it, not because I feel I have to do it.

BESIDE HIM?

Some feminists are puzzled as to why there aren't more black women in feminist organizations. If anything, black women have suffered the most from gender discrimination. They receive less pay and fewer benefits. They have less access to health and social services. Poor black women suffer the most when state and federal governments restrict funds to public hospitals and clinics. Black women are also subjected to sexual assaults and violence. So, again, why aren't they in the front ranks of feminist organizations?

It's a good question. Black women do have much to gain from the fight for women's rights. But many are hesitant to join feminist organizations. They feel their main battle is against racism, not sexism. In this battle, their best ally is still the black man.

CARMEN: *I strongly believe that a couple should make decisions jointly. Two people should be able to sit down and talk about their needs and then come to an agreement. If one person is always making decisions for the other there's bound to be resentment and hostility. This will often come out in ways that the other doesn't see or understand.*

It was a sad spectacle for most African-Americans to watch. A black man and a black woman on national TV, swapping accusations of sexual misconduct. For days, the nation was tantalized by the charges of sexual harassment made by Anita Hill against U.S. Supreme Court Justice nominee, Clarence Thomas.

The issue was not whether Anita Hill was telling the truth. The issue was that a black woman and a black man were at odds. Many black women regard sexual harassment as a serious matter and they support penalties against it. They believe that racism and sexism (even among African-American men) are twin evils, and that both must be fought with equal vigor. But they also looked beyond Hill and Thomas at America.

African-Americans were reeling from a decade of Reagan–Bush administration assaults on civil rights, social services, education and job programs. On top of this, the problems of crime, drugs, gangs and violence were piling higher on the doorsteps of African-Americans. That's why many blacks were alarmed. They thought that the Hill–Thomas fight being played out before the eyes of racially unsympathetic whites could be used by them to further degrade blacks. Many said that this was the time for African-American men and women to unite and not fight each other.

CARLA: *I try to find out what he wants, what will satisfy him. I try to do it without nagging or making him feel like he's on the spot. I don't do this to keep the peace. I do it because I want to make myself happy. If he's not happy, there's no way that I can be happy.*

Still others wondered. If blacks continue to engage in their bruising battle of the sexes, won't this deepen the suspicions of much of white America that there is something "pathologically" wrong with black men AND women? Bigots could then easily ask, If black men and women can't get along with each other, then why should we?

MELANIE: *I think many black men are still caught up in the need to control their women. If a woman voices opinions that may differ from his, he feels threatened, or takes it as a sign that she doesn't love or respect him. Men should stop for a moment and think how they deal with their male friends they disagree with. Do they stop being friends with them? Do they take it as a personal challenge or insult? No, they might end up going for a drink and laughing about it. They can do the same with a woman.*

Malcolm X liked to tell audiences that black people don't catch hell because they are Methodist, Baptist, Catholic or Muslim. They catch hell because they are black. His point: blackness is the great leveler in America. It cuts across all class and religious lines. No matter whether an African-American is a millionaire or a pauper, a supreme court justice or a prison inmate, a surgeon or an indigent patient, a university president or a high school drop-out. If you're black you can still be refused a loan, denied a job or promotion or be harassed by the police. Gender? It makes little difference whether it's an African-American male or female.

ANDREA: *My fianceé and I have been stopped a couple of times by the police. Both times they made us get out of the car. They asked us a lot of questions and ran checks on both of us. It didn't seem to matter to them that our children were in the car. They had these two blacks and they were going to make sure both of us were clean before they let us go.*

She's a highly paid reporter who travels frequently on assignments. On several occasions, this black woman has been frisked and questioned. She's had her purse and luggage searched and her passport inspected. She does not look like a drug dealer or a smuggler. Being a successful career woman means little. Being black means everything.

MELANIE: *In my position as a social worker, I notice that when it comes to single black mothers, case workers will, at the slightest suspicion that a mother is neglecting or abusing her children, recommend that they be placed under protective care. They hardly ever do this with white children.*

I have seen the photo many times. And I am always struck by the determined looks on the faces of Dr. Martin Luther King and his wife Coretta as they marched down the highway locked arm-in-arm. The photo was taken during the famed

March from Selma to Montgomery, Alabama, in 1965. Nearly twenty-five thousand people marched together that day for political justice and economic rights in America. They were the conscience and soul of America.

On that eventful day, there were many other black couples among the marchers. They had their eyes fixed firmly on history. They had their eyes firmly fixed on each other.

CARMEN: *A husband and a wife have to work at compatibility. Even then it can take many years before a couple learns each other's needs, and desires. And it may take even more years before they recognize the ways that a person expresses them. One person doesn't always have to tell the other person, for example, that they want to be held, or comforted, or that they want to be left alone. They can communicate that by a look, a gesture, a smile, a frown, or even silence. When I hear that a couple is getting a separation or divorce, after say 20, 25, or 30 years of marriage, I'm convinced that many of them, despite all those years together, are in some ways probably still strangers to each other.*

I knew instantly that something was wrong. My mother sat immobile in her chair. She stared at the TV. Her eyes were ringed with deep, red circles. She had been crying. She did not look at me as I sat down. It seemed as if she was frozen in time. On the screen was a group of black men, they were hovering over the body of a prostrate man on the balcony of the Lorraine Motel.

The date was April 4, 1968. Dr. King had just been cut down by an assassin's bullet in Memphis, Tennessee. As I watched her staring intently at the TV screen, I thought of the scene following Indian leader Mohandas Gandhi's assassination. At his funeral, distraught women tried to throw themselves on his burning funeral pyre. They had been very much a part of his life and struggle for freedom. And they wanted to be a part of him, even in death.

As King lay prostrate on the balcony with the life ebbing from him, I knew that my mother and millions of other black women were dying inside too. They deeply loved, revered and respected the man. To them, he was more than just a leader, he was a loving black man. He exemplified strength, dedication and purpose.

He was the kind of man that my mother respected and admired. He was the kind of man with whom she would be proud to stand side-by-side. Even though there would be no funeral pyre for King, the embers of the deep respect she had for him as a leader and a man would always burn in her heart.

ROSETTA: *Maybe I'm a little naive. But I want a man that I can give all my trust to. If I'm with someone and he's not worthy of my trust then I know that I won't be with him very long. And I'm pretty sure that he also wants me to be the kind of woman that he can trust too.*

Ana and Frederick Douglass, W.E.B. and Shirley Graham DuBois, Margaret and Booker T. Washington, Marcus and Amy Jacques Garvey, Eslanda and Paul Robeson, Richard and Julia Wright, Ida B. Wells and Ferdinand Lee Barnett, and Malcolm X and Betty Shabazz. Can anyone think of better teams?

CARLA: *I couldn't stay with a man very long that I didn't respect. I want to feel that a man believes in something rather than just talking to hear himself talk.*

History provides no examples of generals winning major battles by leaving half of their army in the rear. The struggle against racism and exploitation are monumental battles. It has consumed the energies of black men and women for four centuries in America.

It is a battle that has been marked by advances and retreats, forward thrusts, and backward marches. At each step, black women nursed their men in battle, offered them their shoulders to cry on in tragedy and crisis, and extended to them their hands to lift them up when they fell. They bolstered their resolve and confidence to continue the struggle.

CARMEN: *Men try to cover up their feelings and not let you know when they hurt, because that's what the world expects them to do. But when a man gets behind the doors of his home, he will show his true feelings. If he's hurting it will come out and his woman will pick up the vibes from him that tell her he needs and wants a pat or a stroke to pick him up.*

Many black fathers understand that manhood is not adulthood. Manhood requires that a male attain responsibility, commitment and wisdom. Adulthood requires only that a male attain legal age. Manhood does not come by luck or chance. It requires patience, hard work and understanding. Many men are prepared to take their sons through the ancient African tradition called the "rites of passage" to reach manhood.

What about their daughters? Should they be left out of the process of self-actualization too? The Sojourner Truth Adolescent Rites Society believes that the same passage is necessary for girls to become women. In their rites of passage they teach:

Family History
Sex Education
History of Our People
Spirituality/Community Spirit
Taking Care of Self
Housekeeping/Finances
Assertiveness/Leadership
Values Clarification/Future Planning
Time Management/Organizational Skills
Art and Dance

First, they want to make girls conscious of their dignity and worth as women. And second, they want to make them aware of their duties and responsibilities to their communities and to their families.

MELANIE: *There's been so much emphasis on the problems of black men, that black women have gotten lost in the shuffle. That's not to say that black men don't have some serious problems, like health, prison and unemployment. But, with black women, the pressures are just as great, maybe even greater, because we're women, too.*

IN FRONT OF HIM?

"Move or Die!" The tone in her voice and the cold steel of the revolver pressed to the frightened slave's head told him that Harriet Tubman meant business. Twenty-five times the frail but iron-willed woman went South. She defied dogs, night riders, slave patrols and posses. She braved the dangers of the swamps, forests and rushing rivers to deliver slaves from captivity. She prided herself on never losing a single passenger. They did not call her Moses for nothing. When a slave signed on with her, there was no turning back.

CARLA: *I can't blindly follow anyone. I know what I want and I am just as capable as anyone of making my own decisions.*

When our daughters are children, we want them to wear pretty little dresses. We want them to help their mothers in the kitchen and around the house. We want them to come home promptly every day from school.

When they are teens, we want to know who their friends are. We want to know what they do every moment they are away from home. We want them to always act in a demure and ladylike manner. We want them to be escorted everywhere they go.

When they are adults we want them to choose the right career. We want them to pick the right husband. We want to protect our daughters from the pitfalls of the male dominated world.

But one day our daughters will be women. They will make their own decisions and lead their own lives. On that day, the things we want may not be the things they want.

CARMEN: *As girls, many women learned how to plan, manage and organize time, money and work. It's a talent they use everyday with their families, children, relationships and on their jobs, oftentimes without knowing it.*

That day came with my daughter. I wanted her to pursue her graduate studies at a college close to home. It had a good curriculum and she would have access to a car. It made perfectly good sense to me, but not to her.

The school she wanted to go to was on the east coast. There, she would not have a car. The courses she wanted to take were chancy, career wise, and she would have to adjust to life in a new city. She wasn't deterred. She visited the campus and liked it and then applied. She even received an academic scholarship.

My daughter loves me and she respects me. She talked to me and she listened to me, but in the end, she followed her heart and her head, made her own decision. She was a winner and so was I.

ANDREA: *A lot of men hate to ask a woman's opinion about something, until a problem or a crisis comes up. Then, they'll ask.*

If there is one word that can sum up the lives of many black women it is RESPONSIBILITY. When they were young girls, they had to follow strict rules and perform duties, often very strict. They had to help their mothers cook, clean, wash and iron. When they were teenagers, they cooked, cleaned, washed and ironed AND worked at jobs outside the home. As adults, they cooked, cleaned, washed and ironed, worked outside the home AND took care of their children and their husbands.

Nearly every moment of their lives, black women have had to make decisions. More often than not, the only ones with whom they had to keep counsel were themselves. This was not by choice. Poverty or broken homes had often forced

them to be both mother and breadwinner. Many saw the role as a challenge. It was almost as if the fate of their people rested on their sometimes broad, sometimes narrow, but always weary, shoulders.

MELANIE: *A woman made decisions about her life long before she met her husband or boyfriend.*

The eight black women profiled in a popular black magazine possessed poise, confidence, talent and plenty of savvy. They were successful as corporate chief executives, public officials, business owners, attorneys and doctors.

I noted one other thing, only two of them were married. The other six were single either by choice or because of failed marriages. Why? Each of the six women clearly stated what they wanted in a mate. I couldn't help but wonder whether the very success they created for themselves made many men wary of them.

ROSETTA: *I think some women do things to push men away without realizing it. It may be their attitude or the way they act. That's why I think it's good to have a close friend who can act as a sounding board. They may be able to point out faults or problems that you may not see.*

"She slapped me" and then she asked me, "How come yuh didn't hide. How come yuh always fightin?" For novelist Richard Wright, the memory of his mother rebuking him for daring to throw rocks at the white boys who had attacked him was painful. In the "Ethics of Jim Crow," Wright pointed to a dilemma that many black mothers and their sons have faced.

They understand that much of American society is hostile to black men. They know that too many black men have been jailed, beaten or killed for fighting back against injustice and racism.

In their tales of growing up, many black men, especially in the South, tell how their mothers scolded or punished them for talking back to whites. Some mothers probably just wanted their sons to show good manners and respect to adults. Others, like Wright's mother, may have been trying to shield them from the danger that could come to a black man who challenges white authority.

But in harnessing their son's aggression and energy, do some women in effect emasculate them? Do they prevent them from becoming the protectors and defenders of their families and communities? Do they pass the mantle of leadership to black women by default?

ANDREA: *I don't know why some men feel challenged when women make decisions. I would think that a man should be glad if a woman for a change plans a trip or activity that he would enjoy. Just like men want women to go with the flow, they should do the same. Who knows, they might like it.*

They go by various names: male bonding, men's consciousness, male self-awareness and so on. Black men form these groups to show their women that men want to be sensitive, caring and nurturing. Many are sincere about wanting to get in touch with the real essence of their manhood. They believe that women have much to show them about these qualities.

That men feel the need to join these groups is a stark admission that male domination and sexism exacts a terrible price on men just as racism does on whites. The emotional stunting from male sexual privilege prevents them from enjoying a productive and meaningful relationship with women as equal persons and equal partners. For many black women this is a welcome turn and may lead to stronger, more productive relationships with men.

CARLA: *I feel that most men are afraid to let themselves go. I have told men friends of mine several times, "Why don't you try hugging." It's OK to touch someone if you feel like it. Nobody will laugh at you or think you're silly.*

Is it enough for men to talk to other men? Is there a danger that men left alone to their own devices may simply reinforce their own biases and stroke their egos? If that happens, they may never discover that it's OK to: hail their woman's successes and triumphs and not feel threatened by them; make decisions with a woman and not for her; cry when they feel joy or sadness, and not suppress their feelings; replace the tattered mantle of aloofness with the cloak of personal warmth; understand that men can be tender, gentle, compassionate and reflective and still be decisive, tough, tenacious and aggressive. They can discover what women have always known, that strength comes in many forms.

ANDREA: *When I am angry or even happy, I want him to acknowledge my feelings. Look at my facial expressions, listen to my voice, see it, recognize it and react to it. I don't want him to pretend or try to ignore that I don't have feelings too.*

Should black women stand behind, beside or in front of their men? There is no one answer. There are times when black women have chosen to do one or the other. There are times when she has chosen to do all three. It does not mean that black women are in competition with black men. Most black women prefer to think of themselves as in partnership with their men. They want their relations with them to be based on mutual respect and sharing.

Many women are still willing to put aside their momentary and emotional needs, to give their man the little extra stroke or pat on the back he needs. They know that black men assaulted for decades by American society are still in the frantic search to discover themselves and their "maleness."

They also don't want men to forget that women have their own physical and emotional needs and personal ambitions, too. Women remind men that the same pat or stroke they are willing to give them, they also need. Women want a level playing field in the relationship game.

1. Why, according to Hutchinson, have black men had a "terrible way to go" historically? How has this affected their masculinity? Have black women's experiences been better?

2. Why aren't there more black women in feminist organizations?

3. Some of the women Hutchinson interviewed admit to "maneuvering" men to get what they want. Is manipulation a necessary ingredient of male/female relationships—regardless of race or ethnicity?

8 Grappling with Changing Gender Roles in Dominican American Families

Patricia R. Pessar

Like many other immigrants, those from the Dominican Republic come to the United States looking for a better life and hoping to advance economically. As Patricia R. Pessar discusses, attaining these objectives usually requires Dominican women to work outside the home. Such employment violates traditional beliefs about gender roles but often empowers women personally and helps a family financially. Working outside the home may also result in tensions, conflict, or divorce.

DOMINICAN FAMILIES BACK HOME

Before they emigrated, most Dominican immigrants lived in a nuclear or extended-nuclear family, either as a child or as a member of a conjugal pair. A smaller number of immigrants resided in single parent or extended–single parent units (Grasmuck and Pessar 1991).

Nuclear families in the Dominican Republic are commonly quite patriarchal, with formal authority residing with the senior male. Publicly, at least, the image of the husband as the authority figure is maintained even though there are numerous, subtle ways that wives exercise a voice in, or

sometimes veto, male decisions (Hendricks 1974). As patriarch, the man is expected to be the primary, if not sole, breadwinner, household head, and representative of the family in public life. In contrast, the woman's "place" is in the home, meeting the needs of the family. As one Dominican refrain expresses it, "el hombre en la calle y la mujer en el hogar" ("the man in the street and the woman in the home"). While this model of gender relations is predicated on a system of reciprocal exchanges between husband and wife, these exchanges are by no means equitable. Rather, men commonly enjoy a host of special privileges including far greater liberty to appropriate household income for their own use, to socialize outside of the home, and to form extramarital relations

(Báez and Taulé 1993). As many of my female informants related, such male privilege could contribute to interpersonal and financial strains within families. Sometimes these pressures lead to marital disruptions. And, it is noteworthy that divorced and separated women are more likely to migrate to the United States (Gurak and Kritz 1987). Nonetheless, women are usually advised to avoid marital discord by reacting to husbands' excesses with patience and resignation. According to one expert on Dominican families, the ideology goes somewhat like this:

> A woman has to marry; she marries, and marriage is like a lottery—you cannot predict what you will get. You cannot tell how a man will turn out. He may be a *gallero* (aficionado of cock fighting), a heavy drinker, or a womanizer. Whatever happens, it is the woman's duty to bear (literally, support) it all and remain faithful and responsible—remain, that is, a "serious woman." If she behaves properly, as she should, one day her husband will stop his irresponsible behavior and dedicate himself to his wife. (Brown 1975: 325).

DOMINICAN IMMIGRANT FAMILIES

With Dominican settlement in New York, many couples have come to fashion a division of authority and responsibilities within the family that is somewhat more equitable. Changes have been most evident in three areas: beliefs about household authority, budgetary control, and the allocation of household members to housework tasks.

For most Dominicans the status of household head is equated with the role of breadwinner. According to a 1981 survey of Dominicans residing in New York, less than one-third (31 percent) of the women had been employed prior to emigration, whereas 92 percent worked for pay at some time since moving to the United States (Gurak and Kritz 1982). As Dominican immigrant women have come to demonstrate their capacity to share material responsibility with men on more

or less equal terms, they have asserted the right to assume the status of household head alongside their husbands. Thus, in response to my questions, Who is the household head now? and, Who was the head previous to your emigration?, many echoed the words of this woman:

> We both are the household heads. If both husband and wife are earning salaries then they should equally rule in the household. In the Dominican Republic it is always the husband who gives the orders in the household. But here when the two are working, the woman feels herself the equal of the man in ruling the home.

Household budgeting is another arena in which women have sought and won greater equality. In interviews in the early 1980s with immigrant women, I found that in the Dominican Republic prior to emigration, men generally controlled the budget in their households even though women often contributed income on a regular or semi-regular basis. Some households followed a traditional, patriarchal pattern in which members gave all or part of their wages or profits to the senior male who, in turn, oversaw the payment of household expenses. In others, the senior male amassed all of the family income and then gave his wife an allowance to cover such basic expenditures as food and clothing. In the United States today far fewer Dominican households follow a male-controlled pattern of budgeting. Indeed, pooling income is now the dominant pattern. That is, the husband, wife, and working children pool a specific amount of their wages or profits for shared household expenses, such as food, rent, and utilities. The rest of their income is usually divided between joint or individual savings accounts and personal consumption items.

Thirty-three-year-old Carmen Rubio and her husband Orlando, 38, explained to me how the transition from a male-controlled form of budgeting to a pooled pattern occurred in their household. Before emigrating in 1978 Carmen had been a housewife. Orlando, then an accountant in a law office in Santo Domingo, provided her with a weekly allowance for the basic items. While they discussed major purchases such as a new automobile, Orlando had the final say on all such expenditures.

Once in New York, it was decided that both would seek employment: Carmen found work in a doll factory and Orlando worked as an accountant in a cousin's supermarket. In Carmen's words, "At first I did what most women did back home. I gave Orlando my pay check to use to pay the bills. He gave me an allowance for food and other essentials." Some months after their arrival Carmen needed a new dress for her niece's wedding, and she asked Orlando for $100. He balked. Carmen, smarting at his refusal, sought advice and help from her female relatives who had lived in New York for many years. It was actually Carmen's brother, a resident in the United States for six years, who intervened after hearing about the dispute. According to Carmen, "He told Orlando that as long as I was bringing in good money I had the right to buy what I wanted, as long as all the pressing bills were paid. He said that here couples put their wages together and shared in paying bills."

For his part, Orlando explained that at the time of the dispute he did not want Carmen to buy such an expensive dress, because they had many debts to repay linked to their emigration. Nonetheless, he recanted, "They told me I was being old-fashioned and not appreciative of Carmen's help. They also told me that women have many more expenses here than at home, like clothes to wear to work. I could see that here, honorable men, like my brother-in-law, were handling affairs differently than they did back home; so I decided I could change too." Significantly, both Carmen and Orlando now claim that they like the pooled pattern of budgeting better than the household allowance mode. "We each know how much the other earns and we discuss how our money is being spent and saved," Orlando explained. "Back home Carmen would sometimes

accuse me of spending my money on vices, like gambling, while she struggled to feed the family. I would tell her she was wrong; my earnings just didn't go as far as they did in the past. Now she sees my pay check; there are no secrets. It's better."

Consistent with research on other working-class families (Hood 1983; Lamphere et al. 1993), I found that many Dominican immigrant women were able to use their wage-earning as leverage to obtain assistance from husbands in housework and child care. In a sense, Dominican women are simply following the logic of what one writer calls the "marketwork/housework bargain" (Hood 1983). An underlying assumption in this "bargain" is that men's principal responsibility is to provide for the family's economic needs, the woman's is to maintain the household. However, if the woman assumes economic responsibility for the family by engaging in wage work, as many Dominican immigrant women have done, then the allocation of other household responsibilities should change as well.

The vast majority of Dominican women and men I met in New York believed that when both partners worked outside the home, the husband should "help" with tasks such as shopping, washing dishes, and child care. Occasionally, they even cook, as in the case of Ernesto Collado, a chef in New York, who assumed that his contribution to running the household should include cooking at home as well. When I visited the Collado apartment, I found Ernesto preparing dinner. He said he would never have been found in the kitchen, let alone cooking, in the Dominican Republic. There, he told me, the kitchen was solely the women's domain—"la cocina se respeta." Yet, on the island, his wife would not be working outside the house; he alone would be the breadwinner. Once both he and his wife were working, they realized that "if both worked outside the house, both should work inside as well. Now that we are in the United States, we should adopt American ways."

There seems to be a direct relationship between the amount of money a woman contributes to the household and the degree to which her spouse is willing or feels compelled to engage in domestic responsibilities. Dominican women who contribute almost half, if not more, to the household budget can usually depend on greater male involvement in domestic tasks than women who make more modest financial contributions. This was the case for Ismelda Nuñez, who explained that when her children were very young she worked a few hours a day at home sewing for a neighborhood garment factory (i.e., industrial homework). "I worked fewer hours than my husband and I wasn't bringing in much money. If he decided to help me bathe the children or do the dishes, that was fine; but I never insisted, not then." Once the children were older and in school, Ismelda began working full-time in a shoe factory. "I work nine or ten hours a day," she stated. "I am bringing in a lot of money to help my husband. . . . He actually does things around the house now without my even asking."

Many of the women I spoke to indicated that they did not explicitly request that their husbands assist them in household labors. Rather, many said, "the changes just happened." Often they were the result of expediency. For example, Ernesto Collado first began cooking for the family when his work schedule permitted him to return home before his wife. "I opened the door on three kids complaining that their school lunch was lousy. They knew I was a chef so they kind of insisted that I start dinner."

Dominican women consistently mentioned male assistance in housework and child care when they compared their life in the United States favorably with that in the Dominican Republic. Yet none of my informants went so far as to suggest that men could or should act as women's equals in the domestic sphere. Indeed, the following woman's words capture the belief of most of the working women I spoke to: "I know of cases where the man assumes the housekeeping and child care responsibilities. But I don't believe a man can be as good as a woman; she is made for the home and the man is made to work."

Such sentiments suggest that women's wage work may have led to greater changes in domestic social practice than in actual gender ideology and norms. On this score the rhetoric with which Dominican women describe changes in traditional gender relations is telling. I often heard women comment favorably on the increased sharing and unity (*unión*) between husbands and wives that wage earning and residence in the United States afforded. In particular, they praised husbands for "helping" their wives in child care and housework. By contrast, women usually described their own wage-earning as "helping" their husbands. In my opinion, both sets of comments reflect women's attempts to reconcile wage work and the changes in domestic life it has occasioned on the one hand, with a more paramount set of enduring values on the other. Despite the acknowledgment that, while in the United States, women may need "to help" husbands earn a livelihood and husbands may legitimately be called upon "to help" working women at home, a more conservative message about the sexes is implied. It is the same message we noted in our earlier discussion of premigration families. It holds that women are persons whose primary interests and responsibilities are rooted in the home, while men are beings who are responsible for maintaining the family by their labors in the workplace. . . .

DISBANDED UNIONS

Women's employment and their major contribution to household budgets have promoted greater gender parity within many Dominican households. Some, like Marta and Margarita, have sacrificed these gains, however, in the name of powerful gender constructs that identify women foremost with the domestic sphere. Still others have seen their struggles to attain more equitable domestic relations and social mobility end in dismantled unions and poverty. Of the fifty-five women I interviewed extensively in New York, eighteen have divorced or separated from a partner while in the United States. Fourteen cited a struggle over domestic authority and social practices as the primary disruptive factor.

Sometimes difficulties arose when the woman lived and worked in the United States prior to sponsoring her mate's migration. Women reported that newly arrived husbands typically became unnerved by what they viewed as an inversion of gender roles. While many men adamantly insisted that their wives return to a more traditional pattern of household authority and budgeting, a few reacted quite differently. Claiming that their wives were trying to wear the pants in the family, these men insisted upon their wives becoming true ("male") breadwinners by assuming responsibility for major fixed expenses, such as food and housing. For several women the breaking point came when the man monopolized his salary for personal expenses, such as entertainment, while at the same time demanding a disproportionate economic contribution from his wife.

Clara Duarte, who sponsored her husband's emigration after residing in New York without him for three years, described several bitter and humiliating fights over the control and allocation of money. When Mario first arrived in New York, he insisted that she hand her pay check over to him; she refused. He then demanded that she continue to pay the rent and utilities, "since the contracts were solely in her name." At first Clara agreed to cover the major household expenses, figuring that she would give Mario a chance both to find a relatively well-paying job and to learn how other Dominican immigrant couples managed household budgeting. "But, still, after two years, he continued to use his money for his philandering and claim he didn't have enough to pay our bills," Clara explained. "I saw he would never change. I was still young, we had no children, and I figured I could find another man who was more

understanding, a better companion." Clara was fortunate to find such a partner a few years after she divorced Mario. Her new husband was a Dominican who arrived in the United States as a youngster. Juan had seen his own parents jointly manage the household budget, and he readily adopted this pattern when he and Clara married.

As these case studies show, immigrant life in the United States equips Dominican women with new material, social, and cultural resources. These resources empower some women to make more demands upon their husbands and to be willing to disband unions in which husbands refuse to compensate them, even minimally, for their involvement in traditional male activities, such as wage-earning. Sadly, though, women's empowerment often carries a price. When household bonds are severed, the goal of the migration project—social advancement for the family—often falters, because the individual resources of single members, especially women, are insufficient to sustain it. The newfound autonomy of many immigrant women may, in the end, lead to poverty.

REFERENCES

Báez, Clara and Ginny Taulé
1993 "Posición socio-cultural y económica de la mujer en la república dominicana." *Género* 1(2): 1–144.
Brown, Susan E.
1975 "Love Unites Them and Hunger Separates Them: Poor Women in the Dominican Republic. In Rayna Reiter, ed., *Toward an Anthropology of Women.* New York: Monthly Review Press.
Grasmuck, Sherri and Patricia R. Pessar
1991 *Between Two Islands: Dominican International Migration.* Berkeley: University of California Press.
Gurak, Douglas and Mary Kritz
1987 "Family Formation and Marital Selection among Colombian and Dominican Immigrants in New York City." *International Migration Review* 21(2): 275–298.
1982 "Dominican and Colombian Women in New York City: Migration Structure and Employment Patterns." *Migration Today* 10(3–4): 14–21.

Hendricks, Glenn
1974 *The Dominican Diaspora: From the Dominican Republic to New York City—Villagers in Transition.* New York: Teachers College Press.
Hood, Jane C.
1983 *Becoming a Two-Job Family: Role Bargaining in Dual Worker Households.* New York: Praeger.
Lamphere, Louise, Patricia Zavella, and Felipe Gonzales with Peter Evans
1993 *Sunbelt Working Mothers.* Ithaca, New York: Cornell University Press.

[?] Think about It

1. In what three domestic areas have Dominican Americans encountered the greatest changes compared with traditional expectations and beliefs about appropriate gender roles?
2. What does Pessar mean when she describes women's and men's family roles as "a dichotomous construct"?
3. Why does Pessar see a relationship between Dominican American women's employment and disbanded unions or divorce?

9 Appropriate Gender Roles in Vietnamese American Families

Min Zhou and Carl L. Bankston III

In their study of low-income, urban, Vietnamese immigrants in Versailles Village, New Orleans, Min Zhou and Carl L. Bankston III examine how the families are adapting to the opportunities and constraints of living in a new country. One of the adaptations involves balancing traditional gender roles with newer, conflicting views—especially in the education of young Vietnamese women.

Studies of the Vietnamese have shown that gender roles among Vietnamese refugees in the United States differ markedly from those in Vietnam, which are characterized by the subordination of women (Freeman 1989; Kibria 1993; Muzny 1989; Nash 1992; Rutledge 1992). The anthropologist Gerard C. Hickey's classic ethnographic

Source: From Min Zhou and Carl L. Bankston III, *Growing Up American: How Vietnamese Children Adapt to Life in the United States* (New York: Russell Sage Foundation, 1998), 171–72, 174–83. Copyright © 1998 Russell Sage Foundation, New York, New York. Reprinted by permission of the Russell Sage Foundation.

study of Vietnamese village life in the late 1950s testified to the second-class status of women in Vietnam (1964). Hickey observed that rural Vietnamese women were expected to marry early, bear children, and serve their husbands. Except for a few Catholics, families widely accepted polygamy. Most of the villagers were poorly educated; but women were four times as likely as men to be illiterate, since in the past only men received a formal education, while woman were taught household arts. Although significant improvements in educational facilities have been made in contemporary Vietnam and more villagers agree that women deserve a basic formal education, educational opportunities for women have remained strictly limited.

With migration to the United States, gender roles have changed in significant ways. We can trace these changes to two sources: necessity and opportunity. The economic situation of Vietnamese families no longer permits men to function as sole providers. At the same time, Vietnamese women encounter many more opportunities for education and employment outside the home, establishing an identity that includes greater independence from their husbands than they had in Vietnam. Vietnamese women's work outside the home has also greatly narrowed the male–female power gap within the home (Kibria 1993). Despite these changes, researchers generally agree that traditional ideas about family and gender have not been completely abandoned by the Vietnamese. The anthropologist James M. Freeman's collection of short autobiographies of the Vietnamese show a people profoundly attached to their family traditions and troubled by challenges to them (1989). And Jesse W. Nash's participant observation in a Vietnamese community portrays the idealization of women as a core value of the community (1992). . . .

In contrast to adult Vietnamese women, handicapped by the educational disadvantages they brought with them from Vietnam, younger-generation Vietnamese women in the United States no longer trail their male peers in schooling. Why is it that these young Vietnamese women seem to have attained levels of education that are at least equal, and possibly superior, to the levels attained by men? Our fieldwork in Versailles Village pinpoints the factors behind this reversal. Since gender roles are fundamentally matters of interpretation of the kinds of behavior considered appropriate to men and women, we focused on how fathers, mothers, young men, and young women themselves have perceived the importance of women's education and how perceptions of women's education may be related to broader views about changes in gender roles. In addressing

the broader views about gender roles, we pay special attention to whether the refuge in the United States has brought about a break from the traditional Vietnamese ways of thinking about men and women or whether these ways of thinking have somehow been adjusted to new circumstances.

THE FATHER'S VIEW

Most of the Vietnamese fathers interviewed considered obedience as the most desired quality and achievement as the second most desired quality to be expected from or desired in their daughters. But the fathers did not view obedience and achievement as mutually inconsistent. From the father's perspective, obedience produced achievement. One father told us:

> It is important that all children obey their parents. But it is more important for daughters to obey. The daughters will be mothers one day and they must be good mothers. So, they must obey their parents today.

Obedience from all children, both sons and daughters, is generally expected in Vietnamese families. In Vietnam, fathers might have expected obedience throughout life, but in the United States, they hoped that it would last until marriage. Fathers worried that the greater level of personal freedom in American life might undermine obedience among daughters and sons, but they overwhelmingly agreed that the perceived need to protect the sexual purity of daughters made the obedience of daughters even more important than that of sons. A father remarked:

> Of course a boy can get away with more than a girl. A boy can do more before he gets a bad name. A boy can get a bad name and still become good later. But if a girl gets a bad name, I don't know what she can do to get over [it].

The fathers whom we interviewed not only tolerated the idea that their daughters would be educated but encouraged it. They pointed out that women had always participated in the household economy in Vietnam, but mostly in agriculture, a pursuit that required little formal education. But farming was not part of the Vietnamese experience in the United States, as one father explained:

> In Vietnam, the girls helped with the rice, sure, but here nobody's a farmer. You got to have a job to get money. A good wife needs to help her husband. She got to have a job to help and she got to go to school to get a job.

Having experienced so much hardship in the United States, fathers knew the importance of a two-income family. Most of the fathers whom we interviewed worked as fishermen or in low-skilled manufacturing; their wives either did not work outside the home or were employed at relatively low-income part-time jobs. As low-wage workers, the fathers realized that their wives' lack of job skills made it all that much harder to get ahead. They had also learned that living well in America, required a relatively high income, a goal that only families with multiple earners could hope to attain. For these reasons, fathers had come to see education as a way that would allow their daughters to contribute to family well-being, as expected by the traditional Vietnamese family, but in a manner suitable to American needs and wants. A father said:

> It is very hard for me being the only one in the family who works. I am a fisherman. I make enough money for us to live, but I worry all the time. My wife, her English is not good, and she cannot work. So, I want my daughter to go to school so that she and her future family will not have these problems. My daughter is good, so she will do what I say and her life will be better than ours.

Fathers struck a clear note when discussing their desire for their daughters to do well in school—namely, the expectation that education would make a young woman an appropriate match for a relatively high-status husband. Several fathers outlined the following contrasting scenarios.

In Vietnam, an uneducated woman had no other options but marriage into a working-class or peasant family; in the United States, an uneducated woman would face a similar option, and she would have a hard time finding a husband with good prospects of doing well. In the minds of most fathers, pushing daughters toward academic achievement did not subvert traditional gender roles, but rather affirmed those roles under changed circumstances. As one father explained:

> I want my son-in-law to be a doctor or an engineer. A doctor or an engineer does not want a wife whom he has to be ashamed of. Say, nursing would be a decent job for my daughter; and she would work with doctors. If she found a husband who's a doctor, she would help him in his job. I always tell my daughter to study hard so that she will be someone who can be part of a good family.

Furthermore, Vietnamese fathers expected personal and familial rewards to accrue from their daughters' success in school. How daughters did made little difference as long as education was largely limited to men, as in Vietnam. But the very availability of education to women in the United States made daughters' education a matter of status competition for the fathers. The educational accomplishments of sons and daughters reflected on the fathers themselves. With daughters there was actually a keener edge; expecting higher levels of obedience from girls, the fathers were more likely to take personal responsibility for their daughters' success or failure in school. With sons, in contrast, fathers generally took a more laissez-faire approach, treating their sons as individual actors rather than as dependents. A father said:

> The daughter of my neighbor finished college last year. I would feel ashamed before him if my daughter had not also finished college. If my daughter does less than the daughter of my neighbor, that means I am a less good father than my neighbor.

On the issue of relative control over sons and daughters, another father explained:

Of course I want both my son and my daughter to do well in school. But my son, he is a man, and if he do not do what I want him to do, others will understand. But my daughter, she must do what I tell her to do, and how can I explain if she does not do good?

Overall, the Vietnamese fathers whom we interviewed voiced support for their daughters' educational pursuits for three important reasons: (1) educated daughters have high earnings potential and can thus contribute to the incomes of their future families; (2) educated daughters can make suitable wives to relatively high-status husbands and ensure quality child-rearing; and (3) educated daughters can be status symbols for their birth families.

THE MOTHER'S VIEW

Gaining access to mothers was more difficult, since fathers were generally presented as the spokesmen of the Vietnamese families. But the mothers opened up when their husbands were not present, and they told us a similar, though distinctive, story. Like the fathers, the mothers whom we interviewed saw their daughters' education and eventual employment as an affirmation, not a rejection, of traditional Vietnamese gender roles. Whereas fathers stressed educational achievement as an outcome of the obedience they required from the daughters, however, mothers usually perceived education as a means of enhancing opportunities and thereby improving their daughters' bargaining position within traditional gender roles. The mothers stressed the importance of academic achievement as did the fathers, but they went even further, linking women's education to a version of the Vietnamese image of feminine virtue as modified by the encounter with American culture.

The mothers whom we interviewed desired independence for their daughters, understanding that dependence on men was not good for their daughters growing up in America. They generally held the idea that men should hold more power in the family than women, but they felt that women should get more involved in family decision making than they did in Vietnam. These mothers reasoned that education would increase their daughters' earnings potential and thereby improve their status within the family, while remaining within "traditional" gender roles. One mother remarked:

If my daughter no have good job and she marry, the husband can go off with other woman and do what he like. Maybe he good, OK, but if my daughter go to school, get good job, make money, then she no have to put up with anything husband do, and he have to be good.

Other mothers whom we interviewed commonly echoed this view. They did not seem to seek complete independence for their daughters, nor did they hope that their daughters would abandon a Vietnamese identity. They universally expected that their daughters would marry and would maintain what was seen as Vietnamese culture through their roles as mothers.

The mothers also shared fathers' views that daughters required greater control than sons. They accepted the sexual double standard and the part that this double standard played in determining the marriageability of young women. One mother reflected a view similar to that of the father cited earlier:

My daughter must be a good girl. That means she must do good in school and she must not go out alone at night with boys. Sometimes my son is bad, but not very bad. He can always do better. But if a girl is bad, people will always see her as bad, so it is very important to be careful with daughters.

The mothers seemed to not only accept but even to expect a certain amount of acting up from their sons. A mother told us that if a boy was "too good," never rowdy or disorderly, she would worry that his excessively unproblematic behavior might suggest a lack of spirit. Parents indulged unruly sons, even at a very early age. As we observed, mothers allowed little boys to play and run around public places, at church functions, or in shops, only admonishing them when their play became excessively energetic. By contrast, little girls and young women often showed a quiet self-discipline, inculcated by parental control. Such parental control may stem from fathers, who are seen as the chief authority figures in these Vietnamese households, but it is exercised primarily by mothers, who have the immediate responsibility for raising children.

Housework illuminated the mothers' divergent expectations of daughters and sons. In the older generation, women were almost exclusively responsible for housework. When wives worked outside the home, their paid work was usually simply added onto their household responsibilities; and these dual responsibilities were carried over to the younger generation, since mothers looked to their daughters for help with the housework. In Versailles Village, as in other Vietnamese communities, when girls came home from school, they were expected first to help with the housework and care of younger siblings and then do their studying. Unlike boys, who were allowed to participate in relatively uncontrolled activities outside the home, girls often had to stay home doing household chores. Thus, mothers' expectations kept girls more tightly bound to their mothers and to the domestic sphere, ensuring that young women spent a greater amount of time under the control of the family.

VIEWS OF YOUNG MEN

Vietnamese adolescent men in Versailles Village generally agreed with the idea of a strict gender separation and accepted the gender double standard that expects young women to be morally superior. Our field observations of young men and young women in the schools and in the community indicated a strong tendency toward gender-segregated friendship groups. One young man expressed a common attitude:

> Yeah, sure, girls are more good than boys. Everybody knows that. Not too many girls smoke or drink. So sure they act better in school and get better grades. It's different [for boys and for girls].

Though often preferring traditional ways, these young men whom we interviewed seemed more flexible in their ideas about gender roles than were the older men. They were acutely aware of the tensions between the Vietnamese ideals presented to them by their elders and the American ideals they adopted from the popular media and from exposure to their non-Vietnamese peers. The young men also frequently expressed allegiance to both sets of ideals. They wanted girlfriends who would dress fashionably and who would be "fun," not stodgy. But as wives, they would desire sexually inexperienced women who would put a priority on motherhood. One young man put it this way:

> I guess I want a girlfriend who is very American but a wife who is very Vietnamese. I think girls can be both of these things, though. They can wear okay clothes and listen to okay music and still be Vietnamese inside.

Young men also explicitly associated the "Vietnameseness" of young women with better school performance. They generally agreed that a "good girl" should do well in school; they also thought doing well in school was more important for girls than for boys, reasoning that girls could not afford to have a "bad name." Thus, the women's identity as Vietnamese has a unique twist. Unlike their mothers and grandmothers in Vietnam, the young women were encouraged to acquire an education, and this encouragement was reinforced by strong family control and pressures from the surrounding community, including those from their male peers.

VIEWS OF YOUNG WOMEN

Not surprisingly, Vietnamese young women themselves showed the greatest awareness of the contradictions, complications, and frustrations inherent in the changing meaning of appropriate gender roles. Like their mothers, many young women voiced a general acceptance of traditional gender roles but felt that role expectations were perplexing and frustrating matters complicated by the pressures to conform. Some young women sought to rebel but found it very difficult to do so, given the authoritarianism of many families and the nature of tightly knit communities.

Almost all the young women with whom we spoke told us that parents enforced discipline more strongly among girls than among boys, even in the use of corporal punishment, the form of parental discipline permitted and commonly practiced in Vietnam. While corporal punishment was considered appropriate for all children, almost all the young people we interviewed who said that they had been spanked or beaten at home were young women. By contrast, the only young man who said that his father had tried to use corporal punishment also reported that he had actively resisted his father's attempt at force.

One young woman, aged 16, whom we spoke with in school and later interviewed in greater depth by telephone, explained that her father allowed her to speak with the interviewer on the telephone because he knew that the interviewer was a non-Vietnamese researcher (also a substitute teacher in the girl's school at the time) who was attempting to learn about Vietnamese people. Cooperating with an outside researcher was seen as working with someone who represented authority and school. Had the interviewer been a young Vietnamese man calling on her socially, she would not have been allowed to speak with him. This girl made it clear that her social life was highly controlled at home. She was permitted to visit with female friends in their homes but was not allowed to "hang out" in local restaurants or other public places. When she disobeyed her father or did anything that did not meet with her father's approval, she said, corporal punishment would follow. If she had had a non-Vietnamese neighbor to whom she could complain about her father's beating, or if she had called 911, her father might have been jailed for child abuse. . . . this Versailles Village girl did not consider corporal punishment as abuse and was therefore not likely to report it as such. When asked how she felt about corporal punishment, she said that she did not like it but that she understood that there were many dangers facing Vietnamese girls in America and that her father used it for her own good. While it is difficult to gauge just how common the use of corporal punishment on girls may be in Vietnamese communities in the United States, the fact that girls are subjected to it more often than boys is an indication of the stricter social controls imposed on young women. These social controls exist because of the importance of the Vietnamese ideal of "the virtuous woman," which calls not only for passive obedience but also for living up to higher behavioral standards than are expected of men.

But these higher behavioral standards have generated greater pressures for academic achievement. One high school teacher, an American Vietnam War veteran who had close ties to the Vietnamese community, candidly discussed the grades of his students with us in an interview. He commented on one particular young Vietnamese woman who almost never made grades below A. "She has to," he explained. "If she brings home a B, her father beats her."

Young women were often frustrated by the stricter parental control to which they were subject and the higher moral standards expected of them. A common complaint was that parents were "old-fashioned" or "too Vietnamese." One girl complained to the interviewer:

> It's just not fair. My brother can stay out all night with his friends and they [the parents] don't say any-

thing about it. But for me, I have to tell them where I am and what I'm doing all the time, and they get real mad at me if I don't.

Another girl added:

They don't understand about life here. They want us to do everything the way they did things when they were in Vietnam. And it isn't the same.

Though uncomfortable with their parents' cultural expectations, our young female interviewees were not prepared for an open confrontation with parental authority. But they were ready for—and indeed often embarked on—challenges of an indirect sort. For example, most of the young women whom we interviewed reported that their parents disapproved of the American custom of dating. Many said that rather than rebel openly against their parents, they would leave the house with a group of female friends and then later go off alone with a young man.

Parents, of course, are not the only source of social control, and they are not the sole object of this frustration. If neighbors and other social contacts do not back up parental authority, young people will be more likely to rebel. But adolescents generally go along with their parents' expectations when the surrounding community echoes these expectations. Many young women spoke about the effect of public opinion in their tightly knit little community. A young woman said:

It's so easy for girls to get a bad reputation here. You really have to watch everything you do. There's gossip all over the place. All my neighbors know everything. They even know some things that never happened.

This observation can help us understand why it is that young Vietnamese women accept gender role expectations that they themselves see as unfair and also why young Vietnamese in general often conform to the expectations of their elders rather than to the expectations of their American peers. As has been discussed in previous chapters, young Vietnamese do not live in isolated families, nor are they surrounded by an alien culture. Instead, they are embedded in a complex system of Vietnamese social relations that reinforces and also enforces parental expectations.

REFERENCES

Freeman, James M. 1989. *Hearts of Sorrow: Vietnamese-American Lives.* Stanford, Calif.: Stanford University Press.

Hickey, Gerald Cannon. 1964. *Village in Vietnam.* New Haven: Yale University Press.

Kibria, Nazli. 1993. *Family Tightrope: The Changing Lives of Vietnamese Americans.* Princeton, N.J.: Princeton University Press.

Muzny, Charles, 1989. *The Vietnamese in Oklahoma City: A Study in Ethnic Change.* New York: AMS Press.

Nash, Jesse W. 1992. *Vietnamese Catholicism.* Harvey, La.: Art Review Press.

Rutledge, Paul J. 1992. *The Vietnamese Experience in America.* Bloomington: Indiana University Press.

? *Think about It*

1. Discuss the three reasons why many Vietnamese fathers support their daughters' educational pursuits.
2. Compare fathers', mothers', sons', and daughters' views about gender role expectations in the Vietnamese American families that Zhou and Bankston studied—especially in terms of obedience, the sexual double standard, parental control, and corporal punishment.
3. Many Vietnamese American parents encourage their daughters to take advantage of educational opportunities in the United States. How might the women's academic pursuits subvert the traditional gender roles that control much of a daughter's behavior?

Coping with Gender Role Strains in Korean American Families

Moon H. Jo

Many Korean American couples are encountering egalitarian principles about gender roles that stand in contrast to traditional family values based on Confucian philosophy. One source of conflict is wives' gaining economic power and independence while their husbands experience downward mobility after immigrating to the United States. *

THE [TRADITIONAL] RELATIONSHIP BETWEEN HUSBAND AND WIFE

In a traditional Korean family the male is superior in almost all spousal relationships. Moreover, a traditional Korean family expects absolute obedience of children to their parents. Respect for their elders, particularly their parents and grandparents, is a fundamental underpinning of traditional Korean family values. These values were mostly derived from philosophical concepts imbedded in the teachings of Confucius and that formed the moral foundation which has prevailed in Korea from the fourteenth century until the early twentieth century of the Chosun Dynasty. Moreover, Korean culture is an eclectic confluence of many ideals and values taken from Buddhism, Taoism, and Christianity, as well as a host of other material and not so material factors. These values, despite sweeping economic, demographic, and social changes that have taken place in Korea in the past few decades, continue to be the dominant influence on Korean families. Reviewing changes

*Moon H. Jo's research is based on in-depth interviews with fifty adult Korean immigrants in Washington, D.C., Los Angeles, and Philadelphia. *Ed.*

Source: From Moon H. Jo, *Korean Immigrants and the Challenge of Adjustment* (Westport, CT: Greenwood, 1999), 101–103, 127–32. Copyright © 1999 Greenwood Publishing Group, Inc. Reproduced with permission of Greenwood Publishing Group, Inc., Westport, CT.

in family values as a result of industrialization and urbanization, scholars such as Park and Cho concluded that these changes have had little or no effect on the social, political, and legal status of women. Thus, the notion of male superiority still persists within the society and the family. The father is the head of the household which he rules with almost unquestioned authority and his wife is his dutiful, obedient assistant. In such a household, sons take precedence over daughters and they also have greater privileges.[1] The hold of Confucianism is quite tenacious and dominates the very approach to life of modern Koreans.

For most Americans who have spent decades listening to the arguments of feminists, it may be rather hard to understand the role of women in Korea, their social position, and their exact function in marriage. The most important part of Confucian philosophy concerns the social position of women, who are taught that they are inferior and are expected to be submissive first to their parents, then to their husbands. Wives must never challenge or question their husbands and under no circumstances are they to act on their own. Nor are women to seek achievements in their own name. There is a Korean proverb which Korean men often cite with approval: "If a hen crows, the household crumbles."

The roles of sons, daughters, even daughters-in-law are clearly delineated by the Confucian concept of family relationships. Dutiful sons discover themselves in their parents through devoting themselves to their parents selflessly. Dutiful daughters, while at home, learn from their mothers how to be submissive and obedient. After marriage, the dutiful bride transfers her obedience and loyalty to her husband and to her parents-in-law if her husband was the first son.[2]

Given the cultural conservatism of Koreans, is it surprising to learn that Korean immigrants, although they may have lived in America many decades, have largely maintained traditional Korean family values? Kinship relations are very important to most Korean immigrants because, among other reasons, their kinfolks are the main sources for financial assistance, but perhaps more importantly, they provide emotional and familial support in a time of turmoil, in a land of strangers. Family also provides all important social support.[3] If their kin are still in Korea, they may fly to Korea frequently to see them, or stay in touch by telephone, or find other means to maintain the all-important family ties. In the absence of family ties, as a substitute for family, they reach out to other members of the Korean-American community in their neighborhood, either by means of Korean social organizations, Korean churches, or even by men sharing in a common interest, such as a round of golf. The more Korean immigrants associate with their kin and other Korean acquaintances in America, the more they reinforce their traditional family values, although doing so may aggravate the tensions and conflicts with members of their family who are trying to fit in the larger community.

The Korean immigrants who have brought their traditional Korean family values to the United States face innumerable conflicts in their family relationships as they cling stubbornly to their beliefs in the traditional Korean authoritarian and male-dominated values so incongruent with current American egalitarian values. Although immigrant husbands' beliefs in rigid sex-role distinctions may yield in the face of the reality of their wives' earning power outside their homes, Korean immigrant women can expect little support from their husbands in pitching in to shoulder some of the household tasks. According to Kim and Hurh, the financial contributions of Korean women, no matter how significant or time consuming, did not lessen the number of household tasks they were expected to perform. A high percentage of Korean immigrant wives not only worked but continued to perform such tasks as grocery shopping, housekeeping, and dishwashing. The presence of children in the home meant that the wives assumed yet another major responsibility. Only in the areas of garbage disposal and the management of the family budget did the men take responsibility.[4] Min also found that full-time Korean immigrant housewives spent 46.3 hours per week on housework compared to 5.2 hours for their husbands. Among dual-earner couples, the wives' time on housework was reduced to an average of 24.8 hours per week while the husbands' time increased only to 6.7 hours.[5] . . .

ASCENDANCE OF WIVES' ECONOMIC ROLE AS A SOURCE OF TENSION AND CONFLICT

[One] element which causes tension in Korean immigrant families is the gradual acquisition of economic power by wives. To many immigrant husbands, the fact that their wives are working outside their home is a troubling, if not baffling, experience. The immigrant husbands are largely unprepared to recognize their wives' earning power, but when their wives begin to demand a voice in the family decision-making processes, ordinarily reserved for husbands in traditional Korean families, they are stunned. In many cases, both husbands and wives work together in their family businesses and in doing so, wives become indispensable economic partners. The more wives participate in the family's economic activity, the more they expect to be treated as equals in not only the workplace, but in the family as well. While some immigrant husbands welcome their wives' contribution to their businesses and family finances, there are many immigrant husbands, already suffering from downward social mobility and sensitive about their current status, who resent the encroachment of the economic power and authority of their wives. A husband half in jest said: "My wife pays a few bills and now she thinks she is making 'a big noise' at home. One of these days, I am going to teach her a lesson about who is the boss." Invariably wives will say their demand for equality is not intended to undermine the traditional Korean husbands' role. A wife put it simply: "I am very sensitive not to hurt my husband's ego and pride. But I work very hard at a factory. Sometimes I must put in overtime and come home late and my husband has to cook. He always resents cooking, doing house chores, and grocery shopping by claiming these tasks are beneath his dignity. But he knows he has to do all of these things if we want to maintain our current economic status." Wives' newly acquired economic power and their assuming some of the traditional male responsibility can become a major source of friction, especially when the husbands feel they are losing their authority, power, and respect in their family.

Playing a dual role as both housewife and wage earner is not easy for Korean immigrant wives who never expected to play such a dual role because they were not accustomed to such a role in Korea. Once in the United States, many immigrant wives were thrust into the labor market out of economic necessity. Once in the work place, they tried their best to balance their obligations to their job with their family obligations. Once launched in the public sphere, at one time an exclusively men's preserve, they found their service was of value to their community. In a study of the activities of Korean immigrant women in the Korean community in southern California, Yu found Korean immigrant women's involvement in various community organizations was extensive. Yu reports they have been particularly active in church committees, education, youth services, literary circles, and journalism.[6] The more Korean immigrant wives gain earning power and assume some of the family responsibilities, the more they are likely to participate in community services, and the more their husbands find it necessary to adjust their thinking to accommodate the changing role of their wives, whether they like it or not.

Some immigrant wives early on have recognized that their newly gained economic power gives them a stronger voice in family decision-making. However, they insist that their reason for going to work was not intended to undermine their husbands' authority in the family, but to contribute to improving the family's financial condition, and perhaps increase their business capital. Furthermore, the influence of close relatives and friends who could give advice on financial matters dwindled once they immigrated to America. As a result, wives have had to become their husbands' advisers. It has been noted that one-third of working wives work in their husbands' stores. Consequently, the operation of the business becomes a joint venture, and it is almost logically inevitable that wives become involved in decisions affecting the business.[7] Some wives also claim that their reason for participating in business and family financial matters is because their husbands are not all that interested in financial matters. A wife in Los Angeles explains: "I run a small ice cream parlor and my husband is a shoe repairman right next to my store. I have a keen interest in running my business and have been doing very well. My husband, who was a school teacher in Korea, is not much interested in business matters or in family finances. Therefore, I make most of the decisions on matters having anything to do with money matters." Another wife, who is a nurse in the Washington, D.C., area, says: "My husband is working toward his doctoral degree in psychology. Although he received a small scholarship from the university, I have been supporting him for many years. I take care of everything ranging from our children's educational expenses, to insurance, home buying, and investments if we have some left over, and other financial matters. Sometimes I resent my husband for his lack of interest in the family finance matters."

Most Korean-American men still manage business and family finances, although their control over these matters has been weakened by their wives' involvement. However, some professional men, such as doctors, engineers, college professors, and researchers, still regard showing any interest in running businesses and dealing with the details of money matters as undignified. Some of these professional people comment disdainfully about the merchants' drive to make a lot of money and show off their expensive houses and cars. An engineer in Albuquerque, New Mexico, proudly comments: "I don't know anything about money. My wife takes care of everything about the family finances. She likes to do that, and she is very good at that." A sociology professor in central Pennsylvania says: "By nature of their discipline, most sociologists are not keen to make or manage money. My wife, who is a physician, makes three times as much as I do. Since my contribution to the family finances is limited, I don't have much to say about how our joint income should be used." A doctor in New York also comments: "My wife takes care of all taxes and investments. She is better [at managing our finances] than most accountants and financial planners. I trust what she is doing with our income."

Although some recent women immigrants may have had some experience running small businesses in Korea, most have had no experience before they came to America. For them running a dry cleaning business, a restaurant, a grocery store, or a fish market is a revelation. In some cases, wives discover their own business acumen when their husbands fumble. As a result, more and more husbands begin to rely on their wives, not only for their wives' labor, but for their advice on running the business itself. A wife in Philadelphia comments: "Running a clothing shop is not easy. My husband is bored working at the store, and he is simply not interested in matters such as overhead and earnings. Although my husband works hard, he should know hard work alone, without business savvy, will not lead to success." Some wives say that their husbands love showing off by buying expensive cars, houses, furniture, and memberships in golf clubs, without knowing too much about the source of their income. Wives believe they have to intervene in matters related to business and family finances because their husbands have a tendency to spend beyond their means.

The more wives step in to manage family finances, the more they influence decisions on expenditure for major purchases, such as houses, automobiles, children's education, vacation planning, and caregiving for their elderly parents. As a result, family financial planning has gradually ceased to be the exclusive domain of men. A working wife in a small town in Pennsylvania comments: "My husband would like to send our son to an Ivy League college, even going so far as to borrow money from a bank. I disagree with him because we simply can't afford such an expensive college. I told him Penn State University is good enough. This has been a constant source of argument between us. Furthermore, I don't believe in this business of sending kids to Ivy League colleges to enhance the status of Korean men." A few husbands observed that they used to make the final decisions with regard to their children's choice of school, buying automobiles, taking trips, and other costly undertakings. Now more and more, husbands wryly observe that their wives are taking the final, decision-making authority away from them. One husband says: "I am not going to fight with my wife over who has the decision-making authority in our family. To do so would give me *golchiapa* (headache)." Husbands also claim their children sense which parent has the authority in the family and often choose not to talk over their plans with their fathers. Women's role in the workplace does have an effect on the balance of authority between husbands and wives in Korean immigrant families, although many wives insist their earning power has nothing to do with the dwindling authority of their husbands.

Some wives, not in the labor market, dislike being completely dependent on their husbands. They would very much like a career and a chance to become more independent. The wife of a physician in a small town in upstate New York remarks:

Unlike in Korea, in America women who have careers are respected by others. Furthermore, when they become single mothers, they can take care of themselves. I came to America to become a pharmacist or a worker in a health field. That dream disappeared when I met my husband who is a physician from Korea. He has always practiced his profession in small towns where physicians are desperately needed. We moved many times but never to a large city where large universities and colleges are located. Now, we live in a town where a university is located fifty miles away from my place. But my husband doesn't like the idea that I go back to school to get a degree and pursue a career. He is very tradition-oriented. He wants me to stay home and take care of the children and "serve" him and his parents. I don't think he understands how I feel about foregoing my career for the sake of his career. Furthermore, as I depend on my husband financially, I don't have much of a voice in deciding anything related to finance. My children's education, the mortgage for the house and car payments, insurance, and everything else is paid by him.

Another immigrant wife regrets the chance she lost to pursue her own career because she had to help her husband with his business while caring for her four children. Now she believes it is time to pursue her own career:

I decided to start a college degree program at this stage of my life to save myself, to save my career. For so many years I had been preoccupied with child care and family survival. But suddenly I realized that I had lost too much of myself. Of course, my study complicates my family life and marital relations. But I am now so determined that my husband cannot stop me.[8]

As Korean immigrant wives have gained more economic power, they have also shed the subservient role of traditional Korean wives. Although many wives still look after their husbands' parents, they are no longer blindly serving their parents-in-law as they once did in Korea. Furthermore, working wives have greater decision-making power on matters related to the welfare of

their parents-in-law and their own parents. One example illustrates this situation perfectly. A man in New York comments: "My mother is being taken care of by my brother in California. I would like to send her some money, but it is difficult to do so without consulting my wife as she controls all family financial matters. My wife keeps on saying that my mother is getting enough SSI (Supplementary Social Security) from the state of California. When my mother had a stroke and became immobilized, I was going to buy a wheel chair for her. Again my wife objected, saying that the social welfare department will provide it for her. Sadly, the idea that daughters-in-law serve their mothers-in-law is no longer applicable in America."

NOTES

1. Insook Han Park and Lee-Jay Cho, "Confucianism and the Korean Family," *Journal of Comparative Family Studies* 24 (1995): 117–134.
2. For an excellent article on the status of women in Confucian society see Yun-shik Chang, "Women in a Confucian Society: The Case of Chosun Dynasty Korea (1392–1910)," in *Traditional Thoughts and Practices in Korea,* eds. Eui-Young Yu and Earl H. Phillips (Los Angeles: Center for Korean-American and Korean Studies, California State University, 1983), 67–93. See also Michael C. Kalton, *Korean Ideas and Values* (Elkins Park, Pa.: Phillip Jaison Memorial Foundation, Inc., 1979).
3. In his study of the level and kinds of kin involvement among Korean immigrant families in Atlanta, Min found that about 53 percent of those 70 respondents reported that they meet kin members once a week or more often. About 29 percent indicated that they meet kin members every month or more often but less often once a week. See Pyong Gap Min, "An Exploratory Study of Kin Ties among Korean Immigrant Families in Atlanta," *Journal of Comparative Family Studies* 25 (1984): 59–75.
4. According to Kim and Hurh, in their sample of 70 families without children in the Los Angeles area, 78 percent of employed wives do grocery shopping while 71 percent of unemployed wives do so; 88.9 percent of employed wives do the housekeeping while 90.5 percent of unemployed wives do so; 82.6 percent of employed wives do laundry while 71.4 percent of unemployed wives do so; and 87 percent of employed wives wash dishes while 81 percent of unemployed wives do so. However, husbands outperformed their wives at such household tasks as garbage disposal and family budgeting. The burden of carrying out household tasks did not change for wives who have chil-

dren. See Kwang Chung Kim and Won Moo Hurh, "Employment of Korean Immigrant Wives and the Division of Household Tasks," in *Korean Women in Transition: At Home and Abroad,* eds. Eui-Young Yu and Earl H. Phillips (Los Angeles: Center for Korean-American and Korean Studies, California State University, 1987), 199–252.

5. Pyong Gap Min, *Changes and Conflicts: Korean Immigrant Families in New York* (Boston: Allyn and Bacon, 1998), 43.

6. Eui-Young Yu, "The Activities of Women in Southern California Korean Community Organizations," in *Korean Women in Transition: At Home and Abroad,* eds. Eui-Young Yu and Earl H. Phillips (Los Angeles: Center for Korean-American and Korean Studies, California State University, 1987), 275–299.

7. According to Kim and Hurh's study of household tasks performed by husbands and wives in Los Angeles, when wives are not employed, 52 percent of husbands dealt with the family budget. On the other hand, when both husbands and wives are employed, 61 percent of wives tended to the family budget. See Kim and Hurh, "Employment of Korean Immigrant Wives and the Division of Household Tasks," 207.

8. Quoted in Min, *Changes and Conflicts: Korean Immigrant Families in New York,* 54.

? Think about It

1. What is the relationship between husband and wife in traditional Korean society? How do traditional gender roles differ from more egalitarian gender roles in the United States?

2. Why, according to Jo, can Korean American wives be described as playing "double roles" in the family?

3. As Korean American wives' economic contributions increase, how does decision-making power between husband and wives change? Also, how do relationships between daughters-in-law and mothers-in-law change?

11 To Be an Asian Indian Woman in America

Monisha Das Gupta

Readings 8, 9, and 10 show how recently arrived immigrants cope and struggle with U.S. gender role expectations that differ from those of their country of origin. Here, Monisha Das Gupta posits that the first generation may play a significant role in constructing a gendered ethnic identity whereby females and males are treated differently because of their sex. The second generation of women may rebel and "reinvent" gender role definitions that establish a sense of their own voice between "American" and "traditional" Indian culture.

In the winter of 1989–1990, I interviewed Indian immigrants living in New York City to grasp what it meant to be Indian in the United States. I talked

Source: From Monisha Das Gupta, "'What Is Indian about You?' A Gendered, Transnational Approach to Ethnicity," *Gender and Society* 11 (October 1997): 572–96. Copyright © 1997 Sage Publications, Inc. Reprinted by permission of Sage Publications, Inc.

to families settled in the city and its suburbs, newspaper vendors in Manhattan, and South Asian shopkeepers in Jackson Heights. Among the stories they shared, the struggles around identity of four second-generation Indian women have haunted me. When I asked them the rather essentializing question, "What is Indian about you?" what emerged was a contested terrain where "Indian" had no fixed meaning. The contestations represented the production of conflicting signifiers about what it meant to be an immigrant Indian *woman* living in a culture that her parents considered alien. . . .

This article draws on the accounts of four second-generation women—Manpreet, Archana, Kamini, and Nidhi.[1] These cases are useful in mapping the transnational invention of "the authentic Indian immigrant family" by the first generation, the second-generation women's rebellion against this invention, and their attempts to reinvent their identity in a going back and forth between at least two cultures. I use Gloria Anzaldua's (1987) powerful conceptualization of "borderlands" to illustrate the realities of borders, physical and cultural, in these women's lives. Each process—invention, rebellion, reinvention—requires an understanding of how these women were expected to signify what was "Indian" about their families and their communities, and how those signifiers were tied to class status and the enforcement of monogamous, endogamous heterosexuality. These codings make "being Indian" not only a question of ethnicity but also of identity, which is broader in scope. I place parental expectations of their daughters within mainstream pressures on these families to assimilate. These pressures served to valorize the parents' need for authenticity.

CENTERING WOMEN

. . . The compelling nature of the information that these women gave me demanded fresh consideration, making me return to my data again and again since 1992. I decided to focus on the four women and deepen my investigation. Along with asking new questions of the old data, I got back in touch with the four women to elicit clarifications and new data to reconceptualize the project. Manpreet, Kamini, and Nidhi had been part of the 10 Indian families in New York City and its suburbs, which were at the core of my 1990 study.[2] Archana, peripheral to the initial study, was a single second-generation woman who had been among the many immigrants in the New York area to whom I had talked in order to get a sense of the social landscape in which I was operating.[3] Returning to the project gave me the chance to foreground her story and document the experiences that she shared informally with me. . . .

Manpreet, Archana, and Kamini's parents immigrated to the United States between 1970 and 1974. Six-year-old Manpreet moved with her family from New Delhi in 1970. They settled in Queens. Her father, after some struggle, found employment as a lawyer. Archana was four months old when her parents brought her over in 1970. Her mother is a pediatrician and her father a biochemist. Kamini immigrated in 1974 at the age of nine. The daughter of a United Nations official, she had already lived in Egypt and Sudan besides India. Only Nidhi's father came in 1959 as a student under a special quota system that had allowed 100 Indians to enter the United States annually since 1946. This concession was granted by the U.S. government in appreciation of India's World War II efforts. Nidhi, newborn in 1959, did not leave India to join her parents in the United States until she was five years old. Her father first worked for American companies and later set up his own business.

When I interviewed the four second-generation women in 1990, they had already spent at least 20 years of their lives in the United States. Manpreet and Kamini, women in their late twenties, had completed their higher education and were established in their professions. According to them, their parents had relocated to the United States specifically with the hope of bettering their children's educational and occupational opportunities. At the time I met them, Manpreet worked as an editor for a legal publishing company, while Kamini was a dietitian at a Long Island hospital. Archana had not yet graduated from college but was contemplating going to graduate school to study either politics or law. Nidhi had a different career trajectory. On completing high school, she worked for a while in her father's business. After her marriage, she got a clerical job in a food-processing company in New Jersey. During this time she attended college part-time. When I spoke to her last in 1994, she was ready to graduate in the spring. Manpreet, Nidhi, and Kamini were married and at the time I met them, Kamini was pregnant, while Nidhi had a young daughter.

INVENTION OF THE "AUTHENTIC" IMMIGRANT FAMILY

To understand the culture of the participants' homes and how that culture came to be authenticated, it is important to realize that the first post-1965 immigrants to the East Coast rarely had a family base, much less a community, to ease their transition to a society that had little to offer them socially.[4] Most of those who entered the United States under occupational preferences during this period came as individuals or nuclear families. They had no social networks to which they could immediately turn to recreate a semblance of home and familiarity. As compared to the substantial concentrations of Indians in the New York tristate area today, immigrants to New York City in the late sixties and early seventies were fewer in number and geographically dispersed.

The various degrees of isolation that the four women felt came from their awareness of being different, feelings that ran the gamut from a vague sense of not being "the same" to hostile encounters. This sense of difference was reinforced at home but with other motivations. Parents carefully cultivated a high, pristine version of Indian culture current among the educated middle class in a newly independent, artificially unified India. In the United States, this interpretation facilitated a stark contrast against their stereotypes of "American" culture, which by their definition was degenerate. In reaching for what Spivak calls "a fantasmatic . . . cultural heritage" (1989, 279), the first generation in many ways drew on colonial and nationalist rewriting of Indian history, which glorified a Vedic past (Chakravarti 1990; Tharu and Lalita 1991). The interpretations of Indian culture promoted by these immigrants reinscribed the antagonism between the East and the West.

Growing up in Queens in the early seventies was a very lonely experience for Manpreet, who was six years old when she arrived. Her memories of the first years of public school are suffused with the pain of being singled out and marginalized on the basis of her ethnicity—as an Indian and as a Sikh. She found no points of contact in the environment outside her home during those first years:

> People were not really being taught about India then [early seventies]. India wasn't even on the map for them. . . . I have suffered to the extent that the kids would wait for me and my brother and sister after school to beat us up. It was very bad because we were Sikhs and my brother would have his hair [knotted up] on top his head. They would wait for him after school just to open up his hair. They would ask him whether he was a girl. . . . My father used to come to pick us up from school because we'd be scared to go home alone. It got so bad that we did not want to go to school. The teachers knew about this. They couldn't do anything or they did not want to do anything. You know, I felt prejudice from everywhere.

She and her family constantly came up against mainstream American caricatures and ignorance about India. Manpreet was often asked why her mother was "wrapped in a cloth." Her father, who kept his hair long—tied up and turbaned in accordance with the tenets of Sikhism, was asked by his potential employers to cut his hair. She recounted an instance when a family acquaintance, also a Sikh, was pressured into cutting his hair after a barrage of questions like, "So who is your guru?" or "What is your cult?"

Her estrangement from her surroundings led Manpreet to seek out other Indians in an effort to link her life at home with life outside it. Making those connections was not easy because of the initial lack of an Indian community in her neighborhood. In the late 1970s, by which time Manpreet was a teenager, more Indian families had moved into Queens. Manpreet described the difference that the demographic change made in her life and how relieved she was to have classmates from South Asia:

> You had to go to the next town [in the early 1970s] to meet an Indian. I felt very happy if I ran across an Indian on the block. You'd make a friend right away. Now, of course, you see them all over the place. Some years later [referring to the late seventies] more Indians started coming. The gurdwara [Sikh place of worship] became a place to meet friends. There were more Indians in school. We had places to go where we didn't have to be with Americans. Now you had another Indian friend to be with. In junior high school when we would sit in the cafeteria there would be Indians, Bangladeshis, Pakistanis all around you.

Kamini, who immigrated with her parents to New York City in 1974, spoke of the extreme insulation of her home as a result of her mother's acute anxieties about the "corrupting" influences of American society. Except for going to school where she made a few friends, the world outside her home was virtually closed to her. Describing how drastically different her life in the United States was from her experiences in Sudan and Egypt where she lived before migrating to New York, she said,

> Our lives completely changed after coming to this country. We withdrew. In the other countries [where] we had been, we had learnt the language, adopted the food. We were so relaxed! But on coming to America, my mother felt our cultural values were being threatened. In Africa, our ideas, our values were never threatened. My mother's paranoia [once they moved to the United States] was so intense that after school we were not allowed to go anywhere, do anything. I hardly had friends. Everything about America was bad. My father is a very liberal person but I think he became conservative under my mother's influence. She would always discourage my father from saying anything positive about the system here. She would either put it down or negate it. We ate Egyptian food when we were in Egypt but

it took her 10 years to taste a pizza and that too after she saw it was okay with one of her Gujarati friends who is extremely conservative.

The other two respondents, like Manpreet, traced their sense of not fitting in back to the lack of an Indian community. Stuck in the suburbs of New York City, Archana said she never lived in a neighborhood with more than two or three Indian families. Nidhi, who went to kindergarten in Pennsylvania and then moved to Edison, New Jersey, met few Indian children in school in the sixties. For her this meant making American friends. "I grew up with them, played with them in our backyard," she recalled, "There were a lot of times when I forgot I looked different."

Not until the mid-seventies to late seventies did communities and institutions start taking shape (Fisher 1980). Newly established places of worship began to serve as secular social spaces for Indian immigrants. Nidhi said that her interactions with other Indians increased once a temple was built near her home. Her mother, although she was not particularly religious, started visiting it with Nidhi on weekends. Corroborating the other respondents' perceptions of these places of worship as community centers, Nidhi said the temple she attended as a teenager served as a social club where people came together to "gossip and search for prospective sons- and daughters-in-law."

The initial isolation, however, had created a disjuncture between the immigrants' private lives and the larger society. For the immigrants, the family continued to serve as the primary space where children were socialized into "Indian" ways of living. It was the site where "traditions," distinct from "American" ways, were produced. Parents, consequently, became the repositories of India's cultural wealth and ethical mores. They were the sole interpreters, upholders, and transmitters of their natal culture. More often than not, their class and regional origins informed their interpretations.

The first generation, in self-consciously distancing themselves from what they perceived to be "American," were in the process of inventing what they understood to be appropriately "Indian." In an attempt to reproduce the dense matrix of relationships in their natal cultures, the parents bound themselves to their children in sentimental systems of rights and duties. They expected their children to respect and obey their judgments about the host society and about India. If children acted without their parents' mandate, their parents defined the children's behavior as alien and undesirable—in short, "American." Daughters often had less flexibility in negotiating parental expectations than sons, as will be discussed in the next section. Explaining how she was reprimanded every time her behavior fell short of her parents' expectations, Nidhi said, "My parents continuously accused me of being too American. They did not have the slightest idea about what they had in mind when they said that!"[5]

The notions of "Indian tradition" that emerged from the tension between cultures ironically bore few resemblances to contemporary middle-class attitudes in India. What the first-generation immigrants rigidly enforced as "Indian" ways were, in fact, specific to the context they were familiar with before they left India. My respondents were only too aware of this museumization of practices. In their visits to India they had noticed the discrepancy between their parents' version of "Indian" and what Indians in India actually did. Manpreet articulated this conservatism when she said her parents and their contemporaries in the United States seemed "frozen in time." Referring to the life I live in India, she laughingly pointed out:

> The difference between you and me is that you can do many more things in India than I can do here. My father's nephews and nieces in India do things he would still say "no" to. They wear their hair short, go out with friends, hold hands [with the opposite sex]. I see my father as a very well-educated man but culturally I find him backward.

When I brought up the issue with Nidhi, she agreed. She wondered about her father's "narrow outlook," which she felt was an anomaly, considering his westernization and the increasing "liberalization" of the Indian middle-class ethos that she noticed during her trips to India. For the first generation, however, this liberalization adds to their sense of authenticity. Developments in India serve as a measure of their success in bringing up their children traditionally. As preservers of culture, they take pride in being more Indian than Indians in India. Amid a polyphony of contestations—those from the immigrant parents, their children, new social institutions, and middle-class Indians in India—tradition becomes an embattled category.

What is "Indian" then, is not automatically what is preserved but what is *constructed* as preserved. The museumization of selected practices by the first generation in my research is not merely a hanging on to defunct tradition. The first generation valorizes and resignifies those practices by claiming full knowledge of contemporary social realities in India. Their sense of authenticity is predicated on the recognition of change in India itself. The ethnicity paradigm, because of its nationalist frame of reference, misses the dynamic process of invention. . . .

TO BE AN INDIAN WOMAN IN AMERICA

The authenticity of Indian culture transplanted in what the first generation perceived as an alien setting depends on the place that immigrant women are expected to occupy in their ethnic community. The policing of women's sexuality lies at the center of defining that place. The ideas of propriety that the immigrants brought with them were generalizations of middle-class Victorian views promoted by the British and reworked by nationalists (Sangari and Vaid 1990). The daughters of immigrants in my study were vulnerable to these controls but they also found ways of contesting them. In doing so, they changed the meanings of their ethnic identity. Thus, the construction of ethnic identities cannot be disaggregated from ascribed gender roles and sexuality (Anderson and Collins 1992; Anzaldua 1990; Asian Women United of California 1989; Moraga and Anzaldua 1983).

The confrontation of cultures sparked generational tensions requiring the women I interviewed to conform to the role of dutiful daughters. The women had no doubt that their gender intensified their parents' anxiety and strictness. This meant their parents expected their daughters to be chaste, obedient, and attentive to the needs of their families. As women, they were expected by their community to be more careful than men about their conduct and in their social interactions. The four women keenly felt the double standard of the restrictions imposed on them. The second-generation men I talked to for my larger study said they too were brought up strictly, especially when compared with American men (Das Gupta 1990). They also were expected to submit to their parents' ideas about their social life, education, and marriage. However, their assertions of independence could be accommodated within the roles ascribed to men because of the status and privilege they enjoy in Indian high culture.

The women were monitored by their parents well into their adulthood, most of them until they got married. They had to put up with strictly imposed curfews. Their parents screened their friends. Kamini was discouraged by her mother from making any American friends. The women recalled needing their parents' permission to go to parties. Activities permitted outside school or their parents' circle of friends were very limited.

Comparing her experiences of growing up with those of her brothers, Manpreet pointed to the gender bias in the expectations her parents had for her. She said,

> After a while, that [the rules that applied to her] does not seem fair. Then you start breaking rules. I was never allowed to go away from home to study. But my brother has got away with a lot. Right now he is away at college. He worked night shifts and returned at three in the morning. Or he goes out at ten at night saying he would be back in half-an-hour but

he stays out until twelve. That does not create a problem!

She was not allowed to attend college outside New York City because that would require her to move out of her home. Her parents expected her to live at home until her marriage.

Archana felt her brother enjoyed greater freedom and was exempted from regulations that circumscribed her life. Although her parents provided both children with the same educational opportunities, they were far more indulgent toward her brother and were not prepared to break down the gender roles they had been socialized into in India. Her mother, a professional, had tried raising her to perform chores like serving food while the men ate to teach her how to express her womanliness. Such tasks were never demanded of her brother. He also enjoyed a freer social life while living at home than Archana did.

All four women told me that dating was forbidden by their parents. The disapproval had to do with the older generation's understanding of the practice. The issue stirred up the parents' worst apprehensions about exogamy and assimilation. Archana, who is single, voicing her parents' fears, said, "With my parents, it's okay if my brother dates and marries someone who isn't Indian. But this is not extended to me."

Dating as a procedure to find a partner threatened the first generation's views on propriety. In India, older generations stigmatize free and unsupervised mixing of the sexes as improper and promiscuous. The rigidity of sex segregation, however, varies with class backgrounds and the particular subculture of a family. For the parents of my respondents, the association of premarital sex with dating added to their fears. Again, the women were much more vulnerable than were men to the strictures about sexual behavior.

Parents felt an urgent need to protect their families, especially their daughters, from the "chaos" and "permissiveness" of the host society. Daughters bore the weight of their family's and community's honor on their shoulders. "From an early age I understood that dating, smoking, drinking, staying out late were simply not done," Manpreet said while telling me what was "Indian" about her upbringing. The taboo on dating was more of an issue for the women than for men since their reputation and marriageability depended on their chastity. The slightest doubt about her could damage a woman's and her family's social standing in their ethnic community.

Most immigrant parents expected to arrange their children's marriage. Thus, they found any initiative on the part of their children to find partners inappropriate. Nidhi and Manpreet upset their parents by exerting their will and choosing their husbands. Even though Nidhi stayed within the cultural and religious boundaries of her community by marrying a Gujarati, her father was extremely displeased with her choice. The marriage strained her relationship with her father, and they were hardly on speaking terms since Nidhi's father saw this as a gesture of disobedience and disrespect. Manpreet, a Punjabi Sikh, chose to marry an Uttar Pradeshi Hindu, crossing barriers of religion and region. Kamini opted for marriage arranged in India having witnessed her mother's anguish at her sons' decision to marry Americans. "To this day, she has not forgiven my brothers for marrying Americans," she said.

THE WOMEN'S WAYS OF RESISTANCE

The women resisted the suffocating aspects of their parents' cultural expectations and tried gaining some control over their lives—their education, their career plans, and marriage. They related bitter confrontations with their parents, who had instituted themselves in authorial positions about the "right" culture. They were under constant pressures to weigh and evaluate, accept or reject the claims that the two cultures—"Indian" and "American"—laid on them. As a generation of Indians who spent most of their formative years in a country different from that of their parents, they found themselves constantly negotiat-

ing their allegiance to their parents' natal culture and the culture of their adopted home.

Sometimes the women openly confronted their parents. "In college," Nidhi said, "I started questioning my father and then we had tremendous fights." Despite much opposition and acrimony, Archana, in her junior year in college, foiled her parents' attempts to plan her career. In keeping with the Indian community's model minority image in the United States, her parents wanted to send her to medical school. They believed a career in medicine would secure their daughter a steady income and her future husband's respect for her profession. Outlining what she thought were her parents' motives, Archana said she had to be a doctor or engineer "so that I'd be seen as a lucrative investment for another Indian family to even consider me for their son." Instead of enrolling as a premed student at the liberal arts school she attended, Archana designed a major in South Asian Studies. That was her way of cherishing and learning more about her Indian heritage, which, she felt, was interpreted too narrowly by her community.

At other times, the rebellions were less direct. Manpreet was determined to become economically independent right after high school. She started working while going to college without the knowledge of her parents. Her parents would have stopped her from working had they known because she felt her father would consider her having to work for extra money a failure on his part to provide for his daughter. They would also not have approved of their daughter beginning to earn money before she entered a profession.

Daughters posed the most serious challenge to parental authority by being assertive about plans for their marriage. Parents considered arranging their children's marriage, especially their daughters', to be one of their basic duties. Manpreet and Nidhi preempted the prospect of arranged marriages. Manpreet had a difficult time communicating to her Sikh parents that she intended to marry a Hindu Uttar Pradeshi. She had not only decided to bypass her parents in choosing her partner but she had also chosen a man who was not Sikh and not Punjabi. In doing so she had gone against some of her parents' deeply held beliefs.

Nidhi chose to marry another Gujarati. The fact that her husband came from the same community as her family did not help assuage her father's anger. Relating the circumstances of her wedding and the painful breach it created, Nidhi said,

I came loggerheads with him [her father] over marriage. I was 26 and he still wanted to direct my life. Though I married within the community, he did not let anyone in the family come to the wedding. No one came. My father called up my relatives asking them not to go since his daughter had gone against his wishes [by not having an arranged marriage].

These gestures of defiance against "Indian" norms did not mean that the women completely rejected their parents' heritage. In fact, they all mentioned that their decision to marry Indian men reinforced their ties with that heritage. The resistances surfaced when they tried to reconcile the realities of their lives with what had been handed down to them by their parents as tradition.

NOTES

1. The names of the women have been changed.
2. The 10 couples who agreed to be interviewed represented a combination of first- and second-generation nuclear families. The definition of "Indian" in selecting participants of my study rested on their acknowledgment of some kind of natal tie with independent and partitioned India. The interviews were open-ended, designed to access the tenor of their lives as Indians in the United States. They were backed up with a questionnaire about the participants' immigration history, income (a category often left unanswered), and occupation. The interviewees responded to the questionnaire in writing. The material I collected from Manpreet, Kamini, and Nidhi in 1990 was very rich. The follow-up interviews, therefore, were aimed at getting a fuller account of their life histories and seeking clarifications.
3. This group of immigrants consisted of individual men and women from different class backgrounds and different parts of South Asia. The majority worked in, or owned, newspaper stands and small businesses in Manhattan and Queens. A few, like Archana, were first- or second-generation college-goers. Although I did not formally interview any of them, in talking about my project, we discussed many of the issues that I raised with the 20 formal participants.
4. At that time, the only sizable Indian community was based in Yuba City/Marysville in California (La Brack 1986; Leonard 1992).
5. Questions of American identity, which form a vast body of literature, cannot be dealt with fully in this article. I only examine the ways in which scholars and immigrants circumscribe the meanings of "America" and "American." In the section, "Borderlands: The Politics of Reinvention" below, I juxtapose Anzaldua's "third country," the borderlands, against the incorporative powers that cultural pluralists lend the term "American." As for the first generation of post-1965 immigrants, its fears about becoming "American" contradicted its economic behavior. This generation vigorously pursued the American Dream but rejected the same ideology of individual autonomy in its social life (Saran and Eames 1980). However, what the first generation left unstated in its characterization of "America" is its association of whiteness with being American. Those who want to assimilate have little doubt about what they want to assimilate into, namely white "America," even in a multi-ethnic metropolis like New York City. Kaizad Gustad's (1993) film, *Corner Store Blues,* about an Indian newsstand worker's efforts to break into the New York City blues scene, comes to mind. The protagonist's so-called benefactor, on finding out about his employee's ambitions, exclaims in disgust and disbelief, "Everyone who comes to America wants to be white and you want to be Black!" (Gustad 1993).

REFERENCES

Anderson, M. L., and P. Hill Collins, eds. 1992. *Race, class and gender: An anthology.* Belmont, CA: Wadsworth.

Anzaldua, G. 1987. *Borderlands/la frontera: The new mestiza.* San Francisco: Aunt Lute.

———, ed. 1990. *Making face, making soul: Haciendo caras: Creative and critical perspectives by women of color.* San Francisco: Aunt Lute.

Asian Women United of California, ed. 1989. *Making waves: An anthology of writings by and about Asian American women.* Boston: Beacon.

Chakravarti, U. 1990. Whatever happened to the Vedic dasi? Orientalism, nationalism and a script of the past. In *Recasting women: Essays in Indian colonial history,* edited by K. Sangari and S. Vaid. New Brunswick, NJ: Rutgers University Press.

Das Gupta, M. 1990. Growing roots in foreign soil: Experience of ten Indian families in New York. Unpublished.

Fisher, M. P. 1980. *The Indians of New York City: A study of immigrants from India.* Columbia, MO: South Asia Books.

Gustad, K. 1993. *Corner store blues.* Film. New York.

La Brack, B. 1986. Immigration law and the revitalization process: The case of the California Sikhs. In *From India to America: A brief history of immigration, problems of discrimination, admission and assimilation,* edited by S. Chandrasekhar. La Jolla, CA: Population Review.

Leonard, K. 1992. *Making ethnic choices: California's Punjabi Mexican Americans.* Philadelphia: Temple University Press.

Moraga, C., and G. Anzaldua, eds. 1983. *This bridge called my back: Writings by radical women of color.* New York: Kitchen Table: Women of Color Press.

Sangari, K., and S. Vaid, eds. 1990. *Recasting women: Essays in Indian colonial history.* New Brunswick, NJ: Rutgers University Press.

Saran, P., and E. Eames, eds. 1980. *The new ethnics: Asian Indians in the United States.* New York: Praeger.

Spivak, G. C. 1989. Who claims alterity? In *Remaking history,* edited by B. Kruger and P. Mariani. Seattle, WA: Bay.

Tharu, S., and K. Lalita. 1991. Introduction. In *Women writing in India: 600 B.C. to the present,* edited by S. Tharu and K. Lalita. Vol. 1. New York: Feminist Press at City University.

Think about It

1. What does Das Gupta mean when she says that an ethnic identity (such as being Asian Indian) has no fixed meaning but is socially constructed?

2. Why did the first generation of parents discourage their daughters from becoming "American"? Did the same rules apply to sons?

3. In what ways did the women in this study resist their ascribed gender role expectations? What were the results—personally, within the nuclear family and the extended family? What similarities, if any, do you see between Das Gupta's findings and those reported in Reading 9?

CHAPTER 3

Cohabitation, Marriage, and Intermarriage

Because 93 percent of all Americans will marry at least once, marriage is still the norm. Increasingly, however, the unmarried population has increased among many groups. In 1999, for example, 34 percent of Asians and Pacific Islanders 15 years old and over had never married. In the same year, 39 percent of black adults over the age of 18 had never married, up from 21 percent in 1970. The proportion of Latino adults over 18 who had never married rose from 19 to 34 percent during the same period.[1] Large numbers of people are postponing marriage, but an even higher proportion—especially of black women and men—may never marry.

Although cohabitation rarely replaces marriage, the number of unmarried-couple households in the United States has increased almost sevenfold since 1970.[2] In Reading 12,

Denene Millner and Nick Chiles, husband and wife, debate some of the merits and disadvantages of black couples "tying the knot" rather than living together. Although most black women want to marry ("We don't want lifetime playmates"), Millner argues, they stay in long-term cohabiting relationships because settling for a "so-so commitment" and "half-happiness" is better than nothing. Chiles claims, however, that black men don't propose because Ms. Right might be just around the corner.

While Millner and Chiles discuss some of the interpersonal reasons for and against marriage, demographic and macro-level variables also influence decisions about marrying rather than cohabiting. When plenty of jobs are available, for example, black men and women are likely to marry and have children. Others attribute the high single rate among black women to the "unavailability" of black men. As you saw in the introduction to Chapter 2, on gender roles, at least a third of young black men are in prison and the death rate among black men is the highest of any race–sex category. In addition, as more black women finish college, enter the labor market, and become financially independent, there's little incentive to "marry down."[3]

The pool of eligible partners narrows, moreover, because every society (and subcultural group within a society) has norms that define the "right" marriage partner. The principle of *endogamy* (often used interchangeably with the term *homogamy*) requires that people marry within a certain group, such as Jews marrying Jews or African Americans marrying African Americans. *Exogamy* (often used interchangeably with the term *heterogamy*) requires marriage outside the group, such as not marrying one's relatives or someone from a social, racial, ethnic, religious, or age group different from one's own.

In the United States, many ethnic groups encourage or practice endogamy. Johanna Lessinger's study of Asian Indians, for example, shows that arranged marriages are not uncommon (Reading 13). Many young Asian Indians find arranged marriages appealing, although others opt for semi-arranged marriages, and a small number prefer an "open" courtship mating process. Some researchers suggest, however, that there is intergenerational conflict and a clash of values between Asian Indian parents who feel they have a right to control their children's behavior and young adults who demand more freedom of choice in exercising their dating, mating, and marriage preferences[4] (see also Readings 9 and 11).

Once people marry, are they happy? Because there is no generally agreed upon definition of "marital happiness," researchers base their descriptions of the success or satisfaction of marriages on the marital partners' own evaluations. Using these evaluations, throughout the 1970s and 1980s many social scientists reported a U-shaped curve throughout the life cycle: marital satisfaction was high right after marriage, declined gradually during parenthood, and then rose again during late middle age and old age after children left home. Most of the research, however, focused on white families or cross-sectional studies (where data are collected at one point in time) rather than across the life course.

In Reading 14, Kyriakos S. Markides and his colleagues report their findings on marital satisfaction in three generations of Mexican Americans. Using a longitudinal approach (in which data are collected two or more times), they found, in contrast to the U-shaped curve, marital satisfaction varying by gender and the duration of the marriage. As you read this article, think about other variables that researchers might use to gauge marital satisfaction among ethnic groups, such as handling conflict, positive sexual experiences, household tasks, and decision-making power.[5]

Interracial and interethnic marriages in the United States have been increasing—from 0.7 percent in 1970 to about 6 percent in 1996.[6] In 1998, almost 39 percent of Latinos were married to non-Latinos, 9 percent of blacks were married to nonblacks, and less than 3 percent of whites were married to nonwhites.[7] About half of the husbands who are American Indians, Eskimos, or Aleuts have interracial marriages.[8] Among second-generation Asian Americans, exogamous marriages range from 36 percent for Chinese Americans to 67 percent for Korean American women.[9] If outmarriage rates included partners who are themselves of mixed ancestry (instead of assigning individuals to a single racial or ethnic category), intermarriage statistics would probably be much higher.[10]

Because the rates of exogamous marriage among many ethnic groups are high (and growing), the last two readings in Chapter 3 consider intermarriage in several ethnic groups. Nazli Kibria examines intermarriage and ethnic identity among second-generation Chinese and Korean Americans (Reading 15), and Barbara Bilgé provides an in-depth look at Turkish American marriages (Reading 16). Both authors show that intermarriage is complex. Bilgé's study, for example, shows that demographic variables such as socioeconomic status affect Turkish men's exogamy and their ability to transmit Turkish values to offspring. Kibria explains how interethnic cultural, religious, and historical "boundaries" influence mate choices across Asian American groups.

Other research also highlights the importance of structural and historical factors on intermarriage rates. Asian groups that are more likely to outmarry have a large pool of eligible partners within the Asian American population. They reside in communities that have large concentrations of Asians from other countries, have lived in the United States a long time, and have established economic and social networks that facilitate intimate social relationships. As many achieve middle-class status, individuals move out of ethnic enclaves and into mixed-Asian and white suburbs. In addition, growing numbers of Asian Americans are attending colleges and universities where they are likely to meet prospective white and ethnic marital partners, including Asian Americans from other countries.[11]

As Kibria discusses in her literature review in Reading 15, one of the most important contributing factors to intermarriage is a growing racial consciousness in U.S. society, which many Asian Americans (and perhaps Latinos) perceive as becoming increasingly racially polarized and stratified. Thus, "race, increasingly more so than ethnicity, shapes the experiences and the development of identity among Asian Americans."[12] As a result, *panethnicity,* "the development of bridging organizations and solidarities among several ethnic and immigrant groups of Asian ancestry,"[13] has emerged in the United States and other multiracial, multiethnic societies.

NOTES

1. Arlene F. Saluter, *Marital Status and Living Arrangements* (Washington, DC: Government Printing Office, 1994); U.S. Census Bureau, www.census.gov/population/socdemo/race/black/tabs99/tab02.txt, www.census.gov/Press-Release/www/2000/eb00ff05.html (accessed July 1, 2000).
2. Arlene F. Saluter, *Marital Status and Living Arrangements: March 1995 Update* (Washington, DC: Government Printing Office, 1996); U.S. Census Bureau, *Statistical Abstract of the United States: 1997* (Washington, DC: Government Printing Office, 1997), Table 58.
3. See, for example, M. A. Fossett and K. J. Kiecolt, "Mate Availability and Family Structure among African Americans in U.S. Metropolitan Areas," *Journal of Marriage and the Family* 55 (May 1993): 288–302; and

Angela D. James, "What's Love Got to Do with It?: Economic Viability and the Likelihood of Marriage among African American Men," *Journal of Comparative Family Studies* 29 (Summer 1998): 373–86.

4. Shehendu B. Kar, Devin Campbell, Armando Jimenez, and Gangeeta R. Gupta, "Invisible Americans: An Exploration of Indo-American Quality of Life," *Amerasia Journal,* 21 (Winter 1995/1996): 25–52.

5. For a discussion of how marital interactions and roles affect marital well-being, for example, see Jean Oggins, Joseph Veroff, and Douglas Leber, "Perceptions of Marital Interaction among Black and White Newlyweds," *Journal of Personality and Social Psychology* 65 (1993): 494–511.

6. The U.S. Supreme Court declared miscegenation laws, which prohibit interracial marriages, unconstitutional in 1967.

7. U.S. Census Bureau, *Statistical Abstract of the United States: 1999* (Washington, DC: Government Printing Office, 1999), based on data provided in Table 65.

8. M. Yellowbird and C. M. Snipp, "Native American families," in *Minority Families in the United States: A Multicultural Perspective,* ed. R. L. Taylor (Upper Saddle River, NJ: Prentice Hall, 1994), 179–201.

9. Sharon Lee and Keiko Yamanaka, "Patterns of Asian American Intermarried and Marital Assimilation," *Journal of Comparative Family Studies* 21 (1990): 287–305.

10. See Teresa Labov and Jerry A. Jacobs, "Preserving Multiple Ancestry: Intermarriages and Mixed Births in Hawaii," *Journal of Comparative Family Studies* 29 (Autumn 1998): 481–502.

11. Sean-Shong Hwang, Rogelio Saenz, and Benigno E. Aguirre, "Structural and Individual Determinants of Outmarriage among Chinese-, Filipino-, and Japanese-Americans in California," *Sociological Inquiry* 64 (November 1994): 396–414; Larry Hajime Shinagawa and Gin Yong Pang, "Asian American Panethnicity and Intermarriage," *Amerasia Journal* 22 (Spring 1996): 127–52.

12. Shinagawa and Pang, 144.

13. Yen Le Espiritu, *Asian American Panethnicity: Bridging Institutions and Identities* (Philadelphia: Temple University Press, 1992), 15.

12 Black Couples and the "Big C": The Ring, the Ceremony, Forever

Denene Millner and Nick Chiles

In the United States today, and especially among African Americans, the median age at first marriage is higher than ever before, the never-married make up the largest and fastest-growing segment of the unmarried population, and, since 1970, the number of cohabiting households has burgeoned. Denene Millner and her husband, Nick Chiles, discuss why many black women want to get married while many black men avoid the "Big C."

FROM A SISTAH

No, see, you don't understand. We want the ring. We may not just come right out and say it, we may not make it immediately clear from the getty-up

(well, some of us just might), but we want to get married—particularly if we've been dating for some time now. It's just logical: we meet, we date, we date exclusively, we get hitched. Simple as that.

For us, at least.

You guys? Well, that's a whole different bag. We sistahs get the distinct impression that you'd rather cross a pit of burning hot coals, with needles stuck in your eyes, butt-naked, in full makeup and a RuPaul wig on national television—preferably in the NBC Thursday-evening 9:00 P.M.-post–Seinfeld slot—with your mama sitting in the center of the front row of the studio audience, rather than work your lips to ask us to marry you. You all get the hives when we look like we're about to bring it up, and start stuttering like baleep, baleep, Pa-pa-porky the Pi-pi-pig when we ask you to discuss your intentions.

"I mean, we've been dating for five years now," the sistah says. "I love you, you know that, and you say you love me. What's wrong with making it official?"

"We-we-well, baby—everything's ga-ga-good between us. You don't na-ne-need a ma-ma-ma—um—a piece of paper to confirm my love for you."

And why not? There is so much more scrutiny in the relationship when you've got the papers. It's like, we've stood before God and said that we will be faithful and true and love each other come what may, and here's the certificate and the ring to symbolize that vow of commitment.

Then there's the kid thing—with the two of us being the parents in a traditional household. Not knocking the single-parent thing, or the live-in thing, for that matter. In fact, I fully advocate the latter, as it's the only possible way, I think, that two people can truly get to know each other before they take such a huge step into the commitment of marriage. But it's got to come to the marriage eventually, or it's like this relationship isn't official. It makes it a helluva lot easier to walk away from a relationship. Marriage? Well, there's no way you can just waltz away from that. It automatically elevates our status, makes us both think and try a lot harder to patch up the not-so-good things and work even more to create better times and a stronger bond for our relationship. If you're thinking about walking away from a long-term relationship, you know all you'll have is a broken heart and a broken lease. You think about walking away from a marriage, and you come to your senses more quickly—realize that it's not so easy to walk away, that you have to try to make it

stick because she is your wife, you are her husband and you told the Lord, the minister and your mama you two were in this for life.

Perhaps the scariest thing that could happen in New York recently was Mayor Rudy Giuliani's decision to let domestic partners receive benefits. The measure, geared toward homosexual couples who can't, by law, get married, allows longtime partners to receive all the benefits of a married couple, without having to tie the knot. If one has good benefits on the job, the other can be covered under that plan. If one dies, the other can inherit the deceased's apartment/house/car et al. There's one catch, though: The domestic partner rule isn't limited to homosexual couples—heterosexual couples can take advantage, too. That means that boyfriend doesn't even have to put a ring on her finger; she'll get dental, free gynecological care and a right to the apartment without him having to "suffer" being married to her. It completely goes against the whole institution of marriage—makes it easier to justify why you don't have to do it.

Figures a man came up with the idea.

You know what? We don't want lifetime playmates; we want for-real commitments, the ring, the Big C—the minister, the flower girl and the aunt singing (albeit a bit off-key) "A Ribbon in the Sky." The whole nine. And we think that you guys should feel the same way about us—particularly if we've invested a ton of time in this relationship and I love you and you claim to love me. **What's up with that? Why are brothers so afraid of the "Big C"?**

FROM A BROTHER

Well, you know what we fear, right? We fear that once we make that commitment and decide once and for all that you're the one, forever and ever, till death us do part and all that, then SHE will walk down the street, stroll right in front of our face, and smile. We'll think SHE is the most beautiful woman to walk the earth and what SHE wanted most in life was to make us hers. But no, we won't be available for SHE because we gotta stay with you or die.

Yes, of course this is stupid and childish and ridiculous. Of course you're the most beautiful woman to walk the earth and certainly if you weren't there's no reason to believe the woman who is would be smiling up in our face. Of course we gotta make decisions and then stick by them, because that's what adults do. We know all that. But then there are the sneakers.

You see, just as our lives have been carefully stage-managed by the gods of fate so that we'd one day be primed and ready for you, we have also spent the other part of our lives in search of the coolest, phattest pair of sneakers. We sauntered into Sneaker World that first time by ourselves, oh, 'bout ten, twenty, thirty years ago, our sweaty palms leaking moisture all over the $20, $50 or (if this was in the past decade) $100 balled up in our pocket. Our eyes fastened lovingly on the Havliceks or Dr. J.s or Penny Hardaways or Air Jordans in the center display. We knew this would be the shoe that would make us happy forever. Not only would we become a whirling, spinning, slam-dunking dervish on the court, but Sharon or Ayesha in the other seventh-grade class would profess her undying love for us once she caught a glimpse of the jewels on our feet. We slide them oh so carefully on our feet the next morning as we head out to school. We can just feel the eyes of the world on our feet; we know there has never been a cooler kid with a cooler shoe since man walked upright. And then disaster strikes. We're leaning against the wall before the bell, chatting with our boys, regaling them with the legend of our solo sneaker purchase, when up walks Tyrone/Raheem, sporting the newer, more expensive, oh-so-much-phatter limousine for the feet that was being sold at the newer, fancier Sneaker World at the mall where white people shop. Our friends all drift over to Tyrone/Raheem, never even giving us or our foot jewels a second glance. All those chores, all that time watching the jar fill up, all that anticipation, comes rushing

back to us, leaving a bitter taste in our mouth. It is a taste we will never forget.

Fast-forward two decades. Every time you bring up the subject of long-term, forever-type commitment, we start tasting a bitterness in our mouths. We blink rapidly, we shake our heads furiously, we take a few deep breaths. Still, we can't get rid of the taste. It won't go away. The sneakers.

How long into the relationship do you start looking at us cross-eyed if we haven't broached the subject of marriage or given you some clue that we're thinking about it?

FROM A SISTAH

For some of us, it's immediate. We will set a deadline for ourselves and cut your black butt off quicker than the jury freed O.J. if you're just sort of carrying on with no firm commitment coming down the pike. Ain't nobody trying to turn gray waiting for you to get your stuff together.

I have a girlfriend who lets guys know up front that she's looking for a husband, and that if he's not looking for a long-term commitment within their first two years of dating, she's not even trying to stick around. She has, after all, a wedding to plan.

For a lot of others, though, it's ridiculously too long. I'd heard some horror stories out on the road that plain turned my stomach—stories about sistahs who'd been in relationships with men for near-lifetimes, y'all, and were still waiting, hoping, praying and begging for that ring. One woman from the D.C. area told me that her brother had this one girl all strung out—had three kids with her, the last one born around the same time as another child homeboy had sired with some other woman he'd been dating on the side of his main squeeze. The couple, according to the woman, had been together fourteen years—fourteen years, y'all—and homegirl was still talking about "I want to get married, but he says I should just sit tight—we don't need a piece of paper to prove we're together."

Right.

Of course, the logical argument here is that homegirl has invested fourteen years in this relationship—and at this point, she's probably not seeing any tangible reason why she should leave. She's got a man (kinda), a father for her three kids, and basic security, as they live together and he, no doubt, pays a sizable sum to keep the family comfortable. Why would she want to start over—give up all of that stability (if you wish to call it that) to put herself back on the market, three kids and all? It would mean that she wasted fourteen solid years of her life—and at that point, it's *easier* to keep him.

Which leads me right to my point: Too many of us figure it's easier to keep him—easier to just go on along with the program rather than to be alone. We'd just as soon settle for fourteen years of so-so commitment, half happiness, big-time disappointment with him just because we can't stand the idea of having to go it alone—as if a man somehow makes us whole. It's a serious problem. We're in an unstable, miserable relationship, it's easy to say, "Girl—you need to just walk away." But doing it isn't all that simple.

There are other sistahs who are simply content dating men—having a companion without the firm marriage commitment thing. They're older, quite set in their ways, quite used to not having to disrupt their quiet, self-centered lives to split everything down the middle with some Negro. Fine if he wants to go to the movies or the museum—out to dinner and perhaps a little sleepover afterward—but, please, no marriage, because marriage will just screw it up.

But there is no science to figuring out which one you're going to get. She may, like my girlfriend, tell you up front that if you're not in it for the commitment, get to stepping. She may let you sit up in her house for a billion years, bear your kids and never make you get out. Or she may just let you stick around for a decent amount of time without talk of "the ring," ask you what's happening if you appear to be moving just a little too slow for comfort, and book up if you don't even-

tually—but in a reasonable amount of time—come around.

I can tell you, however, what you can do to help it along: You can stop playing games and just get to it—tell us if you're seriously considering marrying us, or if you're just sticking around until "SHE" miraculously reveals herself to you. Of course, we could make it even easier than that, and once we figure out if we really want you, we just come on out and ask you for *your* hand in marriage. **How would you respond if we asked you to marry us?**

FROM A BROTHER

Yeah, right. Y'all can't even get up the nerve to ask a brother to dance with you. I'm supposed to believe there are sistahs out there who'd actually ask a brother for his hand in marriage? Are you also gonna slide a nice big diamond ring on my finger? Am I supposed to cry and go call my dad to share the news with him?

Most of the brothers I know would have some problems with getting a proposal from a sistah, even if they had planned on doing it themselves at some point. The circumstances of our proposal—time, place, carat size, knee or no knee, trickery or straightforward—are details that cause a great deal of stress, but it's a good stress because we retain control of the event. We can do it when we're ready to do it, how we want to do it. Sure, you ladies are put in the difficult position of having to wait . . . and wait . . . and wait . . . for us to get around to it, but the last thing you should want is for your man to feel rushed or forced into marriage, trapped into giving the answer he thinks she wants to hear. That's a recipe for disaster. When the sistah proposes to the brother, there's too great a danger that he's not going to be ready yet.

If this is a woman we are growing to love, we don't want to hurt her feelings by saying "No" or, just as bad, "I don't know." We want to make her happy, but we don't want to get roped into something. The weaker, more-eager-to-please brothers among us might say yes before we're ready for that lifelong commitment. What happens then? We feel a growing sense of dread that we've made a mistake. We might even start resenting you.

If we were in no way intending to marry you but we were enjoying the relationship nonetheless, a rejected marriage proposal by the brother is going to instantly push the relationship onto bumpy ground. What are we supposed to do after that?

"Honey, I've been thinking. We've been doing this dating thing for almost two years now," she says, gazing sweetly into his eyes—which have instantly narrowed in suspicion.

"I think it's about time we took the next step," she continues, going on despite his obvious and growing discomfort. "Let's tie the knot. Let's get married. Okay?"

He tries to stay calm and not reveal his shock and anger at being put in this position. And he had really been enjoying his grilled salmon, too. Already she can tell by his response that she has made a bad move. She wants to say something else to ease the coming blow, but she holds herself back.

"Well, damn. That was unexpected," he says, wiping his brow with a napkin. He tries to smile, but it comes off looking like a pathetic grimace. He grows more angry at her for making him look pathetic.

"I, uh, well, I don't know. I'm not sure that I'm ready for that."

Are we expecting the sistah to forget the whole thing in this situation and ask the brother to pass the salt? Clearly, once she asks and gets an answer in the negative, there's a chance the whole relationship will blow apart into thousands of painful little shards—and no one within the explosion's radius will be spared the pain.

The safest thing for both parties is to talk about marriage enough before any proposal is dangled out there that you'd know with confidence what the answer is going to be. Spontaneity and whimsy are great for sex and romance, but in this arena they are usually as welcome as a toddler in a Tiffany store. The marriage proposal is a delicate creature.

We should consider the logistics of the thing, too. You ask, but I'm still supposed to go out and buy the ring? What if I don't have the requisite cash right now for a diamond ring purchase? What if I need a new transmission first, then I was planning on starting to save for a nice ring? If you propose, that takes all my planning and dropkicks it into irrelevancy. I won't like that. But, hey, if you're doing the asking, maybe you're going to buy your own ring. That way, you can be sure of getting one you'd like. I wouldn't even need to be there with you for the shopping. You could bring a girlfriend. Then you could just cart it over to my place—certainly you'd need a wheelbarrow to carry it—to show me what you got. I'd nod and say, "That's nice, honey." Is that what you want?

? Think about It

1. Why, according to Millner, should black couples marry instead of cohabit? Why, according to Chiles, do many black men evade marriage?
2. When discussing domestic-partner benefits, Millner comments, "Figures a man came up with the idea." What does she mean?
3. Do you agree with Millner that women should propose to men? Or do you agree with Chiles, who dismisses the idea as inappropriate? Explain your position.

13 | Asian Indian Marriages—Arranged, Semi-Arranged, or Based on Love?

Johanna Lessinger

Most countries do not have the "open" courtship system common in the United States and other Western nations. Instead, many groups try to preserve cultural consistency, family unity, and friendship ties through arranged marriages. Johanna Lessinger's research on Asian Indians in New York City shows that although arranged marriages are still prevalent in the United States and in India, the second generation has more options than the first generation had in meeting and marrying a suitable partner.

The continued Indian immigrant preoccupation with female chastity is partly an effort to keep women subordinated and partly an effort to maintain an important cultural distinction between "us" and "the Americans." It is also closely connected with the system of arranged marriages. Such marriages, the norm in India, still prevail among Indian immigrants, complete with ostentatious receptions and large dowries provided by the bride's family. As Luthra (1989: 343) points out, the phrase "decent marriage" appearing in the matrimonial ads of immigrant newspapers signals a willingness to give or take dowry.

Arranged marriages are the subject of endless discussion among members of the second generation. Agarwal's sampling of prosperous California immigrants indicates that two thirds of the young people she spoke to rejected arranged marriages, at least in principle, and wanted to select their own mates. (1991: 50). Not all manage to do so.

Raju, an aspiring writer, is somebody who has definitely rejected a marriage organized by his parents. Feeling the responsibilities of an only son he agreed some years ago to let his parents introduce him to one or two eligible girls. The dinner

Source: From Johanna Lessinger, *From the Ganges to the Hudson: Indian Immigrants in New York City* (Boston: Allyn and Bacon, 1995), 119–24. Copyright © 1995 Allyn & Bacon. Reprinted by permission.

parties at which the introductions between the two families took place were, according to Raju, "a farce, a nightmare. Everybody knew what this was for but everyone was pretending this was an ordinary party but silently thinking: 'Fall in love!' I sat there, she sat there, we were paralyzed and couldn't say a word to each other. I told my parents, 'Enough. Stop.'" Raju has since made his own choice, of a non-Indian artist; he and Ellen are not married but live together. His parents still hope this relationship is "just a phase" which Raju will outgrow and that he will eventually marry an Indian. "Well, they also hope I'll outgrow wanting to be a writer." Raju says. "Sorry. No."

Whatever their ideals, not all young people succeed in choosing their own mates. Many submit, if reluctantly, to having parents guide their choices or choose for them. For instance during the summer of Nalini's sophomore year in college, her parents told her that old friends had proposed a marriage between Nalini and their son. Nalini at first protested vigorously. When her parents asked why and suggested she loved somebody else, she insisted she did not. She simply resented the idea of being told whom to marry when. Her parents begged her to at least meet the young man, and promised not to push her if she disliked him. Nalini agreed reluctantly, and traveled with her parents to another state to meet the man, his parents and sister, and to inspect his apartment. Nalini decided that 26-year-old Dipak was handsome, shared her interest in classical Indian music, behaved politely to her parents and seemed kind. She also liked his sister, who lived near him. His apartment was large and modern. Dipak and his parents even promised that they would pay tuition so Nalini could transfer to a nearby college and finish her BA. The two were married at the end of the summer.

A certain number of young people actually view arranged marriages positively, in preference to the possible heartbreak and rejection involved in American-style dating. The Desais had fallen in love and gotten married as students in India. They migrated to the U.S. partly to escape the resulting family uproar and censure of this "love marriage." They were stunned when their own 22-year-old daughter asked their help in finding a husband. The young woman said she was too afraid of the American dating scene, involving pre-marital sex and potential rejection, to take responsibility for getting married. A year later their 24-year-old son asked for similar help in finding a bride.

Arranged marriage stems from a cultural concern with family unity and family cooperation. Indian society considers the background of a potential bride or groom to be just as important as individual personality when the two family circles join through marriage. Furthermore, since most Indians look on marriage as a lifelong commitment and consider divorce a shameful tragedy, it is practical to ask older people in the family to search out, and investigate, potential spouses and their families. Young people are believed to be too befuddled with romantic notions and sexual yearning to choose sensibly.

In a traditional arranged marriage, an all-points bulletin is broadcast through the network of family and friends when young people reach marriageable age, usually after finishing college or in the later years of graduate training. Newspaper advertisements or marriage brokers may be used to broaden the pool of candidates. Traditionally potential spouses were required to be of the

same caste, from the same region of India, of the same general socio-economic status and to be moderately good-looking. Young men are still expected to have employment prospects and young women to have families willing to give good dowries. Within these constraints, the young couple's personal compatibility and common interests were considered, but family elders often put other considerations first.

Today marriage advertisements in U.S. immigrant newspapers like *India Abroad* give indications of how the arranged marriage institution is shifting and adapting in the American context. Phrases such as "no bars" in more and more ads show the declining importance of caste, language group or even religion in mate selection if people are otherwise compatible in terms of education and profession. Additionally, matrimonial notices are beginning to stress personality and interests— such as a sense of humor or an interest in physical fitness—alongside the inevitable height, weight, beauty and professional criteria. The greater attention to individual and personal qualities within the framework of arranged marriages seems to be an adaptive response to American life, which isolates married couples and demands that they be more interdependent, while denying them the support of the extended family.

Even the traditional arranged marriage is not devoid of love and romance. Indians assume that young couples of similar background and interests will gradually develop love and respect for each other after marriage, and that these feelings will be solidified by the responsibilities of parenthood and running a household. In India particularly, gender segregation means that husbands and wives do not necessarily have to become each other's closest friends; that role is taken on by other people of the same sex. In practice Indian arranged marriages, although different in emotional construction from American marriages, are neither cold nor loveless and no more unhappy or likely to fail than marriages elsewhere.

A further adaptation of the arranged marriage to modern life is the emergence of what is often called the "semi-arranged" marriage, both in India and in the U.S. For an urban upper middle class (but not for millions of less fortunate Indians) this is intended to retain parental control while accommodating the youthful yearning for romantic love which is fed by both Indian and American media. Many urban Indian professional families have in the last 15 years begun to introduce suitable, pre-screened young men and women who are then allowed a courtship period during which to decide whether they like each other well enough to marry. (See Narayan 1995 for an insider's account of such a match.) This differs from American-style dating in that parents and friends are still involved in the initial screening, the courtship is much shorter, little or no premarital sex is involved, and there is a pragmatic recognition by both parties that the aim of meeting is marriage. In the U.S. the friendship circles of immigrant adults often operate as informal marriage bureaus, bringing suitable young people into contact so that they choose each other with only minor parental manipulation. Of course even in India there have been, for several generations now, brave individuals who chose for themselves and made love marriages in the face of parental opposition and family ostracism. In the U.S. such marriages are more numerous, since they have support from the larger society and American culture. However, they make many first generation parents uneasy and some try to arrange marriages when their children are young to cut off the possibility of a love marriage.

Immigration has added a complicating factor to the institution of arranged marriage. Indian parents in the U.S. have the option of seeking brides or grooms from India or from other parts of the Indian diaspora, as well as from the U.S. Marriages with the children of Indian immigrants in Canada or Britain are common. Certain Indian immigrants arrange to marry their children to people in India, largely to reenforce their own ties with family and friends there. It is no longer hard to locate potential spouses in India because of the widespread eagerness to migrate. For the parents of Indian-American women, there is a financial incentive in that grooms may accept the green card that comes with marriage to a legal resident or citizen in lieu of an expensive dowry of cash, jewelry or a house. Nevertheless there is great potential for exploitation in such arrangements. There are a number of tragic tales about "green card marriages" which collapsed after legal U.S. residence was established.

The question of marrying somebody from India versus marrying a fellow immigrant divides second generation men and young women. The women, with their American-bred sense of independence, tend to prefer young men raised, like themselves, in the U.S. They know that men from India will demand a kind of service and subservience they are not prepared to give. Many also complain that Indian men are shy, poorly dressed, awkward and unsure in American social situations. "They're totally uncool." (These complaints cut both ways. Young men in India believe immigrant women "have lost their culture" and make bad wives: too assertive toward men, unable to adjust to the demands of others, poor cooks and probably unchaste.)

For their part some young Indian-American men rather like the idea of having a "real Indian wife" who will be quiet, humble and certifiably "pure" and who will cater to them as their mothers did. An irate young Indian woman in New Jersey, thinking over those she knows, reports, "You have these lovely girls from India, really beautiful and educated, with PhDs, getting married off to real losers from here! Ugly guys or guys who haven't even finished high school! . . . The parents do that because they couldn't find anyone here willing to marry those idiots. The girls do it for the green card. Their lives are ruined."

The one point on which Indian immigrants and their children generally agree is that it is important to marry and have children. Even young women headed for careers want a husband and one or two children as well. In general the second generation is almost as family-minded as the first. It is perhaps a tribute to Indian immigrant parents that so many young people want families of their own, even if the process of getting married is one of the most stressful in young Indian-American lives. Additionally, many of the second generation, having been strenuously taught to value Indian culture, also agree with their parents about the desirability of marrying a fellow Indian. Of course, some of the second generation have rejected traditional patterns by choosing to live with or marry Americans; others have opted for lesbian or gay relationships. Yet it is important to realize that these choices do not necessarily imply a rejection of Indian culture and Indian identity, but rather represent a recognition of a range of personal options American life offers. These are options the first generation rarely had.

REFERENCES

Agarwal, Priya. 1991. *Passage from India: Post-1965 Indian Immigrants and Their Children.* Palos Verdes: Yuvati Publications.

Luthra, Rashmi. 1989. Matchmaking in the Classifieds of the Immigrant Indian Press. In *Making Waves: An Anthology of Writings by and about Asian American Women.* Asian Women United of California, eds. Boston: Beacon Press.

Narayan, Shoba. 1995. When Life's Partner Comes Pre-Chosen. *New York Times* May 4: C1, C8.

? Think about It

1. What is the purpose of arranged marriages? Why do many young Asian Indians find arranged marriages appealing? How have arranged-marriage practices shifted and adapted to American life?

2. How do semi-arranged marriages, especially in the United States, differ from American-style dating? Are Asian Indian women and men equally enthusiastic about semi-arranged marriages?

3. In Reading 12, Millner criticized black men for avoiding marriage. Would arranged or semi-arranged marriages increase the possibility that black women would meet and wed like-minded men?

Changes in Marital Satisfaction in Three Generations of Mexican Americans

Kyriakos S. Markides, Jan Roberts-Jolly, Laura A. Ray, Sue K. Hoppe, and Laura Rudkin

We often hear that "children cement a marriage." Because families from Mexico, on average, have more children than do white or other ethnic families (see Reading 1), can we assume that Mexican American marriages are happier than most others? Are such assumptions accurate or simplistic? Kyriakos Markides and his colleagues examine marital satisfaction across three generations of Mexican American spouses. Their findings suggest that marital happiness is a complex feeling that varies by gender and the duration of the marriage.

The literature on marital satisfaction during the 1970s and the 1980s has generally supported a U-shaped pattern over the life course: It is high right after marriage, declines gradually until middle age, and rises during late middle age and in old age (Ade-Ridder and Brubaker 1983; Anderson, Russell, and Schum 1983; Burr 1970; Glenn 1989; Rollins and Cannon 1974). Explanations for the U-shaped curve have focused on the addition of children to the family and stresses associated with raising them, problems with teenagers, responsibilities toward aging parents, and the departure of children from the household. Lower marital satisfaction during the child-rearing years has been found to be more characteristic of women than of men, presumably because they bear more of the burden of raising children (Burr 1970; Rollins and Feldman 1970).

In his review of the literature, Glenn (1990) questioned the common interpretation of the U-shaped curve that focuses on the influence of children and suggested that cross-sectional variation in marital satisfaction also involves the effects

Source: From Kyriakos S. Markides, Jan Roberts-Jolly, Laura A. Ray, Sue K. Hoppe, and Laura Rudkin, "Changes in Marital Satisfaction in Three Generations of Mexican Americans," *Research on Aging* 21 (January 1999): 36–45. Copyright © 1999 Sage Publications, Inc. Reprinted by permission of Sage Publications, Inc.

of the duration of marriage, marital dissolution, and differences among different marital cohorts. Clearly, longitudinal studies would shed light on the complexity of the relationship. Such longitudinal studies conducted during the 1980s found a decline with the transition to parenthood (e.g., Belsky, Lang, and Rovine 1985; Feldman and Nash 1984; Goldberg, Michaels, and Lamb 1985), a decline that was generally greater among women than among men. However, as Glenn points out, such a decline cannot be totally attributed to the transition to parenthood since marital satisfaction declines regardless of the addition of children. This suggests the presence of a duration-of-marriage effect (see also Vaillant and Vaillant 1993).

Although the U-shaped curve has received considerable support, there has been an absence of longitudinal studies in this area. In addition, there has been little research on marital satisfaction in minority populations, especially Mexican Americans. In one study, Bean, Curtis, and Marcum (1977), who characterized Mexican American families as more male dominated and more familistic than Anglo families, found greater marital satisfaction to be associated with egalitarian marriages. Markides and Hoppe (1985) examined levels of marital satisfaction cross-sectionally in three generations of Mexican Americans in San

Antonio and found a slight linear increase in satisfaction from the younger to the older generation, as measured by the negative sentiment dimension of marital satisfaction. However, Markides and Hoppe found that a U-shaped curve in the positive interaction dimension of marital satisfaction was present only in men, with women exhibiting a linear decline from younger to older generations.

In attempting to explain the absence of a U-shaped curve in positive interaction among Mexican American women, and instead why there appears to be a linear decline by generation, Markides and Hoppe (1985) speculated about the importance of cultural factors. They suggested that the role of mother may be especially important in the Mexican American community (see Alvirez, Bean, and Williams 1981), particularly in the older generations, with alternative roles being scarce in comparison to the Anglo community so that the departure of children from the home results in low levels of positive interaction in late middle age and old age. Why these low positive feelings were not accompanied by negative feelings was not clear, except perhaps that older marriages tend to be of the "compassionate" type (Ade-Ridder and Brubaker 1983), characterized by low negative sentiments but not necessarily by a high level of positive feelings (Markides and Hoppe 1985).

These findings, like those of most research, suffer from the limitations of cross-sectional data when attempting to delineate aging or life-course effects. The purpose of this analysis is to employ longitudinal data from an 11-year follow-up of the three-generations study of Mexican Americans on which the Markides and Hoppe (1985) analysis was based. If, indeed, aging brings declining levels of positive interaction in Mexican American women but not in men, as suggested by the cross-sectional data, we should observe such a decline in middle-generation women 11 years later but not in men. Such a prospective analysis that is based on intact marriages only has the advantage of not being contaminated by "survivor" effects that are a problem in cross-sectional analyses.

METHOD

As indicated above, the analysis presented below is based on an 11-year follow-up of the three-generations study of Mexican Americans conducted in the San Antonio area in 1981–82. The original sampling design involved a multistage area probability sample of Mexican Americans age 65 to 80 residing in San Antonio who had children and adult grandchildren (18 years of age or older) living within a 50-mile radius of the city. An eligible grandchild was randomly selected, which also identified his or her middle-generation parent who was the son or daughter of the older generation subject. This process yielded 375 three-generation lineages, amounting to 1,125 subjects (see Markides et al. 1983; Markides and Martin 1990). The sample was disproportionately female (approximately two-thirds) and had median ages of 74 in the older generation, 49 in the middle, and 26 in the younger generation, with minimal overlap in age among adjacent generations. The 1981–82 analysis of marital satisfaction was based on 752 subjects who were currently married, 171 in the older, 287 in the middle, and 284 in the younger generation (Markides and Hoppe 1985).

In 1992–93, the investigators were able to reinterview 624 of the original subjects, or 56% of the original sample. Among the dropouts, 227 were deceased, 199 of them from the older generation. There were 75 subjects who refused to be reinterviewed, 24 had moved out of town or were in prison, 27 were "too ill" to be reinterviewed, and 138 were lost to follow-up.

The analysis reported below is based only on reinterviewed subjects who were married to the same spouses at Time 2. As might have been expected, there were very few eligibles in the older generation. Only 13 men and 12 women out of the original 75 and 91, respectively, were eligible. In the middle generation, there were 62 men (out of 105) and 106 women (out of 171). Finally, there were 47 men (out of 118) and 83 women (out of 163) in the younger generation.

Our measure of marital satisfaction was the

10 item Likert-type scale employed by Gilford and Bengtson (1979) in the Southern California Study of Generations. Respondents were asked to indicate how often certain "things husbands and wives may do together" take place with their spouse (scored from 1 to 5, from *hardly ever* to *very often or all the time*. Scale items included (1) you calmly discuss something together, (2) one of you is sarcastic, (3) you work together at something (dishes, yard work, etc.), (4) one of you refuses to talk in a normal manner, (5) you laugh together, (6) you have an interesting exchange of ideas, (7) you disagree about something important, (8) you become critical and belittling, (9) you have a good time together, and (10) you become angry. Scores of negative items were reversed, and the 10-item scale was subjected to factor analysis at both Time 1 and Time 2. As in the Gilford and Bengtson study, factor analysis yielded two distinct factors: a "positive interaction" dimension and a "negative sentiment" dimension, the first consisting of the five positive items and the second of the five negative items. Time 2 factor analyses with the older generation subjects were not performed because there were only 13 men and 12 women eligible. For the younger subjects, each factor had an alpha reliability coefficient of at least .80.

The analysis presented below simply is aimed at identifying changes in the two dimensions of marital satisfaction over an 11-year period (1981–82 to 1992–93) in subjects married to the same spouses. We compare mean scores at each time separately by gender. Caution is needed in interpreting data for the older generation given the small number of cases and our inability to examine psychometric properties with such small numbers. However, we are mostly interested in changes as well as stability in the middle generation (and the younger) and whether these data are consistent with our cross-sectional findings with the Time 1 data. In particular, do middle-age women show a decline in positive interaction over 11 years while middle-age men do not?

FINDINGS

Table 1 presents data on the positive interaction and negative sentiment dimensions of marital satisfaction at Time 1 (1981–82) and at Time 2 (1992–93) by gender for each generation. Each scale has a potential range from 1 to 5 (sum of the five items divided by five), with higher scores indicating higher levels of satisfaction for both dimensions.

TABLE 1 Positive Interaction and Negative Sentiment at Time 1 and Time 2 by Generation and Gender (means and standard deviations)

	Positive Interaction		Negative Sentiment	
	Time 1	Time 2	Time 1	Time 2
Older generation				
Men (*N* = 13)	3.97 (0.56)	3.45 (0.53)	4.35 (0.48)	4.25 (0.46)
Women (*N* = 12)	3.97 (0.71)	2.95 (1.19)	4.23 (0.70)	4.42 (0.59)
Middle generation				
Men (*N* = 62)	3.84 (0.75)	3.86 (0.67)	4.30 (0.66)	4.37 (0.47)
Women (*N* = 106)	3.87 (0.80)	3.34* (0.84)	4.17 (0.62)	4.15 (0.71)
Younger generation				
Men (*N* = 47)	4.19 (0.62)	3.65* (0.86)	4.29 (0.58)	4.12 (0.56)
Women (*N* = 83)	4.11 (0.68)	3.62* (0.84)	4.18 (0.68)	4.01 (0.67)

*$p \leq .01$.

As noted earlier, only 13 men and 12 women in the older generation (age 65 to 80 at Time 1) were married to the same spouses 11 years later. There is no significant change in negative sentiment in either gender or in positive interaction among males.

In the middle generation, we also observe no change in negative sentiment 11 years later. Again, while middle-generation men show no change in positive sentiment, women show a significant decline in positive interaction over the 11-year period. This finding for middle-generation women entering old age is consistent with our previous cross-sectional findings at Time 1 (Markides and Hoppe 1985), which showed lower positive interaction among older generation than among middle-generation women. Unlike our cross-sectional findings that showed a U-shaped curve among males, the absence of an increase in positive sentiment among middle-generation males does not support an increase in satisfaction in late middle age and early old age that would be consistent with the U-shaped curve hypothesis.

As in the other two generations, there is no change in negative sentiment scores among either women or men in the younger generation over the 11-year study period. However, both younger men and women exhibit significant declines in positive interaction, a decline that is consistent with the U-shaped curve hypothesis, which could very well be associated with a transition to parenthood for most younger subjects but which could also represent what Glenn (1990) calls a duration-of-marriage effect.

DISCUSSION

The primary purpose of this analysis was to replicate with long-term longitudinal data from the same study our previous cross-sectional finding of an absence of a U-shaped curve in marital satisfaction as measured by the positive interaction dimension of marital satisfaction (Gilford and Bengtson 1979) in Mexican American women. Our longitudinal finding of a decline in positive

interaction among middle-generation women over an 11-year period is indeed consistent with the finding of lower positive interaction in older than in middle-generation women at Time 1. No decline (or increase) was observed among middle-generation males. The original cross-sectional finding with respect to women was interpreted (see Markides and Hoppe 1985) as possibly associated with cultural factors related to the role of older women particularly in earlier generations, namely, the great importance of motherhood and relative scarcity of alternative roles after children have left home. That we also find a decline longitudinally among middle-generation women suggests the operation of an aging (or life course) effect that is not unique to the older generation. This suggests the continuation of the importance of motherhood for the next generation of Mexican American women now entering old age, and possibly the continuing scarcity of alternative roles for older women after children have left home, that might be associated with more fulfilling marriages. It is also consistent with the heavy burdens middle-age and older Mexican American women bear in caring for others in the extended family, a burden also observed in other familistic populations such as Italian and Polish Americans (Cohler and Grunebaum 1981).

This finding, along with the finding of no decline in positive interaction among middle-generation males, supports findings from our previous work suggesting that aging has greater negative consequences on the well-being of Mexican American women than on Mexican American men. For example, we have shown that rates of depressive symptoms are very high in older Mexican American women, while they are very low in older Mexican American men (Mendes de Leon and Markides 1988).

We also replicated our cross-sectional finding with the baseline data that negative sentiment did not increase among middle-generation women as they became older, supporting the notion that older marriages are of the compassionate type characterized by little conflict but not necessarily very high positive feelings. This finding also underscores the importance of examining different dimensions of marital quality.

Both younger generation men and women exhibited significant declines in positive interaction over 11 years, a finding that is consistent with the U-shaped curve prediction of declines in marital satisfaction after the early years of marriage. Again, no such change was observed with respect to negative sentiment, possibly because marriages characterized by increasing negative sentiment during the 11-year study period may have been dissolved by the Time 2 follow-up.

Finally, we should point out that longitudinal studies of intact marriages underestimate the negative effects of duration of marriage because of the marriages that end in divorce over time. Given this consideration and our findings over 11 years, there does not appear to be much support for an upturn in marital quality in middle age or later, as cross-sectional studies have shown.

REFERENCES

Ade-Ridder, Linda and Timothy H. Brubaker. 1983. "The Quality of Long-Term Marriages." Pp. 21–30 in *Family Relationships in Late Life*, edited by Timothy H. Brubaker. Newbury Park, CA: Sage.

Alvirez, David, Frank D. Bean, and Dorrie Williams. 1981. "The Mexican American Family," Pp. 269–92 in *Ethnic Families in America*, 2d ed., edited by C. H. Mindel and R. W. Habenstein. New York: Elsevier.

Anderson, Stephen A., Candyce S. Russell, and Walter R. Schum. 1983. "Perceived Marital Quality and Family Life-Cycle Categories: A Further Analysis." *Journal of Marriage and the Family* 45: 127–39.

Bean, Frank D., Russell L. Curtis, and John P. Marcum. 1977. "Familism and Marital Satisfaction among Mexican Americans: The Effects of Family Size, Wife's Labor Force Participation and Conjugal Power." *Journal of Marriage and the Family* 39: 769–67.

Belsky, Jay, Mary E. Lang, and Michael Rovine. 1985. "Stability and Change in Marriage across the Transition to Parenthood: A Second Study." *Journal of Marriage and the Family* 45:567–77.

Burr, Wesley R. 1970. "Satisfaction with Various Aspects of Marriage over the Life Cycle." *Journal of Marriage and the Family* 26:29–37.

Cohler, Bertram J., and H. U. Grunebaum. 1981. *Mothers, Grandmothers, and Daughters: Personality and Child Care in Three-Generation Families*. New York: John Wiley.

Feldman, Shirley S. and S. C. Nash. 1984. "The Transition from Expectancy to Parenthood: Impact of the Firstborn Child on Men and Women." *Sex Roles* 11:84–92.

Gilford, Rosalie and Vern L. Bengtson. 1979. "Measuring Marital Satisfaction in Three Generations: Positive and Negative Dimensions." *Journal of Marriage and the Family* 41:387–98.

Glenn, Norval D. 1989. "Duration of Marriage, Family Composition, and Marital Happiness." *National Journal of Sociology* 3:3–24.

———. 1990. "Quantitative Research on Marital Quality in the 1980s: A Critical Review." *Journal of Marriage and the Family* 52:818–31.

Goldberg, Wendy A., Gerald Y. Michaels, and Michael E. Lamb. 1985. "Husbands' and Wives' Patterns of Adjustment to Pregnancy and First Parenthood." *Journal of Family Issues* 6:483–504.

Markides, Kyriakos S. and Sue K. Hoppe. 1985. "Marital Satisfaction in Three Generations of Mexican Americans." *Social Science Quarterly* 66:147–53.

Markides, Kyriakos S., Sue K. Hoppe, Harry W. Martin, and Dianne M. Timbers. 1983. "Sample Representativeness in a Three-Generation Study of Mexican Americans." *Journal of Marriage and the Family* 45:911–16.

Markides, Kyriakos S. and Harry W. Martin. 1990. *Older Mexican Americans: Selected Findings from Two Studies*. Monograph of the Tomas Rivera Center. San Antonio, TX: Tomas Rivera Center.

Mendes de Leon, Carlos F. and Kyriakos S. Markides. 1988. "Depressive Symptoms among Mexican Americans: A Three-Generations Study." *American Journal of Epidemiology* 127:150–60.

Rollins, Boyd C. and Kenneth L. Cannon. 1974. "Marital Satisfaction over the Family Life Cycle: A Reevaluation." *Journal of Marriage and the Family* 36:271–83.

Rollins, Boyd C. and Harold Feldman. 1970. "Marital Satisfaction over the Life Cycle." *Journal of Marriage and the Family* 32:20–28.

Vaillant, Caroline O. and George E. Vaillant. 1993. "Is

the U-Curve of Marital Satisfaction an Illusion? A 40-Year Study of Marriage." *Journal of Marriage and the Family* 55:230–39.

 Think about It

1. What is a U-shaped curve? What did a U-shaped curve show about marital satisfaction during the 1970s and 1980s? How have many researchers interpreted the U-shaped curve?

2. According to Kyriakos and his colleagues, what are the advantages and disadvantages of longitudinal research in their study and others?

3. Summarize this study's findings about younger, middle-generation, and older spouses. How do the researchers explain the lower levels of marital satisfaction that middle-age and older women reported? What alternative explanations, if any, do the readings on gender roles in Chapter 2 ("Gender Roles") suggest?

15 Intermarriage and Ethnic Identity among Second-Generation Chinese and Korean Americans

Nazli Kibria

What does being "Asian American" mean? Nazli Kibria explores conceptions of ethnicity through an analysis of Chinese and Korean Americans' attitudes and beliefs about marriage across racial and ethnic lines. Kibria discusses how the construction of "Asian American" is a process that involves (1) recognition of the shared personal experiences and orientations of Asian-origin persons, (2) growing up in an Asian home, and (3) adhering to Asian values that emphasize family, education, hard work, and respect for elders.

In this article I explore the forces and processes that underlie the development of an Asian American identity. I focus specifically on the experiences and meanings of "Asian American-ness" among second-generation[1] middle-class Chinese and Korean Americans as revealed by their atti-

Source: From Nazli Kibria, "The Construction of 'Asian American': Reflections on Intermarriage and Ethnic Identity among Second-Generation Chinese and Korean Americans," *Ethnic and Racial Studies* 20 (July 1997): 523–44. Copyright © 1997 Taylor & Francis Ltd. Reprinted by permission. http://www.tandf.cp.uk./journals

tudes and beliefs about intermarriage across racial and ethnic[2] lines. Analysts of the Asian experience in the U.S. have seen the construct of "Asian American" in primarily racial and political terms (Lowe 1991; Espiritu 1992; Espiritu and Ong 1994). That is, brought together by their common racial status in U.S. society, Asian-origin groups form strategic political coalitions in order to protect and advance their interests. My findings suggest that among certain second-generation segments of the Asian-origin population in the

U.S., there is a developing pan-Asian American consciousness, one that extends beyond strategic political considerations. The second-generation Chinese and Korean Americans understood themselves as "Asian American" because of their sense that Asians in the U.S., particularly those who were the children of Asian immigrants, shared certain common experiences and worldviews.

BOUNDARIES, OUTMARRIAGE AND THE RACIAL ETHNOGENESIS OF ASIAN AMERICANS

The notion of "boundaries" is often used in the study of ethnicity as a way of conceptualizing the mechanisms of group differentiation and identity (Barth 1969; Wallman 1986; Nagel 1994). I suggest that for members of ethnic groups, intermarriage often poses a "boundary dilemma" or a conceptual space within which to consider questions about one's ethnic identity. That is, as they reflect on the meaning and consequences of outmarriage for their ethnic affiliation, group members also inevitably confront questions about the definition, meaning and significance of the boundaries that mark their identity. Thus, reflections on outmarriage represent a useful vehicle for understanding conceptions and experiences of ethnic identity. This is particularly so for groups that have both a strong tradition of censure towards marriage with "outsiders" and relatively high rates of outmarriage. By highlighting both the possibility and gravity of exogamy, these conditions encourage conscious reflection about outmarriage among group members.

Among the variety of questions that surround the issues of outmarriage is the fundamental one of how to define one. While deceptively simple at first glance, this question is confounded by the complexity of ethnic boundaries, in particular their situational, multi-layered and emergent character (see Nagel 1994). For example, the weight that is placed on ethnic affiliation in definitions of outmarriage varies across situations, in

response to factors ranging from the social class background of the marriage partner to the local availability of fellow ethnics for marriage partners. Dichotomous conceptions of outmarriage also ignore the multifaceted quality of ethnic identities. In fact, rather than being seen in absolute terms, the definition of outmarriage is most aptly viewed as a continuum on which marriage partners are placed, based on the *degree* to which they are perceived to share ethnic membership. Thus in his study of intermarriage in the U.S., Spickard (1989) notes a "hierarchy of preference" in the attitudes of ethnic groups towards intermarriage. For example, Chinese immigrants to the U.S. in the first half of the century evaluated marriage partners in a gradational manner, considering not just their Chinese or non-Chinese origins but also their particular linguistic and regional affiliations. Marriage partners who shared a greater number of these affiliations were preferred partners, since they represented a greater degree of shared membership. . . .

The micro-level exploration of how Asian-origin persons in the U.S. understand the Asian racial label may provide important insights into the nature and meaning of membership in an Asian American collectivity. As far as racial identity is concerned, one of the crucial differences between black and Asian immigrants to the U.S. is that in the case of the former, racial labelling implies membership in a group—Black American—that has a relatively strong and well-defined sense of collective history and culture. In contrast, Asians confront membership in a community with a less developed sense of its unique history and culture. The very idea of "Asian American" is one that was developed by activists in the 1960s (Espiritu 1992, pp. 31–33). While Asian American Studies programmes and groups have been active in articulating and educating their students and members about a shared Asian American past, it is clear that important questions remain about the substance of Asian American ties.

In this article I use the reflections on intermarriage of second-generation Chinese and Korean

Americans to explore Asian American identity processes. While Chinese Americans and Korean Americans differ in important respects, they are both groups that share the "Asian" racial label.[3] Furthermore, while exogamy is generally not viewed favourably by Chinese and Koreans, rates of Chinese and Korean American intermarriage, especially among the second generation, are substantial[4]—conditions that make reflections on intermarriage a particularly useful vehicle for the analysis of ethnicity. Using 1980 census data, Lee and Yamanaka (1990) report rates of intermarriage among U.S.-born or second-generation Chinese American women to be 36.8 per cent and for second-generation Korean American women, 66.9 per cent.[5] They find that while most of the outmarriages, especially those involving women, were to whites, there were significant numbers of intra-Asian marriages. For example, of U.S.-born Chinese American men in exogamous marriages, 35.1 per cent had spouses of "other Asian" origin.[6]

STUDY METHODS

The materials presented here are drawn from sixty in-depth interviews with second-generation Chinese Americans and Korean Americans in the Los Angeles and Boston areas. The study was limited to second-generation Chinese and Korean Americans between the ages of twenty-one and forty. Interviewees were asked to talk about the role and meaning of their racial and ethnic affiliations in such life spheres as work, family and neighbourhood over the life course. The interviews, which lasted from 1.5 to 4 hours, were tape-recorded and later transcribed. Informants were located through the membership lists and referrals of a variety of churches, professional and social clubs, and college and university alumnae associations.

Although they had been raised in homes that varied greatly in economic standing, all of the informants were college-educated, and many had graduate or professional degrees. In fact, the majority (about three-quarters) were either married to professionals or working in professional occupations. While these characteristics are generally associated with a greater likelihood of involvement in Asian American institutions, about two-thirds of my sample indicated minimal or no involvement with Asian American groups and organizations.

As far as marital status, twenty-eight of the sixty interviewees were married. Of the married group, fifteen were married to persons of the same national ethnic background as themselves. Of the remainder, ten were married to whites, two to other Asians, and one to an African American. In comparison to those who were married, a larger proportion of the single informants were involved in inter-racial and inter-ethnic relationships. Fourteen of the thirty-two single second-generation Chinese and Korean Americans informed me that they were involved in what they described as "serious" and "committed" relationships that might lead to marriage. Of this group, seven were involved with other Asians, three with whites, one with a Latino, and three with those of the same national ethnic background as themselves.

THE "BOUNDARY DILEMMAS" OF OUTMARRIAGE

In their opinions, preferences and behaviours with respect to outmarriage, the second-generation[7] was a diverse group. There were, however, some important themes or threads of commonality in how they experienced and understood outmarriage. Among these was a belief in romantic love, in which partner selection was ultimately a matter of where Cupid's arrow happened to land rather than such considerations as group affiliation. This ideology of romantic love, intermingled with the ideas of individual choice and freedom, served as a constant backdrop to the second-generation's ruminations on the "boundary dilemmas" of outmarriage, even among those who expressed a strong and conscious commitment to limiting their choice of partner along racial and/or ethnic lines. However, these beliefs coexisted with the understanding that partner selection was a matter that had much to do with one's group affiliations. Among the boundaries that were of significance to partner selection was an Asian American one. In what follows I explore the development of a sense of "pan-Asian-ness" among my informants as revealed by their reflections on the "boundary dilemmas" of outmarriage.

Racial Labelling and an "Asian Race"

. . . As Frankenburg (1993, p. 99) observes, when the boundaries between groups are understood as biological in substance, marriage outside the group carries with it the danger of impurity or contamination, as personified by the "mixed-race" child. For the second generation, these dangers were deeply linked to their concerns about family honour. That is, racial crossing by way of outmarriage threatened the purity of the family lineage through the introduction of non-Korean or non-Chinese blood into the family. This impurity threatened family honour and perhaps even the continuity of the family line, as "mixed-race" children were not acceptable carriers of the family name. It is not surprising that men rather than women informants were more likely to articulate these concerns about "lineage purity," given the traditional centrality of sons to the family line of descent. However, these concerns were also present among women. For example, the link between racial continuity and family continuity was emphasized by her father to Sandra, a twenty-nine-year-old Korean American born in the United States. He went to great lengths to establish how important it was for the continuity of the family line that she "marry Korean." His remarks, as recounted by Sandra, are particularly interesting in the light of the fact that in the patrilineal Korean family system, daughters do not carry on the family name but enter, upon marriage, into the family descent group of their husband:

It's extremely important for them that I marry someone Korean. After college my first boyfriend was Jewish American. They liked him but the fact that he wasn't Korean was a big concern. My father talked to me about it. It was very dramatic, but he said if you do marry a non-Korean you will be putting an end to our history. At home we have three volume texts on our family history which go back as far as the fourth century in China. Although I'm not male and I wouldn't be carrying on the family name, women are still included in the family history.

For the second generation, these concerns about lineage purity, along with the conceptions of racial identity that underlay them, interacted with the larger context of U.S. society in complex ways. In the U.S., explicit concerns about maintaining racial purity is widely seen as "racist," since they clash with the popular ideals of a colour-blind society. Because of their connotations of racism, some informants chose to reject traditional concerns of lineage, often invoking the ideology of romantic love and individual choice in the process. But others, such as Jeff, a twenty-three-year-old Korean American, effectively turned this concern on its head. He talked of how the effort to preserve Korean boundaries through endogamy was a response to the fundamental racial divisions of U.S. society, in which the possibilities for integration were limited for non-whites. His words suggest a subtle transformation in the understanding of the relationship of race to ethnic identity. The need to maintain racial boundaries in marriage had moved from being driven by fears of violating lineage purity to a defence against racism. In this shift, ethnic identity was also reinterpreted, from an affiliation that was rooted in a common blood heritage to one that was reactive, a response to the exclusion of U.S. society.

After listening to my parents and thinking about it, I've pretty much decided that I will marry Korean. I want to keep my lineage (pause) . . . I don't want to say pure because that kind of has a negative connotation, but I don't want to mix. I know it sounds racist, but a lot of it has to do with the fact that this society doesn't accept us at some deep level. I feel like it's important to marry Korean because no matter how American you think you are, by the fact that your hair is black and your skin is yellow and you have Korean blood, you are different. Plus biracial children have a lot of problems fitting in.

. . . There was generally a powerful sense of racial commonality with "other Asians" among the second generation, one that seemed to be present for the immigrant generation as well. As recounted by their children, many immigrant parents preferred their children to marry "Asian" if they were not able to marry a Korean or a Chinese (cf. Pang 1994, p. 114). In general, for immigrant parents, Asians tended to rank second in a continuum of outmarriage in which the specific national group of origin was at one end and blacks at the other. The preference for "Asians" stemmed, in part, from a sense of shared race, which was fostered for the immigrant generation by not only the racial labels they encountered in the U.S., but also by the greater racial and ethnic diversity of the U.S. compared with the country of origin, which worked to highlight sources of commonality rather than difference with other Asians.

Wayne, a thirty-year-old Chinese American writer and artist who had grown up in New York, talked of how his mother's initial dismay that he was dating a non-Chinese person evaporated when she learned that he was seeing a Korean American woman. At least part of her comfort with her son's Korean American girlfriend stemmed from her sense that Koreans and Chinese were physically similar, a view apparently related to her understanding that Americans could not distinguish between Koreans and Chinese:

A while back, my mother talked about how I was getting old and I should get married. I said, "I'm thinking I might marry someone who is not Chinese." She got really upset and I was kind of surprised because we haven't talked about this in a long long time. But then I told her I was going out with a Korean woman pretty seriously and she was really happy. She said, "Oh, Korean, Korean. They look

like us, they look just like us. Sometimes you can't tell the difference. Americans can't tell the difference between Chinese and Korean."

For the second generation, the sense of shared race arose not simply from the understanding that Asians were "physically similar," at least in the eyes of the dominant society; it also reflected the understanding of a shared racial history, or a set of common experiences that stemmed from the dynamics of racial assignment as "Asian" by the dominant society. While some (particularly those who had been exposed to Asian American forums) referred to a collective history of racial oppression shared by Asians in the U.S. (for example, anti-Asian immigration laws, hate-crimes against Asians), it was more common for informants to refer to the shared personal racial history of Asian Americans, one that often revolved around common "growing up experiences." As children, for example, they had been teased and taunted with what one informant described as the "generic" Asian racial slurs of "Chink" "Jap" "Gook" "Nip" and "slant eye." They also described how second-generation Asian Americans shared common dating experiences, particularly in their adolescent years.

Virtually all my informants talked of how, for them, as for other Asian Americans, popular American cultural stereotypes and images of Asian sexuality had affected their dating experiences. Men confronted the image of the sexually unattractive, under-sexed and effeminate Asian male, while women faced stereotypes of the "exotic and sensual Asian woman" (see Cheung 1990). Some informants mentioned that while growing up, many Asian Americans went through a "white phase" or a time of wishing they were white—a reaction to experiences of exclusion and negative stereotyping. Meg, a Chinese American in her mid-twenties who had grown up in Las Vegas and was working as an administrator in a large Los Angeles entertainment corporation, talked of this at some length. At the time of the interview she was going out with a Japanese American, although for several years before she had only dated white men:

In high school I went through a white phase. Definitely. I remember saying to my friends, I'm gonna date white guys, I don't care. I turned away from dating Asians. (*I: Why do you think you went through this white phase?*) I think it has a lot to do with being accepted by whites in general. I think all Asian females go through that phase, at least a lot of my friends did. There's so much confusion among Asian Americans about what to be loyal to.

But the widespread sense of a shared Asian race that I found among my informants did not consistently include all Asian-origin groups. In contrast with the inclusive ideals commonly voiced in Asian American organizations, the second generation tended to see some Asian groups as "closer" to them than others. It was not simply "other Asians," but other East Asians with whom there was a particular affinity. The affinity with Japanese Americans that the second generation talked of was particularly striking in the light of the extremely sharp historical animosity of Chinese and Koreans towards Japanese. Some informants did, in fact, talk of how their parents would find it difficult to accept someone of Japanese origin, given the still vivid memories of the brutal Japanese occupations of China and Korea during the first half of the century. But even among their parents, as recounted by the second generation, Japanese and other East Asians were generally seen as closer on the continuum of outmarriage in comparison to other Asians, such as Filipinos, Vietnamese and Cambodians. Greg, a thirty-two-year-old Chinese American engineer who had been born and raised in Boston, talked of his mother's preference that he marry a woman of East Asian origin:

She ran off this list to me in the order of what was acceptable. If not Chinese, then Japanese or Korean. Whites were actually next, and I remember that Filipinos and Vietnamese were not so popular. (*I: Why was that?*) I guess because they look different from us, much more so than Japanese and Koreans. And they're also seen as not so successful. I know that the Vietnamese are recent immigrants. I'm sure that has something to do with it.

As the above suggests, the lower ranking of Asian groups such as Filipinos, Vietnamese and Cambodians emerged out of a sense of greater racial and socio-economic difference with them in comparison to that among East Asians. Similar findings have been noted by Gin Pang (1994, p. 115) in her analysis of the ethnic preferences of Korean immigrant parents for the marriage partners of their children. Pang (1994) notes that Filipino Americans were seen by the Korean immigrant parents as both racially and culturally extremely different from Koreans, due in part to the experience of Spanish colonialism in the Philippines. Vietnamese were distinguished from the East Asian groups by their comparatively low social and economic status, both within the U.S. and in terms of the global stature of Vietnam as a nation.

"Immigrant Stories" and an Asian American History and Culture

The second generation understood the boundary of "Asian American" as not simply racial, but also cultural in substance. The cultural commonalities of Asian Americans were understood within the framework of an "immigrant narrative." As Bacon (1997) notes, in the U.S. the second-generation experience is commonly understood with reference to a classic, prototypical "immigrant story." The story revolves around a series of oppositional dichotomies—immigrant *versus* American, traditional *versus* modern—that help to define the second-generation experience. Two features of the immigrant story are particularly relevant to the second-generation's construction of a pan-Asian American history and culture. The first is the marginal and "in-between" position of the second generation, which is caught within the oppositional pulls of the dichotomies that define the immigrant experience; the children of immigrants are inevitably "cultural conflict-bound" (Puar 1995, 23). For my informants, the fact that they had had "an Asian upbringing" had much to do with their experience of "not fitting in." . . .

The second generation identified their *Asian* upbringing as an important reason for their being different and not fitting in with their non-Asian, particularly their white, peers. That is, as the children of Asian immigrants, they had been brought up in certain, distinctive ways. What I heard most frequently from interviewees was that as Asians, their parents had expected a great deal of them, more so than did non-Asian, particularly white, parents. A high level of achievement at school, for example, was a virtually "given" expectation of Asian parents. Not getting good grades at school could result in what several informants described as "the Asian parent guilt trip," in which family honour and sacrifice were held up as weapons of discipline. There were expectations that revolved around the special emphasis on family among Asians, such as taking responsibility for younger siblings and spending time with older relatives such as grandparents. In general, Asian parents were stricter in the rules of conduct they laid down for children. Especially for women, rules about dating were quite stringent and rigid (cf. Espiritu 1994, p. 267).

It is clear that all these features of their Asian upbringing, as described by my informants, could be understood not only as "Asian," but also as "immigrant," "ethnic," and, more specifically, "Korean" or "Chinese." The emphasis put on the educational achievement of children, for example, is an orientation that is widely prevalent among immigrants in general. However, these and other characteristics of their upbringing seemed to be powerfully related to the second generation's conceptions of what was particularly "Asian American" about them. Jenny, a Chinese American in her early thirties who was working in a clerical job, began to tell me about the distinctive child-rearing style of Chinese parents. But she easily and unconsciously moved on to talk of this style as not simply Chinese, but also as Asian:

> Chinese parents are stricter than American parents. Study hard, no dating till you're in college, that kind of thing. It was different for my friends. (*I: You mean your non-Chinese friends?*) Yeah, all my friends were white when I was growing up. I do know that a lot of other Asian kids go through the same thing, having strict parents and rules. It's an Asian thing. I appreciate it to some extent now, but I hated the rules when I was growing up.

What ultimately underlay the common child-rearing styles of Asian parents were "Asian values." In fact, common Asian values were at the heart of the second generation's understanding of an Asian American culture. These values were defined as an emphasis on family, education, honesty, hard work and respect for elders. Gordon, an unmarried Chinese American medical resident in his thirties, told me that although the women he dated were from diverse backgrounds, he wished to marry a Chinese American woman. His second choice would be an Asian American woman, because of the similarity of Chinese and Asian values. It is worth noting that the ideology of romantic love and individual choice in partner selection meshes easily with the notion that similarities in values between partners can result in a relationship that is both expressive and supportive of one's individuality:

> I date all kinds of women—black, white, Middle Eastern, Latin. I enjoy that. But when it comes to marriage it's different. When you get married, you want to approach your life in the ways that your parents taught you. And for the Chinese, that's education, hard work and honesty. (*I: So you would prefer to marry a Chinese woman?*) Yeah, although I have to admit I have yet to date a Chinese woman! But yeah, I would want to marry either a Chinese or Asian woman because they would share my beliefs about how to live your life.

But while Asians, in general, were associated with the core cultural values, the second generation also differentiated among Asian groups with respect to these values. It was East Asians (Chinese, Koreans and Japanese) who were the most closely associated with them. Soo Jin, a Korean American in her mid-twenties who had just finished law school, was living with her Chinese

American fiancé. She felt that Chinese, Koreans and Japanese shared the core values, but was unsure about just how strongly present they were among other Asians:

> As far as my relationship with Jim [her fiancé], I think it's important that Chinese have the same work ethic and the same sense of family as Koreans. I guess those are pretty much Asian things. (*I: Do you think all the Asian groups share them?*) Well, I think the Japanese do, and the Vietnamese and Filipinos to some extent, but not quite as strongly. It has to do with Confucianism; the countries that are more Confucian emphasize those things more.

Like Soo Jin, a number of informants saw the values of family, education, hard work and respect for elders as a legacy of the historical ties of the East Asian countries, especially the common influence of Confucianism.[8] This understanding of a common Confucian heritage among East Asians was reinforced by perceptions of the similar socio-economic status of East Asians. As I have described, the sense that Chinese, Japanese and Koreans were racially similar, certainly more so than other Asian groups, was supported by their generally favourable and comparable socio-economic image, both in the U.S. and abroad. Similarly, the sense of a shared Confucian heritage was reinforced by perceptions and images of East Asians as a success story, both in the U.S. and abroad. That is, the socio-economic status of East Asians provided positive proof of their association with the values of Confucianism. . . .

Among the variety of reasons that underlay the search for a partner who shared the emphasis on family was the need to affirm, through one's choice of partner, an identity that was distinct from "mainstream America." For many, "mainstream America" was in a state of social and moral decay due to an absence of the core values. George, a Korean American doctor in his mid-thirties who was married to a Korean American woman, felt particularly strongly about this issue. His words suggest that while they could be used

to mark one's Chinese or Korean identity, the core values could also work to define an ethnic identity in more general terms, to ward off the dangers of sinking into "mainstream America" with its lack of distinction and decaying moral fabric:

> The only thing that's really important to me about being Korean, marrying Korean, and raising my son in a home that is connected to Korean culture is family or family values. I think that family values are almost non-existent in general American society, and that's at the heart of a lot of the social problems, like crime and drugs. (*I: What do you mean by family values?*) I'm talking about the divorce rate, and the fact that parents don't spend time with their children. And the value on education and on respecting elders.

CONCLUSION

. . . In general, I found a pervasive sense of shared Asian American culture among the second-generation Chinese and Korean Americans, one that included but went beyond the racial commonality of Asians. In describing the substance of the common Asian culture, the second generation affirmed the popular U.S. stereotype of Asians as a "model minority." They felt that Asian Americans shared the experience of "an Asian upbringing" and socialization into the Asian values of education, family, hard work and respect for elders. This sense of a common Asian cultural background was explicitly constructed in opposition to white dominant U.S. culture. In other words, the second generation worked to create the boundaries of "Asian-ness" by distinguishing it from that of a homogeneously conceived white "mainstream" U.S. culture. . . .

While my findings suggest that forces of pan-Asian ethnogenesis are at work among certain segments of the Asian American population, they also raise questions about the significance and long-term viability of an Asian American identity. For most of my informants, their ethnic identity as

Chinese or Korean American was far more important to them than their Asian American one. Their Chinese or Korean affiliation carried with it membership in a community that had a deep and rich sense of history and culture, and ongoing social ties and networks. In comparison, membership in "Asian America" carried with it less tangible significance. Ultimately, then, the future of pan-Asian ethnicity in the U.S. depends heavily on the fate of the national ethnic identities of Asian-origin individuals.

NOTES

1. I define "second generation" to include those who are the children of immigrants, and have been born and/or raised in the U.S. since the age of twelve or earlier.
2. I define a racial group as one that is socially defined primarily on the basis of physical criteria and an ethnic group as one that is distinguished primarily on the basis of culture or nationality (Feagin 1989, p. 9). These criteria are not mutually exclusive: the boundaries of racial and ethnic groups overlap in significant and complex ways.
3. While an exhaustive comparison of the Korean and Chinese communities in the U.S. is outside the scope of this article, some relevant differences include the longer history of Chinese settlement in the U.S., dating from the early nineteenth century, in comparison to the overwhelmingly post-1965 origins of the Korean-origin population in the U.S. At the same time, both Chinese and Korean immigration have been a substantial part of the post-1965 immigration flow into the U.S. In comparison to Chinese Americans, Korean Americans are more homogeneous in their pre-migration social background and, thus, exhibit more solidarity in their community structure.
4. Rates of intermarriage among Asian-origin groups are lower than for Native Americans and Pacific Islanders, but far higher than for whites and African Americans (Jacobs and Labov 1995). According to Lee and Yamanaka (1990), within the Asian-origin groups, rates of intermarriage are highest for the Japanese, followed by Koreans, Filipinos, Vietnamese, Chinese and Indians. An analysis by Jacobs and Labov (1995) suggests, however, that the reported rates of intermarriage among Koreans and Vietnamese may be somewhat misleading and inflated in that they include "war brides" or foreign-born women who are married to U.S.-born veterans.
5. The comparable figures for native-born Chinese and Korean American men are 37.6 per cent and 69.4 per cent respectively (Lee and Yamanaka 1990).
6. The comparable figures for Chinese American women, Korean American women, and Korean American men respectively are 24.6 per cent, 27.8 per cent and 48.1 per cent (Lee and Yamanaka 1990). Unfortunately these percent-

ages are not broken down to indicate the specific Asian ancestry of the spouse.
7. For ease of presentation, I refer to the subjects of the study—second-generation Chinese and Korean Americans—as "the second generation" throughout the article.
8. While not acknowledged by the informants, Confucianism has also been influential in Vietnam, and, to a lesser extent, in other South East Asian countries.

REFERENCES

Bacon, Jean 1997 *Life Lines: Community, Family and Assimilation among Chicago's Asian Indians,* New York: Oxford University Press

Barth, Fredrik 1969 *Ethnic Groups and Boundaries,* Boston, MA: Little Brown

Cheung, King-Kok 1990 "The woman warrior versus the Chinaman Pacific: must a Chinese American critic choose between feminism and heroism?," in Marianne Hirsch and Evelyn Fox Keller (eds.), *Conflicts in Feminism,* New York and London: Routledge, Chapman and Hall, pp. 234–51

Espiritu, Yen L. 1992 *Asian American Panethnicity: Bridging Institutions and Identities,* Philadelphia, PA: Temple University Press

——— 1994 "The intersection of race, ethnicity and class: the multiple identities of second-generation Filipinos," *Identities,* vol. 1, nos. 2–3, pp. 249–73

Espiritu, Yen L. and Ong, Paul 1994 "Class constraints on racial solidarity among Asian Americans," in Paul Ong, Edna Bonacich and Lucie Cheng (eds.), *The New Asian Immigration in Los Angeles and Global Restructuring,* Philadelphia, PA: Temple University Press, pp. 295–321

Feagin, Joe 1989 *Racial and Ethnic Relations,* Englewood Cliffs, NJ: Prentice-Hall

Frankenburg, Ruth 1993 *White Women, Race Matters: The Social Construction of Whiteness,* Minneapolis, MN: University of Minnesota Press

Jacobs, Jerry A. and Labov, Teresa 1995 "Sex differences in Asian-American intermarriage: Asian exceptionalism reconsidered," unpublished paper presented at the Annual Meetings of the American Sociological Association, Washington DC, August

Lee, Sharon and Yamanaka, Keiko 1990 "Patterns of Asian American intermarriage and marital assimilation," *Journal of Comparative Family Studies,* vol. 21, no. 2, pp. 287–305

Lowe, Lisa 1991 "Heterogeneity, hybridity, multiplicity: marking Asian American differences," *Diaspora,* vol. 1, no. 1, pp. 24–44

Nagel, Joane 1994 "Constructing ethnicity: creating and recreating ethnic identity and culture," *Social Problems,* vol. 41, no. 1, pp. 152–76

Pang, Gin Y. 1994 "Attitudes towards interracial and interethnic relationships and intermarriage among Korean Americans: the intersections of race, gender and class inequality," in Franklin Ng, Judy Yung, Stephen Fugita and Elaine Kim (eds.), *New Visions in Asian American Studies: Diversity, Community, Power,* Pullman, WA: Washington State University Press, pp. 112–19

Puar, Jasbir K. 1995 "Resituating discourses of "whiteness" and "Asianness" in Northern England: second-generation Sikh women and the construction of identity," *Socialist Review,* vol. 24, nos. 1 and 2, pp. 21–54

Spickard, Paul 1989 *Mixed Blood: Intermarriage and Ethnic Identity in Twentieth Century America,* Madison, WI: University of Wisconsin Press

Wallman, Sandra 1986 "Ethnicity and the boundary process in context," in John Rex and David Mason (eds.), *Theories of Race and Ethnic Relations,* Cambridge: Cambridge University Press, pp. 226–45

? Think about It

1. Explain the complexity of outmarriage ethnic boundaries in terms of socioeconomic status, mate availability and a "hierarchy of preference."

2. How do outmarriage boundary dilemmas promote a sense of "pan-Asian-ness"? What role, for instance, do factors such as lineage purity, racism in the United States, racial communality, and Asian American stereotypes play in shaping mate selection?

3. How do immigrant stories as well as Asian American culture, religion, family values, and childhood experiences discourage marriage outside of the Asian American community?

16 Turkish American Intermarriage

Barbara Bilgé

In Reading 15, Nazli Kibria discusses intermarriage among second-generation, middle-class Chinese and Korean Americans. Here Barbara Bilgé examines the family life of affluent Turkish American couples. She provides insights into their relations with kin, the quality of marital bonds, and the transmission of Turkish values to children and grandchildren. *

. . . This study of intermarried Turkish-American couples is derived from my research on variations in family structure and organization within the older and more recent Turkish communities in Michigan and nearby Ontario (Bilgé, 1984). I identified thirty-three heterogamous couples in the post–World War II community; of these, I was able to gather comprehensive data on twenty-six and less complete data on the remaining seven. My association with this ethnic community began as a married-in, foreign insider and lasted twenty-one years, after which I divorced. However, I remain enmeshed in its webs of friendship and retain membership in the Turkish-American Cultural Association of Michigan (TACAM). . . .

Focusing on the intermarried couples, differences in socioeconomic background within the cohort of post–World War II Turkish immigrant men here described, their diverse paths to North America, and their American wives' ethnicities and social class origins have produced significant variations in their family relations. Nevertheless,

*This excerpt is from Bilgé's larger analysis of intermarriage, which includes working-class and middle-class (especially ex-military) Turks and their non-Turkish spouses. *Ed.*

Source: From Barbara Bilgé, "Turkish-American Patterns of Intermarriage," in *Family and Gender among American Muslims: Issues Facing Middle Eastern Immigrants and Their Descendants,* ed. Barbara C. Aswad and Barbara Bilgé (Philadelphia: Temple University Press, 1996), 59–106. By permission of Temple University Press. Copyright © 1996 by Temple University. All rights reserved.

they can be categorized into three major groups: working-class families; middle-class, ex-military Turks and their non-Turkish spouses; and families of affluent doctors and engineers who were civilians when they were students in the United States or Canada. Couples within each category show similar family dynamics but differ significantly in this respect from couples of the other categories.

AFFLUENT FAMILIES

My contacts with purely Turkish and mixed, wealthy couples occurred during large parties at their homes and at TACAM events. However, my close friendships with affluent Turks have been with three purely Turkish families rather than with those of the mixed couples. Gaps in information about the latter were filled by in-depth, ethnographic interviews, genealogies, and life histories of six couples. The section below describes the family life of these six couples. My information about the other seven mixed, affluent couples in the community, though not as complete, shows similar patterns.

Husbands' Backgrounds

Though the nationality and self-stated identity of all the men is Turk, their ancestors include Georgian Turks, Crimean Tatars, Circassians, and Laz. All interview respondents could trace ancestors in their paternal lines back at least three generations and often more, unlike most men in the other two groups, many of whom knew little about their grandparents. Lineages of some affluent men contained nomads who were settled in central and eastern Anatolia in the nineteenth century by the Ottoman government. Their descendants became landowners and government officials. Many were known locally for their piety and charity. Fathers of the Turks in this group included a local administrator in the Turkish republic's postal service, a career military officer, a newspaper editor jailed for leading the liberal opposition against Ataturk in the 1930s, and a Muslim lawyer who also managed a lucrative flour mill. Some of the men's mothers were literate in both Turkish and Arabic in the old Arabic script. All were homemakers. Some, according to their American daughters-in-law, were "liberated women."

The fathers of the intermarried, affluent men were able to support them and some of their siblings, even a few of their sisters, during their completion of professional degrees in Turkey's finest institutions of higher learning, a strategy pursued for family advancement by forward-looking, eastern Anatolian elites in smaller cities and towns as Turkey began to modernize after World War II (Aswad 1971, 1978; and Eberhard 1970). Five of the six male respondents were physicians who came to the United States for advanced training in medical specialties such as plastic surgery or radiology. The sixth earned a B.S., then an M.S. in engineering at the University of Michigan. All were Turkish civilians with student or special visas on arrival.

Wives' Backgrounds

The American wives were born into middle- to working-class families, so the Turks married women of lower socioeconomic class origins than their own. Five women are, ethnically, WASP Americans. One of them was born in Scotland of a mother whose ancestors included sea captains and makers of fine footwear. . . . Her first marriage to a Scotsman produced two children, but ended in divorce. She migrated to the United States, becoming a naturalized citizen in 1958. Another woman's English-born parents migrated to Canada, then to the United States. Her father, a commercial artist, died soon after her birth in Detroit. Her mother worked as an accountant to support her, an only child. The third woman's ancestors left England to settle in Mississippi in the 1730s. She showed me her thick, family history books with genealogical tables and vignettes of her now widely dispersed, numerous kin. Her father had a small, commercially-oriented farm, and her mother was a homemaker. Another woman of English ancestry was born in Missouri, where her father had a tiny farm, which he sold; then he was employed as a truck driver. Her mother worked part time as a motel clerk. The fifth wife had Irish and German ancestors. Her father, a policeman in Massachusetts, left the Catholic church, switching to a Presbyterian congregation; her mother kept house and raised the six children. The only Catholic among the six wives I interviewed is of Polish ancestry. Both her father and mother were born in America of immigrant parents and were bilingual. Both also worked in factories in northern Ohio.

The women were educated primarily in public U.S. or in British schools. Two took a few art courses after graduating from high school, where they majored in the commercial curriculum. Neither pursued a university education. Both were skilled medical secretaries when they met their husbands. A third earned certification in X-ray technology at a junior college. Two women graduated as registered nurses after training in university hospitals. One woman completed her B.A. and M.A. in education at two southern universities and also took classes at a Methodist seminary. While in college, she directed church-sponsored summer programs for children and taught high school social studies at an Appalachian boarding school. In 1951 she was hired as an administrator by the University of Michigan.

Courtship and Weddings

Five spouse pairs met in hospitals where the Turkish doctors were interns and their future wives were nurses, medical technicians, or secretaries. The engineer and his wife met at a weekend social for Turkish students hosted by the University of Michigan, where she worked. In some cases, the women initiated dating. One asked her husband-to-be and his Turkish roommates to dinner in her apartment. In other cases, the men asked the women out. One asked the medical secretary with whom he had interacted at work to a Turkish ball. The time span between first date and marriage proposal ranged from eight to eighteen months. One couple dated, broke off and dated others for about a month, then decided to marry.

Three weddings were conducted by a justice-of-the-peace, with a few friends present. In two, no kin from either side attended. In the third, parents on both sides vehemently opposed the couple's marriage on religious grounds. However, the wife's family came to the modest American wedding, and her parents gave them a small reception afterwards in their home. When the couple went to Turkey to introduce the bride to the husband's family, his parents accepted her completely. To please her husband, she had converted to Islam. His father then held a Muslim wedding ceremony (*nikâh*) for the couple in his home. Two couples were wed in Protestant churches by ministers who did not require the husbands to convert or pledge any children they might have to the church. The Polish Catholic woman and her husband were married in a Catholic church after he completed a course of instructions and promised to bring up their children as Catholics. This couple saved their money to pay for an elaborate church wedding and lavish reception. Her family attended.

Relations with Kin

None of the couples reported any significant tensions between themselves and the wife's relatives.

Before their marriages, four men already had completed their mandatory two-year term of military service required of all Turkish male citizens. One of these couples lived in Turkey the first four years after their marriage. The husband taught medicine at a Turkish university in Izmir while his wife worked as an intensive care nurse at the U.S. air force base there. Their eldest child was born in Turkey during these years. The other three couples lived in the United States. They could freely visit Turkey at any time, but did not make their first trip overseas until four to eleven years after their weddings. The two remaining Turks still had to fulfill their military service. One did so by working as a physician at an American air force base, his wife, meanwhile, was a medical secretary at its commissary. The engineer and his wife, however, actually divorced so he could serve his term. Nevertheless, she lived with his kin, working first as a secretary, then as assistant personnel manager for Mobil Oil Corporation in Turkey. She and her husband remarried in Turkey after he completed his military service, had their marriage registered in the U.S. embassy, and then returned to the United States.

Thereafter, the five doctors' families have visited Turkey every three to six years, in summer, when their children have been on vacation from school. The doctors stay two to five weeks, but leave their wives and children with relatives for two or three months. American wives praised the generous hospitality of their in-laws and spoke of gatherings of many of their husbands' kin at meals in their homes or at restaurants, gift exchanges, shopping excursions, and visits with his relatives to points of interest. One woman explained, "Life there is different (i.e., more gregarious). Here we lead singular lives, cut off even from neighbors. In Turkey, women go out every day to stroll, visit, shop. They see neighbors and friends all the time." These overseas visits also have given the children frequent, prolonged, largely positive experiences in their fathers' homeland and contribute greatly to their pride in their Turkish heritage. Moreover, every three to six years, the doctors have funded, at least in part, trips to America from Turkey by their parents, siblings, cousins, and even nieces and nephews. Only the engineer and his wife did not return to Turkey for a visit until twenty-five years after they left his homeland to settle in the United States. Their vacations, over the years, were confined to the United States. However, after their children left home to attend universities, this couple took in unrelated, college exchange students from Turkey.

Factors Affecting Marital Relations

When interviewed in the early 1980s, both spouses of four couples reported happy marriages, despite occasional disagreements. These couples are so licitous of one another and relaxed wherever I encounter them. Wives of the other two couples reported troubles in their marriages. One of these couples divorced in 1994.

After moving to successively larger homes and more upscale neighborhoods, all couples occupied spacious homes by the later 1970s. Interior decor ranges from American colonial, to eighteenth century French to modern. Turkish heritage is expressed strongly in four houses, hardly at all in the other two. Ornamental Turkish items seen in these homes include fine carpets, brass braziers, etched copper plaques, traditional pottery vases, dishes, and tiles crafted in Kutahya, cut glass tea sets, and dolls wearing regional folk or historical Ottoman costumes.

All six couples, even the two with troubled marriages, do not fight over money. The five doctors were earning between $60,000 and $150,000 annually by the early 1980s; in addition they and their wives had large savings accounts, stocks, and bonds. Four couples owned lots, apartments, condominia, or homes in Turkey, and one had a condominium in Florida as well. One physician and the engineer have no Turkish properties but have other assets.

All couples have joint checking accounts, Three wives write most checks and balance the

family budget. Even where the husbands do the family bookkeeping, their wives said they buy what they please, either charging or writing checks for their purchases. They receive ample household allowances, and their requests for extra money are granted generously. Three spouse pairs shop together and make joint decisions on major purchases such as cars and appliances. Two husbands make financial decisions for the family after consulting their wives. One wife said she makes all major purchases after obtaining her husband's opinion. None of the women were working in the early 1980s, and they had not worked for fifteen to twenty years. Two employ a maid to clean their homes once a week. The others do all their housework themselves.

Each wife learned how to cook Turkish food, which she prepares once a week on average and serves when entertaining both Turkish and American friends. Turkish customs adopted by wives and transmitted to children include respectful behavior toward elders and removing shoes before entering the home. One doctor's wife especially enjoys Turkish hospitality. She commented that none of her relatives ever drop in on kin or friends unannounced, as Turks do. Four of the wives were active in TACAM.

English is spoken predominantly in all households. One couple said they speak Turkish in the presence of their children if they want to keep something secret from them. One doctor periodically ruled that only Turkish be spoken at home, which never lasted more than twenty-four hours before everyone lapsed into English. All the wives know some Turkish. Those who lived in Turkey a year or more can understand most Turkish conversations. Two speak fluent Turkish and read Turkish language magazines and newspapers. All the Turkish husbands speak idiomatic English, two with no trace of an accent.

The men's desire to preserve Turkish identity is reflected most sharply in their attitudes toward becoming U.S. citizens. During the swearing-in naturalization ceremony, immigrants must repudiate citizenship in any other nation. The United

States does not recognize dual citizenship. Two doctors and the engineer were glad to become American citizens. One doctor said he especially values the political freedom Americans enjoy by law. These three men retain their pride in their Turkish ancestry and cultural heritage, but are committed to making a good life for themselves and their children in the United States. The three remaining doctors acquired U.S. citizenship reluctantly, to remain in the United States for the sake of their wives and children. Until 1971 no foreign doctors in America could renew their medical licenses after practicing here for seven years unless they became U.S. citizens. Their seven-year terms expired in the late 1960s and in 1970, so they became U.S. citizens.

The loyalty conflicts the Turkish doctors experienced disappeared in 1982, when Turkey recognized dual citizenship. People born of a Turkish parent, in Turkey or elsewhere, are always Turkish citizens, even if they become citizens of another country. Children with only one Turkish parent, if living outside Turkey, must decide at age eighteen whether or not to become Turkish citizens.

Islam never became an issue among these couples. Four of the men are secularized agnostics. One is a nominal Muslim, and one is best described as a Unitarian-like Muslim. Only these last two expressed a mild interest in making the *haj,* and both of their wives converted to Islam. One is more pious than her husband in most aspects of Islam, but she occasionally accepts an alcoholic beverage at a party. Her husband is the only abstainer from alcohol among the six affluent Turks. Neither the Muslim husbands nor their converted wives pray five times a day. All six families occasionally eat pork. They usually attend TACAM sponsored *bayram* festivities, but do not fast during *Ramadan.*

The secularized doctor who married the Polish-American Catholic woman saw that their children were reared in the Church, as he had promised. Five families celebrated Christian holidays when their children lived at home. Christmas trees, gifts,

and Easter baskets were annual highlights. One Muslim physician whose wife converted to Islam enjoyed celebrating Christmas and Easter with his wife and children, noting that Muslims honor Jesus as a Prophet second only to Muhammad. Only the nominally Muslim doctor forbade Christmas trees and Easter baskets in his house. Despite his wife's conversion to Islam, she wanted to have them for their children's enjoyment. Heated arguments over this issue would erupt between them so she finally kept quiet and yielded to his wishes.

One couple's marriage has been marred by the husband's attempt to dominate his wife, who, according to some Turkish women, never stood up to him. His frequent temper tantrums and occasional physical abuse of her and their children are found in countless purely American marriages and have nothing to do with Islam or Turkish heritage. Turkish men are apt to be more verbally assertive than most American men, quickly ignited but just as quickly cooling off. As one contented wife put it, "We (i.e., Americans) must learn how to cope with the Turkish male disposition, which is difficult to adjust to, but in the end, you learn."

As noted above, one couple divorced in 1994 after some thirty years of marriage. The husband's adultery and belittling of his wife's capabilities finally drove her from him.

Children and Grandchildren

All the affluent couples have children, ranging from one to six per couple. Styles of child rearing and areas of cultural conflict among these couples echo those described previously for the ex-military couples. Four of the Turks were "too strict" with their children and "tended to yell" at them, according to their American wives, three of whom admitted that they too shouted at their naughty offspring sometimes. Only in one family, however, did the children fear and avoid their father who rarely showed them affection. The three other fathers were loving and jovial toward their children when pleased with their behavior.

The engineer and his wife did not tolerate disrespect or disobedience from their children, but rarely shouted at them and always backed one another's disciplinary measures, usually deprivation of something valued, or grounding. These are the ideal middle- and upper-middle class American patterns described above. One woman said her husband was so indulgent, both to his adopted daughter from her first marriage and to their son, that she became the children's primary disciplinarian.

All the Turkish fathers suffered as their daughters began to express interest in boys. The men felt pressured to concede their girls' "reasonable" requests in order to keep their own and their beloved daughters' sanity intact. Mixed gender group activities, known and approved boy friends, curfews, and going to high-school proms, were norms in these families, all well within the mainstream American range of variation. Virginity before marriage was mandatory for daughters, but not as important for sons. Teenage sons were free to date whom they pleased and stay out as late as they wished, as long as they did not get into trouble. The recent divorcée declared, during our interview in the early 1980s, that when her son turned sixteen, her husband would take him out and "teach him the ropes," which she opposed and hoped to prevent.

Today all the children are young adults. All have bachelor's degrees, and some have master's degrees. The young men's occupations include architect, microbiologist, chemist, optometrist, and owner of a small consulting business. The young women include a psychological counselor, school administrator, nurses, an executive secretary, an office worker with her own art studio on the side, a business consultant, and married, full-time homemakers. Many of the children are geographically scattered, living in states other than Michigan, where their parents still reside.

Of the twenty natural children of these couples, five daughters and two sons have married. One girl wed an Italian-American, Roman Catholic law student; another a Puerto Rican medical student; and a third an American whom she met at the university they both attended. Two young women wed Turks; both now are divorced. One of them married a first cousin, with whom she fell in love during a visit to Turkey. The other eloped with a nephew of one of the community's affluent Turkish couples. Her father had opposed the marriage, but allowed them to live in his house . . . while he and his wife took a prolonged trip to Turkey. Her brother married an American of Eastern European ancestry in a Roman Catholic church. The father did not attend the nuptials, nor did his wife, who wished to, but did not for fear her husband would "blow up" and ruin the ceremony. Turks were not invited to the church wedding, which hurt the groom deeply, but his parents and their Turkish friends came to the reception afterwards.

Nine offspring of three doctors have a strong sense of their Turkish as well as American identity. One son, for example, became active on TACAM's Youth Committee while a university student in the 1980s, and he joined a Turkish Student Association. Today he remains active in the TACAM. He and another young man have taken Turkish citizenship, which requires all males to do a term of military service. They both fulfilled this requirement by paying a fee to the Turkish courts, which then reduced their term of service to two months. The failed marriages of the two women who married Turks were not forced upon them, and they remain proud of their Turkish ancestry and heritage. Their many visits to relatives in Turkey over the years and their American mothers' love of and respect for Turkish culture have helped build these women's love of their fathers' homeland.

The first grandchild was born in 1983, and more have arrived since. All are young, but some already have been to Turkey.

REFERENCES

Aswad, Barbara C. 1971. *Property Control and Social Strategies: Settlers on a Middle Eastern Plain.* Anthropological Papers, no. 44. Museum of Anthropology, University of Michigan.

————. 1978. "Women, Class, and Power: Examples from the Hatay, Turkey." Pp. 473–481 in *Women in the Muslim World,* ed. Lois Beck and Nikki Keddie. Cambridge: Harvard University Press.

Bilgé, Barbara J. 1984. "Variations in Family Structure and Organization in the Turkish Community of Southeast Michigan and Adjacent Canada." Ph.D. diss., Department of anthropology, Wayne State University, Detroit.

Eberhard, Wolfram. 1970. "Changes in Leading Families in Southern Turkey." Pp. 242–256 in *Peoples and Cultures of the Middle East,* ed. Louise E. Sweet. Garden City, N.Y.: Natural History Press.

Think about It

1. During courtship and marriage, what was the range of reactions by the couples' parents?
2. How did husbands and wives accommodate their spouses' cultural norms and values?
3. The affluent families in Bilgé's study transmitted a Turkish identity to their offspring. What role, if any, did the husband's socioeconomic status play in his "Americanization" and in the children's internalization of their Turkish heritage?

CHAPTER 4

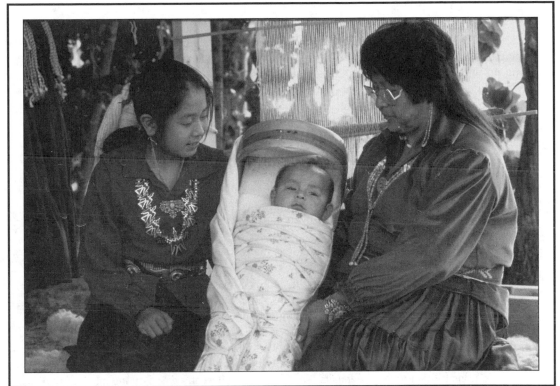

Parenting

This chapter incorporates two themes. First, the material shows how ethnic parents ensure the family's survival and continuity despite numerous obstacles. Second, each reading addresses topics that researchers have largely neglected or issues about which misconceptions are widespread.

We begin with a look at fathers. Only during the last decade have researchers focused on fatherhood and fathers' involvement in child rearing. As a result, we know little about fathering, especially in ethnic families, and often assume that fathers play a minimal role in their children's development. John F. Toth Jr. and Xiaohe Xu show, however, that black, white, and Latino fathers are very involved in raising their children (Reading 17). Toth and Xu's results indicate that there are more similarities than differences across the three groups but that black and Latino fathers surpass their white counterparts in activities such as monitoring and supervising their offspring's behavior. These results are consistent with other recent studies that show that ethnic parents, including fathers, are interested in their children's behavior and in teaching young children skills (such as reading and counting) and responsibility.[1]

There is a wealth of information on black families. Much of the material, however, focuses on mother-headed households, especially those in lower socioeconomic classes or mothers who are on welfare. It's true that black children have a greater likelihood of growing up with only one parent than do children in Latino, Asian American, Mideastern, or white families. In 1999, however, 47 percent of black households were married couples.[2] Why do we rarely hear about parenting in married-couple black families?

Susan D. Toliver fills part of this gap in her study of middle- and upper-middle-class black families (Reading 18). She shows that affluent black parents are better able than many other African Americans to prepare their children for adulthood because the "Baby Bumps" enjoy educational opportunities and benefit from their parents' resources. Toliver argues, however, that these privileged backgrounds create a paradox: growing up in isolated and "race neutral" communities diminishes parents' ability to instill a sense of black identity and protects children from the overt and subtle forms of racial discrimination that they will encounter.

Unlike more isolated middle-class families, many low-income white, American Indian, and Latino parents often depend on family, relatives, and friends for support, especially in buffering stressful child-rearing circumstances. These social networks may provide instrumental support (by loaning money, for example), but more typically they provide emotional support (for example, by providing reassurance and encouragement).[3]

A growing body of research, especially since the 1970s, has documented the existence of extensive kin networks within black communities.[4] These networks include *fictive kin,* close friends who are regarded in kinship terms and who receive the same respect and have the same responsibility as family members (see Chapter 1 and Reading 4). Among many Latino families, fictive kin include *compadrazgo,* close friends who provide child-rearing support.[5] As Rebecca A. López shows (Reading 19), *comadres,* or godmothers, assist mothers in co-parenting. By sharing parenting responsibilities and providing other assistance, *comadres* make critical contributions to the survival of single-mother households otherwise at risk because of the mothers' undocumented status, language, or cultural barriers.

The literature on parenting gay and lesbian children is extensive, but only a modest amount of it examines parent–child relationships—especially outside of black and white families. Often, moreover, the approach is clinical and therapeutic (helping people accept and cope with their homosexuality) rather than descriptive or analytical.[6] Although there are scattered paragraphs about parenting gay and lesbian children in Latino, Asian, American Indian, and Mideast immigrant families, there is a dearth of research in this area. An exception is Alice Y. Hom's exploratory study of Asian American parents' attitudes and reactions to their children's homosexuality (Reading 20). Hom shows that reactions (and not unlike those of black and white parents) vary. Some parents react with horror or outrage; others are accepting. Mothers tend to blame themselves ("What did I do wrong?"). Asian American parents' reactions are particularly complex, Hom suggests, because many live in close-knit ethnic enclaves. The parents worry that their status and reputation in the community will suffer or that family members will stigmatize them as bad parents.

Whether their children are gay or straight, recent immigrants, especially, are sensitive about their gender and parenting roles and responsibilities.[7] In their study of Jordanian mothers, for example, Marianne Hattar-Pollara and Afaf I. Meleis show how and why parents feel pressure to conform to the larger U.S. ethnic community's expectations (Reading 21). Because a child's behavior (or misbehavior) always reflects on the mother, women in the Jordanian family must be "good mothers" both within and outside of the family unit. These pressures are especially stressful because many recent immigrants are also coping with daily living problems such as language barriers, isolation, unfriendly neighbors, and child-rearing values at odds with their traditional or religious beliefs.[8]

NOTES

1. Ruth K. Chao, "Beyond Parental Control and Authoritarian Parenting Style: Understanding Chinese Parenting through the Cultural Notion of Training," *Child Development* 65 (1994): 1111–19; Teresa W. Julian, Patrick C. McKenry, and Mary W. McKelvey, "Cultural Variations in Parenting: Perceptions of Caucasian, African-American, Hispanic, and Asian-American Parents," *Family Relations* 43 (January 1994): 30–38; and Theodore C. Wagemaar and Rodney D. Coates, "Race and Children: The Dynamics of Early Socialization," *Education* 120 (Winter 1999): 220–36.
2. U.S. Department of Commerce News, "Profile of the Country's African American Population Released by Census Bureau," www.census.gov/Press-Release/www/2000/eb00-27.html (accessed June 29, 2000).
3. David MacPhee, Janet Fritz, and Jan Miller-Heyl, "Ethnic Variations in Personal Social Networks and Parenting," *Child Development* (December 1996): 3278–95.
4. For a good review of much of this research, see Linda M. Chatters, Robert Joseph Taylor, and Rukmalie Jay Akody, "Fictive Kinship Relations in Black Extended Families," *Journal of Comparative Family Studies* 25 (Fall 1994): 297–312.
5. Close friends can be important sources of child-rearing support within middle classes as well. For example, in a study of 760 Latino parents, almost 30 percent of whom had at least two years of college, 75 percent of the respondents indicated that they prefer to receive parenting information from friends or family rather than from other sources, such as books. See Karen B. DeBord and Julia T. Reguero de Atiles, "Latino Parents: Unique Preferences for Learning about Parenting," *The Forum for Family and Consumer Issues* 4.1 (1999), www.ces.ncsu.edu/depts/fcs/pub/1999/latino.html (accessed March 14, 2000).
6. See, for example, Joan Laird and Robert-Jay Green, ed., *Lesbians and Gays in Couples and Families: A Handbook for Therapists* (San Francisco: Jossey-Bass, 1996); Joseph F. Aponted and Julian Wohl, eds., *Psychological Intervention and Cultural Diversity*, 2d ed. (Boston: Allyn and Bacon, 2000).
7. See Haideh Moghissi, "Away from Home: Iranian Women, Displacement, Cultural Resistance and Change," *Journal of Comparative Family Studies* 30 (Spring 1999): 207–17.
8. Several other studies provide valuable insights about the problems that immigrant parents encounter when traditional family practices and ideology clash with dominant Euro-American values. See, for example, Lydia De Santis and Doris Noel Ugarriza, "Potential for Intergenerational Conflict in Cuban and Haitian Immigrant Familes," *Archives of Psychiatric Nursing* 9 (December 1995): 354–64; Diane L. Wolf, "Family Secrets: Transnational Struggles among Children of Filipino Immigrants," *Sociological Perspectives* 40 (1997): 457–82; and Yu-Wen Ying and Chua Chiem Chao, "Intergenerational Relationships in Iu Mien American Families," *Amerasia Journal* 22 (1996): 47–64.

17 Fathers' Child-Rearing Involvement in African American, Latino, and White Families

John F. Toth Jr. and Xiaohe Xu

Using national-level data, John F. Toth Jr. and Xiaohe Xu examine fathers' participation in three child-rearing domains—behavioral, affective, and cognitive. They show that fathers' involvement varies considerably across these areas and that black and Latino fathers outperform white fathers in the cognitive domain.

Child-rearing studies have often underemphasized fathers (Phares, 1996). One reason for this neglect historically has been the general cultural belief that women are naturally suited for parenting while men are disinterested in active parenting. During the last decade, increased research attention has focused on fatherhood and fathers' involvement in child care (see Marsiglio, 1993, for a cogent review). At the start of the new millennium, the research on fatherhood continues to spearhead new directions and new insights. Though scholars have moved beyond the theoretical treatment of fathering as a unidimensional phenomenon (e.g., Lamb, 1987; Palkovitz, 1997; cf. Silverstein, 1996), empirical research continues to lag behind theoretical and conceptual developments. Put differently, scholars now think about fathering as an activity that is comprised of many facets of physical and emotional participation in the lives of their sons and daughters. However, the collection of data has not kept pace with this new thinking. Researchers have tended to study only one or two sides of fathering rather than explore the many aspects simultaneously.

In particular, most studies have not incorporated new measures of fathers' involvement. Palkovitz (1997: 208) has noted, for example, that "because [new theoretical developments] are not studied in empirical research, we do not have good descriptions of the ways that men and women are truly involved in parenting." While most discussions emphasize the multidimensional character of fathers' involvement, prior research has not yet clearly identified distinct domains of fathering and then examined them both empirically and quantitatively. Given these gaps, it is important to bridge theoretical and conceptual developments with empirical research.

Specifically, research is needed to explicate racial and cultural/ideological differences in fathers' involvement. There is limited empirical information about racial and cultural variations in fathering and these sources too often follow stereotypical depictions of ethnic minority fathers as less capable than white fathers (see Marsiglio, 1993). Moreover, prior research has often yielded inconsistent or understated findings regarding racial and cultural variables. Cooksey and Fondell (1996), for instance, found significant racial/ethnic variations in their analysis of fathering

Source: Adapted from John F. Toth Jr. and Xiaohe Xu, "Ethnic and Cultural Diversity in Fathers' Involvement: A Racial/Ethnic Comparison of African American, Hispanic, and White Fathers," a revised version of an original article appearing in *Youth & Society* 31 (September 1999): 76–99. Reprinted by permission of the authors.

behavior, but treated race as a control variable rather than as a systemic part of the theoretical perspective and, consequently, gave race limited conceptual notice in their discussion. Indeed, a misconception in the literature on parent–child relations in general and father–child relations in particular is the belief that involvement is theoretically and empirically uniform in a culturally and racially diverse nation (Palkovitz, 1997). Contrary to this common misconception, cultural factors such as fathers' nontraditional gender ideology and commitment to the parenting role result in greater child care participation (Baruch & Barnett, 1981; Minton & Pasley, 1996).

This paper makes several research contributions in this area. First, for the first time, we utilize and test a theoretically up-to-date multidimensional conceptualization of fathers' involvement. It is one of only a few studies which have examined simultaneously more than one fathering domain. Second, we investigate variations in involvement for African American, Latino, and white fathers in a nationally representative sample, with a particular focus on three distinct involvement domains for children aged five to eighteen years old. Third, by examining family and gender ideologies alone and as interconnected with race, we analyze the interplay between culture and race and its effect on men's participation in the fathering role. Finally, we scrutinize commitment to the paternal role, parental values, and the interconnection between these and race, while controlling for relevant sociodemographic factors.

DIMENSIONS OF FATHERS' INVOLVEMENT

Researchers' use of the term "involvement" or "fathers' involvement" has typically lacked conceptual clarity, making it difficult to compare research findings across studies. Lamb (1987) addressed this weakness by conceptualizing fathering in a systematic fashion. His triple-dimensional taxonomy of involvement became an industry stan-

dard: (a) engagement or interaction, the time spent in actual face-to-face contact with the child; (b) accessibility, the time spent in close proximity to the child but not actually interacting one-on-one with the child; and (c) responsibility, a feeling of having a moral obligation to ensure that children's needs are met. Though Lamb's model has served as a catalyst in the development of sophisticated domains of fathers' involvement since the late 1980s, an array of empirical studies tended to focus primarily on only one domain, usually engagement.

In line with Lamb's (1987) early work, Palkovitz (1997) conceptualized three involvement domains: *behavioral,* including overtly observable manifestations of involvement, such as feeding, talking to, teaching, etc.; *affective,* consisting of emotions, feelings, and affection; and *cognitive,* encompassing reasoning, planning, evaluating, and monitoring. For purposes of this study, we emphasize one of Palkovitz's key theoretical assumptions for the model: involvement should vary by race and culture, because these variables affect involvement. This assumption implies that the social environment influences people. And, as part of this larger context, a person's racial or ethnic identity filters how life is experienced as well as how and why individuals interact with others, including their families. Cultural traditions and beliefs about gender roles and family ideology also shape parenting behavior.

RACE/ETHNICITY, CULTURE, AND FATHERING

Based on an extensive review of the literature, we argue that a major shortcoming of past research on fathers' involvement is its limited discussion of race/ethnicity and culture. Simultaneous comparison of fathers' involvement across racial/ethnic groups in the United States are extremely rare (see Bartz & Levine, 1978, and Cooksey & Fondell, 1996, as partial exceptions). This lack of research attention, along with a myopic view of what constitutes involvement, contributes partially to a deficit model of fathering. To move beyond this research confinement, we place central emphasis on racial/ethnic and cultural diversity in American fathers' involvement in child rearing. In the following sections, we examine relevant aspects of African American and Latino family life in comparison to whites to develop a picture of how men's participation in fathering may vary by race/ethnicity.

African American Families and Fathers

African American families, like other minority families in the United States, must deal with the historical legacy and current manifestations of racism. For parents, this means that their children will at some point encounter racism in some form and that parents will have to respond to this fact (LeMasters & Defrain, 1983). In addition, the disproportionate level of economic hardship endured by African American families makes parenting difficult. Regardless of their economic and educational achievement, parents expect their children to reach high in their goals (DeGenova, 1997). Despite these expectations, there exist very real structural and cultural differences within and across economic groups.

In many ways, African American fathers may not "fit" the traditional models of fatherhood discussed in the literature. Ransford and Miller (1983) found, for example, that African American males are significantly more traditional in gender-role outlook than white males. It appears that African American men are more likely than white men to believe that women should remain at home to take care of the children and to maintain the household. Although there is a strong belief in the institution of the family among African Americans, actual family living arrangements often do not match this ideology in large part because many African American men cannot meet the responsibilities of husband and father that society expects of them (Staples, 1985). In fact, a lack of financial resources can heighten African American

men's sense of failure within the family (Madhubuti, 1990). Such an argument has direct implications for studies of fathers' involvement. For example, if African American fathers could not meet traditional responsibilities such as visiting a museum or attending a sporting event, what types of child-rearing activities might be pursued?

For many African American men, a sense of responsibility about involvement may be more present than the actual time spent with children (cf. Hossain & Roopnarine, 1994). This condition may be due to social and structural barriers which foil some African American fathers' aspirations (Allen & Connor, 1997). Indeed Hyde and Texidor (1994) found that 90 percent of the African American fathers in their sample wished they could spend more time with their children and 89 percent indicated that only they as fathers could provide for some of their children's needs.

Of course, it cannot be assumed that time deficits are unique to minority fathers. White fathers are subject to many of the same economic [constraints] on time as well. While conflicting evidence exists as to whether black and white men are more similar or dissimilar in their fathering behavior (see Wade, 1994), no nationally representative samples have supported either claim. Nonetheless, based on the reasoning of blocked economic and social opportunities, some studies suggest that African American fathers may participate in cognitive involvement more than do fathers in other racial/ethnic groups. And because African American men hold stronger traditional gender ideologies than their white counterparts, they may be significantly less affective than whites in their parenting behavior. That is, white fathers may be more likely to show affection toward their children when compared to black fathers.

Latino Families and Fathers

Latino families represent many ethnic and cultural entities, with those of Mexican origin comprising the largest Latino ethnic group. Vega (1990) traced some important issues in his review of research on Latino families. Among the most pertinent is that there appears to be support for the notion of familism in Latino families. *Familism* refers to a set of values that emphasize the importance of family over individual needs. Although these beliefs represent ideals, they influence the behavioral outcomes of Latino Americans (Kane, 1993). This may mean that Latino groups are more family-oriented than white households. Given this interpretation and the fact that Latino groups have generally higher fertility rates than whites (Bean & Tienda, 1987), one might expect Latino families to place greater value on children and on the role of parenting than would white families. Therefore, it would seem logical to expect that the stronger the family ideology, the greater a father's involvement. Bartz and Levine's (1978) study showed little or modest support for different child-rearing practices between Latino and other ethnic groups. However, a recent national-level study found that men of Latino origin were more likely than white or African American men to agree that both sexes should share responsibilities for children (Grady et al., 1996).

For Puerto Rican fathers, gender role beliefs may translate into low direct involvement in child rearing (Sanchez-Ayendez, 1988). While the Mexican-origin home places much emphasis on child rearing when children are young, there seems to be great concern that girls be closely monitored whereas boys are allowed considerable freedom (Locke, 1992). In the end, although Mexican Americans may place greater emphasis on family and children than do Puerto Rican or Cuban Americans, all three groups seem to rank these life issues as more important than do whites generally. Indeed, in a large study of Latinos, Sabogal, Marin, and Otero-Sabogal (1987) found familism to be a core characteristic in the social life of Latinos. Latino subgroups reported similar family-oriented rather than individual needs and attitudes regardless of differences in national origin.

All of these studies indicate that there are racial/ethnic differences in socialization patterns, family, gender, and parenting role beliefs, and parental child-rearing values. Thus, it is important to explore how these factors may lead to variations in men's fathering involvement. Because of the strong, albeit sometimes indirect, evidence which suggests that ethnic identity and ideology may influence paternal involvement, we focus on racial/ethnic diversity, ideology, and the interconnection of the two in separate analyses of three involvement domains for children aged five to eighteen years old. The next section briefly describes the questions we asked and how we conducted the study.

RESEARCH QUESTIONS AND METHODOLOGY

First, because African American fathers hold more traditional gender ideologies and face many structural barriers which prevent them from realizing their paternal goals (Allen & Connor, 1997; LeMasters & Defrain, 1983; Ransford & Miller, 1983), we ask: Are African American fathers less likely than white fathers to be involved in direct behavioral and affective fathering relationships? Second, because of a mismatch between what African American fathers would like to do (cultural ideals) and what they can do (structural barriers), we ask: Are African American fathers more involved in the cognitive domain than are other groups? Next, because Latino groups have also disproportionately experienced adverse socioeconomic circumstances and strong familial attitudes, we expect Latino fathers to be more involved in the cognitive domain than are white fathers. Finally, regardless of fathers' racial/ethnic identity, we ask: Are fathers who hold traditional gender and family values, who are committed to child rearing, and who stress stricter discipline as a child-rearing value more likely to be involved in only one domain or equally involved in all three domains—behavioral, affective, and cognitive? We also examine if there are any interconnections between ethnicity, the two measures of gender and family ideology, paternal role commitment, and paternal child-rearing values. That is, do these factors interact simultaneously to influence child-rearing behavior?

Sample

The data come from the first wave of the National Survey of Families and Households (NSFH; Sweet, Bumpass, & Call, 1988), a national probability sample of 13,017 adults interviewed in 1987 or 1988.[1] For households with children under the age of 19, information was collected about a randomly selected child in the household (the focal child). Although data were gathered from a randomly selected adult (primary respondent) as well as from the spouses or cohabiting partners of primary respondents, we utilize only primary respondent data from male-present households with children. They only exception is for employment and income information of spouses or partners, which was included as a control variable. Thus, the analyses here focus on 1,258 primary male respondents (fathers) with children aged 5 to 18 who provided usable information to all fathering items under study. The final sub-sample consists of at least 915 whites, 210 African Americans, 119 Latinos (a combined group of Cuban, Mexican, and Puerto Rican Americans and other Latinos), and 14 others. (Note that sample size may vary across the dependent variables.)

Dependent Variables: Fathers' Involvement with Children

Corresponding to Palkovitz's (1997) conceptualization, three indexes were created to represent child-rearing behavior. (An index is created when two or more survey questions or items are combined into one measure.) We examine three domains of involvement between fathers and their children: *behavioral, affective,* and *cognitive.* The *behavioral* index contains six measures (or questions). The questions asked men "how many days last week did you eat breakfast or dinner [each

representing one item] with at least one of the children"; "how often do you spend time with the children . . . in leisure activities away from home (picnics, movies, sports, etc.)," "at home working on a project or playing together," "having private talks," and "helping with reading or homework?" The *affective* index includes two items. The questions asked respondents how often they "praise" and "hug" their child. The *cognitive* index contains three items. Respondents were asked the following questions: "Do you restrict the amount of television that (the child) watches," "do you restrict the type of program that (he/she) watches," and "is (he/she) required to complete (his/her) chores before playing, watching television, or going out?"

Independent Variables

Race/Ethnicity. The three major racial/ethnic groups included in our analyses are African American, Latino, and white fathers. Because of the limited cases of different Latino groups (Mexican, Cuban, and Puerto Rican Americans and other Latinos), we combined them into one group. The alternative method was to explore each group separately, but missing values on the parent items would produce too few cases for the analysis.

Gender Ideology. The gender ideology item highlights one gender against another, thereby directing attention to divisions between women (unpaid domestic work) and men (paid employment), and how these differences define them. This item asked respondents about their level of agreement with the statement that "it is much better for everyone if the man earns the main living and the woman takes care of the home and family."

Family Ideology. The family ideology measure focuses more specifically on how men and women should engage in family or marital roles generally. Respondents were asked their level of agreement with the statement: "If a husband and wife both work full-time, they should share housework tasks equally."

Parental Roles. To tap the perceived level of commitment to the parenting role, we included a measure which directly focuses on the paternal role. Respondents were asked about their level of agreement with the following statement: "I often wish I could be free from the responsibility of being a parent." Fathers who seldom wish to escape their parenting role are more likely to be involved with their children at some level than are fathers who often seek to avoid this role.

Parental Values. Two items were used to construct an index of obedience. Respondents were asked: "How important is it to you that your children always follow family rules?" and "Do children always do what you ask?"

Interaction Terms. The intersection between culture and race/ethnicity is a much-discussed but seldom-examined topic. In this paper, we utilized the interaction effects between race and ideology to examine explicitly the intersection between culture and race/ethnicity. (Interaction effects examine whether the relationship between the independent and dependent variables varies under different conditions of a third variable.) We computed interaction terms between race and the measures of gender and family ideology, commitment to the fathering role, and parental values.

Sociodemographics. Our analysis of fathers' involvement included a number of statistical controls. Previous research suggests that men's participation in domestic/family work varies by the socioeconomic positions of their partners, and this may be particularly true for black fathers (McAdoo, 1993). With reference to Latinos, there is some evidence that the wife's employment outside the home spurs Latino fathers to become more involved in child care (Ybarra, 1982). For these reasons, the socioeconomic circumstances of wives or cohabiting partners were statistically

controlled by combining their employment status (i.e., employed or not) and total income. (To maintain as much data as possible, a dummy variable was included to represent missing values). The analyses also included fathers' age, employment status, and education. (A series of dummy codes were created for education [some college or 2-year degree, 4-year degree, and post 4-year degree] where high school or below was used as the reference category.) (For a full description of our methodological and statistical procedures, see Toth and Xu, 1999.)[2]

RESULTS

The Conceptual Dimensionality of Fathers' Involvement

As discussed earlier, we used Palkovitz's (1997) recent conceptualization of fathering to investigate racial/ethnic and cultural diversity in the father's involvement with his children. Our empirical measures from the NSFH for Palkovitz's three domains of fathers' involvement confirm the dimensionality of fathering. The items that we used in this study provide a valid view of actual child-rearing activities of men.

Racial/Ethnic Diversity in Fathers' Involvement

One of the most important findings is that, in comparison to white fathers, black fathers are far more likely to monitor and supervise their children's activities (cognitive domain). This finding is consistent with previous literature that found black parents tend to be more strict, cautionary, authoritarian, and controlling than white parents (e.g., Bartz & Levine, 1978). In terms of how individuals are influenced by their social environment, African American men may approach parenting based in part on their experience with racism (LeMasters & Defrain, 1983; Madhubuti, 1990). That is, they may pattern their involvement with children according to larger social and cultural realities more than white fathers do. We found that, everything else being equal, African American fathers invest considerably more energy in the cognitive domain of child rearing than do white fathers. The evidence suggests that the stereotype of irresponsible and nonsupportive black fathers is inaccurate and should be rejected. In examining the other two domains (behavioral and affective), African American fathers are similar to white fathers in interacting with and expressing affection toward their children, regardless of gender and family ideologies, the level of paternal commitment, child-rearing values, and other socioeconomic factors.

The results for Latino fathers partially support our theoretical expectations. Not only are Latino fathers more likely than their white counterparts to monitor their children, but also to interact and spend time with them. While this finding parallels that of African American fathers for the cognitive domain, the greater involvement in the behavioral domain appears to be unique to Latino fathers. Out interpretations of these findings are twofold. First, our results bolster the traditional notion of familism, which places greater value on the family, child rearing, and family cohesion (Baca Zinn, 1982/1983; Carrasquillo, 1997; Vega, 1990). Also, in contrast to the majority of white parents but similar to black parents, Latino fathers tend to reinforce the norms of family closeness and expect their children to show respect for and conform to authority (Carrasquillo, 1997). Consequently, they monitor and supervise their children more closely than white fathers do. In short, on behavioral and cognitive dimensions, it can be argued that not all fathers participate in child rearing in a similar fashion.

Finally, there appears to be a certain degree of racial/ethnic parity in the affective dimension of fathers' involvement. We found that minority fathers are generally less affectionate toward their children than white fathers, but the statistical results are not strong enough to generalize the findings to a broader population. Therefore, it can be stated that regardless of racial/ethnic origin, fathers are almost equally likely to be expressive, affectionate, and encouraging while rearing their children between five and eighteen.

Cultural Diversity in Fathers' Involvement

Cultural traditions, dominant ideologies, personal beliefs, and parental child-rearing values associated with racial/ethnic groups are vital to our understanding of fathers' involvement. This is not to say that other structural forces, such as social class and wife's labor force participation, are not important in examining paternal involvement. Our findings indicate that, irrespective of racial/ethnic background, those who hold nontraditional gender role and egalitarian family role ideologies, who are reportedly committed to fatherhood, and who value or demand the child's obedience are much more involved parents than are their counterparts, across all three dimensions of fathers' involvement. Also of interest is that, contrary to our expectations, fathers who emphasize children's conformity do not distance themselves from their children. They are actually more emotionally involved than are fathers who endorse children's independence.

To summarize, it can be argued that changing gender and family role ideologies in U.S. society have challenged some, but not all, American males to become involved and nurturing fathers. These results support earlier findings reported by Baruch and Barnett (1981) that fathers' gender role ideology determines the likelihood of their participation in child care, but they also expand those findings by integrating different dimensions of the father's participation in the child-rearing process. Our results strongly suggest that cultural beliefs about gender and family, as well as commitment to fatherhood and paternal child-rearing values, are important determinants of American fathers' involvement with children in the three fathering domains that we analyzed.

The Interplay between Race/Ethnicity and Cultural Beliefs

According to recent studies, in the past few decades both black and Latino men in the United States have voiced more support for the traditional family-provider role than their white counterparts, though the general changing trend is toward egalitarian attitudes (Ransford & Miller, 1983; Rubin, 1994; Wilkie, 1993). In terms of fathers' child-rearing orientations and goals, racial/ethnic differences are also noted (Bartz & Levine, 1978; Kotlowitz, 1991). Our analysis generally supports these prior findings. However, the only notable and systematic findings are associated with Latino fathers' family role ideology and child-rearing orientations. Although fathers who subscribe to traditional family role ideology are generally more detached from child rearing across the three domains, an analysis of the interconnection among the study variables indicates that this is more evident for white fathers than for Latino fathers. In other words, the data suggest that white fathers who hold a traditional family role ideology are less likely than are traditional Latino fathers to participate in the three fathering domains examined here.

In addition, for the affective dimension, the effects of fathers' emphasis on children's obedience are opposite in direction for white and Latino fathers. It appears that strict Latino fathers are less affectionate toward their children than are their white counterparts. Controlling for socioeconomic and other demographic factors does not erase the significance of these effects. The findings show that the decrease in paternal involvement (for all three domains) is greater for white fathers than for Latino fathers if they do not endorse egalitarian family role ideology. This outcome contradicts our expectations that both black and Latino fathers are disproportionately more likely to hold nonegalitarian family orientations. Therefore, the noninvolvement effects should be stronger for Latino fathers than for white fathers. One possible explanation for this finding is that Latino fathers might be more traditional in ideology but egalitarian in actual fathering practices. For example, several recent studies have shown egalitarian family patterns in the behavior of Mexican-origin families, with both wife and husband actively involved in household responsibilities, child rearing, and decision making (Sanchez, 1997). In sum, the results provide some evidence of an interplay between race/ethnicity and cultural forces.

DISCUSSION AND CONCLUSIONS

This paper contributes to the extant fathering literature in a number of ways. First, to our knowledge, this paper represents the first systematic attempt to predict simultaneously the tripartite conceptual domains of fathers' involvement, which was first set forth by Lamb (1987) and then systemized recently by Palkovitz (1997). Of course, we realize that no single research can attempt to encompass the entire gamut of fathers' involvement with child rearing. However, too often prior studies selectively used only one or two but not all three dimensions of fathers' involvement (e.g., Harris & Morgan, 1991; Tuttle, 1994). Though the NSFH empirical measures of the behavioral, affective, and cognitive dimensions of father's involvement are far from comprehensive and ideal, our reliability and correlation (including partial correlation) analyses do not suggest any systematic or conceptual problems for the fathering measurement model. Second, our findings show that the patterns of paternal involvement vary considerably across racial/ethnic groups in the United States. Based on our regression results, deficit models of fathering for minority groups must be questioned. Far from being associated with low parental involvement, the minority fathers in this study clearly participate in the lives of their children. For example, in this study Latino fathers outperformed their white counterparts in both the behavioral and cognitive domains. Perhaps more than other groups in America, Latino men approach fathering based in part on their strong belief in the value of family (Sabogal et al., 1987). Fathers' involvement among Latino men becomes an important contribution to the overall life of the family, whereas for white men parenting may be more of a duty associated with the fathering role itself. However, Latino, white, and black fathers were equally likely to express affection with their children. That the cognitive domain stood out in our analysis may indicate that other social and cultural forces are at play as well. For example, both Latino and black men confront disproportionately more structural barriers to economic success than do white men, which helps to influence fathering behavior.

For African American fathers, the pattern of paternal involvement is less explicit than expected. The findings are in line with McAdoo's (1993) observation that African American fathers differ from fathers in other ethnic groups. However, our analysis also refutes McAdoo's claim in a positive sense. Like their Latino peers, black fathers exceeded white fathers in the cognitive domain. Compared to white fathers, black fathers seem to care more about how much and what their children watch on TV and whether the children finish their chores before playing. African American men parent within a social system that limits traditional fathering such as the amount of direct time spent with their children (Allen & Connor, 1997). Moreover, many African American fathers will have to respond to their children's encounters with racism (LeMasters & Defrain, 1983). In this socio-cultural context, it makes sense that African American fathers are more concerned with the cognitive preparedness of their children than are white fathers in U.S. society. Black fathers must prepare their children not only to deal with the negative personal feelings associated with racism but also to develop the skills necessary to succeed economically in a system that seems to discourage such advancement.

Third, the findings reveal that the nontraditional, committed, and strict fathers are actively engaged fathers. In addition, some of these ideological effects on fathering vary noticeably across racial/ethnic groups. For instance, endorsing non-egalitarian family role ideology is more likely to prevent white fathers (compared to Latino fathers) from getting involved with child rearing in all three domains. With respect to Latino fathers, we speculated that a greater degree of familism may decrease the effect of nonegalitarian family role ideology. In fact, our analysis indicated that Latino fathers outperformed their white counterparts in this regard. These findings provide partial validation for an interconnection between racial/ethnic identity and cultural diversity in determining fathers' involvement with child rearing. In other words, racial/ethnic identity and cultural factors create a mutually reinforcing context that influences men's parenting.

Overall, our results suggest that minority fathers, compared to white fathers, may lag in their acceptance of gender role and family role ideologies, but nevertheless they are involved fathers. In the cognitive domain, they are definitely doing a better job than white fathers. In the other two domains, minority fathers' performances may fall behind or may exceed whites' depending on racial/ethnic identity. It is important to recognize that the racial/ethnic differences identified in the current research do not reflect negative involvement with child rearing for any of the racial/ethnic groups we examined. On the contrary, our findings echo racially differentiated investment given to three distinct domains of fathering and highlight the social and cultural context of parenting in U.S. society. Therefore, we do not suggest that these differences be translated into simplified labels of "bad dads" versus "good dads" based on racial/ethnic identities. In general, the men in our study are actively pursuing their roles as fathers.[3]

NOTES

1. The National Survey of Families and Households was funded by a grant (HD21009) from the Center for Population Research of the National Institute of Child Health and Human Development. The survey was designed and carried out at the Center for Demography and Ecology at the Uni-

versity of Wisconsin–Madison under the direction of Larry Bumpass and James Sweet. The field work was done by the Institute for Survey Research at Temple University.

2. We utilize the Seemingly Unrelated Regression (SURE) technique (Greene, 1990). In order to implement the analysis and estimate the specified SURE models, the LIS-REL program was used for convenience. The models can then be expressed as $Y = \Gamma X + \beta$ (Jöreskog & Sörbom, 1989). It should be pointed out that OLS regression analyses were also performed separately on each dimension of paternal involvement. Not surprisingly, the results are clearly comparable to those derived from the SURE models. However, we feel that for both conceptual and methodological concerns, the SURE models are more appropriate in that the conceptual dimensions of fathers' involvement should be correlated theoretically.

3. Several caveats of this research must be addressed. First, fathers' involvement with child rearing varies by children's gender (e.g., Harris & Morgan, 1991). But due to the complexity of our topic, a separate analysis is called for. Second, because of the small sample size for minority fathers, we knowingly treated Latino fathers as one group by disregarding their specific countries of origin. In addition, other racial/ethnic groups such as Asians and Native Americans were not compared and discussed for the same reason. Finally, the items used to construct the three fathering domains are not a complete list based on Palkovitz's model. Nonetheless, we argue that this paper serves as a starting point for future research on diversity in child rearing.

REFERENCES

Allen, W. D., & Connor, M. (1997). An African American perspective on generative fathering. In A. J. Hawkins & D. C. Dollahite (Eds.), *Generative fathering: Beyond deficit perspectives* (pp. 52–70). Thousand Oaks, CA: Sage.

Baca Zinn, M. (1982/1983). Familism among Chicanos: A theoretical review. *Humboldt Journal of Social Relations, 10*, 224–38.

Bartz, K. W., & Levine, E. S. (1978). Childrearing by Black parents: A description and comparison to Anglo and Chicano parents. *Journal of Marriage and the Family, 40*, 709–19.

Baruch, G. K., & Barnett, R. C. (1981). Fathers' participation in the care of their preschool children. *Sex Roles, 7*, 1043–55.

Bean, F., & Tienda, M. (1987). *The Hispanic population of the United States*. New York: Russell Sage Foundation.

Carrasquillo, H. (1997). Puerto Rican families in America. In M. K. DeGenova (Ed.), *Families in cultural context* (pp. 155–72). Mountain View, CA: Mayfield Publishing Company.

Cooksey, E. D., & Fondell, M. M. (1996). Spending time with his kids: Effects of family structure on fathers' and children's lives. *Journal of Marriage and the Family, 58*, 693–707.

DeGenova, M. K. (1997). *Families in cultural context: Strengths and challenges in diversity*. Mountain View, CA: Mayfield Publishing Company.

Grady, W. R., Tanfer, K., Billy, J. O. G., & Lincoln-Hanson, J. (1996). Men's perceptions of their roles and responsibilities regarding sex, contraception and childrearing. *Family Planning Perspectives, 28*, 221–26.

Greene, W. H. (1990). *Econometric analysis*. New York: Macmillan Publishing Company.

Harris, K. M., & Morgan, S. P. (1991). Fathers, sons, and daughters: Differential paternal involvement in parenting. *Journal of Marriage and the Family, 53*, 531–44.

Hossain, Z., & Roopnarine, J. L. (1994). African-American fathers' involvement with infants: Relationship to their functioning style, support, education, and income. *Infant Behavior and Development, 17*, 175–184.

Hyde, B. L., & Texidor, M. (1994). A description of the fathering experience among Black fathers. In R. Staples (Ed.), *The Black family: Essays and studies* (5th ed.) (pp. 157–64). Belmont, CA: Wadsworth Publishing Company.

Jöreskog, K., & Sörbom F. (1989), *LISREL 7. A guide to the program and applications* (2d ed.). SPSS Inc.

Kane, N. (Ed.). (1993) *The Hispanic American almanac: A reference work on Hispanics in the United States*. Detroit, MI: Gale Research.

Kotlowitz, Alex. 1991. *There are no children here: The story of two boys growing up in the other America*. New York: Anchor Books.

Lamb, M. E. (1987). Introduction: The emergent American father. In M. E. Lamb (Ed.), *The father's role: Cross-cultural perspectives* (pp. 3–25). Hillsdale, NJ: Lawrence Erlbaum Associates, Publishers.

LeMasters, E. E., & Defrain, J. (1983). *Parents in contemporary America: A sympathetic view* (4th ed.). Homewood, IL: Dorsey.

Locke, D. (1992). *Increasing multicultural understanding*. Newbury Park, CA: Sage.

Madhubuti, R. (1990). *Black men: Obsolete, single, dangerous?* Chicago: Third World Press.

Marsiglio, W. (1991). Paternal engagement activities with minor children. *Journal of Marriage and the Family,* 53, 973–86.

McAdoo, J. L. (1993). The roles of African American fathers: An ecological perspective. *Families in Society,* 74, 28–35.

Minton, C., & Pasley, K. (1996). Fathers' parenting role identity and father involvement: A comparison of nondivorced and divorced, nonresident fathers. *Journal of Family Issues,* 17, 26–45.

Palkovitz, R. (1997). Reconstructing "involvement": Expanding conceptualizations of men's caring in contemporary families. In A. J. Hawkins & D. C. Dollahite (Eds.), *Generative fathering: Beyond deficit perspectives* (pp. 200–16). Thousand Oaks, CA: Sage.

Phares, V. (1996). Conducting nonsexist research, prevention, and treatment with fathers and mothers: A call for change. *Psychology of Women Quarterly,* 20, 55–77.

Ransford, H. E., & Miller, J. (1983). Race, sex and feminist outlooks. *American Sociological Review,* 48, 46–59.

Rubin, L. B. (1994). *Families on the fault line.* New York: HarperCollins.

Sabogal, F., Marin, G., & Otero-Sabogal, R. (1987). Hispanic familism and acculturation: What changes and what doesn't. *Hispanic Journal of Behavioral Sciences,* 9, 397–412.

Sanchez, Y. M. (1997). Families of Mexican origin. In M. K. DeGenova (Ed.), *Families in cultural context* (pp. 61–83). Mountain View, CA: Mayfield Publishing Company.

Sanchez-Ayendez, M. (1988). Puerto Ricans in the United States. In C. Mindel, R. Haberstein, & R. Roosevelt (Eds.), *Ethnic families in America* (pp. 173–98). Boulder, CO: Greenwood Press.

Silverstein, L. B. (1996). Fathering is a feminist issue. *Psychology of Women Quarterly,* 20, 3–37.

Staples, R. (1985). Changes in Black family structure: The conflict between family ideology and structural conditions. *Journal of Marriage and the Family,* 47, 1005–13.

Sweet, J., Bumpass, L., & Call, V. (1988). *The design and content of the National Survey of Families and Households (NSFH working paper, No. 1).* Center for Demography and Ecology, University of Wisconsin, Madison.

Toth, J. F., Jr., & Xu, X. (1999). Ethnic and cultural diversity in fathers' involvement: A racial/ethnic comparison of African American, Hispanic, and White fathers. *Youth & Society,* 31, 76–99.

Tuttle, R. C. (1994). Determinants of fathers' participation in child care. *International Journal of Sociology of the Family,* 24, 113–25.

Vega, W. A. (1990). Hispanic families in the 1980s: A decade of research. *Journal of Marriage and the Family,* 52, 1015–24.

Wade, J. C. (1994). African American fathers and sons: Social, historical, and psychological considerations. *Families in Society,* 75, 561–70.

Wilkie, J. R. (1993). Changes in U.S. men's attitudes toward the family provider role, 1972–1989. *Gender and Society,* 7, 261–79.

Ybarra, L. (1982). When wives work: The impact on the Chicano family. *Journal of Marriage and the Family,* 44, 169–78.

? Think about It

1. Describe the behavioral, affective, and cognitive indexes that Toth and Xu used to measure fathers' involvement in child rearing.

2. Toth and Xu found that, at the cognitive level, black and Latino fathers are more involved with their children than are white fathers. How do they explain these findings?

3. How do family role ideologies affect black, white, and Latino fathers' parenting?

18   Parenting in Middle-Class Black Families

Susan D. Toliver

Much of the research on child rearing in ethnic families, especially in black families, fo-
cuses on lower socioeconomic households. In contrast, Susan D. Toliver explores some of
the child-rearing concerns of middle- and upper-middle-class black parents. She examines
the content of good black parenting, emphasizes the importance of instilling a sense of
black identity among privileged black children, and finds that parents' worries about their
youngsters encountering racism are often well founded.

. . . The children of black corporate managers, by nature of their parents' employment, are middle class. They enjoy the benefits gained by the civil rights movement, and their lives are privileged in ways that surpass the life circumstances of recent previous generations of black middle-class youngsters. They are among the first to be born into and grow up in an "integrated" society.

Blacks who have succeeded climbing the corporate ladder, as a variation of the term "Yuppie" (the acronym for "Young Urban Professional"), have been referred to as "Buppies" (Black Urban Professionals"), or "Bumps" (Black Upwardly Mobile Professionals). Their children, who could be called "Baby Bumps," enjoy the multiple fruits of their parents' achievement. They often live in upper-middle-class and exclusive neighborhoods; they attend private schools, or public schools in affluent communities; they enjoy private lessons and other privileges that their parents can afford. Although all of this translates into greater opportunities for these children than those of other (non-middle-class) black youngsters, it usually also means, in reality, that they are growing up

Source: From Susan D. Toliver, *Black Families in Corporate America* (Thousand Oaks, CA: Sage, 1998), 121–38. Copyright © 1998 Sage Publications, Inc. Reprinted by permission of Sage Publications, Inc.

in a predominantly white environment having a predominance of white mainstream experiences in childhood. Although there are obvious educational and economic advantages inherent in the life situations of Baby Bumps, black parents are concerned that there are serious disadvantages for the black child growing up in a mainstream environment and therefore having a predominance of childhood experiences that are race neutral: Black middle-class youngsters may not grow up with a positive sense of self as black, and may not be prepared for adult life in the larger society that is not race neutral, but in which racism persists.

Alternatively, the advantage of children growing up in a black community is that they are more likely to gain a black awareness and self-identity. This is likely to be an expected consequence of the environment. We might say that it is likely to occur almost through osmosis. A drawback to growing up in such an environment is, of course, that it can often, although not always, be equated with poor schools, older housing, and a concern for personal safety.

There are advantages, other than the obvious, however, to growing up in the kind of neighborhoods that Baby Bumps find themselves in— spending one's early years of life free from the concern of physical harm, and growing up with all of the advantages enjoyed by other children of some degree of privilege. These advantages are, however, truly a mixed blessing. The negative side of these advantages is the highly probable fact that black children at some point, usually by their early teens (if not long before), must experience an abrupt departure from their commonality of experience with other nonblack children. As youngsters, they are unable to grasp that when they get older distinctions will be made between them and others. Nor are they as likely as other black children, who grow up in a black environment, to be armed with a strong positive black identity with which to face racism. Thus, they are in for a rude awakening.

The isolated communities that constitute the social world of these corporate black youngsters (school and neighborhood) do not shed light on the realities of what they can expect to encounter in the wider world. This isolated social world gives them no clues as to what lies ahead and therefore cannot and will not prepare these youngsters for their adult (black) experiences (see Banks, 1984). How then are they to be prepared for the future?

If black middle-class youngsters raised in predominantly white communities are to receive the preparation that they need, it must come through interaction with the black community, but, most important, from their parents. (The term "community" as it is used here does not refer to a geographic location or physical place.) An essential element of good parenting for black corporate families in the 1990s is parental projective care that will prepare black youngsters for the realities of racism. . . .

It is difficult to find good instructive literature on parenting in general, and it is almost impossible to find literature on black parenting. Most child-rearing books are geared toward the white middle class. Their patterns and particulars are considered the norm. Furthermore, few books deal with issues of race or race relations.

Often in both professional and lay circles, the discourse on child rearing flows without mention of differences by race. The work of some re-searchers, however, includes race as a major factor in child rearing, child development, and child supports (Banks, 1984; Bartz & LeVine, 1978; Baumrind, 1972; Clark, 1983; Comer & Poussaint, 1975, 1992; Hale-Benson, 1986; Hopson & Hopson, 1990; Hurd, 1995; Jones, 1989; H. P. McAdoo, 1993; McAdoo & McAdoo, 1985; McLoyd, 1990; Peters, 1981, 1988; Spenser, Brookins, & Allen, 1985, 1991; Washington, 1988; Washington & La Point, 1987; Watson, 1988; Willie, 1989). Clark (1983), Comer and Poussaint (1975, 1992), and Hopson and Hopson (1990) believe that there are differences in raising a black versus a white child. Their view is that a white-dominated society, that is sometimes hostile to blacks, makes for special problems for both black parents and black children.

They argue that a sense of belonging in society enables parents to accept its values and pass them on to their children. Racism, however, denies blacks the security of belonging—a sense of "oneness" with society. As a corollary to Comer and Poussaint's (1975, 1992) and Hopson and Hopson's (1990) assessments, I would like to suggest that we view this concept of "belonging" in society as something that is experienced by blacks in varying degrees, so that some are likely to have a stronger or weaker sense of belonging than others. Black middle-class corporate families, to a greater extent than others, because of the intimacy with which they share in mainstream culture, "belong." In this sense then, black corporate parents are better able than many other blacks to prepare their children for adulthood in our society.

Black parents, in rearing their children, have to cope with the same concerns that all other parents have in rearing their children. But, in addition, black parents also have to contend with and accommodate the changing faces of racism and the changing social attitudes and values regarding race. As the nature of race relations changes, so, too, must the content of black parenting.

A part of the message that Comer and Poussaint (1975, 1992) were giving black parents in the early to mid-1970s is somewhat different from the concerns about race and racism that parents have today for their children. Although they strongly advocated instilling black pride in children, they were concerned that race would be used as an excuse for such things as poor achievement. Now the concerns for preparing the child for a healthy future would be different—making the child aware of race and racism, rather than being too preoccupied with race and using it as an excuse. This change has come about in response to changes in contemporary race relations.

Race (and racism) causes special problems; black child-rearing practices must take this into account. Although basic child-rearing practices for all U.S. children, given that they occur within the context of U.S. society and U.S. culture, should likely be fundamentally similar, there will, can, and ought to be differences on the basis of different subcultural values and differences in social experience.

> In providing for the psychological well-being of our children, we, as black parents will occasionally need to act in special ways. (Comer & Poussaint, 1975, p. 23)

This is no different from what other groups (e.g., religious ones) have had to do.

What to Do

What specifically can and should black parents do to instill in their children a sense of self as black, and to prepare them for their future and the likelihood that they will experience racism? The following are some suggestions from Comer and Poussaint (1975):

1. Parents should talk to their children about racial injustice. This enables them to recognize racism and to handle it. Research shows that blacks are better at recognizing racism because white children do not get to talk about race and are not educated about the facts. Let me add that black children have an advantage over others—they are socialized to be aware of social injustice. They are able to critique the social order without

the bias of the status quo. This might suggest a tendency to be more humane and thoughtful, a value we would want cultivated in all children regardless of race. This is especially important to develop in black children because they are more frequently the victims of such injustices.

2. Successful blacks should be pointed out to children. They should see parental respect for black art, music, and other aspects of black culture. That blacks are deserving of respect is proven through the actions of significant others (e.g., parents, teachers).

3. It is important for parents to call situations as they are. If it is an act of racism, tell your child so—"you (parent) aid best by helping your adolescent learn to 'see it like it is'" (Comer & Poussaint, 1975, p. 284).

It is also important that parents then follow through on taking any appropriate action that may be called for.

To these suggestions I would like to add that it is of the utmost importance for parents who believe that racism persists to engage in activities that promote change. Their children will gain more of a sense of the reality of things from their parents' criticisms and assertions that racism is alive and well if coupled with constructive action. Parents spending the time and effort to combat racism will instruct young people that it is a serious matter. . . .

Special Black Parenting Concerns

The black middle to upper-middle class has a special set of concerns as parents. This is a powerful added concern to those of parents in general. That is, black parents have a concern for their children's "blackness."

Because racism continues to persist, being black in U.S. society today continues to affect one's life chances, to affect the opportunities available, and to affect one's life experiences. The nature of racism has shifted to manifest itself in more subtle forms; overt expressions of it are less easily found. Thus, black children today do not on a routine basis experience the same social discrimination, sometimes in forms that were life-threatening, as did perhaps their parents or previous generations of blacks when they were children. In fact, many of today's black middle-class youngsters are relatively old (in their teens) before they experience any of these situations. Furthermore, the media, in particular television and music videos, tend to portray black–white relations in a neutral (although unrealistic) light, giving children a sense of equality between the races. Black musicians and white musicians perform together, rock videos portray romantic encounters with and attraction between opposite-race characters. They give one the sense that race is a nonissue in our society. We know the average number of hours that U.S. children spend watching television (Mann, 1982 reports this figure at 6 hours and 44 minutes per day), and research informs us that the media does influence our views of the world.

Black parents, on the other hand, feel quite differently. They are aware of the persistence of racism and they worry about their children. They are concerned that their children, who grow up in predominantly white neighborhoods and attend predominantly white schools, do not as young people get a realistic view of the larger social world. Their youngsters are insulated from the harsher realities of life that they inevitably will encounter in their teen years and as adults. So, although insulated as youngsters, their parents fear what will face them in the future. . . .

EVIDENCE THAT PARENTAL FEARS ARE WELL-FOUNDED

There is evidence that black parents' fears for their children are well-founded. One can point to the numerous recent racially motivated uprisings on predominantly white college campuses being experienced by college young people today. Displays of antiblack sentiment have recently occurred in the South as well as in the "liberal

northeast" and in California—ranging from name calling to cross burnings to fistfights to brutal beatings to homicide. Many black students say they have been taken by surprise, and social scientists claim that many are unprepared for these attacks. These are examples of some of the incidents of racism that black middle-class parents fear their children are unprepared for.

At a recent Discrimination Forum at a New York City college that was motivated by racist acts perpetrated against a black faculty member, students expressed shock that this kind of thing (writing "nigger" across the professor's office door, and assaulting him with racist graffiti around the urban campus) could happen at their school on the eve of the 21st century. No one quite knew what to do.

Psychologist Ogretta McNeil, professor at the small Worcester, Massachusetts College of the Holy Cross, worries about black youth. An article in the *Black Collegian* (Turner, 1985) states that McNeil "cautions that a campus with a predominantly white student body is not the place for blacks who are uncertain about who they are to find out" (p. 24).

FINDINGS

I pursued the subject of race relations with a group of 21 preparatory school youngsters, 19 of whom were children of black and other minority corporate managers. The fathers of the other two children were physicians, one mother a nurse, and the other a school guidance counselor. Although they are not children of corporate managers, their experiences are appropriate to include in this discussion because their lifestyles are similar by virtue of their upper-middle-class status. It becomes relevant to point out that the parental concern for black corporate children is much the same concern that is held by other black middle-class parents for their children, whose life situations are similar because of their class status. Thus, the phenomenon is largely an artifact of social class affected by parents' corporate managerial employment status and income.

In speaking of prejudice, discrimination, and stereotypes with these children, I was struck by the separation and distinction made by many of the black (and Hispanic) "preppies" between themselves and blacks in general, or "the blacks," as they referred to them. When asked for stereotypes about blacks, they talked about blacks as "they" and "them." When it was explained to the group that stereotypes are based on false assumptions, and, occasionally, on some small kernel of truth, they challenged with statements such as "Well, blacks *do* steal . . . and hang out in gangs . . . and carry 'ghetto blasters'" (large portable radios).

Two of the main points to be concluded from the group session are the following:

1. These black and minority youngsters do not identify with the black community.
2. These youngsters have "bought" a negative image of blacks, such as that presented by the media, which more often shows blacks in the news, being arrested for various types of crime, rather than in any kind of positive light.

These young people seemed to believe that there are two kinds of children: minorities and preppies—and they (blacks) were preppies, just like the other (white) kids who sit beside them in their classrooms. For these youngsters (from their view), class is a more salient divider of people or social groups. They would support William J. Wilson's (1978) thesis of class over race. They also very firmly identified black (or minority) with lower class, something that they very definitely were not. Although this sample of preppies is small, their views regarding race were consistent with those of other children of corporate managers in the sample.

I was struck by the way in which one girl, whom we will call Lisa, talked in a very patronizing way about other blacks who were not "Highlands kids" (the upper-middle-class neighborhood that she lives in that is adjacent to a low-income

area with a fairly large minority population) like she was. She explained to us the differences in their clothing—Highland kids were Benetton, blacks wear Nike sneakers and Sergio Valente clothing—differences in their speech, and so on. She said that she and her mother used to try to "educate" the lower-class black kids by taking them to cultural events and activities (mainstream culture, not black) such as museum exhibits and plays. But she said the other kids "just couldn't absorb it all. They couldn't really take advantage of it." So, she and her mother had given up. No more "cultural enrichment excursions" for the blacks from the nearby area.

Lisa also talked about a former friend whom she described as "really stupid" because she passed up an opportunity to go to private parochial school in favor of the local public school, because she wanted to be with her friends. Lisa had no understanding or tolerance for the former friend—no understanding for the security of being in a familiar environment with friends, the power of peer pressure, perhaps the possible lack of savvy that her friend's mother had about which education would be best for the child, or other possible explanations for the choice of schools. The friend was simply written off, without compassion, as "stupid."

Lisa told the group that black kids from the other neighborhood said she was "stuck up" and that she was turning her back on being black. She says that she is not stuck up and that she is proud of being black—surprising in light of how she talked and her attitude toward blacks who are not like her. But, it seemed likely that this young woman should feel no responsibility to those in her community (black) when she reached adulthood. She had already written them off. Some youngsters never go so far as to make the attempt, although perhaps paternalistic, to "enlighten" others of their race who are less fortunate. It is not their problem, it has nothing to do with them. It was never their concern and it never will be.

They also seemed, in some small way, embarrassed about blacks. Lauren, another young black girl, talked about blacks in an objectified fashion, as a group very much apart from herself and from those with whom she identifies. When she described blacks as "people who play loud music and carry big radios," someone in the room chided her, saying that they had noticed her radio (of course she did not have one). In response she frowned, mumbled a few words, and became defensive in her posture and body language. I think that she was surprised to have the stereotype projected back at her and embarrassed by it. Very vocal up to this point in our group discussion, she became reticent for the remainder of the session. (I spoke privately with Lauren about her feelings after the group session.)

On Racism

Many of the corporate families in this study pointed to recent incidents of racism that their children had experienced. Included are the testimonies of respondent members of three such families. Although the teenage children were more likely to be faced with discriminatory situations, incidents of young children (aged 5 and 6 years) experiencing racism were also reported. The first of the following is an account of one mother and her young child's experience, the second account is a teenager's, the third is of a family with three children of varying ages. They speak of the youngsters' feelings of hurt, shock, anger, and lack of fairness.

Mrs. Robinson, a suburban mother whom I interviewed, spent a great deal of time investigating the private schools in her area to find the one that would offer the best all-around educational opportunity for her children. At first, she was quite satisfied with the school she had chosen and delighted with her children's progress there. But after a couple of racial incidents experienced by her second grader, her oldest child, she became disheartened and angry. The final incident proved to be too hurtful.

One of little Nicole's classmates had a big birthday celebration, complete with gifts of a stuffed animal (valued at about $50.00) for each child, and a performance by a professional marionette company. All of the children in the second-grade class talked on and on about the good time had at the party on the next class day. That is, all but Nicole, who was not invited. Nicole, with hurt feelings and a tear in her eye, asked why she had not been invited. The birthday girl told her, "My mother said we couldn't invite you." Nicole is the only black youngster in her class.

Mrs. Robinson told of her frustration and hurt in trying to explain and soothe the situation for her daughter, who came home that day in tears. "The poor baby was so upset and confused; she couldn't understand why her little friend didn't like her and kept asking, "Why doesn't she like me?" This mother did not expect that her children would experience discrimination so early in life. It was this incident that prompted Mrs. Robinson to enroll her children at another school.

Corporate manager Clifford Jones shares his story. Cliff Jones, from a grassroots family background, had worked his way up to a prestigious upper-middle-management position in corporate America. He told me of an experience had by his teenage son. The boy was raised in a predominantly upper-middle-class community and had less frequent contact with other black youngsters than his father would have cared for.

Michael, aged 16, was a fine student and had always excelled in athletics. Enrolled in one of the nation's top northeastern prep schools, his grades were good and he was a star campus athlete. He was popular and generally well liked.

Ever since he was old enough to recall, Michael's father has told him that he should be proud of his blackness, and never to let anyone mistreat him because of it. Mr. Jones in particular instilled the lesson that, "If anyone ever calls you nigger, you make sure that he's on the ground before he can call you that twice." Michael, who had had few personal exposures to racial injustice, was not quite sure that he understood his father's concern, or why he should hit someone for using that word.

One day, after a game of intramural football, the call of a certain play evoked a confrontation between Michael and his rival, one of the opposing team players. Some words were exchanged. The rival called Michael a nigger. Michael, remembering his father's words, decked the youth with one solid punch.

The "fight" was reported to the assistant headmaster, who called to see Michael immediately and demanded that he explain his behavior. The youngster explained what had happened and also told him of his father's instructions. The assistant headmaster telephoned Michael's father and said that violence was not condoned at their institution and that Mr. Jones would have to rescind his teachings or his son would be expelled. Mr. Jones responded that if the school could promise that Michael would never again be called that name he would promise that Michael would never strike another student. When the headmaster got wind of the incident, a formal letter of apology was sent to Michael's parents and a workshop on racial awareness was given for the full student body. Michael, surprised by the incident, began to understand his father's fear.

Ted Campbell shares a disheartening tale of discrimination. Campbell, a middle-aged corporate manager and father of three children, told me that he was glad when he and his family had an experience of racial discrimination. The occurrence took place while the family was traveling home from visiting relatives in the South. Although the event took Campbell by surprise, his children were amazed with disbelief.

After driving all day en route back to their New York–area home, the Campbells decided to stay the night in a small town in Maryland, just outside of Washington, D.C. They came to a motel whose vacancy sign was lit and the Campbells went in to register. They were told by the person at the desk that there were no vacancies. When Campbell queried about the sign, he was told that someone had forgotten to turn on the "No Vacancy" sign. The sign was then switched on. The family turned away and fortunately found a motel just a short way down the road where they were able to rent rooms for the night.

After taking their bags out of the car and into their rooms, the kids talked their dad into taking them back down the road to a Dairy Queen they had spotted across the highway from the first motel. They piled back into the car in quest of their midnight snack. As they pulled into the Dairy Queen, they noticed that the vacancy sign at the motel was once again lit. As the kids were getting their ice cream, they saw a white family pull into the motel and enter the office. They then left the office, got their luggage from their car, and took it inside one of the motel rooms, obviously to bed down for the night.

The Campbell children thought what they had seen was incredible. They were up in arms with questions and protests. "That isn't fair," exclaimed Campbell's daughter.

To Campbell, who says that his kids think of the civil rights movement as part of a long past era, this was an eye-opening experience for his children to have. He saw it as their introduction to the real world. The family then retired to their motel, where the father tried to explain to his children what had happened and to put the event into the proper context for them.

The event enabled Campbell to use a concrete example based on their own experience to talk to his children about racism and discrimination and provided an opportunity for them to discuss in a constructive fashion how to deal with racism.

Most of the parents in the sample were generally happy about the kinds of opportunities that they could provide for their kids. But these opportunities did not come without fears. The reality of providing youngsters with a wholesome sense of self as black in the context of these privileged environments remains a challenge. It is possible, but it is not easy.

REFERENCES

Banks, J. A. (1984). Black youths in predominantly white suburbs: An exploratory study of their attitudes and self-concepts. *Journal of Negro Education, 53,* 1.

Bartz, K. W., & LeVine, E. S. (1978). Child rearing by black parents: A description and comparison to Anglo and Chicano parents. *Journal of Marriage and the Family,* 40, 709.

Baumrind, D. (1972). An exploratory study of socialization effects on black children: Some black–white comparisons. *Child Development, 43,* 261–67.

Clark, R. (1983). *Family life and school achievement: Why poor black children succeed or fail.* Chicago: University of Chicago Press.

Comer, J. P. & Poussaint, A. F. (1975). *Raising black children.* New York: Penguin.

Comer, J. P. & Poussaint, A. F. (1992). *Raising black children* (2d ed.). New York: Penguin.

Hale-Benson, J. E. (1986). *Black children.* Baltimore, MD: Johns Hopkins University Press.

Hopson, D. P., & Hopson, D. S. (1990). *Different and wonderful: Raising black children in a race-conscious society.* New York: Prentice Hall.

Hurd, E. P. (1995). Quiet success: Parenting strengths among African Americans. *Families in Society, 76,* 434–43.

Jones, R. L. (Ed.). (1989). *Black adolescents.* Berkeley, CA: Cobb & Henry.

Mann, J. (1982, August 2). What is TV doing to America? *U.S. News and World Report,* p. 23.

McAdoo, H. & McAdoo, J. L. (1985). *Black children: Social, educational, and parental environments.* Beverly Hills, CA: Sage.

McAdoo, H. P. (1993). *Family ethnicity: Strength in diversity.* Newbury Park, CA: Sage.

McLoyd, V. C. (1990). Minority children. *Child Development, 61,* 263–66.

Peters, M. (1981). "Making it" black family style: Building on the strength of black families. In N. Stinnett, J. DeFrain, K. King, P. Knaub, & G. Rowe (Eds.), *Family strengths 3: Roots of well-being.* Lincoln: University of Nebraska Press.

Peters, M. (1988). Parenting in black families with young children: A historical perspective. In H. McAdoo (Ed.), *Black families* (2d ed., pp. 211–24). Newbury Park, CA: Sage.

Spencer, M. B., Brookins, G. K., & Allen, W. R. (1985). *Beginnings: The social and affective development of black children.* Hillsdale, NJ: Lawrence Erlbaum.

Spencer, M. B., Brookins, G. K., & Allen, W. R. (1991). Ethnicity, ethnic identity, and competence formation: Adolescent transition and cultural transformation. *Journal of Negro Education, 60,* 366–87.

Turner, R. D. (1985). The resurgence of racism on white campuses. *Black Collegian, 5,* 18–24.

Washington, V. (1988). *Black children and American institutions: An ecological review and resource guide.* New York: Garland.

Washington, V., & La Point, V. (1987). *The cultural foundations of black children: Social status, public policy, and future directions.* New York: Garland.

Watson, M. F. (1988). Black adolescent identity development: Effects of perceived family structure. *Family Relations, 37,* 288–92.

Willie C. (1989). Child development in the context of the black extended family. *American Psychologist, 44,* 380-85.

Wilson, W. J. (1978). *The declining significance of race.* Chicago: University of Chicago Press.

? *Think about It*

1. Who are the "Baby Bumps?" According to Toliver, what are the advantages and disadvantages of growing up as a Baby Bump?

2. In what ways does the raising of black children differ from the raising of white children, including those in middle-class communities?

3. At the end of this selection, Toliver describes three racist incidents that black parents and their children experienced. Do you agree or disagree with the ways the parents handled the incidents?

19 Las Comadres as a Parenting Support System

Rebecca A. López

Many Latinos rely on compadrazgo, *or coparenthood, in raising their children. Rebecca A. López explores the relationships between Latinas and their children's godmothers (comadres). Comadres, an important support system, often provide economic and social resources, especially for households headed by single mothers.*

THE *COMPADRAZGO* SYSTEM

Latinos often maintain networks of mutual assistance with the centuries-old practice of religious ritual and tradition that dictates the inclusion of new members as kin. One such tradition for many Latino cultures is the acquired role that an adult— either male or female—takes on by virtue of his or her religious involvement with another nuclear family unit. Often referred to in the literature as *compadrazgo,* or coparenthood, this system involves reciprocal relationships that are created not by blood ties but by commitment to a mutual religious doctrine (Roman Catholicism) and the sponsorship of ritualized rites of passage (Williams, 1990). Sponsorship is an integral part of Roman Catholic ceremonies of baptism, confirmation, first communion, and traditional marriage. The compadrazgo network is created when a couple with a newborn selects another couple as sponsors (godparents) for their infant. The godparents assume the responsibility of protecting the child and providing him or her with religious instruction. As Williams (1990) noted: "The ritual parents were seen as accepting the responsibility

for taking care of the spiritual and physical needs of the child in the absence of the parents. . . . In the event of the death of the parents, the godparents were expected to rear the child" (p. 26).

The godparents theoretically take on the status of second parents to the newborn and forge a special relationship with the child as he or she grows. Also, new roles with members of the child's extended family are formed. Thus, the godparents become components of an additional family system. Ho (1987) referred to these acquired family members as *fictive kin.*

Just as the child enjoys additional protection and attention from the fictive parents, the child's parents derive benefits from well-selected godparents. The parents acquire an additional support system that may provide emotional support or more tangible benefits like material assistance (Williams, 1990). Often the coparents (the parents and godparents) have a relationship of mutual trust; it was the basis for the offering and acceptance of the godparent role. Some godfathers (*compadres*) and godmothers (*comadres*) establish intimate, lifelong relationships with the children's parents that prevail long after the children have become adults. These relationships often rival the intimate interactions normally found only in the relationships among close siblings in other

Source: From Rebecca A. López, "*Las Comadres* as a Social Support System," *Affilia* 14 (Spring 1999): 24–41. Copyright © 1999 Rebecca A. López, Ph.D. Reprinted by permission of the author.

population groups. As Achor (1978, p. 44) noted, "Both parties were expected to assist each other in times of social or economic need."

Latinos of many countries maintain the compadrazgo system in their social institutions with minor adjustments to the terms used to identify the players. For example, Puerto Ricans may shorten comadre to *comai* and compadre to *compa.* Similar to this, a Puerto Rican child may refer to his or her godmother and godfather, respectively, as *nina* and *nino,* rather than *madrina* and *padrino.* In describing the comadre, Puente (1991, pp. 39–40) stated,

> She is a sister, a friend, a trusted confidante. . . . The comadre is very much part of the whole compadrazgo (kinship) system that characterizes *Latinismo.* . . . You can end up with all these interrelations of people that are not related by blood. . . . Even members of the madrina's family become connected to your family.

Foster (1969, p. 262), who studied the compadrazgo system among the mestizo peasants of Tzintzuntzan, Mexico, referred to it as

> the device par excellence for achieving formal social relationships beyond the nuclear family and the immediate kin. . . . The raison d'être of the compadrazgo [system] and source of its vitality is its ability to structure and validate a wide spectrum of essential social relationships not adequately serviced by kinship, friendship, political, commercial, or other ties. In fact, the most noteworthy aspect of the compadrazgo system is its malleability.

The compadrazgo system also allows its members to expand their kinship networks into more diverse socioeconomic strata (Van den Berghe, 1979). The vertical compadrazgo structure suggests that families may attempt to expand their kinship systems to include persons of different— and perhaps more powerful—socioeconomic classes (Wolf & Hansen, 1972); whereas a horizontal structure is reflected in the selection of compadres who are members of the same class (Foster, 1969; Mintz & Wolf, 1950). Thus,

> the participants in social networks have options, in that they can exercise choices in the preferred associations to a degree not usually characteristic of unilinear kinship systems. . . . Depending on who is selected for godparent roles, the institution can enlarge numerically and spatially the non-kin circle of intimates, or it can reinforce already existing kinship ties. (Foster, 1969, pp. 262–263)

Foster's (1969) analysis of the functional aspects of this system concluded that the compadrazgo system functions on an economic level to form "a kind of social insurance" that is available to families in times of emergency. Ho (1987, p. 127) commented on another functional aspect: "During times of crisis, transferring children from one nuclear family to another within the extended family system is a common practice among Hispanics."

Still another functional area relates to the generative nature of the system for young couples who choose older, more experienced compadres. The anxiety of impending parenthood may be mitigated by having access to trusted, experienced couples who model and guide the new parents through the stress of pregnancy and childbirth and socialize the new parents in child-rearing practices (Telles, 1982; Zambrana et al., 1992). A woman derives particular support from having another woman as a source of support (Salgado de Snyder & Padilla, 1987). Although a comadre may be selected from among a woman's peers, the guidance that an experienced mother can offer may also be a consideration in the selection process.

Although the compadrazgo system may provide additional roles and responsibilities for various family members, it is especially important for helping Latinas respond to traditional child-rearing expectations. As with other cultural groups, a Latina's assumption of numerous tasks as the anchor of the family unit provides the impetus for seeking additional supports, such as a comadre.

EFFECTS OF ACCULTURATION ON COMPADRAZGO

Acculturation is a major factor in the reconfiguration of the Latino American family (Carrillo, 1982) and its retention of religious traditions like baptismal rites and the selection of compadres. In the past, religion played a compelling role in the lives of most Latinos (Williams, 1990). For example, Ramirez and Castaneda (1974) noted that Mexican Catholicism reinforces and supports a myriad of Mexican values and significantly influences many aspects of the family and community. However, there have been many changes in religiosity and religious practices in Latino American communities (Sabagh & Lopez, 1980). Thus, although Catholicism remains the predominant religion among Latinos, significant inroads have been made by the Mormons, Southern Baptists, Pentecostal sects, and other Protestant groups (Moore & Pachon, 1985). Hence, the competition for the souls of Latinos may further diminish the importance of a religion-based institution like the compadrazgo system.

Sabogal, Marin, Otero-Sabogal, Van Oss Marin, and Perez-Stable (1987, p. 397) explored the extent in which acculturation affects the perceptions of familial obligation and family support among Mexican, Cuban, and Central Americans and found that

> the high level of perceived family support, invariable despite changes in acculturation, is the most essential dimension of Hispanic familism. Family obligation and the perception of the family as referents appear to diminish with the level of acculturation, but the perception of family support does not change.

In her study of Mexican Americans in Texas, Achor (1978, p. 44) stated that because of acculturation, "the compadrazgo ceremony no longer serves to sustain the 'fictive kinship system' as it was traditionally defined." Nevertheless, she conceded that despite changes in religious practices, the cultural tradition of establishing compradrazgo networks persists:

> A number of couples . . . are seeking to sustain these ceremonies as part of their cultural heritage, not because of any strong religious conviction. The ritual is part of the Mexican American tradition and has only a vague religious meaning for those participating in it. The emphasis on tradition is more compelling than religion itself. (p. 69)

Poma (1987) and Rueschenberg and Buriel (1989) concluded that Latino families are in various stages of acculturation and that acculturation may interrupt social relations and can threaten established support systems. Others have contended that Catholicism reinforces and supports a variety of familial values and social activities (Gibson, 1983).

Changing practices in acquiring extended kin systems are particularly important when considering the growing population of women who are single parents that are forced to seek all sources of emotional and material support to maintain their households (Ehrenreich & Piven, 1984; Norbeck & Sheiner, 1982). Many have substantiated that single parenthood results in additional strains and the increased risk of dysfunction amid poverty (Sands & Nuccio, 1989). This problem is no less prevalent for Latinas than for other single mothers (Vega et al., 1986). To what extent do Latinas depend on and value their extended kin as sources of support? Do they perceive of themselves and their comadres as mutually vital resources for family stability? The study presented here sought to explore comadres as resources for Latinas.

METHOD

The sample of 38 Latinas was recruited in southern California through a snowball sampling technique.

The data were gathered from self-administered questionnaires completed in Spanish or English. The 38 women met three basic criteria: they were all of Latin American descent, over age 25, and involved in relationships as comadres to other women. The questionnaire elicited demographic data and asked the comadres to respond to a series of statements related to the perceived value and benefits of the comadre relationship. It also included two open-ended questions that asked the women why they selected nonfamily members (nonblood relatives) to serve as comadres and to make additional comments regarding comadres or the compadrazgo system. The reliability and validity of the instrument are not known. Descriptive statistics were used to analyze the data. The mean differences among the respondents' characteristics were explored using *t*-tests.

RESULTS AND DISCUSSION

The women ranged in age from 25 to 85 (mean = 41 and mode = 26.0). The majority (23 women) were married, and the mean number of children was 1.89. . . .

Several demographic questions sought to determine the women's levels of acculturation through their preference for speaking English or Spanish, whether they were first- or second-generation U.S. residents, the birthplace of their mothers, and whether they adhered to the traditional religion of Roman Catholicism. Of the 38 women, 34 were born either in the United States (*n* = 16) or in Mexico (*n* = 18); the remainder were born in Central America (*n* = 2) or an unspecified country (*n* = 1). One woman did not respond. Of the 38, 18 spoke only Spanish at home, 17 spoke both Spanish and English, and 3 spoke only English. Catholicism was the religious preference of 32 of the women; of the remainder, 2 listed Christian, 1 listed Evangelical, and 3 listed another religious preference. The majority (22) described themselves as being only somewhat religious. When asked about the frequency of their attendance at church or religious services, the women indicated a wide range of practices—from rarely ever attending to attending every week.

The number of godchildren (for baptism) that the women had ranged from none (*n* = 3) to 32 (*n* = 1). The mean number of godchildren was 3.55 and the mean number of comadre relationships was 5.21. The women who were born in Mexico had a higher mean number of comadre relationships (5.5), whereas those born in the United States averaged fewer (3.75 comrades). The 38 respondents listed a total of 198 relationships with comadres who were blood relatives (66%) and friends (34%). Sisters and sisters-in-law represented about 37% of the relatives who were comadres. Other relatives included cousins, aunts, nieces, mothers, and grandmothers. On average, the women were in contact with their comadres about once a week.

Table [1] presents the responses to 20 statements about the women's comadres. The greatest agreement among the women was with two statements: "I am always happy to visit with my comadre" . . . and "If my comadre was unable to care for my godchild for 3 months, I would take my godchild into my own home." The greatest disagreement occurred with four statements: "My comadre wouldn't be able to survive without my help," . . . "My comadre and I are not really very close anymore," . . . "My comadre doesn't really care about me," . . . and "My comadre asks too much of me sometimes." . . . Some significant differences among the women were found on the basis of their countries of origin. For example, the comadres who were born in Mexico were significantly happier to visit their comadres . . . and more likely to disagree with the statement that their comadres ask too much of them sometimes . . . than were those who were born in the United States or another country.

With regard to their perceptions of their comadres as coparents, the women agreed at least somewhat that they could entrust their children's lives to their comadres, could be counted on as second moms, and would take their godchildren

TABLE 1   Respondents' Experiences with Their Closest Comadre (*N* = 38)

Statement	Mean	SD
1. My comadre is a person who is always around when I am in need.	4.38	.794
2. My comadre is a person with whom I can share my joys and sorrows.	4.38	1.063
3. I get all the help I need from persons *other than* my comadre.	2.97	1.424
4. I take my role as a godmother seriously.	4.43	1.015
5. I can talk about my most personal problems with my comadre.	4.05	1.201
6. My comadre is willing to help me make tough decisions.	4.22	1.017
7. I am always happy to visit with my comadre.	4.73	.508
8. My comadre doesn't really care about me.	2.32	1.600
9. Sometimes, when I need just a little money to get by, I can count on my comadre to help me out.	3.43	1.365
10. I feel very emotionally close in my relationship with my comadre.	4.23	.942
11. I would entrust my child's life to my comadre, if necessary.	4.17	1.000
12. My comadre and I are not really very close anymore.	2.22	1.548
13. My comadre is a good source of useful information.	4.16	.866
14. My comadre asks too much of me sometimes.	2.38	1.479
15. My godchild can count on me as his or her "second Mom."	4.16	1.365
16. I depend on my comadre for child care sometimes.	2.66	1.434
17. If my comadre was unable to care for my godchild for three months, I would take my godchild into my own home.	4.61	.766
18. I don't really get any support at all from my comadre.	2.68	1.600
19. My comadre wouldn't be able to survive without my help.	1.43	.899
20. If something was to happen to my godchild's parents, I would be prepared to adopt my godchild as mine.	4.42	.937

NOTE: The possible responses were 1 = *completely disagree*, 2 = *disagree somewhat*, 3 = *no opinion*, 4 = *agree somewhat*, 5 = *agree completely.*

into their homes either temporarily or permanently. The single comadres were significantly more likely than the married comadres to agree to take their godchildren into their homes for 3 months, if necessary. . . .

The women's ages contributed to the wide variance in their responses to two statements. The younger respondents (mean = 25 years) disagreed somewhat with the statement, "I feel very close in my relationship with my comadre," whereas the older respondents (mean = 46 years) agreed completely. The younger respondents . . . were also less likely to agree with the statement, "If my comadre was unable to take care of my godchild for three months, I would take my godchild into my own home."

The first open-ended question yielded some interesting comments about why the women selected persons other than family members to baptize their children. Several women stated that it is the custom in their families to have the first child baptized by the child's grandparents and then to look outside the family for compadres. Those who chose close friends rather than relatives said they did so because there were no available family members residing in this country. As one woman put it: "[I chose a close friend] because my family doesn't live in the U.S. and I wanted to have someone who is close by, who could support, counsel, and morally and spiritually guide my children in the event something happened to us." Similar to this, one comadre was able to create a new family for a friend in this country. She noted: "One of my good friends came to this country, but she had no family here, so she became part of our family when she baptized my daughter." Others noted that they chose friends as their compadres on the basis of the friends' personal qualities. One woman said:

> We selected our compadres because we know how they would bring our children up if we were not around. Religious, moral, sensitive and caring persons, they are the type of model persons, and we know they would take [the children] in as their own.

One woman noted that it just made sense to select a nonfamily member in light of the political and economic benefits an outsider could offer. However, another woman took issue with economic motives, stating: "Where I come from, it is not viewed as socially or morally correct for one comadre to use another to get economic benefits. This relationship is based on love, support, confidence, and respect."

The second open-ended question allowed the women to comment on their thoughts about the study, about their relationships with their comadres, or about the compadrazgo practice in general. One woman chose to expand the survey's definition of comadre. She said: "I have many friends who are my comadres, although we do not have any baptized children between us. We carry on the tradition of comadres as a networking and mentoring tool and process." Most of the women noted their delight in being able to express their comments about their valued comadres and reiterated that they derive strength and support from having comadres. As one woman put it, "We are good friends and would do anything for each other. We are closer than sisters."

. . . The inclusion of compadres in kin networks may increase the resources and adaptability of families in meeting environmental demands. This is an important consideration, particularly for women and the inequitable burden they bear in sustaining their families. At a minimum, there is evidence that the compadrazgo system produces greater emotional support for those who participate. The more tangible benefits become critical and have more serious implications for Latino families who have no access to formal supports because of their undocumented status, language, and/or cultural barriers. Because the practice of compadrazgo seems to persist in Latinos who do not necessarily have all the attributes of traditional Latinos (religiosity and Spanish language), it may be a mechanism that newly arrived Latinos can use to facilitate adaptation, acculturation, and eventual stability. The special demands on the Latina head of household to function in new cultural and societal roles may be particularly aided through the assistance of role models provided by a network of comadres. When there is a dearth of available close family members, comadres may provide needed guidance and a sense of extended family with increasing roles for women who become new coparents even in their later years.

More research is needed to explore fully the dynamics of interdependence and networking among comadres, as well as the nuances of the system and its persistence in light of acculturation and migration. For the comadres in this study, the author concludes that the compadrazgo practice perseveres, is viewed favorably, and should be given credence as one durable contributor to the survival of the Latino family.

REFERENCES

Achor, S. (1978). *Mexican Americans in a Dallas barrio.* Tucson: University of Arizona Press.

Carrillo, C. (1982). Changing norms of Hispanic families: Implications for treatment. In E. E. Jones & S. J. Korchin (Eds.), *Minority mental health* (pp. 250–266). New York: Praeger.

Ehrenreich, B., & Piven, F. F. (1984). The feminization of poverty. *Dissent, 31,* 162–170.

Foster, F. M. (1946). Godparents and social networks in Tzintzuntzan. *Southwest Journal of Anthropology, 25,* 261–278.

Gibson, G. (1983). Hispanic women: Stress and mental health issues. *Women and Therapy, 2,* 113–133.

Ho, M. K. (1987). *Family therapy with ethnic minorities.* Newbury Park, CA: Sage.

Mintz, S. W., & Wolf, E. R. (1950). An analysis of ritual co-parenthood (compadrazgo). *Southwestern Journal of Anthropology, 6,* 341–367.

Moore, J., & Pachon, H. (1985). *Hispanics in the U.S.* Englewood Cliffs, NJ: Prentice Hall.

Norbeck, J. S., & Sheiner, M. (1982). Sources of social support related to single-parent functioning. *Research in Nursing and Health, 5,* 3–12.

Poma, P. A. (1987). Pregnancy in Hispanic women. *Journal of the National Medical Association, 79,* 929–935.

Puente, T. (1991, May). Mothers and others. *Hispanic, 1,* 39–40.

Ramirez, M., & Castaneda, A. (1974). *Cultural democracy, biocognitive development and education.* New York: Academic Press.

Rueschenberg, E., & Buriel, R. (1989). Mexican American family functioning and acculturation: A family system perspective. *Hispanic Journal of Behavioral Sciences, 11,* 232–244.

Sabagh, G., & Lopez, D. (1980). Religiosity and fertility: The case of Chicanas. *Social Forces, 59,* 432–439.

Sabogal, F., Marin, G., Otero-Sabogal, R., Van Oss Marin, B., & Perez-Stable, E. L. (1987). Hispanic familism and acculturation: What changes and what doesn't? *Hispanic Journal of Behavioral Sciences, 9,* 397–412.

Salgado de Snyder, V. N., & Padilla, A. M. (1987). Social support networks: Their availablity and effectiveness. In M. Gaviria & J. D. Arana (Eds.), *Health and behavior: Research for Hispanics* (pp. 4–7) (Monograph Series No. 1). Chicago: Simon Bolivar Hispanic American Psychiatric Research and Training Program.

Sands, R. G., & Nuccio, K. E. (1989). Mother-headed single-parent families: A feminist perspective. *Affilia, 4,* 25–41.

Telles, C. (1982). Psychological and physiological adaptation to pregnancy and childbirth in low-income Hispanic women. (Doctoral dissertation, Boston University, 1982). *Dissertation Abstracts International, 43,* B1271.

Van den Berghe, P. L. (1979). *Human family systems: An evolutionary view.* New York: Elsevier.

Vega, W. A., Kolody, B., Valle, R., & Hough, R. (1986). Depressive symptoms and their correlates among immigrant Mexican women in the United States. *Social Science Medicine, 22,* 645–652.

Williams, N. (1990). *The Mexican American family: Tradition and change.* Dix Hills, NY: General Hall.

Wolf, E. R., & Hansen, E. C. (1972). *The human condition in Latin America.* New York: Oxford University Press.

Zambrana, R. E., Silva Palacios, V., & Powell, D. (1992). Parenting concerns, family support systems, and life problems in Mexican-origin women: A comparison by nativity. *Journal of Community Psychology, 20,* 276–288.

? **Think about It**

? **Think about It**

1. Why are godparents considered "fictive kin"? Why does López describe them as "acquired" family members?

2. Describe the functions of the *compadrazgo* system, including the vertical and horizontal dimensions. Are there comparable support systems in other ethnic groups (see Chapter I)?
3. How has acculturation affected the *compadrazgo* system?

20 Perspectives of Asian American Parents with Gay and Lesbian Children

Alice Y. Hom

We rarely read about Asian Americans who are gay because, as Alice Y. Hom observes, "Sexuality is an issue rarely or never discussed among Asian families." Hom describes some Asian American parents' feelings and reactions when they learn about their children's sexual orientation.

Sexuality is an issue rarely or never discussed among Asian families, yet it remains a vital aspect of one's life. What are the implications of alternative sexualities in family situations? Coming out stories and experiences of Asian American lesbians and gay men have had some exposure and publication,[1] however, the voices of the parents are rarely presented or known.

I found the majority of interviewees through personal contacts with individuals in organizations such as Asian Pacifica Sisters in San Francisco, Mahu Sisters and Brothers Alliance at UCLA and Gay Asian Pacific Alliance Community HIV Project in San Francisco. I met one set of parents through the Parents and Friends of Lesbians and Gays group in Los Angeles. Obviously this select group of people, who were willing to

Source: From Alice Y. Hom, "Stories from the Homefront: Perspectives of Asian American Parents with Lesbian Daughters and Gay Sons," *Amerasia Journal* 20 (1994): 19–32. Copyright © 1994 UC Regents. Reprinted by permission of the UC Regents.

talk about their child, might represent only certain perspectives. Nonetheless, I managed to pool a diverse set of parents despite the small size in terms of disclosing time and time lapse—some parents have known for years and a few have recently found out. I did receive some "no" answers to my request. I also offered complete anonymity in the interviews; most preferred pseudonyms. Names with an asterisk sign denote pseudonyms.

I interviewed thirteen parents altogether, all mothers except for two fathers.[2] The interviewee pool consisted of four single mothers by divorce, a widower, two couples, and four married mothers. The ethnicities included four Chinese, four Japanese, three Pilipinas, one Vietnamese, and one Korean. Most live in California with one in Portland and another in Hawaii. All of the interviews occurred in English with the exception of one interview conducted in Japanese with the lesbian daughter as translator. Ten out of the thirteen interviewees are first generation immigrants. The other three are third generation Japanese American. I interviewed four mothers of gay sons including one mother with two gay sons. The rest had lesbian daughters including one mother with two lesbian daughters. Six were told and seven inadvertently discovered about their children's sexual orientation.[3] . . .

ATTITUDES OF PARENTS TOWARD GAYS' AND LESBIANS' PRE-DISCLOSURE

The knowledge of lesbians and gay men in their native countries and in their communities in the United States serves as an important factor in dismantling the oft-used phrase that a son or daughter is gay or lesbian because of assimilation and acculturation in a western context. The parents interviewed did not utter "it's a white disease," a phrase often heard and used when discussing coming out in an Asian American community and context. Connie S. Chan in her essay, "Issues of Identity Development among Asian American Lesbians and Gay Men," found in her study that nine out of ninety-five respondents were out to their parents. Chan suggested that this low number might be related to ". . . specific cultural values defining the traditional roles, which help to explain the reluctance of Asian-American lesbians and gay men to 'come out' to their parents and families."[4]

Nonetheless, the parents interviewed recounted incidents of being aware of lesbians and gays while they were growing up and did not blame assimilating and Anglo American culture for their children's sexual orientation. One quote by Lucy Nguyen, a fifty-three year old Vietnamese immigrant who has two gay sons, does, however, imply that the environment and attitudes of the United States allowed for her sons to express their gay identity. She stated:

I think all the gay activities and if I live at this time, environment like this, I think I'm lesbian. You know, be honest. When I was young, the society in—Vietnam is so strict—I have a really close friend, I love

her, but just a friendship nothing else. In my mind, I say, well in this country it's free. They have no restraint, so that's why I accept it, whatever they are.

This revealing remark assumes that an open environment allows for freedom of sexual expression. Nevertheless, it does not necessarily suggest lesbians and gay men exist solely because of a nurturing environment. Rather lesbians and gay men must live and survive in different ways and/or make choices depending on the climate of the society at the time.

Midori Asakura,* a sixty-three-year-old Japanese immigrant with a lesbian daughter, related an example of lesbianism in Japan. She remembered, while studying to be a nurse, talk in the dorm rooms about "S," which denotes women who had really close friendships with one another. She recalled,

One day you'd see one woman with a certain blouse and the next day, you'd see the other woman with the same blouse. They would always sit together, they went everywhere together. There was talk that they were having sex, but I didn't think they were. . . . People used to say they felt each other out. I thought, "Nah, they're not having sex, why would they?" Everyone thought it was strange but no one really got into it.

When asked what she thought of the "S" women, Midori replied, "I didn't think much of it, although I thought one was man-like, Kato-san, and the other, Fukuchi-san, who was very beautiful and sharp-minded, was the woman."

Another parent, George Tanaka,* a fifty-three-year-old Japanese American who grew up in Hawaii and has a lesbian daughter, remembers a particular person known as *mahu*.[5] Toni Barraquiel, a fifty-four-year-old Pilipina single mother with a gay son, commented on gay men in Manila because of their effeminacy and admission of being gay. Toni asserted these men would be in certain careers such as manicurists and hairdressers. When asked of the people's attitudes toward them she replied, that they look down on those gays and lesbians, they make fun of them. . . . It seems as if it is an abnormal thing. The lesbian is not as prominent as the gays. They call her a tomboy because she's very athletic and well built.

Maria Santos,* a fifty-four-year-old Pilipina immigrant with two lesbian daughters, spoke of gays and lesbians in Luzon. She said, "There were negative attitudes about them. 'Bakla' and 'Tomboy'—it was gay-bashing in words not in physical terms. There was name-calling that I did not participate in."

Lucy Nguyen* had lesbian classmates in her all-girls high school. She said, "They were looked down upon, because this isn't normal. They were called 'homo.'" A common thread throughout the observations of the parents about gays and lesbians lies in stereotypical gender role associations. For example, Margaret Tsang,* a sixty-year-old Chinese single parent who has a gay son, recalled a family member who might possibly be gay, although there was not a name for it. She observed, "He was slanted toward nail polish and make-ups and all kinds of things. And he liked Chinese opera. He behaved in a very feminine fashion."

Similarly, Liz Lee, a forty-two-year old Korean single parent with a lesbian daughter, clearly remembered lesbians in Seoul. "My mother's friend was always dressed like man in suit. She always had mousse or grease on her hair and she dressed like a man. She had five or six girlfriends always come over." Liz related that she did not think anything about it and said they were respected.[6] When asked of people's attitudes toward these women, Liz responded, "They say nature made a mistake. They didn't think it was anybody's choice or anybody's preference."

For the most part the interviewees, aware of gay and lesbians during their growing up years, associated gender role reversals with gays and lesbians. The men were feminine and the women looked male or tomboy with the women couples in a butch–femme type relationship. The belief and experiences with lesbians and gay men who dress and act in opposite gender roles serve as the backdrop of what to compare their children with when faced with their coming out. Most of what these parents see is a part of homosexuality, the dress or behavior. They have not seen the whole range of affectional, emotional, intellectual and sexual components of a person. Although I asked the interviewees if they had any thoughts or attitudes about lesbians or gay men, most said they did not think about them and did not participate in the name calling or bashing. This might not be necessarily true because they were able to relate quite a few incidents of homophobic opinions which might have been internalized. Moreover, once they know they have a lesbian or gay child, that distance or non-judgmental attitude radically changes. As one mother remarked, "the fire is on the other side of the river bank. The matter is taking place somewhere else, it's not your problem."

DISCLOSURE OR DISCOVERY

For the most part, parents experience a wide range of emotions, feelings and attitudes when they find out they have a lesbian daughter or a gay son. Parents find out through a variety of ways, ranging from a direct disclosure by the child themselves, discovering the fact from a journal, confronting the child because of suspicions or by walking in on them.

For example, Liz Lee, who walked in on her daughter Sandy, said, "[it was] the end of the world. Still today I can't relate to anything that's going on with my daughter, but I'm accepting." She found out in 1990 and said,

> I was hoping it was a stage she's going through and that she could change. I didn't accept for a long time. I didn't think she would come out in the open like this. I thought she would just keep it and later on get married. That's what I thought but she's really out and open. . . . I said to myself I accept it because she is going to live that way.

Because Sandy serves as the co-chair of the Gay, Lesbian and Bisexual Association at school, her mother sees Sandy as happy and politically fulfilled from this position, which assists her process in accepting Sandy's sexual orientation. However, like many of the parents interviewed, she initially thought she had done something wrong. "I didn't lead a normal life at the time either. But Sandy always accept me as I was and she was always happy when I was happy and I think that's love. As long as Sandy's happy."

Toni Barraquiel responded differently when Joel told her at an early age of thirteen or fourteen that he was gay back in the mid 1980s. She plainly asked him if he felt happy [to] which he replied affirmatively. Thus her response, "well, if you're happy I'll support you, I'll be happy for you." Their relationship as a single mother and only child has always been one of closeness and open communication so problems did not arise in terms of disclosing his sexual orientation. Toni Barraquiel experienced confusion because at the time he had girlfriends and she did not think of him as a typical feminine gay man, since he looked macho. She also wondered if her single mother role had anything to do with Joel's gay orientation:

Maybe because I raised him by myself, it was a matriarchal thing. I have read now that these gays, there is something in the anatomy of their bodies that affect the way they are. So it is not because I raised him alone, maybe it's in the anatomy of the body. Even if I think that because I raised him alone as a mother, even if he came out to be gay, he was raised a good person. No matter what I would say I'm still lucky he came out to be like that.

In the end she accepted Joel no matter what caused his sexual orientation.

Katherine Tanaka,* a fifty-three-year-old Japanese American from Hawaii, found out about Melissa's lesbianism through an indirect family conversation. George Tanaka* brought up the issue of sexuality and asked Melissa* if she was a lesbian. He suspected after reading her work on the computer. Katherine* remembered her response:

I was in a state of shock. I didn't expect it, so I didn't know how to react. It was the thing of disbelief, horror and shame and the whole thing. I guess I felt the Asian values I was taught surface in the sense that something was wrong. That she didn't turn out the way we had raised her to be.

George Tanaka* recalled, "After we hugged, she went off to her bedroom. As she was walking away from us, all of a sudden I felt like she was a stranger. I thought I knew [her]. Here was a very important part of her and I didn't know anything about it." The idea of not knowing one's children anymore after discovering their sexual orientation remains a common initial response from the interviewees. Because of this one aspect, parents believe their child has changed and is no longer the person they thought they knew. For example one parent said:

The grieving process took a long time. Especially the thing about not being a bride. Not having her be a bride was a very devastating change of plans for her life. I thought I was in her life and it made me feel when she said she was a lesbian that there was no place for me in her life. I didn't know how I could fit into her life because I didn't know how to be the mother of a lesbian.

Upon finding out the parents interviewed spoke of common responses and questions they had. What did I do wrong? Was I responsible for my child's lesbian or gay identity? What will others think? How do I relate to my child? What role do I have now that I know my child is a lesbian or gay man? The emotions a parent has ranged from the loss of a dream they had for their child to a fear of what is in store for them as a gay or lesbian person in this society.

Nancy Shigekawa,* a third-generation Japanese American born and residing in Hawaii, recalled her reaction:

I had come home one night and they were in the bedroom. Then I knew it wasn't just being in the room. My reaction was outrage, to say the least. I was so angry. I told them to come out . . . and I said [to her girlfriend] "I'm going to kill you if you ever come back." That's how I was feeling. I look back now and think I must have been like a crazy lady.

Maria Santos* remembered her discovery.

I found out through a phone call from the parents of [her] best friend. They [Cecilia* and her friend] were trying to sneak out and they had a relationship. I thought it would go away. Let her see a psychiatrist. But she fooled me. In her second year at college she told me she was a lesbian. It broke my heart. That was the first time I heard the word lesbian, but I knew what it meant. Like the tomboy.

She also had a feeling about her youngest daughter, Paulette*:

At Cecilia's graduation I saw them talking secretly and I saw the pink triangle on her backpack. I can't explain it. It's a mother's instinct. I prayed that it would not be so [starts to cry]. Paulette told me in a letter that she was a lesbian and that Cecilia had nothing to do with it. I wanted it to change. I had the dream, that kids go to college, get married and have kids.

Maria Santos* did not talk to anyone about her daughters. She grew up having to face the world on her own without talking to others. However, she said, "But I read books, articles all about gays and lesbians as members of the community. They are normal people. I did not read negative things about them."

In this sense parents also have a coming out process that they go through. They must deal with internalized homophobia and reevaluate their beliefs and feelings about lesbians and gay men. One method in this process includes reading about and listening to gay men and lesbians talk about their lives. Having personal contact or at least information on lesbian and gay life takes the mystery out of the stereotypes and misconceptions that parents might have of lesbian and gay people. What helped some women was the per-

sonal interaction and reading about lesbian and gay men's lives. They had more information with which to contrast, contradict, and support their previous notions of lesbians and gay men.

Yet sometimes some parents interviewed have not yet read or do not seek outside help or information. Some of the parents did not talk to others and have remained alone in their thinking. This does not necessarily have negative effects. Liz Lee said, "Still today I don't think I can discuss this with her in this matter because I can't relate. . . . I can't handle it. I wouldn't know how to talk to her about this subject. I just let her be happy."

MG Espiritu,* a sixty-year-old Pilipina immigrant, believes her daughter's lesbianism stems from environmental causes such as being with other lesbians. Nonetheless, less than a couple of years after finding out about her daughter Michelle, she went with her daughter to an Asian Pacific lesbian Lunar New Year banquet. MG* did so because her daughter wanted it and she wanted to please her. When asked how she felt at the event, MG* replied, "Oh, it's normal. It's just like my little girls' parties that they go to." She speaks of little by little trying to accept Michelle's lesbianism.

PARENTS, FRIENDS, AND THEIR ETHNIC COMMUNITIES

For some parents having a lesbian or gay child brings up the issue of their status and reputation in the community and family network. Questions such as: What is society going to think of me? Will the neighbors know and what will it reflect upon us? Did they raise a bad child?

I told her we would have to move away from this house. I felt strongly neighbors and friends in the community would not want to associate with us if they knew we had a child who had chosen to be homosexual.

The above quote reflected one parent's original reaction. Now she feels differently but is still not quite out to her family in Hawaii.

Some parents have told their siblings or friends. Others do not talk to relatives or friends at all because of fear they will not understand.

The following quote highlighted a typical anxiety of parents:

> I was ashamed. I felt I had a lot to do with it too. In my mind I'm not stupid, I'm telling myself, I know I didn't do it to her. I don't know if it's only because I'm Japanese . . . that's the way I saw it. I felt a sense of shame, that something was wrong with my family. I would look at Debbie* and just feel so guilty that I have these thoughts that something's wrong with her. But mostly I was selfish. I felt more for myself, what I am going to say? How am I going to react to people when they find out?

Despite her apprehension in the beginning, she did disclose Debbie's lesbianism to a close friend:

> I have a dear friend who I finally told because she was telling me about these different friends who had gay children. I couldn't stand it, I said, "You know, Bea, I have to tell you my daughter is gay." She was dumbfounded. I'm starting to cheer her up and all that. That was a big step for me to come out.

Nancy Shigekawa's* quote emphasizes the complexity of feelings that parents have when adjusting to their children's sexual orientation.

If parents are not close to their immediate family, they might not have told them. Others have not spoken because they do not care whether or not their family knows. Some parents do not disclose the fact of their gay son or lesbian daughter to protect them from facing unnecessary problems.

When asked how their respective ethnic communities feel about lesbians and gay men, some parents responded with firm conviction. Liz Lee, who spoke about the Korean community, said, "As long as they're not in their house, not in their life, they accept it perfectly." She mentioned her daughter's lesbianism to a nephew but not to others in her family. "I'm sure in the future I have to tell them, but right now nobody has asked me and I don't particularly like to volunteer." Jack Chan,*

a sixty-one-year-old Chinese immigrant, claimed, "Shame, that's a big factor. Shame brought upon the family. You have to remember the Chinese, the name, the face of the family is everything. I don't know how to overcome that."

Lucy Nguyen* gave this answer about the Vietnamese community, "They won't accept it. Because for a long, long time they say they [gays and lesbians] are not good people, that's why." Lucy felt that by talking about it would help and teach the community to open their minds. The frankness and openness of speaking out about gay and lesbians will inform people of our existence and force the issue in the open. In this way having parents come out will make others understand their experiences and allow for their validation and affirmation as well.

Although most of these parents have negative views about the acceptance level of friends and particularly with ethnic communities, some have taken steps to confide in people. One must also realize their opinion reflects their current situation and opinion, which might change over time. Three of the parents have participated in panels and discussions on Asian American parents with lesbian and gay kids. . . .

NOTES

1. See Kitty Tsui, *the words of a woman who breathes fire* (San Francisco: Spinsters Ink, 1983). C. Chung, Alison Kim, and A. K. Lemshewsky eds., *Between the Lines: An Anthology by Pacific/Asian Lesbians* (Santa Cruz: Dancing Bird Press, 1987). Rakesh Ratti, ed., *A Lotus of Another Color: The Unfolding of the South Asian Gay and Lesbian Experience* (Boston: Alyson Press, 1993). Silvera Makeda, ed., *A Piece of My Heart: A Lesbian of Colour Anthology* (Toronto: Sister Vision Press, 1993).

2. Mothers comprise the majority of the parents interviewed. Perhaps mothers are more apt to talk about their feelings and emotions about having a gay son or lesbian daughter than the father. Mothers might be more understanding and willing to discuss their emotions and experiences than the fathers who also know.

3. I did not interview parents who had a bisexual child. I believe a son or daughter who comes out as bisexual might encounter a different set of questions and reactions, especially since the parent might hope and persuade the

daughter or son to "choose" heterosexuality instead of homosexuality.
4. Connie S. Chan, "Issues of Identity Development among Asian-American Lesbians and Gay Men." *Journal of Counseling and Development,* 68 (Sept/Oct, 1989), 19.
5. *Mahu* does not necessarily mean gay but defines a man who dresses and acts feminine. However, its common usage does denote a gay man.
6. Liz based this respect on this particular woman's election to something similar to a city council and her standing in the community.

? Think about It

1. What were the attitudes toward homosexuality in the home countries of the parents whom Hom interviewed?
2. How did the parents in Hom's study react to the disclosure or discovery of their children's being gay or lesbian?
3. How do ethnic communities affect parental feelings and behavior about having gay or lesbian offspring? Do you think that these reactions differ from those in non-Asian communities?

21 *Parenting and the Stress of Immigration among Jordanian Mothers*

Marianne Hattar-Pollara and Afaf I. Meleis

Parenting can be especially difficult for many immigrants because the new environment is unfamiliar or inhospitable. Marianne Hattar-Pollara and Afaf I. Meleis describe how everyday stresses complicate child rearing as immigrants, especially mothers, settle in, try to maintain their cultural customs and values, and learn how things work in the host society.

THE JORDANIAN FAMILY: WOMEN AND THEIR ROLES

. . . In the Arab culture, the family is the center of all social organizations and constitutes the dominant social institution through which individuals and groups inherit their religious, class, and cultural affiliations (Barakat, 1993; Patai, 1983). "The very concept of family in Arabic (*'aila* or

Source: From Marianne Hattar-Pollara and Afaf I. Meleis, "The Stress of Immigration and the Daily Lived Experiences of Jordanian Immigrant Women in the United States," *Western Journal of Nursing Research* 17 (Spring 1995): 521–39. Copyright © 1995 Sage Publications, Inc. Reprinted by permission of Sage Publications, Inc.

usra) reflects such mutual commitments and relationships as interdependence and reciprocity. The root of the words *'aila* and *usra* means "to support." Although the father's role is defined as provider (*janna*) and the mother's role as homemaker (*banna*), children change from being *'iyal* (dependents) to *sanad* (supporters) once their parents reach old age" (Barakat, 1993, p. 98).

Kin ties mark the Jordanians' strongest loyalty and alliance (Racy, 1970). Through such ties, the individual in each nuclear family, and within the context of the extended kin system of *hammulleh,* receives his or her sense of identity and belonging, as well as security and support in times of individual and societal distress (Barakat, 1993; Patai, 1983). However, with these privileges comes a set of certain duties and obligations that are expected from all single family units and their individual members. There is an essential requirement for the individual to subordinate him/herself to the family and the *hammulleh* with which they are identified (Barakat, 1993; Berger, 1964; Patai, 1983). This subordination involves putting the needs and priorities of the family as a whole ahead of and beyond personal needs and desires. This hierarchical structure is based on gender and age and, as such, requires the young to obey the old and adhere to their expectations. Within these lines of relationships, the success or failure of an individual member becomes that of the family as a whole (Barakat, 1993). Thus failures are not confined to the individual or to the nuclear family; instead, a failed member means a failed family.

Within such a context, women in the Jordanian family occupy a dynamic position in managing role relationships, interpersonal relations, and social interaction within and outside the family unit. In the tradition of the Jordanian family, the father's role as provider and head of the family (*rabb al-usra*) also means that he is the authoritative figure and ultimate decision maker in the family. He expects respect and unquestioning compliance with his instructions. By contrast, the mother is assigned the role of housewife. Although cultural norms assign family power to the father, the wife actually exercises power over the children and is, in effect, entrusted with raising and disciplining them. Hence she also performs the role of mediator between the children and the father. As Meleis and Rogers (1987) indicate, women in developing countries tend to have a negotiating or intermediary role in family interactions which takes the form of advocate for children in decisions made by the husband. Women also have an advocacy role for males in the family to "save face," to maintain their re-

spect, and to protect them from direct confrontations with children, other members of the extended family, or both. Women in the Jordanian family play an equally crucial role in maintaining close kin ties and in negotiating and promoting the position of their family unit in the community. This may take the form of meeting culturally sanctioned social obligations, minimizing situations of conflict, and negotiating problem-solving strategies among other women of the extended family. Although this role of negotiator conveys a great degree of informal power in influencing decisions, it is a burdensome one with the potential to cause emotional distress and family polarization, thus draining one's energy and leading to emotional burnout, according to Meleis and Rogers (1987).

The findings of the few reported studies on Arab Americans and Arab Canadians identify a wide range of adjustment difficulties involving the traditional structure of the family and role relations between spouses and between parents and children (Abu-Laban, 1980; Ahdab-Yehia, 1970; Elkholy, 1966). Therefore, given the cultural background of Jordanian immigrant women, which stands in contrast with the American way of life, and the potential negative consequences of immigration, there is a need to understand and document their daily lived experiences, and the stressors that shape them.

METHOD

This study is part of a larger one, the focus of which was to describe and examine the relationships between immigration-related stress and adolescent rearing-related stress and the physical and emotional health of Jordanian American mothers. This report focuses on an in-depth account of the lived experiences and the perceived stress associated with being Jordanian immigrant women in the United States. A descriptive design was used for this part of the study.

The Setting

The study was conducted in the greater Los Angeles area, which included the city of Los Angeles, the San Fernando Valley, and the San Gabriel Valley. Access to potential subjects in the community was problematic, due to the lack of an established directory of community members. The snowballing technique, in which subjects provide access to potential subjects, was used. This process was a very lengthy and exhaustive one to facilitate access to all potential subjects in the greater Los Angeles area and thus ensure adequate representation of the target population.

Participants

Thirty Jordanian American immigrant women participated in this study. All were mothers and first-generation immigrants (born in Jordan), and they ranged in age from 35 to 59, with a mean age of 45 years. Of the women, 50% were Catholic, 40% were Greek Orthodox, and 10% were Protestant. Approximately 93% were married, one was separated, and one was widowed. Approximately 57% resided in the San Gabriel Valley, and 43% resided in the San Fernando Valley. The subjects had been immigrants to the United States for a minimum of 6 and a maximum of 33 years, with an average of 13.5 years. About 40% had immigrated to the United States to join other family members, 34% came for economic reasons, 20% came to seek a better quality of life, and 6% came for reasons of political instability in the Middle East.

The majority of the subjects (92%) were homemakers, 4% had part-time employment, and 4% were employed on a full-time basis as registered nurses. Of the sample, 20% had less than primary schooling, 37% had primary schooling, 33% had a high school education, and 10% had a junior college education. Approximately 27% of the sample reported an annual family income of $10,000 or less, 40% reported an income of $30,000 or less, 20% reported an income of $50,000 or less, and approximately 13% reported family earnings of more than $50,000.

Procedure

Interviews were conducted with participants in their homes and were 1½ to 2 hours in duration. English and/or Arabic languages were used depending on the participant's preference. . . .

RESULTS

Participants in this study revealed several themes regarding perceived sources of stress. These were conceptualized as (a) the daily living of settling in, (b) the quest for ethnic continuity, and (c) the re-creation of familiarity.

Daily Living, Settling In

The first few years after immigration were particularly stressful for the Jordanian American women in this study. Finding jobs or establishing a steady source of income, enrolling and settling children in schools, and establishing a home, along with feelings of loss of social status, loneliness, and social isolation, were among the frequently cited postimmigration stressors. One woman described her experience as a new immigrant:

> The first 3 years were really hard. I used to cry every day. My husband and I felt like lost. Neither him nor I spoke English. We sold everything we owned in Jordan and we came with what we thought would be a lot of money, but we were so discouraged to find out that we could not even buy a home or start a small business here. My husband, who was a landlord in Jordan, had to take a night job in a factory where speaking English was not required.

Children's education was identified as a top priority for women in this study. However, following and managing their educational requirements was perceived as being difficult. Participants spoke often of the language barrier and of their inability to coach or monitor the learning progress of their children, and of their inability to communicate with school officials. The following quote reflects the typical experience of most participants:

One of the main reasons that pushed us to come to America is children's education. The problem I face, as well as my husband, is the English language. We cannot tell if they are doing well or not. Back home, we could ask the help of a cousin or uncle, but here everyone is to himself.

School also presented other sources of stress to these women. They perceived the school's environment as a threat to their children because of their exposure to the value systems of other children and teachers, which are drastically different from their own. The coeducational system, after-school activities, and school dance parties, among other things, are alien to these Jordanian American women, and they are considered to conflict with the family's values. One woman expressed it this way:

When it comes to the behavior of my children, I am tough. I have to be tough and make sure they know that we are different because, if I do not, who will? The environment of schools, the parties, and the daily interaction between boys and girls, especially teenagers, may influence our kids in ways that go against our culture. I and my husband always keep an eye on them. We take and bring them from school. I also go to school always to find out what kind of friends they have and what the teachers think of them.

Language barriers were also blamed, in part, for feelings of loneliness and social isolation. Difficulties in understanding media news reports, in communicating with others, and in reading newspapers reinforced their sense of loneliness and social isolation. The majority of the participants identified the necessity of having to learn English quickly, but this priority was not without challenges. One woman who completed primary school pointed out the great difficulty she had in trying to make sense of the English vocabulary:

It was a terrible feeling, to be left at home alone without understanding a word of what was being said on television or on the radio. My husband used to leave early for his job and all the children were in school. Many times I felt as if life was being choked out of me. I wanted to talk with people. I wanted to know what was happening in the world around me, but I soon realized that the only way out of this is to learn English. I started by matching the sounds of words in English with words in Arabic, and I would ask the children the meaning of the words I was trying to learn. They used to laugh and say, "Mother, that is not the way it is pronounced," but little by little, I made it, and made my family proud of me.

Other difficulties pertained to managing the household and carrying out essential and ordinary daily tasks, such as shopping for food, using public transportation, writing a check, or paying monthly bills. These tasks were identified as being unusually difficult, and were sources of great fear and anxiety, especially during the first few months following immigration. However, as participants practiced with these activities, confidence and self-reliance replaced fear and anxiety. Women described how believing in the inevitability of having to master these daily living skills forced them to cope with their perceived lack of mastery.

If anyone told me that, within few months, I will be able to do all what I am doing now, I would have died from laughter! Shopping was a major ordeal. I did not know how to take public transportation. I was afraid of getting lost. So I used to walk more than 5 miles with bags of groceries. I also did not know what to buy. It took me months before knowing what is good and what is not.

Shock about the seeming unfriendliness of neighbors, and at times, their perceived outright hostility, was also evident. Women expressed frustration and sadness with the seemingly unfriendly attitudes of their "American" neighbors, which, in turn reinforced their feelings of being foreigners and undermined their sense of belonging. Participants were always reminded that they did not really belong in some subtle and not so subtle ways. There reminders eroded their attempts to become integrated into American society.

> We have been living here for years, and we still do not know the names of our neighbors. I tried to get to know them and invited them over for coffee, but all my attempts were frustrated. I do not know! We grew up among people. People are for people [an Arabic proverb] but, here, each is for himself. [A] few days ago, we were in the house of one of our relatives for a baptism party, and all of a sudden we found out that the police were called by the neighbors because they were disturbed by our noise. Such a thing would never happen in Jordan. People there are a lot more tolerant and, if they have a problem, they would talk to each other, not call the police!

Immigration and the first few years of being an immigrant produce a number of new demands and challenges for these women. Some of the practical and more immediate demands, such as enrolling and settling children in school, finding a steady source of income, and learning about how things worked in the host society, were surmounted and overcome. However, other aspects of settling in appeared to continue beyond the first few years of immigration. Issues pertaining to the lack of integration reinforced their quest for ethnic continuity.

The Quest for Ethnic Continuity

Women felt very strongly about their need to maintain their ethnic identification and their sense of who they are as Jordanian women, wives, and mothers. However, they perceived the sharp contrast between the traditional values governing their family life and the patterns of family life in the larger society as being particularly challenging to their sense of identity as Jordanians and to their roles as wives and mothers. When asked "What has been most stressful to you about living in the United States?" almost all began by asserting that they are Arabs first and foremost, which meant that they are fundamentally very different from Americans. They identified differences in all aspects of family living, including values that govern family relations between husbands and wives, parents and children, and nuclear and extended families, and the larger Jordanian community in the United States and in the home country.

The need to maintain ethnic continuity stems not only from their own and their spouses' strong desires, but also from the need to escape the negative judgment of the larger Jordanian community in the United States and in the home country. The family's livelihood and sense of meaningful social existence depends largely on the kind of social judgment others hold about the family and its members. Such judgment creates pressure for conformity and is inescapable, because of the many implications it has on the family unit as a social entity. First and foremost, the family's derived sense of meaningful social existence is largely defined by the social standing and position of the family in the community. Second, conformity brings honor and social prestige; failure to conform, however, brings shame. Therefore, for these women, maintaining ethnic continuity is not only a personal choice, but also a strong cultural expectation with far-reaching consequences, as one woman explains:

> I spend most of my energy on teaching my kids our customs and norms, and I take every chance to point out to them the right from the wrong. I worry a lot because I see what is going on out there of promiscuity, drugs, and alcohol. I always tell them that their father and I are willing to sacrifice our health and everything we own for their sake as long as they follow our teachings and raise our heads in the community. We just cannot take any chance, and we have to make sure that our name will not be disfigured; otherwise, what is the point of being here? Nothing is worth putting the name of the family in the mud.

The positive effects of family members' conformity include acquiring and being awarded a sense of immense pride for fulfilling, according to tradition, the parenting role. This translates into putting the family as a whole in a highly desirable social position, thus guaranteeing the family's good name, the social support and close social ties, and eventually the marriage of sons and daughters to members of the community. As one woman said:

Our life and the future of our children depends on our position in the community. Everything goes back to the mother. People will say "if the mother is good, then the children will be good." People would then seek us and feel honored to establish close ties and ask for the hand of my daughter for marriage. This would be the same for my sons also because, before any family would expect to marry their daughter off, they would ask about everything pertaining to the family, including the behavior of the parents, grandparents, and even the great-grandparents.

Among other negative consequences of the failure to conform is "bad-mouthing" the family and its name by members of the community. The consequences of this lead to shame, social disgrace, and social isolation.

The most important and biggest hope for us, which we live for, is to live with honor among our people, and to raise our children in a way that will make us feel proud, and help us keep our heads raised high in the community. People here and in Jordan are watching and waiting for a chance to talk. We also care a lot about our customs, and we just cannot let anything touch or implicate the family's name because if this happens, God forbid, we will then blacken our face ["lose face"]. You know, if one's face is blackened, that is it, one is finished, one cannot receive the respect and regard of others and cannot even look at them in the eyes. One will then forever live with the head bent down and looking to the floor; he forever will be shamed.

The women in this study perceived the need for conformity, within the perceived cultural contrast with the mainstream American way of life, as a major challenge that gives them a sense of burden and overload in carrying out their roles. Role overload is defined as the addition of duties and responsibilities to their daily functions, without the relief of already established ones. It also denotes a perceived lack of societal support in fulfilling their role obligations.

Life here is very difficult; everything in this new environment works against us. Back home, life, in and outside the home, is the same. What we teach at home is reinforced by the society, but here we have too much responsibility to keep the family together. My husband works long hours and we basically do not see him much except on Sundays. So it [rests] upon me to raise children according to our customs, and it is essentially my fault if they failed or made mistakes, because the mother and the home environment are the ones that influence children most.

In contrast to the interdependence and cooperation among members of extended families in the home country, participants identified an evolving competitive attitude among single Jordanian immigrant family units here in the United States. This competitive attitude denotes comparing and contrasting the financial success of others in the community, and the efforts made trying to keep up with their apparent success. Financial success was identified as a source of both pride and stress. Families who have "made it" financially are awarded more respect than those who are still struggling. However, the most significant aspect of this competitive attitude is its implication on the patterns of socialization and social relations among families in the community, and the barrier it creates in terms of sharing and exchanging support. Several participants pointed out their hesitancy to share or discuss the problems they face in their daily lives, be it financial or otherwise, because, as one woman put it, "people are waiting to hear one negative thing about you."

The pressure from within to maintain ethnic continuity and to conform, in conjunction with the competitive attitude from the ethnic community, in an environment that does not reciprocate the same value system, seem to be the reasons for a lack of integration in the host society. These reasons can also explain why being Jordanian immigrant women versus becoming American is not a choice, but a strong cultural expectation, due to the potential losses and negative consequences that nonconformity may bring.

The Re-creation of Familiarity

Participants identified a number of stressors that persist, regardless of the passage of time. Among these stressors were persistent feelings of loneliness, nostalgia, being a foreigner, and of a diminished social network. One of the main reasons for experiencing such stressors pertained to how participants viewed the nature of social life in the American society versus what they were accustomed to in their homeland. Issues related to the pace of life in the United States, the intensive involvement of people in their work, their individuality and personal privacy, and the formalities in interactions were identified as factors contributing to their sense of persistent loneliness, their diminished social network, and their failure to feel that they belonged.

> There are many things that I like about life here: the individual freedom, the free speech, the human rights, even the personal privacy sometimes. These are great things in this great country. However, no matter how well we like and try to adapt to these values, we will suffer because we are used to lots of people around us, we are used to sharing our lives. We are spontaneous people, but life here leaves little room for spontaneity. Everybody is busy, the men are busy all day long, the women are consumed by the needs of the family and the children, we cannot socialize like we used to, and now we have to make an appointment to visit a relative or friend. What kind of a life is this when the chances of developing close friendly relationships are not there? I miss the old days so much that sometimes it hurts inside. We used to gather over a morning cup of coffee and talk about everything in life. I never knew how valuable this was, because now I do not find somebody to talk or share with my thoughts and feelings.

Other reasons related to participants' perceived limited ability to relate to how "Americans" conduct their lives, or to feeling misunderstood by members of the host society. Being misunderstood was a theme that ranged from being stereotyped as a category of women who are subordinate and submissive, to classifying the Arab culture as primitive and backward. Accounts of this stereotype were experienced not only by participants, but also by their children at school. One participant gave the following account of an interaction that took place during a group swimming lesson for one of her children at the YMCA:

> I did not realize why all the women, who were sitting by the pool, were shocked when I told them that I got married after one week of engagement. I am proud of that, but after talking with them, I felt like I should be embarrassed. It is really confusing sometimes. I tried to explain to them our ways, but their ideas about life are very different.

The re-creation of familiarity was a theme that emerged from the methods participants used to manage these persistent stressors, and to create an infrastructure within which ethnic continuity could be maintained. It is defined here in terms of the efforts that participants and their spouses made to establish a social network of their own kind, and to re-create a social environment that resembled the social environment of the home country. The re-creation of familiarity was also designed to provide the cultural environment within which children are socialized and taught the ways of the culture. Most of the participants revealed that the only possible way to effectively manage and counteract the daily challenges in their lives was through religion. This strategy was evident by the intense involvement of the women who were residing in the San Fernando Valley in the already established Arab American Eastern Rite Melkite parish. As for the community in San Gabriel Valley, a number of women and their spouses took charge of corresponding with church officials in the home country to help them establish an Arab American parish which would minister to their religious and social needs. After two visits by the Patriarch of Jerusalem and the Bishop of Jordan, a Jordanian priest was assigned to establish an Arab American parish in the Los Angeles area. In one church gathering, which was organized by the Arab parish priest to address the challenges faced by Arab American Christians, one woman stated the following:

> Today, more than ever, there are daily challenges to living within the teachings of our culture. I see challenges in my family and in my social relationships, but what distresses me the most are the challenges faced by my children, which can potentially endanger their lives as well as their souls. In searching for ways to assist, guide, and teach my children to live their lives as they should, I find myself turning to God and the faith I was raised with. Being an Arab American Christian is the core of my motherhood. I cannot imagine life any other way. My faith and culture are synonymous. Living a life of faith is inherent to being Arabic.

Thus religiosity was the common denominator that pulled the majority of Jordanian immigrant women together and strengthened them as a group. This common thread of religion mobilized the resources of the group to establish Arab American parishes, and to bring an Arab priest from the home country to meet their unique religious and social needs. For them, the only available means of maintaining their ethnic continuity while gaining a sense of belonging was through re-creating familiarity. As it is now, a great deal of religious and social activities take place within these parishes. Among these are monthly picnics, dance parties for the whole family, dance parties for the children, and parties designed to celebrate American holidays such as the Fourth of July and Thanksgiving. These social activities, which mimic the social activities of the dominant society, are instituted not only to re-create a social network among those of their own kind, but also to provide a sense of normalcy for the children. As one woman explained:

> We expect a lot from our children. We want them to continue living the same way we are living, but it is important for them to have more or less similar so-

cial activities as their American peers. They need to feel normal. Organizing dance parties is not something we thought we would do because we are not used to this style of life, but we feel a lot better to provide that in a safe, controlled environment and under the supervision of a priest. It is good for them and for us because, this way, they meet with children from the same background.

REFERENCES

Abu-Laban, B. (1980). *An olive branch on the family tree: The Arabs in Canada.* Toronto: McClelland & Stewart.

Ahdab-Yehia, M. (1970). *Some general characteristics of the Lebanese Maronite community residing in Detroit: A sociological investigation.* Unpublished master's thesis, Wayne State University, Detroit, MI.

Barakat, H. (1993). *The Arab world: Society, culture, and estate.* Berkeley: University of California Press.

Berger, M. (1964). *The Arab world today.* New York: Doubleday, Anchor.

Elkholy, A. (1966). *The Arab Muslims in the United States.* New Haven, CT: College and University Press.

Meleis, A. I., & Rogers, S. (1987). Women in transition: Being versus becoming or being and becoming. *Health Care for Women International, 8,* 199–217.

Patai, R. (1983). *The Arab mind.* New York: Charles Scribner's Sons.

Racy, J. (1970). Psychiatry in the Arab East. *Acta Psychiatrica Scandinava, 221* (Suppl.), 1–71.

Think about It

1. In what ways do the gender expectations of Jordanian women place high demands on parenting roles within and outside the family unit?
2. How does maintaining ethnic continuity and conformity to the larger Jordanian community in the United States result in role overload and pressures to be a "perfect" mother?
3. Why, according to Hattar-Pollara and Meleis, does religion play an important role in child rearing?

CHAPTER 5

Work Experiences, Discrimination, and Family Life

Ethnic women, including those who are married, are joining the labor force in ever increasing numbers. In ethnic households, work and family roles become especially intricate because people are coping with racial and economic discrimination. Besides discrimination, the readings in Chapter 5 highlight two other important themes. The second theme is the complex intersections between race/ethnicity, gender, and social class that are at the heart of many work issues. Researchers (in the selections that follow and elsewhere) don't simply describe ethnic families, women and men, or socioeconomic status. They show, instead, how *being* a woman or a man *and* from an ethnic group *and* in a particular social class influences economic realities, social mobility, and interpersonal family relationships. The third important theme is the shaping of individual choices and work experiences by structural factors such as migration prospects.

Commuter marriages demonstrate some of the complex interconnections between race, gender, socioeconomic status, and economic structures. Such marriages are not a new phenomenon. Certain occupations and specific circumstances have often necessitated temporary marital separations (e.g., military service, war, incarceration, frequent business travel, seasonal work by construction or migrant workers). An increasing number of today's couples, however, are opting for commuter marriages to pursue individual career aspirations.[1] According to Anita P. Jackson and her associates, black dual-career commuter marriages are rising in response to exclusionary employment practices (Reading 22). Although commuter marriages increase career options and social mobility, they take a toll on the couple's interpersonal relationships, child–parent interactions, community life, and friendship networks.

The next two readings examine the interstices of work, race, ethnicity, and gender in white-collar and working-class families. Denise A. Segura's study of Chicanas explores the linkages between organizational stereotypes about ethnic groups, occupational segregation, and racial discrimination. Moreover, Segura shows that sexual harassment diminishes women's dignity and effectiveness in the workplace (Reading 23).

Segura found that the Chicanas in her sample adhered to traditional gender roles at home despite work responsibilities. She posits that this seeming contradiction is a rational accommodation to the relatively rigid constraints imposed by both gender and race-ethnicity. Instead of struggling with their husbands and partners over the division of household labor, "Chicanas conform to their community's gendered expectations reaffirming both their womanhood and their culture" (see page 197).[2] Other scholars maintain, however, that ethnic women's "double burden" roles reflect both the wife's and the husband's educational level and occupational achievement. For example, Chicana (and possibly other ethnic) wives who have more income and are employed more hours, and whose occupation is comparable in status to that of their husbands, are the most likely to be considered coproviders financially and to demand help with domestic chores.[3]

In Reading 24, Alex Stepick describes how Haitian immigrants, despite their strong work ethic, have encountered more problems and difficulties than many other groups because they are "triple minorities": "Not only were they foreigners, but also they spoke a language no one else spoke (Haitian Creole) and they were Black."[4] These constraints, according to Stepick, together with the modest human capital most Haitian immigrants— especially the most recent arrivals to the United States—have funneled many Haitians into the secondary employment sector, where wages are low and opportunities for advancement few.

Structural factors also have an impact on which groups of immigrants—in terms of national origin, gender, and socioeconomic status—are actively recruited to the United States. In Washington, D.C., for example, there is an unusual predominance of women among Central American immigrants (see also Reading 1). Is this because Central Americans have personal characteristics—such as level of education, English-language ability, and legal status—that enhance their desirability among some U.S. employers? Not according to Terry A. Repak's research (Reading 25). Instead, Repak maintains, the high proportion of Central Americans in domestic and service jobs in the nation's capital is the result of *gendered labor recruitment.* As many black women moved from service to clerical occupations beginning in the 1970s, international diplomats and U.S. government employees started recruiting Central American women to work as housekeepers and nannies, at very low wages and despite many of the immigrants' possessing no legal documents and little facility in English.

During this time, moreover, El Salvador, Guatemala, and Nicaragua were experiencing civil wars, a decrease in the availability of agricultural work, and a closing of many factories and other businesses. Because of these structural conditions and the cultural acceptance of the idea that women could migrate to find work, many women were available to take jobs as domestic workers and child-care providers in other countries. A construction boom and the proliferation of restaurant industries in the Washington area during the same period also attracted growing numbers of Central American immigrant men.[5]

Besides having an impact on the finding of paid work, ethnicity, gender, and social class also have an effect on the creation of employment for oneself and one's family. Bernard Wong, for example, shows how the interplay of low-paying jobs, an ideology of success, and close kinship relationships has spurred many Chinese Americans to set up their own businesses (Reading 26). Although many in the second and third generations may not be interested in continuing the business because they have more employment options than their parents did, family firms often are able to survive economic recessions because family members pitch in during hard times. In addition, a firm can be kept in the family by employing relatives (such as paternal uncles or cousins) to manage the business. As Wong and others observe, these "economic enclaves" are sometimes exploitative in their treatment of employees, many of whom are women.[6] But despite the problems and some interfamily conflicts, many of these family businesses provide Chinese Americans and other immigrants an opportunity to move up the economic ladder.[7]

NOTES

1. More than half of all married couples are *dual-earner couples* in which both marriage partners are employed outside the home. Such couples are also referred to as *dual-income, two-income, two-earner,* or *dual-worker* couples. Only about 5 percent of dual-earner families are *dual-career couples* in which both marriage partners work in professional or managerial positions that require extensive training and a long-term work commitment and offer ongoing professional growth. For these distinctions and an overview of the literature on dual-earner couples, see Nijole V. Benokraitis, *Marriages and Families: Changes, Choices, and Constraints,* 3d ed. (Upper Saddle River, NJ: Prentice Hall, 1999).

2. Other researchers have also suggested that ethnic women who bear a heavy burden of double roles accept them voluntarily because they see the traditional family role as part of their role obligation. See Kwang Chung Kim and Shin Kim, "Family and Work Roles of Korean Immigrants in the United States," in *Resiliency in Native American and Immigrant Families,* ed. Hamilton I. McCubbin, Elizabeth A. Thompson, Anne I. Thompson, and Julie E. Fromer (Thousand Oaks, CA: Sage, 1998), 225–42.

3. Scott Coltrane and Elsa O. Valdez, "Reluctant Compliance: Work-Family Role Allocation in Dual-Earner Chicano Families," in *Challenging Fronteras: Structuring Latina and Latino Lives in the U.S.,* ed. Mary Romero, Pierrette Hondagneu-Sotelo, and Vidma Ortiz (New York: Routledge, 1997), 229–57. In the same volume, see also M. Patricia Fernández-Kelly and Anna M. Garcia, "Power Surrendered, Power Restored: The Politics of Work and Family among Hispanic Garment Workers in California and Florida," 215–27.

4. Alex Stepick, *Pride against Prejudice: Haitians in the United States* (Boston: Allyn and Bacon, 1998), 4.

5. Although market needs influence immigration paths, even highly educated women scientists and engineers may have difficulty finding jobs or being promoted because they come as "unmarried secondary migrants." See Kimberly Goyette and Yu Xie, "The Intersection of Immigration and Gender: Labor Force Outcomes of Immigrant Women Scientists," *Social Science Quarterly* 80 (June 1999): 395–408.

6. See, for example, Greta A. Gilbertson, "Women's Labor and Enclave Employment: The Case of Dominican and Colombian Women in New York City," *The International Migration Review* 29 (Fall 1995): 657–70.

7. For a comprehensive discussion of enclave economies and other small business enterprises, see Min Zhou, *Chinatown: The Socioeconomic Potential of an Urban Enclave* (Philadelphia: Temple University Press, 1992).

22 | Some Benefits and Costs of Black Dual-Career Commuter Marriages

Anita P. Jackson, Ronald P. Brown, and Karen E. Patterson-Stewart

In a commuter marriage, married partners live and work in different geographic areas and get together only intermittently, such as over weekends. Anita P. Jackson, Ronald P. Brown, and Karen E. Patterson-Stewart take an in-depth look at four black commuter couples. They examine the reasons for setting up commuter marriages, which include the need to counter racial employment opportunities, and they describe the advantages and disadvantages of such arrangements and the reactions of children and friends.

REVIEW OF RELATED LITERATURE

In spite of the many studies concerning husband-wife relations and dual-career families, little research has addressed commuter marriages. The few studies that exist (Anderson, 1992; Anderson & Spruill, 1993; Bunker et al., 1992; Gerstel & Gross, 1984; Groves & Horm-Wingerd, 1991) have focused primarily on European American couples. Furthermore, most of these studies have only examined the commuter in the commuter relationship. This type of relationship is typically composed of one spouse who assumes the role of the commuter and the other spouse who lives at the primary residence and assumes the role of noncommuter. Bunker et al. (1992) noted that past research has not investigated the impact of these varying roles in the commuter relationship on the perception of experiences. Among commuter families, the lifestyle may be experienced differently as a function of one's role as commuter or noncommuter in the commuting relationship. Last, the studies reviewed were mostly quantitative, using self-report semistructured questionnaires. Issues investigated were characteristics of individuals who adopt this lifestyle, stressors they encountered, role strain, satisfaction, and quality of life issues. Although quantitative studies are useful, qualitative inquiry can enhance a deeper understanding of underlying, nonobvious issues and meanings from the lived experiences of the participants.

Previous research findings suggest that benefits of this lifestyle for the commuter are (a) increased sense of autonomy, achievement, and satisfaction; (b) enhanced self-esteem and greater confidence; (c) greater ability to pursue careers without immediate and everyday family constraints; (d) increased opportunity to use one's education; and (e) enhanced opportunity to satisfy the psychological need to develop self-identity and increase self-gratification (Chang & Wood, 1996; Douvan & Pleck, 1978; Groves & Horm-Wingerd, 1991). Benefits for the couple are greater awareness and communication with each other in the spousal relationship (Bunker et al., 1992; Groves & Horm-Wingerd, 1991).

Furthermore, studies have indicated that the commuting lifestyle provides opportunities for greater concentration and more time at work by separating work and nonwork responsibilities (Bunker & Vanderslice, 1982; Farris, 1978). For

Source: From Anita P. Jackson, Ronald P. Brown, and Karen E. Patterson-Stewart, "African Americans in Dual-Career Commuter Marriages: An Investigation of Their Experiences," *The Family Journal: Counseling and Therapy for Couples and Families* 8 (January 2000): 22–36.

instance, according to a study conducted by Bunker et al. (1992), commuters reported greater work-life satisfaction than did dual-career single-residence couples. This is believed by the researchers to occur due to the greater opportunity for commuters to compartmentalize work and family roles. In addition, in another study (Chang & Wood, 1996), women were found to experience less psychological and physical difficulties if they could successfully resolve role conflicts, whereas men reported improved relationships with their children and feeling more effective in the parenting role.

In contrast, challenges to this lifestyle for both the commuter and spouse are (a) stresses from trying to balance family and career responsibilities, (b) loneliness and lack of companionship, (c) lack of understanding or appreciation of this lifestyle by others, and (d) hectic schedules associated with the greater separation of work and family responsibilities (Chang & Wood, 1996; Groves and Horm-Wingerd, 1991). Farris (1978) and Gerstel and Gross (1984) suggested that strain results from the total segregation of work and home and leads to hectic schedules and compartmentalization of each of these aspects. Although compartmentalizing work and family has been identified as beneficial in that the commuter can focus on one or the other without interference, it is also noted as a stressor due to the hectic schedules needed for its management. In addition, Gerstel and Gross (1984) stated that societal and workplace resources have failed to support participants' commitments to this lifestyle, which adds to the strain.

Earlier studies (Farris, 1978; Winfield, 1985) found sex differences in happiness with the commuting marriage, pessimistic attitudes of society in general with regard to marital commuting, and an acceptance of the pessimistic attitudes by commuters. A more recent study by Groves and Horm-Wingerd (1991) found no sex differences and that couples do not perceive themselves as socially isolated. It has been suggested (Groves and Horm-Wingerd, 1991) that changing societal attitudes have assisted in more favorable views of commuters.

African Americans are participating more frequently in this lifestyle as reported in the popular press ("Commuter Couples," 1993). Yet, no empirical research has been employed relative to the realities that African American couples face or to any specific issues they may encounter. The recognition of an increase in African American dual-career commuter marriages and lack of research raises a number of issues. What are the commuter marriage experiences of African Americans? Are these issues specific to them? Are there cultural norms that affect their commuter lifestyle differentially than for non–African American commuter couples? How do they cope with the issues that do arise? What factors contribute to the survival of the couple relationship? What is the influence of this lifestyle on children and friends? These questions were examined throughout this investigation.

METHOD

Considering the lack of research on African Americans in dual-career commuter marriages, a qualitative study was conducted to identify issues and themes that are relevant to their living this lifestyle. A qualitative study was chosen to explore the nature of African Americans' experiences with this lifestyle to see what themes would emerge because so little is known about them specifically. . . . Based in grounded theory, the authors attempted to discover the meaning that the participants gave to their experiences in the commuter lifestyle. Grounded theory is a means of building theory inductively that is derived from the study of the phenomenon it represents. In other words, rather than starting out with a theory to prove, it begins with the area of study and allows what is relevant to the area to emerge. . . .

Participants

The participants in this study were four middle-age, middle-class couples residing in the Midwest region of the United States. Two couples involved African American women, Roxanne and Freda (pseudonyms), who commuted, whereas the other two couples involved African American men, Carl and Manning (pseudonyms), who commuted. Following is demographic information concerning the couples' education, employment, family makeup, and conditions that led to the establishment of a commuter lifestyle. During the interviews, the couples were asked to discuss circumstances that influenced their decision to live a commuter lifestyle.

Wives as Commuters. Roxanne and her husband, Ty, were both college educated at the time of their marriage. They owned a home with considerable acreage on the outskirts of a large city at the time of this study. They had worked in the same or nearby cities and raised their two children to their college years at the time the wife was offered a position in another city. Although Roxanne and Ty were fairly well established in their careers and actively involved in the community, Roxanne had completed her doctorate and was ready to assume other challenges and opportunities. After some discussion with her husband, she decided to assume the position and establish another residence. During the years of the dual-career commuter marriage, the children attended and graduated from college and graduate school and one child married. Ty, who held two positions, resigned from one position during the 4th year of the commuter marriage and is currently employed only in his primary career. Although commuting is seen as a temporary arrangement, the couple was sharing their 8th year of a commuter lifestyle when interviewed.

Freda and her husband, Troy, were both in a second-marriage relationship and held graduate degrees. Freda had obtained a master's degree in business administration and Troy had received his Juris doctorate in law. When Freda and Troy met, they were both heavily involved in their careers. Freda was initially indecisive about moving to the town where her husband-to-be was employed.

She felt it was her obligation to do so as a wife but wanted to maintain her business where it had been established. As a successful lawyer, Troy wanted to maintain his position where it was located. After 4 months of deliberation, they decided to marry and commute. They felt that this was best for each of them. Because Freda lived in a small apartment and Troy owned a home 6 hours away, it was decided that Freda would commute. Both Freda and Troy had two grown children from previous marriages. The four children were either working, attending graduate school, and/or raising families. At the time of this study, Freda and Troy were experiencing their 5th year in a commuter marriage.

Husbands as Commuters. Carl and his wife, Carol, began their marriage living as most nuclear families do—in the same residence. They both had undergraduate degrees from early on in their marriage. They also had two daughters who were 8 years apart. While the girls were very young, Carl began working on his master's degree and doctorate. After completing his doctorate and holding several positions over a period of about 10 years, Carl was offered a position that was going to require him to establish a separate residence. Motivating factors included the fact that the pay was better than his previous positions and he had already held positions where he was away from the family for several days at a time. This new position was 2 hours away. By that time, his oldest daughter was attending a university and Carol was involved in her career. The younger daughter, who was in junior high school, was actively involved in extracurricular activities at school and church. Carl and Carol were experiencing their 5th year of their commuter marriage during this investigation.

Manning and his wife, Kanisha, were previously married and both had one child from their first marriages. During her previous marriage, Kanisha obtained a master's degree. Manning and Kanisha began their life with each other as a dual-career couple sharing the same residence. Soon after marriage, Manning completed his master's degree. Manning's career advancement required considerable involvement in another city. However, his wife did not wish to give up her work or her clients considering the respect she had acquired in the community. The couple discussed establishing an additional residence and felt that they could do this temporarily. Due to the extreme distance, 12 driving hours, Manning flew for the commute. This couple saw each other once a month. One child, age 12, was still living at home at the time the commuting was initiated. During the screening process, Manning stated that he had commuted for 2 years. . . .

Interviews

Data collection involved 2-hour semistructured interviews conducted by the researchers. Additional data collection included a 1-hour session with one child of each couple and a 1-hour session with a friend whom the couple identified for the purpose of triangulating the data. Triangulating data allows for obtaining information from various sources to ensure accuracy and alternative perceptions of participants' information.

Prior to the interview, participants were informed of the purpose of the study (to explore the experiences of African American couples living a dual-career commuter lifestyle), the length of time (screening, 2-hour interview, reading of transcript, review of researchers' patterns and themes identified, follow-up interview to make any necessary changes), and level of involvement (inclusion of child and friend informants) anticipated in the study. The primary question asked of all participants was "Tell us about the commuter lifestyle as you have experienced it and continue to experience it." This strategy enabled the researchers to obtain unstructured ideas and perceptions of the commuter lifestyle. Other questions included "Tell us about the advantages," "Tell us about the disadvantages," "How have your experiences changed over time?" and "Is there anything that you experience specifically as an African

American living this lifestyle?" However, the interview was not limited to the above questions to allow for further probing of responses so that the experiences could be more fully understood.

The primary question asked of each child was "Tell what it is like living with parents who work so far from each other that they have to acquire a separate home." The primary question asked of each friend was "How do you perceive the relationship of your friends who live a dual-career commuter lifestyle?" An additional question included was "How do you personally experience their lifestyle?" . . .

RESULTS

Following is a discussion of the categories and themes discovered relative to the advantages and disadvantages of the dual-career commuter experience for African Americans as well as coping strategies the couples used. Table 1 represents the relevant findings, showing four themes identified as advantages and two themes identified as disadvantages.

TABLE 1 Advantages and Disadvantages of the Commuter Lifestyle in the Lives of African American Couples

Advantages	Disadvantages
Meaningful personal expression	Stress of complex lifestyle
Personal fulfillment	Hectic schedules
Enhanced identity	Driving
Autonomy	Financial hardship
	Sexual advances
Enhanced family dynamics	Alienation and isolation
Effective interactions	Loneliness
Quality use of time	Guilt
	Misperceptions of the lifestyle
	Lack of community
Career advantages	
Combat employment limitations, assumptions, racial stereotypes/ oppression	

Advantages

Theme 1: Meaningful Personal Expression.
The men and women of all four marriages identified the opportunity to engage in meaningful personal expression as a benefit of a commuter
marriage. Meaningful personal expression reflected the importance the participants placed on
having the opportunity to be themselves and
demonstrate their own unique qualities and skills.
Each participant spoke of experiencing a sense of
being lost in each other's identity and/or demands
prior to the commuting in their current relationships. This theme was illustrated through three
categories: (a) personal fulfillment, (b) enhanced
identity, and (c) autonomy. Regarding the first
category, greater work-related opportunities and
challenges enabled all four commuters to experience a greater sense of personal fulfillment. The
four commuters stated that they had educated
themselves beyond their previous jobs and that
their current positions were a better match of their
skills and abilities. Through personally fulfilling
work, they felt that a core part of themselves was
being expressed. "I feel alive, like me. I'm doing
what I enjoy. I'm recognized for what I do and not
just for what my husband does," Roxanne said.
Manning noted, "I am able to focus totally on
my work without attending to the needs of the
family on a daily basis. I can sort of be myself."
The four noncommuters also felt personal fulfillment through their careers, which they were able
to maintain by not having to move. The salient
factor in experiencing a greater sense of personal
fulfillment was furthering one's education and obtaining a position that matched the individual's
knowledge and skills. Thus, employment opportunities and geographical location required some
individuals to commute to obtain the personal
fulfillment that they desired.

The challenges of the commuting lifestyle and
opportunity to make effective decisions and
achievements bolstered the couples' confidence
and contributed to a positive identity. However,
this impact differed based on their gender and

role in the commuter relationship. For instance,
whereas the noncommuting women felt greater
confidence in their home management skills, the
commuting women felt confidence in their ability
to manage their career, travel, car, business, and a
second residence. The two commuting men spoke
of their enhanced identity in the context of a society that has many negative portrayals of African
American men. They noted that the ability to
commute and employ skills in their chosen field
enhanced their opportunity to effectively carry out
their role as family providers, which they emphasized is not always the case for African American
men. They also spoke of the importance of doing
work that was meaningful and that reflected their
skills and abilities against a historical and political reality of not having such opportunities. The
spouses of these two commuters made similar
comments about their husbands. The two men
further stated that the act of commuting provided
an impression that their work was prestigious and
extremely important. The two women who commute also noted the intriguing nature of commuting. "Commuting gives an air of importance that
contributes to one's positive identity . . . and it's
kind of exciting going to another place to work,"
Roxanne commented. Last, one commuter noted
that commuting allowed greater opportunity to
mask one's flaws. People in one setting often do
not know of the weaknesses of the commuter in
the other setting. This allows for an extended
opportunity to look good and keep the identity
intact.

An additional source of meaningful expression
was their sense of autonomy. The women, in particular, spoke of having time to be themselves
without being defined only through family and
spouse. The four commuters appreciated the opportunity to be completely away from the family
when working in order to focus totally on work.
All four spouses of the commuters stated that they
too enjoyed and appreciated some time alone to
do their own things, although they noted that they
had to consider home responsibilities more often
than did their commuting spouses.

Each of the participants noted that having the opportunity to be themselves was extremely important and that temporary separations from their spouses permitted time to do so. The necessary time that the spouses had to spend away from their partners and depend on themselves enabled them to more fully develop their own personhood.

Theme 2: Enhanced Family Dynamics. Two categories developed related to enhanced family dynamics. They included effective interactions among family members and quality use of time when together. All participants stated that they communicated more openly and frequently. Roxanne noted that Ty seldom talked when he was home prior to their commuter relationship. "Now he has all kinds of things to share with me," she said. Several couples made comments about being more open and honest with each other. Freda and Troy, who had been in their commuter relationship for 5 years, appeared to have developed a style of communicating that was frank and to the point. "We really don't have a lot of time to waste, so we tend to be more direct, frank, and honest. You know, to the point," Troy said. "We don't play those silly little power games. We don't have time for it." The couples who lived in a same-residence house before initiating the commuting said that their current conversations seemed to be more interesting than they were when they resided together. Ty, Freda, and Manning noted that their different worlds provided novelty and interesting conversations with their spouses.

Another aspect of effective interactions was seen when two couples noted that they more intentionally engaged in behaviors, activities, and discussions that demonstrated love, respect, trust, and appreciation for each other. "I think because it's so easy to be dishonest or unfaithful, honesty has increased in its importance. . . . I seem to appreciate him more now that I don't have the chance to be with him all the time," Freda said. This was a common statement among all the couples, whether commuter or noncommuter.

Interactions among the couples' children also were described positively. Roxanne, Freda, and their spouses felt that their children became more independent and responsible. The children confirmed this perspective and felt that their acquisition of greater responsibility enabled them to avoid parental confrontation that many of their peers encountered. The children stated that their parents were very frank, open, and honest with them, which resulted in them being more frank, open, and honest with their parents.

Related to enhanced family dynamics, participants noted that time spent with each other had increased in its purposefulness and meaningfulness due to the limited time they had with each other. "It's not that we do a special activity, it's just that our time together, whatever we do, has come to be very special," Carl said. Sometimes the quality time that the couples spent with each other was over the telephone or e-mail. However, this was infrequent so as to avoid expensive bills. During at least part of most weekends, the families or couples spent some meaningful and purposeful time together. Couples who had lived this lifestyle longer believed that their appreciation for one another had grown stronger over the years and felt that commuting helped in this growth.

Theme 3: Career Advantages. The commuting spouses felt that their commuter lifestyle enabled them to engage in careers that brought many advantages. Specifically, employee benefits; enriching experiences; and greater opportunities for further advancement, networking, travel, and consulting. Although three couples reported only slight increases in salary and one reported a decrease in salary, all four couples saw some financial gain through employee benefits.

The commuters also noted increased opportunities to supplement their family incomes through consulting and grant opportunities. Freda stated,

> I didn't like the idea of commuting but this position has opened all kinds of opportunities for me, and commuting provides the autonomy to take advantage of them. I get to travel, meet all kinds of people,

make important decisions, learn new things, enhance my skills, take on new and exciting challenges, and make additional income.

Although none of the four spouses of the commuters relished the idea of a commuter relationship, they "put up with it" due to the employee benefits. One appreciated the higher salary, two appreciated a free college education for their children, and all four noted the improved health plans for the family.

Theme 4: Combat Employment Limitations, Assumptions, and Racial Stereotypes/Oppression. Each of the commuters spoke about their ability as commuters to counter employment limitations, prior assumptions persons have of their abilities, and negative racial stereotypes and oppression. Manning said,

> Job competition is pretty stiff locally. Besides, I got the message that they (employers) felt ethnic quotas were already filled and they didn't need anybody else like me. It meant either unemployment, a job outside my field, or travel. I'm certainly not going on welfare and would not be happy if I can't do the job I trained for. Folks around here think we're [African Americans] all on welfare anyway.

Roxanne stated, "I was a teacher for a long time in this community. It was like the people couldn't think of me as doing anything else." Freda stated, "I think they felt they had enough African Americans [only one] in that position so I chose to stay put where I could utilize my skills and just travel to my husband."

Another aspect of Theme 4 that was interesting was two commuters' recognition that they could confront certain issues, such as racial oppression, in their home community more openly. Due to the fact that their job was not in the local home community, they were not concerned about possible negative consequences to their career objectives. Manning stated,

> I think some African Americans dislike some of the things that occur here but are reluctant to speak out

because they fear their jobs may be on the line. I have a little more freedom in that sense—to speak out on racial issues here at home. I'm not likely to get job pressures since my job is not here and folks at work don't know what I do here.

Disadvantages

Two major themes related to disadvantages were identified. They were (a) a stressful and complex lifestyle and (b) alienation and isolation. Four categories relative to a stressful lifestyle were identified. These include (a) hectic schedules, (b) driving, (c) financial hardship, and (d) sexual advances. Four categories relative to alienation and isolation were identified. These include (a) loneliness, (b) guilt, (c) misperceptions of the lifestyle, and (d) lack of community.

Theme 5: Stress of a Complex Lifestyle. A major disadvantage of a commuter lifestyle as identified by the men and women of all four couples was the complexity of the lifestyle. From hectic schedules, hours of driving, financial hardships, and sexual advances, they viewed their lifestyle as stressful. Freda noted,

> Nothing is easy living like this. It's so hectic. Financial transactions, making decisions about family matters, deciding on major purchases and projects, getting information to and from others, scheduling and meeting obligations are all complicated by commuting. Constantly having to be organized can wear you down. And then, institutions often have policies or practices that do not consider, understand, or appreciate our lifestyle.

Roxanne noted problems pertaining to institutional practices of health care:

> Due to managed care and the institution's insurance carrier, I acquired a primary physician in the city of my employment because the insurance carried by the institution applies only to the area of the state where I work. However, during vacations and holidays when I am in my home city, access to certain

health care needs (appointments, prescriptions) becomes a problem. I had to terminate physical therapy for an injury once because it came during a vacation time when I needed to be in my home city. I was not going to drive that distance for a 1-hour appointment every other day.

Carl stated, "These companies want our employment but sometimes they give so little consideration to families, especially those who commute."

Whether driving or flying, each of the commuters stated that they tire of all the traveling. Road construction and conditions, weather, flight delays, alternate routes, and price fluctuations were cited as stressors. In addition, the commuters had extra work-related obligations that were expected beyond their regular job responsibilities. These individuals were building careers that often called for networking or organizational and public relations responsibilities. Furthermore, they believed that they were often called on because their representation as African Americans was desired. "The banquets, luncheons, speeches, committees, meetings, and extra obligations cut into my leisure and family time because they often demand extra travel," Carl said. The time and scheduling of these events and obligations were critical to the amount of travel that was required. In addition, all four spouses of the commuters spoke of their constant worry about the travel safety of their commuting spouses.

All four couples noted the financial drain of the commuting lifestyle—trying to pay for a second residence as well as extra household items. Although the couples appreciated the employee benefits, none of them saw much long-term gain financially considering the extra cost required to live in two locations. Manning stated, "Whatever gains I made in salary are eaten up by travel and the extra living expenses." Carl stated, "Maintaining a second residence for a short time is not so bad, but over many years, it's not financially beneficial."

Each participant spoke of the stress and conflict they experienced in coping with sexual advances. Because they were alone so much of the time, the frequency of sexual advances increased. This was more common among the commuters because they were not only alone but more likely to be perceived as single. All four couples felt that a commuter relationship requires a high level of maturity, trust, respect, and honesty due to the many hours away from each other.

The spouses of the commuters, both men and women, spoke adamantly about their partners taking on too much work responsibilities and not being home. The four individuals seemed particularly disturbed about their partners' absence during times that assistance or decision making was needed. The two noncommuting women further discussed their frustration with the tiredness of their husbands when they arrived home. In addition, they often found their husbands too distant from the issues that they had to deal with everyday and felt that their husbands did not understand the dynamics of what was happening at home.

Although the spouses were pleased with their partners' happiness, they were stressed by a level of uncertainty concerning the future of the commuter relationship. They pointed out that future goals or objectives had never been discussed so they never knew from year to year how long the commuting would last. As reported by Kanisha, "I have no idea how long Manning is going to continue working so far from home. It leaves me a little anxious because I envision at some point living differently than we are now." Ty also mentioned, "I know she feels good about what she's doing, her work and all, but I'd rather have my wife at home. Right now I have no idea how long this will have to last. I suppose she doesn't either." In general, the commuter couples felt that the strain of this lifestyle was doable for a short period of time but not something that could be maintained over a long period.

Theme 6: Alienation, Isolation. Several categories centered on alienation and isolation. These included loneliness, guilt, misperceptions, and lack of community. Although each of the commuters and their spouses spoke of the loneliness they experienced, the noncommuters appeared to have more difficulty coping. The commuters' hectic schedules were more likely to keep them too busy at times to feel the loneliness. In addition, the four commuters spoke at length about the guilt they experienced for being away from the family so much. Most of the guilt centered on not being able to attend to daily issues or activities of their children. Carl stated, "When I look back on this now, I still sense this as a real loss." Roxanne feels that her commuting lifestyle was forced on her spouse and feels at fault for having made their lifestyle what it is.

Feelings of alienation and isolation also stem from others' lack of understanding about the commuter relationship. The four commuters talked about the assumptions people have of married couples. Freda stated, "When it's known you're married, people automatically think of traditional same-residence marriages. So when scheduling events or discussing situations, most people do not consider your travel time, absence from the area, or that you live in two locations." Demonstrating her frustration, Roxanne loudly proclaimed,

> He scheduled the get-together on Saturday evening. Either I have to stay up here until Sunday or all weekend by that time or not go to the party and if I don't go they think I don't care about them. But I don't want to stay here all weekend. I have obligations at home. I don't want to drive all the way back up here when I have to drive back on Monday.

Being a relatively new phenomenon, misperceptions abound pertaining to a commuter lifestyle. Carl and Manning reported, "Other men view my lifestyle as wonderful. They assume I have women everywhere and that I have it made living married but single." The women commuters, however, reported that their commuter lifestyle was viewed as a negative influence on their families or spouses. Roxanne stated, "Others think that something has to be wrong with me or

my husband for me to spend so much time away from him." Freda stated, "My lifestyle is viewed as abnormal." Three of the noncommuters stated that the misunderstandings of the lifestyle and lack of other commuter couples around them contribute to feelings of loneliness and isolation.

Another experience of alienation and isolation was the commuters' lost sense of community, which became more of a concern with increasing years in this lifestyle. This was noted by those couples who had commuted 5 or more years. The lack of community was salient and the one issue that three commuters spoke most about. Roxanne expressed, "I feel as though I am not a part of any community." Freda commented, "I don't belong anywhere." Roxanne described it as a lost feeling. Freda also stated, "Community is very important among African Americans and it's certainly a strong part of who I am. The lack of community is the hardest for me." Carl stated,

> I'm not at home long enough to be involved with people here. I've really lost track of friends and things that happen here at work. At work, I may do things in the community but since I don't live there, I'm not considered as one of the folks that will be affected by what happens there.

Roxanne stated, "I work hard but I don't seem to have any connections anywhere. Everyone assumes I'm away and too busy with work so friends don't come around."

Because of time constraints and distance from the home community, all four commuters noted limitations to engaging in non-work-related activities they enjoy and that provide personal fulfillment. Time spent away in the work setting limited the commuters' opportunities to get involved in the community and personally meaningful activities. Roxanne, who used to participate in community theater, dance performances, and choir, could never be home for rehearsals. "I really miss expressing this important part of me," she said. Manning could not continue his involvement in a tennis league that met twice a week or in little league with his son.

Noncommuter spouses (both men and women) stated that their friends do not call as frequently as they had before the commuter relationship began. Friends would assume that the couple was not home or that they were too busy. In addition, the spouses spoke of their lack of knowledge and connectedness to their commuter spouses' world of work. They commented that they did not know their spouses' associates or colleagues.

Children of Commuters

In the commuter relationships where the children were in college, they commented that in most cases they were not affected by the commuter relationship of their parents. The daughter of Roxanne stated that she felt neglected by her mom during her first semester of college. "I thought Mom would visit, write, or call more often. I felt kind of left out. As I made more and more friends and adjusted to the college life, it didn't bother me as much," she said. For those relationships where the children were still living in the home, the most salient concern was that the commuter parent seemed uninvolved in their lives. "Sometimes I don't think he cares about me. He missed practically all my games," exclaimed Manning's son. The two children interviewed who experienced this spoke of their disappointments and the anger they felt when their commuter parent did not show up to their events. "I know Dad has a lot to do but I was really expecting him at my volleyball game," noted Carl's daughter. The children said that they did enjoy telling their peers that their parent was far away working and only came home on weekends. They indicated that there was something prestigious about that. Their commuting parents seemed to be really special because they had to be away so much.

Friends of Commuters

The friends of each of the commuter couples indicated that they admired the trust they saw in the relationships but admitted their initial concern about the strain that commuting would place on the relationship. They also expressed sadness in that they could not spend more time with the couple due to the many hours the commuter was away and the couple's need to be alone when they were together. "I really miss their companionship. We're still friends but I used to be able to run over to see them most anytime and we ran around a lot together. I miss the old times," a friend stated. Friends who were the same sex as the commuter indicated that they were uncomfortable visiting at times the commuter was away because of impressions that others might acquire. The friends felt sorry for the male spouse that was home because they believed he was lonely. However, none of the friends mentioned this about the noncommuting women. The friends also believed that the commuting women should not assume too many work obligations in order to spend more time with their husbands. One friend who believed that the couple's marriage would not survive commuting acknowledged that it was one of the strongest and most beautiful relationships she had seen. "Before the commute, they argued a lot. Now they seem so happy together," Roxanne's friend stated.

Coping: Factors That Facilitated This Lifestyle

Learning to cope with stressors has been critical to the maintenance and success of this lifestyle. Factors that appear to reduce stress and enhance maintenance of this lifestyle for the couples include the following: (a) stable relationships and conditions at home, (b) older children, (c) emotional stability, (d) physical energy, (e) commitment to professional goals, (f) involvement in hobbies and other meaningful activities, and (g) participation in the community in a way that serves others, particularly African Americans. All of the participants stated that the commuter lifestyle would not work if their marriages were weak and unstable. Freda captured this perspective when she further iterated,

The reason for the commute is our commitment to each other in the context of our career lives. If the commitment to each other is weakened, there's no need to commute. I know we've had our up and down times but the ups have been more than the downs and that's good because during the difficult times I would have a lot of mixed feelings about leaving or returning home. But over the years we've learned to give and take, and that helps.

The couples' ability to be flexible with one another seemed to help in maintaining strong and stable relationships. Also, they noted that supportive individuals who were not judgmental of their lifestyle were helpful. "When I get support and affirmation of my lifestyle from others it helps me to know I'm not totally crazy for living like this," Roxanne reported. The women also noted their reliance on a higher power to help them through difficult times.

The spouses of the commuters spoke of supportive people that had enabled them to endure the stressors and issues encountered in this type of relationship. The spouses also noted that implementing personal goals was an important factor in dealing with loneliness and uncertainty. "I had to learn to be alone and what to do with myself. It was hard at first. Then I became centered on ways I could continue to develop personally and professionally. Now I do a lot of interesting things," Ty said.

DISCUSSION

Investigation into the lifestyle of four African American couples in dual-career commuter marriages indicated that they experience many of the same advantages and disadvantages noted in studies of others (Chang & Wood, 1996; Douvan & Pleck, 1978; Gerstel & Gross, 1984; Groves & Horm-Wingerd, 1991) living in dual-career commuter marriages. However, with only four couples as participants in this study, care must be taken not to generalize the findings to all African Americans in dual-career commuter marriages. Nevertheless, these findings shed some light on the realities they experience and have implications for further research.

Advantages of a commuter lifestyle for the eight participants, which are supported by the literature (Chang & Wood, 1996; Douvan & Pleck, 1978; Gerstel & Gross, 1984; Groves & Horm-Wingerd, 1991), include greater opportunity for meaningful personal expression, enhanced family dynamics, and career advantages. Commuters obtained their jobs for financial gains and employee benefits that assisted or enhanced family goals as well as for personally fulfilling work. However, recognizing that financial gains were not outstanding considering travel and second residence expense, a driving force for employing a commuter lifestyle was doing meaningful work. As personal fulfillment, self-development, and individual rights has gained importance in our society, so too has obtaining meaningful work opportunities. According to Lerner (1994), individuals want to do meaningful work. They have a need to actualize their capacities and are powerless to the extent that they are prevented from doing so. Commuting is a strategy for engaging in meaningful work when such opportunities are not in close proximity to one's family residence. For African Americans, this opportunity may be of particular significance considering their long history of oppressed employment opportunities and the finding in this study that commuting was viewed as a way to combat obstacles, such as employment limitations, restrictive assumptions about one's skills and abilities, and racial stereotypes and oppression. Throughout history, African Americans have traveled long distances from their families to obtain gainful employment, such as during the large migration of African Americans from the rural south to the northern cities in the early part of the 20th century (Staples & Johnson, 1993). Today, with a greater range of educational and occupational opportunities available to them, coupled with a competitive workforce,

African American men and women may be choosing to commute in order to obtain not only employment but employment that matches their skills and abilities and is personally meaningful.

Of particular interest is the finding that family dynamics were enhanced. In spite of much-discussed tensions in African American male–female relationships (Hare & Hare, 1989) and declining quality of life in African American families, the marriage institution among African Americans is strong (Staples & Johnson, 1993). Sacrifices are frequently made to keep the family together. The establishment of a commuter marriage is evidence of marriage and career as important values. The commuter marriage is an alternative strategy for maintaining a marriage in the face of employment circumstances that prevent the couple from living in the same residence. Furthermore, working conditions have been found to affect the emotional life of families (Johnson, 1990; Piotrowski, 1979). Those who have gratifying careers that affirm self-worth are more emotionally available to family members. The commuting lifestyle seems to provide this opportunity. Because of frequent couple separations, tensions do not have time to build and time together is focused on tasks that build family bonds. This dynamic was described succinctly in Kanisha's statement, "We don't have time to argue." The ability of these families to function effectively in the face of the many disadvantages described speaks to the commitment that these individuals have for maintaining the family.

Last, due to many years of economic hardships, strains as a cultural group, and difficulty in saving financially and building economic resources, African Americans are opting for positions that provide substantial employee benefits. These benefits assist financially in areas that they may be unable to obtain sufficient resources or manage well, such as health care plans and fee waivers for college.

Disadvantages that are supported by the literature include a complex and stressful lifestyle and alienation and isolation. More specifically, hectic schedules, financial hardships, sexual advances, and loneliness were disadvantages for the couples, whereas travel, guilt, and misperceptions of the lifestyle were disadvantages specifically for the individual commuters. These findings concur with other studies (i.e., Chang & Wood, 1996; Groves & Horm-Wingerd, 1991) that indicated that the challenges to this lifestyle for the commuter couple included stresses from balancing family and career responsibilities, loneliness, lack of support from others, and hectic schedules associated with greater separation of work and home responsibilities. Also important, as a perspective that emerged from this study, was that the commuter and the spouse should be investigated individually and as a couple. The role of either commuter or noncommuter in the relationship was a significant factor in the types of stressors experienced. In general, however, the disadvantages contribute to the negative perspectives that those in commuter relationships have of this lifestyle. Nevertheless, their reasons for adopting this lifestyle result from a shared history in which professional involvement is important for both the husband and wife, an egalitarian ideology that legitimates women's pursuance and establishment of careers, and job market realities that undermine the possibility of husband and wife remaining in the same locale (Gerstel & Gross, 1984).

The commuter lifestyle can be a severe drain on the stability of the family. Yet, as demonstrated by this study and supported in the literature (Gerstel & Gross, 1984; Groves & Horm-Wingerd, 1991), family dynamics are often enhanced in spite of the complexity and stress of this lifestyle. Family stability is recognized as a function of work satisfaction (Cheatham & Stewart, 1990). Thus, the acquisition of gratifying work appears to initially enable couples to cope with the disadvantages. Nevertheless, over time, these issues seem to result in a reduced appeal for this lifestyle. Changes in priorities and what is considered gratifying work, increased frequency of disadvantages, and/or reduced energy or desire to continue the strain contribute to the reduced appeal.

Relative to disadvantages, what has not been evident in previous literature is the lost sense of community experienced by the commuters. Although some researchers (Bunker et al., 1992; Gerstel & Gross, 1984) have noted a sense of alienation and isolation experienced by commuters, it has been discussed as a rejection of their lifestyle by others. The lost sense of community discussed here is a feeling that one has lost his or her connectedness to a community. This lost sense of community was especially felt as the duration of living this lifestyle and salience of contributing to the community increased. The lack of opportunity to be in others' presence, involved in their lives, and have knowledge of the everyday situations of friends and the community was experienced as a severe loss. Malidoma Some (1998) and Sobonfu Some (1997) have noted that African wisdom teaches that without community, individuals have no sense of belonging and no place to bring their gifts; neither do they have anyone to support and affirm who they are. This condition then disempowers individuals' psyches. Considering the salience of community in the lives of many African Americans, as noted in the literature, commuting might bring significant issues to the lives of African Americans that will need to be addressed.

In addition, commuters discussed their lack of time to participate in their communities for the service of other African Americans. African Americans are often raised with the notion that the skills and abilities they obtain should contribute to the general welfare of the Black community (Staples & Johnson, 1993). Serving the community is often stated as a primary objective among many African Americans going into their chosen field. Staples and Johnson (1993) stated that Black women college students entering nontraditional fields did so because of a strong drive to serve the needs of Black people. They also stated that satisfaction derived from contributing to the general welfare of the Black community

and financially supporting and nurturing their families outweighed any negative aspects of performing multiple roles (Harrison, 1989). The contribution that women perceive they are making to the community is important (Staples & Johnson, 1993). It appears that those in dual-career commuter marriages find that as the lifestyle continues they are less able to fulfill this role and connect with friends. This was the case for both of the women and one of the men in this study.

Children. The perspective of children is nonexistent in the literature about dual-career commuter marriages. Adult children participants in this study indicated that they did not view the dual-career commuter lifestyle as being problematic for them. In fact, minor children noted a type of prestige associated with telling their peers about their parents' out-of-town careers. However, these children also indicated resentment and anger toward the commuting parents for not being available, particularly for activities and issues in their lives. According to Gerstel and Gross (1984), the least ideal time for commuter lifestyle is when the children are young. Mothers often experience guilt about being away from their children and worry about negative consequences in their children's development. The feelings of guilt are evident when children make statements such as "Come home" and "You missed my program." Although there is a dearth of empirical studies about the children of dual-career commuter couples and findings from this study cannot be triangulated with the literature, the literature (i.e., Wilcox-Matthew & Minor, 1989) on dual-career couples indicates that there are multiple concerns about raising children and child care. Therefore, it is conceivable to hypothesize that adding the strain of commuting to dual-career parenting would be problematic for the children and the couple. Thus, this category certainly warrants further investigation.

Nevertheless, some commuter couples state that they are providing their children with a positive alternative role model and speak of the benefits of the commuter lifestyle to their children's development. Children of dual-career couples have been said to describe their parents as more independent, resourceful, and active contributors to the home. Some dual-career couples see their children's exposure to other caretakers as expanding their opportunity to interact with others and experience other role models (Silberstein, 1992).

Friends. The most significant notion from the couples' friends was the perception that the married couples had a very trusting relationship. Nevertheless, they all stated that they had initially worried about the couples' marital relationship because they viewed commuting as unusual and as a strain on married life. The friends also missed the couples' companionship. It was the perception of the friends that the couples need their limited time to be with each other.

Gender-Specific Issues

A number of gender differences were observed in the issues presented. Enhanced identity centered on the men's role as effective family providers. Regardless of location, employment was important and reflected their strong work ethic. This finding supports several studies (Bowman, 1989; Staples & Johnson, 1993) of African American families that demonstrate that Black husbands who are unable to live up to their image of a good provider are at greater risk of unhappiness and low self-esteem. On the other hand, enhanced identity for the women centered on their confidence acquired in effectively managing home, career, and travel responsibilities. The women commuters particularly enjoyed the opportunity to function autonomously without being defined only through their family and spouses. Staples and Johnson (1993) noted that the work role is important for the psychological and physical well-being of middle-age and older Black women.

The couples believed that there were gender differences in others' perceptions of the commuter relationship. They believed that the commuting

men were perceived as having a wonderful lifestyle that offers great opportunity to engage in extramarital affairs, whereas the commuting women were viewed as abnormal, self-centered, and possessing a negative influence on their family or spouse.

These gender differences may be a result of socialization processes that emphasize women's home and family responsibilities, men's provider role, and a double standard relative to sexual expression (Collier, 1982; Simms & Malveaux, 1986). Autonomy was an extremely important aspect of the dual-career commuter relationship for women.

Issues Specific to Changes over Time

Those who had been in the commuter relationship longer talked about their greater appreciation for each and also their dislike for the back-and-forth travel and their concern about being disconnected from community. These dual-career commuter marriages have survived for at least 2 years, in some cases 8 years, and each of the couples stated that their appreciation for one another had grown stronger over the years. Also, there were differences in the way they spoke of travel, from "tiring" to "hating it," as the duration of this lifestyle continued. Last, there was also an increase in concern about feeling disconnected from the community among those who had experienced this lifestyle longer. Manning, who had been in this lifestyle for 2 years, noted this issue as not being a concern.

Although the couples interviewed recognized advantages in their dual-career commuter marriages, they endorsed findings of other researchers (Gerstel & Gross, 1984; Silberstein, 1992) in that the commuters would have preferred to carry out their career and family responsibilities in a same-resident situation. They viewed their lifestyle as a result of economic, employment, and racial circumstances; a commitment to their careers; and a desire for meaningful personal expression.

In addition, these participants appreciated the

opportunity to discuss and analyze their lifestyle and stated that they learned more about their own functioning as a result. Participation appeared to normalize some of their feelings and provoke thoughts and ideas for more effective coping. They all felt that commuter support groups would be beneficial.

REFERENCES

Anderson, E. A. (1992). Decision-making style: Impact on satisfaction of the commuter couple. *Journal of Economic Issues, 13,* 5–21.

Anderson, E. A., and Spruill, J. W. (1993). The dual-career commuter family: A lifestyle on the move. *Marriage and Family Review, 19,* 131–47.

Bowman, P. J. (1989). Research perspectives on Black men: Role strain and adaptation across the adult life cycle. In R. J. Jones (Ed.), *Black adult development and aging,* Berkeley, CA: Cobb & Henry.

Bunker, B. B., & Vanderslice, V. J. (1982). *Tradeoffs: Individual gains and relational losses of commuting couples.* Paper presented at the American Psychological Association Convention, Washington, DC.

Bunker, B. B., Zubek, J. M., Vanderslice, V. J., & Rice, R. W. (1992). Quality of life in dual-career families: Commuting versus single-residence couples. *Journal of Marriage and the Family, 54,* 399–406.

Chang, C. Y. & Wood, A. M. (1996, April). *Dual-career commuter marriages: Balancing commitments to self, spouse, family, and work.* Paper presented at the National Conference of the American Counseling Association, Pittsburgh, PA.

Cheatham, H. E. & Stewart, J. B. (1990). *Black families: Interdisciplinary perspectives.* New Brunswick, NJ: Transaction Publishing.

Collier, H. (1982). *Counseling women.* New York: Free Press.

Commuter couples. (1993, August). *Ebony, 48*(10), 52–58.

Douvan, E., & Pleck, J. (1978). Separation as support in working. In R. Rapoport & R. Rapoport (Eds.), *Working couples* (pp. 138–40). New York: Harper & Row.

Farris, A. (1978). Commuting. In R. Rapoport, R. N. Rapoport, & J. M. Bumstead (Eds)., *Working couples* (pp. 100–07). London: Routledge & Kegan Paul.

Gerstel, N. & Gross, H. (1984). *Commuter marriage.* New York: Guilford.

Groves, M. M. & Horm-Wingerd, D. M. (1991). Commuter marriages: Personal, family and career issues. *Sociology and Social Research,* 75(4), 212–17.

Hare, N., & Hare, J. (1989). *Crisis in Black sexual politics.* San Francisco: Black Think Tank.

Harrison, A. O. (1989). Black working women: Introduction to a life span perspective. In R. L. Jones (Ed.), *Black adult development and aging.* Berkeley, CA: Cobb & Henry.

Johnson, L. B. (1990). The employed Black: The dynamics of work–family tension. In H. E. Cheatham & J. B. Stewart (Eds.), *Black families: Interdisciplinary perspectives* (pp. 217–35). New Brunswick, NJ: Transaction.

Lerner, M. (1994). *Surplus powerlessness.* Atlantic Highlands, NJ: Humanities Press.

Piotrowski, C. S. (1979). *Work and the family system: A naturalistic study of working-class and lower-middle class families.* New York: Free Press.

Silberstein, L. R. (1992). *Dual-career marriage: A system in transition.* Hillside, NJ: Lawrence Erlbaum.

Simms, M., & Malveaux, J. (Eds.). (1986). *Slipping through the cracks: The status of black women.* New Brunswick, NJ: Transaction Books.

Some, M. P. (1998). *The healing wisdom of Africa: Finding life purpose through nature, ritual, and community.* New York: Penguin.

Some, S. E. (1997). *The spirit of intimacy: Ancient teachings in the ways of relationships.* Berkeley, CA: Berkeley Hills Books.

Staples, R., & Johnson, L. B. (1993). *Black families at the crossroads: Challenges and prospects.* San Francisco: Jossey-Bass.

Wilcox-Matthew, L., & Minor, C. W. (1989). The dual career couple: Concerns, benefits, and counseling implications. *Journal of Counseling and Development, 68,* 194–98.

Winfield, F. E. (1985). *Commuter marriage: Living together, apart.* New York: Columbia University Press.

[?] *Think about It*

1. Using Table 1 as a guide, describe the advantages and disadvantages of black commuter

marriages. How do gender roles and changes over time influence the commuters' experiences and perceptions?

2. How do the children of commuter marriages feel about their parents' arrangements? In the four couples that Jackson and her colleagues interviewed, the youngest child was 12 years old. Do you think that younger children would benefit from or complain about living in commuter marriage homes?

3. As the introduction to this chapter notes, increasing numbers of couples are involved in commuter marriages. What are the differences, if any, between black and white dual-career couples? Also, how might the parents' socioeconomic status affect children's reactions as well as the parents' commuting experiences?

Chicanas in White-Collar Jobs: "You Have to Prove Yourself More"

Denise A. Segura

Most of us spend many of our waking hours in organizations. Besides producing goods and services, organizations also produce social beliefs about gender roles and racial/ethnic relations. Denise A. Segura shows how workplace experiences, sex and racial/ethnic discrimination, sexual harassment, and the female-associated tasks that Chicanas continue to do at home all intensify traditional gender roles as well as reinforce occupational segregation.

Chicanas' movement into white-collar jobs contributes to growing heterogeneity in the work force, although it has eroded neither occupational segregation nor inequality at work and in the family. This paper explores how 152 Chicana white-collar workers in a major public university view their employment experiences and family responsibilities in ways that contribute to the production of gender and gender/race-ethnicity in the labor market and in the larger ethnic community. I explore how job satisfaction among these women reflects one aspect of their reproduction of traditional gender and race-ethnic relations. Specifically, I suggest that work activities can affirm one's gendered relation to the world and reinforce one's gender/race-ethnic sense of self, particularly when the clients are racial-ethnic minorities. I also examine the workplace barriers Chicanas encounter, such as sexual harassment and racial ethnic-discrimination, and how their effects can strengthen a gender/race-ethnic sense of self. Finally, I argue that Chicanas' activities at home and their seemingly irrational satisfaction with the unequal division of household labor actually represent rational ways of accommodating themselves to the relatively rigid constraints imposed by gender and race-ethnicity. These actions and their interpretations offer another lens to view

Source: From Denise A. Segura, "Chicanas in White-Collar Jobs: 'You Have to Prove Yourself More,'" *Sociological Perspectives* 35 (1992): 163–82. Reprinted by permission of the Pacific Sociological Association and the author.

mechanisms critical to the maintenance of the ethnic community, and of gender and labor-market inequality.

REPRODUCING GENDER AND CHICANO ETHNICITY

The theoretical reference point for this paper is the perspective originally developed by West and Zimmerman (1987), and usefully applied to other empirical data on women's work (Berk 1985). This framework views gender and race-ethnicity not just as categorical statuses, but as dynamic, interactional accomplishments. It presumes that in the course of daily affairs—work, for example—we present, reaffirm, and reproduce ourselves as belonging to, and competently representative of, gender and racial-ethnic categories. Thus, the worker not only *is* Chicana, she also "does" Chicana. And, work activities provide ample opportunities for the reaffirmation of membership in good standing of that group.

Female-dominated jobs offer unique occasions for women to "do gender," or enact and thus reaffirm what we take to be the "essential nature" of women (West and Zimmerman 1987; West and Fenstermaker n.d.). When an occupation involves "helping others," or "serving men," etc., women can simultaneously affirm themselves as competent workers, and also reinforce social conceptualizations of their "essential" femininity within the organization, for the clientele, and among themselves. . . .

Within the labor market, Chicano race-ethnicity is reinforced by discrimination (both objective and perceived) and social exclusion from the dominant group (Barrera 1979; Nelson and Tienda 1985). In addition, there are other, less obvious ways that Chicano race-ethnicity may be affirmed. Even as occupations contain a dimension for "doing gender," there may be a dimension for "doing Chicano race-ethnicity" as well. That is, organizations may structure jobs in ways that reaffirm Chicanos'

sense of themselves as members of a unique racial-ethnic group (e.g., using bilingual workers as interpreters without additional pay). Or, Chicanos may themselves act in ways that either consciously or unconsciously serve the Chicano community. As one example of the first possibility, Chicanos who work in jobs structured to "serve" a racial-ethnic clientele (e.g., minority students) may encounter a reward system that affirms their racial-ethnic identification while doing their job. In the second case, Chicanos who work in jobs that are not overtly structured to accomplish race-ethnicity may nonetheless reaffirm their racial-ethnic identity. They often remain in white-collar jobs despite experiencing social isolation or discomfort because they feel that such "success" indirectly enlarges the options for others in the racial-ethnic community.

For Chicanas, accomplishing race-ethnicity is even more complex since their social identity involves gender and embraces the family and the labor market in ways that may have profound implications for Chicano culture. That is, insofar as women's employment is typically viewed as "for the family," such employment may not offer a dynamic avenue for challenging gender inequality or male privilege at home (Zavella 1987; Segura 1989a). This possibility is strengthened when Chicanas work in jobs that affirm both their traditional gender and/or gender/race-ethnic sense of themselves. Also militating against a forceful challenge to gender inequality is women's household work, often eulogized as part of a distinct cultural heritage under assault by outside social pressures (Mirande and Enriquez 1979; Zinn 1982, 1979, 1975; Segura 1989). For Chicanas to challenge traditional patterns involves integrating personal empowerment with the politically-charged issue of culture-ethnic maintenance. Thus, the need or motivation to continue "traditional" patterns may be more complex for Mexican women inasmuch as doing housework or child care is the site of accomplishing not only gender, but culture/race-ethnicity as well. This dilemma adds another dimension to our understanding of the tenacity of Chicana inequality. The following section explores the ways gender and gender/race-ethnicity are affirmed in the lives of Chicana white-collar workers.

METHOD AND SAMPLE

In Fall 1989/Winter 1990, in collaboration with Beatriz Pesquera of the University of California, Davis, I administered a 20-page questionnaire on "women and work issues" to all Hispanic-identified women employed at a large public university in California. The questionnaire included a battery of closed-ended questions concerning work, the intersection of family and work, gender ideology, feminism, ethnicity, and political ideology. One hundred and fifty-two women completed the questionnaire, representing a response rate of 47.5 percent. In addition, we conducted follow-up interviews with 35 randomly-selected informants. The purpose of the interviews was to explore in greater depth the meanings of work, gender, and ethnicity for this group of women. This paper is an exploratory analysis of these survey and interview data for their implications for the reproduction of gender, race-ethnicity, and labor-market stratification.

Background Characteristics

Most of the survey respondents are of Mexican (Chicano) descent (85%) with the rest either Latin American or Spanish (Hispanic) origin. All but fifteen women were born in the United States. All of the women express a great deal of pride in their ethnicity and a majority also feel that maintaining Chicano culture is important. Sixty percent of the respondents are bilingual in Spanish and English.

All but three women received high school diplomas; 118 have educations beyond high school; 43 have a B.A. degree or above. Their educational levels are much higher than the California norm for Chicanas (11th grade). Ninety-four women (61.8%)

are presently married or partnered, 45.8 percent ($n = 43$) are married to Chicano men, 10.6 percent ($n = 10$) are married to "other Hispanic" men, and 40.4 percent ($n = 38$) have non-Hispanic husbands. Three women declined to state their husband's ethnicity. The respondents' ages range from 20 to 60 years old, with an average age of 36.5 years. One hundred and eleven women have children. The mean number of children is 2.1.

Occupations

Chicanas' employment profiles and my textual analysis of their interviews reveal that their experiences at work—their social experiences, discrimination, harassment, or acceptance—all took on gendered and/or racial-ethnic features. By and large, the women work in environments that are both homogeneous in terms of gender (59.2% report all-female coworkers); race-ethnicity (80% report all-Anglo coworkers); and reproduce gender/race-ethnic hierarchies (only 29 women have minority women supervisors).

Of the 152 respondents, 41.4 percent ($n = 63$) work in jobs we classified as "lower-level clerical"; 28.9 percent ($n = 44$) are "upper-level clerical workers"; 5.9 percent are "technical aides and service workers" ($n = 9$); while 19.7 percent are "professional/managerial workers" ($n = 30$).[1] Six women declined to provide information about their occupations. The mean income of the respondents is $23,288 annually.

The informants' average incomes are above those of many women workers.[2] This income profile allows me to explore the intersection of gender and race-ethnicity among Chicanas in the more privileged tiers of the working class. It is important to note, however, that the form and contours the intersection of gender and race-ethnicity take among this group of women probably differs from that of Chicanas in different jobs with lower incomes. The benefit of the present analysis is that it attests the pervasive significance of gender and race-ethnicity to Chicanas' lives.

FINDINGS

Job Satisfaction

. . . In the present study, 70.4 percent of the Chicana workers (n = 107) report being satisfied with their current jobs; only 21.7 percent (n = 33) indicate dissatisfaction. When asked to select three features of their jobs they liked most (out of a list of 10 items), 60.3 percent of the women replied "having control of my own work"; 56.3 percent chose "the pay"; 39.7 percent replied, "it makes me feel good"; 38.4 percent selected "doing different things at work"; 30.5 percent listed "my coworkers"; and 25.8 percent indicated "ability for me to make meaningful changes." I should note that about one-sixth of the women reported that they enjoyed more than three work features while seven replied they liked nothing about their jobs.

There were a few interesting variations by occupational groups. A much higher proportion of lower-level clerical workers and technical aides/service workers listed "coworkers" as important to their job satisfaction (42.9% and 44.4%, respectively) than did either upper clerical (18.2%) or professional workers (17.2%). On the other hand, professional and upper clerical workers were much more likely to indicate their job "makes me feel good" (55.2% and 43.2%, respectively). Few women indicated they valued their jobs because of the "prestige" or "chances for promotions." Professional workers were the least likely to mention promotion as a valued feature of their jobs. Insofar as they esteem the social aspects of the job and place less emphasis on occupational prestige or promotion, survey respondents appear to confirm previous research on women's job satisfaction.

The in-depth interviews provide insight into the meanings women attach to social aspects of work as well as job features that make them "feel good." Women's accounts of their jobs reveal two major patterns. First, women discuss job features and job satisfaction in terms that affirm social conceptualizations of femininity. Second, their accounts reveal a sense of affinity or connection with Chicano ethnicity. For example, when I asked an upper clerical worker what she valued about her job, she replied:

> I need to do that because for your self-esteem to feel that you're doing something and you're helping other people accomplish themselves [is important]. In that sense it's good for my health and also for my kids. I think if they see that you're involved with something, it helps them reach beyond their own world to see that there is an outside world there. And, that there's things that they can pursue that they enjoy.
>
> [upper clerical worker #64a]

This informant values her job for allowing her to "help others," a trait socially ascribed to the "feminine nature." Her commitment to affirm the feminine is captured by her insistence that helping others is "good" for her health and is maternally nurturant. Her subsequent opinion that her job enables her children to "reach beyond their own world" demonstrates solidarity with her racial-ethnic group's politicized view that Chicano youth have limited options (Ogbu 1978; Garcia 1981; Keefe and Padilla 1987). Moreover, gainfully employed in an upper clerical job, she sees herself as a role model for the larger Chicano community. Finally, her words underscore the centrality of "family" among the respondents—a dynamic consistent with the politics of Chicano cultural maintenance (Williams 1990; Keefe and Padilla 1987).

Other respondents worked in jobs structured to do "gender and race-ethnicity," or "help" racial-ethnic minority students or staff. One Chicana professional worker employed in this type of job stated:

> It is very satisfying when you're working with a Chicano student or with a black student who really wants to become a veterinarian. To see them being admitted to a Vet school is really very satisfying and to see them graduate is just incredible. I just gradu-

ated my second class, and every year they'll say, "Thanks!" And, God—the parents will say, "We never thought we'd have a doctor in the family!" So, that's really neat to feel that way, but I'm still limited in that I'm not doing enough.

[professional worker #10]

This informant, like others employed in jobs structured to "help" racial-ethnic minority students or staff, is satisfied when she is able to do the job competently. Critical here is that the gendered act associated with women- that of "helping others" intersects with bettering the racial-ethnic community, thereby allowing the respondent to simultaneously accomplish gender and race-ethnicity.

Many of the respondents (60.3%) reported they liked feeling "in control" of their job. When I explored what this meant, I found that Chicanas filtered their evaluation of their jobs through a gender and/or race-ethnic lens. That is, they valued job control as a means to better help others (a value associated with women) and also expand the job range of Mexican American women (a value associated with the ethnic community and women). As one lower clerical worker (#4) succinctly stated: "You're helping in some ways helping people in helping make a difference." In this way, the preference for on-the-job "control" implies a politicized sense of themselves as racial-ethnic women striving for social change.

About one-fifth of the respondents are dissatisfied with their jobs. Women with children tended to dislike their jobs if their supervisors were inflexible about taking time off and making up work. Since women bore the major responsibility for taking children to doctor appointments or caring for them when they were sick or on vacation, women valued jobs that offered them a degree of flextime. Women employed in lower-level clerical jobs tended to be unhappy with their pay. In general, women disliked their jobs when they felt they were not doing anything they perceived as "helpful" or "useful." As one woman, working in a laboratory setting, said:

I need something that's useful and related to something that is happening in the world now. And what we're doing is really closely related to basic science and, for me has no practical purpose. So, I don't feel—I was going to study plant sciences to save the world and I'm not doing anything now. I find that my research is not useful at all for people so I really want to move out.

[professional worker #212a]

This informant's words imply that not only was doing "useful" work critical to job satisfaction, it also enabled her to affirm her femininity and accomplish gender.

In general, the job characteristics Chicanas enjoy (e.g., "control," and "helping others") are not necessarily engaged in voluntarily, but rather form integral parts of the jobs as structured by this particular organization. Thus, Chicanas who "feel good" about helping minority students obtain information about financial aid or other resources are actually performing tasks essential to their jobs. In helping others, Chicanas affirm their gender and their race-ethnicity. The organization structures this enactment (e.g., specifications of the job description) and they are held accountable for it by their coworkers and clients (e.g., through performance evaluations). Chicanas' impetus to continue this process is intertwined with the process of identity as well as the larger politic of accessing jobs outside the purview of most Chicana workers in the state.

Sexual Harassment and Race-Ethnic Discrimination

Women's gendered and race-ethnic sense of themselves is reinforced by other, unrewarding features of the job. In this study, about one-third of the respondents reported experiencing sexual harassment ($n = 50$), while nearly 44 percent ($n = 67$) said they had encountered discrimination based on gender and/or race-ethnicity. Sexual harassment and discrimination reinforces Chicanas' sense of on-the-job vulnerability and their social inequality. In addition, the way in which women describe sexual harassment and employment discrimination reveals how gender and gender/race-ethnic boundaries are maintained in the organizational setting. While maintaining these boundaries is not the same as the accomplishment of gender on the job, it provides a context in which it occurs.

Women interviewed in this study believe that sexual harassment is one of the most underreported problems of the organization. They aver that women often do not know the definition of sexual harassment and are reluctant to pursue a complaint out of fear of recrimination. Or, as one informant (#155a) put it: "You have to pick your battles."

Sixty percent of the women who indicated having experienced sexual harassment reported "doing something about it." Usually this meant, "telling the person to stop," "talking with friends and family," or "complaining to the appropriate personnel officer." Eleven women did "nothing" and another nine women acted as though nothing had happened.

Chicanas voiced outrage when women (especially themselves) were cast in the role of instigators rather than victims by coworkers and/or supervisors:

> Everyone likes to pretend it [sexual harassment] doesn't happen. When you go from one position to the next in this university it's so small that bosses know each other and say, "hey, this woman—watch out for her." So, you get blackmailed that way. And so you sort of have to be careful in how you handle it—you don't want to give that person a chance to get out of it. So, if you really want to nail him, you'd better go through the proper channels and make sure that when you do it you do it well.
>
> [professional worker #102a]

Implicit in this informant's words is the sense that women who assert themselves in ways that directly confront men risk retaliation by those participating in the interpersonal networks of supervisors and other workers. Bosses warn each other. In her assertiveness, the Chicana worker violates *all* rel-

evant expectations of the group: as a worker, as a woman, and as a Chicana; she becomes a threat to the organization, and especially vulnerable to informal workplace sanctions.

Sexual harassment reinforces Chicanas' sense of vulnerability and subordination to men within the organization. Women express anger when sexual harassment occurs, but view it as a job hazard that needs to be handled with care. Within this constrained setting, women are expected to meet debilitating gender expectations in a way that denigrates their sense of self even as it reconfirms their secondary standing in the institution.

A problem of equal or greater magnitude is discrimination based on Chicanas' combined gender-race/ethnicity. It is noteworthy that with few exceptions ($n = 9$), survey respondents did not privilege one form of discrimination over the other. Rather, they felt their experiences reflected *both* gender and race-ethnicity.

During their interviews, Chicanas spoke passionately of their firsthand experiences with on-the-job discrimination. Almost to a woman, they argued that employers, coworkers, the organization, and society itself maintain pejorative, stereotyped images of Chicana and Hispanic women:

> When people look at us they don't *see us* [her emphasis]. They just see the stereotypes that they have gotten from the movies or somewhere . . . they think we are all uneducated. They have this "indito" under the cactus plant idea. I've had people say, "I didn't know that there were any educated people in Mexico that have a graduate degree." I think we stumble against the wall because they're looking at us across a barrier that is their imagination.
>
> [professional worker #212a]

One lower clerical worker described negative stereotypes more succinctly:

> That we like to be pregnant. We don't like to take birth control. We're "manana" [tomorrow] oriented. We're easy. We're all overweight and I guess we're hot [laughs]—and submissive.
>
> [lower clerical worker #153a]

Chicanas feel they are held accountable or judged in terms of their deviance from or conformity to these one-dimensional stereotypes. Chicanas claim that supervisors, coworkers, and the institution draw on these negative images when they evaluate their credentials or previous work experience:

I think that society as a whole sees Mexican women as the good family role models, but they don't see them as also being just as good in the workplace. Just as capable. So, I think that they have a view that's limiting their role—what they [Chicanas] can do.
[professional worker #176a]

Another Chicana declared:

I think you have to demonstrate that you can do a job—I mean I've seen it! In interviews with a white candidate. They see it written on paper and they say, "isn't this great!" But, when you bring a Latina woman in, it's almost like they're drilled: "Tell us"; "Give us examples"; "How long did you do it?" Some say to prove yourself and that's what I feel. You always have to prove yourself that you are just as good even when it's all there. It's all written. You almost have to fight harder to demonstrate that you can do a job just as well!
[upper clerical worker #64a]

This particular informant told me that she had resisted interpreting her experience as evidence of gender/racial-ethnic discrimination. In this regard, she is very similar to the majority of the women interviewed. Survey respondents typically tried to downplay the salience of gender/racial-ethnic discrimination in their personal lives although most (70%) considered it a feature of the organization and society at large. All the women interviewed believe that women of Mexican descent have a "harder time" getting good jobs than either Anglo men, Anglo women, or Latino men.

Women who believed they had experienced discrimination condemned it and described its nuances at length. Several told of "subtle discrimination," i.e., comments that devalue their culture and/or features of their combined gender/race-ethnicity:

. . . it's subtle discrimination. I haven't gotten a job because of, or I don't know if I have gotten a job because of my color. You know, subtle stuff—that subtle baloney that people pass you over because they think that women of color aren't as brilliant as they [Anglos] are. That sort of thing. Actually, they can be condescending to me.
[upper clerical worker #155a]

Another said:

I'm usually asked because of my accent—they say "you have a funny accent." And, I always say, "I'm Mexican." And people are really surprised. They say, "You don't look Mexican. And so I ask, "how many Mexican people do you know?" And they say, "Oh, just you."
[professional worker #212a]

The Chicana respondents argued that differences in skin color, accents, language skills, and cultural mannerisms shaped their occupational chances. One respondent said: "They want someone to fit the mold, and if you don't fit the mold . . ." (#102a). Interestingly, many of the women reporting that they had not personally experienced job discrimination (although they were careful to note their belief in its importance), attributed it to their fair, or light complexions:

Maybe I haven't felt as much discrimination because I'm not—I'm kind of fair complected. So, a lot of people don't know, or don't even assume that I'm Mexican. They're real surprised when I say, "Yeah, I'm Mexican."
[professional worker #5]

Many women also offered analysis of the consequences of gender-race-ethnicity for Chicana employment inequality. Some women argue that discrimination is the primary reason Chicanas are overrepresented in lower-level positions in the organization. Other women assert that the organization often "punishes" Chicanas who try to "push" their way into a promotion either by denying them the job or actually downgrading it. For example:

This position that I have now, before me was a Word Processing Supervisor. None of them [previous job incumbents] had the work load that I have now. In fact, they just surveyed my job, and it's increased 130 percent. Yet, I'm a Senior Word Processor. I've had to fight tooth and nail to be classified back. Even then, it's been procrastinated. They know it has to be done, but why is it taking so long? It's just obvious. It just makes you think—those were all white women prior to me. What's the difference?

[upper clerical worker #64a]

The Intersection of Family and Work

An analysis of social dynamics that contextualize Chicanas' options and maintain their social inequality would be incomplete without considering the family (Smith 1987; Zavella, 1987). Motherhood is simultaneously a source of joy and a powerful constraint on employment and occupational mobility. Coltrane argues that "the routine care of home and children . . . provide opportunities for women to express and reaffirm their gendered relation to men and to the world" (1989: 473). Among the 111 Chicana respondents with children, family caretaking constrains their chances for mobility in the world of work. It also forms one way they accomplish gender and culture.

One way Chicanas strive to manage the contradictions of overwork is to try carving out two separate worlds where, in reality, there is but one world and one woman trying to meet the expectations of children, coworkers, supervisors, and her own ambitions. As one woman said:

For the most part, my job doesn't interfere too much with home. When I leave work, I leave my work. I switch stations to do whatever I need to do for the family. But, there are times when, yes, work does tend to tire you out and you do carry it home with you in terms of less energy and not having the energy to deal with the family. That's really hard, especially when both of you come in very tired and you sort of want the other one to do something because you're too tired to deal with it. Then it's hard. The poor kids, they don't understand. They just

know that they're hungry and "how come you guys won't feed us?"

[professional worker #102a]

This woman speaks to the dilemma of reconciling what Hochschild refers to as the "competing urgencies" of family and work. Interestingly, women in this study downplayed the spillover between work and family. In the surveys and in their interviews, women consistently reported that their jobs "almost never" (27%) or only "occasionally" (47.7%) interfered with their abilities to manage their family responsibilities. Yet, their discussions of the intersection of family and work reveal they are experiencing considerable tension and stress in this relationship.

Ironically, ideological changes that have expanded the domain of women's competencies may impede women's articulation of their stress meeting family and work responsibilities. As one woman argues:

I think as women, maybe the progress has been kind of negative in some aspects. You know, we go out and say that we can do this—we can work, we can raise a family, and all that. And yet at the same time, I feel like maybe we've hurt ourselves because we can't do it all. I don't believe there is super-woman.

[professional/managerial worker #5a]

An additional constraint felt by many of the Chicana workers is their responsibility to maintain Chicano cultural traditions and forms. One woman said:

In order to be valued we have to be wives and mothers first. That cultural pressure is the most difficult to overcome.

[professional worker #10]

This informant struck a chord that resonated throughout the study: Mexican/Latina women take on much of the caretaking work in the household as an expression of Mexican culture.[3] Charged with cultural socialization of offspring, Chicanas often avoid debating their partners about the household division of labor. An overwhelming majority of our survey respondents reported "little" (39.4%) or "no" (40.4%) difference of opinion on the household division of labor between married women and their spouses. Yet, when asked about the actual division of labor, women reported doing most of the housework and wished their husbands/partners would do more.

Traditional gender roles and gender ideologies are particularly resistant to change when they are framed within what Caufield (1974) terms a "culture of resistance." Consistently, Chicanas refuse to engage in sustained struggle with husbands/partners over the division of household labor even though they admit they are, as one Chicana professional worker (#6) said, "too stressed and torn between career and family responsibilities to feel good about the accomplishments!" Rather, Chicanas conform to their community's gendered expectations reaffirming both their womanhood and their culture:

> I'm just happy [about] who I am and where I come from. Our women, Latino women, do things just a little bit differently because of who we are and where we came from. There are certain things that we do . . . for our husbands that I know that other women, white women, have problems doing . . . for instance—and I've seen it because my brother-in-law was married to a white woman. You're eating and you go to the stove to maybe serve yourself a little more. It's just normal, I think. You're brought up with that real nurturing with, "honey, do you want some more?" . . . And her comment was, "Well, he can get up by himself." Just the real independence on their side, and I think we're brought up a little more nurturing to our male counterparts. Maybe there's more machismo there too—whatever. It's the way you're brought up.
>
> [upper clerical worker #64a]

The desire to affirm their gender and their race-ethnic culture is strengthened in those cases where women work in jobs that value services to other women and/or Chicanos on the campus. As one Chicana professional worker (#6) said:

> Chicanos feel that working—we see ourselves as social change agents. We see it as being done in a partnership basis with our families. We get hurt by things that people in our culture do, but we don't turn against them. Maybe that hurts in the end, but I think we want to keep a forged relationship and a partnership. As painfully as it may be. And that's where I want to be. Yes.

SUMMARY AND CONCLUSION

This study has demonstrated ways in which gender and race-ethnicity are affirmed in the labor market among selected Chicana white-collar workers. By considering both the features of jobs that Chicanas value and dislike and the perceived barriers to success at work that they encounter in the organization, I have identified mechanisms that reinforce occupational segregation by gender and gender-race-ethnicity.

There is, however, another outcome of Chicana employment. Chicanas' job performances and their concurrent fulfillment of family responsibilities mutually reinforce the accomplishment of culture and ethnicity. Whereas traditional Marxist and feminist analyses view market labor as potentially "liberatory" by increasing women's economic clout (e.g., Engels [1884]1968; Smith 1987; Moore and Sawhill 1978; Hartmann 1981; Ferree 1987), this study finds the opposite. That is, while women usually enjoy their jobs, work is not so much "liberatory" as intensifying their accomplishment of gender both in the tasks they do at work as well as the sex-typed tasks they continue to do at home. Moreover, their attachment to family is linked ideologically to the survival of the culture, rendering their accomplishment of gender an overt act of racial-ethnic and cultural politics. This particular finding may well be a neglected truth in many women's lives. . . .

NOTES

1. Our occupational categories were derived in consultation with the personnel manual of the research site and two personnel analysts. In general, lower clerical occupations

(levels 1–3 in this organization) are nonsupervisory. Upper clerical occupations (levels 4–6) are often supervisory. Professional occupations include managers of academic and staff units as well as a variety of specialized jobs that are mainly administrative (e.g., counselor, personnel analyst) or scientific (staff research associate). Service and technicians tended to be lower-paid workers in laboratories (laboratory helper) or custodians. One important limitation of this case study is that relatively few women in the latter category answered the questionnaire ($n = 9$) or answered our call for an oral interview.
2. National median incomes in 1989 for white female full-time workers was $19,873 and $16,006 for Hispanic females (U.S. Bureau of the Census 1991).
3. It is important to note that the literature that focuses largely on samples of white women reports similar findings. Gender, culture, race, and ethnicity are readily and easily invocable to justify an asymmetrical division of household labor. Nevertheless, the Chicanas in this study are unique insofar as they invoke their gendered responsibilities to Chicano culture.

REFERENCES

Barrera, Mario. 1979. *Race and Class in the Southwest: A Theory of Racial Inequality.* Notre Dame, IN: University of Notre Dame Press.

Berk, Sarah Fenstermaker. 1985. *The Gender Factory: The Apportionment of Work in American Households.* New York: Plenum.

Caufield, Mina Davis. 1974. "Imperialism, the Family, and Cultures of Resistance." *Socialist Revolution* 2:67–85.

Coltrane, Scott. 1989. "Household Labor and the Routine Production of Gender." *Social Problems* 36:473–491.

Engels, Frederick. [1884] 1968. *Origin of the Family, Private Property, and the State.* Moscow: International Publishing.

Ferree, Myra Marx. 1987. "The Struggles of Superwoman." Pp. 161–80 in *Hidden Aspects of Women's Work,* edited by Christine Bose, Roslyn Feldberg, and Natalie Sokoloff. New York: Praeger.

Garcia, John A. 1981. "Yo Soy Mexicano . . . : Self-Identity among the Mexican Origin Population." *Social Science Quarterly* 62:88–98.

Hartmann, Heidi, 1981. "The Family as the Locus of Gender, Class, and Political Struggle: The Example of Housework." *Signs: Journal of Women in Culture and Society* 6:366–394.

Keefe, Susan E. and Amado M. Padilla. 1987. *Chicano Ethnicity.* Albuquerque: University of New Mexico Press.

Mirande, Alfredo and Evangelina Enriquez. 1979. *La Chicana.* Chicago: University of Chicago Press.

Moore, Kristin A. and Isabel U. Sawhill. 1978. "Implications of Women's Employment for Home and Family Life." Pp. 201–55 in *Working Women: Theories and Facts in Perspective,* edited by Ann H. Stromberg and Shirley Harkess. Palo Alto: Mayfield.

Nelson, Candace and Marta Tienda. 1985. "The Structuring of Hispanic Ethnicity: Historical and Contemporary Perspectives." *Ethnic and Racial Studies* 8:49–74.

Ogbu, John U. 1978. *Minority Education and Caste: The American System in Cross-Cultural Perspective.* New York: Academic.

Rubin, Lillian B. 1983. *Intimate Strangers: Men and Women Together.* New York: Harper & Row.

Segura, Denise A. 1989. "The Interplay of Familism and Patriarchy on the Employment of Chicana and Mexican Immigrant Women." Pp. 35–53 in *Renato Rosaldo Lecture Series Monograph,* vol. 5. Tucson: Mexican American Studies and Research Center, University of Arizona.

Smith, Dorothy E. 1987. "Women's Inequality and the Family." Pp. 23–54 in *Families and Work,* edited by N. Gerstel and H. E. Gross. Philadelphia: Temple University Press.

U.S. Bureau of the Census, 1991. "Money Income of Households, Families, and Persons in the United States: 1988 and 1989." *Current Population Reports,* Series P-60, No. 172. Washington DC: U.S. Government Printing Office.

West, Candace and Sarah Fenstermaker. n.d. "Power, Inequality and the Accomplishment of Gender: An Ethnomethodological View." In *Theory on Gender/ Feminism on Theory,* edited by Paula England. New York: Aldine.

West, Candace and Don H. Zimmerman. 1987. "Doing Gender." *Gender and Society* 1:125–51.

Williams, Norma. 1990. *The Mexican American Family, Tradition and Change.* New York: General Hall.

Zavella, Patricia. 1987. *Women's Work and Chicano Families: Cannery Workers of the Santa Clara Valley.* Ithaca, NY: Cornell University Press.

Zinn, Maxine Baca. 1975. "Chicanas: Power and Control in the Domestic Sphere." *De Colores, Journal of Emerging Raza Philosophies* 2:19–31.

———. 1979. "Chicano Family Research: Conceptual Distortions and Alternative Directions." *Journal of Ethnic Studies* 7:59–71.

———. 1982. "Mexican-American Women in the Social Sciences." *Signs: Journal of Women in Culture and Society* 8:259–272.

 Think about It

1. What does Segura mean when she says that the workplace affirms gender roles and racial/ethnic relations?

2. How do workplace barriers—such as racial discrimination and sexual harassment—strengthen Chicanas' gender and ethnic identities? What are the positive and negative aspects and consequences of reinforcing gender and racial/ethnic boundaries in the organization?

3. Many of the women in Segura's study experienced stress from juggling work and motherhood responsibilities. Why, then, did the women say that they were satisfied with the unequal division of labor at home?

24 *Struggling to Succeed: Haitians in South Florida*

Alex Stepick

Most immigrants come to the United States because they want to work. Alex Stepick describes how primary and secondary employment sectors and discrimination in south Florida affect Haitian immigrants' job opportunities. Success is difficult to achieve, Stepick finds, even though Haitian immigrants "are willing to work hard, accept low wages, and complain little."

HUMAN AND SOCIAL CAPITAL

Human capital consists of education, skills and work experience that can help one find a job. For both immigrants and native-born Americans, those with a college education tend to obtain better jobs than those who drop out of high school. The socioeconomic status of one's parents also affects an individual's job possibilities—if your parents attended college and became professionals, then you are more likely to complete college and have a good job, too. Furthermore, once individuals enter the job market, the more experience they have the better the chances of finding another

Source: From Alex Stepick, *Pride against Prejudice: Haitians in the United States* (Boston: Allyn and Bacon, 1998), 37–43, 52–54. Copyright © Allyn & Bacon. Reprinted by permission.

job and the more one's income may be expected to rise. Most economists and other social scientists consider human capital the most important variable in determining an individual's economic status (Borjas 1990).

The human capital [that] immigrants have may not be immediately applicable in the United States. Haitians, who are commonly bilingual (French and Haitian Creole) and frequently even trilingual (Spanish, too) enter a land where they do not speak the dominant language and where employers and others may not recognize their educational degrees or previous job experience. In short, much of their human capital becomes irrelevant. Many among the first Haitian immigrant wave in the 1960s came from Haiti's well-educated elite and middle classes. They experienced acute difficulty in making their human capital relevant to U.S. opportunities.

Joel Dreyfuss is the former editor of *PC Magazine,* perhaps one of the most important computer magazines in the United States. In the 1960s he came from Haiti to the United States as a child and he remembers how his relatives and friends, from the most highly respected families in Haiti, took care of other people's children, cleaned other people's apartments, worked in garment factories, or drove cabs. One man had been a Senator in Haiti, but in New York he pushed a hand truck through the bustling traffic of the garment district (Dreyfuss 1993).

Roger Biamby was sixteen when his family of ten fled to New York from Haiti in 1964 after his father Ernst, an army colonel, launched an unsuccessful coup against President Duvalier. The Biambys, once part of the Haitian elite, arrived in New York with only $100. A career military officer with no experience in the civilian world, the former colonel took a job collecting litter at the 1964 World's Fair in Queens. His wife sewed in a garment factory. His son, Roger, washed dishes at a Times Square restaurant, eventually putting himself into a doctoral program in political science. In the late 1970s Roger moved to South Florida, where he has run nonprofit centers in Miami, Fort Lauderdale, and Pompano Beach that provide job placement, legal help, and other services to Haitian immigrants (Grogan 1994).

In the 1960s over one quarter of the immigrants from Haiti to the United States were professionals (Portes and Grosfoguel 1994). In 1980 before most of the second wave of Haitian immigrants had arrived in South Florida, 55.9 percent of all the Haitians nationwide had graduated from high school and nearly 10 percent had completed four years of college (1984 census). In short, many Haitians who had arrived in the first wave of immigration were well educated. Although they could not immediately make use of their human capital when they arrived in the 1960s, by the 1980s they had time to retool or their children had

obtained higher education. Most of the Haitians we hired to conduct interviews, for example, were college students whose parents came from Haiti's small middle class and who made sure their children advanced their education in the United States.

In contrast, most Haitians in the second wave who migrated to South Florida in the 1970s and 1980s had much less human capital that could be immediately used in the United States. My own surveys in the early 1980s revealed that only 5 percent of South Florida's recently arrived Haitians had graduated from high school (Stepick and Portes 1986). Of those Haitians who arrived in the early 1980s, not one whom we surveyed in 1983–1984 had completed four years of college. Later, some did go on to college. But when they first arrived, by U.S. standards they possessed little human capital.

Most of the recently arrived Haitians in the early 1980s did not speak English well. French is the official language of Haiti and Creole is the language of everyday use. While English is becoming more popular as U.S. influence increases, knowledge of English in Haiti is still very limited. Only 18 percent of those we surveyed who arrived in the early 1980s reported speaking English very well, compared with 50 percent of all Haitians in Florida and more than 66 percent for Haitians nationwide according to the 1980 census.

Nevertheless, Haitians who immigrated to South Florida in the early 1980s were generally better educated than those who remained in Haiti and once they arrived they worked hard at improving their human capital. About three-fourths of Haiti's population is illiterate. Until recently, schools did not even exist outside the major cities. With an overall average of nearly five years of schooling, the Haitians who migrated to South Florida in the early 1980s had more education than the average Haitian in Haiti (Stepick and Portes 1986).

The recent Haitian immigrants also seriously worked to improve their knowledge of English once they arrived in the United States. Just two years after arriving, more than 65 percent had taken English or another education course. Adult-education courses in Little Haiti throughout the 1980s always had many Haitian students. Even in the 1990s after federal government cuts made English language classes much less available, Haitians flocked to the few places that offered classes. In the mid-1990s, each weekday night the school at the Haitian Catholic Center in the middle of Little Haiti bustled with activity. Adult Haitian students filled all of the classrooms in what had been a Catholic girls' high school before being converted into the Haitian Catholic Center. The nearby public school, which also offered adult education in the evening, similarly bulged with Haitians seeking to improve their human capital and their chances of finding work by taking English classes.

Human capital is critical, but not sufficient, for economic success. Social capital permits one to make full use of human capital. Social capital consists of friends, relatives, co-ethnics and others who can ease access to economic resources. Immigrants most often obtain jobs through referrals from people they know. Lucy's family and particularly her husband Charlie's experiences at the seafood restaurant exemplify the importance of social capital. Nearly everyone in the immediate family plus more distant relatives obtained jobs because Charlie already had a position in the restaurant. Having the right skills and experience are not irrelevant, but individuals may not have the chance to use them unless they are in the right place at the right time. Social capital, embodied in social networks of relatives and friends, helps them get to the right place at the right time. New immigrants must work at obtaining social capital that native-born Americans usually take for granted because they grew up in America and have relatives and friends living in the United States.

Among recently arrived Haitian immigrants in South Florida in the early and mid-1980s, nearly 70 percent said that friends or kin helped them find their first job. So many Haitians came in such a short time in the early 1980s that they did not have enough social capital to spread around. While they relied on relatives, there just were not enough relatives. On average those who migrated in the early 1980s had only 1.5 relatives already in Miami compared to over twice as many for Cubans who came to Miami from the Cuban port of Mariel in 1980 (Stepick and Portes 1986).

Anti-Haitian prejudice combined with relatively low levels of both human and social capital to impede the economic incorporation and advancement of those Haitians who arrived in the early 1980s. As a result, in the early years of their U.S. residency most of these Haitians vacillated between unemployment, the secondary sector and the informal sector.

SECONDARY SECTOR EMPLOYMENT: THE WORKING POOR

. . . Linase "Lina" St. Fleur, along with her husband and friend, Olga, provide an example of Haitians working in local industry. Lina worked for twelve years in an apparel factory in the Miami suburb of Hialeah. She had worked her way up from seamstress to supervising twelve sewing-machine operators, most of whom were also Haitian. Her good friend, Olga Louis, was in charge of shipping for the same firm. One night, however, thieves pried open a security door, meticulously unscrewed the twelve industrial sewing machines, and carried them off. Lina, Olga, and their friends all lost their jobs. At the same time, Miami's apparel manufacturing was moving overseas, to the Caribbean, Central America and Asia where wages are much lower than in the United States. The stolen sewing machines easily could end up in an overseas factory that produces clothes for the U.S. market.

The newly unemployed Haitian women all try to help each other. "But," says Lina, "only one of them has found a new job. The others keep looking. 'Nothing yet,' they always tell me." The state of Florida Job Service is really trying to help them, Lina says, "but they send you out to a place that has one job open, and they send ten or fifteen people. You're better off going door-to-door or talking to friends."

Meanwhile, it is tough at home. Lina's husband makes $10 an hour in a local bakery. "Even when you both work, it's hard—rent, electricity. When only one works, it's worse," she says. "I have a loan I can't pay back. We can't do things we used to do. We've just cut out fun. We don't go out to eat, to movies. We just stopped all those things." She has to explain to her 18- and 20-year-old daughters and her 13-year-old son that they won't be getting all the new clothes they would like. "I tell them you can't just ask for anything you like. We can't afford it. They see the way it is."

Olga's husband works in a ceiling-tile factory. They, too, have children in Miami—an 11-year-old girl, a 13-year-old boy. They, too, are cutting back on fun, on school clothes. And, they have another worry—a 19-year-old son living in Haiti. "I used to be able to send him something. Now it's hard. I don't know what I'm going to do" (Tasker 1994).

Lina's and Olga's family work experiences mirror those of many recently arrived Haitians in South Florida. Lina, Olga and their husbands each obtained jobs in the secondary sector, that is, jobs that are semiskilled or unskilled, primarily blue collar that offer low wages and benefits and few opportunities for advancement (Averitt 1968). Through hard work, they achieved a small amount of economic mobility, but only by pooling resources within their household did they have an adequate income. When one family member loses a job, the whole extended family, including those back in Haiti, becomes vulnerable. The social relations among friends at work constitute their most important asset in finding another job. Nevertheless, in a local opportunity structure with few openings for unskilled Black immigrants, their social capital has been insufficient to easily overcome unemployment. The trend for U.S. manufacturing firms to move overseas, as exemplified by apparel factories in Miami, exacerbates their economic vulnerability.

Haitian employment experiences in South Florida mirror those of most other immigrant groups where most jobs are either in agriculture or low-wage, low-skilled urban occupations. Ac-

cording to my own surveys, Haitians in South Florida through the 1980s overwhelmingly concentrated in farm work and low-paying factory or service work such as back of the house jobs in hotels and restaurants (such as Lucy and her husband had): hotel maids, janitors and maintenance men, kitchen helpers, bus boys and dishwashers (Portes and Stepick 1987; Stepick and Portes 1986). According to the census, most Haitians hold lower-level positions with the largest segment working in restaurants, over one-third in services (especially in hotels) and over one-fourth working as low-skilled laborers (Kerr 1996; Mompoint 1996).

Lina and Olga's sudden unemployment also reflects two other critical points concerning the incorporation of recently arrived Haitians into the local economy. Lack of opportunity for Haitians in South Florida in the early 1980s meant that in general what human capital Haitians did have could not be readily used. Those with a high-school diploma had no better chance of finding a job and earning money than someone who had never attended school. Likewise, those who had years of experience in a skilled or semiskilled job had no better chance of finding a job and earning money than those who had never worked before. Educated and uneducated, professionals and farmers, those who knew English and those who did not were all equally likely to be unemployed (Portes and Stepick 1985).

Moreover, females had it much worse than males. In the early 1980s among the recently arrived Haitians, women had a 27 percent greater probability of unemployment than men (Stepick and Portes 1986). While education and work experience did not help South Florida Haitians obtain a job, being a man did make more opportunities available. Even when Haitian females had the same education, skills and knowledge of English as men, they still faced much greater difficulty in finding employment. In short, contrary to the theories of economists, human capital was not important in determining Haitian economic success in the early 1980s for the most recently arrived Haitians. Instead, anti-Haitian prejudice embodied, for example, in the tuberculosis and AIDS scares closed the opportunity structure to many Haitians.

Haitians have also been particularly vulnerable to arbitrary, prejudiced management and can easily lose jobs for little reason. At the seafood restaurant where Lucy worked, the manager suspended a Haitian cook for three days after seeing him eat a piece of fried chicken for which he had not paid. When Sue Chaffee, the anthropologist who also worked at the restaurant, arrived, she found Lucy surrounded by a group of co-workers, all visibly upset, angrily discussing the suspension. One Haitian man remarked to Sue, "Bobier (the suspended cook) has worked here for seven years. He worked a ten-hour shift today with no food and no breaks. The man was hungry so he has every right to eat. Vance (the manager who suspended Bobier) is the only person I know who would put a man 'on vacation' for that."

The seafood restaurant received a new management team in mid-1991. They immediately announced a set of cost-saving measures, including reduced hours. Lucy complained, "How am I supposed to feed my children?" Management responded that workers not willing to conform to the changes should feel free to leave and look for another job. In the following weeks, not only did Vance schedule Lucy for reduced hours, but he also frequently asked her to leave an hour and a half before she was scheduled to leave. On two successive Saturdays when told to leave early, she grabbed her bag that stored her walking shoes and personal belongings while angrily talking to herself in Creole, punched out, and proceeded out the front door to catch a bus home. On the third Saturday when ordered to leave early, she ignored the order and continued scooping lettuce out of the bin and filling bowls with salads. Vance soon confronted her, loudly demanding directly in her face, "Punch out immediately!" Lucy later claimed Vance's "having no respect made me crazy." She erupted verbally as best she could in English, telling Vance that he was no good, had no respect

for Haitians, and only wanted White people working in the restaurant. While Lucy was the only one to make these claims publicly, all Haitians working there apparently concurred.

Since the 1980s, South Florida Haitian social service agencies and the Legal Services Corporation have received complaints from Haitians that employers not only paid less than the minimum wage, but some did not pay the Haitian workers at all. Legitimate businesses such as auto body shops or security guard companies would hire a Haitian and not pay him (most cases involved males) for two, three, even four weeks. In other cases, usually involving factories such as a local plastic manufacturer, Haitians would work for eleven months and two weeks. Just before they became eligible for vacation, employers would fire them. In the mid-1980s, one Haitian social service agency registered 500 such complaints in the first four months of its offering legal services.

For those Haitians working in agriculture, conditions were frequently abominable. In 1980 a Haitian dishwasher in a Miami restaurant left his job after a job recruiter promised a good job in South Carolina. He, his wife, and their fifteen-year-old son, along with one other Haitian, worked for this contractor for five weeks. Employment records showed they should have earned $2,500. The contractor actually paid them $540 after deductions for transportation, housing, food, and even a $1.50 charge for each use of the bathroom. The camp where they lived had no electricity and no facilities for cooking, no stove, and no refrigerator. All the thirty or so workers slept in one large room with no partitions. Rats and insects nibbled at everything. When the wife went into advanced labor, the contractor and the foreman of the farm where they were living and working denied them permission to leave the camp and go to the hospital. Finally the contractor and foreman relented. As she was enroute to the hospital, less than one-half mile from the camp, the woman gave birth in the back of a moving truck that was dirty from hauling produce. In this case, Florida Rural Legal Services obtained a $20,000 judgment against the contractor and farmer. However, since the 1980s the U.S. Congress has consistently cut funds to the Legal Services Corporation which offers legal services to those who otherwise cannot afford them. One special target of congressional cuts was services to immigrants. By the mid-1990s immigrants subject to such abuse had very few legal alternatives. . . .

PRIMARY SECTOR EMPLOYMENT: MIDDLE-CLASS PROFESSIONALS AND SKILLED WORKERS

. . . Many Haitians incorporated into the primary sector of the economy are from the Haitian middle classes who left Haiti in the 1960s and lived in northern cities before looping down to Miami. In 1985 when we conducted a census of . . . the approximately 200 businesses in Little Haiti, all of the owners had been in the United States more than 10 years and more than 70 percent had graduated from high school. While Haitian Creole is their native language and nearly all are also fluent in French, all spoke English well and they were thoroughly familiar with American culture. Those under forty-years-old have received a significant portion of their education, frequently including college, in the United States or Canada.

By 1995 the profile had shifted. More and more Haitian professionals, entrepreneurs, and others with stable, middle-class jobs had grown up or at least been educated in South Florida. The Haitian Engineers Association in South Florida, for instance, has a majority of members who graduated from engineering schools in Florida. Social work and nursing schools at universities in Miami, including Florida International University, Barry University, and the University of Miami, have graduated numerous Haitian students. Many of these recent graduates have modest family backgrounds, including some who were the boat people of the 1970s and 1980s who suffered from the negative stereotypes of being illiterate,

unskilled and likely to be a drain on U.S. society. At least the second generation has fulfilled the hopes of their immigrant parents. They have overcome extraordinary prejudices and succeeded through education. They may not represent the majority of the population or even the majority of the second generation, but their numbers are great enough to offer hope and increased respectability to the rest of the community.

REFERENCES

Averitt, Robert 1968. *The Dual Economy.* New York: Norton.

Borjas, George 1990. *Friends or Strangers: The Impact of Immigrants on the U.S. Economy.* New York: Basic Books.

Grogan, John 1994. "South Florida Becomes Home by Variety of Routes," *Fort Lauderdale Sun-Sentinel,* October 30: 6S.

Kerr, Oliver 1996. "Miami Haitians in the 1990 Census," unpublished paper. Miami: Florida International University.

Mompoint, Noe 1996. "Population Characteristics of Haitians Living in Dade County," unpublished paper. Coral Gables: Miami-Dade Water and Sewer Department.

Portes, Alejandro and Ramon Grosfoguel 1994. "Caribbean Diasporas: Migration and Ethnic Communities," *The Annals of the American Academy of Political and Social Science.* May, 533: 48–70.

Portes, Alejandro and Alex Stepick 1985. "Unwelcome Immigrants: The Labor Market Experiences of 1980 Cuban and Haitian Refugees in South Florida," *American Sociological Review,* 50, August: 493–514.

———1987. "Haitian Refugees in South Florida, 1983–1986," *Dialogue No. 77, Occasional Papers Series.* Latin American and Caribbean Center, Florida International University, February.

Stepick, Alex and Alejandro Portes 1986. "Flight into Despair: A Profile of Recent Haitian Refugees in South Florida," *International Migration Review,* Spring 20(2): 329–250.

Tasker, Fred 1994. "Threads of 16 Lives Unravel with Theft of Sewing Machines," *Miami Herald,* July 31: 1j.

Think about It

1. What do social scientists mean by *human capital* and *social capital?* How have human capital and social capital differed across the three waves of Haitian immigration?

2. How do the primary and secondary employment sectors differ? What factors have influenced Haitian employment in each sector?

3. How do prejudice and exploitative work conditions undermine many Haitians' efforts to be upwardly mobile?

---

25   *Central American Workers: New Roles in a New Landscape*

Terry A. Repak

Gender can be a determining factor in influencing the decision to migrate and the choice of a destination. Terry A. Repak describes the key role that gendered labor recruitment played in persuading women from Central America to work in Washington, D.C., and in shaping the immigrants' labor force participation patterns. The settlement process has created both opportunities and problems for Central American men, women, and their families.*

Somehow within a single generation, Washington, D.C., managed to attract entire villages, households, and extended families from El Salvador and other Central American countries, to the point that it could claim the second largest Salvadoran community and the third largest settlement of Central Americans in the United States. In many ways this migration constitutes a departure from the labor migrations of other Latin Americans to the United States, and the Central American immigrants who chose to settle in Washington may be embraced as "new immigrants."[1] Their settlement patterns were profoundly influenced by the fact that women predominated in the initial phase of the migration, by the distinctive gender differences that emerged in labor force participation patterns, and through the assumption of transformed gender roles.

A historical–structural framework was employed here to explain the origins and the directionality of this Central American migration, along with certain facets of the labor market experiences of men and women. Labor recruitment theory also contributed to an understanding of the timing and composition of the migration. But since gendered labor recruitment was primarily responsible for determining the peculiar direction and gender composition of this particular migration, a focus on gender is essential in any analysis of the migration, settlement, and labor force

*Repak's data are based on interviews with 30 representatives of social service agencies, local government, and community-based groups working primarily with Central American immigrants; 50 Central American immigrants chosen randomly from the caseloads of three social service agencies; and 100 Central American households selected randomly from five sites in the District of Columbia and in Maryland and Virginia suburbs with large Central American populations. *Ed.*

Source: Excerpted and reprinted from the Conclusion to Terry A. Repak, *Waiting on Washington: Central American Workers in the Nation's Capital* (Philadelphia: Temple University Press, 1995), 177–90. Copyright © 1995 Temple University Press. Reprinted by permission of Temple University Press. All rights reserved.

participation patterns of recent Central American immigrants in the United States.

GENDER FACTORS IN THE MIGRATION PROCESS

El Salvador serves as a prime example of a country where the forces that propel or cause migrations cannot be separated and neatly compartmentalized as political or economic in nature. The most densely populated mainland country in the Western Hemisphere, El Salvador was a battleground for access to land throughout the twentieth century as more and more land became concentrated in the hands of fewer and fewer families. Earlier studies demonstrated that three-fourths of all emigrants from El Salvador in the 1950s and 1960s came from the excluded population of landless or land-poor peoples, but no studies underlined the gender composition of these movements. To a large extent political-economic transformations—for example, the concentration of land in the hands of wealthy families and the increasing polarization, political repression, and violence in the societies—were occurring simultaneously in Guatemala, in Nicaragua, and (to a lesser extent) in Honduras. In all of these Central American countries, people migrated in response to economic dislocations and changes in the world economy and as a result of war and political persecution.

Women have predominated in migrations from rural to urban areas throughout most of Latin America for a number of years. But beginning in the 1960s Central American women pioneered and dominated the early labor migration to a distant city in the United States—that is, to Washington, D.C. Structural links between the United States and the Central American countries had expanded rapidly since the early 1960s on account of U.S. business, government, and cultural influences. Potential emigrants in Central American countries increasingly were made aware of conditions in the United States through burgeoning communication links (e.g., through radio and television, through consumer goods, and through the medium of social networks). When landless and land-poor peasants who were leaving El Salvador (and other Central American countries) were joined by students and teachers, by workers without jobs, by individuals who were persecuted or targeted for assassination, and by apolitical people who were caught between warring factions, many already had information about or close ties with cities in the United States because of the women who had migrated earlier for work.

The structural conditions that generate emigration from certain countries tend to be gender-specific, especially when linked with cultural norms and ideologies in both sending and receiving countries. In the case of El Salvador, these gender-based structural conditions had a profound impact on women: the nonexistence of paid work for women in rural areas; family traditions of encouraging daughters to depart; low marriage rates along with high rates of female-headed households; the not uncommon pattern where men may have multiple partners and may be linked loosely to several households; and the availability of domestic-service jobs in cities that attracted women with few employment opportunities in rural areas. Similarly, characteristics of labor markets in certain receiving cities may hold more allure for women than for men among those who wish to emigrate. Cultural norms also determine whether women or men are preferred as candidates for certain jobs, particularly in gender-segregated labor markets such as Washington, D.C., with its overabundance of service-sector jobs. The exodus of U.S.-born women out of such gender-stereotyped occupations as domestic service and child care since the 1960s and the increasing demand for low-wage workers to fill these jobs obviously presented more attractive employment opportunities to Central American women than to men.

Because of a high proportion of female-headed households in countries such as El Salvador, women who wished to emigrate were the primary actors in decisions about when and where they desired to move. A majority of women who converged on Washington in the 1960s and 1970s did so as single individuals or as single mothers and heads of households who sought ways to provide for their families, and most of them emigrated without the approval or assistance of men. Gendered labor recruitment was responsible for luring many of these early immigrants to Washington. The testimonies of women like Rosa Lopez, Lucia Herrera, and Rhina Garcia illustrate how over the years Washington's government, diplomatic, and professional workforce recruited immigrants (particularly women) who could furnish basic services as domestic workers and child-care providers.

A constellation of forces prompted the shift from employer-induced to family- or network-based migration in the movement of Central Americans to Washington, D.C. At the same time, the migration pattern shifted from one in which women predominated to a more general movement of men and women. Washington was never a major center of manufacturing, assembly, or production work, and the city did not experience an abrupt shift from a goods-producing to a service-based economy. Instead, its transformation can be attributed primarily to population growth, diversification (i.e., the increase of biotechnology, defense, and research-and-development firms), and gentrification rather than to structural change. The city's phenomenal growth since 1960 resulted in the proliferation of highly skilled jobs, as well as an expansion of low-skilled and service jobs.

An international capital and new "world city," Washington posed an attractive destination for new immigrants, and this attraction was enhanced by the vibrant economic conditions persisting throughout the 1980s. Throughout most of that decade, Washington had the highest average household income of any major metropolitan area in the country, as well as the nation's highest proportion of women in the workforce (69 percent). The city has perpetually suffered from an acute shortage of day-care facilities and a commensurate abundance of high-income families who can afford to procure housekeeping and child-care services. These professionals eagerly sought or recruited the services of domestic workers and child-care providers from other countries to relieve them of day-care and household responsibilities. They also created a demand for the products made and sold by growing numbers of specialty shops (e.g., gourmet foods and fine linen), all of which depended on semiskilled and unskilled workers. A persistent dearth of North Americans to fill low-wage jobs in the Washington area led to a minuscule unemployment figure of 2.9 percent for the region in 1988. Leverage in wages was possible for Central American immigrants, particularly those with documents, because of the tight labor market conditions that persisted throughout the Washington metropolitan area.

These noteworthy features, then, distinguish the migration of Central Americans to Washington from similar movements of Mexicans, Dominicans, and other Latin Americans to major cities in the United States. As primary actors in the decision-making stages, women initiated the migration and pioneered the movement to a city that did not have a well-established Latin American community ready to receive and assist them with support services. Many of the women were recruited to work or had jobs arranged for them in Washington by diplomatic or professional families. Distinct gender differences emerged in the settlement patterns that ensued as a result of a gendered labor migration. Central American women brought more family members along with them (or sent for them in time) than Central American men did, which led to a relatively stable, legal, and permanent immigration. In addition, women had to form their own social networks, which eventually provided job referrals, housing, and other forms of assistance to later arrivals from their countries of origin. As Nestor Rodriguez has observed, women's presence contributes to the rapid development of a thriving community that ensures the continuation of cultural traditions and assists coethnics in the settlement process. Women immigrants "fuel the development of families and, hence, of family-related activities, such as weddings and baptisms, that trigger community social participation."[2]

One final distinction between Central American migration patterns and those of other Latin American migrations is the fact that a substantial proportion of the immigrants were forced to leave their homes because of civil wars and political repression. Many émigrés were highly educated white-collar and professional people who brought their skills and talents to the labor pools of U.S. cities without [imposing] a burden on public resources. Yet the overwhelming majority of immigrants from Central American countries were not recognized as political refugees and encountered a hostile reception by the U.S. government upon arrival in this country. Consequently, family members, social networks, and social service agencies (largely staffed by women) had to mediate for those in need of food, housing, job referrals, and training. Gender-based networks were often the only conduit to safe havens and sanctuaries for later immigrants who fled their countries as a result of political persecution and war in the 1980s. Indeed, networks grew to such an extent that half of the later immigrants from Central American countries chose to go to Washington because they had a family member in that city, and many others went because they heard that there were more jobs and higher wages in Washington than elsewhere in the country. Very few were left to find jobs and housing on their own, without the advice or assistance of seasoned compatriots.

LABOR FORCE PARTICIPATION PATTERNS

From a study of this nature, questions arise about the intrinsic character of gender-based social networks and how they vary when women predominate in a migration. Even larger questions emerge with the striking gender differences in the labor market experiences of Central American men and women: with regard to labor market insertion patterns, wage levels, occupational mobility, and the range of occupations open to immigrant women as opposed to immigrant men. The large disparity in wages and job mobility for Central American immigrants can hardly be attributed to human capital differences between men and women or to any deficiencies on the part of the women. By all human capital measures, Central American women held distinct advantages over men—that is, in length of time in the United States, in level of education, in English-speaking ability, and legal status. Even when comparing social capital, women exhibited stronger ties to social networks and profited from them to a greater extent than men. But the sector of employment in which men worked was more important than any of their background characteristics in determining wage levels and job mobility, and structural factors were clearly in their favor. Central American men found unusually advantageous employment opportunities in the Washington area. A booming construction industry and tight labor market conditions throughout the 1980s translated into higher wages than comparable jobs paid in other cities, regardless of education levels, English proficiency, and legal status. The proportion of the Central American men surveyed in Washington who were employed in construction was far higher (at 61 percent) than the figures for Latin American men in other U.S. cities (such as Mexicans in California, at 18 percent), and wages far surpassed those recorded for Mexican men in California as well as for Central American men in Houston.[3]

Central American women experienced less economic "success" and occupational mobility than Central American men in the Washington area labor market despite their human capital advantages and extensive use of social networks. Women exhibited little mobility in wage levels or job status largely because of structural factors, that is, the narrow range of occupations open to them and the fact that they were confined to informal or secondary-sector jobs. For immigrant women with lower levels of education, domestic service is hardly "transitional work," since they will probably never experience mobility out of the occupation. Domestic service is an occupation with built-in idiosyncrasies that bar women from career advancement and age mobility to an extent that men never experience in the occupational sectors that they dominate. Women in domestic service work in isolation from compatriots; they are insulated from more diverse networks with information on other types of jobs; and they lack the opportunities to learn new job skills (such as word processing or administrative skills). Most domestic workers are unable to organize themselves into unions and thus have no means for redressing grievances or improving work conditions. These circumstances are especially acute for live-in domestic workers, and most of them seek to make the transition to live-out domestic work as early as possible. Few other occupations entail such enormous responsibility (for the lives of children and the welfare of homes) and yet are so poorly remunerated and devoid of vital benefits such as medical and retirement insurance, sick leave, and paid vacations.

A rigid sex-typing of jobs may occur among immigrant women anywhere in the United States as soon as they enter the labor market. But in a service-oriented city such as Washington, semi-skilled women who would most likely move into production-and-assembly jobs in other urban areas in the United States find few opportunities for employment outside of domestic service. Most white-collar jobs are out of reach for Central American women because such jobs generally require fluency in English, higher education levels, and the possession of legal documents. The few women who were able to move into pink- or white-collar jobs (e.g., in secretarial, teaching, and counseling positions) attained higher status but not necessarily higher-paid employment than their counterparts in domestic service. Employment stagnation and wage discrimination are indeed problems for women nationally, regardless of their origins. Several studies have noted that women of all national origins, Anglo and other U.S.-born women in-

cluded, attain far lower proportions of upper-income job categories (in professional and managerial positions) than men do.[4] They stress that the occupational segregation by gender of the triple role that women have to assume as wives, mothers, and wage workers probably account for the fact that human capital variables make little difference in women's earnings.

Gender factors clearly emerge as preeminent in the analysis of immigrant labor market incorporation and render structural and personal characteristics inadequate as explanations for the performance of Central American immigrants in Washington's labor market. Long-term patterns of economic adaptation for Central American men and women are as yet impossible to determine because they are relatively recent immigrants and because their experiences vary widely with the divergent labor markets in different cities. The question that must be answered in time and with further research is whether first-generation immigrant women with high levels of human capital eventually achieve marked improvement in wages and employment mobility, or whether occupational advancement and career opportunities become available only to the generations that succeed them. . . .

SELF-CONCEPTS AND GENDER ROLES

A final area in which Central American immigrants distinguish themselves as "new immigrants" is in the reformulation of gender roles upon settlement in the United States. Many Central American women made the decision to emigrate and actually moved to a distant U.S. city of their own accord and by their own resources, especially if they had jobs arranged for them in the United States. Women who made such decisions and accomplished the arduous move to the United States on their own had already embarked upon a process of transformation in self-perception and gender roles. These immigrants reveal that gender roles are perpetually in a state of flux during the migration and settlement processes and that as a result their relationships are fraught with contradictions. The process of migration and resettlement alters gender roles to an enormous extent, and a majority of Central American women maintain that they enjoy more personal independence and autonomy in the United States, particularly if they work for wages. But the flip side of the coin is that the women have to work much harder than they did at home and that job-related stresses often take a heavy toll on their personal and family lives.

The degree of contentment that Central American women expressed over their lives in the United States depended largely upon whether they experienced a sharp decline in social and occupational status upon migration and whether they had any hope of mobility out of low-status jobs. After several years of work in domestic service, for example, the women who had moved into higher-status jobs as secretaries, teachers, and counselors voiced contentment with their achievements in the United States even though their salaries were far from adequate. Similarly, women with low education levels who held few aspirations to shift out of domestic service expressed a certain satisfaction with their work and personal lives in this country. Most of these women were appreciative of their jobs and glad to be working for "decent" wages. But the women who had experienced an irreversible decline in job status and could find no alternative to jobs in domestic service in the Washington area (generally semiskilled workers who had worked in factories or stores in their countries of origin) displayed a sullen discontentment with their working lives. Most of these women worked hard because they wanted their children to have the opportunity for higher education and the higher status careers that have eluded them.

Other problems in the settlement process that created hardships for both men and women were discrimination from landlords, employers, and neighbors; the language barrier (if they were unable to speak English); the new immigration law, which complicated the search for stable employment for people who were undocumented; and

unemployment or unstable work conditions, particularly for undocumented Central American men. Dealing with discrimination and exploitation by employers or other Americans was an intransigent problem for both immigrant men and women when they settled in the United States. Coming from more homogeneous societies in Central American countries (such as El Salvador), few of those interviewed had experienced the depth of racial or ethnic enmity and discrimination that they encountered in the United States. Isabel Martinez remarked at how deeply she felt the divisions in U.S. society between black, brown, and white people. She feared for her children because they were often subject to nasty forms of discrimination. "Sometimes I feel like a cockroach crawling on the ground because of the way people treat me. And my daughter comes home from school and tells me that other kids are saying things to her, and I feel bad." Such problems may enhance the sense of cultural isolation and low self-esteem that many immigrants must contend with, particularly if they are locked into servile work that is far below their levels of education and expertise.

Most Central American women worked outside the home to contribute to the household's sustenance and as a result they became empowered in their roles as major providers. The extent to which women gained personal freedom, independence, and a sense that they were living more rewarding lives after migrating to the United States often hinged upon personal characteristics such as marital status, education level, socioeconomic background, and urban versus rural origin. But all women who earned wages were able to use that financial independence as a vehicle for gaining control over other areas of their lives, for negotiating more equitable sharing of household responsibilities, and for demanding greater autonomy. They believed that they had earned the right to go where they pleased, to take classes and "develop" themselves, to purchase their own cars, to socialize with friends, and to participate in decisions about household expenditures.

Married and single women alike complained that men changed little in their roles and attitudes toward women after migrating to the United States, and that as a result relationships became more complicated and contentious upon resettlement here. The stresses of working long hours at low-wage service jobs, of adjusting to a strange culture and altered roles within the family, and of dealing with problems related to legal status are often severe enough to cause the break-up of marriages. Even though migration may enable women to augment their independence and power within the family, "the success of the migration project may hinge on the maintenance of household structures that permit the pooling of several rather low incomes. . . . If the new-found autonomy of employed immigrant women leads to marital disruption rather than altered power relations in the traditional household, the collective mobility project is likely to fail, leading to poverty . . . in the United States," as Sherri Grasmuck and Patricia Pessar (1991: 202) observed. Only with time will the actual dimensions of the personal toll that migration entails become clear.

The immigration experience obviously holds different benefits for women and men. Migration and resettlement in the United States has enabled a sizable proportion of women to shirk traditional roles and patterns of dependence so that they may realize aspirations for financial independence, enhanced autonomy, and personal goals for their children.[5] In certain senses they have achieved more than Central American men, who must relinquish some of the privileges of patriarchal cultures. Yet women confront more barriers than men in their pursuit of personal development and career advancement in the United States, particularly in cities such as Washington that are replete with gender-stereotyped jobs from which women may never escape. For both men and women, migration indeed entails a melange of bitter blessings.

NOTES

1. Rodriguez (1987) wrote about the ways in which Central American immigrants in Houston formed new migration patterns in that city.
2. Rodriguez 1987: 9.
3. On California figures, see Cornelius 1988; on Houston, see Rodriguez 1987.
4. Tienda and Guhleman 1985; Zhou and Logan 1989.
5. See Pedraza 1991: 321.

REFERENCES

Cornelius, Wayne. 1988. "Los Migrantes de la Crisis: The Changing Profile of Mexican Labor Migration to California in the 1980s." Paper presented at the conference "Population and Work in Regional Settings," El Colegio de Michoacan, Zamora, Michoacan, November 28–30.

Grasmuck, Sherri, and Patricia Pessar. 1991. *Between Two Islands: Dominican International Migration.* Berkeley and Los Angeles: University of California Press.

Pedraza, Silvia. 1991. "Women and Migration: The Social Consequences of Gender." *Annual Review of Sociology* 17: 303–25.

Rodriguez, Nestor. 1987. "Undocumented Central Americans in Houston: Diverse Populations." *International Migration Review* 21: 4–26.

Tienda, Marta, and Patricia Guhleman. 1985. "The Occupational Position of Employed Hispanic Women." In *Hispanics in the U.S. Economy,* ed. George Borjas and Marta Tienda. New York: Academic Press.

Zhou, Min, and John Logan. 1989. "Returns on Human Capital in Ethnic Enclaves: New York City's Chinatown." *American Sociological Review* 54: 809–20.

? *Think about It*

1. Why does Repak characterize the Central American immigrants in her study as "new immigrants"? How do they differ from other Latin Americans who migrated to the United States?

2. How did gender and structural factors affect the migration process and the occupations of Central American immigrants in the District of Columbia?

3. Why, according to Repak, has migration resulted in "bitter blessings" for both women and men?

Family and Traditional Values: The Bedrock of Chinese American Business

Bernard Wong

Business enterprises owned and operated by Asian Americans have proliferated since the 1970s. Chinese American entrepreneurship ranges from very successful high-technology research and manufacturing firms to modest family operations. Bernard Wong examines the crucial role that tradition, values, and family ties play in establishing and operating family-based businesses in the Chinese American community.

THE ROLE OF KINSHIP IN CHINESE BUSINESS

The family firm has numerous advantages: (1) ease of training family members in business operations; (2) control of information or trade secrets; (3) family members will put in long hours; (4) families are important sources of financing; and (5) kinsmen constitute an important labor pool. In addition to these advantages, Chinese family firms offer the flexibility needed for business survival. This is particularly important in situations with keen competition and fluctuating demands for goods and services like the garment industry. Given the seasonal nature of San Francisco's garment industry, family-run factories tend to have greater endurance and flexibility than others. When business is slow, family members can do the work themselves and cut down on outside help. In adverse situations, family members can forgo a salary temporarily, or reduce the profit for each garment. Low profit margins and reduced production costs in the family firm environment have enabled many Chinese garment factories to survive during slow seasons. Family firms have many of the same benefits in the restaurant trade.

Source: From Bernard Wong, *Ethnicity and Entrepreneurship: The New Chinese Immigrants in the San Francisco Bay Area* (Boston: Allyn and Bacon, 1998), 66–69; 71–74; 79–80. Copyright © 1998 Allyn & Bacon. Reprinted by permission.

In the past several years, Chinese restaurants in the Bay Area have been affected by two major events: the earthquake of 1989 and an economic recession. The reduction of tourists and local customers has caused bankruptcy among some Chinese restaurants. However, family-run Chinese restaurants have been able to survive California's economic recession.

Family firms in the Bay Area today are of three types: (1) firms owned and managed by the nuclear family; (2) firms owned and managed by siblings; and (3) firms owned and managed by a core group of kinsmen with the help of outsiders.

Family Firms Owned and Managed by the Nuclear Family

Firms run by a husband and wife and their children are normally small in size. The nuclear family in this case is both the consumption and production unit. Family members usually are paid only what is needed for daily necessities, and children help out after school or on weekends. Those who work in the firm have meals together in the common kitchen. Eating together saves manpower since one person can do the cooking and shopping. Communal eating also saves money because costly equipment is purchased together and food can be bought in bulk. This kind of family firm can maximize labor resources since everyone who can help will work in the firm. Family businesses also minimize expenditures by not hiring outsiders. Money saved can be used in a flexible manner, such as for the expansion of the business or the purchase of common properties like automobiles and houses.

Authority is structured according to the Chinese kinship system, by generation, age, sex, and birth rank. The family head, usually the oldest effective male, is the major decision maker, although adult children are allowed to make minor decisions without consultation. The division of labor is relatively simple. Day-to-day routine business operations are delegated to family members. Trust permeates the family firm. A mistake by a son or a daughter is tolerated; he or she will be given another chance and is expected to learn from the mistake.

In most cases, the second generation Chinese immigrants are not interested in a career in the restaurant business, despite their immersion in the business from an early age. For example, one family from Taiwan started their restaurant when their children were very young. The children would go to the restaurant every day after school; the family workplace was also their playground. After eating dinner they would return home to do their homework. Now those children are teenagers, and they come to the restaurant only on weekends to help with business. The children have no interest in continuing the family business. The son, now a senior in high school, told me that the restaurant business is too hard. He hopes to find work as a computer scientist in Silicon Valley.

Family firms share common traits. They use kinship relationships for business purposes. Family members are employees, workers, and managers of the family business, and family relationships are intertwined with business relationships. Chinese immigrant family firms are a means to generate family wealth and to lay a foundation for future business ventures. Family businesses are tied to the quest for the American Dream—immigrants involved in them feel that family businesses are the only viable path to social mobility in America. Immigrants are driven to succeed in their new land. "We have spent so much time and energy in our immigration to the United States," one informant told me. "It is a loss of face if we fail in our quest for a better life." Another immigrant put it this way: "Our family business is our only avenue to a better life in America. There is no other method!" In the family firm environment, the ideology of success and the necessity of hard work are deeply ingrained in family members.

Family Firms Owned and Managed by Siblings

As a result of the Immigration Act of 1965, adult siblings of United States citizens became eligible for immigration to the United States. Quite a number of family businesses in the Chinese population are now organized around a sibling group. Compared to family firms owned by the nuclear family, those owned by siblings draw on a larger group of kinsmen, and the father is generally absent. Normally, sibling-based family firms are larger in size than nuclear family–based firms and workers are often hired from outside the family as well. Among siblings who are partners in a family business, the older brother usually acts as the leader or supervisor, though in modern America, the eldest sister might take charge. The leader organizes the family business and delegates responsibilities.

Family Firms Owned and Managed by Kinsmen and Outsiders

In my research I have not come across firms owned by lineages or clans. However, large family firms often hire patrilineal relatives (such as paternal uncles or cousins) or members of a family name association (who, in actuality, may not be blood relatives). This type of family firm is usually so large that it may not be able to function without the help of outsiders.

Personal and family savings seem to be the basis for business financing among the first generation

Chinese (see also Chan and Cheung's 1985 study of Chinese businesses in Toronto, Canada). The informal credit associations or rotating credit associations (hui) of old, as described by Light (1972), B. Wong (1982) and others, in which members made contributions to a fund given to the highest bidder, are now an insignificant source of financing among new immigrant entrepreneurs. Nor is it common for Chinese immigrants to borrow money from banks to finance business ventures. According to one prominent Chinatown banker, all banks consider loans for small start-up businesses too risky. When it is necessary to borrow money, families usually mortgage their homes to obtain cash to start a business.

Pooling family resources adds an extra dimension of solidarity and responsibility to business enterprises. One informant stated: "I can't start or manage the business myself. I need my family members to help me. We pull our money together and everyone in the family feels responsible for the business. It feels closer to do business with family members. We all have the same stake in the business. We are business partners, associates and at the same time we are family."

There is a developmental cycle of family firms so that many start out with members of a nuclear family and expand to include extended kin. According to an argument put forward by S. L. Wong (1985), business partnerships between unrelated Chinese immigrants often lead to family firms. Unrelated business partners sometimes pool resources because their families do not have sufficient resources to help them. Once the partnership amasses enough financial strength, an extended family business can emerge, although nonkin partnership arrangements often disintegrate before this stage because of differences of opinion, accusations of embezzlement, and other conflicts.

FAMILY MEMBERS AS EMPLOYERS AND EMPLOYEES

If enough family members are available to fill the jobs in a Chinese firm, they are the preferred individuals to hire. However, the practice of hiring outsiders is common among Chinese family firms and appears to be on the rise. Both regionalism and dialect similarities are important considerations in hiring. Taiwanese prefer to hire Taiwanese just as the mainland Chinese and the Hong Kong Chinese prefer their compatriots. Nonfamily employees are usually brought in because of the need for special talents and skills that no family member possesses, such as cooking experience or knowledge of herbs. Sometimes family firms hire outsiders because the family's children have taken better paying positions in the American job market and are not interested in working in the family business.

Small family firms such as hardware or electronic stores are often simply run by a husband and wife. However, larger operations often need to hire help from outside the family. Grocers often hire outsiders to manage stock. A chef who is not a member of the family may be given a partnership in a restaurant to encourage his commitment to the business. Similarly, a Chinese herb store may need to hire an outside specialist. Garment factories require many employees and usually use outsiders as seamstresses, though supervisory positions may be held by family members. Even non-Chinese at times are hired for essential positions which cannot be filled by family members or kinsmen. Common examples are managers of banking or financing operations. A trend among Chinese restaurants recently is the hiring of Mexican American busboys and waiters. In suburban Chinese take-out restaurants, it is common to hire white receptionists to take orders and white drivers to do deliveries for the ease of communication.

Thus Chinese enclave businesses are no longer as isolated and culture bound as they used to be. They transcend ethnic lines in their business activities and in their competition for customers and even employees. Their businesses have become more diversified and their circles of customers and employees have enlarged to include whites and other non-Chinese.

There continues to be pressure on family members to help out relatives in need by giving them jobs. Especially after they have established their own businesses, the Chinese are obligated by kinship norms to sponsor relatives from Hong Kong, Taiwan or the mainland to get visas to move to the United States. The impending transfer of the control of Hong Kong from Great Britain to the People's Republic of China has further heightened expectations of sponsorship. Through the visa-sponsoring process, relationships among relatives have become even more complex as employers and patrons often act as sponsors. Newly arrived immigrants feel obligated to their sponsoring relatives and work hard to reciprocate the social debt they have incurred.

In Chinese family firms, family values and kinship ideology are intertwined with the values and ideology of the family business (Wong, McReynolds and Wong 1992). The traditional Chinese values of *ganqing* (sentimental feelings), *yiqi* (personal loyalty), and *renqing* (sympathy) are still highly regarded. In San Francisco's Chinatown, all but two owners of ninety-one family firms I spoke with considered these qualities important in both employer–employee and employee–customer relationships. Traditionally these values have contributed to harmonious relations by instilling feelings of commitment, responsibility, and integrity on the part of family members working together. Ideally, employers are expected to be as concerned about the welfare of the individuals who work for them as if they were family members. In turn, employees are supposed to be loyal and contribute as best they are able to the firm.

Exploitation in Chinese firms does exist. Outsiders who work in the family firms sometimes complain about (1) depressed wages, (2) long hours, (3) the lack of medical benefits, and (4) the lack of *yiqi* (personal loyalty or righteousness). Workers in Chinese garment factories who get paid by the piece complain about how they need to work long hours for a reasonable pay. In Chinese restaurants workers complain that sometimes they have to contribute part of the tips they collect to their employers. Some say that they even have to pay for what they eat in the restaurant. Occasionally, there are cases of embezzle-

ment of workers' contribution to various insurance plans.

However, there are fewer overt conflicts between employers and employees in Chinese firms than in other business establishments in America. One seldom sees demonstrations or strikes in Chinese establishments, except in rare cases. Class conflicts are minimized due to the fact that employers often work side by side with employees. Also, employees today may be employers tomorrow. When I interviewed several employees in the garment factory owned by the Yuan family, I found that they admired the industry and frugality of their employers. When asked whether they felt they were exploited in any way, a typical answer was that "the Yuan family has the righteousness. They are working class people like we are. They really have family spirit!"

CONFUCIANISM, TRADITIONS, AND BUSINESS

Chinese traditions and values play a role in business in the Bay Area today. Indeed, many Chinese restaurants, garment factories, gift shops and even herbal stores have a statue of Guan Gung on their premises. One informant told me that the statue of Guan Gung—the patron deity of justice and wealth—was an effective motivator for the workers in her restaurant's kitchen. Her staff, facing the statue while they work, are constantly reminded of the virtue of justice. According to my informant, the staff tended to be more careful with cooking materials and less wasteful if they saw the statue of Guan Gung in the kitchen.

Confucianism, once considered by Weberian scholars to be a hindrance to economic development, is now thought to be a driving force for the economic success of the five tigers: Japan, Korea, Singapore, Hong Kong and Taiwan. Among immigrants in the San Francisco Bay Area, Confucian values of family are clearly important to Chinese firms in a number of ways. First there is the Confucian emphasis on the importance of the family as the main social unit of society. It is the moral obligation of each individual to care for his or her family. When the family is cared for, it is believed, the society and community are cared for. When the family is right, the community will be right. When the community is right, the nation will be right and when each nation is right, the world will be right. Therefore, it is important to have the family under control, socially, economically, and ethically. When the family is regulated, the community and nation can be regulated. Second, within the family, Confucian rules and discipline stress a hierarchical order, and authority is structured according to generation, age, and gender. Fathers have authority over sons; husbands over wives; and older brothers take precedence over younger ones. Many social scientists believe that this hierarchical structure meshes well with business activities, for it instills discipline and allows tasks to be assigned without confusion about the chain of command. Commitment to family can easily be translated to commitment to the family firm.

The Confucian notion of filial piety is also a factor in children's involvement in Chinese family firms. Children are taught to be respectful to their parents and to their ancestors. To be obedient to one's parents, to be solicitous to their needs, is to practice filial piety. To save family wealth and continue the family business is thought to be an obligation for children, and a form of filial piety. In the family firm environment, children who work hard and dedicate themselves to the family business are held up as examples of filial piety.

The emphasis on ancestral lineage and family continuity also is helpful for family businesses. The success of one's family will bring glory to one's ancestors. Similarly, in order to glorify one's ancestry, one must succeed in scholarship and business. It is a parents' obligation to help one's children obtain higher education, to have a successful business so that children can go to uni-versities. This remains an overarching concern for Chinese immigrants.

REFERENCES

Benedict, Burton 1968. "Family Firms and Economic Development." *Southwestern Journal of Anthropology* 24(1): 1–19.

Chan, J. B. L. and Y. W. Cheung 1985. "Ethnic Resources and Business Enterprise: A Study of Chinese Business in Toronto." *Human Organization* 44(2): 142–54.

Coser, L. 1974. *Greedy Institutions.* New York: Free Press.

Light, Ivan 1972. *Ethnic Enterprises in America.* Berkeley: University of California Press.

Wong, Bernard P. 1982. *Chinatown: Economic Adaptation and Ethnic Identity of the Chinese.* New York: Holt, Rhinehart and Winston.

Wong, Bernard, Becky McReynolds and Wynnie Wong 1992. "Chinese Family Firms in the San Francisco Bay Area." *Family Business Review* 5(4): 355–72.

Wong, S. L. 1985. "The Chinese Family Firm: A Model." *British Journal of Sociology* 361(1): 58–72.

Think about It

1. What advantages do Chinese American firms that are owned and managed by the nuclear family, by siblings, and by kinsmen enjoy? What are some of the problems that Chinese American businesses encounter?
2. How do Confucian values promote successful entrepreneurship in Chinese American family-based businesses?
3. Why, in comparison with Haitian communities (see Reading 24), do Chinese economic enclaves seem more successful?

CHAPTER 6

The Impact
of Social Class

Many scholars describe the United States as a highly stratified society characterized by *structured social inequality:* "a social arrangement patterned socially and historically, which is rooted in an ideological framework that legitimates and justifies the subordination of particular groups of people."[1] As a result of this inequality, many women, people at lower socioeconomic levels, and racial and ethnic groups are systematically excluded from full and equal participation in politics, education, employment, and other social institutions. This exclusion limits *social mobility,* the transition from one social position or social class to another.

The selections in Chapter 6 examine some of the dynamics and consequences of stratification for white and ethnic groups. We begin with an overview of social class. Then we consider one of the wealthiest (Cuban Americans) and one of the poorest (Puerto Rican

Americans) Latino groups. We examine the largest group of poor Americans—never-married, single black mothers. We conclude with a discussion of how members of ethnic groups form their own racial ideologies as they interact with white and ethnic groups. All of this material should give you an idea of the diversity of stratification both across and within ethnic families.

Using broad strokes, Alison Stein Wellner shows that the middle classes in the United States are becoming more diverse and that ethnic households have enjoyed upward mobility during the last few decades (Reading 27). Wellner credits this mobility to factors such as higher educational levels, the infusion of highly skilled immigrants (the "brain drain" phenomenon), and an increase in two-income households (see also Chapter 5). While reading her article, however, keep these three caveats in mind: First, some of the upward mobility has been due to an increase in dual-earner families, and many workers—despite modest educational levels—moonlight, work split shifts (which may have a negative impact on couples with preschool-age and young children), or work unwanted overtime.[2] In other words, many people work very hard and very long hours to reach the middle class or to stay there. Second, although, as one of Wellner's sources notes, "Education is the biggest ticket to the middle class," structured social inequality places numerous barriers in the way of academic achievement.[3] Only the most determined people who have few resources will succeed. Third, national-level figures, though invaluable in presenting a broad view of demographic data, provide little insight about the stratification process (see Reading 30). Even ethnic groups that "make it" to the middle class, for example, may continue to experience prejudice and discrimination.[4]

Although structural factors typically discourage the mobility of lower socioeconomic and ethnic groups, they can be gateways to wealth, influence, and respect. Among Latino subgroups, for example, there is a great deal of social class variation. Many Cuban Americans are faring very well while most Puerto Rican Americans are struggling to survive economically. Does this disparity suggest that one group has endorsed the work ethic and another group has not? No. As Roberto Suro shows in Reading 28, economic success and social mobility depend on a number of interrelated factors, such as U.S. immigration policies and political relations with the country of origin, migration timing, the human capital that immigrants bring with them (see also Reading 24), and the deterioration of major metropolitan areas that are open to development. In the case of Cuban immigrants, all of these variables were "just right." Perhaps one of the most important reasons for the success of many Cuban Americans, Suro maintains, is the "generous welcome" that the U.S. government extended to Cuban exiles. In contrast to its treatment of any other Latino or non-Latino group of immigrants, the United States provided Cubans with government subsidies, magnanimous refugee programs, scholarships for college students, and other resources.[5]

This doesn't mean that all Cuban Americans are wealthy or even middle class. In 1998, 11 percent of all Cuban families lived below the poverty level. In the same year, 24 percent of Mexican Americans, 27 percent of Puerto Rican Americans, and almost 19 percent of the families from Central and South America were living below the poverty level[6] (see also Reading 1). Although the number of middle-class Latino families has increased (see Reading 27), many are struggling. In many cases, according to one researcher, "The [Latino] family that is doing the right thing is still falling behind. We have people working, people married, and yet we see poverty increasing."[7] In Reading 29, Maura I. Toro-Morn examines working-class Puerto Rican American couples who are "falling behind." But instead of giving up, the respondents—especially mothers—developed resistance strategies to circumvent discrimination and accommodation strategies to ensure their families' economic survival.

Robin L. Jarrett shows, similarly, that even the poorest ethnic households in the United States develop survival strategies to ensure the family's continuity and viability (Reading 30). In her study of never-married, low-income black mothers, Jarrett found that black women not only adapted to economic marginality but played active roles in overcoming structural impediments by creating alternative family arrangements to raise their children. Jarrett challenges the notion that poor black mothers constitute an *underclass,* a group that includes households headed by black women who have high unwed motherhood rates, low marriage rates, and "poor values" that lock their families into poverty.[8] Instead, Jarrett argues, many of the families in the lowest socioeconomic echelons are amazingly resilient and innovative while "living poor."[9]

As Readings 28, 29, and 30 illustrate, dominant group stereotypes and institutionalized structural obstacles promote ethnic stratification. In addition, members of ethnic groups and subgroups construct racial and ethnic ideologies that fuel either positive or negative attitudes about "others."[10] Many of these attitudes (and consequent behavior, in many cases) evolve during interactions in schools, neighborhoods, stores, and leisure activities. Most of the interactions that shape self-identity and conceptions of other groups occur in workplaces and may vary by social class. In Reading 31, Kyeyoung Park describes how social class influences Korean Americans' perceptions of other Korean immigrants, blacks, whites, and non-Korean groups. The workplace experiences of Korean Americans who are professionals differ from the experience of those who are small business owners or employees. As a result of such differences, racial and ethnic attitudes and stereotypes about other cultural groups can vary considerably by social class *within* an ethnic group.

NOTES

1. Adalberto Aquirre Jr. and David V. Baker, eds., *Structured Inequality in the United States: Discussions on the Continuing Significance of Race, Ethnicity, and Gender* (Upper Saddle River, NJ: Prentice Hall, 2000), 4. See also Joe R. Feagin and Clairece Booher Feagin, *Racial and Ethnic Relations,* 6th ed. (Upper Saddle River, NJ: Prentice Hall, 1999).
2. For an overview of some of the research on these topics, see Nijole V. Benokraitis, *Marriages and Families: Changes, Choices, and Constraints,* 3d ed. (Upper Saddle River, NJ: Prentice Hall, 1999) 364–66.
3. See Peter B. Wood and W. Charles Clay, "Perceived Structural Barriers and Academic Performance among American Indian High School Students," *Youth & Society* 28 (September 1996): 40–60.
4. See, for example, Edgar Gamboa, "'International Medical Graduates Are Tested Every Step of the Way,'" in *Filipino American Lives,* ed. Yen Le Espiritu (Philadelphia: Temple University Press, 1995), 127–42.
5. Some researchers agree with Suro that Cubans received unprecedented government assistance. Others note that the Cuban community in Miami has been active in the political system—though often motivated by concern about the U.S. policies toward Cuba—in terms of voting and running for office. See Lisandro Pérez, "Cuban Miami," in *Miami Now! Immigration, Ethnicity, and Social Change,* ed. Guillermo J. Grenier and Alex Stepick III (Gainesville: University Press of Florida, 1992), 83–108.
6. Roberto R. Ramirez, "The Hispanic Population in the United States: March 1999," www.census.gov/prod/2000pubs/p20.527pdf (accessed June 29, 2000).
7. M. A. Fletcher, "Latinos See Signs of Hope as Middle Class Expands," *Washington Post,* (July 22, 1997): A8.

8. See, for example, Carl F. Horowitz, "Searching for the White Underclass," *National Review* 47 (September 1995): 52–55.

9. A number of studies show that women, especially, in other ethnic groups and across social classes play an active role in devising strategies to counteract structured social inequality. See, for example, Miriam Ching Louie, "Immigrant Asian Women in Bay Area Garment Sweatshops: 'After Sewing, Laundry, Cleaning and Cooking, I Have No Breath Left to Sing,'" *Amerasia Journal* 18 (1992): 1–26, and Keiko Yamanaka and Kent McClelland, "Earning the Model-Minority Image: Diverse Strategies of Economic Adaptation by Asian-American Women," *Ethnic and Racial Studies* 17 (January 1994): 79–114.

10. For an analysis of how self-identity is influenced by both resistance to and acceptance of class and racial hierarchy in the United States, see Yen Le Espiritu, "The Intersection of Race, Ethnicity, and Class: The Multiple Identities of Second-Generation Filipinos," *Identities* 1 (1994): 249–73.

27 | *Are Ethnic and White Middle Classes Booming?*

Alison Stein Wellner

There is great social class diversity across and among white and ethnic families in the United States. During the last few decades, however, increasing numbers of ethnic households have achieved middle-class status. Alison Stein Wellner discusses how the racial and ethnic composition of the middle class has changed, why many ethnic groups have been upwardly mobile, and how Internet access preserves one's cultural heritage despite acculturation.

Thirty years ago, more than half of all middle-class households were headed by non-Hispanic whites. But as the population as a whole has become more diverse, so, too, has the middle class. Today, the percentage of middle-income households headed by non-Hispanic whites has dropped to 49 percent. And the middle-class diversity trend only accelerated during the 1990s. In 1992, 38 percent of black households had middle-class incomes. Six years later, that number had grown to 41 percent. Hispanic households saw a similar increase during that same time period: from 44 percent to 46 percent. At the same time, the percentage of non-Hispanic white households in the middle decreased by 1 percentage point, and the percentage of Asian households remained flat.

Certainly, the rising tide of the economy has played an important role in the changing make-up of the middle—especially for Americans born in the United States. But immigration has been a key factor as well. Over the past 30 years, there's been an important shift in the demographics of immigrants: They're getting younger. Forty-four percent were aged 25 to 44 in 1997—up from just 19 percent in 1960, when one-third of immigrants were over the age of 65, compared to just 11 percent in 1997. This has been central to the diversification of the middle class, since younger immigrants have a better chance of improving their financial situation over time. And they are bringing a different mentality and a different set of expectations to the middle-class marketplace.

Of course, identifying what we mean by mid-

Source: From Alison Stein Wellner, "The Money in the Middle," *American Demographics* 22 (April 2000): 58–64. Copyright © 2000. Reprinted by permission of Intertec /A Primedia Company.

dle class is a tricky endeavor—not even the U.S. Census Bureau has an official definition. Part of the problem is that the true "middle" is a shifting target. Between 1997 and 1998, for example, the real median income of households in the United States grew by 3.5 percent.

Nevertheless, to some it's simply a matter of income quintiles, and the middle three—or 60 percent of U.S. household income distribution—create the boundaries of the middle [see Figure 1]. In 1998, the middle three quintiles accounted for an estimated 165 million households. But by that definition, households with incomes as low as $16,117 and as high as $75,000 would each be considered middle class. And the poverty threshold for a family of four in 1998, according to the U.S. Office of Management and Budget, was $16,660.

[Gregory] Acs [senior research associate at the Urban Institute in Washington, D.C.,] suggests that the income range of the middle 40 percent of the population is a better way to define middle class. "Middle class is a feeling," he says, as much as it is a numerical paradigm. Using Acs' range, a middle-class income today is roughly between $30,000 to $75,000—a level that spans the third

and fourth quintiles. The absolute lowest limit to be considered middle class may actually be a bit lower, cautions Acs, around $25,000; it depends on the number of people in the household. It also depends on where in the country the household is located, since there are geographic variations in the cost of living.

COMING TO AMERICA

What does it take for a low-income household to cross that $25,000 threshold into middle class? It helps to have two earners in the household, says Acs. And that is a fundamental difference between middle-class hopefuls today and those of years past, points out Toni Horst, an economist with Dismal Scientist and RFA, an economic data analysis company based in West Chester, Pennsylvania. Between 1987 and 1997, households with two earners saw their income increase by 5 percent, according to *American Incomes: Demographics of Who Has Money* (New Strategist). At the same time, households with one earner saw their income decrease by 2.3 percent. Today, having two earners is a requirement to keep up, says Horst.

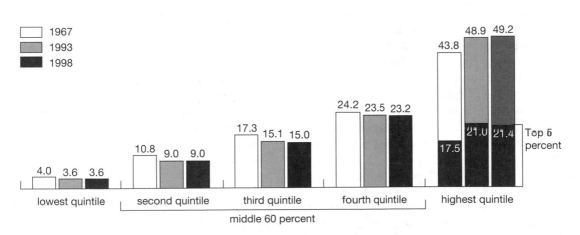

FIGURE 1   Target Practice: Share of Aggregate Household Income by Quintile, 1967, 1993, and 1998

Source: U.S. Census Bureau, Current Population Survey, March 1968, 1994, 1999.

Which is one reason why much of the growth in the middle class today has been fueled by immigration. At 3.32 people per foreign-born household, immigrant families are considerably larger than the 2.56-person average size of native-born households. And these larger households have more earners: 1.6 versus 1.39.

But large household size doesn't tell the whole story. Mexican-born households, the worst off financially of all immigrant groups, also have the largest household size (over four people per household). At the same time, they have low levels of educational attainment. "Education is the biggest ticket to the middle class," says Horst. "Not much happens without it."

There's a sharp difference in income between people who are educated and people who aren't, agrees Frank Stafford, a professor at the University of Michigan and the principal investigator of the Panel Study of Income Dynamics. For example, between 1976 and 1996, the earnings of men with advanced degrees increased by more than a third for non-Hispanic whites and blacks, and by 20 percent for Hispanics. In contrast, earnings for men who did not finish high school fell by 12 percent for blacks and by 20 percent for whites and Hispanics.

And nearly a quarter of all foreign-born residents have their bachelor's degrees, essentially the same proportion as native-born Americans. Even when you control for age (college education is less common among all older people), the difference in college education between natives and immigrants is insignificant.

Of course, the foreign-born population is far from homogenous, and there are important differences by country of origin, including the number of immigrants arriving annually from each nation. In 1998, the largest share of new arrivals by far was from Mexico, according to the Immigration and Naturalization Service, accounting for nearly 20 percent of the 660,000 immigrants legally admitted to the country that year. The next-largest group was from China, at about 6 percent, with another 5.5 percent coming from India. European countries combined contributed about 14 percent of new arrivals in 1998.

The share of America's foreign-born population who are European has dropped sharply over the decades, according to the Census Bureau. In 1970, 62 percent of foreign-born residents were from Europe. By 1997, that number had dropped to 17 percent, while 51 percent were from Latin America, and 27 percent were from Asia.

There are also two distinct groups of immigrants: those who are educated and are already middle class, and those who are struggling to break in with other low-income and less-educated U.S. citizens, points out George Vernez, the director of immigration studies for RAND in California. In 1997, 49 percent of African-born residents had their bachelor's degrees, for example, followed by 45 percent of Asians, and 29 percent of Europeans. That's compared with 10 percent of all immigrants from Latin America, and 4.6 percent of Mexicans. But 43 percent of foreign-born households have incomes below $25,000, and many of then (35 percent) lack even a high-school diploma. This, experts say, will make any transition into middle class an upward struggle at best.

"For those who come from a low level of education, they are unlikely to make it during their lifetime here," says Vernez. "If they have less than a high-school level of education, they don't have much mobility at all." Nor will many of their children, he adds. "They will acquire more education than their parents, and most of them will eventually graduate with a high-school degree or equivalent, but a smaller share of them are expected to go to college," he says. "They will lag behind other groups, at least in the first and second generations."

THE NEW IMMIGRANT MARKETPLACE

Still, nearly half of all foreign-born residents (42 percent of men and 37 percent of women) have middle-class incomes, and 29 percent have incomes over $50,000, according to the Census Bureau. And we're not just talking about those who came here 20 or 30 years ago: A significant portion of even the newest immigrants—those who have been here ten years or less—enjoy middle-class status: 31 percent of men and 25 percent of women. This is the new immigrant contingent of the new middle class.

Asian immigrants lead the pack in terms of median income—$42,900 in 1996, well above the median for native householders. One reason for the Asian earning power is that 36 percent work in a managerial or professional role, a proportion that's topped by Canadian immigrants (46.5 percent) and European-born immigrants (37.8 percent), according to the Census Bureau. Another reason is that there are fewer Asian households aged 65 and over. (Older households tend to have lower incomes.)

Asians aren't the only group of immigrants who are doing well: Median incomes of immigrant households from Europe, Africa, South America, and North America (Canada) are all over $30,000.

But no matter where they are born, these new American consumers share important characteristics, says Felipe Korzenny, co-founder of Cheskin Research, a Belmont, California-based market research firm that focuses on Hispanic and Asian consumers. Regardless of educational attainment, these consumers lack a clear understanding of the consumer culture that defines the United States, he says. On a very basic level, whole product categories could be unfamiliar, and Korzenny cites insurance as an example. Both Asians and Hispanics have strong traditions of younger people caring for the old, for example, so for many, it doesn't make a lot of sense to take out an insurance policy that would protect an adult child. There's also a sense of taboo around thinking about death, adds Korzenny.

For other product marketers, there's a historical experience gap that makes the consumer marketplace bewildering. Growing up with a certain brand of toothpaste or cereal provides an emotional context for choosing a product that these consumers lack. "Marketers that are able to claim a niche tend to stay with these communities for a relatively long time," says Korzenny.

And these new middle-class consumers lack marketing savvy, says Korzenny. "In many ways, the Hispanic and Asian middle class today is almost equivalent to where the mainstream market was in the 1950s, in terms of advertising. They are looking at advertising for advice and guidance. These are consumers who are very educated, have nice incomes, and really do not understand why they should pick one product instead of another."

There's another very important piece of the puzzle to understand when targeting new middle-class immigrants, says Korzenny. Unlike the ideal of a melting pot that was so prevalent at the beginning of the 20th century, today's immigrants are more anxious to preserve their own culture, even as they embrace their American lives. "You don't have to be Anglo to be okay," he says. Korzenny believes that this will continue and be strengthened by Internet penetration in the middle class [see Figure 2].

And computer penetration is on the rise: Among Hispanic households with incomes of $35,000 to $74,999, for example, 49 percent had a computer at home in 1998, a 19-point leap from 1994; and 27 percent used the Internet, according to "Falling through the Net," a study conducted by the National Technology Information Administration. The study also found that nearly 40 percent of middle class "non-Hispanic others," mostly Asians, had Internet access.

Online access has enabled these new residents to customize their acculturation process, says Korzenny. For Hispanics, "It enables them to be connected to the Latin world. You can read newspapers in Latin America, converse with your cousins and grandparents who are still in Mexico City or Guatemala." Within the next five years, to a much greater extent as Internet penetration grows, immigrants of all nationalities will be ordering food from their native countries, downloading movies in their own language, and listening to

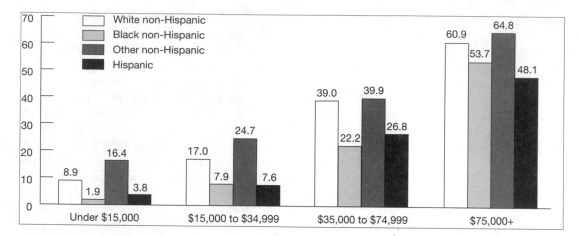

FIGURE 2   Internet Interaction: Percent of U.S. Households Using the Internet, by Race/Origin, by Income, 1998

Source: "Falling through the Net: Defining the Digital Divide," National Technology Information Administration.

radio stations from home. "The marketers that are going to be the most successful are the ones that are customizing your culture the best," says Korzenny.

NATIVE TRANSITIONS

But not all additions to the middle class were born in foreign lands. Among native-born Americans transferring into the middle class, many are African American.

There are several reasons why African Americans are transitioning into the middle class, says Roderick Harrison, director of Databank, the data analysis component of the Joint Center for Political and Economic Studies, in Washington, D.C. Harrison says that many of the gains in income and educational attainment that set the stage for a middle-class transition were made during the 1970s, the era immediately following the Civil Rights movement. During the 1980s, progress slowed for many black households, but in the 1990s, black households began experiencing increases that were greater than that of the general population.

In fact, the percentage of blacks with middle-class incomes has been on the rise over the past three decades. In 1998, 41 percent of black householders had middle-class incomes of $25,000 to $75,000, compared to 35 percent in 1967. In comparison, during roughly the same time period, the percentage of non-Hispanic whites who were middle class declined by nearly 7 percentage points, mostly due to a positive income shift overall. The share of Hispanics with middle-class incomes also decreased, due to an increase in both poor and wealthy Hispanic households.

The economic boom of the 1990s has been an extra bonus for black households, says Harrison, because many are concentrated in the Southern region of the country, which boomed the loudest. In the Rust Belt region, where blacks were disproportionately hit when the nation's manufacturing base left the country, a recovery has also begun, and blacks have enjoyed the gains there as well.

Positive education trends for blacks have also helped the transition to middle class. In 1960, only four in ten blacks completed high school. By 1997, 87 percent did. During the same period, white high-school completion rates rose from about 60 percent to more than 90 percent. Today, 14 percent of blacks have a bachelor's degree or higher, as do 26 percent of whites and 9 percent of Hispanics, according to the National Center for Education Statistics.

Although those education statistics reflect a broader positive trend, it's important to note that black education levels hardly match those of whites, one powerful reason why more black households haven't been able to take full advantage of the economic boom. After all, 49 percent of black households have incomes that are below the middle-class line drawn by the Urban Institute's Acs, compared with 44 percent of Hispanic households and 28 percent of white households.

There's another reason why many blacks have yet to transition into the middle class: It takes money to make it. Or more specifically, it takes wealth, points out University of Michigan's Stafford. The Panel Study of Income Dynamics found that, for every dollar in financial wealth held by the average white household in 1999, the average black household held barely 9 cents. Lower overall home values of black householders and fewer stock holdings account for part of the problem. But the largest stumbling block for many black households is generational wealth. A primary source of wealth for white households is intergenerational transfers in the form of inheritance and gifts.

And unlike new immigrants, African Americans do not have the advantage of household formation on their side. In fact, Harrison says the biggest barrier for transitioning to the middle class for blacks in the United States is the prevalence of African-American single-parent households. "To be comfortably middle class or higher, you need to have a fairly high-paying job, or you need two earners," notes Acs. That is simply not happening among the majority of African-American families: 62 percent of all African-American families are headed by a single parent.

This proportion is twice as large as it is for white families and 75 percent greater than Hispanics. For more blacks to transition into middle-class status, progress on the educational front must continue, and the household formation situation must be resolved.

Of course, there are no easy solutions for lower-income Americans who hope to transition into the ranks of the middle class. Certainly access to education and to technology are key. But one thing is clear: The demographic make-up of the middle class has changed. Forever.

Think about It

1. Why does Wellner feel that defining *middle class* is a "tricky endeavor?" Do you agree with analysts who think that an annual income between $30,000 and $75,000 is a good measure of middle class? What other characteristics besides income might you include when gauging social class?

2. According to Wellner, why have middle-class diversity trends accelerated since the 1970s?

3. Many black households have moved up into the middle class. Why, however, has the rise in middle-class incomes for many black Americans been slower than for many other ethnic and white households?

28 Explaining Cuban Americans' Success

Roberto Suro

Cuban Americans compose one of the most affluent Latino groups in the United States. Roberto Suro argues that much of the economic success that Cuban Americans enjoy is due to factors such as geography, migration timing, politics, immigration policies, and "massive public assistance" in education, housing, and business.

Sometime in the early 1950s, Miami International Airport became the place where the United States and Latin America crossed paths. South-bound travelers had to go there to catch the roaring DC-7s for the long night flights to Panama and beyond. In Miami, these voyagers got their first taste of hot, damp air, their first earful of foreign languages, their first sight of men in starchy white shirts and combed black mustaches. For those headed north, it was the essential gateway to the United States. Once past the formalities of entry, Miami International was the place where everything started becoming neat, orderly, and modern.

In the first months of 1959, shortly after Fidel Castro's triumph, fistfights erupted at the Miami airport as two sets of exiles crossed paths: The first exiles fleeing Castro's revolution debarked flights arriving from Havana and crossed paths with Castro's allies, exiled by the former regime, who were waiting for departing flights to take them home. The angry encounters by the airport gates have become part of the creation myth of Cuban Miami, a fitting legend, because since then, the whole of South Florida has become a massive transit lounge.[1] It is a place of constant arrivals and departures, an entrepôt familiar to people comfortable straddling two cultures without committing themselves to either one.

Source: From Roberto Suro, *Strangers among Us: How Latino Immigration Is Transforming America* (New York: Knopf, 1998), 159–69. Reprinted by permission of Alfred A. Knopf, a division of Random House, Inc.

Nearly half a million Cubans settled in South Florida in the first twenty years after Castro's revolution, and they built the only barrio where a lot of people have become rich, influential, and respected. More than a quarter of those who came in the first two decades had annual incomes of more than fifty thousand dollars by 1990, exceeding the national average, and in the highest brackets, they almost rivaled Anglo affluence. Cuban Miami is the only barrio with country clubs, but, like the others, it remains a place apart from the rest of the country. Well into its fourth decade, Cuban Miami is still a port of entry, a borderland between north and south.

A *Time* cover story about Miami in 1993 proclaimed, "For if the go-go '80s was New York City's and Wall Street's, the globally minded '90s belong to Miami, 'the Hong Kong of Latin America,' perched on the rim of the fastest-growing region in the New World." The article justified its claims by noting that international commerce is a $25.6 billion business in Miami, having grown by 20 percent in 1992 alone. Like Hong Kong, the city is in fact a giant enclave. South Florida has become a destination for the entire Western Hemisphere and for Europeans as well because it is physically attached to the United States but not really a part of it. Miami prospered as a transit lounge for money, people, and ideas, but the city never realized its full economic potential in part because the Cubans remained locked in their glorious barrio.

The Miami Cubans prospered, and they have also remained apart from America. The Cubans' story shows that the separateness of other Latino immigrants is not simply a product of poverty. Their story shows how the migration itself, the ongoing link between north and south, defines the Latino identity in this country today. Like most other barrios, Cuban Miami is not a collection of urban neighborhoods. Cuban Miami is a barrio without borders because it is a frame of mind and a network of relationships that is interwoven throughout South Florida and that stretches across the water down to Cuba itself. Cuban Miami is a place where people reinvent themselves, a marketplace of transactions between an old land and a new land, and in that, it is like all other barrios.

The Miami Cubans are exceptional among Latino immigrants because the initial migrants, the builders of the barrio, came from the upper and middle classes and brought with them high levels of education, business experience, and familiarity with the United States. But that does not entirely explain their success. The so-called golden exiles did indeed arrive with a rich store of human capital—and then, significantly, America showered them with opportunities to make that capital grow.

The anti-Castro Cubans who came after 1959 received a warmer welcome from the United States than any other group of foreigners who have ever come to this country. In addition to economic and political largesse granted them as Cold War heroes, they also benefited from accidents of history and geography. Just as the Puerto Ricans were cursed at almost every turn, the Cubans were blessed in nearly everything they did. In addition to their material success, the Miami Cubans have also enjoyed a demographic triumph of sorts. They are the first Latinos to become the dominant population in an important metropolitan area— the first but not the last. Latinos will become the largest group in metropolitan Los Angeles and many smaller urban areas before long. The Cubans gained the opportunity to govern quickly, within the lifetime of the first arrivals, but they have not bothered to lead Miami. Instead, they have helped fragment the city. Locked inside the mental enclave that is Cuban Miami, they so ignored the op-

portunities around them that they put their success at risk.

The Cubans were able to build a strong barrio and eventually define an entire city because they landed at the right place at the right time. Such coincidences are crucial in the history of immigration.

The European immigrants arrived in New York when it was growing and prospering as a terminus for transatlantic trade. The Puerto Ricans arrived in time to ride the city down as that role declined. Just as New York became the key point of contact between the United States and Europe because steamship routes and telegraph lines ended there, Miami grew starting in the 1960s because it served as the hub for inter-American air travel and telecommunications. Like the European immigrants who helped fuel and define New York's ascent, the Cubans proved the ideal human ingredient for the Miami boom.

"When the Cubans got here, Miami was in a tailspin and ironically that created opportunities for them," recalls Monsignor Bryan Walsh, who directed the Roman Catholic Archdiocese's refugee relief efforts during most of the Cuban influx.

Entering the 1960s, Miami's only substantial enterprise was as a winter resort, and the advent of easy airplane travel had brought killer competition with newly accessible island destinations in the Caribbean. For vacationers, Miami became a place to change planes. Otherwise, it lived off the retirees who had fled from the Northeast and had made Miami the butt of shuffleboard jokes.

In 1961, Walsh remembers, the Miami United Way didn't fulfill 60 percent of its annual fundraising goal. The city had hit bottom. Anybody who could was getting out. Meanwhile, the Cubans were getting in.

Instead of having to fight for a turf like most newly arrived groups, the Cubans found an empty space in a neighborhood just beyond the shadow of downtown where there was a lot of pre–World War II housing interspersed with bakeries, bottling plants, and warehouses. As working-class whites fled the declining economy, the Cubans moved into the stucco bungalows and clapboard salt-boxes. The neighborhood soon became known as Little Havana to outsiders, while the Cubans referred to it as Calle Ocho, after the main commercial thoroughfare, Southwest Eighth Street.

"You had occupancy rates down to thirty percent in Calle Ocho when they [the Cubans] started coming," said Walsh. "It wasn't the nicest place in the world, but it allowed the Cubans to establish themselves as a community right from the beginning."

One of the people who helped build that community is Luis J. Botifoll. An attorney and newspaper editor in prerevolutionary Havana, he became a banker in Miami, rising from loan officer to chairman of the Republic National Bank. When I asked him about the early days, he pointed out of the window of his office atop the bank building. Calle Ocho seemed small and compact and shady compared to the Sun Belt sprawl around it. "If we had been scattered around a big city, we would have been lost. The geography here was essential to our success because it allowed us to concentrate our resources on creating our own economy. Our businesses thrived because our own people provided them with loyal clients and employees."

He was describing the classic formula for the emergence of an ethnic-enclave economy. Little Havana gave the Cubans a place where they could adapt to the United States, build their networks and accumulate capital. Unlike what happened to Puerto Ricans, no one tried to bulldoze them, burn them out, or buy them out. While they got on their feet, no one else moved in to town to compete for housing and jobs. For other Latinos, the barrio has been a place to survive. For the Cubans, the barrio was a means to prosper.

When Cubans progressed enough to seek better housing, they did not have to go far. Miami is sufficiently compact that they were able to move out of Calle Ocho without scattering and losing their sense of community. The Cubans not only created a successful enclave but they managed to avoid one of the great pitfalls that others have suf-fered. Barrios like Magnolia, Washington Heights, and East Los Angeles have remained stuck at a level of working-class poverty in part because the most successful residents are always moving to distant suburbs and breaking off all ties with those who remain behind. Capital, both human and economic, is removed from the barrio, and local businesses lost talent, investment, and clients.

As they expanded out of Little Havana, the Cubans created many new economic enclaves, from the working-class strip malls of Hialeah to the upscale suburban boutiques in Kendal. But, wherever they went, the Cubans stuck together. They remained loyal to one another not only in the choice of a neighborhood store but also in picking car dealers and insurance agents, subcontractors and suppliers, even if that meant driving back to Calle Ocho to make a purchase. In Miami, the Cubans extended the economic benefits of a tight-knit enclave both geographically and across the spectrum of business activities. Meanwhile, Calle Ocho took on a new role. Retaining a run-down fifties look against all the shiny glass and tropical pastels of contemporary Miami, it has become the historic old town of Cuban Miami with its restaurants and bookstores, its ceiba trees and its memorial to those who fell at the Bay of Pigs. Now Calle Ocho is a place of memory and identity.

Most major Latino communities have been stuck on the treadmill of continuous immigration for decades and have constantly expended energy on absorbing the latest arrivals. The Miami Cubans never faced that challenge because two mutually hostile governments limited the human flow, allowing only a few relatively brief blasts of immigration. In between, the Miami Cubans enjoyed stretches of a decade or more when almost nobody arrived. These pauses served as important breathing spaces that allowed them to absorb the newcomers and then continue the work of building a barrio.

In addition, the content of the migration also shifted in advantageous ways over time. As the sociologists Alejandro Portes and Alex Stepick have noted in several studies, the Cubans who came between Castro's takeover in 1959 and the

Cuban missile crisis of 1962, which shut down the influx for the first time, were better educated and more skilled than those who came in the next wave aboard the "freedom flights" of the late 1960s and early 1970s. And they, in turn, surpassed those who came during the four-month Mariel boat lift of 1980. The early arrivals built the barrio and set up the enclave's businesses. Then the "declining social gradient," as Portes and Stepick described it, neatly filled Cuban Miami's growing demands for new workers and new consumers without overburdening it at the onset.

The Cubans had another huge advantage: They received a generous welcome.

"Never in the history of the United States did any immigrant or refugee population receive the kind of help that was made available to the Cubans during their early years here; I am confident that is a very safe statement," said Monsignor Walsh, who helped administer that help.

One federal effort alone, the U.S. Cuban Refugee Program, spent more than $1.5 billion helping settle some 486,000 Cubans who sought assistance during the first twenty years of the migration. Another federal program provided special scholarships for Cuban college students. The University of Miami created a course just to prepare Cuban physicians for the licensing exams that would allow them to practice in the United States and organized a loan fund that helped the doctors while they studied. The Dade County public schools launched a crash program to recertify Cubans who had come with teaching experience. Many were then put to work in the first and some of the most effective efforts at bilingual education undertaken since the days of the European migration. The Miami schools took it as an obligation rather than a burden to help Cuban children make a smooth transition from speaking Spanish to speaking English.

The extra help continued long after the enclave was established. Between 1968 and 1980, for example, 46 percent of the Small Business Administration loans in Dade County went to companies owned by Cubans and other Latinos, compared with only 6 percent for black-owned firms. During the construction of the Metrorail rapid transit system in the late 1970s, half of the contractors were Cuban, while blacks got only about an eighth of the work.

In addition, thousands of Cuban exiles were either fully employed or received extra income from the Central Intelligence Agency. Congressional inquiries conducted in the mid-1970s revealed that the creation of a small army for the failed Bay of Pigs invasion was only the beginning of the agency's expenditures. Building up the Miami station until it became the largest CIA operation outside the agency's Virginia headquarters, the CIA employed its own Cuban legion for many years in an extensive secret war against Cuba, involving sabotage, infiltration, and assassination plots. Even in the late 1960s, the operation was so large and well financed that a single small counterintelligence operation had as many as two hundred Cuban paid informants and a budget of more than $2 million a year, according to congressional testimony.

While the myth of Cuban Miami extols the self-reliant exile who arrived with no more than the shirt on his back and who made a fortune through brains and perseverance, the truth is that the Cubans built their enclave with massive public assistance and then continued to draw government subsidies well after they had established themselves here.

The Cubans also had the law on their side. Until President Clinton changed the policy in 1995, the federal government welcomed all Cubans into the country and automatically granted them permanent legal status after they had been here a year. No matter if they entered the country illegally, they could still live and work in the United States forever. Cubans were allowed in even if they freely admitted that they simply wanted to be with family here or improve their economic condition. And it didn't matter how many showed up, because by "voting with their feet," they testified to communism's failings.

No other nationality received such a ready welcome from the U.S. immigration system. Thousands of Vietnamese languished in refugee camps for years before they could get to the United States. The number of Soviet Jews granted refugee status was subject to specific annual limits. Hundreds of thousands of Haitians and Central Americans were denied asylum on claims of political persecution that were later found valid by the courts, and millions of family-sponsored immigrants from other nations around the world spent as long as a decade on waiting lists before they could get visas.

Finally, the Cubans had a historical advantage. In Miami they never had to adjust to structural changes in the U.S. economy. Latino newcomers elsewhere started out in old-style manufacturing jobs and then had to struggle when these jobs disappeared. The Cubans participated in the creation of a new economy from the ground up and rose with it. During the first twenty years of the exiles' sojourn in Miami, the job market there grew by 74 percent over the national average. No one else was arriving in Miami during those years, and in fact whites were leaving the increasingly Spanish-speaking city. As the unrivaled suppliers of new workers to a hungry labor market, the Cubans prospered.

The Cubans proved doubly fortunate because this new economy based on business services, finance, and tourism has proved exceptionally resilient. During bad times, rich Latin Americans stash their money in Miami, and during good times, they go there to make deals. Miami has another kind of insulation, as well: Drug money is immune to business cycles. When the debt crisis of the 1980s devastated many U.S. businesses that had bet on Latin America, Miami was booming with narcodollars.

This argument is not meant to diminish the many acts of ingenuity and sacrifice by Cuban exiles. But given these advantages of geography, timing, financing, and history, any Latino group—even one with much less human capital—could have done well in Miami. The Puerto Ricans' fate, for example, would undoubtedly have been much different if they had encountered the same circumstances and had enjoyed the same generous handouts as the Cubans. The Cubans, in turn, would have had a

very different experience if they had been wedged into a slice of Harlem and given no help except a welfare check. Though one is a saga of triumph and the other of defeat, both the Cuban and Puerto Rican stories demonstrate that the circumstances encountered by immigrants will influence their ultimate fate every bit as much as the qualities they bring with them.

Aside from the importance of circumstances in the United States, the Cuban experience teaches another lesson, as well: Material success in this country does not guarantee that immigrants will focus their attention on life here. Rich Latinos remain ambivalent toward America just as much as poor ones. In fact, wealth may make it even easier to avoid full engagement with the new land, while poverty sometimes forces attention to one's surroundings. With the Miami Cubans, this is most evident in the political realm. Even though doors were opened to them, they chose not to pass through them.

The Cubans' wealth, the moral authority they carried as Cold War exiles, and eventually their concentrated numbers in an important state added up to tangible political power. That influence could have been exerted on many different types of issues: international trade and telecommunications, overall refugee policy, small-business development, bilingual education, and other matters of immigrant assimilation. The Miami Cubans potentially had interesting things to say on all these matters and were in a position to make their voices heard on a national level. Instead, they have focused their energies almost exclusively on Cuba and an obsessive desire to bedevil Castro. They have created a single organization, the Cuban American National Foundation, that dominates political discourse within the enclave, and its single-minded focus is the liberation of Cuba.

Dissent is not tolerated in Cuban Miami. Even in the 1990s, as the Bay of Pigs veterans head toward old age, anyone who speaks out for accommodation with Castro faces the danger of public denunciation and ostracism. In the past, repeat offenders risked being silenced violently.

Blowing people up in their cars was a favorite sanction, although threats usually sufficed.

The bombs, the weekend warriors who go to the Everglades to train for the next invasion of Cuba, and the anti-Castro protest marches are the most dramatic manifestation of an identity crisis that has preoccupied Cuban Miami from the outset. Like all migrants, the Cubans are battling to prove that an unknown future will be better than a familiar past. It is the same struggle for self-justification that preoccupies anyone who leaves home to make his life elsewhere. Even when an economic or political disaster forces departure, accomplishments in the new land are measured against an idea of what might have happened by remaining in the old country. All migrants are travelers in time as well as in space, going back to their past to justify the future. In the Cuban case, this part of the voyage is starkly defined because it is expressed in political terms. Castro's triumph on January 1, 1959, marks a clear line between the past and the beginning of the migration.

Unlike most other Latinos, the Cubans were unable to return home for visits during most of the time they were building their barrio. That seems to have made them even more preoccupied with their past, even as they gained wealth, position, and power in this country. Achieving prosperity was a way of vindicating their decision to leave, according to Arturo Villar, a publisher and business consultant.

"Once we realized that we were not going to ride right back to Havana, there was a very conscious feeling that we had to do something important here, that we had to show the bastards that had kicked us out that we were better than they were, that we could recoup, that we could build something, and the best part about it is that we ended up believing our own propaganda. It became a conviction that we were chosen for this," says Villar, referring to the material success achieved by those who came in the early era of the exile.

Like many other Latino immigrants, the Miami Cubans began their journey simply thinking of survival, but over time the migration took on other purposes. Building the barrio became a surrogate for defeating Castro. Like other immigrants, the Cubans measured their success in the United States by the amount of admiration and envy it generated back home. Just as Juan Chanax worked overtime in Houston to build a house in Totonicapán that would dispel all the slights inflicted on him as a Maya, the Miami Cubans strove for achievements in the United State to *sobresalir* (surpass) their losses in Cuba.

More than any other Latinos, the Miami Cubans seem to have followed the model defined by the European ethnics, achieving the kind of economic success, social stability, and political influence typical of middle-class white America, but the Cubans did it in a single generation. And yet in other ways, they clearly fit the African-American model, maintaining an identity that marks them as separate from the mainstream, pursuing narrowly focused group interests, and making their sense of shared historical adversity the prime source of political energy.

NOTE

1. The creation myth of Cuban Miami: For accounts of the Cuban migration to Miami see Alejandro Portes and Alex Stepick, *City on the Edge: The Transformation of Miami* (University of California, 1993); Guillermo J. Grenier and Alex Stepick, eds., *Miami Now! Immigration, Ethnicity and Social Change* (University Press of Florida, 1992); David Reiff, *Going to Miami: Exiles, Tourists and Refugees in the New America* (Little, Brown, 1987).

? Think about It

1. How and why did the U.S. government provide an unprecedented and "generous welcome" to Cuban exiles, in contrast to other immigrants?
2. What does Suro mean when he says that Cubans "landed at the right place at the right time?"
3. Why does Suro describe Cuban Americans as living lives apart from the rest of the country?

29 Puerto Rican Migrants: Juggling Family and Work Roles

Maura I. Toro-Morn

Although migration and immigration are always difficult, they can be especially stressful for working-class families with modest economic resources. Maura I. Toro-Morn explains how working-class Puerto Rican migrants in her study worked to maintain family life and to adjust to a new environment despite numerous obstacles. Women, especially, were instrumental in developing both resistance and accommodating strategies to ensure the family's continuity.

. . . This chapter takes a feminist perspective to explore the migration and adaptation of Puerto Ricans in Chicago. The objectives are to examine how working-class women entered the migration process and to study the adaptive strategies they have used to settle in Chicago. Placing women at the center of the analysis allows descriptions of their contributions to family and community life to be heard. This chapter is based on 30 in-depth interviews collected in the Puerto Rican community between March 1989 and July 1990. Different respondents will be identified by pseudonyms.

Drawing on the work of Louise Lamphere (1987), this chapter distinguishes between strategies of resistance and those of coping or accommodation. Strategies of resistance refer to tactics and actions Puerto Ricans use as a group or as individuals to deal with a racially and socially stratified society. Discussion will focus on how these working-class Puerto Ricans confronted and resisted the prejudice and discrimination they encountered in securing a place to live. Strategies of coping and accommodation refer to actions and

Source: From Maura I. Toro-Morn, "The Family and Work Experiences of Puerto Rican Women Migrants in Chicago," in *Resiliency in Native American and Immigrant Families,* eds. Hamilton I. McCubbin, Elizabeth A. Thompson, Anne I. Thompson, and Julie E. Fromer (Thousand Oaks, CA: Sage, 1998), 277–94. Copyright © Sage Publications, Inc. Reprinted by permission of Sage Publications, Inc.

tactics used in the allocation of productive and reproductive labor. In this study, women's work outside the home had become a family strategy for surviving and improving economic position. The second part of this chapter will discuss the coping strategies married working-class women used in different family arrangements to juggle family and work. . . .

PUERTO RICAN MIGRATION TO CHICAGO

Puerto Rican migration to Chicago dates back to the post–World War II wave of migration that brought thousands of Puerto Ricans to the United States (Padilla, 1987). In the late 1940s, the impact of U.S. investment and modernization of the economy transformed Puerto Rico from a predominantly agricultural to an industrial economy. Operation Bootstrap—as the development model is popularly known—attracted labor-intensive light manufacturing industries like textiles and apparel to Puerto Rico by offering tax incentives, cheap labor, and easy access to U.S. markets (Dietz, 1986; Pantojas-Garcia, 1990). These changes in Puerto Rico's economy had profound consequences for Puerto Rican families. The development model was unable to create enough jobs, and working-class Puerto Ricans began to leave the island, heading for familiar places like New York City and new places like Chicago. News about jobs in Chicago spread quickly throughout the island as an informal network of family members, friends, and relatives told people of opportunities and helped families migrate. . . .

The interviews collected for this research suggest that over the years Puerto Rican women and their families have used migration as a strategy for dealing with both economic and personal problems. Working-class married women talk about migration as a family project. The political economy that rendered their husbands unemployable forced them to migrate to Chicago as part of a family strategy. Migration took place in stages. Husbands moved first, secured employment and housing arrangements, and sent for the rest of the family later. Given traditional gender roles in Puerto Rican culture, women left the island to be with their husbands, even though some reported they had been working before they left. Their responsibilities as wives and mothers took precedence over any role as wage earner. In other words, gender relations within the family shaped the migration of married working-class women to Chicago. Some married women went willingly, thinking that the move would improve their families' financial situation. Others resisted, but ultimately their roles as mothers and wives compelled them to follow their husbands to Chicago.

LIVING ARRANGEMENTS

One of the first problems Puerto Rican families faced upon arrival in Chicago was living arrangements. Puerto Ricans who moved to Chicago often had a period of temporary living arrangements with the family members who had facilitated the move. For some working-class women the transition was easy. A crowded apartment with lots of family members provided a sense of continuity and security. When Alicia arrived in Chicago in the 1950s to get married, she shared an apartment with a cousin and her family. In those days, she

recalled, "You rented the apartments with furniture," and "We lived like one big family." Shortly after establishing economic solvency, families moved into their own apartments.

More frequently, working-class migrant women talked about the difficulties adjusting to living with other relatives. Temporary living arrangements ranged from six months to a year, depending on how fast the family could survive on their own and were able to find adequate housing. Within this context, informal reciprocity norms in Chicago dictated that the newly arrived wife would help clean and prepare food for those who were employed. In the 1950s, Rita and her family came to live with her sister-in-law:

> My husband took us to my sister-in-law's house. There *pase la salsa y el guayacan* [popular expression denoting a very hard time]. We had four kids and no house of our own. Imagine? We had to wait to shower after everyone in the other family had taken their shower. If I had my little girl in the bathtub and one of her [sister-in-law] children wanted to shower I had to hurry up and leave them use the shower. For cooking it was worse. I suffered a lot.

At this point, the interview was interrupted because Rita started crying in uncontrollable sobs. She took a deep breath and continued describing that first year of her arrival in Chicago, which for her seemed like a century:

> I used to do everything for her. I cooked, I cleaned the house. You see, because she worked and after work she went to school. She had a house with eight rooms and we rented one room. You had to see all the things that happened to believe it. I shared everything with her, but she did not. She used to buy "cakes" for her children and would not share it with ours. She used to tell me things about my husband that were very hurtful and painful.

Similarly, Victoria described living with her in-laws as the source of numerous problems:

> I stayed home and took care of the children. I cleaned the house. It was very difficult. On top of that I was very shy. I did not dare even to open the

refrigerator to get something to drink. I tried to keep a low profile and not be a bother to them.

Agnes went to live with the relatives who had persuaded her and her husband to move from Puerto Rico. She worked for a while but stopped when she became pregnant. Unemployed, she spent much of her time in the house. She found herself baby-sitting and doing chores as if she were a maid, and the living arrangements that she thought were going to be temporary began to seem permanent. Discomforted, she confronted her husband and proclaimed: "Either you find me an apartment or I'm going back to Puerto Rico." Within the framework of the family structure, these women confronted their husbands in a manner that did not threaten traditional family arrangements. In this context, confrontation becomes a strategy of resistance to deal with inadequate living arrangements.

But finding an adequate apartment was no easy task. Padilla (1987, p. 117) wrote that Puerto Ricans "were trapped in the most run-down residential sections in their communities not only because of poverty but also because of a stringent pattern of housing discrimination." Teresa and her husband experienced the effects of this discrimination and poverty:

> When we went apartment hunting if they saw that we were Hispanics and the rent was $60.00, they asked us $90.00. We could never find an affordable apartment. It was very difficult to find decent housing.

Others were asked, "Are you Puerto Rican?" and were told, "We don't rent to Puerto Ricans." Agnes remembered the kind of problems she confronted:

> When I was looking for apartment around Kildare and Potomac I found a lot of problems. That area was an area where a lot of Europeans lived and when I inquired about apartment openings they closed the door on my face. And you know what? I did not understand why they would do something like that.

As a group, Puerto Ricans devised a number of strategies to resist the housing discrimination they confronted in Chicago. One strategy of resistance families used to deal with discrimination was looking for apartments with more than one unit available. Other family members were told about the vacancies so that they might move together. Some families talked to landlords and found apartments for family or friends who were still in Puerto Rico. Occasionally, members of families pooled their resources to buy a multiunit building, enabling families of brothers and sisters to occupy the same apartment building. Daniela's sister and her family lived on the first floor of a building they share-bought; Daniela and her family lived on the second floor, and her sister's family lived on the third. By living close together, they could help one another more easily.

In addition to these issues, Puerto Ricans struggled with the idea of buying property because it implied a commitment to making Chicago their permanent home. Consequently, families often moved from residences of relatives, to rental properties, to ownership, and back to Puerto Rico.

JUGGLING FAMILY AND WORK

In Puerto Rican culture there is a gender-specific division of labor which consists of men's work (*trabajo de hombre*) as providers and women's work (*trabajo de mujer*) as the caretakers of the home and the children (Rogler & Cooney, 1984). Underlying this gender division of labor is a patriarchal ideology, *machismo,* which emphasizes men's sexual freedom, virility, and aggressiveness and women's sexual repression and submission (Acosta-Belen, 1986). *Machismo* represents the male ideal and plays an important role in maintaining sexual restrictions and the subordination of women. This ideology rationalizes a double standard where a woman can be seen as *la mujer buena o de la casa* (a good woman) or as *una mujer mala o de la calle* (a bad woman and a woman of the streets). Men have to show that *el lleva los pantalones en la casa* (he is the one who wears the pants in the family) and they are free to *echar una canita al aire* (literally meaning, blow a gray hair to the wind, culturally it means to have an affair).

The counterpart of *machismo* is *marianismo,* in which the Virgin Mary is seen as the role model. Within this context, a woman's sexual purity and virginity is a cultural imperative. Motherhood, in Puerto Rican culture, lies at the center of such ideology as one of the important roles a woman plays. A woman is viewed in light of her relationship to her children and, as Carmen, one of the respondents, put it, in her ability to *dar buenos ejemplos* (provide a good role model).

Safa (1976) observed that among working-class Puerto Ricans, gender roles are very rigid. Although industrialization and the entrance of women in the labor force completely contradicts the ideal of *la mujer es de la casa* (women belong to the home), in Puerto Rico the domestic role of working-class women remains intact. Working mothers are primarily responsible for the care of the home and the children.

In Chicago, in keeping with this ideology surrounding family values, some husbands resisted the idea of their wives working and took a double shift so that wives could stay home, take care of the children, and do housework. Most often, economic necessity obliged other husbands to accept women's work roles outside the home. Like Lucy said: "I did not come here to work, but I had to." Alicia elaborated:

> In those days one pay check was like nothing. We put together both paychecks and there were times that we had very little or next to nothing left. By that time there were other relatives living with us and there were lots of mouths to feed.

In the 1950s, Chicago's economy offered new immigrants plenty of job opportunities in the booming manufacturing sector. In fact, the same network of family and friends that helped in the process of migration helped working wives find employment in Chicago factories. . . .

For most married working-class women, employment was a temporary necessity. The way women talked about their work experiences reflected this attitude. In fact, working-class married women often gave in to their husband's wishes of staying home. . . .

Puerto Rican men may have accommodated to their wives' employment but the traditional division of labor within the family did not change. Lucy articulated the problems of working women:

> It was very hard work because I had to take care of the house, the children and the store. Since my husband never learned how to drive I had to learn to drive. I had to go to the warehouse, do the bookkeeping, everything. In the store I used to do everything. My husband helped but I was practically in charge of everything.

Puerto Rican working mothers, regardless of whether they worked outside the home or with their husbands in the family business, were still responsible for the care of the children and housework. Child care first became a problem at the time of migration as they could not afford to travel all at once. Instead, women had to accommodate their roles as working wives and mothers. In Chicago, women developed short-term accommodation strategies to deal with the daily problems of child care. Shift work represented one strategy couples used to allow these women to stay home with the children. The husband worked the day shift and the wife the night shift. Haydee's father worked the day shift in a factory while her mother worked the evening shift as a cook in a hotel. Josefa worked the night shift in a candy factory, and her husband worked the day shift. Josefa was asked if she ever switched with her husband, so he worked nights and she worked days. She replied that they hadn't, because her current work routine allowed her to take care of her daughter during the day.

When children were old enough for school, both husband and wife might be able to work during the day. For wives, however, there was always the added responsibility of returning home to care for the children and do the household chores. Here, girls were introduced to the household responsibilities very early and were left to care for younger brothers and sisters. When Claudia reached age nine she acquired household responsibilities. She was given keys to the apartment, and after school she was expected to clean the kitchen, pick up around the house, and start dinner. This was one way mothers trained their daughters in the traditional gender roles.

Given the ease of migration, other working-class women brought over relatives with them to help care for the children. Lucy and Daniela brought their mothers to help take care of their children. Teresa brought her younger sister to Chicago so that she could help take care of the children.

Sanchez-Korrol (1983, p. 98) found the same kind of informal child-care practices in the early *colonias* in New York City in which "child-care tasks previously undertaken by relatives defaulted to friends and acquaintances outside the kinship network who provided the services in exchange for a prearranged fee." This grassroots system served both those who were employed and those who had to stay at home. The arrangement usually consisted of bringing child, food, and additional clothing to the "mother-substitute" and collecting the child after work. This system provided a practical way to increase family earnings and was an extralegal system with advantages not found in established child-care institutions. These informal child-care arrangements allowed children to be cared for in a familiar environment, in which there was mutual trust, agreement between the adults involved, and flexibility. Children were cared for in a family setting where the language, customs, and Puerto Rican traditions were reinforced.

When Teresa stopped working she became a child-care provider for the women in her building. Now, she no longer cares for other people's children but instead cares for her own grandchildren. Teresa's history represents a typical cycle of care: placing her children with a neighbor while she worked, caring for other neighbors' children while they worked, and finally caring for her own children's children, perpetuating such care practices in another generation.

MARITAL PROBLEMS

In addition to juggling family and work, four married working-class women reported a range of problems with their husbands, including alcoholism, infidelity, and desertion. Rita reported that her husband had started drinking and being unfaithful to her. Rita was aware of his problems but chose not to leave him. Instead, she endured the affairs and her husband's alcoholism. He brought her considerable pain and stress until he died suddenly from his alcoholism in 1980.

Interviewing elderly women in Massachusetts, Sanchez-Ayendez (1986) found that as long as men's behavior did not upset the balance in the household where men are the providers and women the center of the home, married women endured such behavior. Ana, one of her respondents, knew her husband was having an affair but believed that success in marriage depended on the woman's ability "to make it work."

In fact, since her husband was becoming less and less involved with the family affairs, Rita took charge and began to go around her husband's authority. She rationalized her moves in terms of her family responsibilities. She had limitations (a major one being her husband), but that did not prevent her from aggressive action. The home was her domain and it was her right to make decisions about it without the intervention of her husband, who had abdicated his authority anyway because of his drinking. In the absence of her husband's authority, Rita became very resourceful. The story of how she bought a home illustrates the kind of strategies Puerto Ricans forged as individuals and as a group.

> I went to the bank and I asked for a loan. But they would not give it to me without my husband's signature. I kept thinking how can I buy this house? I told my husband again and I asked him to come to the bank with me, I waited all morning long for him and he did not show up. I was so disillusioned. I really liked the house and I saw a lot of potential. I went back to the landlord and I told him that I was really interested and that I wanted to buy the house

if he gave it to me for $10,000. Some people that lived in the building that knew me supported me and told the landlord that I was a good person. I had done a little bit of work and I had some money saved but not enough.

Faced with this problem, Rita took an alternative route: Ask a friend for a loan:

I had this friend and she told me about this Cuban man who could lend me the money. I went [and] talked to him and I asked him to loan me $5,000. But that it had to be through a lawyer. I wanted to do it legal. The lawyer told him how are you going to loan this woman all that money? I was furious. I told the Cuban that I give him my word that if I did not respond that he could take the house from me.

In the process Rita not only had to face the institutional discrimination in the banking industry but also the gender bias from the lawyer who discouraged her friend from lending her the money. Eventually, he lent her the money and with some savings from her children, she bought the house:

Now, the problem was how to tell my husband about it. Well, I fixed the house very nice before we moved. One night he came home drunk laid on the couch and I told the kids that tonight we are moving to the new house. We borrowed a big truck and moved overnight. The following morning when my husband woke up, everything was gone. [Laughing] I was fixing breakfast in the new house and suddenly I remembered that we had left him behind. I rushed to the house, talked to him and told him that this apartment was old, that I did not like it, and that we should sell it. I told him that I had rented out a little house and we had moved overnight. . . . He paid the rent and he did not know the house was ours. He gave me the money for the rent and I invested it. I rented a house in the back and within a year I had the house paid. One day I was going to tell him but he got sick. We took him to the hospital on Friday and by Sunday he had died. Imagine, he died and never knew I had bought the house we were living in.

Years after her husband died, Rita married her husband's best friend (Carlos), whose wife had abandoned him and his children. She had helped him raise his family while he had helped her deal with her husband's alcoholism. Rita and Carlos went through a lot together with their respective families. In old age they found themselves alone and decided to stay together.

Nellie, on the other hand, was conscious of her subordination to her husband and endured it for a good part of her marriage. He was a gambler, even taking her paycheck to pay for his habits, and he turned abusive as his drinking increased. Nellie remembered the fateful day when her marriage came apart:

He picked me up at work and when we got home he wanted me to help him carry some bags. I was very tired and did not want to. He hit me right there in the street. That was it. I left him and went to my mother's place. I lived with my mother for a week. But one day he showed up at work, put a knife to my neck and told me that he was going to kill me if I did not go back with him. So, I told him I would, but first we must go to my mother's to pick up my stuff. That was the trick—when we got there I told him that I was not going with him. That was on Friday, the following Saturday he got in trouble with the police and fled to New York.

Nellie became a single mother and had to take two jobs in order to support herself and her family. She recalled:

It was so hard to find someone to take care of the children while I was at work. One day my mom was gone to New York for a short trip and the police came and took my children. I was lucky because the two ladies that lived next to me went with me to the police station and helped me. They told the police that I was a good and responsible mother. They gave them back to me and I had to leave a job.

The lack of child care was a major barrier to Nellie's search for work and she was forced to rely on the welfare system for survival. Nellie remembered that the day she went to the welfare office, a welfare officer lectured her in English about her responsibilities as a mother. Nellie left the office before the caseworker was finished and took a factory job. This time she asked a woman in her building to help her with her children for a small fee.

Victoria and Agnes had similar problems with their husbands and, like Nellie, became single mothers, having to rely on welfare to survive. Victoria's husband could not hold a job and disappeared for long periods of time. According to Victoria:

> We were legally married for eleven years and in that period we had four children. Within that period he took off more than twenty-five times, leaving me stranded with the children.

She divorced him and in order to support herself she went on welfare. Victoria recalled the day her sister-in-law took her to the welfare office:

> I felt so ashamed. I was not raised to beg for money. In Puerto Rico, we had very little but we never asked for anything. My mother worked and even though she earned very little we stretched it. When I went to the welfare office my English was not very good. That's why my sister-in-law went with me. Social workers were so rude. They asked my sister-in-law whether I knew that there were contraceptives so that I could avoid having so many children. She fought with them. She later told me what had happened.

Victoria lived on welfare for a number of years, but it was not very reliable. She remembered a particular crisis which, in a way, helped her leave welfare. For some reason, the welfare office had started reviewing her case and stopped sending her money. For seven months she had no means to support herself and her family. Finally, she lost control and became very ill, or as she put it, *me enferme de los nervios.* Pelto, Roman, and Liriano (1982) found that Puerto Rican single parents in Hartford also reported suffering from this condition of nervous breakdown. They describe this condition as a mental illness that ranges from mild anxieties, to uncontrollable outbursts, to depressions and suicidal tendencies. *Nervios* is perceived

as a situational illness and is not seen as the fault of the victim. While Victoria was in the hospital, a Lutheran pastor came to see her at her mother's request. According to Victoria, "He spoke Spanish beautifully and perfectly. He seemed to care about Hispanic problems. He rescued me. When I left the hospital, he offered me a part-time job." Since her children were in school, she was able to work her schedule around them and continued taking welfare while working part-time. She attended a GED program with her church and passed the state examination. Victoria reflected on her choices and what they meant to her:

> It is very difficult to raise your family here just working by yourself. I was on welfare but I was able to raise my children without the drug problem or the gang problem. That's what makes me feel good.

Agnes' problems with her husband started after they moved to Chicago. Puzzled by the marital problems, she attempted to rationalize what had happened. Agnes felt that:

> People come here with the dream of working hard, saving some money and returning to one's homeland. But something happens to men. Couples arrive in this country and their marriages fall apart . . . I think it has to do with their work. They come to work in those factories and they lose control. They lose their sense of reality. They think that their only responsibility is to provide for the family. They come put the food on the table and off they go to the streets.

Agnes' husband loved to spend money on automobiles. The family's savings were squandered on cars and car parts. Agnes tried to cope by confronting him about the spending and reminding him of their original goals of saving to return to Puerto Rico. But it was hopeless, and they divorced in 1978. Unable to support herself, she turned to welfare. Her daughters were still very young when she divorced and that was one of her considerations for staying alone and not remarrying. She said:

I always thought of my daughters. I used to tell myself how I am going to allow a stranger to come into our house and take charge of our lives. Sometimes children do not adapt well to a stepfather. Me, no, no, I prefer to raise my daughters alone. I am a person who is very independent I like to depend on my own, and I realized that in order for me to [be] able to move forward and give something to my children I was going to go back to school. I did not want to work all my life in a factory. So, I took public aid and started going to school.

School, however, "was not very stable." So she moved from work to welfare and back to work. At the time of the interview, she worked part-time and received food coupons.

Some husbands abandoned the family altogether. Ivan, now a community leader, and one of the respondents, remembered his mother's struggle to survive on her own. Within a year after relocating to Chicago, his family was abandoned by his father. It was the most traumatic event in his life:

After my father abandoned us my mother was left with the responsibilities of taking care of us. It was the most difficult time of our lives. We were so poor. Really, I don't have words to describe the kind of situation we lived in. But my mother suffered the most. She was a very proud woman. Even in the most difficult situations, she always found happiness and pride. She always tried keeping us clean and neat—that was her pride.

As these cases reflect, when confronted with marital problems, working-class Puerto Rican women develop a number of strategies. They divorced their husbands, but unable to support themselves, they had to rely on welfare. These interviews show how migration affects family relations, resulting in the emergence of single-headed households. . . .

REFERENCES

Acosta-Belen, E. (1986). *The Puerto Rican woman: Perspectives on culture, history, and society.* New York: Praeger.

Dietz, J. L. (1986). *Economic history of Puerto Rico: Institutional change and capitalist development.* Princeton; NJ: Princeton University Press.

Lamphere, L. (1987). *From working daughters to working mothers: Immigrant women in a New England industrial community.* Ithaca: Cornell University Press.

Padilla, F. (1987). *Puerto Ricans in Chicago.* Indiana: University of Notre Dame Press.

Pantojas-Garcia, E. (1990). *Development strategies as ideology: Puerto Rico's export-led industrialization experience.* Boulder, CO: Lynne Rienner Publisher.

Pelto, P., Roman, M., & Liriano, N. (1982). Family structures in an urban Puerto Rican community. *Urban Anthropology, 11(1),* 39–57.

Rogler, L., & Cooney, R. S. (1984), *Puerto Rican families in New York: Intergenerational processes.* Maplewood: Waterfront.

Safa, H. (1976). Class consciousness among working-class women in Latin America. In J. Nash & H. I. Safa (Eds.), *Sex and class in Latin America.* New York: Praeger.

Sanchez-Ayendez, M. (1986). Puerto Rican elderly women: Shared meanings and informal supportive networks. In J. Cole (Ed.), *All-American women: Lines that divide, ties that bind.* New York: The Free Press.

Sanchez-Korrol, V. (1983). *From colonia to community: The history of Puerto Ricans in New York City, 1917–1948.* Westport: Greenwood Press.

[?] *Think about It*

1. How do "strategies of resistance" and "strategies of accommodation" differ? What strategies did Puerto Rican migrants in Toro-Morn's study use to resist housing and work discrimination?

2. How did gender roles shape Puerto Rican men's and women's experiences during and after migration—especially in family/work roles and marital problems?

3. Why, during marital conflicts, didn't most of the wives simply divorce their husbands?

Living Poor: Family Life among Single-Parent African American Women

Robin L. Jarrett

Like the working-class Puerto Rican families described in Reading 29, many poor black households also develop coping strategies to maintain their families' viability. Using data from focus group interviews, Robin L. Jarrett explains how and why low-income, single-parent black mothers adapt to economic marginality and rely on alternative family arrangements to mediate the effects of poverty.

This paper is divided into four sections. Section One provides an overview of the current issues regarding family life and poverty among African Americans. Substantive themes and explanatory frameworks derived from the "underclass debate" are critically discussed and compared to earlier discussions of poverty in the United States. Section Two describes the qualitative group interviews that were conducted with a sample of never-married African-American mothers. These data are used to examine issues raised in Section One, concentrating on unmarried women because they figure so prominently in the underclass debate. Section Three presents empirical findings from the focus group interviews. Verbatim excerpts from these discussions are used to examine key components of the structural argument. Observations from the focus group study are also compared with earlier ethnographic and qualitative research to explore continuity in family patterns. Finally, Section Four explores the broader theoretical implications of the research. . . .

Source: From Robin L. Jarrett, "Living Poor: Family Life among Single-Parent African American Women," *Social Problems* 41 (February 1994): 30–49. Copyright © 1994 The Society for the Study of Social Problems. Reprinted by permission of the University of California Press and Professor Robin L. Jarrett of the University of Illinois at Urbana Champaign.

FAMILY STRUCTURE, RACE, AND POVERTY: "FEMALE HOUSEHOLDER, NO HUSBAND PRESENT"

. . . Two conceptual frameworks, the cultural and the structural, provide competing arguments to explain changes in family patterns. The cultural explanation maintains that changing household and family formation patterns among low-income African Americans are the result of deviant values. Researchers cite various factors generating distinctive values, but cultural formulations that stress the role of liberal welfare reforms in exacerbating deviant values have been particularly influential (Mead 1986; Murray 1984). The basic argument is that ghetto-specific norms differ from their mainstream counterparts, positively endorsing single motherhood, out-of-wedlock childbearing, welfare dependency, male irresponsibility, criminal behavior, low mobility aspirations, and, more generally, family instability (Auletta 1982; Lemann 1986; Mead 1986; Murray 1984; see also Cook and Curtin 1987 for an overview).

The structural explanation argues that demographic shifts in household and family formation patterns reflect larger economic trends. Researchers cite macro-structural changes in the economy—including the decline in entry-level jobs, the relocation of jobs away from the inner-city, and the mismatch between job requirements and employee skills—and parallel declines in rates of male employment, marriage, and childbearing within marriage as evidence of external or situational pressures on family life. The fundamental thesis is that economic factors impede the construction and maintenance of mainstream family patterns: they encourage poor African-American women to forego marriage, bear children out-of-wedlock, head their own households, and rely on welfare income (Darity and Meyers 1984; Joe 1984; Staples 1985; Testa et al. 1989; Wilson 1987).

Current discussions about poverty and the underclass are similar in two ways to the poverty discussions that took place from the early 1960s to the mid-1970s when such issues were last seriously discussed. Then, as now, both structural and cultural arguments were the dominant explanatory frameworks as researchers debated the competing role of economic and cultural factors. Furthermore, recent and past studies concentrate on family structure or, more precisely, household structure. During both periods, structural and cultural perspectives focused on the idea that particular family arrangements—either as a consequence or as a cause—were associated with poverty status (Lemann 1986; Lewis 1965, 1966; Mead 1986; Moynihan 1965; Murray 1984; Garfinkel and McLanahan 1986; Wilson 1987). . . .

Yet, both recent and past poverty research are similar in that they both rely on cultural and structural frameworks as the dominant explanations. They also demonstrate a continued concern with family structure as a key causal or explanatory variable. As a consequence of their differences, poverty researchers today know more about the demographic profiles of poor African-American families than about their internal dynamics; they more frequently respond to journalistic conceptualizations of cultural processes than those of anthropologists and sociologists; and they possess a wealth of quantitative data and a dearth of qualitative and ethnographic research to explore the issue of family life and poverty. . . .

SAMPLE AND METHODOLOGY: "RESEARCH TOUCHED BY HUMAN HANDS"

. . . The data reported in this paper derive from a series of focus group interviews (see Jarrett 1993 for a detailed methodological discussion). The interviews were broadly conceived as an exploratory examination of how women in poor families adapt to conditions of poverty. I concentrated on various aspects of family life, including family formation patterns, household living arrangements, childcare and socialization patterns, intergenerational relations, male-female relations, and welfare, work, and social opportunities.

Ten focus groups, comprised of a total of 82 low-income African-American women, were conducted between January and July 1988. Each focus group session lasted approximately two hours and was held with groups of no more than 8–10 women. The tape recorded discussions were relatively unstructured but topically oriented, allowing for comparisons across groups. . . .

The criteria for selection of the women was based on the profiles of women discussed in the current underclass debate. They included: (1) never-married mothers, (2) who received AFDC, and (3) lived in high poverty or economically transitional neighborhoods in the city of Chicago. Most of the women were in their early to middle twenties and began their childbearing careers as adolescents. A purposive sample was drawn from Chicago-area Head Start programs since such programs are located in low-income communities and serve women fitting the above profile.

A team of research assistants transcribed and coded the interviews thematically by topical area. The initial codes were based on the broad topical areas guiding the research but were expanded to include unanticipated information that emerged in the discussion. Once this task was completed, key issues and themes were identified for each area.

THE EMPIRICAL DATA: "IN THEIR OWN WORDS"

. . . In this section, I present empirical data that offer insights on the lives of real women and that address the limitations of the structural framework. As a point of departure, I examine the normative and behavioral dimensions of familial roles among the sample of never-married African-American mothers. The concentration on the conflict between norms and behaviors provides a dynamic example of how women who hold conventional aspirations concerning family patterns respond in their daily lives. Around this broad topic, I explore four issues: (1) Marriage, the ideal; (2) Marriage, the reality; (3) Economic impediments to conventional marriage; and (4) Alternatives to conventional marriage.

Marriage, the Ideal: "Everybody Wants to Be Married"

Women consistently professed adherence to mainstream patterns. For virtually all of the women interviewed, legal marriage was the cornerstone of conventional family life. Marriage represented a complex of behaviors, including independent household formation, economic independence, compatibility, and fidelity and commitment that were generally associated with the nuclear family. Representative excerpts from group members illustrate:

Independent Household Formation
We were talking about marriage and all of that. . . . We was staying with his mother. . . . I told him we'll get married and we'll get our own place."

He lives with his grandmother. I don't want to move into his grandmother's home. I live at my mother's. I don't want him to move in there. When we get married, I want us to live in our own house, something we can call ours.

Economic Independence
. . . Charles [my boyfriend] be half-stepping [financially]. That's why I'm not really ready for marriage.

I plan on getting married. But I would rather wait. He said he wanted to wait until he made 22. He works two jobs, but he said he want to wait until he gets a better job, where he can support both of us. . . .

Compatibility
I think a person should never get married unless it's for love. . . . [If] you want to spend the rest of your life with that person, you all [should] have a good understanding. If you marry somebody just because you pregnant, just because you have four or five kids by them, or because society or whoever pressured you into it, you goin' to become mean and resentful. And if that person turns out to not be what you thought or that marriage turns out to be something less than you hoped it would be, it's not goin' to be worth it. . . .

A lotta' time you can't get along with the children's father. . . . Me and Carmen's father could not get along, point blank. [I]t wasn't the money. It's not 'cause I didn't have a father; he had a father. We came from good homes. We just could not get along. We don't even know how we made the baby. [laughter]

Fidelity and Commitment
If I get married, I believe in being all the way faithful.

I want you to take care of me. I'm not looking to jump into bed and call this a marriage. I want you to love me, care for me, be there when I need you because I'm going to be there for you when you need me.

As soon as [men] get married and things change and he's looking for somebody else. Man! Why didn't they find that person before they marry you and you start going through all those changes.

Nita, a mother of two children provided one of the most eloquent statements on the meaning of marriage. She said:

I would love to be married . . . I believe I would make a lovely wife. . . . I would just love to have the experience of being there married with a man. I imagine me and my children, my son a basketball player . . . playing for the [Chicago] Bulls. My daughter . . . playing the piano, have a secretary job and going to college. . . . Me, I'm at home playing the wifely duties. This man, not a boy, coming home with his manly odors. . . . My husband comes home, takes off his work boots and have dinner. . . . I would like to have this before I leave this earth, a husband, my home, my car.

Likewise, Charmaine, who despite her own unmarried status, firmly asserted:

I think everybody wants to get married. Everybody wants to have somebody to work with them . . . and go through life with. . . . I would like to be married. . . . I want to be married. I'm not gonna lie. I really do.

Women, despite their insistent statements concerning the importance of marriage as the cornerstone of mainstream family life, were well aware of the unconventionality of their actual behaviors. Women openly acknowledged that their single status, non-marital childbearing, and in some cases, female-headship, diverged from mainstream household and family formation patterns. Tisha said with a mixture of humor and puzzlement:

Is this what it's supposed to be like? So, I'm going backwards. Most people say: "Well, you go to school, you get married, and you have kids." Well, I had my kids. I'm trying to go to school and maybe, somewhere along the line, I'm going to catch up with everybody else.

Natty, the mother of an active preschooler who periodically appeared at the door of the meeting room, further observed:

I really would like to have two children but I'm not married . . . and I would like to be married before I do have another child. . . . So maybe one day we might jump the broom or tie the knot or whatever.

Sherry's comments were similar:

I wanted to marry him because we had talked about it so long. . . . We always talked about it . . . gettin' married, then have our kids and stuff and everything.

Tisha's, Natty's, and Sherry's observations indicate that the desired sequence of events entails economic independence, then marriage, and, finally, childbearing. . . .

Marriage, the Reality: "That's a Little White Girl's Dream"

Women were pessimistic about actually contracting family roles as defined in the mainstream manner. Their aspirations for conventional family roles were tempered by doubt and, in some cases, outright pessimism.

Karen's comment reflected her sense of uncertainty:

I would like to get married one day . . . to somebody that's as ready as I am. . . . But it's so scary out here. You scared to have a commitment with somebody, knowing he's not on the level. . . . They ready to get their life together; they looking for a future.

Denise and Chandra were more pessimistic about their chances for a conventional and stable family life:

I used to have this in my head, all my kids got the same daddy, get married have a house. That's a little white girl's dream. That stuff don't happen in real life. You don't get married and live happily ever after.

It doesn't work that way. Just because you have a baby don't mean they gone stay with you. . . . Even if you married, that don't mean he gone stay with you; he could up and leave.

Even Dee Dee's initially firm assertions were laced with doubt:

I'm goin' to get married one day. I'm goin' to say I know I'm gettin' married one day, if it is just for a month. I'm gettin' married, I know that, [laughter] I know I am . . . well maybe.

Earlier in their lives most of these women assumed that their household and formation patterns would follow conventional paths. Remaining single, bearing children outside of marriage, and heading a household were not foregone conclusions. Rather, pessimism about the viability of mainstream patterns grew out of their first-hand experiences. Women related conflictual and depriving situations that caused them to reassess their expectations.

Andrea described her attempt to forge a long-term relationship and its disappointing outcome:

> I would rather live by myself, me and my two kids, because I used to stay with somebody. . . . Me and him did not work out. We used to have to go scrape up some food to eat. I would rather stay by myself.

Both Pat and Lisa recount similar tribulations:

> It makes me angry to think about it. . . . I go through changes [with him] and . . . sometimes I just throw up my hands in the air—excuse the expression—I just say "Fuck it! Had it! I'm tired!" Sometime I say: "Man disappear!"

> [Men cause] a lot of headache and heartache. . . . All the time you taking to set that man straight you could be spending with your child. . . . Instead of having time with your kids, you got to get him together. . . .

Women's experiences were augmented by the experiences of others. Through the processes of observation of and comparison to older women in the community, younger women gauged their chances of contracting ideal family forms . . . :

> I don't think I'll ever find a husband because of the way I feel. I want it like my mother had it. [My father] took care of us. She been married to him since she was sixteen. He took care of her, took her out of her mother's house. She had four kids, he took care of all the kids.

These comments suggest that even as younger women compare themselves with older women, conventional patterns remain their reference point. Women's views also signal their awareness of declining opportunities for attaining mainstream family patterns within impoverished African-American communities. . . .

Economic Impediments to Marriage: "I Could Do Bad by Myself"

The women's own interpretations concerning changes in household and family formation patterns are consistent with the structural explanation of poverty. Economic factors, according to women, played a prominent role in their decision to forego marriage, bear children outside of marriage, and, in some cases, head households.

Iesha described how economic factors influenced her decisions. She said:

> I had a chance to get married when I first had my two [children]. We had planned the date and everything, go down to city hall. . . . When the day came along, I changed my mind. Right today I'm glad I did not marry him because he still ain't got no job. He still staying with his sister and look where I am. Ever since I done had a baby I been on my own. I haven't lived with no one but myself. I been paying bills now.

Renee, who was considering marriage to her current companion, also recounted how economic considerations influenced her decisions:

> I could do bad by myself. . . . If we get married and he's working, then he lose his job, I'm going to stand by him and everything. I don't want to marry nobody that don't have nothing going for themselves. . . . I don't see no future. . . . I could do bad by myself. . . .

Tina, who was currently uninvolved ("on my own"), further described the link between male economic marginality and marriage:

> I wanted to get married when I first found out I was pregnant, but he didn't want to get married. And I'm glad that he didn't. . . . It would have been terrible; he wasn't working. Maybe that was one of the reasons why he did not want to get married.

Other qualitative and ethnographic studies also describe the depressing effect that economic pressures have on marriage among poor women and men (Aschenbrenner 1975; Liebow 1967; Hannerz

1969; Rainwater 1970; Stack 1974; Sullivan 1985). The absence of legal marriage or economically stable partnerships, however, did not preclude the formation of strong and stable male-female relationships. Many of the women were involved in a variety of unions. As previously described, some of these relationships were indeed conflictual. Others were remarkably stable, considering the economic constraints that both women and men faced. Several women described long-term relationships, some of which had endured for over a decade.

One said:

> I'm not married. I got three kids. But their father is there with the kids. He been there since I was 16. . . . I been with the same guy since I was 16 years old and I'm still with him now. I only had really one man in my life. . . .

Still another one underlined:

> I been with my baby's father for 12 years. We still not married. So maybe one day we might jump the broom or tie the knot or whatever.

These comments are important because they identify the existence of strong alternative relationships that are not detected in demographic profiles that recognize only legal marriages. They also confirm the results of earlier ethnographic studies that identify a variety of male-female arrangements that exist outside of marriage (Aschenbrenner 1975; Jarrett 1992; Liebow 1967; Rainwater 1970; Schulz 1969; Stack 1974; Sullivan 1985). Such arrangements varied from casual friendships to fully committed partnerships. The information gathered from the focus groups and the detailed accounts resulting from ethnographic case studies suggest the need to explore the spousal and parental roles that men assume outside of marriage. These arrangements have significant implications for the support and well-being of women and children.

Women's decisions regarding household and family formation patterns were not surprising in light of the economic profiles of potential marital partners. Even when men worked, their employment options were limited. The prospective mates of the women interviewed were generally unemployed, underemployed, or relegated to the most insecure jobs in the secondary labor market. Within the context of the larger discussion on perceptions of social and economic opportunities, women described the types of jobs their male companions and friends assumed. They included: car wash attendants; drug dealers; fast food clerks; grocery store stock and bag clerks; hustlers; informal car repairmen; lawn workers; street peddlers; and street salvage workers.

The focus group data thus confirm the structural explanation of poverty and its emphasis on economic factors, such as joblessness. But they also go beyond the primary concentration on the economic instability of men and its consequences for family maintenance. The focus group interviews indicate that women also considered their own resources in addition to those of the men. They assessed their own educational backgrounds, job experiences, welfare resources, and childcare arrangements. For example, women reviewed their educational qualifications, and assessed their potential for economic independence.

Educational Attainment. . . . Now I'm trying to go back to school 'cause when I dropped out . . . I was in the 11th grade and was pregnant. . . . I was pregnant with her then, so I had to leave school. . . . Now I'm trying to go back to school for nursing assistant, so I can get off all public aid; find somethin' else to do 'stead of being on welfare all my life.

> I try to do what I can. And it's hard out there when you dropped out of high school or you may have a G.E.D. And you have a child . . . and then go and try to find a job.

Work Experiences. Contrary to common stereotypes, many of the women had worked. Women's past work experiences served to clarify the limitations of using the types of jobs available to them as a strategy of mobility. The women's comments focused on low wages, job access, and job inflexibility.

Low Wages
It don't make sense to go to McDonald's to make $3.35 an hour when you know you got to pay 4 dollars an hour to baby-sit and you got to have bus fare. . . .

Job Access
It was too far. . . . I would have to get up at 4 o'clock in the morning in order to be at work at seven. [I] leave work at 3:30 and still wouldn't make it home until 8 o'clock. And it was too far when I wasn't making anything. . . . I didn't have no time for my kids, no time for myself.

Job Inflexibility
[I] miss[ed] a day on the weekend and they fire[d] me. I didn't understand. They call me, but I wouldn't go back, because ain't no telling when I get sick like I was sick then. I told them no I didn't want it. And I been looking, putting in applications hoping that somebody call.

Welfare Experiences. Welfare, like low-wage jobs, also represented an institutionalized impediment to mobility. The women's comments highlighted the need for benefits, the stigma of public aid, welfare regulations, and their need for childcare.

Need for Benefits
If [public aid is] going to do something, I prefer if they would take me off but leave my kids on. Because they would need it more and I figure I can take care of myself a little bit more than they can. You need that medical for them. . . .

Stigma of Public Aid
You got to go out there on your own not using [your] public aid background . . . because a lot of companies not going to hire you because you coming from public aid.

Welfare Regulations
They give you the runaround for nothing. . . . This money not coming out . . . their pockets. . . . [I]t's not like it's coming out they paycheck every week. . . . It's coming from your parents paying they state taxes. . . . You trying to take care of your children the best way you can and this is one of the ways that you can take care of your children. . . .

They make you go through so many changes . . . so many changes for nothing. . . . When I was goin' to school, they call [me for an appointment. I said:] "Can I come after I get out of school?" [They said:] "No, come now." [I said:] "I have finals." [They said:] "So, come or you will be cut off."

Childcare Needs. Women, unlike men, had to factor children into their work schedules.

Well, I want to wait until my kids get about 5 [to work], so if something's going on [at the babysitter's] they can tell me. I don't want to be worried. I don't have nobody. I keep my own kids.

If I want to go out and get a job, I ain't going to pick any daycare in the city, because they ain't so safe either. . . .

As a result of their limited educational attainment, low-paying jobs, welfare disincentives, and childcare needs, most women came to perceive their economic options as severely limited. Consequently, when women sought other opportunities, they took both men's economic limitations and their own into account.

Alternatives to Conventional Marriage: "You Can Depend on Your Mama"

The focus group interviews expand on the structural explanation of poverty in yet another way. They serve to identify the strategic processes and sequences of events that follow women's decisions to forego marriage, bear children as single mothers, and in some cases, head households. Women responded to their poverty in three ways: they extended domestic and childcare responsibilities to multiple individuals; they relaxed paternal role expectations; and they assumed a flexible maternal role.

Domestic Kin Networks. The extension of domestic and childcare responsibilities beyond the nuclear family represented a primary response to economic marginality. Extended kin networks that centered around women provided assistance to single mothers and their children. For example, LaDawn, whose unintended pregnancy interrupted her plans to leave home, attend college, and get "real wild," described how living with her mother provides valuable support for her:

When your money is gone and you at home with your mama, you don't have to worry about where you getting your next meal from because mama is always going to figure out a way how you can get your next meal. . . . And your mama would be there to depend on; you can depend on your mama.

Likewise, Rita, who currently lives alone with her son, also receives assistance from her mother and other female kin. She described the complex, but cooperative pattern, that characterizes the care of her child:

Well, on the days Damen has school, my mother picks him up at night and keeps him at her house. And then when she goes to work in the morning, she takes him to my grandmother's house. And when my little sister gets out of school, she picks him up and takes him back to my mother's house. And then I go and pick him up. . . .

Diane also described the childcare benefits of living with her mother. She further hinted how her mother's assistance facilitates Diane's role as the primary caregiver:

My mother gives me good advice . . . if something's wrong. [My twins] had the chicken pox. What am I gonna do? . . . They itching. What should I put on them? She helps me out that way. And I stays with my mother. Me and my mother sit down and talk. We don't have no kind of problems as far as her trying to raise [my kids].

The women's accounts in these focus group interviews are paralleled in similar ethnographic studies. Aschenbrenner (1975), Jarrett (1992), and Sullivan (1985), in their works, highlight the im-

portance of grandmothers, as well as other women kin, in the lives of poor women and children. Grandmothers provide money on loan, childcare on a daily basis, and help with cooking and cleaning. These services allow some young mothers to finish school and get a job, staying off public assistance. Other qualitative studies provide comparable descriptions of supportive kin who provide care for poor children (Anderson 1990; Burton 1991; Holloman and Lewis 1978; Liebow 1967; Stack 1974; William and Kornblum 1985; Zollar 1985). These examples are important in another way. They indicate that households labeled as female-headed are often embedded in larger kinship networks. Interhousehold family arrangements and the domestic activities shared between them are usually overlooked in quantitative studies. Conscquently, female-headship as a living arrangement and family as a set of social relationships that may transcend household boundaries are often confounded (Jarrett 1992; Stack 1974; Yanagisako 1979).

Expansion of the Paternal Role. Living in poverty issued yet other strategies. A second type of strategy concentrated on paternal role performance. Women lowered their expectations of men and extended the paternal role to non-biological fathers as ways of facilitating the involvement of men in childcare. Evaluations of paternal role performance that hinged on providing for the family economically were replaced by assessments that centered on men's efforts to find work and assist with day-to-day child welfare (see also Rainwater 1970). For example, Jaleesa, an ebullient mother of one child, said of her daughter's father:

Even though he don't have a job, sometimes what counts is he spends time with his child. That child will think about that: "Well, my father's here when my mother's not here." [That child will] have someone else to turn to. And the father say: "Well, I ain't got no job. I ain't going to be around a child." That's not all to it.

Anna, who openly proclaimed her strength in the face of many obstacles, echoed Jaleesa's sentiments:

> I got three kids all by him and he try to help out when he can. He's not working now but [he] did try to help. And . . . he be going out looking for a job. I don't try to pressure. [Men] care about their kids. They wanna try to help. . . .

The way that poor unmarried fathers assist in the care of their children, both directly and indirectly, is also exemplified in Sullivan's (1985) ethnographic study. Men in his study provided food, clothing, and supervision for their children. Women's willingness to lower their expectations of their children's fathers reflected a fundamental reality. Most men lacked the resources to fully support their children. Yvette summarized this point aptly: "If they don't have it, they just don't have it. You can't get blood from a turnip."

Additionally, women extended the paternal role to men other than the biological fathers of their children. This strategy ensured that there was a male who provided nurturance and discipline, as well as economic support. For example, Alisha, asserted:

> It's not a father, but a male image. . . . My daughter will mind my brother better than she do me. I will tell her to sit down, whereas I would probably have to tell her four or five times; whereas my brother will come in with that manly image and will say sit down one time and she be sitting down. . . .

Several ethnographic studies also provide examples of how non-biological fathers supply support for poor African-American children (Aschenbrenner 1975; Burton 1991; Holloman and Lewis 1978; Liebow 1967; Schulz 1969; Stack 1974; Sullivan 1985). These studies identify an array of male figures, such as uncles, grandfathers, neighbors, fictive kin, and male companions who played significant roles in the lives of many children.

Expansion of the Maternal Role. A third strategy used by women to facilitate the care of

children entailed the expansion of the maternal role. Women, when necessary, broadened their role repertoire to include both expressive and instrumental role responsibilities. Irrespective of the presence or absence of men in the home, women expressed similar views about role flexibility. Under conditions of economic marginality women understood that at some point in their lives they would assume extensive household and family obligations.

Ethnographic research has consistently found that strong and competent mothers are greatly admired in low-income African-American communities (Aschenbrenner 1975; Ladner 1971; Rainwater 1970; Stack 1974). The focus group interviews provided corroboration. Women's comments illustrated their strength and competence as mothers. For example, Jeannie and Connie, who were currently living with the fathers of their children, respectively claimed:

> It does not take a man to make those kids strong. When I tell my kids to do something, they going to look at me first.

> I can be their mother and father and teach them values, teach them the right things. . . . I don't think they have to have a father in the home to teach them the right things.

Crystal, Sharon, and Shelly, who currently were not living with male companions, individually asserted:

> I can discipline [my children] myself. I have that bass in my voice. . . . I raise my voice and they'll . . . sit down. They'll mind me; they'll mind my mother.

> I think a father should be around. But it can't always be. I'm raising my children by myself.

> [My daughter] is well taken care of and I feel good about myself that I can give her everything she needs without his help.

In addition to describing how poor African-American women respond to conditions of poverty, the interviews highlighted the meanings that women attributed to the alternative family roles that they assumed. Motherhood, irrespective of women's single marital status, conferred them with a valued role. Moreover, women's ability to garner scarce resources, provide care for children, and in some cases, maintain households under stark conditions of poverty led to enhanced self-esteem. For example, Diane, mother of twin daughters, expressed her views on motherhood:

> It's some fun parts in it and then you got some down parts when you got to do this and got to do that. But I enjoy my daughters. . . . They make me happy. . . . They're what get me up in the morning. . . .

Contrary to common assumptions, women's accounts described some of the positive consequences of heading one's own household. Tammy, who shares a small apartment with her mother, two sisters, and her children mused:

> I never had a place of my own . . . [but] I'm ready for responsibility. I'm ready to raise my family by myself without my mother or sisters telling me: "Well, you shouldn't do this, and you should do that" . . . I'm ready to do it by myself, now. . . .

Lareesa, who described how she had been labeled "slow" in school, offered one of the most articulate statements on the relationship between household independence and personal development:

> I [and my son] live with my grandmother. . . . She says I have to listen to what she says because as long as I'm living under her roof, I got to obey her rules. . . . I'm not saying I'm *grown* [emphasis], grown [sic], but I want responsibility. That's just like taking an exam. If somebody gives you the answers, that's cheating me out of my life, if I can't do what I want, learn from myself.

DISCUSSION: "BRINGING PEOPLE BACK IN"

. . . The primary goal of this paper is to expand on the structural explanation of poverty. The struc-

tural perspective correctly documents changes in household and family formation patterns and the relationship of these changes to economic factors. Nevertheless, it ignores alternative family arrangements and omits the role of personal agency in understanding poverty among the poor. The focus group data address these two limitations by concentrating on African-American women's first-hand accounts of their lives. Women's narratives describe family arrangements that were, indeed, different from mainstream patterns but that were viable, nonetheless. Significantly, these differences in household and family formation patterns do not represent abandonment of conventional aspirations (see also Rainwater 1987; Staples 1985; Williams 1992). Further, women's accounts highlight the active roles that they played in caring for children and maintaining households. Women do not mechanistically respond to economic forces. Rather, they assess their options and make choices that allow them to forge meaningful lives despite the harsh economic conditions in which they and their children find themselves.

REFERENCES

Anderson, Elijah. 1990. *Streetwise: Race, Class, and Change in an Urban Community.* Chicago: University of Chicago Press.

Aschenbrenner, Joyce. 1975. *Lifelines: Black Families in Chicago.* New York: Holt, Rinehart and Winston.

Auletta, Ken. 1982. *The Underclass.* New York: Random House.

Burton, Linda M. 1991. "Caring for children." *The American Enterprise* May/June: 34–37.

Cook, Thomas D., and Thomas Curtin. 1987. "The mainstream and the underclass: Why are the differences so salient and the similarities so unobtrusive?" In *Social Comparison, Social Justice, and Relative Deprivation: Theoretical, Empirical, and Policy Perspectives,* eds. John C. Masters and William P. Smith, 218–264. Hillsdale, NJ: Erlbaum Associates.

Darity, William A., and Samuel L. Meyers. 1984. "Does

welfare dependency cause female headship? The case of the black family." *Journal of Marriage and the Family* 46: 765–79.

Garfinkel, Irwin, and Sara McLanahan. 1986. *Single Mothers and Their Children: A New American Dilemma.* Washington, D.C.: The Urban Institute.

Hannerz, Ulf. 1969. *Soulside: Inquiries into Ghetto Culture and Community.* New York: Columbia University Press.

Holloman, Regina, and Fannie E. Lewis. 1978. "The 'clan:' Case study of a black extended family in Chicago." In *The Extended Family in Black Societies,* eds. Dimitri Shimkin, Edith Shimkin, and Dennis A. Frate, 201–38. The Hague: Mouton.

Jarrett, Robin L. 1992. "A family case study: An examination of the underclass debate." In *Qualitative Methods in Family Research,* eds. Jane Gilgun, Gerald Handel, and Kerry Daly, 172–97. Newbury Park, Calif.: Sage.

———. 1993. "Focus group interviewing with low-income minority populations: A research experience." In *Conducting Successful Focus Groups,* ed. David Morgan, 184–201. Newbury Park, Calif.: Sage.

Joe, Tom. 1984. *The 'Flip-Side' of Black Families Headed by Women: The Economic Status of Men.* Center for the Study of Social Policy, Washington, D.C.

Ladner, Joyce. 1971. *Tomorrow's Tomorrow: The Black Woman.* New York: Anchor Books.

Lemann, Nicholas. 1986. "The origins of the underclass." *The Atlantic Monthly* 258: 31–55.

Lewis, Oscar. 1965. "The culture of poverty." *Scientific American* 215: 3–9.

———. 1966. *La Vida.* New York: Random House.

Liebow, Elliot. 1967. *Tally's Corner: A Study of Negro Street Corner Men.* Boston: Little, Brown.

Mead, Lawrence. 1986. *Beyond Entitlement: The Social Obligations of Citizenship.* New York: Free Press.

Moynihan, Daniel P. 1965. *The Negro Family: The Case for National Action.* Washington, D.C.: Office of Policy Planning and Research. U.S. Department of Labor.

Murray, Charles. 1984. *Losing Ground: American Social Policy, 1950–1980.* New York: Basic Books.

Rainwater, Lee. 1970. *Behind Ghetto Walls: Black Families in a Federal Slum.* Chicago: Adline Publishing Company.

———. 1987. *Class, Culture, Poverty, and Welfare.* Unpublished manuscript.

Schulz, David. 1969. *Coming Up Black: Patterns of Ghetto Socialization.* Englewood Cliffs, NJ: Prentice Hall.

Stack, Carol. 1974. *All Our Kin: Strategies for Survival in a Black Community.* New York: Harper and Row.

Staples, Robert. 1985. "Changes in black family structure: The conflict between family ideology and structural conditions." *Journal of Marriage and the Family* 47: 1005–13.

Sullivan, Mercer. 1985. *Teen Fathers in the Inner-City.* New York: Ford Foundation.

Testa, Mark, Nan Marie Astone, Marilyn Krogh, and Kathryn M. Neckerman. 1989. "Employment and marriage among inner-city fathers." *Annals of the American Academy of Political and Social Sciences* 501: 79–91.

Williams, Brett. 1992. "Us and them," *The Nation* 255: 371–72.

Williams, Terry, and William Kornblum. 1985. *Growing Up Poor.* Lexington, Mass.: Lexington Books.

Wilson, William J. 1987. *The Truly Disadvantaged: The Inner City, the Underclass, and Public Policy.* Chicago: University of Chicago Press.

Yanagisako, Sylvia J. 1979. "Family and household: The analysis of domestic groups." *Annual Review of Anthropology* 8: 161–205.

Zollar, Ann C. 1985. *A Member of the Family: Strategies for Black Family Continuity.* Chicago: Nelson-Hall.

Think about It

1. How do cultural and structural frameworks differ in their explanations of poor, single-parent households? Why does Jarrett maintain that qualitative research studies (like hers) provide depth in understanding structural constraints?

2. Why does Jarrett argue that poor, never-married black mothers have conventional (rather than "deviant") attitudes and aspirations about marriage and family life?

3. What strategies and coping processes did women in Jarrett's study use to maintain their families despite poverty and absent biological fathers?

31

Social Class, Interaction, and Perceptions about Other Ethnic Groups: The Case of Korean Americans

Kyeyoung Park

Ethnic families don't function in isolation. They interact with the dominant culture and with other ethnic groups. Are there social class similarities and differences in these interactions? Kyeyoung Park explores the question of how workplace encounters structure the racial ideologies that Korean immigrants—especially small business proprietors, workers, and professionals—have about white and ethnic groups across different social class segments.*

In analyzing the ethnic encounters involving Koreans in workplaces, I found that class differences produce different ethnic conceptions. The class segments of Korean Americans—worker, businessperson, and professional—are each associated with distinct ideologies of race and ethnicity derived from differences in their workplace interactions. For example, African American allegations of Korean racism apply mostly to small business proprietors; Korean American professionals and workers are almost never mentioned. These Koreans' ethnic attitudes, in fact, stand in contrast to those of small business proprietors. Professionals are more involved in the American mainstream and are more likely to experience direct racial discrimination by white Americans. Even more than professionals, Korean workers in American businesses experience discrimination. Nevertheless, small business proprietors are the pivotal group because they are the main agents in developing a Korean immigrant racial ideology.

*Park's study was based on in-depth interviews with 109 Korean immigrants in New York City. Ed.

Source: From Kyeyoung Park, *The Korean American Dream: Immigrants and Small Business in New York City* (Ithaca, NY: Cornell University Press, 1997), 144–54. Copyright © 1997 Cornell University Press. Used by permission of the publisher, Cornell University Press.

SMALL BUSINESS PROPRIETORS

For Koreans in small businesses, ethnic encounters arise in their day-to-day operations. For the most part, these businesses provide a setting in which Koreans serve non-Korean customers. Both business proprietors and workers are aware of their subordinate position to white Americans in the U.S. system of ethnic stratification. They understand their role in replacing white American small business proprietors via "ethnic succession" and know that whites are aware of this as well.

After the Immigration Reform and Control Act of 1986, Korean business proprietors began to hire more non-Koreans, the majority of them immigrants from Latin American countries, who now compose more than one-third of their work force.[1] These circumstances have made Koreans more aware of which ethnicities they can consider subordinate to themselves. Korean small business proprietors also encounter various ethnic groups at their workplaces as suppliers and customers. White Americans are said to be problematic—difficult to please and sometimes even threatening lawsuits. Some shopkeepers are too ready to suspect African Americans of being potential shoplifters, primarily because of rumor or bad experiences. This has created situations of conflict.[2]

Latin Americans as the Best Customers

Many Korean small business proprietors in Queens say that Latin Americans are their best customers. Some express it even more precisely: They define the best business area as half Latin American and half African American. It is evident that their choice of business neighborhood is by and large restricted by their amount of capital; however, it is unclear why they prefer these minority neighborhoods. They admit that one can make more money in a white neighborhood but say that they prefer the friendliness of Latin Americans and African Americans. They do not feel the same warmth from white customers. Another reason I have heard is the claim that Latin Americans and African Americans are easier to deal with as customers. They do not take as much time to buy goods, are not difficult to please, and make fewer complaints than white customers do. Clearly most Korean/African American relationships are seen by Koreans as cordial rather than hostile.

In the following examples, I reproduce ethnic characteristics as they were presented to me. In Elmhurst, most white customers are older persons and in many cases less prosperous than new immigrants. Two Elmhurst Korean business operators identified Latin Americans as the best customers and whites as the most difficult, but each has a different explanation for this opinion.

Mrs. Choi runs a grocery. Among her customers, she said, "Latin Americans are the best. They are easier to deal with, without complaints. I have customers such as Colombian, Puerto Rican, German, Italian, and Jewish. Colombians just buy what they want, whereas Germans are very particular and bargain over even one penny." Mrs. Lee runs a dry-cleaning store. She said:

> Seventy percent of my customers are Latin Americans, and the rest are Asians. Spanish people are good customers: They behave as gentlemen and are kind and friendly. They are people with whom I feel intimacy. Among Asians, Indians are difficult: They bring filthy clothes; they bargain over prices. Fil-

ipinos are clean. There are also some Chinese and Japanese. Among the Latin Americans, Colombians are a majority. But those elderly whites who could not leave this neighborhood—they are very difficult to please. They are stingy. At first they ignore you. Later, if you perform well, they accept it but even give back advice. In the past I was made to feel inferior to them because of their racism. Now I do not care any more.

Mr. Chung who runs a fish market in Washington Heights, Manhattan, and lives in Sunnyside, shared his experience: "Now I have hired two black workers. Both of them are very good. Because my store is in Washington Heights, 60 percent of my customers are Dominican; 25 percent are Puerto Rican; 10 percent are black; and the rest include Chinese, Japanese, or Korean. From my observation, Dominicans are a little richer than Puerto Ricans. Dominicans are moody people. There are a few Greek and Jewish customers, but I do not like to deal with them because they are very particular."

Mr. Kim, who has operated businesses in different neighborhoods on his trajectory to establishment, mentioned his wariness in dealing with both white and African American customers: "I used to run a shoe repair shop in the Bronx. I could make $550 or $600 per week. However, as it was in a Jewish neighborhood, people were very stingy. Even now, I do not want to run any business in such a neighborhood. After that, I ran a general merchandise store in an African American area in Brooklyn for one year. Although it was a good business area, I was always worried that they would quarrel with me and that someone would attack me. Now I operate an automobile body shop in Corona."

Differences in Business Practice

In some cases, Korean business proprietors arrive at their evaluations of various ethnicities through their experiences with customers in different types of businesses. For instance, Koreans do not ask for discounts at beauty salons, but they do at drugstores.

Accordingly, Koreans are considered the best customers by hair stylists but the worst by pharmacists. Perhaps this is due to the history of different business practices in Korea. In general, merchants have a positive view of customers who are big spenders. There is no doubt that Koreans buy much more than any other group at Korean groceries, and in those stores they are preferred customers.

Mrs. Nam, a hairdresser who owns a beauty salon, commented on ethnic differences: "Seventy percent of my customers are Korean, and the rest are Hispanic, Jewish, Chinese, and Indian. Among them, the Jews are usually elderly, and Hispanics are both young and old. [When I asked more questions, she clarified that most Hispanics are Colombians.] Koreans are the best customers because they are very generous, and they are not difficult to please. Hispanics are fine, too. Jewish people often bargain over the price. Those who bargain over the price also tend to complain a lot about other things."

I asked Mr. Kim, who runs a drugstore, why Koreans are good customers at Korean-run beauty salons yet the worst at Korean-run drugstores. He shared his experiences: "Eighty percent of my customers are Korean, and the rest are Hispanic and white. In my opinion, there is little difference between any of them. However, Koreans are used to bargaining over prices and want to buy things on credit. If it is too high, Koreans simply do not buy it. Other ethnic groups accept my price. Besides, Koreans ask for medicine without a doctor's prescription. They do not know that in American there is a strict division of labor between doctors and pharmacists. My suppliers from pharmaceutical companies and medicine wholesalers are Jewish or Italian."

Mr. Rim, who runs a Korean supermarket, noted: "Eighty-five percent of my customers are Korean, and the rest are Japanese, Chinese, Indian, and Hispanics. Non-Korean customers do not tend to buy a lot, unlike Korean customers. But they do not complain and greet me in a friendly way."

Another situation is more complicated. Korean sewing factory owners often ask, Why don't Latin Americans work as hard as Koreans do? Asians, they say, are better educated than non-Asians. Mr. Won remarked:

> At the present time, there are forty-five workers, including those who do home work only, who are around ten. Among them, thirty are Korean, eight Chinese, five Spanish, two Indian. Usually those who want work come directly to us, and then we screen them. I hire workers of different ethnic groups. Chinese are very diligent, working patiently. Spanish do not seem to accept heavy pressures of work, working exactly eight hours a day and five days a week. They do not seem to be quick in understanding the work either. On the contrary, in my experience, Koreans are very quick to learn the work, making fast progress. But they are not faithful: if it is no longer in their interest, they leave this job immediately. However, as members of the same ethnic group, they are sympathetic to their employer, working more than they are required.

Mr. Pai sees economic interests as more important than primordial attachments in defining his relations with other Koreans. What matters to him is profit, not ethnicity. "I distribute beer and other drinks to 150 or 200 retailers. Half are American stores, and the other half are Korean ones. If I make a comparison, although there seems to be a little difference, more Korean store owners tend to write bad checks, buy on credit, or get nervous about prices. This is because of their lack of capital."

WORKERS

Workers have ideologies of ethnicity markedly different from those of their employers. Among other things, they emphasize the differences between Korean and American workplaces. They often state that Korean employers exploit their workers more than Americans do. Nevertheless, they experience paternalistic or more reciprocal relationships with their Korean employers. One important reason to work for Korean employers is to learn how to run small businesses.

American Workplaces

Although most Korean immigrants work in Korean business establishments, an increasing number work for other Americans. In addition to experiencing language and cultural barriers, Korean workers often feel that they are not trusted by white employers. Mr. Chun, who worked at an automobile body shop, and recalled: "I was skilled and worked hard, so they treated me well because they needed me. I had both white and black American colleagues. The whites were very cool and suspicious of me as a tongyanggye.[3] The blacks were very friendly and got along well with me. In my analysis, white Americans only know themselves and their own kind, and they are ethnocentric and arrogant."

To make matters worse, some Koreans feel that they are not respected when working for non-Koreans. Mr. Chung, now a fish market owner, told me: "When I was working at an American business, the boss lost something. From then on I was treated peculiarly. I was investigated three times. That did not happen to the other workers. I felt dishonored. And I was very upset. Finally, I called the police and asked them to investigate me and search my residence. How else could I clear myself from dishonor? Eventually I quit the job."

Although some report bad experiences with other minority workers, many Korean workers describe friendly relations. Mr. Nam is an example:

Ordinary Americans seem to be backward. They have too many payments to make and concentrate on trying to enjoy their weekends. On the contrary, Koreans toil sixteen or eighteen hours per day in order to build up savings. For this, Americans make fun of us. At the bakery, I saw a second-generation Puerto Rican who had both a strange inferiority feeling and American pride. When I used to work hard, including overtime, he used to say, "Damn Chinese, you never know how to rest." But on the weekends he would spend all his money. Then he would ask me to lend him $10 or $20. I did, but I used to say, "You see, I am not a slave to money. I

make an effort to work hard in order to save for the future. Don't you understand?"

Korean Workplaces

In many Korean workplaces, employers hire non-Koreans, usually for specific jobs. There is, however, a difference in wage scales based on ethnicity as well as gender. One often observes job hierarchy: Koreans and sometimes white Americans hold a more central position than other workers do. Korean workers frequently become sympathetic to the lives of their non-Korean co-workers by talking about problems of immigrant life and sharing work, meals, and leisure time. One Korean worker expressed relief that he was not born a Mexican because they are paid less and exploited more by employers. At the Korean greengrocery where he worked, he and his Mexican fellow worker shared the 8 P.M. to 8 A.M. night shift, six days a week. While he was paid $350 a week as cashier, the Mexican worker was paid $200.

Mr. Ha told me that there are different job descriptions and wages based on gender and ethnicity at the Korean wholesale store where he works. "Besides the employer and his wife, there are twelve workers: Three are Spanish, and two are [Korean] female accountants. [All were paid less than Korean male workers.] Whereas Spanish workers only do sales for Spanish-speaking customers, Korean workers do many tasks. I am supposed to do various jobs, such as sales, shipping, and arranging stock."

Mr. Kim explained the different pay systems for Koreans and non-Koreans at a Korean garment factory, where he worked after leaving an American firm: "Americans are fair about working hours and payment. But in my opinion, Koreans just try to exploit other Koreans, taking advantage of them. As soon as I started to work, I was immediately covered with cloth dust. Koreans are too cold toward each other, compared with the Chinese and Japanese I see on the subway. As I see it, Korean women seem to remain at garment factories almost forever. I see that Spanish workers work only for an hourly rate, not piecework. Although they are less enterprising, they are kinder than Koreans. As I spoke English better, they became friendly to me."

In Korean small businesses, Korean workers are often directed by their employers to deal with suspected shoplifters. Ironically, customers often believe that these workers have negative attitudes toward them. These Korean employees often complain that their employers force them to watch customers more than is really necessary. Some workers do not see any ethnic or racial differences in the behavior of customers. Mr. Lee's first job was at a greengrocery in Brooklyn, where most customers were African Americans. After that job, he worked for his uncle in a grocery, doing odd jobs. At this store, most customers were Italian. When I asked him to compare these customers with the African Americans at the other greengrocery, he said there was little difference. He complained only that he had to work harder for his uncle than he did at the other store.

PROFESSIONALS

Interestingly, two doctors I interviewed, a pediatrician and a physician, arrived at differing evaluations of their Korean and other patients. This may be related to their specialization. While the pediatrician deals primarily with mothers of babies and young children, the physician deals with adults of both sexes.

The pediatrician, Dr. Choi, said that 80 percent of her patients are Korean and 20 percent are "American," which she said included whites, Indians, Latin Americans, and others. According to her, "American" patients tend to ask why they have to take a prescribed drug, but Koreans patients do not. Korean patients do not directly question their doctors, even if they have questions. In her analysis, Koreans are deferential to authority, unlike her other patients.

About 75 percent of Dr. Park's adult patients are African American, 10 percent white, and the rest Korean and Latin American. Comparing his non-Korean patients with Koreans, he said, "They do not call the doctor for matters other than treatment, whereas Koreans call me for personal advice." Thus, he has to spend more time than is medically necessary with Korean patients. This is also no doubt true for Korean professionals such as lawyers, accountants, and teachers. Due to the language barrier, however, Dr. Park also needs to spend more time treating non-Korean patients. For a thorough examination, he has to ask more questions and examine them more carefully than he does Korean patients. Ironically, his non-Korean patients like Dr. Park's predicament because they feel they are getting a very careful examination.

Many doctors run their own clinics catering to fellow Koreans. Dr. Song, a gynecologist, is one such case. He came to America in 1974. Three years ago he opened his own office in Elmhurst. Now he works both at his office and Flushing Hospital and Medical Center. His wife helps him with work in his office. They have hired a Korean receptionist and Korean nurses. He compared his work at the hospital with his office work: "As I work at my own office, I take more responsibility, besides being kind to patients and more diligent." He described Korean patients that he sees in Elmhurst: "They are not punctual. They should follow the American way, for example, making appointments about seeing the doctor. Nevertheless I feel bad about patients without health insurance. I cannot hospitalize patients or give adequate medical treatment without insurance. In Korea I could do everything, including operations, by myself, and I could take their circumstances into consideration. Here I am limited by the system." In his overall evaluation about his life in America, he stated, "I can have my own private life as a medical doctor. Life here is rather simple. In Korea my family and I were bothered a lot due to the complicated social life, particularly social expectations for a medical doctor, such as service to the community."

Dr. Lee, an herb doctor and acupuncturist, finds Korean patients to be more argumentative than his non-Korean ones. This situation reflects doctor-client interaction in the Korean system of medicine, where patients are expected to interact with their doctor. This dialogue, however, seems to be limited to Korean folk medicine. His non-Korean patients, who usually present neck and back problems, respond well to his instructions and keep returning for treatment. But, his Korean patients do not pay enough attention to what he says. They also stop treatment suddenly or arrive at his office without any appointment. Like Korean lawyers and insurance brokers, who also complain that Korean customers are more argumentative, he now prefers non-Korean clients.

Ms. Ahn works as a registered nurse for a private Queens hospital. She commented on her job:

> My colleagues are quite international: five Indians, three Filipinos, two Koreans, one Thai, one Jewish American, one Irish, one Israeli, one black American, two Italian Americans, and one Cuban. I have worked for five years as an operating room nurse. Half of my colleagues are very experienced. Most nurses work in the ward, taking care of patients in need of intensive care. They have a shift from seven to three. Nurses in the operating room have a nine-to-five shift. Nurses with the same shift socialize together. In terms of hierarchy in the nurses' world, there are supervisors (always more supply than demand); head nurse (it takes several years to move from staff nurse to head nurse); staff nurses, who are R.N.s; nurses' aides; and porters, who are male. For operating room nurses, promotion is very slow. Besides nurses, there are M.D.s, physicians' assistants, surgeons' assistants, and medical technicians.

She has no problems with her supervisor. Regarding M.D.s, she said, "If they get on my nerves, I try to get on their nerves." Because of their high status, the doctors socialize only among themselves. At her hospital, 80 percent of the M.D.s are Jewish. Many medical technicians are U.S. citizens, some Latin American immigrants, and a few Chinese immigrants. About 70 percent of her patients are white. "In general, Asian patients are

passive and more cooperative and have a good reputation at the hospital," she stated.

James, a certified public accountant, commented that Korean clients expect more than just his professional services; and for the extra service that they demand, he accordingly charges higher fees. Most of his clients are Koreans; only a few are not. He estimates that more than half the work he does for his Korean customers is beyond a certified public accountant's normal services—for example, helping them open a bank account or explaining the American educational system.

Korean professionals who work in large American firms, unlike those in private practice, often encounter ethnic discrimination from Americans—or what is called the "glass ceiling." Mr. Suh, a medical technician, explained: "Although there is racism, things remain calm on the surface. Employers prefer Americans educated in the United States when they are considering promotion. Korean professionals tend to advance quickly, which makes people of other ethnicities jealous. However, other Asians who face less language difficulty, like Filipinos or Indians, get better treatment than Korean and Chinese professionals."

THE IMPORTANCE OF PRACTICE IN CONSTRUCTIONS OF ETHNICITY

As Koreans in America modify their ethnic conceptions through experience, some unfortunately transfer the negative treatment they receive from the white majority to other minorities. Others, however, are sensitive to the plight of other minorities. Some Koreans who have experienced racial discrimination from white Americans apparently transfer this racism to African Americans. Mr. Kim, a pharmacist, said: "From my own experience, I feel a kind of discrimination as a minority, visibly or invisibly. When I lived in Yonkers, a white store owner assumed that kind of attitude, seeing me only as a tongyanggye. When I worked as a pharmacist at the hospital, I was treated as a professional but only in the workplace. Beyond that, they knew nothing about me. They even thought that Chinese, Japanese, and Koreans speak the same language. Now I feel that sometimes I myself imitate that kind of attitude toward black customers, suspecting them all of shoplifting, which is a shame."

Mr. Suh, a sewing machine store sales worker, had a negative opinion of Latin American customers because he was told they were potential thieves. Later, when operating his own store, he was helped a great deal by the Chilean former owner and also patronized by Latin American customers, whom he now appreciates. "The local Latin Americans here do not speak English well either. I have few problems dealing with them. Furthermore, I feel that Colombians are better customers than Koreans, who often bargain over price."

The move to New York has given Korean immigrants a new awareness of being Asian in America (tongyanggye mikukin), a heightened consciousness of themselves as a minority enclosed within a sometimes menacing, sometimes friendly, world of more powerful whites. This racial consciousness provides a potential bond with other Asian immigrants. But Korean encounters with other ethnicities are complex, and their attitudes reflect diverse workplace experiences in diverse neighborhoods. These new ethnic encounters and ethnic constructions also depend on class. Different class segments within the Korean immigrant community develop different constructions of ethnicity.

NOTES

1. This is due to more availability of Latin American undocumented workers than Korean workers as well as changes in immigration laws, such as employer sanctions.
2. Since the early 1980s, there have been increasing complaints, tensions, and dissatisfaction toward Korean immigrant merchants in African American neighborhoods.

Some residents have initiated boycott campaigns against Korean stores in New York, Philadelphia, Washington, D.C., Chicago, Atlanta, and Los Angeles. (See E. Chang [1990] for details.) The 1990 African American boycott of Korean grocers in Brooklyn is the most widely publicized example: "Since January, 1990, Brooklyn's Flatbush section had been embroiled by a black boycott of two Korean grocers that began after a Haitian woman accused the Koreans of assaulting her in an argument over a dollar worth of fruit" (*Time,* 28 May 1990).

3. As Korean immigrants spend time in a racially divided America, they learn that being Asian American and immigrant, *tongyanggye mikukin* (people in the United States but from the Asian continent) is a stigma. Literally, it means those Americans who can be traced to Asia. *Tongyang* means "east," indicating countries such as China, Korea, and Japan. It is unclear if this term also includes Indians, Filipinos, Thais, and so on.

REFERENCES

Chang, Edward Tea. 1990. "New Urban Crisis: Korean–Black Conflicts in Los Angeles." Ph.D. diss., University of California, Berkeley.

? *Think about It*

1. How do small business proprietors perceive their white and ethnic customers? How do these evaluations vary across different types of businesses?
2. According to Park, "Workers have ideologies of ethnicity markedly different from those of their employers." Describe these differences in white and Korean workplaces.
3. How do professional Korean Americans evaluate their Korean and non-Korean patients and clients? Do you think that the evaluations of the business owners, workers, and professionals in this study are generalizable to other Korean immigrants in similar settings?

CHAPTER 7

Violence and Other Family Crises

This chapter provides some of the research on family-related problems across the life course in diverse households. Both the literature in general and the readings in Chapter 7 reflect two themes in explaining youth and adult violence, drug use, and other difficulties in ethnic families. The first theme, evident in previous chapters, is that many of the difficulties confronting ethnic families arise from structural factors such as discrimination, poverty, and unemployment. The second theme is that *acculturation*—the process of adapting to the language, values, beliefs, roles, and other characteristics of the host culture—triggers family conflict and tension, especially among recently arrived and second-generation immigrants.

In their study of adolescents in public schools, Enid Gruber, Ralph J. DiClemente, and Martin M. Anderson found that problem-prone behavior was high for all groups. However,

American Indian youth—especially American Indian females—engaged in risk-taking behavior (violence, sexual behavior, substance abuse) at much higher rates than black or white adolescents (Reading 32).[1] In this and other studies, researchers have found that troubles in the home affect adolescents greatly. American Indian adolescents who report that they often worry about the economic survival of their family, about domestic abuse, and about their parents' use of drugs have especially poor levels of health and more involvement in risk behaviors.[2] Black children with emotional and behavioral problems are more likely to have been raised in homes where one or both parents have engaged in crime, have a history of psychiatric or substance abuse problems, or have been victims of violence.[3] In addition, black, Latino, and American Indian youth may engage in self-destructive behavior because of low self-esteem and sexual abuse, a sense of alienation from their communities, or feelings of helplessness in the face of racism and discrimination.[4] Thus, a combination of interpersonal, family, and structural factors explains why white, black, and ethnic children engage in problematic behavior.

Acculturation also seems to have a negative impact on adolescent behavior. In a study of second-generation Asian Indian adolescents, Gauri Bhattacharya maintains that the acculturation process creates intergenerational conflict, which, in turn, contributes to adolescents' use of alcohol, tobacco, and other drugs (Reading 33). In a study of Asian Indian adults, different researchers reached a similar conclusion: intergenerational conflict (especially issues relating to the children's dating and marriage choices) "was the single most important source of concerns adversely affecting the quality of life."[5] There is also some evidence that acculturation increases drug use among Latino adolescents as teenagers (and adults) socialize more frequently with dominant group members who go to bars, clubs, and parties and who are substance users.[6] In contrast, maintaining one's cultural identity and being attached to one's ethnic affiliation through family and friends can decrease the risks of drug use.[7] Some of the most sobering and startling data on black and ethnic adolescents (as well as adults) show that acculturation difficulties, poverty, discrimination, family turmoil, parental substance abuse, disturbed parent–child relations, and a lack of social supports can even lead to suicide.[8]

In addition to drug use and other risky behavior, the National Association of Anorexia Nervosa and Associated Disorders estimates that at least 7 million women and 1 million men between age 10 and the early 20s suffer from anorexia nervosa and bulimia.[9] Most anorexics and bulimics are believed to be young white women of relatively high socioeconomic status who suffer from low self-esteem and a negative body image and tend to be perfectionistic in whatever they undertake.[10] Becky W. Thompson argues, however, that eating problems also affect black women and Latina, lesbian and heterosexual (Reading 34). She maintains that rather than being obsessed with their looks, many girls and women develop eating problems as a response to the demands of acculturation, structural factors (such as racism, sexism, classism, and heterosexism), and interpersonal traumas (such as sexual, emotional, or physical abuse). In effect, Thompson contends, eating disorders reflect survival strategies instead of personal frailties.

Domestic violence is another widespread problem across both white and ethnic households. Although women are abusive (at least in white and black households, according to the available research), they are far less likely than men to use lethal weapons such as knives and guns. Moreover, they are more likely than men to sustain serious physical injuries because they are usually smaller than their partners or because they are attacked when they are pregnant and especially vulnerable.[11] Although most of the research and attention on domestic violence has focused on white, middle-class women, the literature on women of color has been increasing. In Reading 35, for example, Doris Williams Campbell, Beckie Masaki, and Sara Torres present some recent data on the prevalence of and reasons for domestic violence in black, Latino, and Asian American communities. They conclude that domestic violence is a widespread problem in many black and ethnic households.

Other recent research echoes these conclusions. Among Latino subgroups, for example, wife assault rates of Mexican-Americans and Puerto Rican Americans are similar to those in Anglo-American families (while reports of wife assault in the Cuban community are nearly nonexistent). Structural factors including unemployment and poverty underlie much of the abuse. Drug or alcohol abuse, with or without work-related stress, is also associated with increased risks for assaults by husbands against wives in Latino and American Indian families.[12]

Campbell and her colleagues also found some differences across white, black, Latino, and Asian American communities. For example, Latino and Asian American spouses were more likely than their white and black counterparts to see domestic violence as a private matter rather than a public issue. As a result, the wives are less likely to report abuse or to seek help—especially in the presence of language barriers, fear of deportation, and concern about being ostracized by extended families or the community.[13] Thus, low acculturation might discourage leaving an abusive situation.

Toward the end of the life course, many older family members benefit from loving relationships with their children, grandchildren, and other family members (see Chapter 9). In some cases, however, spouses or children abuse older family members. There is a paucity of research on elder abuse among ethnic families. One of the recent exceptions is Quyen Kim Le's study of the prevalence and characteristics of mistreatment of the elderly in Vietnamese families (Reading 36). Although Le found no physical abuse, she suggests that both acculturation stress and the traditional emphasis on filial piety[14] influence other forms of abuse. In a study of one hundred elderly Korean Americans in Los Angeles County, Janet Chang and Ailee Moon found only two cases of physical abuse (the daughter-in-law was the perpetrator in both instances). There was a wide range of other forms of mistreatment, but financial abuse was the most common, such as a son's taking his elderly parent's Supplemental Security Income (SSI) benefits.[15] Most of the reported neglect cases reflect adjustment problems experienced by both the adult children and the elderly parents. While children are adapting to language barriers, cultural differences, and employment difficulties, many elderly parents remain dependent on their children for transportation, making doctor appointments, and taking care of other personal business. As a result, parents are vulnerable to mistreatment by children who feel overburdened by the increased responsibility.

NOTES

1. Problem-prone behavior is a much more serious problem for adolescents who have dropped out of high school. See Frederick Beauvais, Ernest L. Chavez, Eugene R. Oetting, Jerry L. Deffenbacher, and Greg R. Cornell, "Drug Use, Violence and Victimization among White American, Mexican American, and American

Indian Dropouts, Students with Academic Problems, and Students in Good Academic Standing," *Journal of Counseling Psychology* 43 (1996): 292–99.

2. *The State of Native American Youth Health,* www.cyfc.umn.edu/Diversity/nativeamer.html (accessed June 9, 2000). See also Ann Marie Machamer and Enid Gruber, "Secondary School, Family, and Educational Risk: Comparing American Indian Adolescents and Their Peers," *Journal of Educational Research* 91 (July/August 1998): 357–69.

3. Hector F. Myers and Sylvie Taylor, "Family Contributions to Risk and Resilience in African American Children," *Journal of Comparative Family Studies* 29 (Spring 1998): 215–29.

4. See Katherine Fennelly, Patricia Mulkeen, and Carina Giusti, "Coping with Racism and Discrimination: The Experience of Young Latino Adolescents," in *Resiliency in Native American and Immigrant Families,* ed. Hamilton I. McCubbin, Elizabeth A. Thompson, Anne I. Thompson, and Julie E. Fromer (Thousand Oaks, CA: Sage, 1998): 369–82; Anthony E. O. King, "Understanding Violence among Young African American Males: An Afrocentric Perspective," *Journal of Black Studies* 28 (September 1997): 79–96; Robert W. Robin, Barbara Chester, Jolene K. Rasmussen, James M. Jaranson, and David Goldman, "Prevalence, Characteristics, and Impact of Childhood Sexual Abuse in a Southwestern American Indian Tribe," *Child Abuse & Neglect* 21 (August 1997): 769–87; and Gloria J. Romero, Gail E. Wyatt, Tamra Burns Loeb, Jennifer Vargas Carmona, and Beatriz M. Solis, "The Prevalence and Circumstances of Child Sexual Abuse among Latina Women," *Hispanic Journal of Behavioral Sciences* 21 (August 1999): 351–67.

5. Snehendu B. Kar, Armando Jimenez, Kevin Campbell, and Felicia Sze, "Acculturation and Quality of Life: A Comparative Study of Japanese-Americans and Indo-Americans," *Amerasia Journal* 24 (Spring 1998): 129–42.

6. See Saki Cabrera Strait, "Drug Use among Hispanic Youth: Examining Common and Unique Contributing Factors," *Hispanic Journal of Behavioral Sciences* 21 (February 1999): 89–103.

7. Judith S. Brook, Marin Whiteman, Elinor B. Balka, Pe Thet Win, and Michal D. Gursen, "Drug Use among Puerto Ricans: Ethnic Identity as a Protective Factor," *Hispanic Journal of Behavioral Sciences* 20 (May 1998): 241–54.

8. See Chapters 9 through 12 in Silvia Sara Canetto and David Lester, eds. *Women and Suicidal Behavior* (New York: Springer, 1995).

9. Anorexia nervosa is characterized by fear of obesity and the conviction that one is "fat" despite normal body weight. As a result of this fear, anorexics starve themselves. Bulimia is characterized by a cyclical pattern of eating binges followed by self-induced vomiting, fasting, excessive exercise, or the use of diuretics or laxatives.

10. X. P. Szabo and M. J. T. Blanche, "Perfectionism in Anorexia Nervosa," *American Journal of Psychiatry* 154 (January 1997): 132.

11. Richard J. Gelles, "Violence and Pregnancy: Are Pregnant Women at Greater Risk of Abuse?" *Journal of Marriage and the Family* 50 (August 1988): 841–47.

12. Glenda Kaufman Kantor, Jana L. Jasinski, and Etiony Aldarondo, "Sociocultural Status and Incidence of Marital Violence in Hispanic Families," *Violence and Victims* 9 (1994): 207–22; Jana L. Jasinski, Nancy L. Asdigian, and Glenda Kaufman Kantor, "Ethnic Adaptations to Occupational Strain: Work-Related Stress, Drinking, and Wife Assault among Anglo and Hispanic Husbands," *Journal of Interpersonal Violence* 12 (December 1997): 814–31; U.S. Department of Justice, Bureau of Justice Statistics, *American Indians and Crime* (Washington, DC, February 1999); Joe Gorton and Nikki R. Van Hightower, "Intimate Victimization of Latina Farm Workers: A Research Summary," *Hispanic Journal of Behavioral Science* 21 (November 1999): 502–07.

13. Kimberly A. Huisman, "Wife Battering in Asian American Communities: Identifying the Service Needs of an Overlooked Segment of the U.S. Population," *Violence against Women* 2 (September 1996): 260–83; Susan B. Sorenson, "Violence against Women: Examining Ethnic Differences and Commonalities," *Evaluation Review* 20 (April 1996): 123–45.

14. One aspect of filial piety is the expectation that when parents become old, sons will care for parents physically, emotionally, and financially. Filial piety dictates that an adult son, especially the oldest, and his family live with his parents in the same household and that the daughter-in-law perform all household tasks and caregiving for her parents-in-law with respect, politeness, and sincerity.

15. Janet Chang and Ailee Moon, "Korean American Elderly's Knowledge and Perceptions of Elder Abuse: A Qualitative Analysis of Cultural Factors," *Journal of Multicultural Social Work,* 6, no. 1/2 (1997): 139–54.

32 Risk-Taking Behavior among American Indian, Black, and White Adolescents

Enid Gruber, Ralph J. DiClemente, and Martin M. Anderson

Concern about the physical and emotional health of U.S. adolescents has generated much research among government agencies, nonprofit organizations, and health providers. Enid Gruber, Ralph J. DiClemente, and Martin M. Anderson examine the rates of risk-taking behavior among American Indian adolescents—within and outside of reservation lands—in comparison with rates among their black and white counterparts.

INTRODUCTION

Native American adolescents have consistently been reported to have high rates of morbidity and mortality attributable to risk-taking behaviors.[1-3] Unfortunately, native Americans have not been identified as a separate ethnic grouping in national health or nutrition studies.[1,4] Most available information comes from research conducted at native American reservations or boarding schools[2,5-7] or through the resources of the Indian Health Service.[8] Ethnic group comparisons are usually made to national incidence rates from census data or risk appraisal surveys.[4]

Only one recent survey of a national convenience sample, conducted by the National Adolescent Health Resource Center (NAHRC),[4] has examined the full range of risk-taking behavior and its consequences in young native Americans and Alaska natives. Topics covered included substance use, sexual behavior, delinquency, diet and exercise. The study utilized a survey instrument validated in a number of adolescent populations,

allowing for incidence comparisons to be made to earlier samples. While the NAHRC study made a long needed contribution to our understanding of the health of native American youth, reliance on data collected on or near reservation lands may not be representative of the 75–78% of the native American population who reside away from the reservation setting.[9]

To gain a better understanding of native American adolescent risk behavior outside of the reservation environment as well as its comparability to the behavior of other ethnic groups, native American adolescents should be examined in non-reservation settings along with other youth. This paper reports the results of a secondary analysis of data from a public school–based adolescent health survey from the state of Minnesota which compares rates of native American risk-taking behavior to that of black and white adolescents, as well as to available national statistics on reservation youth.

METHODS

The Minnesota Student Survey (MSS) was developed as a state-level response to the Drug-free Schools and Communities Act of 1986 to evaluate

Source: From Enid Gruber, Ralph J. DiClemente, and Martin M. Anderson, "Risk-Taking Behavior among Native American Adolescents in Minnesota Public Schools: Comparisons with Black and White Adolescents," *Ethnicity & Health* 1 (September 1996): 261–67. Copyright © 1996 Taylor & Francis Ltd. Reprinted by permission. http://www.tandf.cp.uk/journals

school-based alcohol and drug prevention programs. The survey was designed to gather data about student substance use, sexual activity, health knowledge and attitudes, as well as other risk-related behaviors. The MSS was administered in 1989 to 67% of the 6th, 9th and 12th grade students in 390 of Minnesota's 433 school districts. The questionnaire consisted of 149 questions taking approximately 35 minutes to complete, and participation was anonymous and voluntary. Items were drawn from several established measures for adolescents, including the annual national survey, "Monitoring the Future,"[10] Substance Use Disorder Diagnostic Schedule or SUDDS,[11] and the CATOR Adolescent History.[12] A 10% random sample was generated and cross-validated, and that sample of 9th and 12th graders became the subject matter of this study.

Our analyses utilized demographic data, self-reports of risk-taking behavior over the prior year including substance use and delinquency, and recollections of the age of initiation of sexual activity. Our analyses focused on three categories of risk: antisocial behavior, sexual behavior and substance use. We examined gross rates of risk taking by gender and age group, and used contingency table analyses to evaluate the significance of proportional differences between gender and ethnic groups. Then, comparisons were made with other delinquency data collected in a national convenience sample of reservation-based native American adolescents.[2,4]

RESULTS

Of the 6159 9th and 12th grade respondents to the MSS questionnaire (52% male), about 7% were black and 8% native American, with the remainder white non-Hispanic. Rates of risk-taking behavior were high; 38% reported engaging in vandalism in the past year and 39% acknowledged the use of physical violence. Shoplifting was reported by more than 31% of the respondents, with 9% running away from home in the past 12 months. With respect to substance use, about 30% report a pattern of binge drinking, the consumption of five or more drinks per sitting on most drinking occasions; 22.4% drink or use drugs before driving, or drive with friends who first drink or use substances. More than half the sample smoked and lifetime prevalence of marijuana use was 29%.

Fifty-six percent of the sample was sexually active, with more than 10% of that group reporting first intercourse by age 12. Almost 200 male adolescents (3%) acknowledged having forced someone into engaging in sexual activity, and while the numbers were statistically insignificant when comparing ethnic groups, more than 40 females also acknowledged some use of sexual aggression. When trends in sexual initiation are compared by ethnicity and gender (Figure 1), minority adolescents of both sexes are identified as initiating sexual activity at earlier ages relative to white adolescents.

Ethnic differences in all risk taking areas were striking (see Table 1). Native American adolescents reported the highest rates of antisocial behavior and substance use, with black youth tending to have the highest rates of sexual activity. Black and native American young women were twice as likely as their white counterparts to initiate sexual activity by age 13, with black and native American males being twice as likely as whites to have an early sexual debut and to have a history of coercing a partner into sexual activity. As expected, native Americans far exceed the rates of their peers in binge drinking, with native American females falling only 3% behind white male consumption. In addition, native American adolescents have the highest rates of smoking, reporting 25–50% greater use than their white and black counterparts. Low alcohol use in black adolescents of both genders is consistent with other reports, as is lower use of tobacco.[10] The native Americans in the sample also reported higher rates of lifetime marijuana use, with native American females edging out native American males, and doubling the rate of white females.

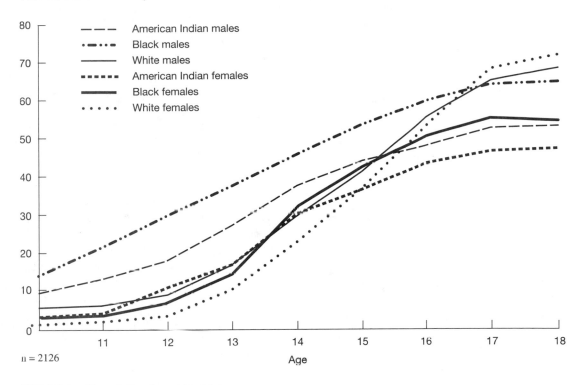

FIGURE 1   Cumulative Age at First Intercourse

The native Americans in the sample were then compared to similar adolescents in a national convenience sample from reservations and rural areas (see Figures 2 and 3). Our comparisons indicate that the MSS sample exceeds most rates of risky activity reported in the NAHRC national sample. Adolescents in the MSS are more likely to report engaging in antisocial activities like violence and vandalism, and report similar rates of sexual activity and marijuana use, giving the comparisons reasonable face validity.

CONCLUSIONS

Comparisons of risk taking behaviors indicate that, in general, native American adolescents have a significantly higher prevalence of risk behaviors relative to white and black peers. Gender-specific

analyses indicate that among females, native Americans reported higher rates of risk taking on nine out of 11 risk measures. Similarly, among males, native Americans reported higher rates of risk taking on eight out of 11 risk indicators. Native Americans were more likely to have engaged in vandalism, violence, shoplifting and running away than their same-sex peers, with shoplifting in native American females exceeding that of both white and black males. Native American females were also approximately two to four times as likely to run away as all other adolescents. More than half of the native American and black males had initiated sexual activity by age 13, compared to a quarter of the white males. For females, native Americans engaged in early intercourse at twice the rate of whites and a quarter more than blacks.

The results are strengthened by the consistency of findings across risk indices. Native Americans

TABLE 1   Rates of Risk-taking by Gender and Ethnicity

Risk-taking activity	Males (%)				Females (%)			
	White	Black	Native American	p	White	Black	Native American	p
Antisocial behavior								
Vandalized	49.9	42.9	60.5	0.00001	24.0	22.0	30.1	0.01
Used violence	48.9	51.6	68.1	0.00001	28.5	34.5	44.0	0.001
Shoplifted	37.2	36.0	42.0	0.01	23.6	20.3	39.6	0.00001
Ran away	6.5	12.5	17.2	0.00001	8.4	8.7	24.0	0.00001
Sexual behavior								
Sexually active	49.2	76.4	68.1	0.00001	41.1	58.7	55.4	0.00001
Early sexual debut	24.4	57.5	50.7	0.00001	15.3	27.1	34.0	0.00001
Ever forced sex	4.6	11.7	10.6	0.00001				
Substance use								
Use cigarettes	54.4	38.7	66.8	0.00001	48.8	44.6	68.3	0.00001
Drink ≥ 5 drinks/setting	38.6	23.1	49.4	0.00001	21.9	5.3	35.7	0.00001
Drive after use	25.3	16.2	27.4	0.01	21.0	5.1	20.5	0.0001
Use marijuana	29.1	40.8	47.9	0.00001	24.2	32.6	48.5	0.00001
n	2680	254	258		2570	173	224	

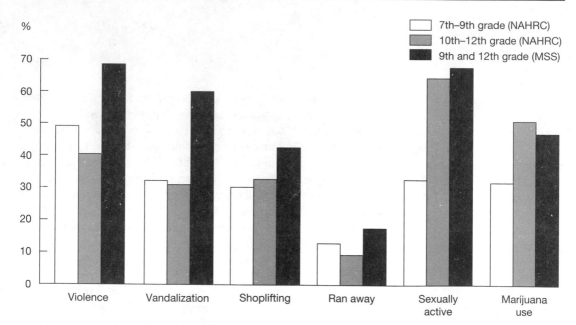

FIGURE 2   Risky Behaviors among Adolescent Native American Males

NAHRC = National Adolescent Health Resource Center; MSS = Minnesota Student Survey.

Source: Adapted from National Adolescent Health Resource Center, *The State of Native American Health,* University of Minnesota. 1992: 23.

%

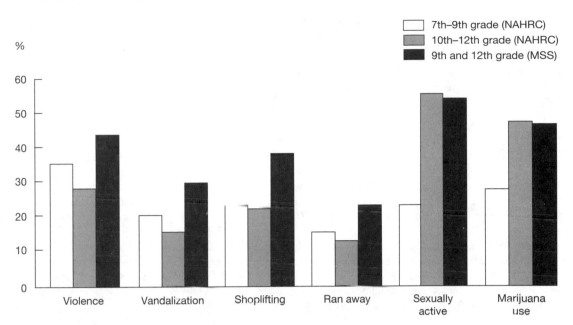

FIGURE 3   Risky Behaviors among Adolescent Native American Females

NAHRC = National Adolescent Health Resource Center; MSS = Minnesota Student Survey.

Source: Adapted from National Adolescent Health Resource Center, *The State of Native American Health,* University of Minnesota, 1992: 23.

of both genders generally report high rates of risk in all three risk categories, with American Indian females often reporting double the rates of other subgroups of both sexes.

When the minority group composition of grade levels is compared, native American representation drops from 10.8% in 9th grade to 4.8% in the 12th grade group, and black representation declines from 8.5% to 5.5%. This would imply that rates of risk in both minority groups may actually be underestimated due to higher high school dropout rates. Risk-related morbidity is an important contributor to overall dropout statistics.[13]

Even when compared to another national sample of native American adolescents[4] taken from reservation settings, these native American adolescents report an exceedingly high rate of risk taking behavior, especially in the area of antisocial activities. This leads us to consider that their

residence and attendance at schools off of the reservation may make them more vulnerable to "acculturation stress"[6] and engaging in behaviors which endanger their health.

While our results appear to be strong, our conclusions should be viewed as cautious and limited. The native American subgroup in the study is sizeable but still represents less than 10% of the total sample. While the original researchers sought a random cross-section of the state's adolescent public school population, issues of geographic distribution remain unclear. Census data also indicate that native American youth in Minnesota are primarily descendants of one tribe (about 97% identify as Chippaqua), so our results may not generalize to other native American groups. Despite these limitations, this study provides a rare comparison of the prevalence of health risk behavior among native American youth relative to black and white peers attending the same public schools. Additional research is needed to understand the social, psychological and cultural determinants of risk taking among native American youth to develop behavioral interventions designed to prevent or reduce risk-related morbidity.

REFERENCES

1. Beauvais F, Oetting ER, Wolf W & Edwards RW. American Indian youth and drugs, 1976–87: a countinuing problem. *Am J Pub Health* 1989; 79: 634–6.
2. Blum RW, Harmon B, Harrish L, Berguisen L & Resnick, MD. American Indian–Alaska native youth. *JAMA* 1992; 267: 1637–44.
3. McShane D. An analysis of mental health research with American Indian youth. *J Adolescence* 1988; 11: 87–116.
4. National Adolescent Health Resource Center (NAHRC). *The State of Native American Health.* University of Minnesota, February 1992.
5. U.S. Congress, Office of Technology Assessment. *Adolescent Health—Volume II: background and effectiveness of selected prevention and treatment services. OTA-H-466* Washington, DC: U.S. Government Printing Office, 1991.
6. Yates A. Current status and future directions of research on the American Indian child. *Am J Psych* 1987; 144: 1135–42.
7. Broussard BA, Johnson A, Himes JH, Story M, Fichtner R, Hauck F, Bachman-Carter K, Hayes, J. Frohlich K, Gray N, Valway S & Fohdes D. Prevalence of obesity in American Indians and Alaska natives. *Am J Clin Nutr* 1991; 53: S1535–42.
8. Dick RW, Manson SM & Beals J. Alcohol use among male and female native American adolescents: patterns and correlates of student drinking in a boarding school. *J Stud Alcohol* 1993; 54: 172–7.
9. U.S. Bureau of the Census, *General population characteristics, American Indian and Alaska native areas (1990 CP-1-1A).* Washington, DC: U.S. Government Printing Office, 1992.
10. Johnston LD, O'Malley PM & Bachman J. *Smoking, drinking and illicit drug use among American secondary school students, college students and young adults, 1975–1991. Vol. 1: Secondary school students. National Institute on Drug Abuse, NIH Pub. No. 93-3480.* Washington, DC: U.S. Government Printing Office, 1992.
11. Davis LJ Jr, Hoffman NG, Morse RM & Luchr IG. Substance use disorder diagnostic schedule (SUDDS): the equivalence and validity of a computer administered and an interviewer administered format. *Alcoholism Clinical and Experimental Research,* 1992; 16: 250–4.
12. Hoffman, NG & Miller NS. Perspectives of effective treatment for alcohol and drug disorders. *Psych Clinics of North America,* 1993; 16: 127–40.
13. Centers for Disease Control. Health risk behaviors among adolescents who do and do not attend school—United States, 1992. *MMWR* 1994; 43: 129–32.

Think about It

1. What are the risk-taking prevalence rates across all the measures of antisocial behavior and substance use for American Indian, black, and white adolescents? How do the rates of specific behaviors vary by gender?
2. Compare the risk-taking behavior of American Indian youth who reside and attend public schools within and outside reservation lands.
3. Why do the researchers feel that their study probably underestimates risk-taking behavior rates, especially among American Indian adolescents? Can you think of other reasons why problem-prone behavior may actually be higher than this study found?

33 Intergenerational Conflict, Acculturation, and Drug Use among Asian Indian Adolescents

Gauri Bhattacharya

The authors of Reading 32 suggest that acculturation stress among American Indian youth might explain the high likelihood of engaging in behaviors that endanger their health. In this selection, Gauri Bhattacharya discusses how the acculturation process can create intergenerational conflict, which, in turn, contributes to the use of alcohol, tobacco, and other drugs. Although Bhattacharya focuses on second-generation Asian Indian adolescents, her discussion includes comparisons with other ethnic groups.

INTRODUCTION

The increasingly multicultural composition of American society underscores the need to understand acculturation issues. Studies have indicated that the acculturation process may create intergenerational conflict. Intergenerational conflict surrounding role expectancies and individual behavior, in turn, tends to destabilize family relations. Thus, family conflict polarizes parents and children, which may lead to deviant behavior and alcohol, tobacco, and other drug (ATOD) use by these children (Szapocznik & Hernandez, 1988; Szapocznik & Truss, 1978; Vega et al., 1993). The primary goal of this paper is to examine intergenerational conflict as a contributing factor in ATOD use among second-generation Asian-Indian adolescents (Asian Americans whose parents emigrated from India).

Demographics

Between 1980 and 1990, the Asian-Indian population grew by 126%, as compared with 108% for Asian Americans overall (U.S. Bureau of the Cen-

Source: From Gauri Bhattacharya, "Drug Use among Asian-Indian Adolescents: Identifying Protective/Risk Factors," *Adolescence* 33 (Spring 1998): 169–84. Copyright © 1998 Libra Publishers, Inc. Reprinted by permission of Libra Publishers, Inc.

sus, 1990). Asian-Indians are now the fourth largest Asian-American group. However, there are significant differences among Asian-Indian, Chinese, and Japanese Americans (U.S. Bureau of the Census, 1990). While the national average for completing four or more years of high school is 66.5%, it is 80.1% for Asian-Indian, 71.3% for Chinese, and 81.6% for Japanese Americans. Also, while 51.9% of Asian-Indian, 36.6% of Chinese, and 26.4% of Japanese Americans have completed four or more years of college, the national average is 16.2%.

ATOD Use

Empirical data on drug use patterns among Asian-American adolescents are limited (Chi, Lubben, & Kitano, 1989); Kitano & Chi, 1990; Sue & Nakamura, 1984; Takaki, 1989). However, studies indicate that as second-generation Asian Americans integrate into society, they may begin using increasingly more alcohol and drugs (Austin, Prendergast, & Lee, 1989; Chi, Lubben, & Kitano, 1989; Fong, 1992; Ross-Sheriff, 1992).

There is little research on intergenerational conflict and ATOD use among Asian-Indian adolescents. Government statistics do not usually break down information by ethnic subgroup. Although it is generally believed that ATOD use is low among Asian-Indian adolescents, low prevalence rates may be a function of underreporting. This underscores the need for valid and culturally sensitive instruments. Another theory is that protective factors may prevent initiation into ATOD use among Asian-Indian adolescents, which underscores the importance of investigating the individual, familial, and systemic factors that bolster resistance to ATOD use.

Multiple sources (e.g., films, literature, anecdotal evidence, case studies, newspaper reports) show increasing identity-related problems within Asian-Indian families, specifically as a result of intergenerational conflict (Jain, 1990; Jindal, 1989; Naipaul, 1990; Saran, 1985). Recognizing the urgency of the problem, community organizations have addressed intergenerational conflict, especially in the areas of family relationships, socialization, drug use/abuse, identity formation, and social perception about the host country. The hope is to eradicate the problem before it becomes endemic, leading to deviant behavior including drug use.

Acculturation

Acculturation has been described as an accumulative social learning process that involves assimilating the values of the host culture while retaining the values of the original culture (Oetting, 1993; Padilla, 1980; Szapocznik & Kurtines, 1980). Studies have identified intergenerational conflict as just one of the stressors of acculturation (Recio Adrados, 1993; Vega et al., 1993). Other stressors include language problems, perceived/ real discrimination, and differences in values and cultural orientations. For this reason, the impact of intergenerational conflict must be studied in the context of the entire acculturation process.

Research has further stressed the need to study the process of acculturation not only from an intraindividual perspective, but also from the broader socioecological context of population subgroups.

Stressors due to acculturation need to be investigated from multidimensional and multidisciplinary perspectives, focusing on the interrelatedness of risk parameters in real-life contexts (Berry & Kim, 1988; Giddens, 1984; Recio Adrados, 1993).

The majority of immigrant Asian-Indian parents aspire to better educational and job opportunities for their children. The discrepancy between anticipated and actual situations can affect the adaptation process (Giddens, 1984). Thus, the relation between intergenerational conflict and ATOD use must consider "time-space" (Wittgenstein & Turner, 1987, cited in Giddens & Turner, 1987, p. 208)—that is, expectations related to surroundings—in intrafamilial relationships in the host country (De La Rosa et al., 1993; Mendoza, 1989; Recio Adrados, 1993).

THE ANALYTIC MODEL

The structural model described here is grounded in systems theory, which holds that behavior is dynamic and must be studied in context (Germain & Gitterman, 1980). According to systems theory, behavior must be viewed in relation to the family system, the community, and macro social systems. Systems theory is especially relevant for studying acculturation processes because of its emphasis on family system (traditions, kinship, values, and cultural beliefs), peer group (behavior patterns, drug use norms), and ecological (institutional sanctions) and community (accessibility and availability of drugs) contexts. From this framework, acculturation and susceptibility to ATOD use are recognized as processes rather than static qualities of individuals or groups. The interactions between these factors are reciprocal, dynamic, and may have synergistic effects on mediating or contributing to the problem. For example, alienation between parents and child may lead to delinquency, ATOD use, and further alienation from parents (Hawkins et al., 1987).

Researchers have found that intergenerational

conflict (sometimes referred to as "the generation gap") makes family interactions stressful and leads to weakened family bonds and increasingly deviant peer bonding, potentially resulting in drug use among youths (Connor, 1977; Ishisaka & Takagi, 1982; Masuda, Hasegawa, & Masumoto, 1973). All second-generation adolescents experiencing this stress do not, however, become drug users. The question arises: What are the intervening or protective factors that distinguish these adolescents from others who do succumb to ATOD use?

Background Characteristics

Empirical studies have shown that ATOD initiation generally occurs during adolescence (Catalano et al., 1992; U.S. Substance Abuse and Mental Health Services Administration, 1993). Difficulties with identity development also occur at this stage, which are compounded by cultural, familial, and ecological conflicts (Rodriguez et al., 1993; King & Thayer, 1993; Ross-Sheriff, 1992, Kitano & Chi, 1990; De La Rosa et al., 1993).

Studies have also shown that, regardless of ethnicity, ATOD use by female adolescents is lower than that of their male counterparts (Wallace & Bachman, 1993; Kitano & Chi, 1990). The differences are attributed to ethnically derived behavioral values and norms concerning the female's role in the family (e.g., subordinated position, conformity with rules of elders).

Low socioeconomic status is also viewed as an environmental risk factor in ATOD initiation among adolescents. Thus, having low-paying jobs and living in high-crime areas may particularly put them at risk (Wallace & Bachman, 1993; Recio Adrados, 1993; Yen, 1992; Ross-Sheriff, 1992).

Psychological Factors

Psychological factors (e.g., self-esteem, self-confidence, assertiveness, risk-taking behavior) have been found to be important in ATOD use among adolescents (Recio Adrados, 1993; Brook, 1993; Brook et al., 1990; Vega et al., 1993; Castro et al., 1994). Minority status and acculturation stressors are viewed as risk factors for all self-esteem deficits and initiation into ATOD use.

Parental Drug Use

Parental drug use has been found to have significant effects on children's perceptions of parental permissiveness toward ATOD use. Parents play an important role in defining drinking norms, both through their own alcohol use and through their attitudes about the harmfulness of alcohol (Barnes & Welte, 1986; Kandel & Andrews, 1987). It has also been reported that the presence of one smoker at home doubles the probability of a child's use of cigarettes.

Family Relationships

The relation between disruptive family relationships and deviant behavior among adolescents, including ATOD use, is well recognized (Brook, 1993; Vega et al., 1993; Castro et al., 1994; Recio Adrados, 1993; Newcomb & Bentler, 1986). Stress resulting from adaptation to a new country may increase the conflicts between parents and children, leading to alienation, deviant peer bonding, and ATOD use. On the other hand, Vega et al. (1993) found that adequate family functioning mediates the negative influence of acculturative stressors and thus protects against initiation into ATOD use.

Peer Bonding

Peer bonding has been found to explain deviance leading to ATOD use, especially when there is weak bonding to family and school (Elliott & Voss, 1974; Kandel, 1982; Jessor & Jessor, 1977; Hirschi, 1969). The problem of meeting the normative demands of two cultures (host country and country of origin) has been linked to adolescents' drug use behavior as a way to cope with conflicts with parents (Rogler et al., 1991; Szapocznik & Kurtines, 1980; Fitzpatrick, 1990).

Cultural Identity[1]

Szapocznik's biculturism model states that those competent in negotiating the contradictory demands of two cultures would be less likely to engage in drug use (Szapocznik et al., 1978; Szapocznik & Kurtines, 1980). Felix-Ortiz and Newcomb (1995) found that among Latinos and Latina adolescents, certain components of cultural identity are associated with increased drug use (e.g., defensive Latino activism), whereas others are associated with decreased drug use (e.g., traditional family role expectations for Latinas).

Ecological Factors

A social environment that sanctions drug use and ensures easy availability of drugs is recognized as a contributing factor in deviant behavior and ATOD use among adolescents (Johnson et al., 1990; De La Rosa et al., 1993). Availability of

drugs, accompanied by disadvantaged socioeconomic status (low income, lack of employment opportunities), facilitates initiation as well as greater use of drugs among minority youths (De La Rosa et al., 1993).

LINKAGE AMONG ACCULTURATION FACTORS, INTERGENERATIONAL CONFLICT, AND ATOD USE

Given the ethnic and cultural diversity of America, it is clear that a single model would not sufficiently address the complex issues related to acculturation and ATOD use for diverse adolescent subgroups. However, a generic multirisk model can be adapted to depict accurately the unique characteristics of specific population subgroups, within and across risk categories in an ever-changing multidimensional context (Brook et al., 1990; Newcomb & Bentler, 1988; Castro et al., 1994). Figure 1 presents a generic model showing risk factors associated with intergenerational conflict and ATOD use. Hypothesized risk factors are

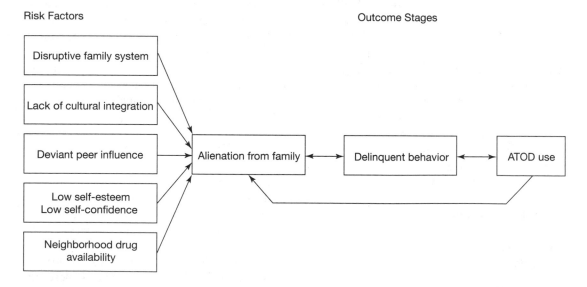

FIGURE 1 Linkages and Temporal Sequelae of Selected Risk Factors and Alcohol, Tobacco and Other Drug (ATOD) Use among Adolescents

delineated on the left and the three outcome stages representing the consequences of acculturation stress and intergenerational conflict are to the right. The model emphasizes not only the impact of individual (e.g., self-esteem) and environmental (e.g., drug availability) factors, but also the reciprocal interplay of these factors on adolescent drug use. The linkage and temporal sequelae of the three outcome stages follow.

Alienation from Family.   Disruptions in family dynamics (e.g., parent-child bonding) may lead to adolescent defiance and loss of family cohesiveness. Weakened family bonds and, in turn, lack of communication create further alienation between parents and children (Elliott & Voss, 1974; Hirschi, 1969; Jessor & Jessor, 1977; Kandel, 1982).

Delinquent Behavior.   A low level of family connectedness is associated with adolescents seeking approval and support from peers. Thus, weak family bonding may also directly influence peer association and deviant behavior. Unhealthy practices (e.g., ATOD use) are negative reinforcements that adolescents use to establish connections with peers. Peer identification, peer influence, and peer drug use behavior are recognized as significant contributing factors in ATOD initiation and use among adolescents (Oetting & Beauvais, 1990; Farrel et al., 1992; Castro et al., 1987).

ATOD Use.   Bonding with deviant peers often leads to ATOD use among adolescents, further alienating children from their parents and increasing the risk of greater drug abuse (Kandel, 1982; Simpson & Sells, 1990; Castro et al., 1994).

ASIAN INDIANS: UNIQUE CHARACTERISTICS

While the generic model is applicable to all immigrant groups in general, the following characteristics may further increase intergenerational conflict and ATOD use among Asian-Indian adolescents.

1. Family Role, Responsibility.   The family is the vehicle for cultural identification and is considered central in Asian society. For understanding different aspects of intergenerational conflict, it is important to understand family structure in the Asian-Indian community.

There are significant differences between Asian-Indian culture and American society, including language (primarily Hindi), food and eating habits, religion (primarily Hinduism), and recreational activities such as dance and music. The greatest difference, however, relates to the *concept of self* (Roland, 1984). For individuals of Asian descent, the self exists as an integrated gestalt in which the familial self predominates. Each person occupies a position within a system of interpersonal and intergroup relations (in the family and community) and is not expected to behave in a totally individuated way (Chung, 1992). The relationship between parents and child is vertical, with power and status determined hierarchically (Fong, 1992; Ross-Sheriff, 1992). The child is expected to maintain family traditions and fulfill family obligations (such as getting good grades, which enhances family reputation).

In contrast, Euro-American culture is individual-centered. Individuation has been described as a part of the normal developmental transition from adolescence to adulthood (Erikson, 1968; Jessor & Jessor, 1977). Asian cultures emphasize "deindividuation" and place value on family/kin responsibilities, hierarchical power structure, obligations, and filial piety (Ross-Sheriff, 1992). The cultural distance between host and original countries further intensifies the stress of acculturation and adaptation. This can lead to family conflict and communication deficits, leading to alienation between parents and children, which, in turn, often manifests itself in delinquency and drug use (Catalano et al., 1992; Kandel, 1982; Paton & Kandel, 1978).

2. Feelings of Failure. Recently, Mohan (1989) associated Asian-Indian parents' expectations (often unrealistic from the developmental perspective of their children) with ATOD use. Asian-Indian adolescents face tremendous pressure to keep up the image of "whiz kids" and to meet the expectations of their parents (i.e., parents choosing children's careers—e.g., medicine, law, teaching—overriding individual aptitude and choice). This creates anxiety and frustration, leading to failure and resentment against parents. This may dispose adolescents to use drugs as a palliative coping strategy to relieve tension or to reduce stress (Juon et al., 1995).

3. Gender-Specific Roles. Gender-specific role expectancies prevail cross-culturally; however, they are particularly strong in Asian-Indian culture. For example, in Asian-Indian families, females are expected to maintain a subordinate role and not assume decision-making power (Kakar, 1982). While American culture encourages development of personal identity and social independence, such behavior, if practiced by Asian-Indian adolescents within the family context, may generate intergenerational and between-gender conflict (Jain, 1990). Socializing with or dating peers from other ethnic groups is not acceptable behavior (Sikri, 1989). Parents are especially overprotective of their female children. Marriage is considered a collective family decision, and the female's opinion is rarely solicited.

Cultural conflict may lead to family conflict, especially when female children challenge parents' differential treatment of male siblings. Studies have shown that disagreement between parents' and female children's socializing norms alienates children from parents and leads to their seeking peer approval and support. This, as explained previously, may lead to ATOD use (Felix-Ortiz & Newcomb, 1995).

4. Economic Stress.[2] Researchers have concluded that social and environmental conditions (e.g., poverty, unemployment, low education level, limited job opportunities) are related to family management and relationships. These structural factors (e.g., overcrowding, less time for supervision) often contribute to family stress, leading to parent–child conflict and hostility, which, in turn, may lead to ATOD use (Jones & DeMaree, 1975). Thus, socioeconomic disadvantages have been linked, indirectly via family management processes, to ATOD use.

Economically, Asian-Indians are a diverse and heterogeneous group. Adolescents in socioeconomically disadvantaged families are at higher risk, within the Asian-Indian population, for ATOD use.

5. Norms for Substance Use. Alcohol use is accepted among older Asian-Indians. Marijuana use is also widespread and culturally acceptable in India (Dornbush & Fink, 1977). Nevertheless, ATOD use is stigmatized as a moral problem contributing to family shame and dishonor (Kim et al., 1995). However, the issues related to ATOD use are seldom discussed, and adolescents in Asian-Indian families often lack information. Family prestige and pride shroud the harmful consequences of ATOD use (Mohan, 1989), putting Asian-Indian adolescents at increased risk (Connor, 1977; Ishisaka & Takagi, 1982; Masuda et al., 1973).

6. Acculturation Level. Studies indicate that the magnitude of intergenerational conflict is highest for first-generation immigrants from a "distant" culture and their second-generation children, who were born and socialized in the host culture. Szapocznik and Kurtines (1980), in their study on Cuban-American adolescents, suggested that discrepancies between parents' and adolescents' levels of acculturation may cause conflict for the adolescents and, therefore, greater dependency on the peer group for rewards, which may lead to drug use. Asian-Indian adolescents may similarly be at higher risk.

EXPERIENCE OF OTHER ETHNIC GROUPS

Since empirical data on acculturation and its influence on Asian-Indian adolescents are not available, studies of other ethnic groups may aid in understanding the impact of the acculturation process and intergenerational conflict on ATOD use. According to Oetting (1993), American-Indian youth who lose their cultural identity are more susceptible to drug abuse than are those who do not. In a study of Puerto Rican youth, investigators linked level of acculturation to drug abuse but not to delinquency. In contrast to the study by Szapocznik and Kurtines (1980), biculturism was not found to be a protective factor (Rodriguez, Recio Adrados, & De La Rosa, 1993), Brook (1993) examined the impact of acculturation on African-American and Hispanic adolescents' drug use. Parent–adolescent relationships were found to affect an adolescent's personality, influencing peer selection, which in turn has an impact on drug use. Brook also indicated that acculturation is complex, multidimensional in nature, and must be examined in interaction with other factors associated with drug use.

Two descriptive studies of intergenerational conflict among Asian-American ethnic groups are noteworthy. Huang (1988) described Chinese Americans as maintaining the cultural ideal of a family built around ancestor worship, filial piety, and patriarchal authority. Even in the host country, this ethnic group was found to maintain a closely knit nuclear family as the central agency of socialization. Gang activity among second-generation Chinese youth was related more to intergenerational conflict than to socioeconomic status. Loss of cultural identity was identified as the primary factor leading to delinquent behavior. Kitano and Kikumura (1988) reported that Japanese culture, particularly with its emphasis on collective idealism and group cohesiveness, has produced a family life-style that reflects high de-grees of ethnic solidarity and identification. The authors stated that acculturation has influenced the family system; yet, they argued, the Japanese culture, in combination with the low power and high visibility of the group, has essentially remained intact even in later generations.

DISCUSSION

The myth of Asian-Indians as a "model" minority group—overachieving, high-economic status, perfect family relationships—has been challenged (Fong, 1992; Kitano & Chi, 1990; Sue & Nakamura, 1984). In addition to the stress of identity development during adolescence, Asian-Indian adolescents' problems are confounded by conflict with parents over family roles and behavior norms. The interactions among these factors are reciprocal, dynamic, and may have synergistic effects on mediating or contributing to their problems. For example, alienation between parents and children may lead to delinquency, drug use, and further alienation. Thus, family conflict and ATOD use among the Asian-Indian adolescents are emerging phenomena that warrant additional scientific inquiry.

It should be noted, however, that intergenerational conflict is only one in a spectrum of factors that may lead to ATOD use among adolescents. It is important to understand the dynamic relationships among genetic, biological, and social forces. Also, the risk-factor approach to ATOD abuse must assess the impact across four groups: individual, family, peer group, and community, which includes school and neighborhood. The interactions within these groups are also dynamic and interrelated (Cazares, 1994).

NOTES

1. The term "culture" is used to describe the customs, beliefs, social structure, and activities of any group of people who share a common identification and would label themselves as members of that group (Oetting, 1993). "Identity" refers

to group behavior, influenced by value orientation, that is accepted as normative for members of that culture.

2. Asian-Indians are broadly divided into two economic groups: professionals and working-class newcomers. Often, they have to support not only their immediate family in the host country, but also extended family members in India, putting additional economic pressure on them.

REFERENCES

Austin, G. A., Prendergast, M. L., & Lee, H. (1989). *Substance abuse among Asian American youth* (Prevention Research Update No. 5, pp. 1–13. Portland, OR: Northwest Regional Educational Laboratory.

Barnes, G. M., & Welte, J. W. (1986). Patterns and predictors of alcohol use among 7–12th-grade students in New York State. *Journal of Studies on Alcohol, 47,* 53–62.

Berry, J. W., & Kim, U. (1988). Acculturation and mental health. In P. Dasen, J. W. Berry, & N. Sartorius (Eds.), *Health and cross-cultural psychology: Toward applications* (pp. 207–236). Newbury Park, CA: Sage.

Brook, J. S. (1993). Interactional theory: Its utility in explaining drug use behavior among African-American and Puerto Rican youth. *NIDA Research Monograph, 130,* 79–101.

Brook, J. S., Brook, D. W., Gordon, A. S., Whiteman, M., & Cohen, P. (1990). The psychosocial etiology of adolescent drug use: A family interactional approach. *Genetic, Social, and General Psychology Monographs, 116* (No. 2).

Castro, F. G., Harmon, M. P., Coe, K., & Tofoya-Barraza, H. M. (1994). Drug prevention research with Hispanic populations: Theoretical and methodological issues and a generic structural model. In A. Cazares & L. A. Beatty (Eds.), *Scientific methods for prevention intervention research* (NIDA Monograph 139, pp. 203–224). Rockville, MD: National Institute on Drug Abuse.

Castro, F. G., Maddahian, E., Newcomb, M. D., & Bentler, P. M. (1987). A multivariate model of the determinants of cigarette smoking among adolescents. *Journal on Health and Social Behavior, 28,* 273–289.

Catalano, R. F., Morrison, D. M., Wells, E. A., Gilmore, M. R., Iritani, B., & Hawkins, J. D. (1992). Ethnic differences in family factors related to early drug

initiation. *Journal of Studies on Alcohol, 53*(3), 208–217.

Cazares, A. (1994). Prevention intervention research: Focus and perspective. In A. Cazares & L. A. Beatty (Eds.), *Scientific methods for prevention intervention research* (NIDA Monograph 139, pp. 5–29). Rockville, MD: National Institute on Drug Abuse.

Chi, I., Lubben, J. E., & Kitano, H. H. J. (1989). Difference in drinking behavior among three Asian-American groups. *Journal of Studies on Alcohol, 50*(1), 15–23.

Chung, D. K. (1992). Asian culture commonalities: A comparison with mainstream American culture. In S. M. Furuto, R. Biswas, D. K. Chung, K. Murase, & F. Ross-Sheriff (Eds.), *Social work practice with Asian Americans* (pp. 27–31). Newbury Park, CA: Sage.

Connor, J. W. (1977). *Tradition and change in three generations of Japanese Americans.* Chicago: Nelson-Hall.

De La Rosa, M., Recio Adrados, J-L., Kennedy, N. J., & Milburn, M. (1993), Current gaps and new directions for studying drug use and abuse behavior in minority youth. In M. R. De La Rosa & J-L. Recio Adrados (Eds.), *Drug abuse among minority youth: Advances in research and methodology* (NIDA Research Monograph 130, pp. 321–340). Rockville, MD: National Institute on Drug Abuse.

Dornbush, D., & Fink, P. J. (1977). Recent trends in substance abuse. *International Journal of the Addictions, 2,* 143–151.

Elliott, D. S., & Voss, H. (1974). *Delinquency and dropout.* Lexington, MA: D. C. Heath.

Erikson, E. (1968). *Identity: Youth and crisis.* New York: Norton.

Farrel, A. D., Danish, S. J., & Howard, C. W. (1992). Risk factors for drug use in urban adolescents: Identification and cross-validation. *American Journal on Community Psychology, 20,* 263–286.

Felix-Ortiz, M., & Newcomb, M. D. (1995). Cultural identity and drug use among Latino and Latina adolescents. In G. J. Botvin, S. Schinke, & M. A. Orlandi (Eds.), *Drug abuse prevention with multiethnic youth* (pp. 147–165). Newbury Park, CA: Sage.

Fitzpatrick, J. P. (1990). Drugs and Puerto Ricans in New York City. In R. Glick & J. Moore (Eds.), *Drugs in Hispanic communities* (pp. 103–126). New Brunswick, NJ: Rutgers University Press.

Fong, R. (1992). A history of Asian Americans. In S. M. Furuto, R. Biswas, D. K. Chung, K. Murase, & F. Ross-Sheriff (Eds.), *Social work practice with Asian Americans* (pp. 18–23). Newbury Park, CA: Sage.

Germain, C., & Gitterman, A. (1980). *The life model of social work practice.* New York: Columbia University Press.

Giddens, A. (1984). *The constitution of society: Outline of the theory of structuration.* Berkeley, CA: University of California Press.

Giddens, A., & Turner, J. H. (1987). *Social theory today.* Stanford, CA: Stanford University Press.

Hawkins, J. D., Lishner, D. M., Jenson, J. M., Catalano, R. F. (1987). Delinquents and drugs: What the evidence suggests about prevention and treatment programming. In B. S. Brown & A. R. Millstein (Eds.), *Youth at high risk for substance abuse* (DHHS Publication No. ADM 87-1537, pp. 81–133). Washington, DC: U.S. Government Printing Office.

Hirschi, T. (1969). *Causes of delinquency.* Berkeley, CA: University of California Press.

Huang, L. J. (1988). The Chinese American family. In C. H. Mindel, R. W. Habenstein, & R. Wright (Eds.), *Ethnic families in America* (pp. 124–147). New York: Elsevier Press.

Ishisaka, H., & Takagi, C. (1982). Social work with Asian- and Pacific-Americans. In J. Green (Ed.), *Cultural awareness in the human services.* Englewood Cliffs, NJ: Prentice-Hall.

Jain, A. (1990). "Brown" outside and "white" inside. *India Abroad, 20*(28), 33.

Jessor, R., & Jessor, G. L. (1977). *Problem behavior and psychosocial development: A longitudinal study of youth.* New York: Academic Press.

Jindal, P. (1989). Asian American or American Indian? *Sanskriti, 1,* 3–5.

Johnson, B., Williams, T., Dei, K., & Sanabria, H. (1990). Drug abuse and the inner city: Impact on drug users and the community. In M. Tonry & Q. Wilson (Eds.), *Drugs and crime* (pp. 9–67). Chicago: University of Chicago Press.

Jones, A. P., & DeMaree, R. G. (1975). Family disruption, social indices, and problem behavior: A preliminary study. *Journal of Marriage and the Family, 37,* 497–504.

Juon, H-S., Shin, Y., & Nam, J. J. (1995). Cigarette smoking among Korean adolescents: Prevalence and correlates. *Adolescence, 30*(119), 631–641.

Kakar, S. (1982). *The inner world.* New York: Oxford University Press.

Kandel, S. (1982). Epidemiological and psychosocial perspectives on adolescent drug use. *Journal of the American Academy of Clinical Psychiatry, 21,* 328–347.

Kandel, D. B., & Andrews, K. (1987). Processes of adolescent socialization by parents and peers. *International Journal of the Addictions, 22,* 319–342.

Kim, S., Coletti, S. D., Williams, C., & Hepler, N. A. (1995). Substance abuse prevention involving Asian–Pacific Islander American communities. In G. J. Botvin, S. Schinke, & M. A. Orlandi (Eds.), *Drug abuse prevention with multiethnic youth* (pp. 295–323). Newbury Park, CA: Sage.

King, J., & Thayer, J. F. (1993). Examining conceptual models for understanding drug use behavior among American Indian youth. In M. R. De La Rosa & J-L. Recio Adrados (Eds.), *Drug abuse among minority youth: Advances in research and methodology* (NIDA Research Monograph 130, pp. 129–140). Rockville, MD: National Institute on Drug Abuse.

Kitano, H. H. L., & Chi, I. (1990). Asian-Americans and alcohol use. Exploring cultural differences in Los Angeles. *Alcohol, Health and Research World, 2*(2), 42–47.

Kitano, H. H. L., & Kikumura, A. (1988). The Japanese American family. In C. H. Mindel, R. W. Habenstein, & R. Wright (Eds.), *Ethnic families in America* (pp. 41–60). New York: Elsevier Press.

Masuda, M., Hasegawa, S. R., & Masumoto, M. (1973). The ethnic identity questionnaire—A comparison of three Japanese age groups in Tachikawa, Japan, Honolulu, and Seattle. *Journal of Cross-Cultural Psychology, 4,* 229–245.

Mendoza, R. H. (1989). An empirical scale to measure type and degree of acculturation in Mexican-American adolescents and adults. *Journal of Cross-Cultural Psychology, 20*(4), 372–385.

Mohan, B. (1989). Ethnicity, power, and discontent: The problem of identity reconstruction in a pluralist society. *Indian Journal of Social Work, 50*(2), 199–212.

Naipaul, V. S. (1990). Naipaul seeking his roots. *India Abroad, 20*(4), 7.

Newcomb, M. D., & Bentler, P. M. (1986). Substance use and ethnicity: Differential impact of peer and adult models. *Journal of Psychology, 120,* 83–95.

Newcomb, M. D., & Bentler, P. M. (1988). *Consequences of adolescent drug use: Impact on the lives of young adults*. Newbury Park, CA: Sage.

Oetting, E. R. (1993). Orthogonal cultural identification: Theoretical links between cultural identification and substance use. In M. R. De La Rosa & J-L. Recio Adrados (Eds.), *Drug abuse among minority youth: Advances in research and methodology* (NIDA Research Monograph 130, pp. 32–56). Rockville, MD: National Institute on Drug Abuse.

Oetting, E. R., & Beauvais, F. (1990). Adolescent drug use: Findings of national and local surveys. *Journal of Consulting Clinical Psychology, 58*(4), 385–394.

Padilla, A. (1980). The role of cultural awareness and ethnic loyalty in acculturation. In A. Padilla (Ed.), *Acculturation, theory, models, and new findings* (pp. 47–84). Boulder, CO: Westview Press.

Paton, S. M., Kandel, D. B. (1978). Psychological factors and adolescent illicit drug use: Ethnicity and sex differences. *Adolescence, 8*(50), 187–200.

Recio Adrados, J-L. (1993). *Acculturation: The broader view. Theoretical framework of the acculturation scales.* In M. R. De La Rosa & J-L. Recio Adrados (Eds.), *Drug abuse among minority youth: Advances in research and methodology* (NIDA Research Monograph 130, pp. 57–78). Rockville, MD: National Institute on Drug Abuse.

Rodriguez, O., Recio Adrados, J-L., & De La Rosa, M. R. (1993). Integrating mainstream and subcultural explanations of drug use among Puerto Rican youth. In M. R. De La Rosa & J-L. Recio Adrados (Eds.), *Drug abuse among minority youth: Advances in research and methodology* (NIDA Research Monograph 130, pp. 8–24). Rockville, MD: National Institute on Drug Abuse.

Rogler, L. H., Cortes, D. E., & Malgady, R. G. (1991). Acculturation and mental health status among Hispanics: Convergence and new directions for research. *American Psychology, 46*(6), 585–597.

Roland, A. (1984). The self in India and America: Toward a psychoanalysis of social and cultural contexts. In V. Kavolis (Ed.), *Design of selfhood* (pp. 170–184). London: Associated University Press.

Ross-Sheriff, F. (1992). Adaptation and integration into American society. In S. M. Furuto, R. Biswas, D. K. Chung, K. Murase, & F. Ross-Sheriff (Eds,), *Social work practice with Asian Americans* (pp. 45–83). Newbury Park, CA: Sage.

Saran, P. (1985). *Asian Indian experience in the United States.* Massachusetts: Schenkman.

Sikri, A. (1989). Dating: A scary cultural gap. *India Abroad, 20*(2), 17.

Simpson, D. D., & Sells, S. B. (1990). *Opioid addiction and treatment: A 12-year follow-up.* Florida: Kreiger.

Sue, S., & Nakamura, C. Y. (1984). Integrative model of physiological and social/psychological factors in alcohol consumption among Chinese and Japanese Americans. *Journal of Drug Issues, 14*(2), 349–364.

Szapocznik, J., & Hernandez, R. (1988). The Cuban American family. In C. H. Mindel, R. W. Habenstein, & R. Wright (Eds.), *Ethnic families in America.* New York: Elsevier Press.

Szapocznik, J., & Kurtines, W. (1980). Acculturation, biculturism, and adjustment among Cuban Americans. In A. Padilla (Ed.), *Acculturation, theory, models, and new findings* (pp. 139–159). Boulder, CO: Westview Press.

Szapocznik, J., Scopettea, M. Kurtines, W., & A. Arnalde (1978). Theory and measurement of acculturation. *Inter-American Journal of Psychology, 12,* 113–130.

Szapocznik, J., & Truss, C. (1978). Intergeneration sources of conflict in Cuban mothers. In M. Montiel (Ed.), *Hispanic families.* Washington, DC: Coalition of Spanish Speaking Mental Health Organizations.

Takaki, R. (1989). *Strangers from a different shore: A history of Asian Americans.* Boston, MA: Little, Brown.

U.S. Bureau of the Census. (1990). *Statistical abstract of the U.S.* Washington, DC: U.S. Government Printing Office.

U.S. Substance Abuse and Mental Health Services Administration, Office of Applied Statistics. (1993). *National household survey on drug abuse: Main findings* (DHHS Publication No. SMA 93-1979). Rockville, MD: Author.

Vega, W. A. Zimmerman, R., Gil, A., Warheit, G. J., & Apospori, E. (1993). Acculturation strain theory: Its application in explaining drug use behavior among Cuban and other Hispanic youth. In M. R. De La Rosa & J-L. Racio Adrados (Eds.), *Drug abuse among minority youth: Advances in research and methodology* (NIDA Research Monograph 130, pp. 144–166). Rockville, MD: National Institute on Drug Abuse.

Wallace, J. M., Jr., & Bachman, J. G. (1993). Validity of self-reports in student-based studies on minority populations: Issues and concerns. In M. R. De La Rosa & J-L. Recio Adrados (Eds.), *Drug abuse among minority youth: Advances in research and methodology* (NIDA Research Monograph 130, pp. 169–170). Rockville, MD: National Institute on Drug Abuse.

Yen, S. (1992). Cultural competence for evaluators working with Asian/Pacific Island–American communities: Some common themes and important implications. In M. A. Orlandi (Ed.), *Cultural competence for evaluators: A guide for alcohol and other drug abuse prevention practitioners working with ethnic racial communities* (DHHS Publication No. ADM 92-1884). Rockville, MD: Office of Substance Abuse Prevention.

? Think about It

1. Define and describe systems theory. Why does Bhattacharya use this perspective in her analysis?
2. What is acculturation? Describe the linkages between intergenerational conflict, acculturation, and alcohol, tobacco, and other drug (ATOD) use.
3. Why does Bhattacharya posit that many of the risk and protective factors in ATOD use are unique to Asian Indian adolescents? Are female and male children equally vulnerable to ATOD use?

---

34 Eating Problems among African American, Latina, and White Women

Becky W. Thompson

Becky W. Thompson challenges the widely accepted belief that eating problems are largely limited to white, middle- and upper-class, heterosexual women. Instead of accepting the notion that women are anorexic and bulimic because of a "culture of thinness," Thompson argues that eating problems are a response to poverty, sexual abuse, racism, heterosexism, social class inequality, and acculturation.

EXISTING RESEARCH ON EATING PROBLEMS

There are three theoretical models used to explain the epidemiology, etiology, and treatment of eating problems. The biomedical model offers important

Source: From Becky W. Thompson, "A Way Outa No Way: Eating Problems among African American, Latina, and White Women," in *Race, Class and Gender: Common Bonds, Different Voices,* ed. Esther Ngan-Ling Chow, Doris Wilkinson, and Maxine Baca Zinn (Thousand Oaks, CA: Sage, 1996), 52–69. Copyright © 1996 Sage Publications, Inc. Reprinted by permission of Sage Publications, Inc.

scientific research about possible physiological causes of eating problems and the physiological dangers of purging and starvation (Copeland 1985; Spack 1985). However, this model adopts medical treatment strategies that may disempower and traumatize women (Garner 1985; Orbach 1985). In addition, this model ignores many social, historical, and cultural factors that influence women's eating patterns. The psychological model identifies eating problems as "multidimensional disorders" that are influenced by biological, psychological, and cultural factors (Garfinkel and Garner 1982). While useful in its exploration of effective therapeutic treatments, this model, like the biomedical one, tends to neglect women of color, lesbians, and working-class women.

The third model, offered by feminists, asserts that eating problems are gendered. This model explains why the vast majority of people with eating problems are women, how gender socialization and sexism may relate to eating problems, and how masculine models of psychological development have shaped theoretical interpretations. Feminists offer the *culture of thinness model* as a key reason why eating problems predominate among women. According to this model, thinness is a culturally, socially, and economically enforced requirement for female beauty. This imperative makes women vulnerable to cycles of dieting, weight loss, and subsequent weight gain, which may lead to anorexia nervosa and bulimia (Chernin 1981; Orbach 1978, 1985; Smead 1984).

Feminists have rescued eating problems from the realm of individual psychopathology by showing how the difficulties are rooted in systematic and pervasive attempts to control women's body sizes and appetites. However, researchers have yet to give significant attention to how race, class, and sexuality influence women's understanding of their bodies and appetites. The handful of epidemiological studies that include African American women and Latinas casts doubt on the accuracy of the normative epidemiological portrait. The studies suggest that this portrait reflects which particular populations of women have been studied rather than actual prevalence (Anderson and Hay, 1985; Gray, Ford, and Kelly 1987; Hsu 1987; Nevo 1985; Silber (1986).

More important, this research shows that bias in research has consequences for women of color. Thomas Silber (1986) asserts that many well-trained professionals have either misdiagnosed or delayed their diagnoses of eating problems among

African American and Latina women due to stereotypical thinking that these problems are restricted to white women. As a consequence, when African American women or Latinas are diagnosed, their eating problems tend to be more severe due to extended processes of starvation prior to intervention. In her autobiographical account of her eating problems, Retha Powers (1989), an African American woman, describes being told not to worry about her eating problems since "fat is more acceptable in the Black community" (p. 78). Stereotypical perceptions held by her peers and teachers of the "maternal Black woman" and the "persistent mammy–brickhouse Black woman image" (p. 134) made it difficult for Powers to find people who took her problems with food seriously.

Recent work by African American women reveals that eating problems often relate to women's struggles against a "simultaneity of oppressions" (Clarke 1982; Naylor, 1985; White 1991). Byllye Avery (1990), the founder of the National Black Women's Health Project, links the origins of eating problems among African American women to the daily stress of being undervalued and overburdened at home and at work. In Evelyn C. White's (1990) anthology, *The Black Woman's Health Book: Speaking for Ourselves,* Georgiana Arnold (1990) links her eating problems partly to racism and racial isolation during childhood.

Recent feminist research also identifies factors that are related to eating problems among lesbians (Brown 1987; Dworkin 1989; Iazzetto 1989; Schoenfielder and Wieser 1983). In her clinical work, Brown (1987) found that lesbians who have internalized a high degree of homophobia are more likely to accept negative attitudes about fat than are lesbians who have examined their internalized homophobia. Autobiographical accounts by lesbians have also indicated that secrecy about eating problems among lesbians partly reflects their fear of being associated with a stigmatized illness ("What's Important" 1988).

Attention to African American women, Latinas, and lesbians paves the way for further research that explores the possible interface between facing multiple oppressions and the development of eating problems. In this way, this study is part of a larger feminist and sociological research agenda that seeks to understand how race, class, gender, nationality, and sexuality inform women's experiences and influence theory production.

METHODOLOGY

I conducted eighteen life history interviews and administered lengthy questionnaires to explore eating problems among African American, Latina, and white women. I employed a snowball sample, a method in which potential respondents often first learn about the study from people who have already participated. . . .

Demographics of the Women in the Study

The 18 women I interviewed included 5 African American women, 5 Latinas, and 8 white women. Of these women, 12 are lesbian and 6 are heterosexual. Five women are Jewish, 8 are Catholic, and 5 are Protestant. Three women grew up outside of the United States. The women represented a range of class backgrounds (both in terms of origin and current class status) and ranged in age from 19 to 46 years old (with a median age of 33.5 years).

The majority of the women reported having had a combination of eating problems (at least two of the following: bulimia, compulsive eating, anorexia nervosa, and/or extensive dieting). In addition, the particular types of eating problems often changed during a woman's life span. . . .

Two-thirds of the women have had eating problems for more than half of their lives, a finding that contradicts the stereotype of eating problems as transitory. The weight fluctuation among the women varied from 16 to 160 pounds, with an average fluctuation of 74 pounds. This drastic

weight change illustrates the degree to which the women adjusted to major changes in body size at least once during their lives as they lost, gained, and lost weight again. The average age of onset was 11 years old, meaning that most of the women developed eating problems prior to puberty. Almost all of the women (88 percent) considered themselves as still having a problem with eating, although the majority believed they were well on the way to recovery.

THE INTERFACE OF TRAUMA AND EATING PROBLEMS

One of the most striking findings in this study was the range of traumas the women associated with the origins of their eating problems, including racism, sexual abuse, poverty, sexism, emotional or physical abuse, heterosexism, class injuries, and acculturation.[1] The particular constellation of eating problems among the women did not vary with race, class, sexuality, or nationality. Women from various race and class backgrounds attributed the origins of their eating problems to sexual abuse, sexism, and emotional and/or physical abuse. Among some of the African American and Latina women, eating problems were also associated with poverty, racism, and class injuries. Heterosexism was a key factor in the onset of bulimia, compulsive eating, and extensive dieting among some of the lesbians. These oppressions are not the same nor are the injuries caused by them. And certainly, there are a variety of potentially harmful ways that women respond to oppression (such as using drugs, becoming a workaholic, or committing suicide). However, for all these women, eating was a way of coping with trauma.

Sexual Abuse

Sexual abuse was the most common trauma that the women related to the origins of their eating problems. Until recently, there has been virtually no research exploring the possible relationship between these two phenomena. Since the mid-1980s, however, researchers have begun identifying connections between the two, a task that is part of a larger feminist critique of traditional psychoanalytic symptomatology (DeSalvo 1989; Herman 1981; Masson 1984). Results of a number of incidence studies indicate that between one-third and two-thirds of women who have eating problems have been abused (Oppenheimer et al. 1985; Root and Fallon 1988). In addition, a growing number of therapists and researchers have offered interpretations of the meaning and impact of eating problems for survivors of sexual abuse (Bass and Davis 1988; Goldfarb 1987; Iazzetto 1989; Swink and Leveille 1986). . . .

Among the women I interviewed, 61 percent were survivors of sexual abuse (11 of the 18 women), most of whom made connections between sexual abuse and the beginning of their eating problems. Binging was the most common method of coping identified by the survivors. Binging helped women "numb out" or anesthetize their feelings. Eating sedated, alleviated anxiety, and combated loneliness. Food was something that they could trust and was accessible whenever they needed it. Antonia (a pseudonym) is an Italian American woman who was first sexually abused by a male relative when she was four years old. Retrospectively, she knows that binging was a way she coped with the abuse. When the abuse began, and for many years subsequently, Antonia often woke up during the middle of the night with anxiety attacks or nightmares and would go straight to the kitchen cupboards to get food. Binging helped her block painful feelings because it put her back to sleep.

Like other women in the study who began binging when they were very young, Antonia was not always fully conscious as she binged. She described eating during the night as "sleep walking. It was mostly desperate—like I had to have it." Describing why she ate after waking up with nightmares, Antonia said, "What else do you do? If you don't have any coping mechanisms, you eat." She said that binging made her "disappear,"

which made her feel protected. Like Antonia, most of the women were sexually abused before puberty; four of them before they were five years old. Given their youth, food was the most accessible and socially acceptable drug available to them. Because all of the women endured the psychological consequences alone, it is logical that they coped with tactics they could use alone as well.

One reason Antonia binged (rather than dieted) to cope with sexual abuse is that she saw little reason to try to be the small size girls were supposed to be. Growing up as one of the only Italian Americans in what she described as a "very WASP town," Antonia felt that everything from her weight and size to having dark hair on her upper lip were physical characteristics she was supposed to hide. From a young age she knew she "never embodied the essence of the good girl. I don't like her. I have never acted like her. I can't be her. I sort of gave up." For Antonia, her body was the physical entity that signified her outsider status. When the sexual abuse occurred, Antonia felt she had lost her body. In her mind, the body she lived in after the abuse was not really hers. By the time Antonia was 11, her mother put her on diet pills. Antonia began to eat behind closed doors as she continued to cope with the psychological consequences of sexual abuse and feeling like a cultural outsider.

Extensive dieting and bulimia were also ways in which women responded to sexual abuse. Some women thought that the men had abused them because of their weight. They believed that if they were smaller, they might not have been abused. For example, when Elsa, an Argentine woman, was sexually abused at the age of 11, she thought her chubby size was the reason the man was abusing her. Elsa said, "I had this notion that these old perverts liked these plump girls. You heard adults say this too. Sex and flesh being associated." Looking back on her childhood, Elsa believes she made fat the enemy partly due to the shame and guilt she felt about the incest. Her belief that fat was the source of her problems was also supported by her socialization. Raised by strict German governesses in an upper-class family, Elsa was taught that a woman's weight was a primary criterion for judging her worth. Her mother "was socially conscious of walking into places with a fat daughter and maybe people staring at her." Her father often referred to Elsa's body as "shot to hell." When asked to describe how she felt about her body when growing up, Elsa described being completely alienated from her body. She explained,

> Remember in school when they talk about the difference between body and soul? I always felt like my soul was skinny. My soul was free. My soul sort of flew. I was tied down by this big bag of rocks that was my body. I had to drag it around. It did pretty much what it wanted and I had a lot of trouble controlling it. It kept me from doing all the things that I dreamed of.

As is true for many women who have been abused, the split that Elsa described between her body and soul was an attempt to protect herself from the pain she believed her body caused her. In her mind, her fat body was what had "bashed in her dreams." Dieting became her solution but, as is true for many women in the study, this strategy soon led to cycles of binging and weight fluctuation.

Ruthie, a Puerto Rican woman who was sexually abused from 12 until 16 years of age, described bulimia as a way she responded to sexual abuse. As a child, Ruthie liked her body. Like many Puerto Rican women of her mother's generation, Ruthie's mother did not want skinny children, interpreting that as a sign that they were sick or being fed improperly. Despite her mother's attempts to make her gain weight, Ruthie remained thin through puberty. When a male relative began sexually abusing her, Ruthie's sense of her body changed dramatically. Although she weighed only 100 pounds, she began to feel fat and thought her size was causing the abuse. She had seen a movie on television about Romans who made themselves throw up and so she began doing it, in

hopes that she could look like the "little kid" she was before the abuse began. Her symbolic attempt to protect herself by purging stands in stark contrast to the psychoanalytic explanation of eating problems as an "abnormal" repudiation of sexuality. In fact, her actions and those of many other survivors indicate a girl's logical attempt to protect herself (including her sexuality) by being a size and shape that does not seem as vulnerable to sexual assault. . . .

Poverty

Like sexual abuse, poverty is another injury that may make women vulnerable to eating problems. One woman I interviewed attributed her eating problems directly to the stress caused by poverty. Yolanda is a Black Cape Verdean mother who began eating compulsively when she was twenty-seven years old. After leaving an abusive husband in her early twenties, Yolanda was forced to go on welfare. As a single mother with small children and few financial resources, she tried to support herself and her children on $539 a month. Yolanda began binging in the evenings after putting her children to bed. Eating was something she could do alone. It would calm her, help her deal with loneliness, and make her feel safe. Food was an accessible commodity that was cheap. She ate three boxes of macaroni and cheese when nothing else was available. As a single mother with little money, Yolanda felt as if her body was the only thing she had left. As she described it,

> I am here, [in my body] 'cause there is no where else for me to go. Where am I going to go? This is all I got . . . that probably contributes to putting on so much weight cause staying in your body, in your home, in yourself, you don't go out. You aren't around other people. . . . You hide and as long as you hide you don't have to face . . . nobody can see you eat. You are safe.

When she was eating, Yolanda felt a momentary reprieve from her worries. Binging not only became a logical solution because it was cheap and easy but also because she had grown up amid positive messages about eating. In her family, eating was a celebrated and joyful act. However, in adulthood, eating became a double-edged sword. While comforting her, binging also led to weight gain. During the three years Yolanda was on welfare, she gained seventy pounds.

Yolanda's story captures how poverty can be a precipitating factor in eating problems and highlights the value of understanding how class inequalities may shape women's eating problems. As a single mother, her financial constraints mirrored those of most female heads of households. The dual hazards of a race- and sex-stratified labor market further limited her options (Higginbotham 1986). In an article about Black women's health, Byllye Avery (1990) quotes a Black woman's explanation about why she eats compulsively. The woman told Avery,

> I work for General Electric making batteries, and, I know it's killing me. My old man is an alcoholic. My kids got babies. Things are not well with me. And one thing I know I can do when I come home is cook me a pot of food and sit down in front of the TV and eat it. And you can't take that away from me until you're ready to give me something in its place. (p. 7)

Like Yolanda, this woman identifies eating compulsively as a quick, accessible, and immediately satisfying way of coping with the daily stress caused by conditions she could not control. Connections between poverty and eating problems also show the limits of portraying eating problems as maladies of upper-class adolescent women.

The fact that many women use food to anesthetize themselves, rather than other drugs (even when they gained access to alcohol, marijuana, and other illegal drugs), is partly a function of gender socialization and the competing demands that women face. One of the physiological consequences of binge eating is a numbed state similar to that experienced by drinking. Troubles and tensions are covered over as a consequence of the body's defensive response to massive food intake. When food is eaten in that way, it effectively works like a drug with immediate and predictable effects. Yolanda said she binged late at night rather than getting drunk because she could still get up in the morning, get her children ready for school, and be clearheaded for the college classes she attended. By binging, she avoided the hangover or sickness that results from alcohol or illegal drugs. In this way, food was her drug of choice since it was possible for her to eat while she continued to care for her children, drive, cook, and study. Binging is also less expensive than drinking, a factor that is especially significant for poor women. . . .

Heterosexism

The life history interviews also uncovered new connections between heterosexism and eating problems. One of the most important recent feminist contributions has been identifying compulsory heterosexuality as an institution which truncates opportunities for heterosexual and lesbian women (Rich 1986). All of the women interviewed for this study, both lesbian and heterosexual, were taught that heterosexuality was compulsory, although the versions of this enforcement were shaped by race and class. Expectations about heterosexuality were partly taught through messages that girls learned about eating and their bodies. In some homes, boys were given more food than girls, especially as teenagers, based on the rationale that girls need to be thin to attract boys. As the girls approached puberty, many were told to stop being athletic, begin wearing dresses, and watch their weight. For the women who weighed more than was considered acceptable, threats about their need to diet were laced with admonitions that being fat would ensure becoming an "old maid."

While compulsory heterosexuality influenced all of the women's emerging sense of their bodies and eating patterns, the women who linked heterosexism directly to the beginning of their eating problems were those who knew they were lesbians when very young and actively resisted heterosexual norms. One working-class Jewish woman, Martha, began compulsively eating when she was 11 years old, the same year she started getting clues of her lesbian identity. In junior high school, as many of her female peers began dating boys, Martha began fantasizing about girls, which made her feel utterly alone. Confused and ashamed about her fantasies, Martha came home every day from school and binged. Binging was a way she drugged herself so that being alone was tolerable. Describing binging, she said, "It was the only thing I knew. I was looking for a comfort." Like many women, Martha binged because it softened painful feelings. Binging sedated her, lessened her anxiety, and induced sleep.

Martha's story also reveals ways that trauma can influence women's experience of their bodies. Like many other women, Martha had no sense of herself as connected to her body. When I asked Martha whether she saw herself as fat when she was growing up she said, "I didn't see myself as fat. I didn't see myself. I wasn't there. I get so sad about that because I missed so much." In the literature on eating problems, *body image* is the term that is typically used to describe a woman's experience of her body. This term connotes the act of imagining one's physical appearance. Typically, women with eating problems are assumed to have difficulties with their body image. However, the term body image does not adequately capture the complexity and range of bodily responses to trauma experienced by the women. Exposure to trauma did much more than distort the women's visual image of themselves. These traumas often jeopardized their capacity to consider themselves as having bodies at all. . . .

Racism and Class Injuries

For some of the Latinas and African American women, racism coupled with the stress resulting from class mobility related to the onset of their eating problems. Joselyn, an African American woman, remembered her white grandmother telling her she would never be as pretty as her cousins because they were lighter skinned. Her grandmother often humiliated Joselyn in front of others, as she made fun of Joselyn's body while she was naked and told her she was fat. As a young child, Joselyn began to think that although she could not change her skin color, she could at least try to be thin. When Joselyn was young, her grandmother was the only family member who objected to Joselyn's weight. However, her father also began encouraging his wife and daughter to be thin as the family's class standing began to change. When the family was working class, serving big meals, having chubby children, and keeping plenty of food in the house was a sign the family was doing well. But, as the family became mobile, Joselyn's father began insisting that Joselyn be thin. She remembered, "When my father's business began to bloom and my father was interacting more with white businessmen and seeing how they did business, suddenly thin became important. If you were a truly well-to-do family, then your family was slim and elegant."

As Joselyn's grandmother used Joselyn's body as territory for enforcing her own racism and prejudice about size, Joselyn's father used her body as the territory through which he channeled the demands he faced in the white-dominated business world. However, as Joselyn was pressured to diet, her father still served her large portions and bought treats for her and the neighborhood children. These contradictory messages made her feel confused about her body. As was true for many women in this study, Joselyn was told she was fat beginning when she was very young even though she was not overweight. And, like most of the women, Joselyn was put on diet pills and diets before even reaching puberty, beginning the cycles of dieting, compulsive eating, and bulimia.

The confusion about body size expectations that Joselyn associated with changes in class paralleled one Puerto Rican woman's association between her eating problems and the stress of assimilation as her family's class standing moved from poverty to working class. When Vera was very young, she was so thin that her mother took her to a doctor who prescribed appetite stimulants. However, by the time Vera was eight years old, her mother began trying to shame Vera into dieting. Looking back on it, Vera attributed her mother's change of heart to competition among extended family members that centered on "being white, being successful, being middle class, . . . and it was always, 'Ay Bendito. She is so fat. What happened?'"

The fact that some of the African American and Latina women associated the ambivalent messages about food and eating to their family's class mobility and/or the demands of assimilation while none of the eight white women expressed this (including those whose class was stable and changing) suggests that the added dimension of racism was connected to the imperative to be thin. In fact, the class expectations that their parents experienced exacerbated standards about weight that they inflicted on their daughters.

EATING PROBLEMS AS SURVIVAL STRATEGIES

My research permits a reevaluation of many assumptions about eating problems. First, this work challenges the theoretical reliance on the culture-of-thinness model. Although all of the women I interviewed were manipulated and hurt by this imperative at some point in their lives, it is not the primary source of their problems. Even in the instances in which a culture of thinness was a precipitating factor in anorexia, bulimia, or binging, this influence occurred in concert with other oppressions.

Attributing the etiology of eating problems primarily to a woman's striving to attain a certain beauty ideal is also problematic because it labels a common way that women cope with pain as essentially appearance-based disorders. One blatant example of sexism is the notion that women's foremost worry is about their appearance. By focusing on the emphasis on slenderness, the eating problems literature falls into the same trap of assuming that the problems reflect women's "obsession" with appearance. Some women were raised in families and communities in which thinness was not considered a criterion for beauty. Yet they still developed eating problems. Other women were taught that women should be thin but their eating problems were not primarily in reaction to this imperative. Their eating strategies began as logical solutions to problems rather than problems themselves as they tried to cope with a variety of traumas.

Establishing links between eating problems and a range of oppressions invites a rethinking of both the groups of women who have been excluded from research and those whose lives have been the basis of theory formation. The construction of bulimia and anorexia nervosa as appearance-based disorders is rooted in a notion of femininity in which white middle- and upper-class women are portrayed as frivolous, obsessed with their bodies, and overly accepting of narrow gender roles. This portrayal fuels women's tremendous shame and guilt about eating problems—as signs of self-centered vanity. This construction of white middle- and upper-class women is intimately linked to the portrayal of working-class white women and women of color as their opposite: as somehow exempt from accepting the dominant standards of beauty or as one step away from being hungry and therefore not susceptible to eating problems. Identifying that women may binge to cope with poverty contrasts the notion that eating problems are class bound. Attending to the intricacies of race, class, sexuality, and gender pushes us to rethink the demeaning construction of middle-class femininity and establishes bulimia and anorexia nervosa as serious responses to injustices.

NOTE

1. By trauma I mean a violating experience that has long-term emotional, physical, and/or spiritual consequences that may have immediate or delayed effects. One reason the term *trauma* is useful conceptually is its association with the diagnostic label Post Traumatic Stress Disorder (PTSD) (American Psychological Association 1987). PTSD is one of the few clinical diagnostic categories that recognizes social problems (such as war or the Holocaust) as responsible for the symptoms identified (Trimble 1985). This concept adapts well to the feminist assertion that a woman's symptoms cannot be understood as solely individual, considered outside of her social context, or prevented without significant changes in social conditions.

REFERENCES

American Psychological Association. 1987. *Diagnostic and statistical manual of mental disorders.* 3rd ed. rev. Washington, DC: American Psychological Association.

Andersen, Arnold, and Andy Hay. 1985. Racial and socioeconomic influences in anorexia nervosa and bulimia. *International Journal of Eating Disorders* 4:479–87.

Arnold, Georgiana. 1990. Coming home: One Black woman's journey to health and fitness. In *The Black women's health book: Speaking for ourselves,* edited by Evelyn C. White. Seattle, WA: Seal.

Avery, Byllye Y. 1990. Breathing life into ourselves: The evolution of the National Black Women's Health Project. In *The Black women's health book: Speaking for ourselves,* edited by Evelyn C. White. Seattle, WA: Seal.

Bass, Ellen, and Laura Davis. 1988. *The courage to heal: A guide for women survivors of child sexual abuse.* New York: Harper & Row.

Brown, Laura S. 1987. Lesbians, weight and eating: New analyses and perspectives. In *Lesbian psychologies,* edited by the Boston Lesbian Psychologies Collective. Champaign: University of Illinois Press.

Chernin, Kim. 1981. *The obsession: Reflections on the tyranny of slenderness.* New York: Harper & Row.

Clarke, Cheryl. 1982. *Narratives.* New Brunswick, NJ: Sister Books.

Copeland, Paul M. 1985. Neuroendocrine aspects of eating disorders. In *Theory and treatment of anorexia nervosa and bulimia: Biomedical, sociocultural and psychological perspectives,* edited by Steven Wiley Emmett. New York: Brunner/Mazel.

DeSalvo, Louise. 1989. *Virginia Woolf: The impact of childhood sexual abuse on her life and work.* Boston: Beacon.

Dworkin, Sari H. 1989. Not in man's image: Lesbians and the cultural oppression of body image. In *Loving boldly: Issues facing lesbians,* edited by Ester D. Rothblum and Ellen Close. New York: Harrington Park.

Garfinkel, Paul E., and David M. Garner. 1982. *Anorexia nervosa: A multidimensional perspective.* New York: Brunner/Mazel.

Garner, David. 1985. Iatrogenesis in anorexia nervosa and bulimia nervosa. *International Journal of Eating Disorders* 4:701–26.

Goldfarb, Lori. 1987. Sexual abuse antecedent to anorexia nervosa, bulimia and compulsive overeating: Three case reports. *International Journal of Eating Disorders* 6:675–80.

Gray, James, Kathryn Ford, and Lily M. Kelly. 1987. The prevalence of bulimia in a Black college population. *International Journal of Eating Disorders* 6:733–40.

Herman, Judith. 1981. *Father–daughter incest.* Cambridge, MA: Harvard University Press.

Higginbotham, Elizabeth. 1986. We were never on a pedestal: Women of color continue to struggle with poverty, racism and sexism. In *For crying out loud,* edited by Rochelle Lefkowitz and Ann Withorn. Boston: Pilgrim.

Hsu, George. 1987. Are eating disorders becoming more common in Blacks? *International Journal of Eating Disorders* 6:113–24.

Iazzetto, Demetria. 1989. When the body is not an easy place to be: Women's sexual abuse and eating problems. Ph.D. diss., Union for Experimenting Colleges and Universities, Cincinnati, OH.

Masson, Jeffrey. 1984. *The assault on the truth: Freud's suppression of the seduction theory.* New York: Farrar, Strauss & Giroux.

Naylor, Gloria. 1985. *Linden Hills.* New York: Ticknor & Fields.

Nevo, Shoshana. 1985. Bulimic symptoms: Prevalence and ethnic differences among college women. *International Journal of Eating Disorders* 4:151–68.

Oppenheimer, R., K. Howells, R. L. Palmer, and D. A. Chaloner. 1985. Adverse sexual experience in childhood and clinical eating disorders: A preliminary description. *Journal of Psychiatric Research* 19:357–61.

Orbach, Susie. 1978. *Fat is a feminist issue.* New York: Paddington.

———. 1985. Accepting the symptom: A feminist psychoanalytic treatment of anorexia nervosa. In *Handbook of psychotherapy for anorexia nervosa and bulimia,* edited by David M. Garner and Paul E. Garfinkel. New York: Guilford.

Powers, Retha. 1989. Fat is a Black women's issue. *Essence,* Oct., 75, 78, 134, 136.

Rich, Adrienne. 1986. Compulsory heterosexuality and lesbian existence. in *Blood, bread and poetry.* New York: Norton.

Root, Maria P. P., and Patricia Fallon. 1988. The incidence of victimization experiences in a bulimic sample. *Journal of Interpersonal Violence* 3:161–73.

Schoenfielder, Lisa, and Barbara Wieser, eds. 1983. *Shadow on a tightrope: Writings by women about fat liberation.* Iowa City, IA: Aunt Lute Book Co.

Silber, Tomas. 1986. Anorexia nervosa in Blacks and Hispanics. *International Journal of Eating Disorders* 5:121–28.

Smead, Valerie. 1984. Eating behaviors which may lead to and perpetuate anorexia nervosa, bulimarexia, and bulimia. *Women and Therapy* 3:37–49.

Spack, Norman. 1985. Medical complications of anorexia nervosa and bulimia. In *Theory and treatment of anorexia nervosa and bulimia: Biomedical, sociocultural and psychological perspectives,* edited by Steven Wiley Emmett. New York: Brunner/Mazel.

Swink, Kathy, and Antoinette E. Leveille. 1986. From victim to survivor: A new look at the issues and recovery process for adult incest survivors. *Women and Therapy* 5:119–43.

Trimble, Michael. 1985. Post-traumatic stress disorder: History of a concept. In *Trauma and its wake: The study and treatment of post-traumatic stress disorder,* edited by C. R. Figley. New York: Brunner/Mazel.

What's important is what you look like. 1988. *Gay Community News,* July, 24–30.

White, Evelyn C., ed. 1990. *The Black women's health book: Speaking for ourselves.* Seattle, WA: Seal Press.

———. 1991. Unhealthy appetites. *Essence,* Sept., 28, 30.

Think about It

1. How do the biomedical, psychological, and feminist models differ in explaining eating disorders?

2. Why does Thompson argue that eating problems are survival strategies for coping with sexism, heterosexism, and emotional, sexual or physical abuse?

3. Thompson maintains that women's eating problems are a response to poverty, racism, acculturation, and social class inequality. How, then, might we explain the low rates of eating disorders among black, ethnic, and low-income men?

35 Domestic Violence in African American, Asian American, and Latino Communities

Doris Williams Campbell, Beckie Masaki, and Sara Torres

Families can be warm, loving, and nurturing. They can also be cruel and abusive. Nationally, family members are more likely than outsiders to assault or kill other family members. Doris Williams Campbell, Beckie Masaki, and Sara Torres show that domestic violence is a pervasive problem in many ethnic communities. *

Domestic violence is a serious and pervasive problem in all three ethnic populations discussed in this chapter, and in every community in the United States. Each of the three communities is different, with varying cultural norms related to domestic violence and varying perceptions about its occurrence. Without an understanding of the specific norms and perceptions, efforts to change community perceptions and decrease violence cannot succeed. . . .

IMPACT OF RACISM AND ANTI-IMMIGRANT SENTIMENT

The experience of being a minority group member in the United States is qualitatively different

*The focus groups that participated in this study consisted of five groups of white respondents, three groups of African Americans, two groups of Latinos, and two groups of Asian Americans in Connecticut, Arkansas, Texas, and California. The EDK survey/poll mentioned in this selection was a national random telephone survey of 1,000 people ages 18 and older, plus 300 Latinos, 300 African Americans, and 300 Asian Americans. It was conducted by EDK Associates, a New York–based public opinion research firm. Ed.

Source: From Doris Williams Campbell, Beckie Masaki, and Sara Torres, "Water on Rock: Changing Domestic Violence Perceptions in the African American, Asian American, and Latino Communities," in Ending Domestic Violence: Changing Public Perceptions/Halting the Epidemic, ed. Ethel Klein, Jacquelyn Campbell, Esta Soler, and Marissa Ghez (Thousand Oaks, CA: Sage, 1997), 64–87. Copyright © 1997 Sage Publications, Inc. Reprinted by permission of Sage Publications, Inc.

from that of being a member of the dominant culture (Asbury, 1993). The experience and effects of racism are daily, insidious, interactive, and incalculable. Immigrant women are members of all three of the ethnic groups discussed here, and immigrants as well as those born in the United States face racism, anti-immigrant sentiment, and a dominant culture that is unfamiliar and sometimes in direct conflict with the cultural values of their countries of origin. Immigrant battered women and their children suffer the same barriers as all domestic violence survivors, but they face additional barriers if they do not speak English, do not know the law or their rights, lack job and educational opportunities, and lack access to language- and culture-competent services. Their immigrant status is an additional source of stress. If the woman is in this country illegally, she may be afraid to seek help. Also, immigrant women may have left family and friends, their major sources of psychological and financial support.

Male batterers use race, culture, and immigration status to control their partners. Batterers frequently accuse their partners of "becoming too Americanized," "betraying their culture, family, and community," and "not being a good Filipina/Japanese/Korean/Mexican/Cuban/Puerto Rican/Guatemalan/Haitian—and so on—woman." Other controlling behavior includes males "forbidding" female partners to learn English, access public transportation, or acquire independent skills necessary to negotiate life in a new country. Immigrant battered women who are dependent on U.S.-citizen spouses for their immigration status are often threatened with deportation by the batterer. Whether threats regarding immigration status are real or perceived by the batterer, a battered woman often has no access to accurate information about her rights. Anti-immigrant legislation and general sentiment in the United States feed into a dynamic of reduced access to alternatives and a rising sense of hopelessness for immigrant battered women. Batterers will attempt to excuse their abusive behavior as "culturally acceptable" or as a consequence of racism, immigrant stresses, or other forms of victimization.

Domestic violence crosses all lines, but services and responses designed to address the needs of battered women do not reach all segments of the population. The severe lack of services and information for and/or specific to battered women from marginalized communities renders the women extremely vulnerable. Without alternatives, battered women of color are not safe to speak out or escape violent relationships. Racism, anti-immigrant sentiment, and strategies that do not match the needs of women of particular ethnic groups create an environment that effectively silences battered women and obstructs the potential for change in public perceptions of domestic violence in those communities. . . . .

DOMESTIC VIOLENCE IN THE AFRICAN AMERICAN COMMUNITY

Some scholars write that the historical literature fails to find any evidence of ill treatment of African women by their male partners. During the entire reign of the pharaohs in Egypt, African women purportedly enjoyed complete freedom, in contrast to the condition of segregation experienced by European women of ancient and medieval times. If these accounts are true, the pattern of spouse abuse as reported in the recent literature (where African American males are more likely to batter their wives or girlfriends than are white males) did not originate in African tradition (Dennis et al., 1995). These authors suggest that the tradition of abuse is part of the American experience. Thus we must examine the American experience of African American males when trying to interpret and intervene in the problem of spouse abuse in African American families.

Numerous attempts to explain the prevalence of domestic and other forms of violence in the black community have been offered, primarily by sociologists and criminologists. The belief that a high rate of violence among blacks is inevitable and "normal" is partly grounded in a racial stereotype. It is also a product of observations made by Eurocentric social scientists who have sought to explain disproportionate levels of violence within the black community. Historically, black women and children have been afforded less protection from abuse in the family than those in any other groups in American society. White women and children have also been underprotected, but much less so than blacks. Unless we confront and challenge persisting ideological and environmental constraints, increasing official intervention in domestic violence will merely result in an unequal race-of-victim pattern of intervention similar to that found in the handling of nonfamily criminal violence. That is, black and poor victims of family violence may be ignored, and most prevention efforts will be targeted at the white middle class.

Research also shows that other forms of violence occur all too frequently in the African American community. Community violence and homicide are both frightening forms of violence confronted by many African Americans. African American women and men and their children in inner-city areas are at greater jeopardy than their counterparts in other environments for witnessing the homicide of their adolescent sons, their spouses, or other family members and friends. African American women may also be at greater risk for battering and homicide by a spouse or male partner than are women in other settings. A dominant factor associated with homicide is

poverty. Poverty appears to be more strongly associated with killings of family members and
friends than killings of acquaintances. Spousal
homicides tend to be associated with a belief in
male dominance. Other factors associated with
homicide of all types, except child homicide, are
the consumption of alcohol, abuse of illicit drugs,
and the presence of a gun in the home (Rosenberg
et al., 1986).

The problem of interpersonal violence is
clearly not unique to African American communities, but homicide is considered a major health
problem in numerous black communities with a
high rate of black-on-black murders. This problem is addressed only rarely in the research literature. The lack of data has led to the common
misconception that violence in the black community is connected only with crime, and thus it is considered a legal rather than a health or community
problem.

Several recent studies suggest that black
women victims of domestic violence are more
likely than white women victims to report abuse
to police and to call police to resolve conflict
within their intimate relationships (Hutchison et
al., 1994; Miller, 1989). They are also more likely
to report all types of violent crime to police, compared with white women (Bachman, 1994; Bachman & Coker, 1995). This finding may be related
to economic resources and social class. Women
with higher incomes likely have greater access to
resources to assist them in keeping their abuse private because they can afford private medical care
and safe shelter. The result, according to Miller
(1989), is that they are able to escape detection by
law enforcement, hospital emergency rooms, or
social service agencies. Thus the significance of
race in the analysis of domestic violence rates
may have more to do with access to resources
than with race (Hampton & Gelles, 1993; Miller,
1989).

Coker (1992) reported that police were more
likely to make an arrest when victims had sustained injuries, when the offender did not have a
history of violence, and when black offenders

were victimizing black victims (compared with
white men who had victimized white women).
Women who experienced repeated victimizations
by the same assailant were more likely to sustain
injuries than women who reported no prior history of violence by their attacker (Coker, 1992).
Bachman and Coker (1995) suggested that unre-
ported incidents not only eliminate the opportunity for offenders to receive formal sanctions but
also place women at an increased risk of sustaining injury. However, because the efficacy of police and/or the judicial system in protecting women
is still unproved, more research is needed to delineate systematically and carefully the effectiveness of alternative police responses in deterring
incidents of domestic violence.

Sampson (1987) conducted conceptual work
on exploring the relationship between African
American male joblessness and urban violence of
all forms. Unemployment is a risk factor for domestic violence that has been found consistently
across studies (Hotaling & Sugarman, 1986; Tolman & Bennett, 1990). The extent to which negative attitudes held by whites become self-fulfilling
in relation to minority groups (e.g., having more
of a predilection toward violence) is also an important area for future investigation. Peterson-
Lewis, Turner, and Adams (1986) suggested that
African American women may attribute the
causes of their abuse to the larger society but not
to the abuser. They may rationalize that the abuse
they have endured from mates reflects the treatment the partner received from the dominant culture. If true, this dynamic may reinforce the myth
of the "strong black woman," willing and able to
tolerate abuse and other indignities to protect her
family and her mate. These authors concluded
that African American females may believe that
African American males are more likely than
white males to be arrested if police intervene in
domestic violence incidents and to be the victims
of police maltreatment. Therefore, the women
may feel terrible conflict when making decisions
about calling the police.

One exceptional preventive/intervention model

for dealing with black women's health problems is the National Black Women's Health Project (NBWHP). This program was initiated by the activist and advocate Billye Y. Avery, an African American grassroots organizer who has worked tirelessly since the early 1980s to help black women improve their mental and physical well-being through empowerment, healing, and self-love. The NBWHP uses a highly acclaimed model of community-based self-help programs, community-based health centers, retreats, educational films, and publications. The organization deals directly with black women's health concerns within the context of black culture. The number one health issue the project addresses is violence against black women of all ages. The NBWHP program can be duplicated anywhere. It is represented by 96 self-help groups in 22 states and 6 groups in Kenya, Barbados, and Belize (White, 1994). . . .

Survey Findings Specific to African Americans

One of the overall EDK survey findings specific to African Americans is important to note as it relates to community action and education. Comparing attitudes about domestic violence by gender in the three ethnic categories, the survey found that only African American women and men appeared almost equally worried about family violence. This finding appears unrelated to education or income; thus it may be an important shared cultural perspective to consider when planning ethnic-specific interventions. African American women and men may already view this problem through the same lens (in contrast to the denial of domestic violence among many white males). One must first recognize and accept the reality that domestic violence is a serious problem before addressing solutions. Thus African American women and men may both be ready to consider specific interventions that might be relevant within their communities.

DOMESTIC VIOLENCE IN THE LATINO COMMUNITY

The culture and current realities of Latino families also have complex interactions with domestic violence. *Marianismo* is a concept describing the expectation that Latinos will emulate the qualities of the Virgin Mary, such as moral integrity and spiritual strength. The spiritual strength should engender self-sacrifice, including tolerating her husband's bad habits, submitting to males of the family, complying with her husband's decisions, and supporting her husband unwaveringly. Family tradition and family unity are important values in the Latino community, and family loyalty is essential. Typically, Latinos value the family's well-being over an individual's (*familialism*). Divorce is less acceptable than among Anglo populations. Traditional Latino families are hierarchical, with the elderly, parents, and males holding power and authority. Male and female roles are separated at an early age and often strictly delineated. The male is the head of the family and is expected to be strong and dominant. He assumes the role of protector of the family—particularly of females. The female is expected to be the family nurturer and submit to males. She is expected to sacrifice for the family. Family matters are handled with privacy, and serious matters such as domestic violence are often handled from within rather than from outside the family. The family, including extended family members, is seen as a source of support at all times.

The concept of *machismo* is also still present in some Latino families and communities. Machismo refers not only to the dominant role of the male but to the sense of responsibility and perhaps pride in the male role. It also represents the investment of strength in males and the need to avoid any signs of weakness.

The focus group conversations in this study revealed aspects of the machismo concept. Some Latinas strongly supported the cultural argument that men who assault their wives are actually living up to cultural perceptions encouraged by our society. They described violence as part of the macho culture. The Latinas felt that deep-rooted traditions of male dominance still exist. Latinas noted a difference between men from Mexico and those born in the United States: They felt the former were more rigid, punitive, and domineering toward women, and many attributed men's violent behavior to lack of education. Latinos were least likely to agree that the use of force was a means of compensating for the lack of other forms of power or sources of self-esteem. This again may be a result of machismo and Latino men's reluctance to admit that they use force to control women, because they view themselves as protective of women.

Many Latinos believe the universe is controlled by external forces and so is an individual's destiny. The attitude of *que sera, sera* or "what will be, will be" is widespread. Even the structure of the Spanish language protects the speaker from accepting full responsibility for unpleasantness. For example, the construction of a sentence that suggests "I missed my plane" becomes "The plane left me." The phrase avoids direct personal responsibility. The feeling that events are meant to be and cannot be changed is often strongly related to religious belief. External events are thought to be "God's will" or externally controlled. Religion has a major influence on behavior and is a source of conflict, particularly in times of stress. Religious beliefs, customs, and superstitions form an intrinsic part of family culture. Material suffering is compensated for by spiritual reward. Suffering on earth is often seen as a way to attain Heaven. Forgiveness of the offender may be perceived as mandated by God or the church.

Catholicism is historically and presently the predominant religious affiliation for Latinas. This religion considers maintaining the family unit as primary, even at the expense of a woman's well-being (Molina et al., 1994), which affects how Latinas may react to abuse. In one study, a higher percentage of Latinas sought assistance from religious organizations before going to a shelter (Torres, 1991). In addition, some Latinas practice *curanderismo,* which is the art and science of us-

ing herbs, prayers, and rituals to cure physical, spiritual, and emotional ills. Some who sought help from agencies had practiced curanderismo first.

Torres (1991), in one of the few ethnic group comparative studies to date, found cross-cultural differences between Latinas and Anglo-American women in terms of their attitudes toward wife abuse and their perceptions of what constitutes wife abuse; Latinas were more tolerant of wife abuse than were Anglo women. Some acts, including hitting or verbal abuse, had to occur more frequently to be considered abusive by Latinas. Furthermore, Latinas had a slightly different perception of what constitutes wife abuse. Some acts perceived as abusive by the Anglo women were not considered abusive by Latinas: for example, verbal abuse or failure to provide adequate food and shelter. The nature of abuse experienced by both groups of women was basically the same for acts considered to be physical abuse. For acts considered to be emotional abuse, Latinas showed more tolerance than Anglo-American women. However, in spite of these findings, there was no significant difference between the two groups in the severity and frequency of abuse.

The choices Latinas have in response to being abused are similar to what most Anglo women have. If a Latina leaves her home, she encounters the same problems basic to all women. Torres's (1991) study showed that culture, family, and religion were the major factors affecting how Latinas reacted to being battered.

The same study found that Latinas pointed to the family as the most important factor influencing their decision to leave or stay in a battering relationship (Torres, 1991). Latinas were more likely than Anglo women to report that they stayed in a relationship because of their children and threats to family members, whereas Anglo women reported staying because of love or not having a place to go. Some 40% of Latinas, compared with 20% of Anglo women, said they left because of their children. The reason most frequently given by Latinas for going back to their spouses was "the children." Compared with Anglo women, Latinas in the Torres study tended to stay longer in the relationship with their abusive spouses before seeking assistance, because of family pressure and "for the sake of the children." The study also found that Latinas were hit more frequently in front of family members than were Anglo women. Latinas left and came back to their spouses more times than Anglo women. Thus it is important not to assume that because a battered Latina has asked for help that she will want to leave her home.

Therefore, advocates and professionals working with battered Latinas should be aware of the family roles, traditions, and expectations idiosyncratic to the Latino culture. The attitudes a woman's culture holds about sex roles affect a woman's self-image. In addition, the study reported that Latinas were especially sensitive and reacted to criticism or nonacceptance (perceived or imagined) of themselves, or their family, culture, language, husband (or other male relative), economic situation, level of education, consciousness, and/or degree of dependence/independence.

Survey Findings Specific to Latino Culture

. . . There has been minimal involvement by Latino men and women in the battered women's movement. However, the EDK survey found more overall similarities than differences among ethnic/ racial groups regarding perceptions of the extent of domestic violence in their own personal experience. Two areas of findings regarding concern about the growth of family violence in the Latino community deserve specific comment.

First, in the EDK study, Latinas were the group most worried about the growth of family violence. One could speculate several causes, such as exposure to violence, the media, or education. Latinas in the United States have a lower educational level than Caucasian women, and education level was found to be related to concern about domestic violence in this study.

Second, Latinas were more concerned about the growth of domestic violence than were Latino men (43% vs. 35%), a difference similar to but smaller than that between Caucasian women and men in the EDK poll. Although both men (64%) and women (70%) acknowledged that men beat women, Latinas were more likely than their male counterparts to say that it happens often (42% vs. 28%). However, Latinos were least likely to deny that men rarely beat women (26% compared with 62% of Caucasians, 53% of African Americans, and 43% of Asian Americans). Thus it is possible that even though Latinos were willing to admit that violence occurs in the home, these men might minimize it, whereas women were more apt to admit the frequency of the abuse. Perhaps the minimizing is part of the macho image and the protective role that Latinos assume over Latinas. In addition, Latinas were more likely than their male counterparts to agree that men beating women is a behavior learned in the home (41% vs. 27%).

Although the majority of every group agreed that a man threatening a woman constituted a public matter, there were significant racial/ethnic differences. Caucasians were most likely to say it is a public matter (67%), whereas Latinos (51%) were least likely. Again, this is indicative of the Latino culture, where family matters are handled in privacy.

Across race, class, and ethnic groups, there was strong agreement with the statement that beating up a woman is often learned in the home. There were significant gender differences among Caucasians (57% of women vs. 44% of men strongly agreed) and among Latinos (41% vs. 27%).

In the focus groups, most men and women agreed with the statement that domestic violence is an attack on women's dignity and freedom; women tended to agree strongly more often than men. In the EDK survey, there were also significant gender differences among Caucasians (59% of women vs. 39% of men strongly agreed) and Latinos (43% vs. 24% strongly agreed). There were also differences across racial/ethnic groups. White women were most likely to agree strongly with this statement (59% compared with 43% of Latinas, 38% of African Americans, and 25% of Asian American women). Among men, Latinos were significantly less likely to agree strongly with this statement than were men from other racial and ethnic groups. Latinas agreed with the statement, but blamed the victim for letting the man rob her of her self-esteem. Similarly, several Latinos said the loss of a woman's confidence depended on her spirit.

In summary, these findings suggest that Latinas are more open than Latinos to revealing the issues and circumstances related to domestic violence. As a group, this population is also less likely than others to be concerned about domestic violence or to think it should be a public issue.

DOMESTIC VIOLENCE IN THE ASIAN AMERICAN COMMUNITY

Asia is home to some of the oldest continuous civilizations in the world. In China, India, and other Asian countries, patriarchal relationships define women's roles in society and are reinforced through language, laws, religion, daily customs, and beliefs. Both the Asian community and outsiders view Asian culture as it was defined by men centuries ago, without regard to the views of women from those cultures nor to the reality that culture undergoes constant change and evolution.

In developing strategies to change perceptions about domestic violence among Asian Americans, understanding the deep roots of Asian belief systems is key to creating a strategy that both incorporates culture and challenges traditional values that condone domestic violence.

In an attempt to be culturally sensitive, some experts mistakenly incorporate a stereotypical, static view of Asian culture and beliefs to inform their analysis or strategy for addressing domestic violence. One example of this can be seen in the Dong Lau Chen case, in which a Chinese immigrant man in New York beat his wife to death with a hammer in 1987. Dong Lau Chen defended his actions by stating that in China, if a man believes his wife to be unfaithful, he has the right to kill her because she has brought shame upon him. Professor Pasternak from Hunter College provided expert testimony to verify that Chen's statement and actions under the circumstances were that of a "reasonable Chinese man." The judge in this case sentenced Chen to 5 years of probation, with no jail time or fines (Volpp, 1994).

Many Asian Americans protested the sentence. No experts were called by the prosecution, and if more research had been done on current Chinese laws against domestic violence, it would have come to light that the beliefs Chen described reflected *feudal* China. In present-day China, strict laws exist that make domestic violence, from battery to murder, a crime.

The author and other Asian American domestic violence workers from the Asian Women's Shelter in San Francisco and the New York Asian Women's Center attended the NGO Forum and United Nations Fourth World Conference on Women in Beijing, in August 1995. At a bilingual workshop, the Asian American women shared the story of the Dong Lau Chen case with the Chinese women there, and the Chinese women were shocked. They reported that the same type of domestic violence murder in China would likely draw a severe sentence, and that laws against domestic violence have been in effect in their country since 1949.

The first shelters for battered women appeared in the United States during the 1970s; the earliest shelter probably existed in 13th-century Japan. Kakekomidera (refuge temple) in the city of Kamakura, Kanagawa Prefecture, was a safe refuge where women could flee their husbands. Divorce in medieval times was virtually unheard of, but if a woman served in the temple for 3 years, she could be officially granted a divorce (Kanagawa Women's Council, 1995).

One of the few small-scale societies with *no* wife beating, according to anthropological evidence reported in Levinson's (1989) study of family violence across cultures, exists in central Thailand. Levinson attributed the lack of family violence to the group's practice of nonviolence throughout their society and to the equal distribution of labor and power without differentiation along gender lines.

. . . Sanctions against battering are seen to be important deterrents to the escalation of domestic violence. Many examples can be drawn from traditional Asian communities throughout history, continuing to the present day. A modern example of public sanctions is Jagori, a single women's group in a village near New Delhi, India; members of the group have held protests in front of the homes of batterers to shame them publicly and raise community awareness and support. Another example is in Beijing, where batterers are held accountable through sanctions from their neighborhood block captains, work unit, and/or the criminal justice system.

Historical examples of public opposition to domestic violence among Asians are important in demonstrating not only that domestic violence is a global problem, but that efforts to prevent domestic violence are global as well. The seeds of changing public perception about domestic violence are rooted in every cultural history.

Survey Findings Specific to Asian Americans

In terms of saliency of domestic violence, . . . Asian Americans were the least likely of the ethnic groups to be "very worried" (20% of women and 26% of men) about the growth of family violence and the most likely of any ethnic group to be "not worried" (30% of women and 28% of men).

This low rate of concern for the growth of family violence among Asian Americans could be attributed to the lack of public awareness about the issue. Asian Americans have traditionally kept problems within the family. Extended families are common in Asian cultures and are an excellent network of support when they operate in healthy

ways. When family violence exists, however, the extended family can be a further barrier for a battered woman to seek outside help and for outside community members to become aware that the problem of family violence exists.

Contributing to the invisibility of family violence within the Asian American community is the severe lack of resources for Asian American battered women who want to escape violent relationships. Racism, the lack of bilingual/bicultural programs, and anti-immigrant sentiment all contribute to silencing Asian American battered women.

Once appropriate resources are made available, Asian American battered women respond as much as battered women from other ethnic groups. The Asian Women's Shelter in San Francisco turns away about 75% of the battered women who call in need of shelter because of lack of space. Some 80% of the shelter's residents choose to end their relationship with the batterer and rebuild their lives as single women and mothers. The few other shelters (New York Asian Women's Center; Center for the Pacific Asian Family, Los Angeles) in the United States that provide bilingual/bicultural services to Asian American battered women and their children report similar numbers of Asian American women requesting services and choosing to end relationships with the batterer.

Although the difference was not statistically significant, Asian American women in the EDK survey were the only group of women "not worried" about the growth of family violence at a higher percentage than men of the same ethnicity (30% compared with 28%), and Asian American women were the only group of women to have fewer "very worried" responses than the men in their same ethnic group (20% compared with 26%).

Asian Americans in the EDK survey also differed from their ethnic counterparts along gender lines in their responses to the statement that domestic violence is an attack on women's dignity and freedom. While in other ethnic groups, women tended to agree with this statement more often than men, for Asian Americans, the men were more likely than the women to agree strongly with this statement (39% compared with 25%). A possible insight into the women's relatively low degree of agreement with this statement was revealed in focus group conversations in which Asian American women did not think most Asians focused on words like *self-esteem* and *self-confidence.* Perhaps they felt that words such as *freedom, independence,* and *self* place too much emphasis on individualism. Asian cultures and languages often express values of interdependence and interconnection. This does not necessarily mean that Asian American women do not believe in concepts such as self-esteem and freedom, but words such as women's *confidence, strength,* and *rights* might resonate more clearly among Asian American women.

The EDK survey was among the first to include Asian Americans in a breakdown of responses by ethnicity. Further research is important to gain more comparison data about Asian Americans' perceptions about family violence and to provide more insight into the responses by Asian Americans in this study, particularly when they differed from the responses from all other ethnic groups.

COMMUNITY RESPONSES TO BATTERED WOMEN OF COLOR

Some ethnic minority communities encourage the victim to keep silent and to deny her abuse. However, this also happens in some white families; comparative proportions are unknown. One often hears of the family of color in which people are abused, and one way they deal with it is to encourage the victim to remain silent. In Latino communities, if a wife is abused, she will often say "My mother told me, 'You married him. You made your bed; you lie in it,' and I will have to stay in it."

The resulting embarrassment and perceived stigma might keep the family from doing any-

thing. This is especially true if the family tried to get assistance in the past and was unsuccessful, or if the family was met with discrimination. In some cases, women who are abused by their husbands won't tell their family or won't tell anybody else for fear their family or their brother or someone close would get into a fight with the husband. Therefore, they will often pretend there is nothing going on. This can also happen when a person is abused by someone outside of the family or by a coworker.

Thus discrimination against the subgroup occurs as an outcome modifier. Studies have found that special populations of women tend to be abused over and over. These victims are often minority women, the homeless, the mentally ill, and other multiply stigmatized women.

Some victims experience secondary injuries. When they are abused and go to the health care system or call the police for assistance, they often experience discrimination. Women of color can often be especially sensitive and reactive to criticism or perceived nonacceptance of themselves, their family, culture, and language because of prior experience with racist or insensitive mainstream institutions.

REFERENCES

Asbury, J. (1993). Violence in families of color in the United States. In R. L. Hampton, R. P. Gullott, G. R. Adams, E. Potter, II, & R. P. Weissberg (Eds.), *Family violence: Prevention and treatment* (pp. 159–175). Newbury Park, CA: Sage.

Bachman, R. (1994). *Violence against women: A national crime victimization survey report.* Washington, DC: U.S. Department of Justice.

Bachman, R., & Coker, A. (1995). Police involvement in domestic violence: The interactive effects of victim injury, offender's history of violence and race. *Violence and Victims,* 10(2) 91–106.

Coker, A. (1992). *Effect of injury on police involvement in intimate violence.* Paper presented at the 44th Annual American Society of Criminology Meeting, New Orleans, LA.

Dennis, R. E., Key, L. J., Kirk, A. L., & Smith, A. (1995). Addressing domestic violence in the African American community. *Journal of Health Care for the Poor and Underserved, 6*(2), 284–293.

Hampton, R. L., & Gelles, R. J. (1993). Violence toward Black women in a nationally representative sample of Black American families. In R. L. Hampton, T. P. Gullotta, G. R. Adams, E. Potter, II, & R. P. Weissberg (Eds.), *Family violence: Prevention and treatment* (pp. 113–139). Thousand Oaks, CA: Sage.

Hotaling, G. T., & Sugarman, D. B. (1986). A risk marker analysis of assaulted wives. *Journal of Family Violence, 5,* 1–14.

Hutchison, I., Hirschel, J., & Pesackis, C. (1994). Family violence and police utilization. *Violence and Victims, 9*(4), 299–313.

Kanagawa Women's Council. (1995). *For the elimination of violence against women.* Kanagawa, Japan: Kanagawa Prefecture.

Levinson, D. (1989). *Family violence in cross-cultural perspective.* Newbury Park, CA: Sage.

Miller, S. L. (1989). Unintended side effects of pro-arrest policies and their race and class implications for battered women: A cautionary note. *Criminal Justice Policy Review, 3,* 299–317.

Molina, C. W., Zambrana, R. E. & Aguirre-Molina, M. (1994). The influence of culture, class, and environment on health care. In C. W. Molina & M. Aguirre-Molina (Eds.), *Latino health in the U.S: A growing challenge.* Baltimore, MD: Victor Graphics.

Peterson-Lewis, S., Turner, C., & Adams, A. (1986). Attributional processes in repeatedly abused women. In G. W. Russell (Ed.), *Violence in intimate relationships* (pp. 107–130). New York: PMA.

Rosenberg, M., Stark, E., & Zahn, M. (1986). Interpersonal violence: Homicide and spouse abuse. In J. Last (Ed.), *Public health and preventive medicine* (12th ed., pp. 1399–1426). Norwalk, CT: Appleton Century-Crofts.

Sampson, R. (1987). Urban black violence: The effect of male joblessness and family disruption. *American Journal of Sociology, 93*(2), 348–382.

Tolman, R. M., & Bennett, L. W. (1990). A review of research on men who batter. *Journal of Interpersonal Violence, 5*(1), 87.

Torres, S. (1991). A comparison of wife abuse between two cultures: Perceptions, attitudes, nature, and extent. *Issues in Mental Health Nursing, 12,* 113–131.

Volpp, L. (1994). (Mis)identifying culture: Asian women and the "cultural defense." *Harvard Women's Law Journal, 17,* 57.

White, E. C. (1994). *The black women's health book: Speaking for ourselves.* Seattle, WA: Seal Press.

Think about It

1. What do the researchers mean when they state that "male batterers use race, culture, and immigration status to control their partners"?

2. What are the risk factors of domestic violence in the black community? According to this study, why did some of the battered women tolerate abuse instead of reporting it to the police?

3. How do cultural values and resources in Latino and Asian American communities affect women's responses to physical and emotional abuse?

36 | Mistreatment of Vietnamese Elderly by Their Families in the United States

Quyen Kim Le

Most of the research on elder abuse has focused on older family members in white households rather than on elderly minorities. Using in-depth interviews in this exploratory study, Quyen Kim Le examines cultural factors—such as dependency and filial piety—that are associated with elder mistreatment in Vietnamese American families. Le also describes the definitions and perceptions of abuse, the characteristics of the perpetrators, and the vulnerable status many immigrant elders and their families experience in a new environment.

HISTORICAL BACKGROUND

To understand the phenomenon of elder maltreatment within the Vietnamese community, it is important to trace the presence of Vietnamese refugees and immigrants in the United States. The history of immigration began in April 1975 when people with higher levels of education and professional skills fled Vietnam at the fall of Saigon, mostly by air. This first group of refugees admitted to the U.S. was almost all Vietnamese. They were from families with wealthy backgrounds or with relationships to the American government and were generally intact. This group acculturated more easily in the U.S. and became financially self-sufficient.

From 1977 to 1986, a second wave of refugees emerged. It was composed of a variety of different ethnic people (Hmong, Mien Khmer, Chinese, and Vietnamese) known as "boat people" who escaped on their own to seek freedom. Some were enlisted men in South Vietnamese armed forces, fishermen, or merchants. They were generally less well-educated and less literate, of rural origin, and much more traumatized during their escape. Many experienced serious multiple traumas such as being raped, robbed, incarcerated, and tortured. Many died at sea and many spent years in refugee camps under intolerable conditions before coming to the U.S.

The third group of Vietnamese refugees began coming to the U.S. in 1985. They were part of the Orderly Departure Program (ODP) or sometimes called the Family Reunification Program, created to allow Vietnamese immigrants in the U.S. to sponsor their immediate family members for reunification with them. Priority was first given to spouses, then children, then parents, and finally to siblings. The sponsoring process could take from five to ten years. Because they arrived first and because of their ability to adapt, refugees from the first wave became well-settled after a few years and had the capability of sponsorship. Born and raised in Vietnam, they still preserved some traditional culture. Since it was normal in Vietnam to live in a multigenerational household, they decided to sponsor their parents to reunite with them.

STUDY PROBLEM

While still actively mourning their losses and recovering from migration stress, many Vietnamese

Source: From Quyen Kim Le, "Mistreatment of Vietnamese Elderly by Their Families in the United States," *Journal of Elder Abuse & Neglect* 9, no. 1 (1997): 51–62. Copyright © 1997 The Haworth Press, Inc. Reprinted by permission of The Haworth Press, Inc.

refugees also had to cope with many cultural barriers and acculturation stresses (Murase, 1982). Through personal observations, this author has noted that the disintegration of the traditional family structure and loss of cultural values are having great psychological impact. The role of the elder is changing. Elders may no longer hold the traditional position of respect in the family. The younger generations of these families are quickly becoming assimilated into American society and developing new sets of values. Holding onto cultural traditions may not be important for them. Caring for an older family member may not be a personal priority for many. The older adults, coming from a culture where elders are respected and cared for by the younger members of their families, often feel neglected and experience a kind of isolation from their own families. This estrangement in combination with the feeling of isolation from their own community as a whole can exacerbate feelings of depression and irrelevance (Nguyen, 1982).

Reflecting the teachings of Confucius, Vietnamese elders have a strong sense of family preservation and self-reliance. They feel an obligation to the family to confine family problems to the four walls of the home. They have faith in fate and filial piety, so disclosure of abusive or neglected situations may be regarded as bringing shame to the family. When compared to the losses of life during evacuation either by air or by boat, losses of identity, status, and family values, as well as the dislocations which they were compelled to live through, concerns such as elder abuse were almost mundane and benign to these older immigrants.

No information regarding elder abuse within this community was available. However through consultations and interviews with professionals at mental health centers which Vietnamese elders utilized, psychological intimidation was reported to be the most prevalent type of maltreatment. In particular, they often experienced "silent treatment" by their children. Within the Vietnamese context, not to speak to someone is an extreme form of punishment. The use of silence and avoidance may be more emotionally devastating than

physical abuse; for example, the abuser may stop talking suddenly, leave the room, refuse to sit with the elder, look right through the elder, or treat the elder as if he or she did not exist. Financial abuse was probably non-existent since the elders became immediately dependent on their offspring as soon as they came to the U.S. However, there were a few cases where the elders' Supplemental Security Income (SSI) or General Assistance (GA) income was "confiscated" by the elder's family. Physical abuse was the least reported, according to interviews with Adult Protective Services in San Jose.

The lack of awareness by the elder and their families that some behaviors constitute abuse or neglect or of services available to help families resolve difficulties tend to make this problem even more hidden than it is in the mainstream population. Cultural traditions, a language barrier, and unfamiliarity with Western culture also contribute to abuse by preventing elders from seeking help.

The questions addressed in this study were: (1) How are Vietnamese elders treated by their families and (2) Is there evidence of abuse or neglect in these families? If mistreatment is evident, (a) How are they abused or neglected; (b) What is the most prevalent type of abuse or neglect; and (c) How do they react to the situation?

METHODS

The study was carried out at the John XXIII Multi-Service Center and the Vietnamese American Cultural and Social Council, both located in downtown San Jose, California. The criteria used for sample selection were:

- The elder person was Vietnamese, 60 years and older.
- The family shared a residence, and the elder was not a house guest or visitor.
- The adult child performed some tasks for the elder which indicated that there was some degree of dependency; for example, the child provided

help with shopping, banking, transportation, translation of documents, and/or applications for services.

- The caregiver was the adult responsible for the household.

Due to the sensitivity of the subject being researched, the sample size was small (n = 20). The age of the respondents ranged from 63 to 96 years of age; the mean age was 75 years.

It became obvious that Western measurement tools of domestic violence were not culturally adequate to capture the intricacies of elder abuse in the Vietnamese community. Therefore, the author developed a questionnaire designed for this special population. Because the findings of this study were based on the experiences of a very small number of participants, they may not reflect the perceptions of the Vietnamese elders in general. In addition, the assessment was based entirely on interviews with elders. Family members' perspectives were not considered, and there was no way to verify the elders' views. The outcome of this research cannot be generalized to other populations due to ethnic and cultural differences. The reliability and validity of the instrument used in this research have not been determined since the tool was developed and tested only this one time.

FINDINGS

Since the purpose of this research was to gather information about the possibility of elder abuse or neglect in Vietnamese families, a topic in which no previous study had been done, the project was considered a pilot effort and exploratory. The interview process began with questioning the elders about their feelings concerning their current living situations. Then, it moved to the areas of verbal and emotional abuses, followed by financial and physical mistreatment. It also inquired about their behaviors and their reactions to abuse if they thought that they were abused.

The general questions about their current liv-ing situations focused on the degree of stress, depression, anxiety, regret, anger, fear, or loneliness perceived by the participants when living with their children or relatives. The results showed that 17 people were depressed; 16 were fearful about future lack of help when they would become frail; 15 felt stressed; 15 reported loneliness; 14 were uncomfortable about their dependency on their children; and 14 were anxious about their future.

Four specific areas of abuse were explored: verbal, emotional, financial, and physical abuses. No physical abuse was identified in the 20 interviews. Only one case of financial abuse was reported. Verbal and emotional abuse were reported most often. Verbal abuse referred to insult, coercion, threat with a weapon, or being asked to leave the house. There were 13 cases where the elder was encouraged to leave the house if they were unhappy, 10 cases of coercion to stay in the house, 9 cases of insult, 1 case of eviction without advance notice, but no cases of threat with a weapon. The majority of the reported coercion cases were related to situations where the elderly women were confined all day in the house. They stated that their daughters-in-law did not want them to learn English or how to use public transportation. Therefore, they were forced to stay in the house to do house chores. One elderly lady reported that she knew a lot of elders in her situation. Their children were using them as free workers.

Emotional abuse refers to harassment, threats of nursing home placement, social isolation, silent treatment, or ignoring the presence of the elder in the house. As a consequence of these actions, the elders acknowledged that they lived in fear. Some elderly women reported that their daughters-in-law gave them more difficulty than sons-in-law. Five cases involved harassments from daughters-in-law. The elders reported that the daughters-in-law were jealous about the filial piety that their husbands exhibited toward their mothers. There was one case where the daughter-in-law always made sure that she was present when the mother and her son were talking. Fourteen cases of silent treatment were mentioned. They were mostly initiated by the adult children toward their parents. Instead of arguing, the children opted not to talk. Nine cases of avoidance were reported. Two of these 9 cases are worth mentioning because of the children's interracial marriages. In one case, the American son-in-law avoided talking to the elder because the latter did not understand English. In another case, an elderly woman reported that her American son-in-law stated that he did not believe in extended families and that he only cared for his wife and children. The woman felt uncomfortable when he ignored her presence in the house.

The results of the interviews indicated that mistreatment of elderly people did occur in Vietnamese families. However, most cases could be considered as moderate rather than severe mistreatment. Of interest is the fact that the elders who reported having no problem at home were the ones who came to the U.S. at the same time as their children. Since they had to go through the same adjustments when starting their new lives in the U.S., parents and children understood each other's struggles. Filial piety was still preserved; therefore their lives were more in harmony. Some other parents were not as fortunate. There were instances when some of them were expected to be babysitters for their grandchildren in exchange for room and board. They also had to do light housework. The elders felt that there was no appreciation for what they had done, but only reproaches.

The people who had severe problems were the newcomers; most had arrived in the previous five years. They reported that their children were insensitive to their feelings. They were yelled at for the slightest mistakes, from damaging gadgets or equipment in the house because they were unable to read the instructions on how to use them, to confiding their feelings of being homesick. They stated that their children did not want to hear their complaints and often suggested that they should go back to Vietnam if they were unhappy here.

A change in behavior of the elders was also worth noting. The respondents were asked whether they had experienced any sleep disturbance, anxiety, irritability, change in eating habits, loss of interest in life, or had any suicidal thoughts in the previous three months as a result of the stress, anxiety, depression, guilt, fear, or loneliness that they had expressed earlier. Twelve elders reported that they had difficulty sleeping, 6 had lost their interest in life, 5 reported changes in their eating habits, and 4 had occasional suicidal thoughts.

Regarding behavioral changes, responses varied according to the degree of mistreatment the elders felt. The greater the extent of the mistreatment, the more the elder's behavior was affected. When asked if they would react to mistreatment, 16 did not know how to report it, 16 wished they could move to another domicile, 15 did not know where to go and whom to ask for help, and 14 did not want to complain to anyone about the mistreatment. For the most part, the respondents preferred to keep their problems to themselves because of their reluctance to reveal family problems to others and risk potential embarrassment and fear of raising conflicts among their children or relatives.

The overall assessment indicated that emotional abuse was the most prevalent among all kinds of abuses, followed by verbal abuse. Financial and physical abuses were non-existent within this sample of Vietnamese elders. Mistreatment was usually inflicted toward female rather than male elders. According to comments from some elderly women, if they could still offer help around the house or be a babysitter for their grandchildren, they were not mistreated as much. But they believed that when they became frail and could not help anymore, the treatment toward them might become worse. Half of the participants in this study lived with their married sons. This arrangement follows the Vietnamese tradition since sons are expected to take care of their parents in old age. The other half lived with daughters or other relatives. Ironically, the findings revealed that these elders encountered more trouble with daughters-in-law in "traditional" households than with relatives in the less traditional settings.

A relationship did exist between the ability to speak English by the parents and the abuse. Those who were able to understand and speak English could mingle with the host society without asking for help from their children. This fact also commanded respect from their grandchildren because they could communicate with each other. One elderly man was proud to tell the writer that his grandchild was so impressed with him because he could speak English, French, and Vietnamese.

Income also played an important role in abuse. It appeared that the more the older person was financially dependent on the children, the more that person was prone to abuse. For example, there were instances when the elderly person was not able to get assistance from the government because of his/her immigration status or the person was too old to find employment; he/she had to rely on the assistance of the family. This situation indirectly triggered inter-generational conflict which occurred when both spouses were employed and their income barely met their daily living needs, let alone supported older parents.

Older Vietnamese immigrants also lacked preparation for their adjustments to the host society. . . . Some elders indicated that they had greater difficulty integrating themselves into the new society. A few used the phrase "blind, deaf, crippled, and dumb" to describe how they felt while living in the U.S. They thought of themselves as blind because they could not read, deaf and dumb because they could not understand English, and crippled because they needed someone to drive them around.

Other comments often heard during the interviews were about the stress in Vietnamese tradition on filial piety, respect for elders, and family closeness. Elderly Vietnamese immigrants usually followed their children to this country in an attempt to maintain the traditional value system of the extended family. However, upon arrival to the U.S., many of the older immigrants found that they had less kinship support than they anticipated. Many were unable to live in the home of their children and, for the first time, had to look beyond traditional family support to formal organizations, particularly to help in locating affordable housing.

DISCUSSION

In mainstream America, the typical, reported elder abuse victim is a woman of poor to modest means over 75 years of age. She is generally widowed, living with relatives, frail and vulnerable due to physical and/or mental disabilities (Steinmetz, 1988). The typical abuser is often afflicted with profound disabling conditions such as addiction to alcohol or other drugs, serious psychiatric disturbances, mental retardation, or chronic inability to make appropriate judgments about the care of the dependent elderly (Quinn & Tomita, 1986).

The typical Vietnamese elder abuse victim is a woman over 60 years old, recently settled in the U.S., who does not speak English and is unfamiliar with Western culture. She is usually in good health, living in a multi-generational household, and financially dependent on her children. The typical abuser is a daughter-in-law who usually works outside the house and has young children at home.

Elder abuse in the Vietnamese population has some unique characteristics. Many studies have examined young and middle-aged immigrants in contrast to elderly Vietnamese immigrants as they settled into new communities. In the literature, there are few references to the problems that elderly Vietnamese people might encounter when coming to this new country. It has been suggested that they have major problems learning the new language and often quickly became dependent on their children and grandchildren (Nguyen, 1982). It was also noted that different family members adapt to the new way of life at different rates. The elders, hoping to bring with them the traditions and the way of life from Vietnam to instill in their children in the U.S., found out that their children had already become more and more acculturated to the American lifestyle. They felt neglected because the younger generations were too busy adapting to a more American way of living, and the elders perceived themselves as an interference in the children's busy lives. Consequently, the elder may repress feelings to preserve harmony in the family. These elders also feel a sense of indebtedness toward their children for bringing them over here.

Many of the Vietnamese elders were relatively unhappy living in the U.S. Even those not subjected to any kind of mistreatment did not feel at home. Most of them longed to live again among their familiar neighborhoods. They missed their customs, the slow pace of life in Vietnam, and the understanding of their countrymen. Even though they felt more secure living in the U.S., could acquire more material possessions, and could receive better health care than in Vietnam, they still felt a void inside them. Most of them felt depressed and a sense of estrangement in this country. They longed to go back home.

The needs of the Vietnamese elders may be a bit different than those of the Caucasian elders, and sometimes it poses a challenge to service providers to recognize them. For example, it is often difficult to detect the presence of depression in Vietnamese elders. Without the tradition of self-revelation, as in Western counseling, they are not accustomed to discussing their personal feelings openly with others. Instead, at times of distress or loss, they often complain to their doctors of physical discomforts such as fatigue, headaches, backaches, or insomnia. Therefore, depressed Vietnamese elders are less likely than white elders to be identified by service providers and less likely to receive treatment. Because the abuse could be subtle, in addition to the elder's attempt to conceal it, it is not always easy to detect. An elderly monolingual woman, confined at home, without government assistance, and totally dependent on the family is more prone to abuse.

Vietnamese elders used significantly fewer public benefits than others. The greatest barriers were lack of transportation, lack of understanding of procedures, and lack of English proficiency. Adding Vietnamese [signs] to help them use public transportation, exposing them to Western culture, and promoting the learning of English will speed up the acculturation of the Vietnamese elders to the host culture.

It was also reported that indigenous healers were still being utilized in refugee communities for both physical and mental health problems. The sick person believes there is a supernatural power and his sickness can be cured through the very power of his faith. Vietnamese elders were never taught about health promotion. They may delay seeking medical care for an illness until it is quite advanced. This occurs because the patient may be trying to decide from whom he should seek care (indigenous healers or health professionals). Vietnamese elders need to know about diet, exercise, preventive check-ups, and, most importantly, about their rights to refuse a treatment or to have a second or third opinion. Most of them think of doctors as gods.

Although duration of residence in this country might be expected to be positively associated with an elder's acculturation level, this assumption may not be true for Asian-American elders, as illustrated in a 1980 study by Salcido, Nakano, and Jue. Among the 100 low-income Asian subjects aged 55 years and over who resided in Asian ethnic communities (Vietnamese, Chinese, Korean) in Los Angeles, 75 percent still spoke only their native language although 77 percent indicated that they had resided in the U.S. for more than 20 years. Therefore, to effectively communicate with non-English speaking clients, service providers need to find an interpreter who can speak the client's dialect and understand the client's cultural background. It is important to be aware of the ethnic/age/sex/class differences between the client and interpreter. In the absence of a professional interpreter on site, telephone interpreter services should be obtained if at all possible, unless the elders express a preference to use their own family members.

Another important aspect for service providers to recognize when working with Vietnamese older people is the potential for depression that they are experiencing in their American homeland. Older refugees have suffered greater losses, are less able to learn English, and often become dependent on other family members. These situations result in loss of self-esteem and isolation, which could lead to being abused. . . .

REFERENCES

Murase, K. (1982). *Indigenous healers in Southeast Asian refugee communities.* San Francisco: Pacific Asian Mental Health Research Project.

Nguyen, S. (1982). The psycho-social adjustment and the mental health needs of South-East Asian refugees. *Psychiatric Journal of the University of Ottawa, 7*(1), 26–35.

Quinn, M. J., & Tomita, S. K. (1986). *Elder abuse and neglect.* New York: Springer Publishing Co.

Salcido, R. M., Nakano, C., & Jue, S. (1980). The use of formal and informal health and welfare services of the Asian-American elderly. *California Sociologist, 3*(2), 213–229.

Steinmetz, S. K. (1988). *Duty-bound: Elder abuse and family care.* Newbury Park, CA: Sage Publications.

? *Think about It*

1. What was the most common form of elderly mistreatment in Le's study? How does the "typical" victim differ in white and Vietnamese families?
2. Why does Le suggest that there is a relationship between acculturation stress and elder mistreatment and between filial piety and elder mistreatment?
3. Why do many Vietnamese elderly refuse to disclose their mistreatment experiences to other family members or seek professional help?

CHAPTER 8

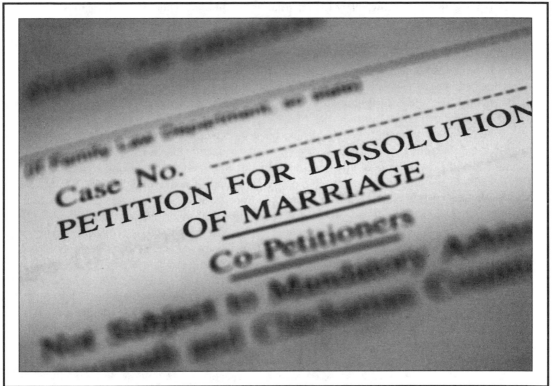

Marital Conflict,
Divorce, and Remarriage

In the United States, about 43 percent of all first marriages end in divorce. Since 1960 divorce rates among African Americans have been more than 75 percent higher than divorce rates among either whites or Latinos, and since 1980 they have been nearly twice as high as the national rate. These differences persist at all income, age, educational, and occupational levels.[1] Nearly half of the marriages of black women are expected to terminate by the end of 15 years, compared with 17 percent of the marriages of white women. Not only are black women more likely to experience divorce, but they do so sooner after marriage than their white counterparts. By the end of five years of first marriage, for example, 20 percent of black women are expected to divorce, compared with only 6 percent of white women.[2] In 1998, 11 percent of African Americans, 10 percent of whites, 7 percent of Latinos, and 5 percent of Asian Americans were divorced.[3]

As these numbers show, many U.S. marital ties don't bind. There is a voluminous literature on black and white divorces, and the material on white remarriages, especially, has been increasing in recent years. In contrast, relatively little research has been done on separation, divorce, and remarriage in other ethnic groups or subgroups. Despite such gaps, the selections in this chapter present a vivid snapshot of the divorce process experienced by various ethnic groups—specifically, changing attitudes about gender roles and their impact on divorce, the effects of migration on marital instability, the divorce experience, divorce mediation, and child support.

We begin by looking at the relationship between acculturation (see Chapter 7), a shift in gender role attitudes, and high divorce rates. As Mohammadreza Hojat and his associates show, the divorce rate of first-generation Iranian immigrants in the United States is estimated to be as high as 66 percent (Reading 37), compared with only 10 percent in Iran.[4] Why is marital instability so high among immigrants from a society where the marriage bond is sacred and divorce is viewed as a "calamity"? Traditional Iranian culture imposes oppressive constraints and heavy restrictions on women. Hojat and his colleagues show that, during acculturation, Iranian women's and men's attitudes about marriage gradually diverge. Iranian women become more liberal in their attitude toward marriage, including divorce. In contrast, Iranian men's attitudes about gender roles, marriage, and divorce remain relatively traditional. The high Iranian immigrant divorce rates might reflect the greater acceptance and accessibility of divorce in U.S. society.[5] In effect, Iranian women appear to enjoy the greater autonomy and share more egalitarian attitudes about gender roles in the United States.

Other scholars also have suggested that there's a relationship between divorce, immigration, and women's greater sense of personal and economic autonomy. In her study of Brazilians in New York City, Maxine L. Margolis found that economic incentives rather than family considerations spurred many women's migration to the United States (Reading 38). Gendered labor recruitment practices (see Reading 25) encouraged many single women from Brazil to seek employment and to live independently. Married women who worked outside the home enjoyed their economic autonomy and started challenging their husbands' traditional breadwinner roles and decision-making authority. For example, one of Margolis's respondents, who earned somewhat more than her husband, purchased expensive items (such as a dining room table and a color TV set) without consulting her husband. She also went out to restaurants and nightclubs with her friends on weekends while her husband preferred to spend his time listening to his CD collection and stayed home with their son. These role shifts led to friction and eventually to divorce. Although such role reversals may be atypical, Margolis notes that even less drastic transformations in gender relations can result in marital breakups.[6]

Statistics at the beginning of this chapter show that black divorce rates are higher than those of other ethnic or non-Latino white families. Being black does not "cause" individuals to divorce, of course. Various demographic, structural, and interpersonal factors are at work. Erma Jean Lawson and Aaron Thompson explore some of the micro and macro reasons for high black divorce rates (Reading 39). Although their study is based on divorced black men (a group that has garnered little research attention in the past), their discussion provides valuable insights about black women's decisions to get a divorce. Numerous self-help books give the impression that divorce is usually due to sexual incompatibility or to meddling in-laws. In reality, among white and black families, financial and communication problems are typically at the top of the list of difficulties promoting marital conflict, arguments, and divorce.[7] Note, also, that the economic consequences of divorce are much more devastating for women and children than for men, regardless of race, ethnicity, or occupational level.[8]

During divorce proceedings, many couples turn to mediation (as a personal choice or because mediation is ordered by the court) in hopes of reaching a settlement as civilized adults. *Divorce mediation* is a process in which a person trained in resolving disputes helps the divorcing couple come to an agreement on issues such as custody arrangements, child support, and the division of marital property. The marital property might include a house, furniture, stocks, savings accounts, pets, retirement accounts, pension plans, debts, medical expenses, and self-employment income. Traditional divorce proceedings are costly, as well as usually bitter and antagonistic, and the participants are rarely satisfied with the results.

Because divorce rates are increasing among second-generation Asian Americans and other ethnic groups, Roger R. Wong predicts that divorce mediation will increase as ethnic families become acculturated (Reading 40). Such predictions may be accurate. Latino couples, for example, are expressing interest in education programs designed to assist separating and divorcing parents.[9] Although divorce mediation can be effective for divorcing ethnic couples, Wong observes that the outcome of mediation often is far from adequate. The mediator (usually white) may not be impartial because of stereotypes and *ethnocentrism* (the tendency to view one's own culture as superior to the culture of others). Moreover, mediation training typically does not emphasize sensitivity to the needs of people from many different cultures.

Most U.S. couples, regardless of race or ethnicity, don't utilize mediators in divorce proceedings. In about 72 percent of the cases, the mother gets custody of the child. White husbands are more likely to be awarded custody than are black husbands.[10] There is scant information about Latino, Asian American, American Indian, and Middle Eastern fathers who want custody of their children after a divorce. Even when ethnic fathers don't seek custody, father–child relationships may be impaired. As Kimberly A. Folse shows, many Latino fathers (especially compared with their white and black counterparts) want to maintain ties with their children (Reading 41). Their good intentions, however, are often stymied by child enforcement systems that penalize fathers who don't have steady employment. The divorced fathers in Folse's study also complained that child support bureaucracies are sympathetic to mothers but ignore fathers. In addition, many noncustodial Latino fathers have argumentative relationships with their ex-wives, who sabotage the men's efforts to see their children. As a result, Folse suggests, even well-intentioned ethnic fathers may lose contact with their children after a divorce.

NOTES

1. L. K. White, "Determinants of Divorce," in *Contemporary Families: Looking Forward, Looking Back,* ed. A. Booth (Minneapolis: National Council on Family Relations, 1991), 150–61; A. F. Saluter and T. A. Lugaila, *Marital Status and Living Arrangements: March 1996,* U.S. Census Bureau, Current Population Reports, P20-496, www.census.gov/population/www/socdemo/ms-la.html (accessed April 29, 1998).
2. Augustine J. Kposowa, "The Impact of Race on Divorce in the United States," *Journal of Comparative Family Issues* 29 (Fall 1998): 529–48.
3. Terry A. Lugaila, *Marital Status and Living Arrangements: March 1998 (Update),* U.S. Census Bureau, Current Population Reports, P20-514, www.census.gov/prod/99pubs/p20-514.pdf (accessed August 8, 2000).

4. E. Sansarian, "The Politics of Gender and Development in the Islamic Republic of Iran," *Journal of Developing Societies* 13 (1992): 56–68.

5. Mohammadreza Hojat, Reza Shapurian, Habib Nayerahmadi, Mitra Farzaneh, Danesh Foroughi, Mohin Parsi, and Maryam Azizi, "Premarital Sexual, Child Rearing, and Family Attitudes of Iranian Men and Women in the United States and Iran," *The Journal of Psychology* 133 (1999): 19–31.

6. Another reason for the high disruption rates among married and unmarried couples may be that migrants and immigrants have weak ties with friends and relatives in their homelands who might provide social support when there are problems and might discourage divorce. See Nancy S. Landale and Nimfa B. Ogena, "Migration and Union Dissolution among Puerto Rican Women," *The International Migration Review* 29 (Fall 1995): 671–92.

7. See, for example, J. Patterson and P. Kim, *The Day America Told the Truth: What People Really Believe about Everything That Really Matters* (Upper Saddle River, NJ: Prentice Hall, 1991), and L. A. Kurdek, "Predicting Marital Dissolution: A Five-Year Prospective Longitudinal Study of Newlywed Couples," *Journal of Personality and Social Psychology* 64 (1993): 221–42.

8. See Pamela J. Smock, "Gender and the Short-Run Economic Consequences of Marital Disruption," *Social Forces* 73 (September 1994): 243–62, and Atlee L. Stroup and Gene E. Pollock, "Economic Consequences of Marital Dissolution for Hispanics," *Journal of Divorce & Remarriage* 30 (1999): 149–66.

9. Maria Serrano Schwartz, "Bringing Peace to the Latino Community," *Family & Conciliation Courts Review* 34 (January 1996): 93–111.

10. S. C. Clarke, "Advance Report of Final Divorce Statistics, 1989 and 1990," *Monthly Vital Statistics Report* 43, no. 9(S) (March 22) (Centers for Disease Control and Prevention, 1995).

37 Divorce and Iranian Immigrants' Attitudes about Gender Roles and Marriage

Mohammadreza Hojat, Reza Shapurian, Danesh Foroughi, Habib Nayerahmadi, Mitra Farzaneh, Mahmood Shafieyan, and Mohin Parsi

In traditional Iranian culture, marriage is an important rite that symbolizes commitment between a woman and a man and bonds their families. What happens if the woman's beliefs and ideas about marriage change after immigration? The research of Mohammadreza Hojat and his colleagues shows that attitudinal disparities between male and female immigrants can provide an explanation for interpersonal conflict and the high divorce rates among Iranians in the United States.

Despite the increasing number of the Iranian-born population in the United States, published research on their sociocultural adaptation is scarce and they

Source: From Mohammadreza Hojat, Reza Shapurian, Danesh Foroughi, Habib Nayerahmadi, Mitra Farzaneh, Mahmood Shafieyan, and Mohin Parsi, "Gender Differences in Traditional Attitudes toward Marriage and the Family: An Empirical Study of Iranian Immigrants in the United States," *Journal of Family Issues* 21 (May 2000): 419–34. Copyright © 2000 Sage Publications, Inc. Reprinted by permission of Sage Publications, Inc.

are one of the misunderstood ethnic groups in this country. The misunderstanding of Iranians and their culture is exacerbated not only by the scarcity of research but also by the distorted view given by the public media, particularly after the hostage crisis, that portrayed Iranians as anti-Western religious fanatics—bearded men and veiled women with stiff upper lips—chanting slogans against the civilized world. Added to the mistaken identity is a view usually held by some lay people in the United

States who incorrectly consider Iranians as Arabs with Arabic culture. . . .

Marriage and the Family in Iranian Culture

The family network (*khanevadeh, tayefeh, khanevar,* and *eel-o-ashireh*) in Iranian traditional culture is considered as the most important factor in bonding people together. Family ties in traditional Iranian culture take precedence over all other social relationships (Nassehi-Behnam, 1985).

Marriage is viewed not only as the sole socially approved pathway to sexual access (Shapurian & Hojat, 1985) but as an everlasting commitment that bonds not only two individuals but their two families together. A strong cultural stigma is attached to marital dissolution. Divorce is viewed as a calamity (*bala*) to the family and is therefore equated with an "unfortunate fate" (*badbahkti*) on the part of those who fall into its trap.

Sex before marriage, which is a norm rather than the exception in the mainstream American society, is still a rare exception to the rule in Iranian culture. In contrast, virginity (*bekarat*), chastity (*nejabat*), and authenticity (from a family with good reputation, *esalat*) are among the gold standards employed in embarking on a search for a future spouse.

It is obvious that these culturally rooted norms provide a sense of identity and belonging that are in sharp contrast with those in the mainstream American society. It is therefore plausible to suspect that for a considerable number of Iranian immigrants in the United States, incompatibility of traditional Iranian cultural values and the norms in mainstream American society regarding basic social institutions of marriage and the family could generate serious intrapersonal and interpersonal tension.

Immigration of Iranians to the United States

. . . Although there is no consensus on the exact number of Iranians in the United States, according to the 1990 census, 1.8 million Iranian-born

immigrants were estimated to live in the United States (as cited in Bozorgmehr et al., 1993). Reported statistics indicate that at least 40% of Iranians in the Untied States hold a college degree, a proportion higher than that of any other foreign-born ethnic group in the United States (Bozorgmehr et al., 1993).

Acculturation, Intra-, and Interpersonal Conflicts

. . . At the intrapersonal level, the acculturation process during the transitional period can be likened to the unpleasant experience of *cognitive dissonance* (Festinger, 1957, 1964). In a cognitively dissonant situation (e.g., collision of two incompatible norms), an unpleasant tension arises that motivates the person to make every effort to reduce the dissonance and achieve consonance. Changing one's attitude to become consistent with the social norms of the host culture is one approach to reducing dissonance (Sherif et al., 1965). The other alternative is to maintain the norms of the home culture and leave the social expectations of the host culture out of consideration. . . . As the norms and expectations in the home and host cultures stand face-to-face rather than dancing in harmony, cognitive dissonance becomes greater, synchronization becomes more difficult, and acculturation becomes more stressful.

If the tension sustains long enough, then it can gradually diminish the sense of belonging to a particular culture and foster a sense of alienation and *marginality* (Park, 1928). Such a marginal person will experience stress and uncertainty known as *cultural shock* accompanied by a threat to the individual's identity (Ticho, 1971). A culturally shocked individual will experience an initial stage of denial followed by confrontation with reality that often generates anger, depression, and loneliness (symptom formation) and finally leading to a willing or unwilling acceptance or rejection of the norms of the host culture (Chen, 1978; DeSole et al., 1968). These stages of acculturation ironically seem similar to those described by Kubler-Ross (1973) as stages of mourning and also described by Bowlby

(1982) as stages of separation protest and detachment from a significant caregiver. Despite these conceptual formulations, scant attention has been given to empirical scrutiny of intra- and interpersonal conflicts in the acculturation process among immigrant populations. . . .

The way in which individuals view social institutions such as marriage and the family is heavily guided by social norms, gender roles, ethnic identification, and religious faith (Johnson et al., 1994). Men and women from different cultures may react differently to the new cultural environment by adopting the new norms and values at different paces and in different degrees. It has been reported, for example, that immigrants to England who came from Pakistan, Bangladesh, and India, especially women from these countries, were much less likely than their Western counterparts to engage in early sexual relations (Johnson et al., 1994). The effects of acculturation can also be different for men and women. For example, Mavreas and Bebbington (1990) found that among Greek immigrants in the United States, high acculturation was related to increased psychopathology in men but decreased psychopathology in women. Prislin, Suarez, Simpson, and Dyer (1998) reported that acculturation of Mexican mothers in the United States contributed to inadequate immunization of their children because of their diminished sense of maternal responsibility. Acculturation of Mexican female immigrants made them more vulnerable to illicit drugs than their male counterparts (Vega et al., 1998). A similar pattern of gender difference was observed in alcohol consumption among Hispanic immigrants in the United States (Polednak, 1997). Acculturated Mexican female teenagers in the United States were younger at their first sexual intercourse and had a higher rate of pregnancy (Reynoso et al., 1993).

Research has shown that women immigrants from Hispanic and oriental cultures adapt to the mainstream American society at a faster pace than their male counterparts (Chia et al., 1985; Espin, 1987; Salgado de Snyder, 1987; Tharp et al., 1968; Vazquez-Nutall et al., 1987). The women's faster adaptation of liberal sexual and marital attitudes has also been observed among American-born (Robinson et al., 1991) and British-born populations (Johnson et al., 1994).

Anecdotal reports indicate that female Iranian immigrants in the United States are more likely than their fellow countrymen to adopt egalitarian attitudes toward gender roles at a faster pace (Ghaffarian, 1989; Tohidi, 1993). However, empirical support is lacking to verify these speculations. The issue of gender incongruity in attitudes toward marriage and the family deserves more serious empirical attention because of its direct implications in the quality of marital and familial relationships.

Purposes of the Present Study

This study was designed to compare Iranian male and female immigrants in the United States on their attitudes toward marriage and the family. In particular, the extent of attitudinal discrepancy (from a traditional stand typical of the prevalent Iranian culture to a liberal stand typical of the mainstream American society) between Iranian men and women in the United States was examined.

METHOD

Participants

The study sample consisted of a total of 205 Iranian immigrants in the United States who responded to an attitude survey. Of the total sample, 45 were excluded because of incomplete questionnaires, unusual response patterns (e.g., acquiescence response set), or because they were not between 20 and 50 years of age. Therefore, the final sample with useable data for statistical analyses in the present study consisted of 160 Iranians (61 men, 99 women) aged between 20 and 50 years. Fifty-five percent of the respondents were residents of California, and the remaining 45%

were mostly from Pennsylvania, New York, New Jersey, and Indiana. Fifty-five percent were married, 14% were divorced, 4% were remarried, and the rest were never married. The average age of the respondents was 37 years, and women were 2 years younger than men.

Research Instrument

A scale of traditional attitudes toward marriage and the family was developed that consisted of 10 items addressing issues related to premarital sex, marriage, divorce, and parental roles (see Table 1). Respondents were asked to specify if they agreed or disagreed with each of the items. They could also choose the "undecided" or "don't know" option if they so desired. The items of the scale were selected from a longer inventory of premarital sexual, marital, child-rearing, and family attitudes given to British (Schofield, 1965, 1973) and Iranian samples (Hojat & Shapurian, 1980; Hojat et al., 1999; Shapurian & Hojat, 1985). . . .

Procedures

As part of an attitude survey of Iranians in the United States and in Iran (Hojat et al., 1999), a questionnaire consisting of 25 items was distributed to a convenience sample of Iranians in the United States in Iranian communities and cultural gatherings through a network of acquaintances. Also, the questionnaire was printed in one Iranian magazine (*Ispand*), with subscribers mostly in the Northeast, particularly in Pennsylvania. Participants were informed in a cover note that the purpose of the study was cross-cultural comparisons. They were asked to complete, seal, and return the questionnaire. It was emphasized in the instructions that answers to the items should reflect the respondent's own opinion regardless of whether such answers were socially desirable or undesirable. Questionnaires were answered anonymously and the return address was provided on the other side of the questionnaire. . . .

RESULTS

Descriptive statistics of the 10-item scale of attitudes toward marriage and the family are presented in Table 1.

The means of the scale of traditional attitudes toward marriage and the family for men and women were 3.1 and 2.3, respectively (corresponding standard deviations were 2.5 and 1.7). Results of the *t* test indicated that the gender difference was statistically significant. . . . The effect size estimate of the difference was 0.39, which approaches a moderate effect size according to the operational definitions suggested by Cohen (1987). An effect size estimate of this magnitude indicates that attitudinal disparity between Iranian men and women found in this study should not be considered trivial. . . .

Also, we compared the attitude scores of the married respondents to those who never married, remarried, or divorced. Married respondents scored significantly higher . . . than the other group . . . , indicating that married participants were more likely to hold a traditional stand on marriage and the family than their other counterparts. Because of this finding, we . . . [examined] the interaction effect of marital status and gender on the attitude scores. No significant interaction effect was obtained, indicating that marital status did not influence the findings regarding the main effect of gender on the attitude scores.

DISCUSSION

Findings of the present study showed that Iranian male immigrants were more likely than their female counterparts to view premarital sex, marriage, and the family from a traditional stand prescribed by the Iranian culture. Conversely, Iranian female immigrants in the study sample were more likely than their male counterparts to take a stand on premarital sex, marriage, and the family more similar to those in the mainstream American society.

These findings seem to support some anecdotal reports (Ghaffarian, 1989; Tohidi, 1993) about Iranian women immigrants' greater acceptance of egalitarian and liberal attitudes toward marriage and the family. The underlying reasons for this gender difference need to be further examined. Probably the heavy restrictions and social pressure imposed on women in traditional Iranian culture is among the reasons for explaining their greater acceptance of liberal attitudes of the mainstream American society.

Oppressive constraints in traditional societies naturally prompt women to be more eager than men to depart from traditional norms. Such departure, if not accompanied at a similar pace by men, can jeopardize the dynamics of mate selection and conjugal relationships. For example, an Iranian woman who has adopted the mainstream Ameri-

can social norms is often viewed by a traditional Iranian man as "Americanized" or "poisoned by West" (*gharbzadeh*) and one who has lost her originality. This negative image of an acculturated Iranian woman is sometimes exaggerated out of proportion and makes it difficult for her to be seriously considered as a future spouse by some of her male Iranian counterparts. Because of this mangled view of modern Iranian women in the United States, some Iranian men through the system of arranged marriages (*khastegari*) ask their parents or relatives to find them a match in Iran who can then be brought to the United States as a "domestic spouse." Many single Iranian women in the United States, who naturally are not happy with these types of long-distance mate selection by their fellow countrymen, in turn characterize this kind of Iranian traditional man as old-fashioned

TABLE 1   The Scale of Traditional Attitudes toward Marriage and the Family and Descriptive Statistics

Item[a]	Agree	Disagree
1. Homosexuals should be punished.	*	
2. Birth control should be taught to young people.		*
3. Premarital sex for girls leads to a bad reputation.	*	
4. There is no need for sex education in schools.	*	
5. It should be made easier to get a divorce.		*
6. Sexual intercourse before marriage is wrong.	*	
7. Men want to marry a virgin.	*	
8. Sexual intercourse before marriage is acceptable for boys but not for girls.	*	
9. If a boy gets a girl pregnant, he should marry her.	*	
10. Parents should stay together for the sake of children, even if they don't get along.	*	

	Descriptive Statistics		
	Men (n = 61)	*Women (n = 99)*	*Total (n = 160)*
Mean[b]	3.1	2.3	2.6
Standard deviation	2.5	1.7	2.1
Median	3.0	2.0	2.0
Range	1 to 9	0 to 8	0 to 9
Reliability[c]	.76	.72	.74

[a] The items are listed by descending order of the magnitude of differences in agreement responses between a sample of Iranian immigrants in the United States and a sample of Iranians in Iran (Hojat et al., 1999). A point is given to each response identified by an asterisk (*). The sum of these points is the total score of the traditional attitude scale.
[b] Mean difference between men and women is statistically significant ($t_{(158)} = 2.21$, $p < .05$).
[c] Reliability estimate by Kuder-Richardson Formula 20.

(*ommol*), regressive, and retarded in adjusting to the new cultural environment and to the social realities (*aghabmondeh*).

Family conflict can arise when some family members represent more of the host cultural values and other members represent more of their original cultural norms (Pawliuk et al., 1996). The high rate of marital instability among Iranians in the United States (and intergenerational discords between Iranian parents and their young children) that are often anecdotally discussed in Iranian local newspapers published in the United States could be a reflection of a disharmonious pace of acculturation among family members, particularly between spouses. For example, divorce has been reported to hover around 10% in Iran (Sanasarian, 1992). Its rate is drastically higher among Iranian immigrants in the United States (estimated to be as high as 66%) (Tohidi, 1993) and other Western countries.

The aforementioned speculation regarding divorce and attitudinal disparity is supported by research findings that people are more attracted to those with similar values, attitudes, and opinions, especially among those who make a long-term commitment (Rubin, 1979). A popular saying, amazingly similar in both American and Iranian cultures (birds of a feather flock together in American and *kabootar ba kabootar, baaz ba baaz* in Persian), confirms this research finding. An empirical study of intra- and interculturally married Iranians in the United States (Rezaian, 1989) also confirmed the findings of the present study. In that study, it was found that cultural differences and attitudinal disparity between couples could lead to less mutual understanding, less marital satisfaction, and more interpersonal disharmony in the family.

Iranian women's faster pace of acculturation is a challenging accomplishment. They are caught up in the midst of a psychosocial drama. Their "double bind" conflict (Tohidi, 1994) requires difficult adjustments in bringing together two incompatible attitudes regarding the roles of a domestic housewife as opposed to a modern woman in the family. This role conflict exacerbates the Iranian

women's cognitive dissonance. The clash of opposing attitudes not only generates an intrapsychic conflict but also adds to the frustration of the couples in dealing with inconsistencies and adjusting to the changes.

The Iranian women's rising expectation and their demands for a more egalitarian gender role is perceived by their Iranian male counterparts who stand on a traditional ground as a stereotypical tendency of women to easily change color and to the women's superficiality in judgment that is deeply rooted in Islamic culture. In some cases, the flame of conflict is further fueled by the increasing women's financial power as a result of their marketable skills (e.g., tailoring, cooking, hair styling, and secretarial skills). In traditional Iranian culture, a stigma is attached to the inability of the man who is the head of the family to bring home more money than his wife (Ardehali & Backer, 1980). Such a powerless head who is supposed to be the main breadwinner of the family is viewed from the traditional stand as a castrated chief (*akhte*).

A divided house would be the inevitable outcome of such a puzzling drama. A marriage counselor or a family therapist who is unaware of these cultural peculiarities would be lost in the midst of this gender drama brought to his or her office (Tohidi, 1993). The therapist's awareness of these peculiarities and understanding of the roles and expectations prescribed by cultural norms can certainly facilitate communication with the client and improve the therapeutic outcomes. . . .

A serious limitation of the study is its nonprobabilistic sampling design that precludes generalizing the findings to a broader population of Iranian immigrants in the United States. The study sample represents the first-generation immigrants and precludes those who could not read and understand their native language. Considering the link between more acculturation and proficiency in English language among refugees in the United States (Nicassio et al., 1986; Nwadiora & McAdoo, 1996), it can be assumed that those Iranians who were unable to answer the survey in Persian have probably adopted the mainstream American society more than the study sample. The gender gap in attitudes could be narrower among Iranian immigrants who are unable to understand their native language, although this assumption awaits empirical verification.

Despite this limitation, we believe that for the sake of helping the first-generation immigrants, serious research attention should be given to the process and outcome of attitudinal changes in the new cultural environment. Such research not only could help to determine factors that contribute to the immigrants' adjustment to the new cultural environment but also could help in improving their mental (and physical) health and to better restore their family relationships and their social interactions. Also, research on acculturation issues can help to reduce or alleviate the intra- and interpersonal conflicts, the inevitable outcome of attitudinal incompatibility, that can lead to a better understanding of the immigrants by those in the host society.

REFERENCES

Ardehali, P., & Backer, D. (1980). Stress and the Iranian patient. *Behavioral Medicine, 6,* 31–35.

Bowlby, J. (1982). *Attachment and loss: Attachment* (Vol. 1, Rev. ed.). New York: Basic Books.

Bozorgmehr, M., Sabagh, G., & Der-Martirosian, C. (1993). Beyond nationality: Religio-ethnic diversity. In R. Kelley, J. Friedlander, & A. Colby (Eds.), *Irangeles: Iranians in Los Angeles* (pp. 59–89). Berkeley: University of California Press.

Chen, R. M. (1978). The education and training of Asian foreign medical graduates in the United States. *American Journal of Psychiatry, 135,* 451–453.

Chia, R. C., Chaung, C. J., Cheng, B. S., Castellow, W., Moore, C. H., & Hayes, M. (1985). Attitudes toward marriage roles among Chinese and American college students. *Journal of Social Psychology, 126,* 31–35.

Cohen, J. (1987). *Statistical power analysis for the behavioral sciences.* Hillsdale, NJ: Lawrence Erlbaum.

DeSole, D. E., Singer, P., & Roseman, J. (1968). Community psychiatry and the syndrome of psychiatric

culture shock. *Social Science and Medicine,* 1, 401–408.

Espin, O. (1987). Psychological impact of migration on Latinas. *Psychology of Women Quarterly,* 11, 489–503.

Festinger, L. (1957). *A theory of cognitive dissonance.* Chicago: Row & Peterson.

Festinger, L. (Ed.). (1964). *Conflict, decision, and dissonance.* Stanford, CA: Stanford University Press.

Ghaffarian, S. (1989). *The acculturation of Iranian immigrants in the United States and the implications for mental health.* Unpublished doctoral dissertation, California School of Professional Psychology, Los Angeles.

Hojat, M., & Shapurian, R. (1980). Multiculture–multiresponse matrices of correlations as a measure of construct validity of a premarital and sexual attitude inventory given to Iranian and British subjects. *Psychological Reports, 47,* 335–338.

Hojat, M., Shapurian, R., Nayerahmadi, H., Farzaneh, M., Foroughi, D., Parsi, M., & Azizi, M. (1999). Premarital sexual, child rearing, and family attitudes of Iranian men and women in the United States and in Iran. *Journal of Psychology, 133,* 19–31.

Johnson, A. M., Wadsworth, J., Wellings, K., Field, J., & Bradshaw, S. (1994). *Sexual attitudes and lifestyles.* Oxford, UK: Basil Blackwell.

Kubler-Ross, E. (1973). On death and dying. In E. Wyschogrod (Ed.), *The phenomenon of death: Faces of mortality* (pp. 14–40). New York: Harper & Row.

Mavreas, V., & Bebbington, P. (1990). Acculturation and psychiatric disorder: A study with Greek Cypriod immigrants. *Psychological Medicine, 20,* 941–951.

Nassehi-Behnam, V. (1985). Change and the Iranian family. *Current Anthropology, 26,* 557–562.

Nicassio, P. M., LaBarbera, J. D., Coburn, P., & Finley, R. (1986). The psychological adjustment of the American refugees: Findings from the personality inventory for children. *Journal of Nervous and Mental Diseases, 174,* 541–544.

Nwadiora, E., & McAdoo, H. (1996). Acculturation stress among American refugees: Gender and racial differences. *Adolescence, 31,* 476–487.

Park, R. E. (1928). Human migration and the marginal man. *American Journal of Sociology, 5,* 881–893.

Pawliuk, N., Grizenko, N., Chan-Yip, A., Gantous, P., Mathew, J., & Nguyen, D. (1996). Acculturation style and psychological functioning in children of immigrants. *American Journal of Orthopsychiatry, 66,* 111–121.

Polednak, A. P. (1997). Gender and acculturation in relation to alcohol use among Hispanic (Latino) adults in two areas of the Northeastern United States. *Substance Use and Misuse, 32,* 1513–1524.

Prislin, R., Suarez, L., Simpson, D. M., & Dyer, J. A. (1998). When acculturation hurts: The case of immunization. *Social Science and Medicine, 47,* 1947–1956.

Reynoso, T. C., Felice, M. E., & Shragg, G. P. (1993). Does American acculturation affect outcome of Mexican-American teenage pregnancy? *Journal of Adolescent Health, 14,* 257–261.

Rezaian, F. (1989). *A study of intra- and inter-cultural marriages between Iranians and Americans.* Unpublished doctoral dissertation, California Institute of Integral Studies, San Francisco.

Robinson, I., Ziss, K., Ganza, B., Katz, S., & Robinson, E. (1991). Twenty years of the sexual revolution, 1965–1985: An update. *Journal of Marriage and the Family, 53,* 216–220.

Rubin, Z. (1979). *Liking and loving.* New York: Holt, Rinehart & Winston.

Salgado de Snyder, V. N. (1987). Factors associated with acculturative stress and depressive symptomatology among married Mexican immigrant women. *Psychology of Women Quarterly, 11,* 475–488.

Sanasarian, E. (1992). The politics of gender and development in the Islamic Republic of Iran. *Journal of Developing Societies, 13,* 56–68.

Schofield, M. (1965). *The sexual behavior of young people.* Boston: Little, Brown.

Schofield, M. (1973). *The sexual behavior of young adults: A follow-up study to the sexual behavior of young people.* Boston. Little, Brown

Shapurian, R., & Hojat, M. (1985). Sexual and premarital attitudes of Iranian college students. *Psychological Reports, 57,* 67–74.

Sherif, C. W., Sherif, M., & Nebergall, R. E. (1965). *Attitude and attitude change: The social judgment–involvement approach.* Philadelphia: W. B. Saunders.

Tharp, R. G., Meadow, A., Lennhoff, S. G., & Scatterfield, D. (1968). Changes in marriage roles accompanying the acculturation of Mexican-American wives. *Journal of Marriage and the Family, 30,* 404–412.

Ticho, G. (1971). Cultural aspects of transference and countertransference. *Bulletin of the Menninger Clinic, 35,* 313–334.

Tohidi, N. (1993). Iranian women and gender relations in Los Angeles. In R. Kelley, J. Friedlander, & A. Colby (Eds.), *Irangeles: Iranians in Los Angeles* (pp. 175–217). Berkeley: University of California Press.

Tohidi, N. (1994). Modernity, Islamization, and women in Iran. In V. Moghadan (Ed.), *Gender and national identity* (pp. 110–147). London: Zed Books.

Vazquez-Nutall, E. V., Romeo-Garcia, L., & Deleon, B. (1987). Sex roles and perceptions of femininity and masculinity of Hispanic women: A review of the literature. *Psychology of Women Quarterly, 11,* 409–425.

Vega, W. A., Alderete, E., Kolody, B., & Aguilar-Gaxiola, S. (1998). Illicit drugs among Mexican Americans in California: The effect of gender on acculturation. *Addiction, 12,* 1839–1850.

[?] *Think about It*

1. What are the traditional Iranian attitudes about premarital sex, gender roles, and marriage?

2. Why does acculturation produce cognitive dissonance and a sense of marginality among Iranian immigrants? Why do Hojat and his associates feel that acculturation fosters interpersonal conflict among Iranian women and men?

3. Why—according to this reading, Readings 7 through 11, and your own reflections or experiences—do many Iranian immigrant women's attitudes about gender roles and marriage change while the attitudes of many Iranian men remain traditional?

38 Separation and Divorce in Brazilian Immigrant Families

Maxine L. Margolis

As you saw in Reading 37, immigration can spark changes in attitudes about gender roles that increase Iranian marital dissolution rates in the United States. Maxine L. Margolis suggests, similarly, that traditional Brazilian gender role expectations and behavior "soften under the sway of migration" and often the result is divorce. *

GENDER SNAPSHOTS

Like racial stereotypes, gender role traditions also soften under the sway of migration. To cite one pertinent example: although women are traditionally seen as migrating for family reasons—to join a male breadwinner or to reunite the family—my own and other research challenges this common notion (Simon and DeLey 1986; Zentgraf 1995). Less than one-third of the Brazilian women I studied were married at the time I interviewed them, and even fewer were married when they first arrived in the United States. In other words, contrary to conventional wisdom, family considerations did not spur most of these women to migrate to the United States. In fact, I found that Brazilian women came to New York for exactly the same reason that Brazilian men did—to take jobs that paid far more than any they could ever find back home.

When women migrate abroad to seek work, gendered labor recruitment is often involved. That is, the particular labor market needs of specific cities in the United States or other host countries may require more female (or male) migrants (Repak 1995). For example, male immigrants might readily find employment in a certain locale if workers for low-wage construction jobs were in demand there. Domestic service is another case of gendered labor recruitment since the call for live-in housekeepers, day maids, nannies and babysitters is almost entirely a demand for *female* labor.

Employment in this sector of the labor market may have given immigrant women an advantage of sorts. Since 1986 when the U.S. Congress passed the Immigration Reform and Control Act tightening penalties on employees who hire undocumented workers, immigrant women have been able to find work somewhat more easily than immigrant men. The reason is that employers of babysitters, housekeepers, and nannies are less likely than others to ask about their employee's legal status or to require that they have a green card (Repak 1995).

NEW LAND, NEW ROLES

Whether they work as nannies, maids, street vendors or gogo dancers, Brazilian women's employment is the primary catalyst for shifts in gender roles. What is crucial is the earning power of women immigrants, not the type of job they hold. Women's greater financial autonomy is what sets

*Margolis's study of Brazilians in New York City is based on 50 informal surveys using open-ended questions, 100 structured interviews, and informal discussions with 250 respondents using participant observation. *Ed.*

Source: From Maxine L. Margolis, *An Invisible Minority: Brazilians in New York City* (Boston: Allyn and Bacon, 1998), 107–12. Copyright © 1998 Allyn & Bacon. Reprinted by permission.

the stage for a reformulation of traditional Brazilian gender roles. Many immigrant women, particularly married women, contend that their former dependence is replaced by the "executive power" (*poder executivo*) they acquire from their new role as breadwinners. They take jobs and for the first time in their lives they earn as much or even more than their husbands. And this, in turn, gives them more familial decision-making power. Indeed, I found no evidence that the conventional Brazilian world view that the street (*a rua*) is a male preserve and the home (*a casa*) a female's negated the power bestowed by women's financial contribution to the household (Da Matta 1991).

To be sure, Brazilian women are not unique in their new found independence as international migrants. Other research has cited the effects of paid employment on women's status and role within the context of international migration (Pessar 1995; Haines 1986; Hondagneu-Sotelo 1994). A study of the migration of Dominicans to New York, for example, noted that since immigrant wages in the city were low—at least in the early years of migration—most Dominican households were incapable of maintaining the traditional male-wage earner/female-dependent division of labor. Men's wages simply were insufficient to support a household, making it essential that women contribute to basic living expenses (Grasmuck and Pessar 1992). Similarly, Haitian women who held jobs in New York were found to have far greater economic autonomy than they had back home, particularly women who had not been employed in Haiti or whose earnings only supplemented their husband's (Buchanan 1979). Along the same lines, Jamaican women spoke of the "independence" and "financial control" that migration to New York afforded them. Central American women in Los Angeles were said to feel "more independent in the United States" because they had more options, particularly in terms of wage labor, than they did back home (Foner 1986; Chinchilla and Hamilton 1995). All of these studies suggest, then, that a realignment of economic responsibilities can moderate the time-worn patriarchal ideology that asserts men should be a family's lone or, at least, its primary breadwinner.

But women's greater autonomy within the context of migration sometimes comes at a price. While women's employment lessens their dependence on men and may enhance self-confidence, research suggests that women's new financial authority also can lead to greater discord between the sexes, particularly among wives and husbands. Ironically, for some immigrant women the achievement of economic parity has not led to more egalitarian households but to the break up of their marriages (Grasmuck and Pessar 1992). Here is a case in point from my own research on Brazilian immigrants in New York City. It illustrates just how a reordering of traditional roles can transform lives and gender relations:

Veronica and Claudio had been married for ten years. They had one son and lived in an apartment in Astoria, Queens. They had been living in New York for two years when I met them and both had jobs cleaning apartments. Veronica was earning somewhat more than Claudio and she purchased whatever she pleased with her wages—a dining room table, a color TV set—without consulting Claudio. On weekends Veronica often went out with friends to restaurants and nightclubs. Claudio, who preferred to spend his time listening to his large CD collection, stayed home with their son.

This lifestyle contrasted sharply with what they were used to in Brazil. Claudio was an assistant bank manager there as well as the lone family breadwinner and Veronica was a full-time housewife. Having no income of her own, Veronica never made a major purchase without her husband's approval. On weekends Claudio went out with his friends to bars or to the beach, while Veronica stayed home with their young son. She would make dinner and sometimes Claudio came home to eat it, other times he would not.

After several months in New York Veronica was clearly enjoying her heady new financial independence and the partial reversal of her family's traditional division of labor. Claudio was far less pleased. At this point, Veronica began telling Claudio that he was simply "paying for his past sins" in Brazil—not showing up for dinner, going out with friends and leaving her at home. As a result of these role shifts, a great deal of friction was evident between the two. They have since divorced and Veronica, who continues to live with her son in Queens, is now married to an American of Puerto Rican ancestry. Claudio has returned to Brazil.

A number of Brazilians told me that this scenario was not uncommon and that many marriages broke up after couples moved to New York. Most credited the breakups to the fact that married women were far more likely to be employed in the United States than they were in Brazil and that with a job came greater economic autonomy and a renegotiation of traditional gender roles. One Brazilian even told a friend who had just arrived in New York that, if he valued his marriage, he should discourage his wife from going to work. He then bet him that they would get divorced if she took a job. She went to work at a restaurant and, indeed, within two months they separated.

This case and that of Veronica and Claudio point to one factor that seems to be critical in a couple's willingness and ability to moderate conventional gender roles: whether or not they married or began living together before or after they came to the United States. Brazilian immigrants suggested that couples who meet in New York and then marry are less likely to wind up separated or divorced than those who were married before leaving Brazil. In New York, the reasoning goes, the woman was already employed when the couple first met, so her work and the economic clout that goes with it was a given from the start of the relationship. This seems to be true of Brazilian immigrants in Boston as well, since evidence suggests that divorce rates are higher among couples who emigrated there together. Said one member of Boston's Brazilian immigrant community:

> To tell the truth there are many separations between couples here. These couples aren't able to stay together because it is so liberal here. In Brazil, the man works and the woman stays home. It is rare that a woman works. Here a woman has to work just like a man and everything is split up. It seems that people become . . . I don't know . . . selfish. I think that here everyone has equal rights and this brings on many problems (quoted in Badgley 1994:84–85).

The time and place of marriage also may play a critical role in the explosive issue of the household division of labor—who cleans, who makes dinner and washes the dishes, and who takes care of the kids, if there are any. Social class and education also seem to affect the domestic division of labor. Research suggests that better educated couples who are both employed come closer to an "egalitarian model of conjugal relations" than do those with less education and a dependent spouse (Safa 1995:46).

The renegotiation of who does what at home can be a volatile question that impacts the health and longevity of marital and other intimate relationships. A Brazilian woman said that while her boyfriend "never did anything domestic back in Brazil," he had changed quite a lot since immigrating to the United States and they now had a more equitable division of labor at home. One male immigrant noted his own updated ideology:

> You lose a lot of preconceived notions about the relationship between men and women. Here in the United States, the man participates more in the life of the house and the woman has much more dialogue with the husband. The man allows [sic] the woman to work out of necessity. A man who helps the woman in domestic chores begins to appreciate what housework is like and he gives it more value.

Once again, studies of other immigrant groups in the United States suggest parallels with the Brazilian case. For example, Salvadoran women in Washington D.C. who formed attachments to men after migration were somewhat more successful in getting them to participate in domestic work than those whose relationships predated their arrival in this country (Repak 1995). Jamaican men were more likely to "help" their wives with housework and child care in New York than they were back home and many Jamaican immigrants, both male and female, began questioning "the legitimacy of the traditional division of labor that assigns only women to housework" (Foner 1986:152). And when women from the Dominican Republic who had moved to New York were asked how relations between husbands and wives had improved since leaving home, the response was a more equitable division of household responsibilities. For most of these women, in fact, an "improvement in gender relations had been an unintended outcome of the immigrant experience" (Grasmuck and Pessar 1992:155). It is precisely this "improvement" in gender relations that makes some Brazilian immigrant women reluctant to return home. What, they wonder, will become of the greater equality they enjoyed in New York? What will happen to the increased freedom and autonomy that comes with a paycheck once they are back in Brazil?

REFERENCES

Badgley, Ruey T. 1994 "Brazucas in Beantown: The Dynamics of Brazilian Ethnicity in Boston." Senior Honors Thesis in Anthropology, Connecticut College, New London, Connecticut.

Buchanan, Susan H. 1979 "Haitian Women in New York City." *Migration Today,* VII (4): 19–25, 39.

Chinchilla, Norma Stoltz and Nora Hamilton 1995 "Sojourners, Settlers or Returnees: Factors in Decisions of Central Americans to Remain or Return." Paper presented at the 19th International Congress of the Latin American Studies Association, Washington, DC.

Da Matta, Roberto 1991 *Carnivals, Rogues, and Heroes, An Interpretation of the Brazilian Dilemma.* John Drury, trans. Notre Dame, IN: University of Notre Dame Press.

Foner, Nancy 1986 "Sex Roles and Sensibilities: Jamaican Women in New York and London." In *International Migration: The Female Experience.* Rita J.

Simon and Caroline B. Brettell, eds., Totowa, NJ: Rowman & Allanheld, pp. 133–151.

Grasmuck, Sherri and Patricia R. Pessar 1992 *Between Two Islands: Dominican International Migration.* Berkeley: University of California Press.

Hondagneu-Sotelo, Pierrette 1994 *Gendered Transitions: Mexican Experiences of Immigration.* Berkeley: University of California Press.

Pessar, Patricia R. 1995 "The Elusive Enclave: Ethnicity, Class, and Nationality among Latino Entrepreneurs in Greater Washington, D.C." *Human Organization* 54 (4): 383–92.

Repak, Terry A. 1995 *Waiting on Washington: Central American Workers in the Nation's Capital.* Philadelphia: Temple University Press.

Safa, Helen I. 1995 "Economic Restructuring and Gender Subordination." *Latin American Perspectives* 22(2): 33–51.

Simon, Rita J. and Margo Corona DeLey 1986 "Undocumented Mexican Women: Their Work and Personal Experiences." In *International Migration: The Female Experience.* Rita J. Simon and Caroline B. Brettell, eds., Totowa, NJ: Rowman & Allanheld, pp. 113–132.

Zentgraf, Kristine 1995 "Household Composition, Decision to Settle and the Changing Political Economic Context: Central Americans in Los Angeles." Paper presented at the 19th International Congress of the Latin American Studies Association, Washington, DC.

Think about It

1. According to Margolis's research, why is women's employment a "primary catalyst" for shifts in gender roles?

2. Why do you think that changes in women's and men's economic roles are likely to transform traditional Brazilian but not Iranian patriarchal ideology (see Reading 37)?

3. Margolis notes that Brazilian women's greater economic autonomy comes at a price—divorce. Should immigrant women be counseled, then, to continue to endorse traditional gender roles to avoid marital breakups?

39 Black Men and the Divorce Experience

Erma Jean Lawson and Aaron Thompson

Statistics in the introduction to this chapter show that African Americans have the highest divorce rates in the United States. Erma Jean Lawson and Aaron Thompson examine some reasons for these high rates from the black male's perspective. The most important factors contributing to marital dissolution, they found, are financial strain, a clash in spending habits, personal incompatibility, failure to resolve conflict, and differences in religious values and practices. *

The following section explores both macro and micro factors that resulted in marital dissatisfaction and subsequent divorce.

FINANCIAL STRAIN

Table 1 shows the rank order of factors that the respondents attributed to divorce including working too much, consumerism incompatibility, incompatible personality characteristics, failure to negotiate conflict, and differences in religious behavior.

The family was an important source of satisfaction for men in our study. The following example of Carl and Rita illustrates the absence of shared time as an important factor that influenced the stability of their marriage. . . .

Carl and Rita's lives became routine. They occasionally entertained family and friends. Carl always shared domestic chores including the laundry, grocery shopping, and housecleaning. After 8 months of marriage, Rita missed her period. She looked squarely at Carl and said, "I'm pregnant."

"Pregnant?" Carl said. "I thought you were taking birth control pills."

*The researchers used a snowball sample to identify and interview fifty black men in the northeastern United States. *Ed.*

Source: From Erma Jean Lawson and Aaron Thompson, *Black Men and Divorce* (Thousand Oaks, CA: Sage, 1999), 58, 60–66, 71–73, 79–89. Copyright © Sage Publications, Inc. Reprinted by permission of Sage Publications, Inc.

"How could this have happened? This wasn't supposed to happen," Carl thought. According to the script that Carl had written for himself, he was supposed to attend law school and to live the rest of his life trouble free. He somehow felt that the baby was Rita's fault, although he was aware that rationally this idea was ridiculous.

The company for which Rita worked did not like a Black pregnant woman in its office and fired her when she was 3 months pregnant. It was then, Carl reported, that the pregnancy symbolized the ending of his personal goals. His life from then on was owned by another person. He explained,

I gave up my dreams of becoming a lawyer. I would have been a great public defense attorney, but all I could think of for years was putting food on the

TABLE 1 Frequency of Causes of Divorce (*N = 50*)

Factor Contributing to Divorce	Number of Respondents
Financial strain	50
Consumerism incompatibility	40
Personality incompatibility	35
Failure to negotiate conflict	30
Religious behavior incompatibility	25

Note: Child-rearing issues, in-law problems, and sexual incompatibility were mentioned by fewer than 20 respondents.

table. I do not believe in abortion, and Rita equated abortion with murder.

Carl received a raise and moved his family to a one-bedroom apartment, a place with a bedroom, living room, and kitchen. Rita became pregnant again with twins, and Carl worried constantly about money. Rita resumed working 6 weeks postpartum, and life seemed a little better because material circumstances had improved. Carl purchased a home with three bedrooms, a living room, and a separate dining room in a neighborhood designed to isolate Blacks. When Blacks moved in, Whites moved out, leaving a stable Black working class.

With a factory job, working part-time, and Rita working, Carl's life was a little easier. Carl painted, wallpapered, refinished furniture, and washed and waxed the floors of his house; it was his pride and joy. In talking about this period in his life, he stated,

Owning the house seemed surreal, like an out-of-body experience, like maybe I was daydreaming and might be awakened any moment because I had achieved more than my parents. At least I owned a home and my kids would not grow up in the projects. I grew up in the projects, where I saw people who had no goals but to get a fix or to wait until the next party. On the building walls where I walked everyday [was] old graffiti with slang and curse words. I could smell the stink of urine in the hallways of the building. I shared a room with my two brothers as long as I remember and heard daily fights from the people who lived upstairs.

With little warning, Carl was laid off. Rita worked two full-time jobs, while Carl remained at home. He checked the employment agencies daily to no avail. Recalling this period in his life, Carl explained,

I felt like a failure, especially since I had a college degree. The kids were growing so fast and needed so many things I could not give them. The lack of money was hard with three children, but the lack of self-respect caused by unemployment was worse. I

hated for my kids to see me unemployed, sitting around the house and feeling miserable.

Following 3 years of unemployment, Carl decided to leave the city and look for work in a midwestern city. He explained, "My family would be better off without me, and I promised to send for them after finding work." Carl felt guilty for failing to maintain a home for his children and, therefore, perceived unemployment as lessening his ability to command respect from his children. Elaborating on his move, Carl said,

When a White worker migrates, it is often because he had a job offer or a transfer. When a Black man migrates, it is most often because he is currently unemployed or working irregularly, which has been the experience of Blacks since slavery.

Carl moved to Detroit, found work, and lived with seven relatives in a one-bedroom apartment. Two years later, he sent for Rita and the kids. One year after the move, Rita filed for a divorce. In explaining the cause of the divorce, Carl stated, "I was consumed with work. I was never home. I worked a full-time job, a part-time job, and played in jazz clubs at night. I directed a church choir on Sundays and spent virtually no time at home." Remembering the marriage, Carl remarked,

I strove to make ends meet, and I wanted to have enough money saved for hard times. Plus, I wanted to have enough money saved so I could help my older daughter go to graduate school. I wanted to help my kids more than my parents were able to help me. The more I worked, the less I thought of Rita's needs, but I had to work because we lost everything before and were starting all over.

At the time of the interview, Carl lived with his 78-year-old mother in the same apartment and neighborhood in which he grew up. In commenting on his divorce, Carl said,

What's a Black man to do? I've tried to do all the right things, like get an education and work hard—

and look where it has gotten me. I wanted to save my marriage, but there were so many things influencing it, like having to work so hard to support my family. Society is about keeping the Black man down.

Carl repeatedly returned to the events of his marriage, trying to identify what went wrong and speculating about how he could have worked differently to pay bills and give Rita the attention she needed. He also recalled the humiliation of working two and sometimes three jobs, only to have the marriage end. He reported feeling persecuted by his inability to earn $40,000 annually without several jobs. He also left the area for 2 months, hoping that by doing so, he also could leave the memories. However, his mind was fixed on Rita's excruciating words: "I want a divorce. This is not the marriage I want because you are never home; all you do is work. I need more out of marriage than this."

Although an inverse relationship between income and the likelihood of divorce has been documented extensively, in this study the level of wages per se was not as centrally related to marital dissolution as were the respondents' efforts to prevent the devastating effects of intermittent and sporadic unemployment. Among Black males employed in the labor force, one out of three will experience unemployment in a given year (Staples, 1985). . . .

CONSUMERISM INCOMPATIBILITY

Evidence suggests that divergent attitudes about money are the most frequent areas of marital disagreement (Spanier & Thompson, 1987). Without exception, men complained that their former wives spent too much money on children, and some resented their wives' spending money on extravagant items such as fur coats and expensive jewelry. In their opinion, these spending habits made their marriages irrevocably unsalvageable. For example, Curtis, whose marriage ended after 6 years, reported that his wife, Julie, spent considerably more money on clothes than he could accept. Cur-

tis always had worked and believed that hard work and saving money were virtues. His comments illustrate the influence of divergent spending practices on marital stability:

I married my high school sweetheart and best friend, Julie. I would have been married to her today if we could agree on money issues. We both worked two jobs because we had two children to raise. Julie had a daughter when I married her. When I received a better job, Julie got overboard with spending money. The marriage changed drastically.

Although Curtis's family operated on a small income even after he received a "better" job, the family still was faced with numerous spending decisions. In fact, he said,

Our arguments were always about money . . . and the money was not enough for Julie. She wanted my 5-year-old son to wear tennis shoes that cost over $100, and we purchased a large-screen television set that cost over $3,000. We were over our heads in debt.

Lennie, a 41-year-old high school teacher, also revealed that divergent values about consumerism subsequently led to divorce. Despite his former spouse's desire for a fur coat, he refused to invest money in an item he considered extravagant. Although he admitted that his former wife had expensive tastes and grew up in an "upper class southern family," Lennie's opposition to the purchase of a fur coat led to intensive marital distress and subsequent divorce:

I made it clear that I was not going to buy my ex-wife, Cheryl, a mink because it seemed extravagant. We had numerous arguments about this. I had no qualms about spending $3,000 or $4,000 on her, but I would not spend that much money on a mink coat.

In explaining his values in regard to consumerism, Lennie noted,

I would spend a couple of thousand dollars on something that we could get some pleasure out of—like a boat—whereas a mink coat represents that I am better than other folks. I would not contribute to that. My marriage deteriorated because Cheryl was unhappy about my refusal to buy her a mink coat.

For Lennie, the fur coat represented bragging of one's economic accomplishments, which symbolized superiority over others and offended his basic sense of egalitarianism. Lennie believed that a fur coat would elevate him to a higher plane and would remove him from the community of Black brotherhood. Lennie's tie to Blackness here rarely was perceived as the militant self-conscious pride of being Black; rather, it was perceived as deeper, more profound ties to beloved figures of childhood.

On the other hand, Cheryl believed that the fur coat represented social status in the context of social marginality. Thus, the conflict in Lennie's marriage involved dissimilarity in consumerism values. Other men also reported marital conflict involving divergent views about the purchases of houses, automobiles, and furnishings. . . .

PERSONALITY INCOMPATIBILITY

According to the men, the jealous behavior of former spouses was the most frequent behavioral characteristic that created marital distress. Actions characterized by jealousy were associated with pervasive distrust in the relationships. Gerald depicted the following pattern: "Molly always accused me of seeing other women, but she could not tell me who those women were. As a result, I stopped playing tennis or jogging to counteract her unreasonable jealousy."

Prior to the divorce, Gerald separated for 1 year, thinking that Molly's jealousy would cease. However, Gerald looked out of his window one day and saw Molly standing across the street watching him. On another occasion, Molly showed up unannounced at midnight to see whether he had been dating someone else. Over time, the behavior of Molly developed into a disturbing pattern, and he subsequently filed for divorce because he felt imprisoned by Molly's "insane" jealousy.

Other men also reported that former spouses doubted their commitment to marriage. For example, Maurice reported,

The bottom line is that I'm a Black male, and Black women frequently believe the stereotypes society have about Black men such as being womanizers who are by nature destined to be uncommitted to marriage. So, Elaine often became jealous when I had business meetings with women, talked to them on the phone, and consulted about buying cars.

In assessing the situation, Maurice stated,

The truth was, I felt obligated to Elaine and my son and daughter in a way I can't explain. I felt an obligation so strong that I would feel ashamed sneaking around with other women, so Elaine's irrational ideas frightened me.

Constant surveillance of the men's movements by former spouses also demonstrated the lack of trust in their relationships. Todd explained the actions of his former spouse, Rachael: "To determine if I was at work, Rachael called constantly. This drove the secretary crazy. Even if I was in a meeting, Rachael expected me to answer the phone to confirm my presence and to have long conversations with her." Other men reported that former spouses called restaurants to determine whether they were in business meetings, secured friends to spy on their behavior after work, and doubted their fidelity. Black women's perceptions of their husbands' betrayal might be explained, in part, by the sex ratio hypothesis. The imbalanced sex ratio (i.e., the number of men per 100 women) remains about 5 points below that of Whites, even when corrected for an undercount of Black men. In other words, there are approximately 1.4 million more Black females than Black males in the United States. For those Black women in the 22- to 25-year age range, the male-to-female ratio is as low as 85.6 males per 100 females, compared to 100.5 for Whites in the same age range.

The imbalance in the sex ratio is due to a number of factors. Black young men have comparatively high mortality rates, and many are confined to prisons. The high homicide rate affecting Black men, combined with the disproportionate number of deaths of Black males from cancer, heart disease, strokes, cirrhosis of the liver, and accidents, also contributes to the severe Black sex ratio imbalance. The increased number of Black men who are attracted to non-Black women for potential mates further reduces the pool of available men for Black women. In 1985, the number of Black male–White female couples in the United States was more than eight times greater than that of Black female–White male couples (Williams, 1990). Moreover, Black men constitute approximately 6% of the general population but represent 50% of male prisoners in local, state, and federal jails. Approximately 46% of Black men between 16 and 62 years of age are not in the labor force, and 32% of Black working men have incomes below the poverty level (Staples, 1985).

Considering the number of Black men who are gay, already married, or unacceptable as mates, the male-to-female ratio for Blacks is further reduced. In fact, Staples (1978) suggests that in practical terms, there might be no more than one Black man for every five single Black women in the United States. Divorce rates are higher when the ratio of women to men is higher. The male shortage in the Black population has been a major contributor to marital decline, adultery, out-of-wedlock births, and less commitment among Black men to relationships.

One presumable consequence of the low supply of Black men is the erosion of basic trust in marriages that erupts through possessive jealousy. A Black jealous wife might be conforming to societal pressure for a monogamous marriage while expressing resentment and frustration with the shortage of Black men as well as the lack of desirable men with whom to form monogamous marriages.

It is possible that, given the quality of the Black marriageable pool, the respondents' wives might have felt pressured to "hold onto" their employed husbands. As Larry poignantly expressed, "Black women are depressed because there aren't nearly enough eligible and sane Black men to go around, and that critical shortage is making them desperate and jealous." . . .

FAILURE TO NEGOTIATE CONFLICT

Violent solutions to marital problems have been incorporated into the mainstream culture of the United States. One terrifying aspect of this fact of American life is that the incidence of domestic violence increases every year. In Atlanta, Georgia, a predominantly Black city, 60% of all police calls on the night shift are domestic disputes. Black male–female conflict leads to the assault and murder of Black females at a greater rate than do the intimate relationships of any other racial/ethnic group in the United States (Gullattee, 1979). Black women are more likely to strike back at their abusive husbands, whereas Black husbands are more likely to assault their wives and cause bodily harm (Plass, 1993).

Identifying the correlates of intimate violence among Blacks, Gullattee (1979) points to the escalating violence in the general population. Violent acts intrude into Black homes through television. Surveys show that acts of violence occur every 3½ minutes on television. During primetime evening hours, Blacks have their choices of endless depictions of death and violence. According to Gerbner (1990), Blacks watch television 39% more than do all other American households. The cumulative message of television is that solutions to marital disputes should involve violence.

In this study, the most common violent situation involved both partners and included verbal and physical abuse. The following represents a typical case. Alvin, a 36-year-old auto mechanic, emphasized that his ex-wife, Maria, was a "loving, intelligent woman who overreacted to trivial events." He viewed his race as creating a particular stress for his Puerto Rican wife because her family objected to the marriage. "The first 2 years of my marriage were really good because Maria was willing to do whatever needed to be done," he asserted. Alvin described an act of violence that centered around a car. To Alvin, a new car symbolized achievement of the American dream:

> We had just bought a $15,000 car. I had experienced layoffs for the past 3 years of my marriage. I worked two jobs, and sometimes three jobs, so that we could have a new car. I wanted a car that was loaded with everything —a CD player, sunroof, you know, the works.

Alvin suffered from a legacy of deprivation and remembered begging for food at a local grocery store as a regular part of his childhood. He quit school to work and to provide for his younger siblings. For a period in his life, he said, "I went crazy, got a girl pregnant who later had an abortion, and hung in the streets." One day, he realized that "I didn't want to end up like my friends in the neighborhood who were in prison or dead. I knew I had to set my own direction." Alvin received his high school GED and became an automobile mechanic. To Alvin, a new car symbolized achievement of the American dream.

Alvin recalled reactions when his ex-wife, Maria, broke the high beams in the car:

> Maria flickered the high beams of the car off and on. She finally broke it. Since I'm paying for this car by working two full-time jobs, I asked her not to do that car like that. Maria grabbed my shirt and was fighting. I hit her. Maria called the police, and we separated for 1 month, then later got back together.

Alvin reported that he felt guilty about beating Maria and was conciliatory the following 6 months. Although they still had arguments, he stated, "I never laid a hand on her again." Two years later, when the couple had a heated argument in the kitchen, Maria grabbed a knife and stabbed him, resulting in Alvin being disabled. Other men pointed to scars and bruises caused by domestic violence. Several men referred to scars on their foreheads; others revealed old bullet wounds, described swollen eyes, and revealed lost teeth.

In several cases, minor attacks escalated into major physical assaults, and experiencing domestic violence once often made it easier for couples to do it again. For example, Vince recalled an abusive incident in which his ex-wife, Sandy, threw a model airplane, one of his cherished possessions, at him. He recalled,

> Sandy and I were arguing, then she threw my model airplane and broke it. Few Blacks or Whites own that model. She grabbed me and tore off my shirt. Afterward, I grabbed her by the throat, lifted her off the ground and threw her. I felt so bad, I felt like an animal. I cried and cried because I was taught never to hit a woman. I grew up around five sisters and was taught never to hit a woman. So, I knew at this point that the marriage was over.

Then Vince told Sandy, "I plan to file for a divorce." He left town to visit relatives in another state—without her. Sandy packed up their 7- and 8-year old daughters and took them to stay with relatives for a few days. On Vince's return, Sandy met him at the door and shot him in the shoulder. In analyzing the incident, Vince said,

> Sandy shot me to show me that she really did not love me. I wanted the marriage to work, but she wanted to get out of the marriage. That was the only option Sandy believed she had. Sandy just couldn't tell me she didn't want to be married anymore.

. . . Domestic violence in the Black community can be viewed as an attempt to cope with long-term frustration associated with social subordination. Black men and women often believe the promise that if they make sure they are qualified and work twice as hard as Whites, then Blacks can be anything they want to be in mainstream America. However, the promise often is not kept, even though some Black men change their appearances and personalities to try to assimilate. Thus, Black men often feel that although they are unable to control how society treats them, they should be able to control their women. A large number of Black men view violence as a means by which they can demonstrate their masculinity because most conventional channels of achievement are blocked.

Gelles (1984) notes that in most cases, a marriage license also functions as a hitting license. As John noted, "Some of my friends told me to give Rita a good beating to put her in her place." Numerous incidents of violence between married partners often are considered by couples to be normal, routine, and generally acceptable. Moreover, the patriarchal system allows a man the right of ownership to some degree over the property and people that comprise his household. John remarked, "It is scary because it is almost normative for Black men to use physical force to control Black women, and until Black men redefine what it means to be a man, there always will be domestic violence."

Similarly, Millette (1993) reports that among West Indian men who migrated to the United States, some use threats of violence, withhold economic support, and/or employ blackmail to control their wives. . . .

DIFFERENCES IN VALUES

Spiritual Incompatibility

According to the respondents, differences in religious practices also affected marital stability. For example, Ben's desire for spiritual freedom and autonomy clashed with his wife's emphasis on church attendance as an expression of spirituality. Ben, who also described himself as a religious person, explained,

> I realized that I had selected a mate not taking into account whether or not my spiritual values would conflict with her values. In fact, when I reclaimed a higher spiritual consciousness, the marriage ended.

I saw that materialism was the basis for Etta's values versus the religious values in my life.

Solomon, who evaluated his former wife, Kaye, on her potential to mother, stated,

> I have God in my life, but Kaye did not; therefore, she did not know how to treat someone like me, who really loved her. Our differences in commitment to God and what that means certainly strained the marriage.

Willy, who married because it was something to do, also illustrated the dissimilarity of religious commitment and its effects on marital stability:

> When Donna joined a fundamental religious sect, the Church of God, she stopped socializing and wanted me to stop smoking and drinking and [to] join the church. I felt frustrated, like I was giving up my life, which created a number of arguments. One day, I got tired of her nagging me to go to church and moved out.

Church attendance historically has been an important source of support for a number of Blacks. The Black church has reinforced values and behaviors. Blacks also share a religious tradition dating to Africa, where the sacred and secular are inseparable. However, the inability of spouses to appreciate differences in spiritual expressions and practices contributed to disagreements and marital disruptions.

VALUE INCOMPATIBILITY

In addition, some men expressed a lack of personal fulfillment and marital happiness because their value systems differed vastly from those of their spouses. Stanley, who stated . . . that he assessed a woman's maternal potential as a characteristic in a future mate, said,

> The only concern Paula had was raising children. She occupied her mind with the latest makeup and

fashions. She could not or did not want to understand the world around her. We were two different
people. We had arguments about this, and she could
not understand my need to read, to visit art galleries,
and to visit libraries, and I could not understand her
need to watch TV talk shows, wear the latest fashion
trends, and dance at trendy nightclubs. We drifted
further and further apart, battling against extreme
differences.

In commenting on value differences in his marriage, Clyde noted, "I am a very ambitious person.
I believe a woman should always strive to better
herself, and Betty did not want to do that. So, we
ended up not wanting the same things." Variations
on this theme expressed by other men included "I
grew professionally and knew where I was going
in life, and my ex-wife did not."

On the other hand, Vance, who viewed love as
no hassles, could not understand Ella's need to engage in political and sociological discussions, to
visit the library, and to read. Ella accused him of
having no knowledge of his potential to grow and
to expand intellectually. He explained,

My main goal was to finish high school and go to
trade school to be a hospital technician. As far as the
future was concerned, I had no desire to go to college, and Ella wanted a college-educated man. She
wanted a "buppie," a single Black heterosexual male
with a job, a white-collar job, so she left me.

In assessing his divorce experience, Vance said,

Ella talked about her career all the time, like [it was]
all there was to life. She liked to hang around her
White friends, dress up, go to fancy restaurants, and
drink white wine. I liked to barbecue, invite people
over, drink beer, and watch TV westerns. I socialized mostly with my family, and she socialized with
people from work. We started going out alone, and
that heightened tensions even more in our home.
Our clash in values caused frequent arguments and
distress, and one day we both realized that we were
making each other miserable. There was nothing we
could talk about, and I think that my ex-wife just got
tired of me, so she took the kids and left.

Similarly, Ernell, who retired from the military,
reported,

My marriage ended due to conflicts over values.
Dee devoted a lot of energy to get me to cooperate
with her game plan, that is, how to get me secured in
some professional career that included a Ph.D. and
relocating to the East Coast with a lifestyle that included designer furniture and a vacation home. She
was recruiting me for certain middle class qualities
that included an Ivy League education and a high-
status professional career. We argued about this because I was happy being a sergeant in the military.

Although a spouse with a college degree has
been highly desirable, a generation of Black men
and women have married from varying class backgrounds. This situation has been attributed to the
importance placed on teaching as an ideal career
for Black women and the lack of professional career opportunities for Black men. In fact, during
the Jim Crow era, a number of Black men with
professional law degrees worked in the post office, and great promising Black talent was locked
out of professional careers.

Whereas few Blacks in the past expected to
marry doctors or lawyers, their ideal mates were
"good" men or women who worked in stable blue-
collar jobs. In fact, during segregation, Black couples often married each other with no money and
few resources, believing that the capacity to appreciate and give love was the legitimate measure
of a person's worth. As Blacks assimilated into
the economic market, similar status has become a
prerequisite to forming and continuing an intimate
relationship.

REFERENCES

Gelles, R. J. (1984). *The violent home*. Beverly Hills,
CA: Sage.

Gerbner, G. (1990). *Violence profile*. Philadelphia: An-
nenberg School of Communication.

Gullattee, A. (1979). Spousal abuse. *Journal of the National Medical Association, 71*, 335–342.

Millette, R. E. (1993). West Indian families in the United States. In H. E. Cheatham & J. B. Stewart (Eds.), *Black families: Interdisciplinary perspectives* (pp. 301–317). New Brunswick, NJ: Transaction.

Plass, P. S. (1993). African American family homicide: Patterns in partner, parent, and child victimization, 1985–1987. *Journal of Black Studies, 23,* 515–538.

Spanier, G. B., & Thompson, L. (1987). *Parting: The aftermath of separation and divorce* (rev. ed.). Newbury Park, CA: Sage.

Staples, R. (1978). Masculinity and race: The dual dilemma of Black men. *Journal of Social Issues, 34,* 183–196.

Staples, R. (1985). Changes in Black family structure: The conflict between family ideology and structural conditions. *Journal of Marriage and the Family, 53,* 221–230.

Williams, M. W. (1990). Polygamy and the declining male to female ratio in Black communities: A social inquiry. In H. E. Cheatham & J. B. Stewart (Eds.), *Black families: Interdisciplinary perspectives* (pp. 171–193). New Brunswick, NJ: Transaction.

Think about It

1. What do Lawson and Thompson mean by "consumerism incompatibility"? Why, in their study, did consumerism incompatibility contribute to the black men's decisions to seek a divorce?

2. Lawson and Thompson describe other incompatibility issues (such as personality and religious differences) that strain marriages and create marital instability. Do these findings suggest that we should dump the old "Opposites attract" adage and instead encourage dating and mate selection based on "Birds of a feather flock together"?

3. What, according to this research (and your own observations), are some of the similarities and differences in the experiences of black and white men that appear to increase marital disruption rates?

40 Divorce Mediation among Asian Americans

Roger R. Wong

Mediation offers divorcing couples the opportunity to negotiate their divorce settlement with the assistance of a neutral third-party facilitator. Roger R. Wong explores the use of mediation in Chinese American and Japanese American families. He examines mediation across cultural settings, analyzes particular problems facing the mediator and culturally diverse clients, and discusses the need for regulations and training programs that incorporate cross-cultural perspectives.

INTRODUCTION

The steady increase in divorce rates within this society has changed the traditional view of court-based divorce proceedings. For court-weary spouses seeking alternatives to traditional divorce litigation, mediation is an attractive option. Mediation basically offers divorcing spouses the ability to negotiate their own divorce settlement with assistance from a neutral third-party facilitator, while assisting the mental and psychological transition of the marital breakup.

. . . Mediation may absorb many ethnic couples in the process of terminating their marriage. This article examines divorce mediation within a cross-cultural setting, specifically with Asian American clients. The term "Asian" represents a vast number of subgroups. There are at least 29 subgroups that comprise the Asian population in the U.S. (Sue & Sue, 1988). The two largest Asian groups are the Chinese and Japanese, with varying levels of acculturation within each.

For this article, cross-cultural mediation is analogized to cross-cultural counseling because they share common structural and substantive elements. Most mediation models evolve from

Kessler's four-stage approach, which defines the mediation process as: (a) setting the stage for the parties, (b) defining the issues, (c) processing the issues, and (d) resolving the issues (Kaslow, 1988).

Taylor's (1988) seven-stage mediation model is an example incorporating Kessler's basic design. Stage 1 introduces the parties to the process and sets out their responsibilities. Stage 2 encompasses fact finding and isolation of the issues for mediation. Stage 3 creates the options and alternatives available to the parties; Stage 4 refines the negotiating and decision making of these options. Stages 5 and 6 include drafting the agreement and presenting it to outside attorneys for review. Stage 7 implements the plan and allows for adjustments and follow-up visits if necessary.

Kessler's four stages are intuitively mirrored in counseling agendas. Ho (1987) discusses counseling ethnic minorities in a three-phase approach. In the beginning phase, the parties are engaged, data are collected, and goals are set. Problem solving is the second phase, and the third phase is evaluation and termination of therapy (Ho, 1987). Thus mediation and counseling structures embrace similar design requirements.

Besides the structural likeness, mediation adopts counseling background in other areas. Many mediation practitioners originate from the mental health field. Likewise, the intimate setting of mediation

Source: From Roger R. Wong, "Divorce Mediation among Asian Americans: Bargaining in the Shadow of Diversity," *Family and Conciliation Courts Review* 33 (January 1995): 110–28. Copyright © 1995 Sage Publications, Inc. Reprinted by permission of Sage Publications, Inc.

parallels the counseling approach. In a counseling context, communication normally flows from the patient to the counselor. Similarly, in mediation the spouses initially direct communication to the mediator. Moreover, divorce is a highly traumatic and stressful experience. This naturally incorporates some degree of emotional processing for the spouses within the private mediation setting.

The most likely cross-cultural counseling situation describes an Anglo counselor and minority clients (Dillard, 1983). This article follows suit and discusses the mediation dynamic of an Anglo mediator and Asian clients. Here, Asian refers to both Chinese and Japanese because the two groups share similar cultural values in the structure of personal and family relations (Ho, 1987). Cross-cultural mediation is discussed in [two] main parts. First, the benefits of divorce mediation and its usefulness for Asians are discussed. Second, the article analyzes particular problems and issues facing the mediator and culturally diverse clients. Within this section are the issues of the mediator's cultural awareness, Asian norms and values, cross-cultural communication aspects, and a survey of some current mediation training programs and regulations.

THE MEDIATION ALTERNATIVE TO DIVORCE LITIGATION

The incidence of divorce indicates its acceptance as a common event in society (Milne & Folberg, 1988). In a 10-year period from 1975 to 1984 there were more than 1 million divorces in each of those years. The annual divorce rate since 1975 has been at least 45% of the number of marriages (Morrison, 1987). Divorce exacts a heavy emotional burden upon the parties that the formal divorce process cannot accommodate. Mediation is at the forefront of the shift away from the "winner take all" approach of traditional litigation. Mediation moves toward a divorce settlement respectful of each party's needs and desires. This section

defines mediation and its application for Asian participants.

Dissatisfaction with Traditional Divorce Proceedings

Traditionally, a couple seeking a divorce had few options. Marital ties were severed through the formal adversarial process, with attorneys representing each spouse's best interests. In costly litigation, spouses battled each other "in a competitive struggle for the material spoils" (Simmons, 1985). The formal structure of divorce left no room for the emotional and psychological needs of the embattled parties.

Dissatisfaction led to changes in traditional divorce proceedings. No-fault divorce and the availability of . . . divorce kits emphasized reduced judicial intervention and became alternatives to traditional divorce proceedings. Though less dependent on the adversarial process, no-fault divorce still requires the use of attorneys and courts to determine the final property and financial arrangements and, if there are children, the custody and visitation arrangements. Thus reliance upon an advocate to arrange affairs still exists. Mediation offers a solution because it is a juncture of legal and mental health professions and operates within the "shadow of the law" (Milne & Folberg, 1988). The parties communicate directly and actively control the settlement issues of division of the marital property, child support, spousal maintenance, and custody (Grebe, 1988).

Oregon defines mediation as "a process in which a mediator assists and facilitates two or more parties to a controversy in reaching a mutually acceptable resolution of the controversy" (Oregon Revised Statutes, 1989). Mediation is a cooperative process using a neutral third party to resolve parenting, financial, and property issues. It can empower the parties to control the settlement and gives them satisfaction for creating a workable solution.

Mediation is first and foremost a process that emphasizes the participants' responsibility for making decisions that affect their lives. It is thus a self-empowering process. The process minimally consists of systematically isolating points of agreement and disagreement, developing options, and considering accommodations through the use of a neutral third-party mediator whose role is described as that of a facilitator of communications.... (Milne & Folberg, 1988)

Mediation recognizes that "feelings become facts," and the emotions associated with divorce are internalized in the process unlike the adversarial approach (Milne & Folberg, 1988). By requiring the parties to participate and communicate directly with each other instead of through attorneys, mediation can instill competence and esteem in the negotiations. Moreover, for post-divorce relations, the parties may learn positive communication strategies and skills useful for future interactions and problem solving.

Mediation for Asian Americans

The advantages of mediation are equally applicable to Asians seeking an alternative to traditional divorce litigation. Cultural differences are not recognized in the formal court process any more than the emotional overlays of divorce.

> [C]ultural and religious responses to divorce are irrelevant in the formal court process. Many divorcing couples, adrift in a sea of conflicting emotions, feel that the court is not interested in what is fair, only what is the law. (Meierding, 1992)

Historically, Asian cultures favored mediation for resolving disputes (Cohen, 1966). Chinese Confucian values emphasized harmony and the community over the individual (Wall, 1993). Preserving harmony and the functioning of the social order was the ideal social norm. The term "jang" meant compromising to restore harmony if it became disturbed or unbalanced. Mediation was favored because

> [A] lawsuit symbolized disruption of the natural harmony that was thought to exist in human af-

fairs.... [L]itigation led to litigiousness and to shameless concern for one's own interest to the detriment of the interests of society. (Cohen, 1966)

The first generation of Chinese immigrants transplanted the community style of mediation practiced in their native land. Mediation resolved disputes within the Chinese communities and was controlled by the family associations, or "benevolent associations," that governed activities within Chinatown (Doo, 1973). Benevolent associations were created to remedy the hostilities imposed by the dominant culture and the need for social cohesion:

> [Chinese Consolidated Benevolent Associations] provided an internal structure in the Chinese community and facilitated relations with the white society by acting as a spokesman for members who needed help in dealing with the outside world. (Doo, 1973)

Today, many Asians are far displaced from their traditional roots and have embraced the dominant culture values. Although the level of acculturation is high, traditional cultural values still are present among the later generations (Sue, 1983). Indeed, many Asians are essentially bicultural, operating successfully within both Anglo and Asian cultures. Therefore, seeking outside counseling for mental problems is normally accepted in the dominant culture; however, to the traditional Asian mindset, it brings shame upon the individual and family. Strong family values emphasize problem solving strictly within the family unit and preserving harmony (Dodd, 1982). In addition, cultural orientation and unfamiliarity with legal processes keep the divorce rates of Asians low (Ho, 1987).

Thus divorce mediation correlates to traditional Asian cultural norms preferring mediation for dispute resolution (Pedersen, 1993). Mediation better fits divorcing spouses because it avoids the guilt pressures of traditional divorce. They are less stigmatized, and the families save "face" when litigation is avoided. In sum, mediation's ability to account for the emotional and mental process of divorce makes it equally beneficial for dealing with the impact of cultural differences in divorce.

ISSUES FOR CROSS-CULTURAL DIVORCE MEDIATION

A successful mediation is dependent on the mediator's ability to cajole the parties to an agreement that is mutually satisfactory. The general theory of mediation prescribes a process carried out through stages that relies on the mediator's ability to manage conflict and educate the parties of their legal entitlements. Because the parties rely on the mediator for guidance and information regarding the settlement issues, establishing a trusting relation is essential. The participants speak the same language, but cultural filters may obscure the cognitive understanding. Thus racial and cultural differences add a unique dimension to mediation.

This section analyzes the problems and unique challenges in a cross-cultural context with an Anglo mediator and Asian disputants. The issues addressed include effects of mediator biases: racism, stereotyping, and ethnocentrism; cultural references to conflict management and fairness; verbal and nonverbal communication patterns; and training for cross-cultural mediation.

Mediator Biases

Racism is the most likely source of problems in counseling diverse clients (Ridley, 1989). Because mediation is practiced in a private setting similar to counseling, culturally motivated tension and misunderstanding hampers the process. This section looks at racial problems that are foreseeable for Anglo mediators working with Asian clients.

Ethnocentrism is the attitude of viewing one's own culture as superior to others. Ethnocentric perceptions undermine the mediation process when these beliefs preclude a fair exchange of cultural values. This promotes bias and creates problems because "racial differences trigger perceptual differences that cut off potential communications before communication attempts have been made" (Dodd, 1982). As presenting the image of a neutral facilitator, the mediator must remove attitudes of cultural superiority from the mediation.

Ethnocentric attitudes can be minimized if the mediator responds to the diverse parties with a "global" view. Internalized cultural references are examined and adjusted. By attempting to understand different cultural customs, the mediator gains insight to the salient cultural values that are often at the core of the dispute.

Ethnocentric attitudes also can permeate the mediation if the overriding concern is on obtaining settlement of all the issues. In this situation, the negotiations will invariably conform to the mediator's preferences and motivations. The client's cultural values become secondary to the arduous task of obtaining an agreement. Alleviating the emphasis on agreement reduces the mediator's influence. Without the pressure to obtain settlement of all the issues, the mediator can be more responsive to the client's cultural orientations.

Similar to ethnocentrism, stereotyping is the practice of generalizing and categorizing social groups (Ridley, 1989). Some stereotyping is useful because it gives a mental reference for the complexities of diverse cultures and a common ground for those belonging to similar cultural groups (Rubin & Sander, 1991). However, stereotyping becomes abusive when it leads to negative referencing of ethnic minorities. Once these negative references become adopted, they are resistant to change.

Stereotyping cultural groups indiscriminately prevents accounting for situational differences; that is, not all persons of a similar ethnic group exhibit the expected behavior in all situations, and much is dependent on the individual's degree of acculturation (LeResche, 1992). Stereotyping dangers are manifest when they achieve a "self-fulfilling prophecy," and the parties behave in accordance to the generalizations exhorted upon them. Ridley (1989) admonishes counselors to "analyze their stereotypes of other people and relinquish their inaccurate ones." It is apparent the mediator needs to relinquish his or her own attitudes of cultural superiority that restrict the client's potential to negotiate and disrupt the process.

Requiring perfect impartiality and neutrality is much like a white elephant—there is no such animal. Human nature involves likes and dislikes, values and differences. Perceptions are shaped by life experiences. Likewise, a mediator is influenced by the surrounding community and its social values. The concept of true impartiality is elusive because "it is based on the notion of an observer without a perspective" (Grillo, 1991).

Therefore, attitudes of ethnocentrism and stereotyping that distort the mediator's impartiality are harmful if left unchecked. For instance, one of the mediator's tools is power balancing, or equalizing the parties' bargaining positions (Haynes, 1988). This is dependent on the mediator's perception of fairness. Neglecting the parties' cultural influences, the mediator takes an active role in deciding that there is a power imbalance without considering any possible cultural implications causing the perceived imbalance. The problem is exacerbated if the imbalance itself originates from the client's anxieties in relating to an Anglo mediator (Grillo, 1991).

To illustrate, an impasse on spousal support develops between the mediating Asian spouses. The husband has little desire to support his wife because he believes the divorce is her fault and is angry for the shame brought upon his family. The wife is reluctant to assert her needs because the husband dominated the marital relation and she is fearful of a confrontation with him over financial issues. They are confused about their inability to resolve the problems within the family structure and still are apprehensive about mediating.

If the mediator presses for a settlement, the parties' cultural values are subsumed by the mediator's perceptions of fairness and quest for agreement. On the other hand, if the mediator takes no active role, the ensuing agreement is unbalanced and detrimental to the wife. An alternative approach acknowledges the parties' cultural attitudes.

The mediator can reframe the issue in cultural terms, defining a resolution that restores harmony and is mindful of family honor. Thus a middle ground is reached by "helping the parties protect themselves and their own interests by assisting them in understanding the consequences of their agreement, while respecting the cultural values and norms that the parties bring to the table" (Meierding, 1992).

In sum, when the mediator impresses a personal agenda upon the process without altering perceptions based on the parties' cultural and racial backgrounds, the result easily can lead to dissatisfaction for both mediator and clients. As Grillo (1991) explains, "the mediator, due to her own internal processes, may not in fact have a sufficiently clear vision of the interaction between the divorcing spouses to make a considered decision about if and how the power needs to be balanced."

Asian Cultural Influences

Another problem arises when the subjective cultural framework of the parties is not accurately assessed. This section asserts that for mediation to satisfactorily resolve conflicts cross-culturally, it is necessary for the mediator to be informed about the cultural norms and values of the parties.

> Given the diverse population of the United States, it is important for mediators to become familiar with each party's cultural and religious perspective of fairness, in order to assist the parties in creating an agreement that will give them long-term psychological and substantive satisfaction. (Meierding, 1992)

The general Asian personality is traced to Confucianism (Pedersen, 1977). This ideology favors unity and harmony in furtherance of the family and societal relations over selfless individualism. Because family and community relations take precedence, shame is an effective tool to coerce proper behavior within the community structure. In conjunction with shame is the concept of "face." Losing face means being ostracized from the important community structure because of behavior against the community or family. Similarly, causing a person to lose face is the ultimate discourtesy for the individual (Wall, 1993). Thus the threatened loss of community and family support is sufficient to restrain individual behavior and save face.

The traditional Asian persona is reserved and unexpressive. Anonymity is favored and Chinese are "taught to remain silent and inconspicuous and not to attract attention to themselves" (Dillard, 1983). Sue (1983) summarizes that "traditional Asian values emphasize reserve and formality in interpersonal relations, restraint and inhibition of strong feelings, obedience to authority, obligations to the family, high academic and occupational achievement and use of shame and guilt to control behavior." In marriage relations, the male is deemed the dominant spouse and the wife is submissive. Thus a primary source of conflict can occur when the wife demands a more egalitarian posture to her husband (Ho, 1987).

Divorce among traditional Asian cultures is not encouraged because it upsets the harmony of the family, causing great shame. The traditional importance of the family structure creates reluctance to use formal divorce proceedings. For marital problems, many Asian couples eschew the use of outside problem solvers, relying instead on the family structure to resolve the conflict. This reluctance on seeking outside intervention requires a culturally sensitive mediator. Counseling research confirms that if this sensitivity is lacking, the sessions will ultimately fail (Ho, 1987).

Asian values and norms are in contrast to Anglo cultural values of assertiveness, spontaneity, and independence (Sue, 1983). Anglo culture is typically direct and to the point. In negotiations, time is a precious commodity not to be wasted. Janosik (1987) terms this preference the "John Wayne" approach because "American negotiators prefer short, informal negotiations that emphasize the equality of the participants." Asian cultures prefer an indirect approach and view these behaviors as crude and inappropriate. Moreover, time is

perceived fluidly, with less demand on producing a quick resolution.

Asian conflict negotiation is rooted in traditional norms and values. As a result, a mediator can feel confident that a fair agreement is made, but without examining the degree of cultural influences, may equate passive compliance with affirmative acceptance.

Verbal and Nonverbal Behavior

Donohue and Weider-Hatfield (1988) surmise, "[I]f the mediator and the disputants are from different cultures that use very different modes of communication, accurate interpretation is quite difficult." Besides the cultural background and biases, mediation between Asians and Anglos presents a challenge to the communication process. Misunderstandings can be attributed to the cultural influences on the communication process between the mediator and clients. Both have different "speech communities" where communication patterns are developed within the set group (Donohue, 1985); that is, both parties share the same language, but the words and actions represent differences in the parties' cultural basis. Culture is more than custom; it is the foundation of cognitive thought processing (Dodd, 1982). This section identifies some concepts of cultural organization that influence communications verbally and nonverbally.

One method of how different cultures organize communication is based upon built-in societal expectations and procedures. These are categorized as high-context or low-context cultures. For high-context cultures, individuals in social interactions are predisposed to know what is meant and what is expected in typical communication patterns. High-context cultures "provide information to equip members with procedures and practices in a number of situations." Conversely, low-context cultures do not provide these assumptions and the expectations are explained as part of the communication process. Here, "information is abundant, procedures explicitly explained, and expectations are discussed frequently" (Dodd, 1982).

Homogeneous cultures are generally high-context cultures because the members all share the same norms and values. Asian countries like Japan, China, and Southeast China are high-context cultures. Low-context cultures like the U.S. and European countries "value individual orientation, over communication codes, and maintain a heterogeneous normative structure . . . " (Ting-Toomey, 1985). Cross-cultural communication is most likely to run afoul when one person acts out of high-context approach and makes certain assumptions, although the other party operates from a low-context condition and expects an explanation.

To illustrate, negotiations between an Asian couple reach impasse on the issue of visitation rights. Analyzing the conflict, the mediator refocuses the discussion on what the individual parents ultimately seek, or the real interests of the disputants. The mediator is operating from a low-context approach because the conflict is defined and explained according to the individual's explicit interests. The mediator also attempts to familiarize each parent with the other's positional interests.

Conversely, the Asian parents may analyze the conflict from a high-context approach. The spouses share the Asian cultural values of maintaining harmony within the wider scope of family relations and community context. The conflict may stem from outside pressures that both parents anticipate when negotiating for visitation rights. Crafting a satisfactory visitation agreement requires a strategy facilitating these assumed converging social expectations and pressures.

Adding to this, LeResche (1992) studied differences between community-based mediation centers in the U.S. with the informal dispute resolution processes used in Korean American communities. She noted the mediation centers emphasized the parties' opportunity for full and open expression of their views of the conflict, although the Korean model of dispute resolution did not mention this goal at all.

Thus categorizing communication through a cultural basis has useful applications for cross-cultural mediation. Asians communicate in an evasive and non-confrontational style because much information is already shared internally. The Anglo mediator typically works from individualistic values and communication is likewise direct. Ting-Toomey (1985) summarizes "in the high context culture system what is not said is sometimes more important than what is said. In contrast, in the low context culture system words represent truth and power."

Cultural effects of the time organization is another communication issue for cross-cultural mediation. In mediation, "[r]eaching closure can be very difficult and frustrating, however, if the parties have different perceptions of time" (Meierding, 1992). Dodd (1982) discusses time in cultural contexts as monochronic and polychronic. Monochronic cultures organize time as linear and in segments, completing one task before beginning the next. Anglo cultures are characterized as monochronic because time is very compartmentalized and tasks are completed sequentially. Polychronic cultures view time as nonlinear and manage a number of tasks simultaneously.

The implication of time organization is relevant to cross-cultural mediation. The mediator seeks a systematic process between both parties. Conversely, the parties may bring a polychronic approach and discuss many diverse issues simultaneously with no real emphasis on agreement. Communication between monochronic and polychronic individuals is imbalanced unless the communication strategy is altered accordingly.

One suggestion is to avoid requiring completion of present issues before continuing to the next; otherwise, a monochronic structure is effectively imposed. Lack of progress on the issues at hand can signal a need to shift the discussion to other areas. Dogmatic reliance on a task-oriented approach can forestall progress when the parties seek discussion on a different issue and may result in frustrating the overall mediation process.

Another suggestion recognizes the different communication requirements of polychronic and monochronic cultures. Ordinarily, the mediator's listening skills are emphasized in the mediation because the parties are communicating directly about the settlement. In contrast, a polychronic approach may consider several issues simultaneously. Here, clear communication efforts are paramount to keep the discussions manageable and centered. As LeResche (1992) observes, "for east Asians, communication cannot be compartmentalized; it is an ongoing, infinite process of interpretation between people. The North American orientation, on the other hand, is to perceive communication as the transfer of messages during a short-term discontinuous relationship."

Much of the communication occurring in a counseling context, besides being verbal, is also nonverbal (Dillard, 1983). Nonverbal communication and behavior is defined as that which transcends the written and spoken word. Since the divorcing spouses are well accustomed to nonverbal behavior among themselves, the task is for the mediator to uncover these nonverbal cues and understand their effects.

In certain situations, nonverbal communication is a better indicator of the truth because it operates at the unconscious level.

> Since nonverbal behavior is more primitive in the sense that it functions in revealing emotions, feelings, and so on, it is more difficult to control than words, and therefore it can be assumed that nonverbal behavior is more powerful than words in revealing emotions, attitudes, degrees of warmth–coldness and so on. (Wolfgang, 1985)

Body language is equally expressive for many cultures. In Anglo cultures, social distance is usually farther than other cultures. Anglo cultures are normally expressive, whereas silence in different cultures signals internalizing of information. Wolfgang (1985) notes some ethnic minorities are wary of white middle class assumptions of nonverbal behavior such as "increased eye contact, smiling

and positive head nods as positive nonverbal reinforcers. . . . " Blind adherence to familiar nonverbal behaviors may create negative impressions upon the divorcing parties.

In sum, communication patterns ultimately arise from cultural influences. Mediation succeeds more easily when there is a shared understanding of the communication process. Therefore, the mediator needs to meld verbal and nonverbal communication patterns to avoid misinterpreting the parties.

Cultural Training and Requirements

The previous sections discussed issues of ethnocentrism, cultural influences, and communication patterns in cross-cultural mediation and affirmatively concluded that mediators must have awareness of the cultural influences brought by their clients. This next subsection examines to what extent current regulations and training programs incorporate cross-cultural issues.

The majority of mediator training takes place in workshop settings (Stulberg & Montgomery, 1987). The workshops normally consist of at least 25 hours of orientation and training that include lectures, role playing, demonstrations, and exercises (Milne & Folberg, 1988). Most mediators are either lawyers or mental health professionals with specialized training in divorce mediation (Haralambie, 1990).

Presently, few mediation training programs include communication skills (Donohue & Weider-Hatfield, 1988). In Oregon, training for court-based mediators includes different standards for court-connected mediation and mediators serving on court panels. The training requirements for court-connected mediators are controlled by administration regulations (Oregon Administration Resolutions, 1992). Because it is included as part of the required curriculum for a mediation training program, Oregon recognizes the importance of communication skills (OAR, 1992). Additionally, the statute requires mediation training to address "[s]ensitivity and awareness of cross-cultural issues" (OAR, 1992). Moreover, for continuing training requirements, mediators must undertake cultural diversity education if it was not part of their prior training (OAR, 1992). There are no similar counterparts for training regulations governing court panel mediators or private practice mediators.

In her study, Schultz (1989) examined four conflict resolution training models taught in large metropolitan cities. She concludes that while these programs effectively teach the basics of conflict resolution in a "hands on" approach, much theory work is left out. Similarly, in another study on mediation training programs, Grebe (1988) found programs lacked much theoretical foundation, providing for more practical applications, or the "cookbook approach." Although all four programs provided some communication skills, Schultz (1989) criticized the lack of interpersonal skills that are important "for dealing with such complex issues as the interaction relationship of the parties to a conflict." Schultz concluded that an effective program should include emphasis on the relation of conflict management styles to understanding the different perspectives of the parties in conflict.

One common complaint of these training programs is the lack of education about specific differences of culturally diverse clients. Interpersonal relation skills are important in mediation. However, many training programs neglect development of this skill in favor of teaching a practical, "hands on" approach. This is especially harmful for programs in large metropolitan cities with a greater likelihood of mediation among culturally diverse participants. Although some states such as Oregon require court-connected mediators to undergo cultural diversity training, many programs do not include this as part of the curriculum. As Schultz (1989, p. 309) points out,

> Explorations of the broader issues of ethnicity and race, politics, and social class could also significantly enhance one's comprehension of the multiple forces affecting a willingness to change. Moreover,

demonstrations of how one's use of language can foster greater trust and influence the choice of remedies might instill in trainees a greater understanding of the underlying principles of conflict resolution.

In assessing mediation training programs, regulations for court-connected mediators recognize the value of training that includes communications and cultural awareness skills. The private sector should follow this lead and provide training that encompasses further development of these skills. . . .

Providing a formal and unambiguous structure furthers negotiations in cross-cultural mediation. When impasse occurs, the mediator should consider problem solving in reference to traditional cultural values. Also, the technique of caucusing individually with clients can advance the stalemate, but should be used judiciously to avoid compromising objectivity.

SUMMARY

If divorce mediation is in its infancy, then cross-cultural divorce mediation is still in gestation. This article discussed the contours of cross-cultural mediation, issues of mediator biases, and cultural influences; assessed some training programs for cross-cultural skill development; and concluded with some possible solutions. The supporting research was culled from different disciplines. Data from the counseling profession are the most viable comparison at this point, but specific research on cross-cultural mediation needs to validate the observations within this paper.

Clearly, divorce mediation will be used with ethnic minority couples. Without fail, the most commonly propounded solution in all the cross-counseling literature affirms the need for a culturally sensitive mediator. Removing racial misperceptions frees the mediator from interjecting biases, promotes neutrality, and eliminates distracting behaviors. Acknowledging and understanding cultural influences on the issues encompassed within the mediation gives all parties a common ground.

Although there are some challenges to cross-cultural divorce mediation, they are not insurmountable. The trick is resolving these challenges as mediation grows out of infancy.

REFERENCES

Cohen, J. A. (1966). Chinese mediation on the eve of modernization. *California Law Review, 54,* 1201–1266.

Dillard, J. (1983). *Multicultural counseling; toward ethnic and cultural relevance in human encounters.* Chicago: Nelson Hall.

Dodd, C. H. (1982). *Dynamics of intercultural communication.* Dubuque, IA: Wm. C. Brown Publishers.

Donohue, W. (1985). Ethnicity and mediation. In W. Gudykunst, L. Stewart, & S. Ting-Toomey (Eds.), *Communication, culture and organizational processes* (pp. 134–154). Beverly Hills, CA: Sage.

Donohue, W., & Welden-Hatfield, D. (1988). Communication strategies. In J. Folberg & A. Milne (Eds.), *Divorce mediation: Theory and practice* (pp. 297–315). New York: Guilford.

Doo, L. W. (1973). Dispute settlement in Chinese-American communities. *The American Journal of Law, 21,* 627–663.

Grebe, S. C. (1988). Structural mediation and its variants: What makes it unique. In J. Folberg & A. Milne (Eds.), *Divorce mediation: Theory and practice* (p. 231). New York: Guilford.

Grillo, T. (1991). The mediation alternative: Process dangers for women. *Yale Law Journal, 100,* 1545–1610.

Haralambie, A. (1990, Summer). Mediation and negotiation, alternatives to litigation. *Family Advocate, 52.*

Haynes, J. (1988). Power balancing. In J. Folberg & A. Milne (Eds.), *Divorce mediation: Theory and practice* (p. 277). New York: Guilford.

Ho, M. K. (1987). *Family Therapy with Ethnic Minorities.* Beverly Hills, CA: Sage.

Janosik, R. J. (1987). Rethinking the culture–negotiation link. *Negotiation Journal, 3,* 385–388.

Kaslow, F. W. (1988). The psychological dimensions of divorce mediation. In J. Folberg & A. Milne (Eds.),

Divorce mediation: Theory and practice (pp. 83–103). New York: Guilford.

LeResche, D. (1992). Comparison of the American mediation process with a Korean-American harmony restoration process. *Mediation Quarterly, 9,* 323–339.

Meierding, N. R. (1992). The impact of cultural and religious diversity in the divorce mediation process. *Mediation Quarterly, 9,* 297–305.

Milne, A., & Folberg, J. (1988). The theory and practice of divorce mediation: An overview. *Divorce Mediation,* 3–4.

Morrison, A. S. (1987). Is divorce mediation the practice of law? A matter of perspective. *California Law Review, 75,* 1093–1155.

Pedersen, P. B. (1977). Asian personality theory. In R. Corsini (Ed.), *Current personality theories* (pp. 367–397). Itasca, IL: F. E. Peacock Publishers.

Pedersen, P. B. (1993). Mediating multicultural conflict by separating behaviors from expectations in a cultural grid. *International Journal of Intercultural Relations, 17,* 343–353.

Ridley, C. R. (1989). Racism in counseling as an adverse behavioral process. In P. Pedersen, J. Dragons, W. Lonner, & J. Trimble (Eds.), *Counseling across cultures* (pp. 55–77). Honolulu: University of Hawaii Press.

Rubin, J. Z. & Sander, F. E. A. (1991). Culture, negotiation, and the eye of the beholder. *Negotiation Journal, 7,* 249–250.

Schultz, B. (1989). Conflict resolution training programs: Implications for theory and research. *Negotiation Journal, 5*(3), 301–311.

Simmons, N. L. (1985). Ethical considerations of divorce mediation: Formal ethics opinion No. 488. *Willamette Law Review, 21,* 645–662.

Stulberg, J. B., & Montgomery, B. R. (1987). Design requirements for mediator development programs. *Hofstra Law Review, 15,* 499.

Sue, D. (1983). The impact of two cultures on the psychological development of Asians in America. In D. Atkinson, G. Morten, & D. Sue (Eds.), *Counseling American minorities: A cross cultural perspective* (pp. 85–96). Dubuque, IA: Wm. C. Brown Publishers.

Sue, D. W., & Sue, D. (1988). Asian Americans. In N. Vace, J. Wittmer, & S. DeVaney (Eds.), *Experiencing and counseling multicultural and diverse populations* (pp. 239–262). Muncie, IN: Accelerated Development Inc.

Taylor, A. (1988). A general theory of divorce mediation. In J. Folberg & A. Milne (Eds.), *Divorce mediation: Theory and practice* (pp. 61–82). New York:
Guilford.

Ting-Toomey, S. (1985). Toward a theory of conflict
and culture. In W. Gudykurnst, L. Stewart, & S. Ting-
Toomey (Eds.), *Communication, culture, and organizational processes* (pp. 71–86). Beverly Hills,
CA: Sage.

Wall, J. A. (1993). Community mediation in China and
Korea: Some similarities and differences. *Negotiation Journal, 9,* 141–142.

Wolfgang, A. (1985). The function and importance of
nonverbal behavior in intercultural counseling. In P.
Pedersen (Ed.), *Handbook of cross cultural therapy*
(pp. 99–105). Westport, CT: Greenwood.

[?] *Think about It*

1. How is cross-cultural mediation analogous to cross-cultural family and marital counseling?
2. What are the advantages of mediation for Asian Americans as an alternative to traditional divorce litigation?
3. Describe the problems of cross-cultural divorce mediation in terms of the following: language barriers, mediator biases and Asian American cultural values, ethnocentrism and stereotyping, cultural perceptions of time, and the inadequacies of culturally insensitive divorce mediation training programs.

41 | Latino Fathers and the Child Support Enforcement Experience

Kimberly A. Folse

We often hear about "deadbeat dads" who don't provide economic or emotional support to their children after a marital breakup. Kimberly A. Folse shows, in contrast, that many noncustodial fathers—especially Latino fathers—try to see their children as often as possible and pay child support when they're employed. The fathers maintain ties with their offspring despite financial difficulties, hostile relationships with their ex-wives, the responsibilities of providing for two families, and what the fathers perceive as an unfair and unsupportive child support enforcement system.

. . . Evidence suggests that the social circumstances of Hispanics, especially their labor market experience which contributes to high poverty, is unique (Tienda, 1995) and deserves special attention. Additionally, what needs to be acknowledged is the link between labor market experience and child

Source: From Kimberly A. Folse, "Hispanic Fathers and the Child Support Enforcement Experience," *Journal of Multicultural Social Work 6; no. 3/4 (1997): 139–58.* Copyright © The Haworth Press. Reprinted by permission of Haworth Press, Inc.

support enforcement. Parents who cannot work, or who work at low-wage, unstable jobs, have a harder time paying support. Thus, the Hispanic father's ability to pay child support and his child support enforcement experience are of special interest.

This paper presents the results from a survey on child support enforcement conducted in Texas (Folse, 1995) for the Office of the Attorney General. Hispanics, who are 27.6% of the population in Texas (Texas Department of Health, 1995), accounted for 54% of the child support enforcement caseload for the six counties selected to be surveyed. Sixty-four percent of the respondents to the survey were Hispanics. Admittedly, the results presented here are not representative of all Hispanics and are specific to Texas. However, this research addresses the gap in the literature, both with respect to Hispanic labor market participation and child support enforcement by providing information regarding the labor market experience of the non-custodial parent and the connection of this experience to the ability to pay child support.

Quantitative data can obscure real-life-experience. The data presented here emphasize the qualitative aspects of the child support experience for Hispanic fathers. Some quantitative data, however, are also presented as a context for the qualitative analyses. Presented are non-custodial parent (NCP) comments regarding personal experience and perceptions of the child support enforcement program (CSE). These comments were elicited as an open-ended question at the end of the survey. . . . The term Hispanic is used rather than Latino, mainly because that is the category most compatible with the U.S. Census Bureau categories and was the ethnic identifier used in the survey.

METHODS

The Sample

The data used for this study come from a survey conducted in 1995 (Folse) to better understand why some non-custodial parents fulfill their child support obligation and others do not. The anonymous survey, written in both Spanish and English, was sent in two waves, approximately one-and-a-half months apart. The two-waves were sent to all non-custodial parents, as there was no way of determining which parents had responded on the first wave. A stratified random sampling procedure was used to identify 4,200 non-custodial parents, or 26% of the child support population of 16,279 cases in the six selected counties. A mini-

mum of 462 cases was needed for the sample to be accurate within ±4 percentage points with a 95 percent confidence level (Kalton, 1983); a total of 477 valid responses were received. The AFDC [Aid to Families with Dependent Children] sample portion (N = 178) represents 43% of the valid respondents for ethnicity and county (N = 412) and 30% of the population of obligated cases (there were 64 observations missing due either to missing ethnicity or missing county). The non-AFDC sample portion represents 57% (N = 235) of the valid responses and 70% of obligated cases.

The primary focus of the research was to determine what factors discriminate between payors and non-payors. As would be expected, those who responded to the survey were disproportionately in the paying category. Thirty-nine percent of AFDC sample respondents were in the non-paying category whereas 89% of the population were in the non-paying category. Twenty-one percent of the non-AFDC sample were in the non-paying category, whereas 71% of the population were in the non-paying category. The ethnic background of the sample closely resembles the population except for the category "Other," which represented 10% of the AFDC population, but 3% of the sample, and 16% of the non-AFDC population and 2% of the sample.

Forty-nine percent of self-identified Hispanics (N = 144 out of 291) wrote additional comments to the survey. A selection from these comments is used here. Some of the responses were in Spanish and had to be translated. Selection for inclusion in this paper was based on comprehensiveness or directness of the comment.

DIMENSIONS OF CHILD SUPPORT ENFORCEMENT

The original study identified four key areas of concern or dimensions related to child support enforcement [CSE]. The four dimensions of child support are: the Financial Dimension, including the employment and occupation characteristics of the NCP; the Inter-Relational Dimension, that is, the relationship between the NCP and the mother including perceptions of visitation and how the custodial parent is spending child support; the Extra-Relational Dimension, which addresses other social circumstances that could affect child support payment such as financially supporting another family and the legal status of the parents when the child was born, that is, married or not; and, the fourth dimension, the Programmatic Dimension. This area is concerned with NCP perceptions of the child support enforcement program, including perceptions of fairness. These dimensions are a tool for organizing data and are, therefore, not always mutually exclusive. Many comments addressed a combination of two or more dimensions. For example, a parent may be having a visitation problem (Inter-Relational Dimension) and having a problem communicating with the CSE program about visitation (Programmatic Dimension). Or, a parent may be supporting another family (Extra-Relational Dimension) and may complain that his order is too high for his income and that he has been unable to get the CSE program to change their order (Programmatic Dimension).

FINDINGS

Financial Dimension of the Child Support Experience

In the larger study (Folse, 1995), steady employment was the most significant factor in determining if the NCP paid his child support in full and on time. According to the data, Hispanic fathers were more likely than White or African American fathers to report being unemployed in the last year. Over 15% of the Hispanic fathers reported being unemployed. Having only one place of employment in the last year, however, was comparable for Hispanic and White fathers. Fifty-nine percent of the Hispanic respondents reported one place of employment last year compared with 57% of White and 65% of African American respondents. More White than Hispanic respondents reported

two places of employment, 23% [for White] versus 16% [for Hispanic] and 12% for African American respondents.

Unemployment is a key factor in non-payment of child support. The structure of the child support enforcement agency is such that changes in employment status are not a factor in what support is owed. What a father owes in child support is determined at the time of the order based on the employment circumstances at the time of the order. Changed circumstances are "the problem of the father," not the child support agency.

The earning capacity of Hispanic fathers in this study is significantly less than for White fathers. Of the parents in the survey earning $20,000 or less a year, 70% were Hispanic. Of those parents in the survey earning $10,000 or less (17%), 75% were Hispanic. Hispanic fathers, therefore, are more likely to have very low incomes and thus difficulty paying child support. One reason why they may have greater difficulty in paying support is because the support obligation constitutes a higher proportion of their incomes; that is, child support enforcement is regressive. On average, non-custodial fathers who pay child support pay about $3,400 a year or 15% of their income. Poor fathers pay an average of 28% of their income for support (Sorensen as cited by Office of Child Support Enforcement, 1997, p. 8).

Because child support is so monetarily focused, it is of no surprise that financial and programmatic concerns represented the most frequent problem identified with paying child support. Of the 144 comments, 34% were concerned with the financial aspect, 63% were concerned with the CSE program. In a third of comments, financial concerns stem from enforcement concerns, that is, programmatic concerns; parents who are having difficulty making child support payments are held accountable by the CSE program. Parents are primarily concerned with survival issues; three-fourths of the comments express the extreme difficulty they have in paying support because they earn so little that they cannot live on what is left after they pay the amount owed. The remaining one fourth of comments address concerns related to supporting two families, being denied access to the children, and what is considered unfair treatment by the CSE agency in determining order amounts.

Parents who have very low incomes or lose jobs, for whatever reason, are still expected by the child support enforcement program (CSE) to make monthly payments at the ordered level. Presented are comments of fathers (verbatim) that testify to their financial dilemma:

> I have been laid-off since May of this year. When I was working I was only making $192.00 every 2 weeks. Which is $398.00 every month, and I had to pay $240.00 for 2 orders of child support because I have 2 girls with two different mothers and it was very hard to make it with only $149.00 every month. . . .

> [When] I have money I send the child support. But when it rains or it's very cold I don't because I don't work. I don't even have for rr [recreation] only my household bills.

> My comment is that there are times when I cannot send my child support payments because I do not have a permanent job. . . .

Child support orders can be adjusted, but only after the order has been in effect for 36 months. The most recent legislation no longer calls for automatic review, but review only at the request of either of the parents. During the three-year time-frame, spates of unemployment can mean that a father can accrue a substantial arrears balance. Arrears are reported to credit bureaus and incur interest charges.

These comments indicate that some fathers feel powerless. They are required to support their children, but sense that the enforcement program is one-sided, that enforcement of financial support is the only concern of the CSE. In part, the sense of powerlessness comes from having a sense that there is nowhere to turn for help except for hiring an attorney, an option that is expensive and beyond the financial reach of many fathers. A father addresses this circumstance, "I have nothing against paying child support cuz I love my son. . . . I just wish there were more laws for the paying fa-

ther always needs an attorney and I can't afford it." Another father, disgruntled about having been taken to court by his ex-wife and ordered to pay more per month, plus insurance and back support, says that he has only two choices: "(1) I just agree with it because I don't like going to court, and (2) I can't miss much work." Not only is hiring an attorney expensive, the time spent away from work is a cost to the father.

Inter-Relational Dimension

One of the key areas of the Inter-Relational Dimension of child support is visitation. Visitation is also a key national issue and a focal point of the 1984 Child Support Enforcement Act (P.L. 100-485). Fifty-eight percent of Hispanic parents in the sample indicated in the survey that they did not have a problem with visitation, that is, visitation went smoothly. Apparently when visitation was not an issue, parents did not feel compelled to document the positives. Only one parent made a comment on positive visitation, stating he lived two houses away from his children and that his new wife and ex-wife were good friends. Hispanic parents were least likely (39%) to indicate that there was a problem with visitation, whereas 43% of White parents and 49% of African American parents indicated a problem.

Distance from one's children can be a factor in visitation; those parents who live closest to their children are more able to visit them. Hispanic (48%) and African American (61%) fathers are more likely than White fathers (37%) to live within 30 minutes of their children. Thirty-seven percent of White fathers live more than three hours away, compared with 15% for Hispanic and 18% for African American fathers. Only 2% of White fathers, 5% of Hispanic fathers, and 8% of African American fathers in the sample do not visit their children. One can infer that living closer means more visitation. The data confirm this assumption; Hispanic (29%) and African American (38%) fathers indicated that they visited their children at least once a week compared with 15% for White fathers. White fathers are far more likely to visit only two to three times a year (30%), compared with Hispanic (11%) and African American (14%) fathers.

Thirty-one percent of the comments expressed concerns related to visitation or interaction with the custodial parent. Ninety percent of the visitation comments were to complain that they were denied access to their children. Two comments indicated that the custodial parent, usually the mother, could deny or absolutely refuse visitation or move and not give the father a new address. Three fathers stated that they have visitation rights, too, but that their only recourse was to hire an attorney; one father indicated that he was told by the CSE program to hire an attorney if he wanted help with visitation problems. The responses are varied, but many indicate a desire for visitation with their children:

Every time the case has gone to court the state represents them, but if they don't abide by the courts order to let me see my children I have to foot the bill for myself and them also. When I call or go by to talk about the problem of not being allowed to see my children, it is as if I don't exist. Men or fathers should I say don't have any right in the state's eyes and this is very unfair, we have as much love for our children too. . . .

I don't know where my daughter lives yet, I am ask to support. I would like to see her and be able to [have] some kind of relationship with her. I would like to know how she is.

Collecting child support is the focus of the CSE program, not visitation enforcement. Public pressure, especially from fathers' rights groups, has been somewhat effective in getting the CSE program to address the issue of visitation. Public Law 104-193 includes grants to help states establish programs that support and facilitate visitation and access to their children. What states will do, and how effective these access visitation programs will be, remain to be seen. Visitation is obviously of concern to some parents, but 58% of Hispanic parents indicate visitation is not a problem. For those expressing concerns with visitation, denied access was the major problem.

Another issue of child support is concern over how the custodial parent spends child support. The majority of all three ethnic groups, 59% of the White fathers, 65% of the Hispanic fathers, and 71% of the African American fathers, felt that the child support they sent was not spent on their children. NCPs have no control over how child support is spent. Whether the allegations are true or not, feelings of powerlessness and perceptions of unfair treatment are represented by these comments. The comments of NCPs point to a perception that the CSE program is one-sided, that there is little accountability on the part of the custodial parent, and that this is not fair:

I find the law totally one sided, yet it should be strict about it should investigate that the children are being taken care of with the money paid. I believe that a father should pay child support for his kids, but how come the Attorney General Office *Always* come after the father, but they never go after the mother when she doesn't spend the money on the kids. The kids always tell me that they go to the mall and she only buys something for herself, and nothing for the kids (there should be a law to go after the mother).

Extra-Relational Dimension of Child Support Enforcement

Only 5% of the comments related specifically to extra-relational concerns, that is, concerns with having to support two families or issues regarding paternity status. Research indicates that most adults go on to form another family after divorce (e.g., Coleman & Ganong, 1991) or are likely to form another relationship after separation. The burden of supporting two families can be significant. In this study 59% of all parents were supporting another family. Sixty-two percent of the White fathers, 57% of the Hispanic fathers, and 62% of African American fathers were in new families and providing financial support to them. Supporting another family is a financial burden for NCPs and makes paying child support to the first children all the more difficult. Here are the three NCP comments on this experience:

> I pay two child support payments; one for one child and one for the other. 1st one is $150.00 and the other $125.00. I make $4.25 an hour. Me and my live in woman support her children. That's very hard.

> With what I earn at times it isn't enough to support my other family. I have 2 sons that live with me and the other for who I pay support that is 13 years old.

> I pay child support for a son I have in California. I also have a son here in Texas and have custody of him. My ex-wife was ordered to pay $100.00 a month and has not paid a cent. She has 2 other children from two different men and has applied for child support. She works nights and receives AFDC. I don't think this is fair. The *system* has failed ME!!

Another possible issue for parents could be the legal status of their child. Alfasso and Chakmakas (1983) found that parents were less willing to pay support if they were never married. In this study, 18% of the White fathers, 38% of the Hispanic fathers, and 60% of African American fathers were not married when the child for whom they owe support was born. Only one Hispanic parent made a comment about paying support for a child that was born out of wedlock. His concern was over being served paternity papers eight years after his child was born; he had no idea that there was a child. He expressed how this revelation caused problems for his current marriage. Apparently, in this study, the legal status of the child, that is, if the child were born out of wedlock, is not an issue for parents. In the larger study, the legal status of the child was not a predictor of payment compliance.

Programmatic Dimension

The programmatic dimension of child support, that is, the CSE program itself, was the focus of the majority of parent comments; 63% of the comments were programmatic concerns. While financial concerns and inter-relational concerns such as visitation were expressed, many of these comments also addressed the CSE program.

Because the program sets orders, monitors payment including reports of arrears, assesses interest, and reports delinquent payment to credit bureaus, NCPs are very aware of the presence of the CSE program in their everyday lives. Sixty-four percent of the Hispanic respondents, 75% of the Black respondents, and 68% of the White respondents claimed that they did not think the CSE program was fair.

There were two primary areas of parent concerns, but both address what fathers perceive as the one-sidedness of the program. The CSE program represents the child and indirectly the mother. Hispanic fathers' (22%) comments indicate that no one listens to them or their plight. They claim, for example, that if they call the CSE agency for help (irrespective of whether the CSE program can help them) they are looked down upon. The second key issue area for Hispanic fathers is that they claim they do not have access to comparable legal representation (27%). These fathers state, for example, that they are told by the CSE agency to hire a lawyer if they want to be heard regarding visitation, order adjustment, and hearings where orders are set. A lawyer may help with visitation, but orders are set at the time of support hearing and are not reviewed again for 36 months:

> Men have few–no rights. If you cannot afford a lawyer you are at the mercy of the courts. The people at CSE will treat you like you are the scum of the earth. It's not fair. I love my kids more than life itself. But who will bat for me, us–men.

> Totally unfair, giving men no chance to speak and standing behind the woman about 90%. Totally unfair. . . .

> I had to pay a private attorney to represent me and my ex-wife had free representation through the Attorney General's office—my visitation is cut down drastically and there was nothing I could do. Their (sic) should be equal benefits for fathers who have been treated unfairly. . . .

The perception that the program is one-sided is a very real one, and indeed, the NCP is bombarded with strong state enforcement tools which are one-sided; the focus is on collecting support from the father. Under the current system, with the focus on financial support, there is little opportunity for father input. The process is relatively cut and dried, with financial support based on income as the bottom line. The real world complexity of the everyday lives of the NCP is of little concern to the program. The comments of the fathers presented here exemplify the one-sidedness of CSE:

I pay $210 a month for medical insurance (court ordered). If they don't have a job, the program doesn't care. . . . all it knows is that you must pay. However, if you do have a job, then the program does care, because it comes after you for as much as it can.

I am still driving my 1974 vehicle, because overtime I report the money the child support division take more away. I do not understand why no one will listen to the parent paying support. I got so depressed one day, I sat around the back shed and was thinking of killing myself because I am so backed into a corner. Our house is falling apart because it needs repairs. . . .

The remainder of comments regarding the program are fairly equally divided among the following: Miscellaneous concerns (9%), accountability (8%) (fathers feel mothers should be accountable for the money that is paid and the CSE program

should be the one to monitor mother's spending); visitation enforcement (14%) (some fathers apparently believe that the CSE program should assist them in access to their children); and tax relief (8%). What the parents mean by tax relief is that they believe that the support they pay should be recognized by the Internal Revenue Service as a deductible expense.

A summary table is offered to capture the picture of the non-custodial Hispanic father child support enforcement experience [Table 1].

DISCUSSION

The child support enforcement experience, from the perspective of the non-custodial parent, is a relatively new area of research. There is scant information about the Hispanic non-custodial parent experience. Because minorities, especially Hispanic and African American populations, are more likely to be poor, many of the concerns related to child support enforcement have special meaning for these populations. For example, to qualify for welfare, parents are mandated to participate in the child support enforcement program. With an increased emphasis on personal responsibility under welfare reform (Personal Responsibility and Work Opportunity Reconciliation Act of 1996, Public Law 104-193), child support enforcement will take a more central role in welfare policy as part of a cost avoidance strategy of moving welfare recipients off of welfare and transferring

TABLE 1   Dimensions of the Hispanic Non-Custodial Parent Child Support Enforcement Experience

Financial Dimension	*Inter-Relational Dimension*	*Extra-Relational Dimension*	*Programmatic Dimension*
Percent of comments: 34%	Percent of comments: 31%	Percent of comments: 5%	Percent of comments: 63%
Key Theme:	Key Theme:	Key Theme:	Key Themes:
Extreme difficulty paying support given very low income	Denied access	NA	Lack of resources for legal representation
			The CSW Program doesn't listen to fathers

Note: Percents add up to more than 100 because for any one comment there may be multiple issues addressed.

support to the parents. If the policy to enforce CSE program participation by welfare recipients is strictly enforced, and more welfare recipients will be required to name fathers or lose benefits, Hispanic involvement in the CSE program is likely to increase since the Hispanic population presently is the least likely to have child support awards (Garfinkel et al., 1992).

Stricter enforcement allows states to implement enforcement techniques such as expanded wage garnishment, assets seizure, and revocation of driver's and professional licenses. In addition, Congress has authorized and provided for CSE access to state and federal databases such as state motor vehicle and law enforcement, local tax and revenue records, records concerning real and titled personal property, and records maintained by public utilities and cable television companies (*Children Today,* 1997).

The Hispanic non-custodial parent's experience is more like the experience of the African American than the White non-custodial parent. However, it is not the same in all respects, and, therefore, deserves special attention for at least two reasons. The first reason is the Hispanic labor market experience. The majority of Hispanic fathers in this sample (52%) were unskilled or semi-skilled. The occupations associated with unskilled labor are often seasonal, and this population is subject to sporadic unemployment. In this study, 15.5% of Hispanic fathers were unemployed at the time of the survey. Unemployment is not conducive to regular payment of child support. Moreover, child support is due irrespective of unemployment. Under the current system, if a monthly payment is not made, that amount owed accrues as "arrears" and arrears accrue interest. In a relatively short time, the arrears balance grows substantially relative to the father's resources. The circumstance can be addressed at a future date, but the father must wait three years for a case review. Child support enforcement procedures look at income at one point in time, when the child support order is determined. Case reviews are supposed to be conducted at three years, as man-

dated by law; however, under the new Personal Responsibility and Work Opportunity Reconciliation Act of 1996, reviews no longer have to be conducted at three years unless one of the parents requests it. In either case, that is, the old law or the new law, the interim period can be characterized by loss of employment and inability to pay support. Despite the fact that some studies (Kost et al., 1995) have found that reviews lead to adjustments in only 21% of cases, the experience of Hispanic (and African American) non-custodial parents needs a closer look. The labor market circumstances of the Hispanic parents can be obscured by data collected after three or more years. Hispanic fathers are more likely to experience sporadic unemployment. After three years, the employment circumstances may have stabilized, but during the three-year period employment is likely to have been unstable and thus interfered with the parent's ability to pay support. In addition, it appears, at least based on this study, that Hispanic parents have the lowest incomes. Seventeen percent of the sample indicated making $10,000 or less a year. Hispanic respondents made up 75% of this income group. Three-fourths of the comments express extreme difficulty in paying child support. Another problem with the setting of orders is that they are regressive; the lowest income fathers are hardest hit by orders determined on a percentage basis.

The second social circumstance unique to the Hispanic population is the closeness of the family members. Hispanic (and African American) fathers are more likely to live closer (within 30 minutes) and to visit their children more often (weekly) than are White fathers. Increased interaction likely increases parental expenditures associated with both recreation and basic living requirements above the ordered amount. Several fathers in this study stated that they often spend money on their children beyond support owed and that their children spent time with them on weekends. The Hispanic child appears to be getting more, financially (assuming full payment) and emotionally, if visitation frequency is a good indicator. The CSE program is not set up to acknowledge financial contributions outside of child support payments, and this leaves fathers little opportunity to personally contribute to their children during visitation; even small expenditures for a movie can be too much.

For many fathers, denied access is the significant issue; the majority of the parent comments (90%) about visitation indicated that they were being denied access. These fathers have no way to enforce visitation other than the legal system, and given that Hispanic fathers tend to have very low incomes, hiring an attorney is out of their economic reach. . . .

REFERENCES

Alfasso, H. & Chakmakas, J. (1983). *Who Are We Missing: A Study of the Non-Paying Absent Parent.* Washington, DC: U.S. Department of Health and Human Services.

Children Today. (1997). Volume 24, No. 2. Washington DC: U.S. Department of Health and Human Services.

Coleman, M. & Ganong, L. H. (1991). Remarriage and Stepfamily Research in the 1980s: Increased Interest in an Old Family Form. In Alan Booth (Ed.), *Contemporary Families: Looking Forward, Looking Back* (pp. 192–207). Minneapolis: National Council on Family Relations.

Folse, K. A. (1995). *Factors Affecting Compliance with Orders for Support.* For the Office of the Attorney General of Texas, Child Support Division. Austin, TX.

Garfinkel, I., Meyer, D. R., & Sandefur, G. D. (1992). The Effects of Alternative Child Support Systems on Blacks, Hispanics, and Non-Hispanic Whites. *Social Service Review 66:* 505–523.

Kalton, G. (1983). *Introduction to Survey Sampling.* Newbury Park, CA: Sage.

Kost, K. A., Meyer, D. R., Corbett, T., & Brown, P. R. (1995). *Revising Old Child Support Orders: The Wisconsin Experience.* Discussion Paper #1070-95. Madison, WI: Institute for Research on Poverty.

Office of Child Support Enforcement. (1997). *Child Support Report, Vol. XIX,* No. 6 (May). U.S. Department of Health and Human Services.

Texas Department of Health 1994 Vital Statistics. (1995). Statistical Services Division, Bureau of Vital Statistics, Austin, TX.

Tienda, M. (1995). Latinos and the American Pie: Can Latinos Achieve Economic Parity? *Hispanic Journal of Behavioral Sciences 17:* 403–429.

? Think about It

1. What specific problems do noncustodial Latino fathers encounter in terms of the four dimensions that Folse delineates? Are your state's child support enforcement systems similar to or different from the ones that Folse describes?

2. Do you feel that the fathers' complaints about each dimension are justified or not? How do you think custodial mothers might respond to the fathers' criticisms?

3. Describe the two ways in which the experiences of the Latino noncustodial fathers are unique compared with the experiences of their black and white counterparts.

CHAPTER 9

Grandparenting, Aging, and Family Caregiving

The United States is graying. As Robert Bernstein shows in his overview, the elderly population will more than double by 2050 (Reading 42). By the same year, non-Hispanic whites may account for only 55 percent of the centenarian population, compared with 20 percent Latino, 13 percent black, 11 percent Asian and Pacific Islander, and 2 percent American Indian, Eskimo, and Aleut.[1] As people live longer, the numbers of *frail elderly* (those who show some mental or physical deterioration and depend on others for carrying out their daily activities) will increase across all ethnic groups. Despite the emergence and availability of professional formal services for disabled and dependent elders, families and friends are still the main caregivers of instrumental as well as emotional support. Family and friends rather than the formal service sector provide an estimated 80 percent of all care for frail elders in the United States.[2] This does not mean, of course, that all people 65 years of age and older are frail or that they always receive, and do not give, support. As the last two readings in this chapter show, some ethnic grandparents have become surrogate parents, and others participate actively in family life and their grandchildren's socialization.

In general, research on older Latinos remains scarce. Social scientists have given little attention to this population in part because of misperceptions and stereotypes that the extended Latino family protects the elderly from a "hostile" world and provides all necessary support.[3] Using a large national data set, Tracy L. Dietz found that Mexican American families provided much affective support of their elderly. However, the elders reported a variety of instrumental needs—such as financial support or help to overcome some physical limitations—that were not being met by their families (Reading 43). A literature review of caregiving in the Latino population concluded that Latino providers are as distraught as Anglo caregivers about coping with elder care. Much of this strain is due to Latino elders' being more at risk for specific diseases such as diabetes (and its medical and psychosocial complications), being disabled at earlier ages than their white counterparts, and having less access to long-term care services because of poverty or meager retirement incomes.[4] In effect, then, although Latino and other ethnic elderly receive intergenerational assistance, some much-needed services lie outside the extended family's informal support networks.

Catherine Hagan Hennessy and Robert John caution that caregiver stress should be measured within a sociocultural context instead of from the assumption that caregiving is synonymous with the elderly person's being a "burden" (Reading 44). In their study of Pueblo Indians, Hennessy and John found that the providing of care to dependent elders was a reflection of the caregivers' view of themselves as a people who value interdependence, connectedness, and reciprocity with the members of the extended family and with the tribe as a whole, even into dependent old age.[5] Like Mexican American caregivers (Reading 43), however, Pueblo Indian caregivers experienced anxiety and felt frustrated with the lack of formal services. For many ethnic elderly, even when services are available, access may be limited because of transportation problems, insufficient numbers of staff who provide services, and cultural values that equate outside support with "handouts."[6]

Readings 45 and 46 present examples of ethnic elderly who provide caregiving to their families or who play an important role in transmitting a cultural heritage to their grandchildren (see also Reading 6). An emerging grandparent role is that of *surrogate,* in which the grandparent provides regular care or replaces the parents in raising the grandchildren. In 1997, an estimated 4 million children lived in grandparent-headed households. For almost 1.3 million children, a grandparent, often the grandmother, is the primary caregiver and no parent is present. Nearly 36 percent of these 1.3 million children are black, 42 percent are white, 17 percent are Latino, and 5 percent are American Indian, Asian or of another racial/ethnic background.[7]

As Antoinette Y. Rodgers-Farmer and Rosa L. Jones show, many black grandmothers are assuming the parenting role to their grandchildren as a result of substance abuse by the grandchildren's parent (Reading 45).[8] Many of the grandmothers indicated that raising their grandchildren provided rewards such as companionship and feeling useful.[9] For the most part, however, surrogate parenting was hard work because the grandmothers dealt with personal, financial, and familial stressors. Some research indicates that many black grandparents are well integrated in informal social-support networks—composed of close and distant kin, friends, church members, and neighbors—that provide much support throughout the life course and especially in later life.[10] Despite such support, black and white grandparents at lower socioeconomic levels, especially in cases of divorce or other crises, sometimes experience frustration and need information to assist their grandchildren who live in stressful environments.[11] The need for information and other support services is even greater, Rodgers-Farmer and Jones maintain, when grandmothers are already experiencing economic hardships but must step in and care for one or more grandchildren.

Even if grandparents aren't surrogate parents, they can have an important influence on their grandchildren's lives. Although Asian grandparents have much in common, Yoshinori Kamo shows that there is great diversity in grandparent-grandchild ties due to differences in the country of origin, immigration and assimilation history, and interaction styles between grandparents and grandchildren (Reading 46). In addition, grandparenting styles may vary because of distance, coresidence, and language skills.[12] Even though the ability to speak English may hinder communication, Kamo observes that "it is absurd to assume that there is no transmission of ethnic values, culture, and heritage from grandparents to grandchildren" (see page 392). Chinese-American grandparents, for example, help to develop their grandchildren's ethnic identity by teaching them Chinese, transmitting traditional practices and customs during holidays, and reinforcing cultural values. One mother commented that "My father taught [my children] well. Since he lived with us and had time to look after the children at home, he often told them to show filial piety towards their parents because parents worked very hard outside the home."[13]

Intergenerational cooperation also generates intergenerational conflict. As you saw in Readings 33, 35, and 36, acculturation can produce strains that lead to elder abuse, domestic violence, and risk-taking behavior among youth. In a study of Asian Indians, for example, the researchers found that parents, their children, and grandparents experienced conflict over gender role expectations, the need to show respect while expressing disagreement about normative behavior, and how to balance Western and Indian values.[14] Nevertheless, despite intermittent discord, the elderly often play a critical role in strengthening intergenerational relationships and enriching family life.

NOTES

1. Constance A. Kratch, *Centenarians in the United States: 1990* (July 1999), www.census.gov/prod/99pubs/p.23-199pdf (accessed June 10, 2000).
2. Ada C. Mui, Namkee G. Choi, and Abraham Monk, *Long-Term Care and Ethnicity* (Westport, CT: Auburn House, 1998).
3. Elisa Facio, "Chicanas and Aging: Toward Definitions of Womanhood," in *Handbook on Women and Aging,* ed. Jean M. Coyle (Westport, CT: Greenwood Press, 1997), 335–50.
4. Maria P. Aranda and Bob G. Knight, "The Influence of Ethnicity and Culture on the Caregiver Stress and Coping Process: A Sociocultural Review and Analysis," *The Gerontologist* 37 (1997): 342–54.
5. Maintaining cultural identity may be especially important for recent elderly refugees who depend on the extended family to compensate for the loss of daily contact with friends in the country of origin. See S-Gay Becker and Yewoubdar Beyene, "Narratives of Age and Uprootedness among Older Cambodian Refugees," *Journal of Aging Studies* 13 (Fall 1999): 295–314.
6. See Debra Tzuling Tsai and Rebecca A. Lopez, "The Use of Social Supports by Elderly Chinese Immigrants," *Journal of Gerontological Social Work* 29 (1997): 77–94. Among Asian families, provision of support for an elderly parent is influenced by financial and structural factors. See Masako Ishii-Kuntz, "Intergenerational Relationships among Chinese, Japanese, and Korean Americans," *Family Relations* 46 (1997): 23–32.
7. Ken Bryson and Lynne M. Casper. 1999. *Coresident Grandparents and Grandchildren,* U.S. Census Bureau, Current Population Reports, p23–128, www.census.gov/prod/99pubs/p23-198.pdf (accessed October 28, 2000).
8. Other reasons for grandparents' raising their grandchildren include the parent's incarceration, death, desertion, or mental illness. See, for example, Denise Burnette, "Grandparents Raising Grandchildren in the Inner City,"

Families in Society 78 (September–October 1997): 489–99; and Kathleen M. Roe, Meredith Winkler, and Rama-Selassie Barnwell, "The Assumption of Caregiving: Grandmothers Raising the Children of the Crack Cocaine Epidemic," *Qualitative Health Research* 4 (August 1994): 281–303.

9. See also Linda Burton and Cynthia Devries, "Challenges and Rewards: African American Grandparents as Surrogate Parents," *Generations: The Journal of the Western Gerontological Society* 16 (Summer 1992): 51–54.
10. Judith C. Barker and Joelle Morrow, "Gender, Informal Social Support Networks, and Elderly Urban African Americans," *Journal of Aging Studies,* 12 (Summer 1998): 199–222; Andrea G. Hunter and Robert J. Taylor, "Grandparenthood in African American Families," in *Handbook on Grandparenthood,* ed. Maximiliane E. Szinovacz (Westport, CT: Greenwood Press, 1998), 70–86.
11. Jeffrey A. Watson and Sally A. Koblinsky, "Strengths and Needs of Working-Class African-American and Anglo-American Grandparents," *International Journal on Aging and Human Development* 44 (1997): 149–65.
12. For a discussion of grandparenting styles among American Indians, see Robert John, Patrice H. Blanchard, and Catherine Hagan Hennessy, "Hidden Lives: Aging and Contemporary American Indian Women," in Szinovacz, *Handbook on Grandparenthood,* 290–315. For a description of the roles of American Indian, Japanese, and black grandmothers, see Ruth Dial Woods, "Grandmother Roles: A Cross-Cultural View," *Journal of Instructional Psychology* 23 (December 1996): 286–92.
13. Vicky Chiu-Wan Tam and Daniel F. Detzner, "Grandparents as a Family Resource in Chinese-American Families: Perceptions of the Middle Generation," in *Resiliency in Native American and Immigrant Families,* ed. Hamilton I. McCubbin, Elizabeth A. Thompson, Anne I. Thompson, and Julie E. Fromer (Thousand Oaks, CA: Sage, 1998), 243–63.
14. Gregory L. Pettys and Pallassana R. Balgopal, "Multigenerational Conflicts and New Immigrants: An Indo-American Experience," *Families in Society* 79 (July–August, 1998): 410–22.

42 Sixty-Five Plus in the United States

Robert Bernstein

Not too far in the future, the rate of growth of the U.S. elderly population will accelerate. By the middle of the twenty-first century, there are likely to be more persons who are elderly (65 or older) than young (14 or younger). Robert Bernstein also describes other trends: The elderly are becoming more racially and ethnically diverse. Elderly women will continue to outnumber elderly men. Increasing numbers of people will have to care for very old and frail relatives. And more and more of the ethnic elderly—especially women—are likely to live in poverty.

The elderly population has grown substantially in this century . . .

During the 20th century, the number of persons in the United States under age 65 has tripled. At the same time, the number aged 65 or over has jumped by *a factor of 11!* Consequently, the elderly, who comprised only 1 in every 25 Americans (3.1 million) in 1900, made up 1 in 8 (33.2 million) in 1994. Declining fertility and mortality rates also have led to a sharp rise in the median age of our Nation's population—from 20 years old in 1860 to 34 in 1994.

Source: From Robert Bernstein, "Sixty-five Plus in the United States," Bureau of the Census, *Statistical Brief* (May 1995), www.census.gov/apsd/www/statbrief/sb95_8.pdf (accessed June 12, 2000).

... and will continue to rise well into the next century ...

According to the Census Bureau's "middle series" projections, the elderly population will more than double between now and the year 2050, to 80 million. By that year, as many as 1 in 5 Americans could be elderly. Most of this growth should occur between 2010 and 2030, when the "baby boom" generation enters their elderly years. During that period, the number of elderly will grow by an average of 2.8 percent annually. By comparison, annual growth will average 1.3 percent during the preceding 20 years and 0.7 percent during the following 20 years [see Figure 1].

... especially for the oldest old.

The "oldest old"—those aged 85 and over—are the most rapidly growing elderly age group. Between 1960 and 1994, their numbers rose 274 percent. In contrast, the elderly population in general rose 100 percent and the entire U.S. population grew only 45 percent. The oldest old numbered 3 million in 1994, making them 10 percent of the elderly and just over 1 percent of the total population. Thanks to the arrival of the survivors of the baby boom generation, it is expected the oldest old will number 19 million in 2050. That would make them 24 percent of elderly Americans and 5 percent of all Americans.

We're living longer.

Back when the United States was founded, life expectancy at birth stood at only about 35 years. It reached 47 years in 1900, jumped to 68 years in 1950, and steadily rose to 76 years in 1991. In 1991, life expectancy was higher for women (79 years) than for men (72 years).

Once we reach age 65, we can expect to live 17 more years. During the 1980s, post-65 life expectancy improved for all race/sex groups. The biggest improvement (a rise of over 1 year) belonged to White men.

The elderly are becoming more racially and ethnically diverse.

In 1994, 1 in 10 elderly were a race other than White. In 2050, this proportion should rise to 2 in 10. Similarly, the proportion of elderly who are Hispanic is expected to climb from 4 percent to 16 percent over the same period.

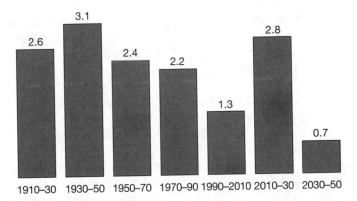

FIGURE 1   Average Annual Growth Rate (in Percent) of the Elderly Population: 1910–30 to 2030–50

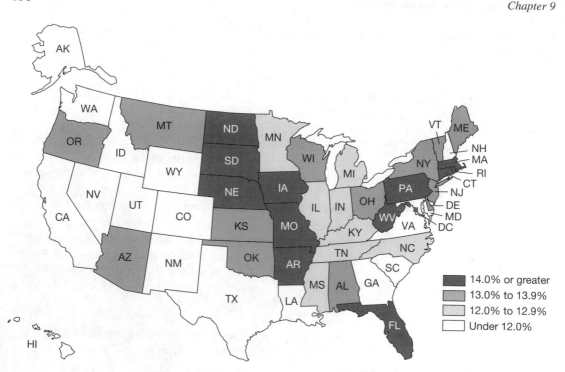

FIGURE 2   Percentage of the Population That Is Aged 65 Years and Over, by State: 1993

California has the largest *number* of elderly, but Florida has the highest *percentage.*

Our most populous States are also the ones with the largest number of elderly. In 1993, nine States had more than 1 million elderly. California, with 3.3 million, led the way, followed by Florida, New York, Pennsylvania, Texas, Ohio, Illinois, Michigan, and New Jersey.

Meanwhile, the States with the greatest *proportion* of elderly are generally different from those with the greatest number. Two exceptions, however, were Florida, where 19 percent of residents were elderly, and Pennsylvania, where 16 percent were. These 2 States led the Nation percentage-wise and, as just mentioned, ranked in the top 4 numerically. In-migration of the elderly contributed to Florida's high rankings. Joining

Florida and Pennsylvania in having high proportions of elderly (14 percent or more) were 10 other States, including several sparsely populated Farm Belt States, such as North Dakota and Nebraska [see Figure 2]. Out-migration of the young contributed to the high proportions in these States and in Pennsylvania.

During the 1980's, the greatest percentage increases in elderly population were mostly in Western States and Southeastern coastal States.

Elderly women outnumber elderly men . . .

Men generally have higher death rates than women at every age. As a result, elderly women outnumbered elderly men in 1994 by a ratio of 3 to 2—20 million to 14 million. This difference grew with advancing age. At ages 65 to 69, it was only 6 to 5. However, at age 85 and over, it reached 5 to 2. As more men live to older ages over the next 50 years, these differences may narrow somewhat.

. . . consequently, while most elderly men are married, most elderly women are not.

In 1993, noninstitutionalized elderly men were nearly twice as likely as their female counterparts to be married and living with their spouse (75 percent versus 41 percent). Elderly women, on the other hand, were more than three times as likely as elderly men to be widowed (48 percent versus 14 percent). The remaining men and women were either separated, divorced, had never married, or had absent spouses. Thus, while most elderly men have a spouse for assistance, especially when health fails, most elderly women do not.

Many elderly live alone.

Another consequence of the relative scarcity of elderly men is the fact that elderly women were much more likely than men to live alone. So much more likely, in fact, that 8 in 10 noninstitutionalized elderly who lived alone in 1993 were women. Among both sexes, the likelihood of living alone increased with age. For women, it rose from 32 percent for 65- to 74-year-olds to 57 percent for those aged 85 years or more; for men, the corresponding proportions were 13 percent and 29 percent.

More of us may face dependency . . .

Many assume health among the elderly has improved because they, as a group, are living longer. Others hold a contradictory image of the elderly as dependent and frail. The truth actually lies somewhere in between. Poor health is not as prevalent as many assume. In 1992, about 3 in every 4 noninstitutionalized persons aged 65 to 74 considered their health to be good. Two in three aged 75 or older felt similarly.

On the other hand, as more people live to the oldest ages, there may also be more who face chronic, limiting illnesses or conditions, such as arthritis, diabetes, osteoporosis, and senile dementia. These conditions result in people becoming dependent on others for help in performing the activities of daily living. With age comes increasing chances of being dependent. For instance, while 1 percent of those aged 65 to 74 years lived in a nursing home in 1990, nearly 1 in 4 aged 85 or older did. And among those who were *not* institutionalized in 1990–91, 9 percent aged 65 to 69 years, but 50 percent aged 85 or older, needed assistance performing everyday activities such as bathing, getting around inside the home, and preparing meals [see Figure 3].

. . . and increasing numbers of people will have to care for very old, frail relatives.

As more and more people live long enough to experience multiple, chronic illnesses, disability, and dependency, there will be more and more relatives in their fifties and sixties who will be facing the concern and expense of caring for them. The parent-support ratio gives us an approximate idea of things to come. This ratio equals the number of persons aged 85 and over per 100 persons aged 50 to 64. Between 1950 and 1993, the ratio tripled from 3 to 10. Over the next six decades, it could triple yet again, to 29.

Heart disease, cancer, and stroke are the leading causes of death among the elderly.

Of the 2.2 million Americans who died in 1991, 1.6 million (or 7 in 10) were elderly. Seven in 10 of these elderly deaths could be attributed to either heart disease, cancer, or stroke. Though death rates from heart disease have declined for the elderly since the 1960's, this malady remains the leading cause of death among them. Death rates from cancer, on the other hand, have increased since 1960.

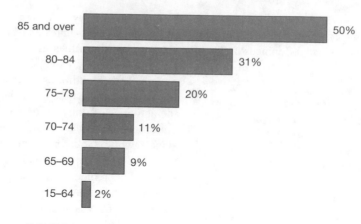

FIGURE 3   Percentage of Persons Needing Assistance with Everyday Activities, by Age: 1990–91 (Civilian Noninstitutional Population)

Poverty rates vary greatly among subgroups . . .

The perception of "elderly" and "poor" as practically synonymous has changed in recent years to a view that the noninstitutionalized elderly are better off than other Americans. Both views are simplistic. There is actually great variation among elderly subgroups. For example, in 1992—

- The poverty rate, 15 percent for those under age 65, rose with age among the elderly, from 11 percent for 65- to 74-year-olds to 16 percent for those aged 75 or older.
- Elderly women (16 percent) had a higher poverty rate than elderly men (9 percent).
- The rate was higher for elderly Blacks (33 percent) and Hispanics (22 percent) than for Whites (11 percent).

As Figure 4 shows, poverty became less prevalent during the 1980's for every elderly sex/race/ethnic group. In addition, within each race/ethnic group, poverty was more common for women than for men at both the decade's beginning and end.

. . . as does median income.

In constant 1992 dollars, the median income for elderly persons more than doubled between 1957 and 1992 (from $6,537 to $14,548 for men, from $3,409 to $8,189 for women).

However, income disparities persist among various elderly subgroups. Age, sex, race, ethnicity, marital status, living arrangements, educational attainment, former occupation, and work history are characteristics associated with significant income differences. For instance, elderly White men had much higher median incomes than other groups. In 1992, their income was more than double that of elderly Black and Hispanic women ($15,276 versus $6,220 and $5,968, respectively).

The elderly of the future will be better educated.

Research has shown that the better educated tend to be healthier longer and better off economically. In 1993, noninstitutionalized elderly were less likely than those aged 25 to 64 to have completed

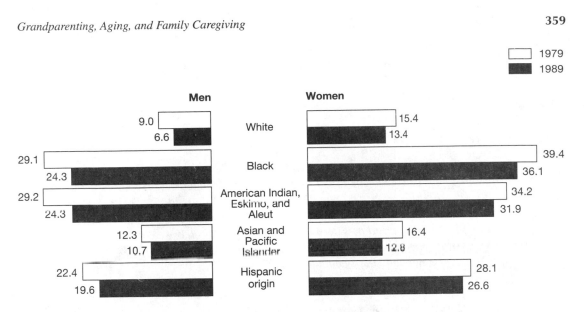

FIGURE 4   Percent of Persons Aged 65 and Over Who Were Poor, by Sex, Race, and Hispanic Origin: 1979 and 1989

Note: Persons of Hispanic origin may be of any race. This graph is based on 1980 and 1990 census sample data.

at least high school (60 percent versus 85 percent) and more likely to have only an eighth-grade education or less (24 percent versus 6 percent). The percent with less than a 9th-grade education rose with age for the elderly.

Fortunately, the proportion of elderly with at least a high school education will increase in the coming decades. That's because nearly 8 in 10 persons aged 55 to 59 in 1993 had at least a high school education; the same was true for nearly 9 in 10 persons aged 45 to 49. Additionally, while only 12 percent of the elderly had college degrees, 20 percent of 55- to 59-year-olds and 27 percent of 45- to 49-year-olds did.

Think about It

1. Why is the elderly population growing? Which age group is expected to increase the most rapidly?

2. How do elderly women and men differ in life-span, marital status, living arrangements, and poverty rates?

3. Family sociologists often describe "baby boomers" (people born between 1946 and 1964) as the "sandwich generation" (people who care for their own children as well as for their elderly parents). How is the parent-support ratio expected to change by around 2050? How do you think this ratio will affect the sandwich generation?

43 Intergenerational Assistance within the Mexican American Family

Tracy L. Dietz

Social scientists have debated the extent to which older Mexican Americans rely on their families to meet their needs. Some argue that the Mexican American family is available to care for the aging Mexican American population. Others disagree, maintaining that this notion is simply a romanticized and stereotypical view. Tracy L. Dietz examines formal and informal support systems and discusses the policy implications of assisting the rapidly growing Mexican American elderly population.

. . . Mexican Americans compose the largest subgroup of the Hispanic population and the second-largest ethnic minority group in the United States. In addition, Mexican Americans tend to be, generally speaking, one of the most economically and educationally disadvantaged groups in the United States (House Select Committee on Aging, 1988; Williams, 1991). Thus, the issue of intergenerational or familial support of elderly Mexican Americans is critical.

Historical Characteristics of the Mexican American in the United States

According to Maldonado (1985), the history of Mexican Americans has molded their experiences and expectations. Five critical experiences have affected their lives and helped to determine the resources they have available to them. First, nearly 50% of older Mexican Americans were born in Mexico, and the older Mexican American population demonstrates many Hispanic[1] traits, with many speaking only Spanish and belonging to the Catholic religion. In addition, expectations like those about familial responsibilities are very much affected by their Mexican heritage. The second characteristic affecting older Mexican Americans is their minority status in the United States. As a result most were offered only limited education, and they often lived in segregated neighborhoods. Hence, career and employment opportunities were also limited, along with future economic success.

Third, many Hispanics served in the U.S. military during World War II, becoming eligible for veterans' programs. Many received a higher education as a result of the GI Bill and moved out of the poor neighborhoods where they had lived prior to the war. Although they have made some progress in the educational and employment arenas, the graduation rates for Mexican Americans remain much lower than for Anglos. A fourth characteristic of Mexican Americans is related to the Civil Rights movement of the 1960s, which also had positive effects for Mexican Americans. Maldonado (1985) indicates that this may have had a significant effect on the lives of older Hispanics because their children and grandchildren have experienced more upward mobility and have moved away from their old neighborhoods, leaving behind the aging. Thus, the family may not be able or willing to care for older family members as they once did.

Source: From Tracy L. Dietz, "Patterns of Intergenerational Assistance within the Mexican American Family: Is the Family Taking Care of the Older Generation's Needs?" *Journal of Family Issues* 16 (May 1995): 344–56. Copyright © 1995 Sage Publications, Inc. Reprinted by permission of Sage Publications, Inc.

Although many Mexican Americans have benefited from a variety of programs and movements, their socioeconomic status continues to be lower than that of Whites. Several dynamics significantly affect that status. Maldonado (1985) indicates that a national strategy of nonservice has emerged. For example, financial support for some programs that help older Hispanics has been drastically cut and other programs have been eliminated, making it harder to access or provide eligibility for services. In recent years, some of the gains made by and for Hispanics during the civil rights era have been rolled back. A resurgence of anti-Hispanic attitudes has rekindled fear among other Hispanics, who witnessed severe discrimination in the past. The result of this, he asserts, is that older Hispanics may become increasingly isolated and withdrawn from public services.

SUPPORT SYSTEMS OF THE ELDERLY

Cantor (1979) distinguishes between the formal and informal support systems on which the elderly can rely in times of need. Formal social support services are those administered by bureaucratic governmental and voluntary organizations. Informal social support systems are the more individualized and nonbureaucratic services that are usually provided by family, friends, neighbors, and people within the community. The degree to which these two types of support systems are available to and used by the Hispanic elderly has been a topic of tremendous debate, with much of the discussion focused on the effectiveness of informal support systems, especially the family.

Caregiving and the Informal Support Network

The literature reveals a controversy over the extent to which older Mexican Americans can and do rely on their families to meet their needs. The research questions that are the foci of this research project become, then:

1. To what extent do older Mexican Americans need assistance?
2. Are their families meeting those needs?

Data obtained from the National Survey of Hispanic Elderly People were used to address these critical questions (Davis, 1990).

The culture of the Hispanic in the United States has included strong commitment to familism (Maldonado, 1985). Consequently, it is not surprising that researchers as well as policymakers have the idea that Mexican American families, grounded in familism, take on the responsibility of caring for their elderly. Most of these studies, which romanticize the extended Mexican American family, were conducted in the 1970s and 1980s (Starrett et al., 1983; Rosenthal, 1986). The cultural aversion hypothesis, which states that older minorities tend to underuse formal social services because their needs are already met by members of their family or community, has been strongly challenged (Sanchez, 1992; Weeks & Cuellar, 1981; Yeo, 1991).

The challengers have concluded that the strong belief in an informal support network among Mexican Americans, composed of family, friends and neighbors, is nothing more than a myth. For example, Lacayo (1980, 1992) indicates that although many Mexican American elderly live within the embrace of an extended family, only 10% of minority elderly live with family members. Furthermore, Weeks and Cuellar (1981) demonstrate that although Mexican American elders who live alone in the San Diego area were four times more likely than Anglos to have extended kin in the geographic area, they were less likely to turn to them and less likely to receive help from them than were the elders in other racial or ethnic groups.

Other researchers have concluded that the Mexican American community continues to use the informal support network for the elderly, but the services provided tend to be affective rather than instrumental. That is, rather than giving concrete assistance such as financial help, the children provide emotional support or advice (Cuellar, 1980). Several social scientists report that children are unable to provide financial assistance to their elderly relatives because they have been restricted to a low socioeconomic position (Becerra, 1983; Cuellar, 1980; Hines et al., 1992; Markides & Krause, 1986). One study of the caregivers of mentally ill elders concluded that although Hispanic families continued to be strong and dedicated, more than 40% of the Hispanic caregivers reported a family income of less than $10,000 per year. Many of these caregivers were forced to quit their jobs in order to care for their ill relatives. Consequently, the caregiving role became a severe financial stressor. As a result, these caregivers expressed a strong need for formal services to relieve them, not only of some of the physical burden, but also of the financial burden (Guarnaccia et al., 1992). This study was limited to caregivers of mentally ill relatives, but it is probably relevant to other caregiving situations as well. For example, Trevino (1988) states that additional services that address the specific needs of the Hispanic elderly should be developed and that the gap between health care and human services should be bridged.

Moreover, Purdy and Arguello (1992) suggest that when elderly Hispanics rely heavily on their kin and friendship networks, they not only drain the financial resources of their already poor children but they may also have needs the family cannot meet. They see a correlation between reliance on informal familial support and depression among elderly Hispanics. Another dimension is suggested by Hines et al. (1992) and Sotomayor and Curiel (1988), who note that intergenerational conflict often occurs between aging Mexican Americans who see their well-being as their children's responsibility and the younger generation who, for whatever reason, cannot or does not want to fulfill those expectations.

Several sociologists have identified other reasons for the lack of support from the informal network. Hernandez (1992) indicates that familism is declining due to geographical separation of family members within the Cuban American population. The Cuban population is quite different from the Mexican American population, yet the finding supports Maldonado's (1985) contention that younger cohorts in Hispanic communities are experiencing upward social mobility. As they attain this social mobility, they may move, leaving behind their elderly. For example, Hall (1987) argues that minority elders are more likely to live alone and to have no immediate family contact than nonminorities and that the support system of Hispanics is less well-developed than that of all other groups studied. He found that 80% of the Hispanics in his sample did not have a family caregiver at all.

Furthermore, in many young couples, both the man and the woman work outside of the home, which makes it difficult to care for aging relatives. In one study, Mexican Americans were more likely than either Anglo or African Americans to be low exchangers of support (Hogan et al, 1993). Other studies that have made systematic comparisons between minority families and nonminority families show similar results: Assistance from kin is not greater within minority communities (Eggebeen, 1992; Eggebeen & Hogan, 1990; Hogan et al., 1990). However, the informal network of Mexican American elders can serve as an information broker for older family members, informing them of the available services that are provided by formal agencies (Henderson & Gutierrez-Mayka, 1992).

In light of these various studies, several authors have concluded that the tendency of policymakers and some researchers to assume that extended Mexican American families are caring for their aging parents is a grave mistake. Cuellar (1980), for example, cautions against overromanticizing and stereotyping the strength of the extended Mexican American family because it is unable to provide the financial resources that older Mexican Americans need so desperately. Yeo (1991) further argues that the public's inclination to believe that Mexican American families care for their own virtually ensures that policymakers and service providers will ignore the needs of these elders and the barriers that they confront in attempting to access formal services.

METHODOLOGY

The present study is . . . based on [a] secondary analysis of the 1988 National Survey of Hispanic Elderly People, which was sponsored by the Commonwealth Fund Commission on Elderly People Living Alone as an extension of its Survey on Problems Facing Elderly Americans Living Alone (Davis, 1990). Its purpose was to obtain information about the economic, health, and social status of Hispanic elders in the United States.

Westat, Inc., screened 48,000 households through telephone interviews to locate Hispanic households. Random-digit dialing of exchanges in areas known to have large Hispanic populations was used in order to increase the possibility of selecting elderly Hispanic households or households that included elderly Hispanics. This selection method created a potential bias by eliminating elderly Hispanics who did not have a telephone. Minimum sample sizes for four Hispanic populations—Mexican American, Puerto Rican, Cuban American, and Other Hispanics—were established prior to the interviews, which were conducted between August and October 1988. Bilingual interviewers were available and most interviews were conducted in Spanish.

After contacting households and obtaining cooperation from a resident, screening questions were used to determine if the household could be identified as Hispanic and if it included residents who were 65 years of age or older. All people who were Hispanic and over the age of 65 were included in the sample, but detailed surveys could not be completed for all of them for a variety of reasons, including refusal and mortality. The overall response rate was 80%, and the overall sample size for the survey was 2,299. For the purposes of this research only those elderly who identified themselves as Mexican Americans were included in the analysis. . . . The *N* for this subsample was 773.

RESULTS

Frequency distributions were calculated on demographic variables. Of the Mexican Americans included in the survey, 63% were female. About 60% were between the ages of 65 and 74, 32% were ages 75 to 84, and 7% were 85 years of age or older. About 51% were married at the time of the survey, 36% were widowed, 5% were divorced, 5% had never been married and 2% were separated. Strikingly, 59% had incomes below the poverty line, and 43% said that not having enough money was a serious problem for them. Whereas 31% were living with their spouse at the time, 22% were living alone, and 14% lived with both a spouse and at least one adult child. The remaining 33% had some other living arrangement. More than 80% of the respondents had less than an eighth grade education. About 70% reported that they spoke English poorly, nearly 58% said their reading ability in English was poor, and more than 65% said that their writing ability in English was poor.

Respondents were asked a series of questions to determine the extent to which they had trouble with various activities of daily living (ADL) and instrumental activities of daily living (IADL). Only those who provided responses for the various questions are included in the following analysis.

As shown in Table 1, more than 50% of the respondents reported having trouble performing heavy household chores. Nearly one third were unable to walk without experiencing problems, and more than one fifth experienced trouble getting in and out of bed, getting outside, and/or shopping. Less than 20% reported difficulty bathing/showering, dressing, using the toilet, handling their finances, using the telephone, preparing meals, and performing light household chores. Less than 5% reported trouble eating.

TABLE 1   Reported Trouble with ADL and IADL

Limitation	N	Percentage
Bathing/showering	125	16.2
Dressing	87	11.3
Eating	38	4.9
Getting in/out of bed	176	22.8
Walking	234	30.3
Getting outside	157	20.3
Using the toilet	65	8.4
Meal preparation	138	17.9
Handling money	107	13.9
Using the telephone	126	16.3
Shopping	171	22.1
Heavy housework	396	51.2
Light housework	116	15.0

Note: N = 773.

In addition to the needs implied by the above percentages, the Mexican American elderly reported having a variety of financial and social/recreational needs. As Table 2 illustrates, more than one third of the respondents reported a need for food stamps, and more than 20% reported a desire for church programs, home health aid, phone checks, homemaker services, senior meals programs, meals on wheels, senior transportation, and/or senior center participation. In addition,

TABLE 2   Social Support Services Mexican American Elders Need or Desire

Service	N	Percentage	Total N
Senior transportation	174	24.9	698
Senior center	170	25.4	669
Meals on wheels	171	24.4	702
Senior meals	153	23.4	653
Homemaker service	161	22.3	721
Phone checks	169	23.1	731
Visiting nurse	130	18.6	699
Home health aid	149	20.2	737
Food stamps	224	34.7	646
Church programs	149	21.3	699

18% wanted to have a visiting nurse come to check on them.

Familial Exchange

Although many minority kinship networks include fictive kin, only those individuals identified by the respondents as relatives were included in the analysis of family contact. This study supports the conclusions of researchers such as Cuellar (1980), Becerra (1983), Markides & Krause (1986), Hines et al. (1992), and Hogan et al. (1993), who have found that the Mexican American elderly have frequent contact with their children. Nearly 80% of respondents in this study said they live with an adult child or have a child living within minutes of their home (37%). An additional 19% said that their children could be there within hours. Moreover, of those who do not live with an adult child, 47% see their children on a daily basis and another 30% see them weekly. About 13% said they see their children monthly, and 8% see them yearly. Of those who do not live with an adult child, 47% speak to their children on the telephone every day, whereas another 32% speak to them weekly.

Despite the amount of contact, relatively small percentages of Mexican American families help their aging family members with their needs. Table 3 illustrates that of all the elders surveyed, 31% reported that their family helped with heavy household chores. For all other IADL and ADL, less than 20% of the respondents received aid from their family.

When the analysis is restricted to elders who report having difficulty with a specific activity, the results indicate that some get help from their family but others do not. About 57% of respondents did not receive any help with any of the activities being discussed, but 10% were receiving help with at least six of the activities. Another 35% reported that they do not need any help with these activities, but 20% need help with five or more. Table 3 shows that family members assist 44% of those who need help getting in or out of bed and 37% of those who have trouble walking.

TABLE 3   Elders Reporting That Their Family Helps with Specific Activities

Activity	Received Help from Family		Elders Needing Help Who Received It	
	N	Percentage	N	Percentage
Bathing/showering	66	8.5	124	53.2
Dressing	51	6.6	86	59.3
Eating	12	1.6	38	31.6
Getting in/out of bed	77	10.0	175	44.0
Walking	87	11.3	233	37.3
Getting outside	102	13.2	156	65.4
Using the toilet	37	4.8	65	56.9
Meal preparation	95	12.3	138	68.8
Handling money	92	11.9	107	86.0
Using the telephone	97	12.5	126	77.0
Shopping	146	18.9	171	85.4
Heavy housework	242	31.3	304	61.4
Light housework	82	10.6	116	70.7
Total reporting	332	42.9	331	66.7

Note: Total $N = 771–773$.

Of the respondents who reported trouble eating, 31% received help from their family. Moreover, 53% received bathing assistance from their family. About 60% received support from their family when they were unable to dress themselves, and 61% received help with heavy chores. Elders who needed help with light housework were assisted by their family 70% of the time. Less than 60% of those having trouble getting to the bathroom were able to call on their family for assistance, and 65% received help to get outside. Moreover, nearly 70% received family assistance with meal preparation, 77% received help with the phone, and about 86% received help with their finances and/or shopping.

Cross-tabulations using chi-square reveal that one third of those respondents reporting a need for assistance with activities do not get help from their family members. In addition, respondents who were living alone were less likely to receive assistance from their family ($p < 0.001$). Moreover, of those respondents reporting a need for assistance, those who were living alone were less likely to have those needs met ($p < 0.0005$). Put differently, because at least two thirds of the respondents were living with a spouse or an adult child, it is obvious that living arrangements were critical to meeting their needs.

Although many Mexican American families are evidently providing some of the needs of their aging relatives, elders are also providing assistance in return. Table 4 shows that more than one third of the respondents baby-sit for their younger family members and more than one half help their family members make decisions. Although only 6% receive money from their family members, more than 12% give money to their family members—even though 59% had incomes below the poverty line and 43% found their incomes too low. Moreover, considering the needs reported by these individuals, it is surprising that almost 60% of the respondents said they did not receive any help from their family.

TABLE 4   Intergenerational Exchange between Mexican American Family Members

Assistance by/to Elder	N	Percentage	Total N
Baby-sits for family	267	34.6	772
Helps with decisions	401	51.9	766
Gives money to family	96	12.4	765
Receives money	49	6.3	765
Receives ADL/IADL help	332	42.9	771

CONCLUSIONS

The elders in this study reported high levels of need, with most of them living on low incomes and nearly 20% reporting difficulty with at least 7 of the 20 activities studied. Interaction between younger Mexican American family members and the older generation is strong. Most of the adult children speak with or see their parents daily. However, many of the Mexican American elders included in this survey reported a variety of needs, some of which are not being met by their families. Consequently, although most families are maintaining contact with aging relatives, many are not providing instrumental support, such as financial support or help to overcome limitations. This appears to be especially true with some of the physical activities of daily living, such as eating, transferring, and walking.

The Mexican American family has been unable to provide for all of the needs of its older population. This is especially true of financial support, with nearly 60% of these elders living below the poverty line and less than 10% receiving any financial assistance from their family. In fact, more Mexican American elders in the survey were giving rather than receiving money from their family.

Moreover, the respondents surveyed expressed desires for more services targeted toward the older population. With nearly one fifth to more than one third reporting the need for specific formal social services, it becomes evident that more services, of a more innovative kind, need to be created to provide for the needs of this rapidly growing population.

As Andrews (1989) states, "Problems of inadequate resources and services can only become more serious as the Hispanic population grows, unless appropriate changes are made in public policies and programs" (p. 26). As growth continues, increased awareness of the needs and experiences of this group is crucial. Moreover, if the informal network is unable to meet those needs, it is imperative that government-sponsored and formal, community-based programs be developed and existing programs be expanded to meet them.

NOTE

1. The tremendous cultural diversity that exists among the various groups included in the category of Hispanic is well recognized by the author. However, in order to maintain consistency with the terminology used in the literature discussed, the term Hispanic will be used when discussing literature that uses this term. In addition, in some instances, it is recognized that some similarities between Mexican Americans, Puerto Ricans, Cuban Americans, Central and South Americans, and Other Hispanics do exist.

REFERENCES

Andrews, J. (1989). *Poverty and poor health among elderly Hispanic Americans.* Baltimore: The Commonwealth Fund.

Becerra, R. M. (1983). The Mexican American aging in a changing culture. In R. L. McNeely & J. L. Colen

(Eds.), *Aging in minority groups* (pp. 108–118). Beverly Hills, CA: Sage.

Cantor, M. H. (1979). The informal support system of New York's inner city elderly: Is ethnicity a factor? In D. E. Gelfand & A. J. Kurtzik (Eds.), *Ethnicity and aging: Theory, research and policy* (pp. 153–174). New York: Springer.

Cuellar, J. (1980). El senior citizens' club: The old Mexican American in the voluntary association. In B. Meyerhoff & A. Simic (Eds.), *Life's career—aging* (pp. 207–230). Beverly Hills: Sage.

Davis, K. (1990). *National survey of Hispanic elderly people.* Ann Arbor, MI: Interuniversity Consortium for Political and Social Research.

Eggebeen, D. J. (1992). Family structure and intergenerational exchanges. *Research on Aging, 14,* 427–447.

Eggebeen, D. J., & Hogan, D. P. (1990). Giving between generations in American families. *Human Nature, 1,* 211–232.

Guarnaccia, P. J., Parra, P., Deschams, A., Milstein, G., & Argiles, N. (1992). Si Dios quiere: Hispanic families' experiences of caring for a seriously mentally ill family member. *Culture, Medicine and Psychiatry, 16,* 187–217.

Hall, P. A. (1987). Minority elder maltreatment: Ethnicity, gender, age, and poverty. *Ethnicity and Gerontological Social Work, 9,* 53–72.

Henderson, J. N., & Gutierrez-Mayka, M. (1992). Ethnocultural themes in caregiving to Alzheimer's Disease patients in Hispanic families. *Clinical Gerontologist, 11,* 59–74.

Hernandez, G. C. (1992). The family and its aged members: The Cuban experience. *Clinical Gerontologist, 11,* 45–57

Hines, P. M., Garcia-Prieto, N., McGoldrick, M., Almeida, R., & Weltman, S. (1992). Intergenerational relationships across cultures. *Families in Society: The Journal of Contemporary Human Services, 73,* 323–338.

Hogan, D. P., Eggebeen, D. J., & Clogg, C. C. (1993). The structure of intergenerational exchanges in American families. *American Journal of Sociology, 98,* 1428–1458.

Hogan, D. P., Hao, L. X., & Parish, W. L. (1990). Race, kin networks and assistance to mother-headed families. *Social Forces, 68,* 797–812.

House Select Committee on Aging (1988). *Demographic characteristics of the older Hispanic population.* Washington, DC: Government Printing Office. (ERIC Document Reproduction Service No. ED 304 506)

Lacayo, C. G. (1980). *A national study to assess the service needs of Hispanic elderly—final report.* Los Angeles: Asociacion Nacional por Personas Mayores.

Lacayo, C. G. (1992). Current trends in living arrangements and social environments among ethnic minority elderly. In E. P. Stanford & F. M. Torres-Gil (Eds.), *Diversity: New approaches to ethnic minority aging* (pp. 43–46). New York: Baywood.

Maldonado, D. (1985). The Hispanic elderly: A sociohistorical framework for public policy. *The Journal of Applied Gerontology, 4,* 18–27.

Markides, K. S., & Krause, N. (1986). Old Mexican Americans: Family relationships and well-being. *Generations, 10* (4), 31–34.

Purdy, J. K., & Arguello, D. (1992). Hispanic familism in caretaking of older adults: Is it functional? *Journal of Gerontological Social Work, 19* (2), 29–43.

Rosenthal, C. (1986). Family supports in later life: Does ethnicity make a difference? *Gerontologist, 26,* 19–24.

Sanchez, C. D. (1992). Mental health issues: The elderly Hispanic. *Journal of Geriatric Psychiatry, 25,* 69–84.

Sotomayor, M., & Curiel, H. (1988). *Hispanic elderly: A cultural signature.* Edinburg, TX: National Hispanic Council on Aging.

Starrett, R. A., Mindel, C. H., & Wright, R. (1983). Influence of support systems on the use of social services by the Hispanic elderly. *Social Work Research and Abstracts, 19* (4), 35–40.

Trevino, M. C. (1988). A comparative analysis of need, access, and utilization of health and human services. In S. R. Applewhite (Ed.), *Hispanic elderly in transition: Theory, research and policy* (pp. 61–72). New York: Greenwood Press.

Weeks, J., & Cuellar, J. (1981). The role of family members in the helping networks of older people. *Gerontologist, 21,* 388–394.

Williams, N. (1991). *Utilization of social services among the Mexican American elderly.* Unpublished final report, the Gerontological Society of America and the American Association of Retired Persons, Dallas, TX.

Yeo, G. (1991). Ethnogeriatric education: Need and content. *Journal of Cross Cultural Gerontology, 6,* 229–241.

? *Think about It*

1. What five historical characteristics have shaped Mexican American lives and the availability of resources for the elderly?
2. Using the data that Dietz presents, what would you conclude about the debate on whether ex-

tended Mexican American families are caring for their aging parents and grandparents?
3. To what extent do family members help the elderly with daily (ADL) and instrumental (IADL) living activities? What kind of assistance do aging relatives provide to younger family members?

44 *Elder Care in Pueblo Indian Families*

Catherine Hagan Hennessy and Robert John

"Caregiver burden" is a key concept in gerontological research. Catherine Hagan Hennessy and Robert John argue that the measures of burden are value-laden: the measures reflect Western social structures and cultural values such as individualism, independence, and nuclear-family relationships that may not pertain to many ethnic and cultural groups. Hennessy and John examined Pueblo Indian perspectives on the burdens involved in caregiving. The researchers found the Pueblos perceive the burden as the constraints that limit their ability to care for elderly family and tribal members, rather than as any limitation of the caregiver's individual freedom and/or increase in responsibilities.

CAREGIVING AMONG AMERICAN INDIANS

. . . Despite a dramatic increase in life expectancy at birth for American Indians over the past 40 years, American Indian elders have the highest proportion of health impairments among the aged population—73 percent experience limitations in their ability to carry out basic activities of daily living (National Indian Council on Aging 1981). Because of inadequate federal funding and an emphasis in federal health policy on meeting the acute care needs of American Indians,

Source: From Catherine Hagan Hennessy and Robert John, "The Interpretation of Burden among Pueblo Indian Caregivers," *Journal of Aging Studies 9*, no. 3 (1995): 215–29. Copyright © 1995. Reprinted with permission from Elsevier Science.

the lack of long-term care services for this population is well recognized (Stuart and Rathbone-McCuan 1988; Indian Health Service 1993; Manson 1989).

For reservation-dwelling elders, in particular, the extended family is the primary and often sole provider of long-term care for functionally dependent relatives (John 1988). This situation is consistent with tribal values that emphasize familial obligations and interdependence (Red Horse 1980). However, in the absence of formal long-term care services, family members often undertake extreme demands in caring for and preventing the institutional placement of an elderly relative (Manson 1989; 1993). As John points out:

It is true that American Indian families continue to provide most of the care elders receive, but American Indian families are not immune to the stresses and strains that can compromise their ability to care for American Indian elders. Indeed, there are a variety of threats to the informal support system among American Indians (1991b, p. 46).

The question of how the problems and stresses of caregiving are construed in light of American Indian cultural norms and expectations for elder care and the general lack of formal support services for frail elders and their caregivers is largely unanswered. In a single, small-scale qualitative study that compared the perceptions of caregiving burden and coping among 10 Northwest Indian and 10 white caregivers matched by sex, income, and rural residence, Strong (1984) suggested that the experience of caretaking responsibilities and stresses did indeed differ between the two groups. In comparison to white caregivers, the responses of the Indian caregivers suggested that they perceived themselves as having less control over the caregiving situation and they also placed more emphasis on the positive dimensions of managing the needs of a dependent elder. Indian caregivers used a copying strategy that Strong characterized as "passive forbearance," that is, emphasizing acceptance of and adaptation to the caregiving situation rather than attempting to actively control it. These findings suggest that at least some of the domains of caregiver burden typically measured by existing scales may have limited or different relevance for American Indians.

The only other research on caregiving in American Indian families (Hobus 1990) is a single case study that describes the intermediary role played by a nurse in helping a family prepare to provide care to a frail Lakota elder during her periodic home visits away from an off-reservation Anglo nursing home. Hobus identified seven major problems that emerged during the family assessment process including knowledge deficits in how to provide care to the elder, lack of knowledge about how to obtain outside help, lack of familiarity with the consumer rights of nursing home patients, guilt related to not providing care to the elder at home, fear about the eventual death of the elder in an alien surrounding, resentment toward previous health care providers, and concern for the health of the primary family caregiver during the elder's home visits. Because the family had provided in-home care to the elder prior to her placement in the nursing home, some of these problems were based on the experience of full-time, in-home caregiving, although these issues were not investigated during the research. Hobus reported that each of the problems was improved through planned interventions developed through a participatory process of family meetings.

Although the literature on caregiving among American Indians is limited, these studies lend support to research with other non-white groups that have suggested the salience of cultural factors in the experience of burden. Studies comparing African American and white caregivers (Lawton et al. 1992; Mui 1992), for example, have emphasized the more favorable orientation of black caregivers to providing assistance, less subjective burden associated with caregiving, and less sense of intrusion on their lives from caregiving responsibilities than among whites. As the authors of these studies assert, research is needed to identify cultural values and social norms that influence such inter-ethnic differences in caregiver burden.

METHODS

The present study was conducted as part of an assessment of the needs of family caregivers of older adults, in conjunction with a project to advise the Indian Health Service about the types of long-term care services needed in northern New Mexico. In order to establish the content validity of a burden scale to be used in a large-scale survey of Indian primary family caregivers within the project's target area, three focus groups were conducted with caregivers from five area pueblos. . . .

Focus group participants were recruited by local senior services program directors who also co-moderated the focus group discussions with the researchers. The 33 participants included primary and other caregivers of functionally dependent elders, who ranged in age from 24 to 79 years and who had been providing care from less than 1 year to over 20 years. These participants included both men and women and a variety of nuclear and extended family members of care recipients.[1]

The group discussions, which lasted from one and a half to three hours, were organized so that participants first responded to a general question about the experience of caregiving and the kinds of problems they had encountered as caregivers of elders with health problems. The second part of the discussion involved an item-by-item review of the caregiver burden scale (Table 1). The 22-item scale is an adaptation of Zarit et al.'s (1980) Burden Interview, which measures several domains of the subjective problems associated with caretaking. This scale was selected for use because of its comparatively concrete phrasing and because of the greater face validity of items for this population than other candidate scales. The focus groups were asked to indicate, for each item, whether the question reflected the situation and concerns of caregivers such as themselves, and whether the question was worded "in the Indian way" (i.e., was culturally appropriate).

All group discussions were tape recorded. The transcribed material was analyzed using the constant comparative method (Strauss and Corbin 1990). This method involves the systematic scrutiny of the text to define and code units of meaning. The text is examined and re-examined to identify these thematic categories and associations among the categories that emerge from the data. The focus group findings are presented below in terms of these qualitative themes that describe the cultural framework within which respondents evaluated the burden scale items. The responses of the participants to the specific scale items are discussed within the context of this framework.

RESULTS

The Family System and Personal Costs of Caregiving

The overall organizing principle in the participants' responses about providing care to dependent elders concerned the sociocentric nature of Pueblo society in which the needs of the group are emphasized rather than those of the individual (Manson 1992; Baines 1992). From this perspective, caregiving was regarded as a reflection of the cultural ethos of interdependency (Red Horse 1980) and reciprocity among the generations (Shomaker 1990). Participants expressed this orientation in terms of their identity as American Indians:

> As you grow up you learn to respect your elders, then they took care of you when you used to be younger, so you sort of have the obligation inside of you to where you should take care of them. And I think that follows for all Indians.

Respondents also described efforts to socialize younger family members into the ethos of family interdependency and the value of caregiving:

> We talk to our kids and tell them that Grandpa needs our help. There's things he can't do by himself and we need to be there with him. And it kind of helps them see the future. Where we make them see that we won't all be healthy all the time. You just have to talk to them and teach them that there's that responsibility that you have for the elderly . . . any elderly person.

Clearly, the end of this comment implies a commitment to elders that is broader than a family responsibility and endorses traditional American Indian cultural norms.

Within the family system, the importance of female kin, particularly daughters and sisters, was especially emphasized. Although male family members were often described as contributing to caregiving efforts, female kin were seen as being

TABLE 1   Caregiver Burden Scale[a]

1. Do you feel that your relative asks for more help than he/she needs?

2. Do you feel that because of the time you spend with your relative, that you don't have enough time for yourself?

3. Do you feel pulled between caring for your relative and trying to meet other responsibilities for your family or work?

4. Do you feel embarrassed over your relative's behavior?

5. Do you feel angry when you are around your relative?

6. Do you feel that your relative currently affects your relationship with other family members or friends in a negative way?

7. Are you afraid of what the future holds for your relative?

8. Do you feel your relative is dependent on you?

9. Do you feel strained when you are around your relative?

10. Do you feel your health has suffered because of your involvement with your relative?

11. Do you feel that you don't have as much privacy as you would like because of your relative?

12. Do you feel that your social life has suffered because you are caring for your relative?

13. Do you feel uncomfortable about having your friends over because of your relative?

14. Do you feel that your relative seems to expect you to take care of him/her as if you were the only one he/she could depend on?

15. Do you feel that you don't have enough money to care for your relative in addition to the rest of your expenses?

16. Do you feel that you will be unable to care for your relative much longer?

17. Do you feel you have lost control of your life since you've become a caregiver?

18. Do you wish you could just leave the care of your relative to someone else?

19. Do you feel uncertain about what to do about your relative?

20. Do you feel that you should be doing more for your relative?

21. Do you feel you could do a better job in caring for your relative?

22. Overall, how often do you feel burdened in caring for your relative?

[a]All items are measured on a five-point scale ranging from "Never" (1) to "Nearly always" (5).

crucial to successful caregiving. The lack of availability of female relatives was seen as putting a dependent elder in a potentially vulnerable position, as well as creating a difficult situation for a solo caregiver. For example, one respondent offered her evaluation of the situation of a young caregiver who had been taking care of both of her grandparents since she was a teenager:

> In Indian I would tell her, "There's nobody else to take over your job. You're it." And that's the way it stands. If you had a sister, maybe one or two sisters, they could take turns. But there's nobody.

Several female respondents also discussed the experience or the expectation of being a serial caregiver, that is, providing assistance to more than one elder during their adult lives. The competing demands of multiple responsibilities within the family system were readily acknowledged, the respondents endorsed the scale items having to do with feeling pulled between caregiving and other duties (Item 3), not having enough time for oneself (Item 2), and feeling like one's health had suffered as a result of caregiving (Item 10). However, the stresses associated with caregiving responsibilities were defined as constituting a burden (Item 22) in a manner that, again, was consistent with the Pueblos' sociocentric orientation. That is, the nature of the burden was interpreted as the fact that outside responsibilities impinge on one's ability to be a good caretaker, rather than caregiving impinging on outside activities and personal interests. As one respondent expressed it:

Sometimes I say "Mom, I just wish I could stay home with you all day long." But I have a job and [have to] keep up my standard of living. And sometimes I wish I could just stay home with her, and I think it becomes a burden when you have a job and have to tend to her, too. I work with the public school, so I have the whole summer. So, we're just on a countdown now. Three months, then I'll be home all day long during the summer with her. But having to hold a job and taking care of a homebound person is a big burden.

Caregiving and Social Relations

The sociocentric orientation of these caregivers was also evident in their evaluation of the scale items involving possible negative effects of caregiving on social space and social opportunities, or dealing with social improprieties. Feelings of embarrassment about the relative's behavior (Item 4), feelings of lack of personal privacy (Item 11), or social discomfort at having friends visit (Item 13), were all seen as of less concern to Pueblo Indian caregivers. In terms of potential embarrassment over inappropriate behaviors, a respondent stated, "I don't think this concerns the Indians." The daughter of a man with an unidentified form of dementia ("confusion") explained:

> Maybe if there were Anglos coming in, because I've seen it in hospitals or other places where I see elderly people in the same situation or almost the same as my Dad's case, and they get after them, they get mad, and they just treat them like little kids. Out here I think we grew up having them to teach us respect for your elders. And I think all the communities, all the Pueblos have the same feelings.

Likewise, in response to the item on lack of personal privacy, a caregiver explained:

> That one there, it would be hard for us here, because as far as our family living in a community, we have large extended families, and things that we do are not just by ourselves. We're not that private . . . a lot of things we do, we do as a group and it's open.

Possibly this feeling may be less true of the youngest caregivers who have not settled into or accepted the routine characteristic of the families of middle-age and later life. For example, after several probes about the issue of privacy, another caregiver observed that privacy was "not so much a problem for me, but I know for my girls, they're still teenagers. They want their privacy. They want to be in their own room and shut out others and that." This comment makes clear several of the finer points regarding privacy. First, it is something that immature individuals think is important and that hopefully it is also something that they will outgrow. Moreover, the desire for privacy is not an attitude that is directed toward the dependent elder but toward everyone in the family.

This emphasis on the importance of social acceptance, inclusion, and group participation was also expressed in the caregivers' reactions to the item on the possible detrimental effects of caregiving responsibilities on one's social life (Item 12). One participant remarked:

> There again, I think that's not really geared toward Native Americans because social life as far as our social life and your [non-Indian] social life are sometimes two completely different things.

Respondents explained that many social activities involved extended family members getting together, and that elders would often be brought along so that they would not be left at home alone or feel left out of the group's activities. None of the respondents viewed the inclusion of elderly family members as impinging on their social participation but the younger and unmarried caregivers acknowledged that caregiving requires the curtailment of one's social life.

Sources of Caregiver Satisfaction

Satisfaction with the job one was doing as a caregiver, which was another domain addressed in the scale (Items 20 and 21), was expressed in general as being able to successfully fulfill the cultural prescription to provide care to one's elderly family member with the resources available within the family. Two themes in the participants' responses were related to this ability. The first was the ability to organize caregiving tasks into a predictable routine with a known magnitude of demands; the second was the ability to stabilize family relationships around the caregiving situation.

Caregivers acknowledged fear and uncertainty in the early phases of their caregiving career or after a change in the elder's health or functional status. Uncertainty was especially evident in having to learn how to provide care to amputees or deal with other complications of diabetes or with high-tech medical equipment in the home. This learning process was often described as being hindered by the lack of availability or access to services or to caregiver training on the reservations or through the Indian Health Service. Most long-time caregivers, however, expressed that, often through trial and error, they had achieved a predictable and acceptable caregiving routine. The scale items concerning feelings of uncertainty (Item 19) and fears about the care recipient's future (Item 7)—especially his or her future medical status—were thus considered to accurately reflect aspects of the caregiving experience, and in particular, problems associated with the initial stages or new phases of caretaking.

Creating an acceptable division of labor and managing other family members' expectations of the primary caregiver were seen as key to stabilizing the family system around caregiving. The goal of these strategies, as one daughter-in-law caregiver put it, was to "try to get your own family happy plus whoever you take care of." Another participant described her own situation in which responsibilities for caring for her father had been successfully apportioned:

Several of us in the family take turns. Like tonight is my night to spend the night with him and we all take turns, each one, so it's not so hard on one person all the time. For bathing him we take turns. So, as far as we're concerned we don't see it as a problem. Be-

cause we have it worked out where we all get our fair share of taking care of him.

In contrast, other caregivers were less successful in involving other family members in caretaking activities and, as illustrated below, were often confronted with and had to manage the expectations of others about the amounts of care that they would provide:

It was in the beginning, all the responsibility fell on me . . . I told my husband, "You know, it's getting to be too much. They're expecting us to do all these different things for her." And it seemed like when she got her amputation, everything just went. . . . So, I told him, "I can't do this any more. I can't do it by myself. I need help."

As the next quote illustrates, family members do not always understand the caregiver's predicament or day-to-day responsibilities.

I feel like I need to do whatever I can for her so I spend as much time as I need to at her house and then I go and I do whatever I need to do. And sometimes, it's an all day thing and I get a little bit of feedback from my husband when he comes home and he'll say, "Well, what did you do today? You didn't clean the house, and you didn't do this and that." And that's the burden, I feel like I'm being pulled two ways. He expects me to do certain things, and then I'm expecting me to do what I can for my mother-in-law.

In addition to the need to reach an understanding within the family on the extent of assistance to be provided vis-a-vis other responsibilities, caregivers also discussed the necessity of managing the elder's expectations of what the caregiver's role should be. This need was often described as being related to efforts to successfully motivate the elder to care for him or herself and regain and maintain greater independence.

In American Indian families, total dependence is no more valued than total independence. With a highly dependent elder sometimes family harmony can be reestablished through encouraging greater personal autonomy and ability to contribute to the group that are the central features of family interdependence. As seen in the following quote, the solution to the problem of an elder's overdependence was framed within the values of personal initiative and ability to contribute to the group:

> My mom used to be at this stage where she just wanted help, help, help, help all the time. But then, I reversed the role and I told her to help me. So I put the dishes on the table and tell her, "Mom, set the table for me." And she does it . . . She'll wheel herself around in her wheelchair. I tell her "Mom, you can start making your way down to the bathroom." And she'll do it. And sometimes I say, "Mom, do you think you can get on your chair by yourself?" And she'll do it . . . And it's to the point where she's going to do it. I won't do it for her . . . She's taking the initiative now to do some of the things.

The focus group participants affirmed that interpersonal aspects of the caregiving experience were represented in the scale items measuring perceived negative effects of caregiving on relationships within the family (Item 6), caregiver feelings that the care recipient is dependent on him or her (Item 8), care recipient expectations for exclusive dependence on the caregiver (Item 14), requests for more help than needed (Item 1), and feelings of strain when around the elder (Item 9). However, our respondents made it clear that the feeling of strain, however, was not directed to the elder or their relationship with the elder but was defined as strain caused by concern for the elder.

Negative Emotions and the Limits of Family Caregiving

Discussion of the scale items indicating that a caregiving situation could provoke negative feelings towards the care recipient produced only tentative responses from the focus groups. For example, no direct replies were elicited in response to questions about the scale item (Item 5), "Do you feel angry when you are around your

relative?," despite several attempts by the focus group moderator to prompt discussion on this issue.

Likewise, discussion about items having to do with the limits of family caregiving, such as feelings of being no longer able or willing to provide care (Items 16 and 18), feeling out of control of one's life (Item 17), or lacking sufficient financial resources (Item 15), provoked responses in which the general unacceptability of institutional alternatives to American Indians was emphasized. In discussing potential reasons for discontinuing caregiving, one respondent in her sixties who had had a stroke herself, admitted having a plan for placing her mother in a nursing home if her own health ever reached the point where she could no longer provide care. However, although discussion about the limits of family caregiving included many examples of the frequent and sometimes extreme difficulties involved in caring for a functionally dependent relative, institutional alternatives were unacceptable to these American Indian caregivers:

> Whites, I think they can just put their relatives away in a home as long as they have money. Indians have more compassion for them. They would rather take care of them at home. None of us would really want [to put someone in a nursing home] . . . just 'cause they're unable to take care of themselves.

The remark of one respondent acknowledged the disparity between the Pueblo cultural ideal for caregiving and the reality that not every situation can meet that ideal, as well as implying the shared sentiment of these caregivers that they were trying to realize this ideal, however imperfectly:

> Like I said, we're extended family and we all take turns. Not as much as we'd like, but in a sense we do take care of one another, either way.

DISCUSSION

In examining Pueblo Indian family caregivers' views of burden, this study addressed the need for greater attention to ethnic variations in informal care of the elderly as highlighted by Malonebeach and Zarit (1991) and Hernandez (1991). In particular, it has responded to recommendations for a reappraisal of concepts included in commonly used measures in gerontological research as they are applied to minority populations (Padgett 1990).

The discussions of the focus group participants about their caregiving experiences and their responses to the specific burden scale items demonstrated both similarities and differences with sources of perceived burden reported for non-Indian caregivers. These Pueblo caregivers confirmed experiences of role strain, interpersonal tensions and conflict within the family, feelings of apprehension and uncertainty about managing care, perceptions of detrimental effects on personal health, and feelings of burden. On the other hand, they did not attribute feelings of social constraint, limitations on personal freedom, or embarrassment to caregiving responsibilities.

Furthermore, these caregivers' valuations contrast, for example, with the findings of Steinmetz's (1988) study in which the stresses experienced by a predominantly white sample of family caregivers were ranked by frequency of occurrence. Lack of privacy was among the most frequently reported stressors, with caregivers citing care recipients' intrusions on household space and on social interactions with other family members and friends as particularly burdensome.

Our focus group discussions elicited only one affirmative response to the privacy issue in which the caregiver admitted that her teenage daughters desired privacy. However, this caregiver stated that this was not a problem for her, presumably the girls would outgrow it, and the desire for privacy was not directed toward the care recipient but toward everyone. We believe that because Pueblo social norms emphasize group activities and interactions, individual privacy does not have the cultural emphasis and connotations of independence and personal autonomy ascribed to it by the caregivers in Steinmetz's study, and the Pueblo caregivers did not interpret sharing space and time with an elder as a source of burden.

Instead, these Pueblo caregivers' reactions to the burden-scale items demonstrated the salience of extended family relationships and responsibilities to perceptions of burden. The findings that the social context of the extended family shapes the activities, meanings, and feelings associated with caregiving for these informal helpers is consistent with survey results concerning family extension among the Pueblo Indians. In examining the situation of elders in 11 Pueblo tribes in New Mexico, John (1991a) found that among these communities, the frequency of coresidence with one or more children ranged between 35% to 84%, and that between 20% and 84% lived with one or more grandchildren. Accordingly, rates of living alone varied from 0% to 25% in these communities, and coresidents often included a wide range of kin. Thus, scale items that reflect the consequences and repercussions of caregiving responsibilities on extended family interactions were interpreted by these caregivers as being highly relevant to the experience of burden.

One possible explanation for the lack of response by the focus group participants to the scale items that indicate negative feelings toward the elderly care recipient is the existence of a cultural norm among American Indians that discourages the direct expression of emotions such as anger (Brant 1990). Brant describes this norm as part of a larger cultural strategy for conflict suppression and the promotion of harmony within the family and the tribe. Consequently, caregiver burden-scale items that query respondents about experiences of anger or closely related negative feelings may have limited usefulness with American Indians.

It is also possible, however, that a group context is a difficult setting in which to admit anger or resentment toward the elder. Clearly, a number of caregivers were distressed by the caregiving situation, were upset with noncontributing family members, and were unhappy with one or more family members for what was perceived to be unwarranted criticism, interference, or indifference to the difficulties of the caregiving situation.

Because of the social unacceptability of expressing negative feelings about others among American

Indians, unobtrusive strategies for capturing negative emotional consequences of caregiving should be considered. Such strategies could include, for example, the construction of items that focus on a lack of personal and interpersonal harmony. Since focus group participants did express a variety of *frustrations* with the caregiving situation including family members not contributing to the caregiving effort or criticizing the primary caregiver's efforts, frustration with care recipient's lack of cooperation or what were considered unreasonable and unneeded demands for care, and frustration with lack of service resources, we recommend that "frustration" replace "anger" in Item 5. It would also be helpful to fully explore the means by which these disquieting situations were resolved.

Indeed, the perceived importance of creating harmony as a means of coping with family illness and dependency has been highlighted in other studies of how American Indians manage health problems and their consequences (Wuest 1991). Moreover, efforts to use caregiver burden instruments with American Indian groups should also consider relevant cultural perspectives on interdependency. . . .

NOTE

1. We do not identify the family relationships by the focus group participants because the data we collected underrepresents the number of spouses in the group who are primary caregivers. During the first two focus group sessions, we discovered the fact that several attendees who did not define themselves as "caregivers" were indeed providing care to a spouse. As a result, we decided to hold a third focus group in order to adequately represent the perceptions of this important class of caregivers. Keeping in mind this caveat, the main caregivers who reported their relationship to the person for whom they provided care consisted of daughters (38%), daughter-in-laws (23%), spouses (15%), and a granddaughter, sister, and cousin (8% each).

REFERENCES

Baines, D. R. 1992. "Issues in Cultural Sensitivity: Examples from the Indian Peoples." Pp. 230–233 in *Health Behavior Research in Minority Populations,* edited by D. M. Becker, D. R. Hill, J. S. Jackson, D. M. Levine, F. A. Stillman, and S. M. Weiss, Rockville, MD: National Institutes of Health.

Brant, C. C. 1990. "Native Ethics and Rules of Behavior." *Canadian Journal of Psychiatry* 35: 534–539.

Hernandez, G. G. 1991. "Not So Benign Neglect: Researchers Ignore Ethnicity in Defining Family Caregiver Burden and Recommending Services." *The Gerontologist* 31: 271–272.

Hobus, R. M. 1990. "Living in Two Worlds: A Lakota Transcultural Nursing Experience." *Journal of Transcultural Nursing* 2: 33–36.

Indian Health Service. 1993. *Consensus Statement of the Roundtable on Long Term Care for Indian Elders.* Rockville, MD: Indian Health Service.

John, R. 1988. "The Native American Family." Pp. 325–363 in *Ethnic Families in America,* 3rd edition, edited by C. H. Mindel, R. Habenstein, and R. Wright, Jr. New York: Elsevier.

———. 1991a. *Defining and Meeting the Needs of Native American Elders: Applied Research on Their Current Status, Social Service Needs, and Support Network Operation.* Final report to the Administration on Aging, 13 Volumes. Lawrence: University of Kansas.

———. 1991b. "The State of Research on American Indian Elders' Health, Income Security, and Social Support Networks." Pp. 38–50 in *Minority Elders: Longevity, Economics, and Health.* Washington, DC: The Gerontological Society of America.

Lawton, M. P., D. Rajagopal, E. Brody, and M. H. Kleban. 1992. "The Dynamics of Caregiving for a Demented Elder among Black and White Families." *Journal of Gerontology* 47: S156–S164.

Malonebeach, E. E., and S. H. Zarit. 1991. "Current Research Issues in Caregiving to the Elderly." *International Journal of Aging and Human Development* 32: 103–114.

Manson, S. M. 1989. "Long-Term Care in American Indian Communities: Issues in Planning and Research." *The Gerontologist* 29: 38–44.

———. 1992. *Chronic Physical Health Problems among Older American Indians.* Warrenton, VA: National Institute on Aging Summer Research Institute on Minority Aging.

———. 1993. "Long-Term Care of Older American Indians: Challenges in the Development of Institutional Services," Pp. 130–143 in *Ethnic Elderly and Long-Term Care,* edited by C. M. Barresi and D. E. Stull. New York: Springer.

Mui, A. C. 1992. "Caregiver Strain among Black and White Daughter Caregivers: A Role Theory Perspective." *The Gerontologist* 32: 203–212.

National Indian Council on Aging. 1981. *American Indian Elderly: A National Profile.* Albuquerque, New Mexico.

Padgett, D. K. 1990. "Consideration of the Ethnic Factor in Aging Research—The Time Has Never Been Better." *The Gerontologist* 30: 723–724.

Red Horse, J. G. 1980. "American Indian Elders: Unifiers of Indian Families." *Social Casework* 61: 490–493.

Shomaker, D. M. 1990. "Health Care, Cultural Expectations and Frail Elderly Navajo Grandmothers." *Journal of Cross-Cultural Gerontology* 5: 21–34.

Steinmetz, S. K. 1988. *Duty Bound: Elder Abuse and Family Care.* Newbury Park, CA: Sage.

Strauss, A., and J. Corbin. 1990. *Basics of Qualitative Research.* Newbury Park, CA: Sage.

Strong, C. 1984. "Stress and Caring for Elderly Relatives: Interpretations and Coping Strategies in an American Indian and White Sample." *The Gerontologist* 24: 251–256.

Stuart, P., and E. Rathbone-McCuan. 1988. "Indian Elderly in the United States," Pp. 235–254 in *North American Elders: United States and Canadian Perspectives,* edited by E. Rathbone-McCuan and B. Havens. Westport, CT: Greenwood Press.

Wuest, J. 1991. "Harmonizing: A North American Indian Approach to Management of Middle Ear Disease with Transcultural Nursing Implications." *Journal of Transcultural Nursing* 3: 5–14.

Zarit, S. H., K. E. Reever, and J. Bach-Peterson. 1980. "Relatives of the Impaired Elderly: Correlates of Feelings of Burden." *The Gerontologist* 20: 649–655.

? *Think about It*

1. How is Pueblo society "sociocentric" in providing care to dependent elders? What are the implications of sociocentric views for decisions about seeking institutional or medical care for elderly relatives and family members?

2. In what ways do Pueblo and Anglo caregiving orientations differ in their perceptions of personal privacy, social space, and potential embarrassment over the elders' inappropriate behaviors?

3. What are the major sources of Pueblo caregivers' satisfaction? How do the providers cope with feelings of strain or stress?

45 Black Grandmothers Raising Their Grandchildren

Antoinette Y. Rodgers-Farmer and Rosa L. Jones

Historically, black grandmothers have played a crucial role in holding their kin networks together, and black grandparents, especially grandmothers, increasingly are postponing or changing their retirement plans to raise their grandchildren. Unlike foster parents, however, most grandparents are either not eligible for or not informed about community assistance programs. Antoinette Y. Rodgers-Farmer and Rosa L. Jones explain the reasons for the rise in black grandparenting, examine the rewards and stressors of these surrogate parenting roles, and suggest how social service agencies could be more responsive to grandparents who are caring for their grandchildren.

The type of involvement grandparents have in the lives of their grandchildren is changing. No longer are grandparents, especially grandmothers, caring for the grandchildren on an as-needed basis. They are often assuming full-time caregiving responsibilities for their grandchildren. This full-time assumption of the caregiving role usually comes during the time when the grandparents are looking forward to retirement. Many of these grandparents have difficulty diverting their energies from retirement planning to the care of their grandchildren (O'Reilly & Morrison, 1993). Furthermore, it has been noted that they are experiencing role confusion, stress, legal, and financial difficulties (Morrow-Kondos et al., 1997).

Grandparents raising their grandchildren is not a new phenomenon. What is new, however, are the reasons why they are raising their grandchildren. Increasingly, grandparents are taking on this responsibility because of the parents' substance abuse. It has been estimated that between 20% and 50% of the inner city children who live with

their grandparents or other relatives are there because of the crack cocaine epidemic (Gross, 1991; Minkler & Roe, 1993). Death and illness of grandchildren's parents, child abuse and neglect, adolescent pregnancy, poverty, and unemployment have also been noted as reasons.

The U.S. Bureau of the Census (1991) estimates that 3.3 million children under the age of 18 live with their grandparents or other relatives, a 40% increase since 1980 (Minkler, 1992). In 1991, comparative data across ethnic groups indicated that grandparenting is particularly prevalent in African American communities. Census data indicated that 12% of African American children live with their grandparents, compared to 5.8% of Hispanic and 3.6% of European American children (U.S. Bureau of the Census, 1991).

Grandparents have always played a strong role in keeping the family together (Morrow-Kondos et al., 1997). This is especially true in African American families where grandmothers often reared their own grandchildren and other children of extended kin, so that families could stay intact. Consequently, African American grandmothers have been described as the "glue" that holds the family together (Seamon, 1992).

Recent studies have presented data that chal-

Source: From Antoinette Y. Rodgers and Rosa L. Jones, "Grandmothers Who Are Caregivers: An Overlooked Population," *Child and Adolescent Social Work Journal* 16 (December 1999): 455–66. Copyright © 1999 Kluwer Academic/Plenum Publishers.

lenge traditional perceptions about African American grandmothers. For example, Burton (1992) found that although grandmothers enjoyed raising their grandchildren, they also were experiencing psychological distress and economic hardship. More often than not these grandmothers indicated that they could use social services to help them continue providing care for their grandchildren. This finding is noteworthy given that African American grandmothers are often described in the literature as having extended kin support.

The purpose of this report is to provide additional data that challenge traditional perceptions about African American grandmothers raising their grandchildren. It presents the findings of a qualitative study of 22 African American grandmothers raising their grandchildren, most of whom have assumed the parenting role to their grandchildren as a result of substance abuse by the grandchildren's parent. Five questions were addressed: (1) Why did you decide to raise your grandchild? (2) What are the challenges and rewards of raising your grandchild? (3) What types of social services do you and your grandchild need? (4) What do you think prohibits social service agencies from adequately meeting your needs and the needs of your grandchildren? and (5) What can social service agencies do so that they can be more responsive to the needs of families in similar situations?

METHOD

Sample and Procedures

The convenience sample consisted of 22 grandmothers (17 maternal grandmothers, 4 paternal grandmothers, and 1 great-grandmother), who were recruited from referrals by two local social service agencies and one church. One of these social service agencies specifically provided services to grandmothers who are raising their grandchildren. The ages of the participants ranged from 47 to 74.

The majority (55%) had between a ninth and twelfth grade education. The income for these families was low, with at least 59% of the families indicating that their income was between $10,001.00 and $20,000.00 per year. The number of grandchildren being raised ranged from one to five. Their ages ranged from 2 to 15 years. The majority of the grandmothers (63%) had cared for their grandchildren since birth. Additional demographic information related to the sample can be found in Table 1.

All participants were interviewed using a 26-item interview schedule, which was developed by the researchers. The items addressed the following areas: reasons for raising their grandchildren; challenges of caregiving; rewards of caregiving; unmet needs for self and grandchildren; interactions

TABLE 1 Demographic Characteristics of the Sample (N = 22)

Variables	Percentages
Marital Status	
Single	14%
Married	32%
Divorced	27%
Widowed	27%
Employment Status	
Employed	27%
Retired	36%
Disabled	14%
Did not specify employment status	23%
Sources of Income	
SSI	55%
AFDC	59%
Salary	27%
Food Stamps	41%
Retirement Benefits	23%
Disability Benefits	14%
Custody Arrangement	
Permanent Custody	41%
Temporary Legal Custody	18%
No Custody	32%
Did not specify custody arrangement	9%

with social service agencies; and suggested changes in social service agencies to make them more responsive to the needs of families in similar situations. The interviews were conducted in the participants' homes or over the telephone by the researchers or a trained research assistant. They lasted from 1½ to 2½ hours. Each interview was audio taped.

RESULTS

Five themes emerged from analysis of the data. First, these grandmothers were raising their grandchildren out of sense of obligation. Moreover, the grandmothers experienced both rewards and stressors in their surrogate parenting role. They identified three types of stressors incurred—role transitional, financial, and familial. The data on social service needs indicated that they needed more financial assistance. They also indicated that they wanted to know how and where to obtain additional social services. Social service agencies did not adequately address the needs of the grandmothers and their grandchildren because of a lack of follow through on the part of staff, and a lack of perceived respect of the grandmothers by staff. Grandmothers suggested that social service agencies could be more responsive to families in similar situations if staff made more contact with these families, and services were provided to the grandchildren to help them deal with parental loss, with an emphasis on helping grandchildren realize that their grandmothers are doing the best that they can.

Obligation

The majority of the grandmothers (68%) stated that they felt obligated to raise their grandchildren. As one grandmother stated:

> I decided to take care of them because they are my grandchildren. If I could take care of my six chil-

dren, I can take care of my own grandchildren. I don't want my grandchildren to be raised in that home or this home. My grandchildren will be raised in no other home but mine.

In discussing their reasons for raising their grandchildren, it was not only quite evident that these grandmothers chose to raise them out of a sense of obligation, but they also did so because they did not want their grandchildren raised in foster care. As one grandmother stated:

> I would not feel comfortable with them in a foster home. That would never happen.

Another grandmother concurred:

> I don't believe in children living place to place . . . foster care.

In an effort to better understand why these grandmothers were raising their grandchildren, participants were asked to indicate why their grandchildren were living with them as opposed to the biological parents. Several reasons were given: biological mother was abusing drugs (45%), death of a parent (23%), maturity level of the parent (14%), abandonment (9%); incarceration of parent (5%), and child abuse (4%).

Grandparenting Rewards

While many of the grandmothers indicated that raising their grandchildren was a challenge, several stated that the role had its rewards. Some of the positive aspects were satisfaction that their grandchildren were well-taken care of, the enjoyment of the companionship, the meaning it put back into their lives (i.e, making them feel useful again or making them feel younger).

Grandparenting Stressors

All the grandparents experienced some type of stress associated with their surrogate parenting role. The stressors they incurred can be grouped into three categories—role transitional, financial, and familial. Three grandmothers reported that raising their grandchildren caused them to experience changes in their lifestyles that they were not quite ready to undertake. One grandmother stated:

> There are a lot of us now who have grown children who are now raising their grandchildren. We are doing it all over again. I had great plans, then she comes.

Another stated:

> I would like to get up when I like. I have gone through this before with my own kids. When you want to sleep, you have to watch the children. I deserve to sleep because I have certainly worked hard and provided . . . Now that I am old and retired, I don't think I should have to take my money and buy food or whatever. I would like to do what I want with my money.

Yet another stated:

> Well, I can't go and come when I want to. I would like to travel to see my relatives and friends more often.

Financial Stress. The most difficult stress these grandmothers experienced was related to the additional expenditures they have incurred as a result of taking care of their grandchildren. Several grandmothers strongly stated that they were experiencing economic hardship. One eloquently stated:

> All of my bills have increased including water, doctor, electric, and dental. I have had difficulty getting financial assistance. One social service agency wanted to know all of our assets, and I felt it was none of the worker's business. I feel we should not have to use our money to care for them. If the children were in foster care, the foster care parents would receive money to care for these children.

Familial Stress. The participants noted that raising their grandchildren had affected their relationship with other family members, namely, other grandchildren not living in their home, their spouse, and their own adult children. Many grandmothers were surprised by the behavior of their own adult children. One stated:

> Instead of them (my own grown children) being helpful, they are resentful.

Another concurred:

> One of my sons told me that I have other grandchildren besides the ones I am raising in my home. He got angry with me because I didn't give his children things. Now he does not speak to me.

The effects of raising grandchildren on the marital relationship are illustrated by one grandmother:

> It puts a lot of stress on my marriage. This is my second husband. He is not related to my grandchildren by blood. At the time that he came into my life, he not only had to accept my children from another marriage, but had to accept a household where there were grandchildren. He has been able to accept them and he cares for them as if they were his own children, but sometimes when we want to do something, we have to make sure that they are taken care of before we can proceed on our trip, or we have to make arrangements to take them along with us, which means that we have to take them out of school. So I have to make arrangements for them to be secure while I am away, or come up with funds so that I can carry everyone with me. This puts stress on my husband sometimes. He feels like I need to return those kids to their mother and let her be responsible for them.

Another stated:

> My husband and I can't spend a lot of time together.

Social Service Needs for Grandparents and Grandchildren

The grandmothers described a variety of services that they or their grandchildren needed. The most frequently cited services needed were financial assistance and day care. Additional service needs included respite care, clothing allowance, support groups for themselves and their grandchildren, and medical assistance for themselves.

In discussing their need for more financial assistance, it became quite apparent that their need was not only related to their current income level, but also to the age of the child. A grandmother of a 13-year-old stated:

> I really need more financial assistance. My granddaughter is at a point where she likes to go places and I can't afford to do that. So, that is one service I really need for her.

Surprisingly, a number of grandmothers reported that they did not know how or where to get additional entitlements/services. One frustrated grandmother stated:

> I don't know much about what is out there. I don't know what I am entitled to.

Another stated:

> There are a lot of organizations out there, but families don't know about them. We need to know what is out there.

Grandparents' Perceptions of Social Service Agencies

The grandmothers identified several problematic issues that they perceived affected social service agencies' ability to provide them with needed services. These issues included high turnover of staff, lack of contact/visitations by staff, uncoordinated services, lack of follow through on the part of staff, and lack of perceived respect of the grandmothers by staff. Concerning the lack of follow through, one grandmother stated:

> I had to call a worker's supervisor because she didn't follow-up on a referral for an evaluation.

Several of these grandmothers reported that staff treated them differently because they were not the biological parents. One grandmother stated:

> Some agency people feel we (grandmothers) are not the "real parents," and they seem to want to make decisions for us.

Another added:

> I had a problem obtaining treatment for my grandchild in an emergency room. Her mother had to sign guardianship over to me to rectify the situation.

How Social Service Agencies Can Be More Responsive

When asked what aspects of social service agencies should be changed so that they might be more responsive to the needs of families in similar situations, the majority of the grandmothers (40%) reported that social service agencies needed to have more contact with the families. One grandmother stated:

> Agencies need to provide workers to come out to the home to see how things are going, counsel the family, and help them cope with the changes and difficulties. I always had my only daughter living with me, but now I must adjust to having four grandchildren.

Several grandmothers felt that services needed to be provided to help grandchildren deal with parental loss. One grandmother stated:

> There needs to be programs where grandchildren learn to cope with the problems their parents have. These grandchildren need a program where they learn their parents are gone, but their grandparents are doing all they can.

DISCUSSION

The results of this study highlight some of the needs and stressors faced by African American grandmothers who are raising their grandchildren. As the results revealed, one of the most frequently cited needs was day care. This finding is consistent with the findings of Jendrek (1994) and Minkler and Roe (1993).

Like the respondents in both the Minkler and Roe (1993) and the Jendrek (1994) studies, these grandmothers also indicated that they were treated like "second-class citizens" because they were not the biological parents. Being treated like "second-class citizens" affected their ability to get services for their grandchildren.

The decision to provide care was based on obligation. The sense of being obligated to care for their grandchildren may be due to fear. In several studies (e.g., Jendrek, 1994; Minkler et al., 1992) the main reason cited for raising the grandchildren was the fear that they would be placed in foster care. Additionally, this sense of being obligated may be due to their perception about their role within the family. Historically, African American grandmothers have played a pivotal role in holding the kin network together. In this role, they have taken on the responsibility of raising their own grandchildren and the children of extended and fictive kin (Hagestad & Burton, 1986; Wilson, 1986). Although the grandmothers may be fulfilling their perceived role in the family, they are in need of further supports to help them carry out this role effectively. The demands for additional social services by African American grandmothers challenge our perceptions about older African Americans using their extended kin support network for help.

Although some of the grandmothers reported that caring for their grandchildren presented them with life style changes they were not ready to accept, they also reported that caring for their grandchildren put meaning back into their lives. This finding is similar to the results obtained by Burton (1992) and Minkler and Roe (1993).

The results of this study not only revealed that caregiving affected the marital relationship, but the relationship between the grandmother and her own grown children who lived outside of the home as well. The former is consistent with the findings of Minkler, Roe, and Robertson-Beckley (1994), and extends earlier works demonstrating that caregiving in general has implications for the marital relationship of the caregiver (e.g., Biegel et al., 1991; Cook et al., 1992).

An unexpected finding was that some of the grandmothers were not aware of the available services and entitlements. One reason is perhaps the lack of consistent contact by staff with the grandmothers. Because staff do not meet with the grandmothers on a regular basis, they do not have the opportunity to tell them about the available services and entitlements.

A word of caution regarding the findings should be noted. As previously stated, some of the participants were recruited from a social service agency that specifically provided services to grandmothers who are raising their grandchildren. It is possible that these grandmothers could have experienced less stress in their relationship with their grown children and their spouses and reported more positive experiences related to care giving than grandmothers who did not receive services from this particular agency. Because there were too few participants in each group, no analyses were performed to assess for differences between the groups. Furthermore, since the grandmothers who were recruited from the social service agency voluntarily sought out their services, this may mean that they have better help-seeking skills and can better appraise potential stress events than those grandmothers who did not receive services from this particular agency. . . .

REFERENCES

Biegel, D., Sales, E., & Schulz, R. (1991). *Family caregiving and chronic illness.* Newbury Park, CA: Sage Publications.

Burton, L. M. (1992). Black grandparents rearing children of drug-addicted parents: Stressors, outcomes and social service needs. *The Gerontologist, 12,* 744–751.

Cook, J. A., Hoffschmidt, S., Cohler, B., & Pickett, S. (1992). Marital satisfaction among parents of the severely mentally ill in the community. *American Journal of Orthopsychiatry, 62,* 552–563.

Gross, J. (1991, April 21). Help for grandmothers caught up in the drug war. *New York Times.*

Hagestad, G., & Burton, L. (1986). Grandparenthood, life context, and family development. *American Behavioral Scientist, 29,* 471–484.

Jendrek, M. P. (1994). Policy concerns of white grandparents who provide regular care for their grandchildren. *Journal of Gerontological Social Work, 23,* 175–200.

Minkler, M., & Roe, K. M. (1993). *Grandmothers as caregivers: Raising children of the crack cocaine epidemic.* Newbury Park, CA: Sage Publications.

Minkler, M., Roe, K. M., & Price, M. (1992). The physical and emotional health of grandmothers raising their grandchildren in the crack cocaine epidemic. *The Gerontologist, 32,* 752–761.

Minkler, M., Roe, K. M., & Robertson-Beckley, R. J. (1994). Raising grandchildren from crack-cocaine households: Effects of family and friendship ties of African-American women. *American Journal of Orthopsychiatry, 64,* 20–29.

Morrow-Kondos, D., Weber, J. A., Cooper, K., & Hesser, J. L. (1997). Becoming parents again: Grandparents raising grandchildren. *Journal of Gerontological Social Work, 28,* 35–46.

O'Reilly, E., & Morrison, M. L. (1993). Grandparent-headed families: New therapeutic challenges. *Child Psychiatry and Human Development, 23,* 147–159.

Seamon, F. (1992). Intergenerational issues related to the crack cocaine problem. *Family Community Health, 15,* 11–19.

U.S. Bureau of Census (1991). Current population reports: Marital status and living arrangements, March 1990 (Series P-20 No. 450). Washington DC: Author.

Wilson, M. N. (1986). The black extended family: An analytical consideration. *Developmental Psychology, 22,* 246–256.

? Think about It

1. According to Rodgers-Farmer and Jones, what are the traditional perceptions about older African Americans and kin support networks? How does their research challenge the traditional perceptions?

2. What rewards did the grandmothers report in raising their grandchildren? What specific role transition, familial, and financial stress did they encounter?

3. Describe the range of services that the grandmothers said they needed to raise their grandchildren more effectively.

46 Variations in Asian Grandparenting

Yoshinori Kamo

The historical and cultural backgrounds of Asian American immigrants have shaped grandparent–grandchild relations in the United States. Although Asian grandparents have much in common, Yoshinori Kamo identifies many differences across Asian subgroups. Some of the differences reflect diverse demographic characteristics, coresidence patterns, filial piety principles, the degree of assimilation and acculturation, and grandparents' varied roles in transmitting knowledge about traditional values and customs.

Grandparents of Asian origins have diverse backgrounds. They come from different countries of origin; some were born in the United States and many others immigrated; some grandparents have strong ties with their countries of origin while others do not. Although there is diversity among Asian grandparents, they still have much in common. Most, if not all, come from Confucian backgrounds and many are Buddhists. Past research has found that both elderly Japanese and Chinese Americans are more likely to live with their adult children than their non-Hispanic white counterparts (Kamo & Zhou, 1994), and this pattern may be common to elderly Asians of many different countries of origins.

Research on grandparenthood entails diverse aspects of grandparent–grandchild contacts, including association, affection and consensus, exchange of services, and kin expectations (Bengtson & Harootyan, 1994; Kamo, 1995a; Kivett, 1993; Mancini & Blieszner, 1989). This chapter will focus on demographic and social psychological factors surrounding Asian grandparents. They include immigration and assimilation history, the notion of filial piety based on Confucianism, living arrangements, interaction styles between grandparents and grandchildren, and socialization of grandchildren.

Source: From Yoshinori Kamo, "Asian Grandparents," in *Handbook on Grandparenthood,* ed. Maximiliane E. Szinovacz (Westport, CT: Greenwood, 1998), 97–112. Copyright © 1998 Greenwood Publishing Group, Inc. Reproduced with permission of Greenwood Publishing Group, Inc., Westport, CT.

HISTORICAL AND CULTURAL BACKGROUNDS OF ASIAN FAMILIES

To examine issues surrounding Asian grandparents, we need to look at cultural backgrounds in their countries of origin. While Buddhism has been widely practiced in East Asian countries such as China, Japan, Korea, and Vietnam, Christianity has been popular in the Philippines, Vietnam, and Korea, and Hinduism has been dominant in India. These religions, however, have not contributed much to form unique characteristics and social norms among Asians. A more common influence was Confucianism, which originated in China as one of its moral codes. Many countries in East Asia such as China, Taiwan, Korea, and Japan adopted Confucianism. Expressed in books compiled for collections of sayings by Confucius (551–479 B.C.), Confucianism has become the center of ethics in many Asian countries.

Confucian ethics emphasize status differences among persons based on gender and age, and stress family life. One of the major parts of Confucianism is the notion of filial piety or filial responsibility. Filial responsibility is defined as "the responsibility for parents exercised by children. The term emphasizes duty rather than satisfaction and is usually connected with protection, care, or financial support" (Schorr, 1980: 1). Normatively, filial piety prescribes respect for and a sense of obligation toward one's parents and ancestors. The second verse of the Analects (or Lun Yü in Chinese), which is mostly a collection of Confucius' sayings, states, "Those who in private life behave well towards their parents and elder brothers, in public life seldom show a disposition to resist the authority of their superiors" (Waley, 1971: 83).

When parents age, filial responsibility is enacted through personal contact with and financial and physical support for these elderly parents. Even in the Philippines, where Confucianism is not considered particularly strong among Asian countries, filial responsibility is emphasized and practiced (Blust & Scheidt, 1988).

Confucianism emphasizes not only filial responsibility but also hierarchy by gender. Thus, elderly fathers/grandfathers rather than mothers/grandmothers possess the final authority of the family. Family membership and family property are most often inherited through the paternal line, from father to son (called patrilineal descent). Married women belong to their husbands' family, rather than their own.

Derived from filial responsibility and gender hierarchy, another related and dominant theme among Asians and Asian Americans is coresidence with elderly parents, particularly husband's parents (called patrilocality). Combined with patrilineal descent, this living arrangement has helped husbands or their mothers dominate their wives or daughters-in-law, strengthening gender hierarchy in Asian countries. These extended-family households often include grandchildren. . . .

The expectation and practice of coresidence with elderly parents seem to vary by countries and time periods. While coresidence seems to be less commonly practiced in such industrial countries as Japan, it is far from having disappeared (Kojima, 1989; Tsuya & Martin, 1992). Parental coresidence with adult children is probably most strictly enforced in Korea (De Vos & Lee, 1993; Martin, 1989; Min, 1988), but it also is widely practiced in China (Tu et al., 1989), Taiwan (Freedman et al., 1982; Tu et al., 1989), the

Philippines (Martin, 1989), Vietnam (Gold, 1993), and India (Ram & Wong, 1994). . . .

For coresidence with elderly parents, whether the adult child is married or not is irrelevant, and whether the elderly parent is still married, widowed, or divorced is not relevant either. Coresidence is usually not for any tangible needs such as caretaking of the elderly parents or assisting the adult children in their economic insufficiency; rather it is a normative arrangement, derived from patrilocal residence rules.

Elderly parent–adult child (and grandchild) coresidence, however, is not entirely the result of filial responsibility. It is facilitated by economic factors also. Retirement pensions are either very small or nonexistent in Asian countries, and this often forces elderly parents to depend on their adult children. Yang and Chandler (1992) describe elderly parents' financial dependence on their married sons and resulting intergenerational tensions in rural China. On the other hand, grandparents in Asian countries may play an active role in their three-generation households in household work and child care. Olson (1990: 144), for example, quotes an elderly Chinese man as follows: "She (my wife) does all the cooking and also takes care of the two grandchildren while my daughter-in-law goes off to work. . . . I usually spend a little time playing with the grandson who is three."

IMMIGRATION AND ASSIMILATION OF ASIAN GRANDPARENTS

. . . Because several immigration waves occurred fairly recently, many Asian and Hispanic elderly were born outside the United States. Many others are children of immigrants. Before they immigrated to the United States or when they were raised by immigrant parents, their life styles and/or cultural values were much different from those of mainstream Americans. Even now, many Asian grandparents speak languages other than English, eat their traditional foods, believe in non-

Christian religions, and/or have different values from white grandparents on many issues (Ishii-Kuntz, 1997; Kitano & Daniels, 1995). This is particularly true among Korean, Vietnamese, Cambodian, and Laotian grandparents who came to the United States recently. Even among such "traditional" Asian Americans as Chinese and Japanese, many grandparents are immigrants themselves or children of immigrants (second-generation Asian Americans). In sum, many Asian grandparents are not fully acculturated to the American society.

On the other hand, some young Asians, particularly Japanese, Filipino, and Asian Indians, have been well assimilated into the mainstream society through education, occupation, residential assimilation, and intermarriages (Kitano & Daniels, 1995). Thus, normative and/or cultural changes associated with modernization (Goode, 1963) may be reflected within each immigrant's family as grandparents live by more traditional values while their grandchildren are more attuned to "modern" American values. Such value and life style differences most likely have profound effects on the interaction between grandparents and grandchildren as we will see later.

. . . The majority of elderly Asian Americans (except for Japanese Americans) were born outside the United States. Only a minority of Asian Americans in the grandchildren's generation share this characteristic of foreign birth. Except for Vietnamese Americans, the majority of young Asian persons were born in the United States.

. . . Among Asian Americans (and some Hispanic Americans), grandparent–grandchild relationships will not only be characterized by the "generation gap," but also by differences in immigration status. Once again, there are pronounced differences among the various Asian groups. Comparison of the percentages of foreign-born individuals in grandparents' and grandchildren's generations indicates that Japanese American families are least likely to experience differences in immigration status between the two generations. Only a minority of both older and younger

Japanese Americans were born in Japan. Among all other Asian American groups there are large differences in the percentages of foreign-born persons between the old and young generations, suggesting that two-fifths to two-thirds of non-Japanese Asian families include foreign-born grandparents and U.S.-born grandchildren.

How much grandparents' foreign-born status impacts on their relationships with grandchildren may vary for different Asian American groups. I would expect that Chinese, Korean, and Vietnamese grandparents have a tougher time dealing with their grandchildren due to cultural differences than do their Japanese, Filipino, and Asian Indian counterparts. Most of Vietnamese Americans are political refugees who may have been forced to emigrate from their country. They thus may not have prepared to assimilate to American society, unlike some other immigrants who chose to come to the United States. Koreans and Chinese, on the other hand, chose to come to this country, but they strongly adhere to their traditional cultures which are quite different from the American mainstream culture. In their own country, they probably practiced filial responsibility more strictly than did Japanese, Filipino, and Asian Indians. Given larger gaps between their own culture and American culture, Chinese and Korean grandparents are likely to have more difficulty with their grandchildren, many of whom are completely assimilated. Poor command of English language may also contribute to difficulty in their relationships with grandchildren among Chinese, Korean, and Vietnamese grandparents. When percentages of people 55 years or older who speak English only, very well, or well (rather than not well or not at all) are calculated from the census data, they are 33% for Vietnamese, 37% for Korean, and 49% for Chinese, compared to 73% for Asian Indians, 82% for Filipinos, and 88% for Japanese.

Setting these inter-ethnic differences in assimilation and relationships with grandchildren aside, there are a couple of characteristics common to most Asian Americans that distinguish them from non-Hispanic whites. These are the notion of filial piety and coresidence between grandparents and grandchildren. These two characteristics may help facilitate interactions and enhance value consensus between grandparents and grandchildren. I will discuss these in the next sections.

CORESIDENCE WITH GRANDCHILDREN

When Asians immigrated to the United States, they brought with them their traditional culture, including the notion of filial piety and the ideal of elderly people living with their adult children, particularly adult sons (Sokolovsky, 1990). Table 1 indicates the proportions of people 55 years or older who live with their grandchildren and the proportions of people 19 years or younger who live with their grandparents for various Asian American groups and other races. Except for Japanese Americans, between 20% and 40% of Asian Americans 55 years or older live with their grandchildren. This proportion is much smaller among their non-Hispanic white counterparts at 4.5%, and somewhat smaller among blacks and Hispanics (19% and 16%, respectively).

Similarly, Asian Americans 19 years old or younger, except for Japanese and Vietnamese Americans, are more likely to live with their grandparents than are their non-Hispanic white and Hispanic counterparts (Table 1). The relatively low incidence of coresidence among Japanese Americans is particularly striking if we consider that they are the only racial/ethnic group with more older people (55 or older) than younger people (19 or younger). The ratio of the former over the latter is 1.20 . . . compared to the second largest ratio among the Asian groups, Chinese, which is .58. This means that young people of Japanese origin are less likely to live with their grandparents, despite the fact that there are more Japanese grandparents around. Thus, factors other than availability of grandparents must account for the low coresidence rate of Japanese Americans.

Japanese Americans are known to be the most assimilated Asian American group in the United States when we consider high-school graduation rate, occupational distribution, unemployment rate, median income, and poverty rate (Kitano & Daniels, 1995). This is primarily due to their unique immigration history. . . . Roughly 70% of Japanese Americans 55 years or older were born in the United States, compared to 2%–17% among other

TABLE 1   Distribution by Race and Ethnicity of Elderly and Young Persons Who Live with Grandchildren and Grandparents

	Total	55 or Older Living with Grandchildren		Total	19 or Younger Living with Grandparents˜	
Non-Hispanic White	2,890	130	(4.50%)	3,715	226	(6.08%)
Black	1,988	385	(19.37%)	4,585	768	(16.75%)
Hispanic	1,919	310	(16.15%)	4,938	445	(9.01%)
All Asians	1,922	421	(21.90%)	4,437	578	(13.03%)
Chinese	538	110	(20.45%)	984	120	(12.20%)
Japanese	473	28	(5.92%)	396	27	(6.82%)
Filipino	426	121	(28.4%)	857	168	(19.60%)
Korean	162	56	(34.75%)	477	76	(15.93%)
Asian Indian	135	52	(38.52%)	542	79	(14.58%)
Vietnamese	87	23	(26.44%)	467	31	(6.64%)

Sources: 1990 Census of Population and Housing; Public Use Microdata Samples; U.S. Bureau of the Census (1992).

Asian American groups. Although they share a common label of "Asian Americans," older Japanese Americans are different from their Asian American counterparts in their nativity status and, as will be shown later, language use.

Like Japanese American children, few Vietnamese children live with their grandparents. This, however, does not indicate more complete assimilation to the mainstream culture as it does for Japanese Americans. This is probably because they or their parents are recent immigrants who left their grandparents or parents in Vietnam (Gold, 1993). Indeed, the ratio of people 55 or older over those 19 or younger among Vietnamese is the smallest among all Asian American or any other racial groups at .16.

Though I have been focusing on a normative trait of Asian Americans (filial responsibility), there are other factors we should consider in examining coresidence between grandparents and grandchildren. Goldscheider and Goldscheider (1989) argue that there are three factors that influence family extension—desirability, availability, and feasibility. Desirability refers to preferences for family extension, availability concerns the presence of eligible family members, and feasibility refers to economic factors.

For one thing, elderly Asian Americans are more likely to be married, have children, and have grandchildren than non-Hispanic whites (Lubben & Becerra, 1987). That Asian grandparents are more likely to live with their grandchildren is partly explained by these demographic characteristics, or kin availability. However, differences in coresidence rates between various Asian American groups and non-Hispanic whites are so large that they cannot be fully explained by differences in the availability of grandchildren or grandparents.

Is grandparent–grandchild coresidence among Asian Americans a result of "feasibility" or of economic consideration? The answer is yes for some families. Many new immigrants have struggled to make a living in the United States, and no doubt opted for coresidence because of economic considerations. Research indicates, for example,

that elderly Chinese and Japanese Americans with low incomes are more likely to live with their married children, and probably with their grandchildren, than Chinese and Japanese Americans with higher incomes (Kamo & Zhou, 1994).

When Asian grandparents live with their grandchildren, they tend to live in "upwardly extended households" (Kamo, 1995b; Szinovacz, 1996) or in households headed by their adult children rather than by themselves or by their spouses. Except for Japanese Americans, the majority (60%–85%) of Asian grandparents who live with their grandchildren do so in their children's households, and young Asian Americans who live with their grandparents are more likely to do so in their parents' households (in 75%–92% of these cases) rather than their grandparents'. Once again, Japanese Americans are an exception. This is in stark contrast to other racial/ethnic groups, particularly blacks, whose grandchildren are more likely to live in "downward extended households" (i.e., households headed by the grandparents). This unique pattern among Asian Americans reflects Confucian ideals and patrilocal norms of coresidence. Once they have established themselves, adult children of Asian origins often bring their elderly parents into their households. Confucian ethics, which stresses age and gender hierarchy, would suggest that most of these adult children are sons, particularly the oldest son in the family, but census data do not allow us to confirm this point.

On the other hand, coresidence between grandparents and grandchildren among Japanese Americans and other racial/ethnic groups is more likely to occur in the grandparents' household (Kamo, 1995b). In many of these cases, adult children's or grandchildren's needs are the primary reason for coresidence (Ward et al., 1992), and it is often a temporary arrangement. In these coresidence arrangements, adult children are often daughters, many of them single mothers. This pattern is particularly common among black households (Flaherty et al., 1987; Szinovacz, 1996, 1998).

While young Japanese Americans and Vietnamese Americans are both less likely to live with their grandparents, there is a clear difference when they do so. Grandparent–grandchild coresidence is much more likely to occur in the grandparents' house (downward extension) among Japanese Americans, but is much more likely to occur in the parents' house (upward extension) among Vietnamese Americans as is the case with all other Asian American groups. While Japanese Americans seem to closely follow the pattern of non-Hispanic whites, Vietnamese Americans still adhere to the "traditionally Asian" pattern of coresidence.

INTERACTION BETWEEN GRANDPARENTS AND GRANDCHILDREN

. . . Many young Asian Americans such as Vietnamese, Cambodians, and Laotians . . . were born outside the United States and have their grandparents living in their home countries. In these cases, it is obvious that grandparent–grandchildren interactions have become minimal. This is exacerbated by the fact that many Asian Americans are political refugees, and, therefore, cannot communicate with family members still living in their countries of origin, including their grandparents (Gold, 1993; Uba, 1994). Likewise, many Asian grandparents, particularly those from Southeast Asia, left their grandchildren in their countries of origin in the turmoil of fleeing (Detzner, 1996).

In contrast, when grandparents live with their grandchildren in the same household (in the United States), there must be some interactions between them. Confucian ethics stress age seniority, that grandparents are to be respected and honored by their offspring, including their grandchildren. Asian grandchildren are thus expected to interact with their grandparents in a more deferential manner, use a more formal conversational style, and use more polite language. Describing Asian Americans' interactions between family members, Uba states "they (many Asian Americans) can not remember the last time that one of their parents hugged or kissed their grandchildren"

(Uba, 1994: 38). Thus, expected among Asian Americans are more formal interactions between grandparents and grandchildren than among other racial/ethnic groups.

When Asian grandparents do not live with their grandchildren, do they maintain more frequent interactions than do grandparents of other races/ ethnicities? Frequent interactions could be expected, given the emphasis on filial piety among Asian cultures. Lubben and Becerra (1987), however, show that elderly Chinese in California are not more likely to see their grandchildren on a regular basis, particularly compared to Mexican and black Americans. This may suggest that enactment of filial responsibility may not be as common as it used to be, or it may be in effect only in more formal aspects such as coresidence. There is a possibility that Asian Americans do not practice filial responsibility when it comes to such spontaneous behaviors as visiting and/or keeping in contact with elderly family members including grandparents.

Even when grandparents and grandchildren see each other, their primary languages may differ. Table 2 indicates [the] proportions of elderly (55 or older) and young (between 5 and 19) persons who primarily speak languages other than English at home. The majority of Asian Americans of both young and old generations primarily speak non-English languages at home, except for young people of Filipino and Japanese origins. Nonetheless, there are intergenerational differences in the proportions of young and old people who primarily speak non-English languages among each Asian American group. These differences are particularly pronounced among Filipinos, followed by Asian Indians and Japanese. Thus, many Asian grandparents and their grandchildren may not share the most fundamental method of communication, language. Such language barriers will inevitably affect communication between grandparents and grandchildren in an adverse fashion. This situation parallels that among immigrant families from Europe at the turn of the century. For example, in Cherlin and Furstenberg

TABLE 2   Percent Who Speak Non-English Languages at Home

	55 or Older	*Between 5 and 19*
Non-Hispanic White	7.61	8.41
Black	3.87	6.30
Hispanic	86.71	71.15
All Asians	80.96	70.17
Chinese	88.29	77.12
Japanese	92.72	41.20
Filipino	51.59	36.59
Korean	88.15	66.84
Asian Indian	93.21	83.14
Vietnamese	98.85	92.53

Sources. 1990 Census of Population and Housing; Public Use Microdata Samples; U.S. Bureau of the Census (1992).

(1986: 37) a Polish grandmother describes the relationship with her own grandmother as follows: "Well, see, my grandmother was Polish, and she couldn't speak English. But she used to come every Sunday. . . . And she'd try to speak to us— it was hard. It was hard for her to speak to us, because we all spoke English and she was Polish."

Kennedy (1992) has shown that grandchildren's feelings that they are known and understood by the grandparents and that they know and understand the grandparents are critical for successful relationships between grandparents and grandchildren. If they do not share the same language, it is rather difficult to "know" each other. Thus, speaking different languages most likely inhibits the development of close relationships between grandparents and grandchildren.

The content of grandparent–grandchild communications among Asian Americans may also differ from that of non-Hispanic white Americans as a result of the immigration history of both generations. We may conceptualize the effect of modernization on grandparent–grandchild relationships as a shift from bonds of obligation to bonds of sentiment (Cherlin & Furstenberg, 1986). Burgess and Locke (1960) characterize this shift

as that from "family as institution" to "family as companionship." . . .

. . . Due to the notion of filial responsibility, relationships between Asian grandparents and grandchildren are likely to be characterized by bonds of obligation to a greater extent than are found among white Americans. Furthermore, many Asian American grandparents are immigrants themselves, and they may possess an insufficient English-speaking ability and thus may not have acquired enough retirement income or pension, rendering them economically dependent. As shown by Anderson (1977), economic dependence of one generation on the other promotes bonds of obligation, and their economic dependence might be an extra factor leading to more formal relationships between Asian grandparents and their grandchildren.

Cherlin and Furstenberg (1986) distinguish three styles of grandparent–grandchild relationships: remote, companionate, and involved. They argue that the companionate style is the most common among American grandparents, followed by the remote, and then involved ones. Out of the respect to the parent–child relationship, grandparents usually adhere to the "norm of noninterference" and do not get involved in raising, socializing, and disciplining their grandchildren. They, however, prefer to maintain their relationships with grandchildren and thus the companionate relationship becomes the most prevalent. This is a useful classification system to describe Asian grandparents. As discussed above, many Asian grandparents live outside the United States, and this inevitably leads to the remote style of grandparenting. As Cherlin and Furstenberg claim, great geographical distance is the most common cause for the remote grandparenting style.

At the other extreme, many Asian grandparents live in the same household as their grandchildren, as shown above. In addition, under the Confucian ethics, children (and grandchildren) belong to the entire extended family, not just to their parents, as is the case among white American households. The "norm of noninterference," described by Cherlin and Furstenberg, which inhibits many grandparents from playing a surrogate parent's role, may not be as strong among Asian Americans. The combination of these factors probably leads to more "involved" grandparents among Asian Americans than among their white counterparts.

Although the companionate style is the most common type of relationship among white Americans, this style may be less common among Asian grandparents. For one thing, this type may be squeezed by the two other types, remote and involved, which are more prevalent among Asian than white American families. Also, this type of relationship requires good communication skills, affectionate expressions, and the notion of equal status between grandparents and grandchildren. Asian grandparents may not be the best candidates for these qualities. Due to the insufficient English language skills, they may not be able to communicate well with their grandchildren. Traditionally, more reserved expressions among Asians may prohibit Asian grandparents from expressing love and affection to their grandchildren (Ishii-Kuntz, 1999), and Confucian ethics and age seniority may lead them to regard their grandchildren as unequals. Thus, companionate relationships between Asian grandparents and their grandchildren are probably less common than among their white counterparts. However, there are as yet no reliable data to support this claim.

It should be noted that some studies suggest that the moderate levels of contact between grandparents and grandchildren typical for the companionate style may be better for the quality of the relationship than either high or low levels of contact (Tinsley & Parke, 1984). For this reason also the relationship between Asian grandparents and their grandchildren may suffer since they often live either in separate countries or in the same household.

Whereas Asian grandparents may ignore the "norm of noninterference" because of their adherence to extended-family ideals and norms of filial piety, this norm may be cherished by their children, who are more assimilated to American society (Holmes & Holmes, 1995). This disagreement may also contribute to a more strenuous and perhaps remote relationship between Asian grandparents and their children and grandchildren. . . .

SOCIALIZATION OF GRANDCHILDREN

One of the possible roles grandparents may play is that of "historians" (Kornhaber & Woodward, 1985). They may transmit "values, ethnic heritage, and family traditions" (Tinsley & Parke, 1984: 172) to their grandchildren either through the middle generation or through direct contacts. This is particularly important among ethnic minorities who face the duality between the adopted culture of American society and their traditional culture. Foreign-born grandparents may be able to tell their grandchildren what their countries of origin were like and what kind of life they lived before immigrating to this country.

Among Asian Americans, however, grandparents' role as family historians may differ from that of other ethnic groups. First, given their limitations in English language ability and communication skills, Asian grandparents may not transmit their values and traditional culture to their grandchildren well. Nevertheless, it is absurd to assume that there is no transmission of ethnic values, culture, and heritage from grandparents to grandchildren, particularly given the strong notion of filial piety among Asian Americans.

Second, among whites and some minorities, if certain values are transmitted from grandparents to grandchildren, this transmission often occurs through the middle generation. In contrast, anecdotal evidence indicates that the third-generation Asian Americans learned Asian culture directly from their grandparents (Ishii-Kuntz, 1997; Phinney, 1990). This generation-skipping value transfer occurred in historical context among Japanese Americans. After the second-generation Japanese tried hard to fully assimilate themselves into the mainstream American society during the 1930's and 1940's, the third-generation Japanese Americans wanted to restore their cultural identity during the 1960's and 1970's, probably affected by general sentiments to preserve cultural heritages.

Asian American grandparents' role in the socialization of grandchildren may be limited to that of family historians. Many Asian American grandparents may not be able to contribute to the general socialization of their grandchildren because their cultural values are based on their original society rather than on American society. To the extent that grandchildren are immersed in mainstream society, their grandparents' perspectives may be irrelevant. On the other hand, their knowledge of the Asian culture and its heritage may be cherished, and grandparents may become a specialized source of knowledge about the traditional Asian culture. In so doing, Asian grandparents play a role in developing and preserving ethnic identity among young Asian Americans. Their cultural heritages, both tangible and intangible, and the history of struggles in the past often serve to solidify ethnic identity among Asian Americans. While grandparents' values, norms, and even behaviors may be out of touch, they still offer a reference point for their young family members, including grandchildren. Thus, Asian American grandchildren learn to be Asians mostly from their family members including grandparents, while they learn to be Americans mostly from people outside their family.

REFERENCES

Anderson, M. (1977). The impact on the family relationships of the elderly of changes since Victorian times in governmental income-maintenance provision. In E. Shanas & M. B. Sussman (Eds.), *Family, bureaucracy, and the elderly* (pp. 36–59). Durham, NC: Duke University Press.

Bengtson, V. L., & Harootyan, R. (Eds.). (1994). *Hidden connections: A study of intergenerational linkages in American society.* New York: Springer.

Blust, E. P. N., & Scheidt, R. J. (1988). Perceptions of filial responsibility by elderly Filipino widows and their primary caregivers. *International Journal of Aging and Human Development, 26,* 91–106.

Burgess, E. W., & Locke, H. J. (1960). *The family: From institution to companionship* (2nd ed.). New York: American Book Company.

Cherlin, A. J., & Furstenberg, F. F. (1986). *The new American grandparent.* New York: Basic Books.

Detzner, D. F. (1996). No place without a home: Southeast Asian grandparents in refugee families. *Generations, 20,* 45–48.

De Vos, S., & Lee, Y. (1993). Changes in extended family living among elderly people in South Korea, 1970–1980. *Economic Development and Cultural Change, 41,* 377–393.

Flaherty, M. J., Facteau, L., & Gurver, P. (1987). Grandmother functions in multigenerational families: An exploratory study of black adolescent mothers and their infants. *Maternal-Child Nursing Journal, 16,* 61–73.

Freedman, R., Chang, M., & Sun, T. (1982). Household composition, extended kinship, and reproduction in Taiwan. *Population Studies, 36,* 395–411.

Gold, S. J. (1993). Migration and family adjustment: Continuity and change among Vietnamese in the United States. In H. P. McAdoo (Ed.), *Family ethnicity: Strength in diversity* (pp. 300–314). Newbury Park, CA: Sage.

Goldscheider, F. K., & Goldscheider, C. (1989). Ethnicity and the new family economy. In F. K. Goldscheider & C. Goldscheider (Eds.), *Ethnicity and the new family economy: Living arrangements and intergenerational financial flows* (pp. 185–197). Boulder, CO: Westview.

Goode, W. J. (1963). *World revolution and family patterns.* London: Free Press.

Holmes, E. R., & Holmes, L. D. (1995). *Other cultures, elder years* (2nd ed.). Thousand Oaks, CA: Sage.

Ishii-Kuntz, M. (1997). Japanese American families. In M. K. DeGenova (Ed.), *Families in cultural context* (pp. 131–153). Palo Alto, CA: Mayfield.

Kamo, Y. (1995a). Grandparenthood. In D. Levinson (Ed.), *Encyclopedia of marriage and the family* (pp. 432–436). New York: Macmillan.

Kamo, Y. (1995b). *Racial differences in extended family households: A comprehensive approach.* Paper presented at the 90th Annual Meeting of the American Sociological Association. Washington, DC, August 1995.

Kamo, Y., & Zhou, M. (1994). Living arrangements of elderly Chinese and Japanese in the United States. *Journal of Marriage and the Family, 56,* 544–558.

Kennedy, G. E. (1992). Quality in grandparent/grandchild relationships. *International Journal of Aging and Human Development, 35,* 83–98.

Kitano, H. H. L., & Daniels, R. (1995). *Asian Americans: Emerging minorities* (2nd ed.). Englewood Cliffs, NJ: Prentice-Hall.

Kivett, V. R. (1995). Racial comparisons of the grandmother role: Implications for strengthening the family support system of older black women. *Family Relations, 42,* 165–172.

Kojima, H. (1989). Intergenerational household extension in Japan. In F. K. Goldscheider & C. Goldscheider (Eds.), *Ethnicity and the new family economy: Living arrangements and intergenerational financial flows* (pp. 163–184). Boulder, CO: Westview.

Kornhaber, A., & Woodward, K. (1985). *Grandparents/grandchildren: The vital connection.* New Brunswick, NJ: Transaction.

Lubben, J. E., & Becerra, R. M. (1987). Social support among black, Mexican, and Chinese elderly. In D. E. Gelfand & C. M. Barresi (Eds.), *Ethnic dimensions on aging* (pp. 130–144). New York: Springer.

Mancini, J. A., & Blieszner, R. (1989). Aging parents and adult children: Research themes in intergenerational relations. *Journal of Marriage and the Family, 51,* 275–290.

Martin, L. G. (1989). Living arrangement of the elderly in Fiji, Korea, Malaysia, and the Philippines. *Demography, 26,* 627–643.

Min, P. G. (1988). The Korean American family. In C. H. Mindel, R. W. Habenstein, & R. Wright, Jr. (Eds.), *Ethnic families in America: Patterns and variations* (3rd ed.) (pp. 199–229). New York: Elsevier.

Olson, P. (1990). The elderly in the People's Republic of China. In J. Sokolovsky (Ed.), *The cultural context of aging: Worldwide perspectives* (pp. 143–161). New York: Bergin & Garvey.

Phinney, J. (1990). Ethnic identity in adolescents and adults: Review of research. *Psychological Bulletin, 108,* 499–514.

Ram, M., & Wong, R. (1994). Covariates of household extension in rural India: Change over time. *Journal of Marriage and the Family, 56,* 853–864.

Schorr, A. (1980). . . . Thy father & thy mother . . . : A second look at filial responsibility and family policy. Washington, DC: U.S. Government Printing Office.

Sokolovsky, J. (1990). *The cultural context of aging.* New York: Bergin & Garvey.

Szinovacz, M. E. (1996). Living with grandparents: Variations by cohort, race, and family structure. *International Journal of Sociology and Social Policy, 16,* 89–123.

Szinovacz, M. E. (1998). Grandparents today: A demographic profile. *The Gerontologist, 38,* 37–52.

Tinsley, B. J., & Parke, R. D. (1984). Grandparents as support and socialization agents. In M. Lewis (Ed.), *Beyond the dyad* (pp. 161–194). New York: Plenum.

Tsuya, N. O., & Martin, L. G. (1992). Living arrangements of Japanese elderly and attitudes toward inheritance. *Journal of Gerontology: Social Sciences, 47,* S45–S54.

Tu, E. J., Liang, J., & Li, S. (1989). Mortality decline and Chinese family structure: Implications for old age support. *Journal of Gerontology: Social Sciences, 44,* 157–168.

Uba, L. (1994). *Asian Americans: Personality patterns, identity, and mental health.* New York: Guilford Press.

U.S. Bureau of the Census. (1992). *1990 Census of population and housing: Public use microdata samples, United States.* Technical Documentation. Washington, DC: U.S. Government Printing Office.

Waley, A. (1971). *The analects of Confucius.* London: Allen & Unwin.

Ward, R. A., Logan, J., & Spitze, G. (1992). The influence of parent and child needs on coresidence in middle and later life. *Journal of Marriage and the Family, 54,* 209–221.

Yang, H., & Chandler D. (1992). Intergenerational relations: Grievances of the elderly in rural China. *Journal of Comparative Family Studies, 23,* 431–453.

?

Think about It

1. Which grandparenting characteristics distinguish most Asian American families from their white counterparts?

2. What are some of the most pronounced differences across Asian American groups in the ways grandparents see their grandchildren, the content of grandparent–grandchild communications, and grandparenting styles?

3. Do Asian American grandparents play a role in socializing their grandchildren or not? How do language barriers affect grandparents' socialization efforts?

Internet Resources

There are many valuable resources on the Internet. We begin with some suggestions for search engines, in case your search skills are still "under construction."

Search Engines and Directories

You probably are familiar with Yahoo! (**www.yahoo.com**), Excite (**www.excite.com**), Lycos (**www.lycos.com**), Infoseek (**www.infoseek.com**), and Alta-Vista (**www.altavista.com**). For other good search engines, try Google (**www.google.com**), Fast Search (**www.alltheweb.com**), Northern Light (**www.northernlight.com**), Oingo (**www.oingo.com**), Dogpile (**www.dogpile.com**), Ixquick Metasearch (**ixquick.com**), All-in-One (**www.allonesearch.com/all1www.html#WWW**), and InfoPeople (**www.infopeople.org/finding.html**). For a good list of search engines, see Parliamentary Library Research Guides (**www.aph.gov.au/library/intguide/searchen.htm**).

For directories, access the Librarians' Index to the Internet (**lii.org**) and the Open Director Project (**www.dmoz.org**).

For good women-focused search engines, try Femina (**femina.cybergrll.com**) and WWWomen (**www.wwwomen.com**).

Some General Social Science Sites That Include Ethnic Families Topics

Social Science Information Gateway
scout18.cs.wisc.edu/sosig_mirror

Social Science Search Engine
sosig.ac.uk/harvester.html

The Scout Report for Social Sciences Current Awareness Metapage
scout.cs.wisc.edu/report/socsci/metapage

Family Science Network
www.uky.edu/HES/gwbrock/fsn

American Studies Web
www.georgetown.edu/crossroads/asw/index.html

Immigration History and Research
www.umn.edu/ihrc/profiles.htm

Asian Studies WWW Virtual Library
coombs.anu.edu.au/WWWVL-AsianStudies.html

Asian American Studies Center, UCLA
www.sscnet.ucla.edu/aasc

Asian / Pacific Islander Minority Links
www.census.gov/pubinfo/www/apihot1.html

Asian American Culture Homepage
**asianamculture.about.com/culture/
asianamculture/mbody.htm**

Asian American Resources
www.ai.mit.edu/people/irie/aar

Hmong Homepage
www.hmongnet.org

Viet-Net WWW Server
www.vnet.org

Asian American Links
www.AArising.com/aalink

Asia Observer
www.asiaobserver.com

The Premier Website for Asian American News
and Entertainment
www.abcflash.com

Gateway to African-American History
www.usia.gov/usa/blackhis

Black/African Related Resources
**www.sas.upenn.edu/African_Studies/Home_Page/
mcgee.html**

Black/African American Minority Links
www.census.gov/pubinfo/www/afamhot1.html

Black History Month (includes statistics on African
Americans)
www.infoplease.com/spot/bhm1.html

Arab-American Affairs Homepage
www.arab-american-affairs.net

Hispanic/Latino American Minority Links
www.census.gov/pubinfo/www/hisphot1.html

Latino Web
www.latinoweb.com

Chicana and Chicano Studies
www.unm.edu/~chicanos

Latino Culture Homepage
**http://latinoculture.about.com/culture/latinoculture/
mbody.htm**

The Latino Virtual Gallery (offers different exhibitions
each year)
latino.si.edu/virtualgallery

Julian Samora Research Institute (JSRI) (offers publications and reports on Latino communities in the Midwest)
www.jsri.msu.edu

Index of Native American Resources on the Internet
hanksville.phast.umass.edu/misc/NAresources.html

WWW Virtual Library: Index of Native American Resources on the Internet
www.hanksville.org/NAresources

American Indian Studies Center, UCLA
www.sscnet.ucla.edu/esp/aisc/index.html

American Indian History and Related Issues
www.csulb.edu/projects/ais/index.html#north

National Indian Justice Center (includes many excellent *Resources* links)
nijc.indian.com

Literature on Race, Ethnicity, and Multiculturalism
ethics.acusd.edu/race.html

The Ethnic Minority Section of the National Council
on Family Relations
www.asn.csus.edu/em-ncfr

Racial and Ethnic Minority Families (National Council
on Family Relations)
web.missouri.edu/~c539613/ncfrgrps.html

FamilyScholar.com
www.familyscholar.com

ACLU Annual Report: The Year in Civil Liberties, 1999 (includes material on immigration)
www.aclu.org/library/ycl99

State Department: Perspectives on Race Relations in the United States (includes sites on race and ethnic diversity)
www.usia.gov/usa/race

INTERracialWeb.com (describes itself as "The largest directory of interracial/intercultural resources on the Web")
www.interracialweb.com

Diversity and Cultural Competence
bluehen.ags.udel.edu/strength/resources/diversity.htm

Family Support America
www.frca.org/fam_issues/supp_topics/culture/Culture_default.htm

The Image Archive on the American Eugenics Movement (includes material on justifications to restrict immigration from some countries)
vector.cshl.org/eugenics

Socialization and Family Values

U.S. Society and Values: Contemporary U.S. Literature: Mutlicultural Perspectives (devoted to "Arab American, Asian American, black American, Hispanic American and Native American writing")
www.usia.gov/journals/itsv/0200/ijse/ijse0200.htm

Life Is Belonging: An American Indian Photo Album (includes maps of American Indian settlements and photos of family life)
www.health.org/pubs/lifebelong/map.htm

Gender Roles

Women's Studies/Women's Issues WWW Sites
www.umbc.edu/wmst/links.html

International Gender Studies Research
globetrotter.berkeley.edu/GlobalGender

The Men's Bibliography
online.anu.edu.au/~e900392/mensbiblio/mensbibliomenu.html

Women's Studies Database
www.inform.umd.edu/EdRes/Topic/WomensStudies

Profile of the Nation's Women
www.census.gov/Press-Release/www/2000/cb00-47.html

Women's Studies/Feminist Journals (identifies 1,000 journals and links to full-text journals)
www.nau.edu/~wst/access/periodichome.html

Women of Color Web (provides access to writings and online resources created by and about women of color in America)
www.hsph.harvard.edu/grhf/WoC

Parenting

Connect for Kids Web (for "insights on pressing issues facing Latino children and families")
www.connectforkids.org

Codetalk, Office of Native American Programs (includes material on children's issues and numerous links)
www.codetalk.fed.us/American_Indian.html

Directory of Children's Issues on the World Wide Web
www.dnai.com/~children/links.html

Children, Youth and Family Consortium
www.cyfc.umn.edu

Forum on Child and Family Statistics
childstats.gov

Family Connections
www.bccf.bc.ca

Child and Youth Health
www.cyh.com

Child Care Resources Services
www.aces.uiuc.edu/~CCRSCare

National Network for Child Care
www.nncc.org

National Child Care Information Center
www.nccic.org

Child Care Bureau
www.acf.dhhs.gov/programs/ccb

YouthInfo
youth.os.dhhs.gov

Child Trends, Inc.
www.childtrends.org

The Impact of Social Class

Inequality.org (features news and analysis of the economic and cultural ramifications of the wide divide between the haves and the have-nots in America)
www.inequality.org

Welfare Information Network (offers a long list of links to sources such as the Welfare Law Center, the Urban Center, and the Center on Budget and Policy Priorities)
www.welfareinfo.org

The Urban Institute (provides many reports on family poverty)
newfederalism.urban.org

Violence and Other Family Crises

National Institute of Drug Abuse
www.nida.nih.gov

Center for Substance Abuse Treatment
www.treatment.org

National Institute on Drug Abuse: Monitoring the Future
monitoringthefuture.org

Resource Guide: American Indians and Native Alaskans (numerous resources and links on health and drug abuse)
www.health.org/pubs/resguide/native/native.htm

National Criminal Justice Reference Service (has an excellent search engine for materials on American Indians, Latinos and other groups' violence, crime, and gangs)
www.ncjrs.org/database.htm

U.S. Department of Justice, Office of Justice Programs (access to information about American Indians and Alaska Natives)
www.ojp.usdoj.gov/aian

U.S. Department of Justice, Office of Violence Against Women
www.ojp.usdoj.gov/vawo

Femina: Health and Wellness, Domestic Violence
www.femina.com

Men against Domestic Violence
www.silcom.com/%7Epaladin/madv

Women and Heart Disease: An Atlas of Racial and Ethnic Disparities in Mortality
www.cdc.gov/nccdphp/cvd/womensatlas

Children's Bureau Express (provides much information and links on child abuse and neglect, child welfare, and adoption)
www.calib.com/cbexpress

Links to Hispanic Health Resources
www.haa.omhrc.gov

Initiative to Eliminate Racial and Ethnic Disparities in Health
www.raceandhealth.gov

Minority Health Initiative
http://www1.od.nih.gov/ormh

Drugs and Crime Facts
www.ojp.usdoj.gov/bjs/dcf/contents.htm

The State of Native American Youth Health
www.cyfc.umn.edu/Diversity/nativeamer.html

Urban Institute: Reports on Teen Risk-Taking Behavior (includes material on race and ethnicity)
www.urban.org/family/TeenRiskTaking.pdf

www.urban.org/news/pressrel/pr000606.html
www.urban.org/family/TeenRiskTaking.html
www.urban.org/family/at-risk/changes.pdf
www.urban.org/family/at-risk/multiplethreats.html
www.urban.org/family/at-risk/reachingout.html

The National Clearinghouse on Child Abuse and Neglect Information (also provides information on the link between domestic violence and child abuse)
www.calib.com/nccanch/pubs/reslist
familyviolence.htm
www.calib.com/nccanch/pubs/bibs/cadv.htm

Marital Conflict, Divorce, and Remarriage

The Divorce Support Page
www.divorcesupport.com

Divorce Net
www.divorcenet.com

The Academy of Family Mediators
www.igc.apc.org/afm

Single Fathers
www.census.gov/Press-Release/www/1999/cb99-03.html

Fathers Receiving Child Support
www.census.gov/Press-Release/cb98-228.html
www.census.gov/Press-Release/www/1999/cb99-77.html

The Stepfamily Association of America
www.stepfam.org

Grandparenting, Aging, and Family Caregiving

Programs and Resources for Native American Elders (American Indian, Alaskan Native, and Native Hawaiian Programs)
www.aoa.gov/ain/default.htm

"America's Demography in the New Century: Aging Baby Boomers and New Immigrants as Major Players"
www.milken-inst.org/pdf/frey.pdf

Access America for Seniors
www.seniors.gov

Administration on Aging
www.aoa.dhhs.gov

National Institute on Aging
www.nih.gov/nia

AARP Webplace
www.aarp.org

Seniors-Site
seniors-site.com

SeniorLaw Home Page
www.seniorlaw.com

Family Caregiver Alliance
www.caregiver.org

Guide to Retirement Living Online
www.retirement-living.com

Photo Credits

Page 15: Bill Bachmann/PhotoEdit.
Page 55: Laima Druskis/Pearson Education/PH College.
Page 93: Fabian Falcon/Stock Boston.
Page 127: Rick Browne/Stock Boston.
Page 171: Corbis Digital Stock.
Page 217: Schamburg Center for Research in Black Culture.
Page 259: Michael Newman/PhotoEdit.
Page 307: Jack Star/PhotoDisk, Inc.
Page 351: D. Young-Wolff/PhotoEdit.